TEXAS
SHALL
BE
OURS

THE ANNALS
OF
AMERICA

THE ANNALS OF AMERICA

Volume 7

1841 - 1849

Manifest Destiny

William Benton, *Publisher*

ENCYCLOPÆDIA BRITANNICA, INC.

Chicago London Toronto Geneva Sydney Tokyo Manila

The editors wish to express their gratitude for permission to reprint
material from the following sources:

The Arthur H. Clark Company for Selections 5, 32,
48, 62, 73, 74, 101, 113, from *A Documentary History
of American Industrial Society*, ed. by John R. Commons *et al.*

Harvard University Press for Selection 15, from *This
Was America*, ed. by Oscar Handlin, Cambridge,
Mass.: Harvard University Press, Copyright 1949 by
the President and Fellows of Harvard College.

Norwegian-American Historical Association for Selection 91, from *America in the Forties: The Letters of Ole
Munch Raeder*, tr. and ed. by Gunnar J. Malmin.

Swedish Pioneer Historical Society for Selection 4,
from *Pioneer in Northwest America 1841-1858. The
Memoirs of Gustaf Unonius*, tr. by Jonas Oscar Backlund, ed. by Nils William Olsson, Vol. I.

The University of Minnesota Press for Selections 2,
49, 107, from *Land of Their Choice: The Immigrants
Write Home*, ed. by Theodore C. Blegen, Minneapolis:
The University of Minnesota Press, © Copyright 1955
by the University of Minnesota.

CODED SOURCES IN THIS VOLUME

Allen

Cowboy Lore. Edited by Jules Verne Allen. San Antonio, 1933.

Blegen

Land of Their Choice. Edited by Theodore C. Blegen. Minneapolis, 1955.

Commons

A Documentary History of American Industrial Society. Edited by John R. Commons *et al.* In 10 vols. Cleveland, 1910-1911.

Globe

Congressional Globe. A record of the proceedings of Congress from 1833 to 1873, arranged by number of Congress and by session. In 46 vols. Washington, 1834-1873.

Globe, App.

Appendix to the Congressional Globe. A supplement to the *Congressional Globe* (see above), paged separately and also arranged by Congress and session. Washington, 1835-1873.

OSL

Old South Leaflets. Published by the Directors of the Old South Work, Old South Meeting House. In 8 vols. (Documents 1-200). Boston, n.d.

Richardson

A Compilation of the Messages and Papers of the Presidents 1789-1897. Edited by James D. Richardson. In 10 vols. Washington, 1896-1899. New edition extended to 1908. Washington, 1909.

Statutes

The Public Statutes at Large of the United States of America from the Organization of the Government in 1789, etc., etc. In 79 vols. as of August 1966. 1845 *et seq.* Vol. 5 edited by Richard Peters. Boston 1854.

TWA

This Was America. Edited by Oscar Handlin. Cambridge, 1949.

Contents

Index of Authors, 564

MANIFEST DESTINY
In Pictures

Growing Urbanization 29-42

The burst of economic expansion that followed the Panic of 1837 spurred
the sudden growth of towns located at transportation crossroads all
across the country. Most people still lived on the land and commerce
in agricultural goods, more than the products of industry, fed the growth
of cities, particularly those along the Midwestern waterways.
Photography, introduced in 1840, begins to enhance the visual record.

Patents and Industry 133-142

In response to the challenges of a vast land and the material rewards
awaiting the successful inventor-entrepreneur, numerous products of "Yankee
ingenuity" that would eventually transform the economy were brought to market.

Wagons West 251-260

During the 1840s many small farmers and businessmen answered the call
of the Far West sounded by early settlers. These beginnings of the
great migration westward were encouraged by expansionists anxious
to populate and eventually to acquire California and Oregon.

A Native Vision 351-358

A "school" of genre painters emerged, expressing an explicitly democratic feeling for the common man. By painting with humor and affection the everyday activities of their neighbors, they sought to record their unqualified confidence in the people and values of rural America. At the same time, New England writers produced the body of work that is America's classic literature.

Problems of Diversity 445-458

Widening democracy, large-scale immigration, and a general sense of self-assurance began to alter the texture and tone of political and social discourse. A dark vein of religious and political intolerance was opened, along with the appearance of a suddenly pronounced jingoist world view.

Politics and War 525-536

The excitement of expansionist politics, puffed into crusading righteousness by notions of "manifest destiny," overcame the inhibitions of sectional rivalry and triggered a distinctly imperialist war with Mexico. Though labeled a war for expansion of slavery in the beginning, the flush of victory and the vast lands acquired overwhelmed the moralist's objections and elected Zachary Taylor President.

Introduction

A key decade in American history, this of the 1840s; and one that, taken all in all, gives the impression of great opportunities missed, of littleness triumphing over largeness of soul, of the failure to live up to promises made in a brighter day. In short, a somber decade, that sowed the seeds, or perhaps cultivated the young plants, of discord and conflict. For if there had been no Mexican War, as many modern historians have observed, there would have been no Civil War — "at least," as Samuel Eliot Morison added, "not in 1861." And if there had been no Civil War — well, it is best not to dwell on such possibilities!

The view expressed in the previous paragraph would have been opposed by many at the time, and might be opposed by some at the present day. To the Democrats, to their President James K. Polk, to the expansionists and the apologists of Manifest Destiny, the 1840s was a glorious decade, during which the United States gained territory of great value and even greater promise — California alone could well be considered to have been worth all the trouble and shame of the Mexican War — and established its claim to that part of the North American continent that it occupies to this day (with the single exception of Alaska, which was acquired two decades later). If success is the only measure of achievement, then this argument is incontrovertible. For there is no denying the success.

At the same time, there are other kinds of success, and this decade was rich in examples of those other kinds. First and particularly notable was the emergence during these years of modern ideas considered — this is the important point — in a modern way. Two or three of these require special comment here. One is the impulse to utopia, the flight from "laissez-faire civilization," that is so much a part of the intellectual atmosphere of our own day. There are few signs of such feelings before the 1840s, but many in the decade itself. For example, four selections in the volume describe four of the utopian communities that sprang up in America during the two or three decades before the Civil War (the four were Brook Farm, the Sylvania Association, the Oneida Community, and the Wisconsin Phalanx, and the Selections are numbers 7, 22, 92, and 113). This is but four out of many; such ventures were numerous. In a sense, these communities, the very isolation of which was intended to insure their virtue, were an outgrowth of the eighteenth-century cult of the primitive and of the noble savage, but there was more to them than mere escapism. They reflected a positive dislike of "modern" civilization, which seemed inevitably to join together convenience, comfort, conformism, and cruelty, that is recognizable today. The young people who have been called twentieth-century "drop-outs" — not from school but from society itself — are the heirs of these earlier exiles.

The members of the communities included some distinguished figures. Brook Farm, for example, in West Roxbury, Massachusetts, and only nine miles from Boston, numbered among its participants Hawthorne, Charles A. Dana, Theodore Parker, Orestes Brownson, Margaret Fuller, Bronson Alcott, and W. E. Channing, although only Hawthorne and Dana, of those named, actually lived there. (Emerson, although he was somewhat sympathetic and visited Brook Farm, was the most articulate critic of the communitarian movement.) The communities in general were deeply influenced by the utopian socialism of such writers as the Englishman Robert Owen (see Selections 48 and 62) and the Frenchman Charles Fourier; they made the mistake (if mistake it is) of assuming that men are naturally good and benevolent, and that human beings require only to have an auspicious social environment to act according to their nature.

The 1840s also saw a new interest in the humane treatment of outcasts from society — as distinguished from voluntary exiles — for example, the insane, and the inmates of penal institutions. Lydia M. Child objected to capital punishment in 1842 (see Selection 14), and Isidore Löwenstern described in the same year the conditions in the Philadelphia penitentiary (see Selection 15); but the most memorable statement of these views is Dorothea Lynde Dix's plea for humane treatment of the insane, which she delivered to the Massachusetts legislature in 1843 (see Selection 21). "I come to present the strong claims of suffering humanity," she declared. "I come as the advocate of helpless, forgotten, insane, and idiotic men and women; of beings sunk to a condition from which the most unconcerned would start with real horror; of beings wretched in our prisons, and more wretched in our almshouses." Her eloquence had an immediate effect, and others joined her in inaugurating a crusade that is still being carried on today.

Another great American crusade also saw its official inception (although its roots went back a generation) during the period covered by this volume. Margaret Fuller urged the emancipation of women in 1845 (see Selection 64), Samuel May advocated their enfranchisement the next year (see Selection 77), but again it was the eloquence of one statement among many that had the real effect. This was the Seneca Falls (N.Y.) Declaration of Women's Rights of 1848 (see Selection 98), in which two gallant ladies, Lucretia Mott and Elizabeth Cady Stanton (they were later joined by Susan B. Anthony) rewrote the Declaration of Independence to include women.

The debate about America's technological progress, which seems to grow all the hotter the more marvels science provides, was fully launched in the period covered here. Earlier writers had either applauded the technical ingenuity of Americans or ignored the subject, but now, almost for the first time in the

Western world, the gifts of technology and, more important, its promise of almost infinite future riches, began to be called in question. A notable statement in this connection is Thoreau's review of a book by one J. G. Etzler, whose enthusiasm for scientific progress would not be out of place on Madison Avenue today (see Selection 29 — and see also Selection 35). However, unlike the selections mentioned in the previous paragraphs, Thoreau's anti-progress manifesto had no effect at all.

It had no effect, of course, because Thoreau was trying to oppose the dominant movement in American history during the nineteenth century, namely, what W. W. Rostow called, in his *Stages of Economic Growth,* the "take off" in American economic development. Somewhere around 1840 the United States made the transition from an agrarian self-subsistence economy to an economy of self-sustaining industrial and economic growth. The critical factor in this transition was the New England textile industry, not simply because it was a manufacturing enterprise but because it had what economists now call "backward and forward linkages." The textile industry created behind itself (the "backward linkage") a need for machine shops and the development of all kinds of metal fabrication, and it created ahead of itself (the "forward linkage") the clothing industry and the sewing machine.

In this movement America led the world. Blessed with unparalleled resources and "an imperial domain within its own borders," the United States created, within the short space of a century, an affluence, based not only on resources but also on "know how," that was envied by all. Important as the movement was in our history, however, there was little if any self-consciousness about it at the time. Nevertheless, a few prophetic writers discussed the change as they saw it, and expressed their vision of what it might mean in the future. (See, for example, Selections 6, 28, 33, 46, 55, 62, 90, and 101.)

The presidential succession starting with the election of 1840 reveals much about the events leading up to the Mexican War. Martin Van Buren was his Democratic Party's candidate for reelection; the Whigs nominated General William Henry Harrison for President, and John Tyler, an anti-Jackson states' rights Democrat, for Vice-President. Harrison won, and named a Whig Cabinet; but he died a month after being inaugurated, Tyler became President, and the Whigs were out again within less than a year. In 1844, however, Tyler had no support from either party, and Henry Clay became the candidate of the Whigs, James K. Polk, the candidate of the Democrats. Polk, like most of his followers, was an expansionist, and the party platform took an aggressive stand, demanding the acquisition of both Texas and Oregon. Clay's election seemed assured, but he and his advisors began to worry about the "patriotic" appeal of the Democratic position, and in July he issued a pair of statements implying qualified support of the annexation of Texas. The statements were carefully phrased; had he won he could have gone either way, and probably would have been able to avoid war. But the statements were not read as carefully as they had been written, and a handful of antislavery Whig votes in New York were diverted to the otherwise unremembered candidate of the Liberty Party. As a result, Clay lost one of the closest races in American political history, and one of the most important for the country's future.

Polk not only was unable to avoid war; he did not want to. What he wanted was California, and he was willing to go to almost any lengths to acquire it. Oregon, too, of course, and the present New Mexico, Arizona, Nevada, Utah, and parts of Colorado, and Wyoming — but it was California, the "lazy paradise" that Polk knew next to nothing about except what he had read in Dana's *Two Years Before the Mast*, that was the prize of prizes. Wars always require at least two antagonists, and the Mexicans were not wholly without responsibility for this one, but it was Polk who was the main culprit — or hero, depending on one's view. It is true enough that he tried to get California without war, by offering to buy it; but when this effort failed he provoked Mexico by moving General Zachary Taylor's army south of the Nueces River and then asked Congress to declare war when the Mexicans attacked. Congress did, and the war was on.

The odds were not as unequal then as they would be now, and there were even some Europeans who felt that Mexico would win. She never even came close, mainly because America had, comparatively speaking, almost unlimited funds and was able, and willing, to spend $100 million (Polk's original offer to the Mexicans had been about $30 million). The war lasted only about a year and a half, beginning with Taylor's foray in April 1846 and ending with the capture of Mexico City in September 1847. Officially, the war ended on February 2, 1848, when the United States Mexican border was fixed at the Rio Grande.

Probably no war in American history, not even the war in Vietnam, has been so deeply disapproved by so many American citizens (nevertheless, they were probably not a majority). Emerson summed up the feelings of New Englanders in his "Ode Inscribed to W. H. Channing" (Selection 79):

> Who is he that prates
> Of the culture of mankind,
> Of better arts and life?
> Go, blindworm, go,
> Behold the famous States
> Harrying Mexico
> With rifle and with knife!

New Englanders not only felt that the war was barbarous but also believed that it was a badly disguised effort on the part of the Southern interest to extend slavery to new territory, and to perpetuate the institution that they hated above all in American life.

Others disapproved, too, including Clay and one of his young Whig followers in Congress, Abraham Lincoln. But the American people have never refused to support a war once it actually began, and even Polk's fiercest opponents did not fail to support this one. And there were others, as well, who had no qualms.

In their view, the war, far from being the calamity that New England considered it, was a triumph, a necessary conflict having full justification in America's "manifest destiny," as they never tired of putting it, to occupy the continent from sea to sea. Indeed, the more aggressive Democrats demanded, after the war's end, the absorption of all of Mexico into the United States; and their slogan after 1846 was "Fifty-four Forty or Fight," a mnemonic that helped them remember that United States territory "rightly" extended northward to the border of the present Alaska, thus taking in half of the present Canadian province of British Columbia. President Polk was content, however, with less than that, and settled for the 49th parallel on the north, for the Rio Grande on the south. After all, that included California. (For Selections in this volume dealing with the Mexican War, see, among others, numbers 18, 20, 38, 39, 53, 60, 61, 78, 80-85, 95, 117, and 118; and see the Chronology for the years 1846-1848 for a more detailed account of the events of the conflict.)

Polk refused to run for a second term in 1848, but one of his last acts as President was fraught with significance for the future. Gold was discovered by one James M. Marshall, a mechanic in the employ of J. A. Sutter, on Sutter's property in the Sacramento Valley on January 28, 1848. At first no one knew how much gold was actually there, but news of the find spread rapidly, as such news does; nevertheless, there might not have been a Gold Rush if Polk had not mentioned the discovery in his last annual message to Congress on December 5. The stampede of '49 began almost immediately. Polk had thus not only acquired California, but also populated it. (For discussions of events in California, see Selections 60, 61, 66, 69, 70, and 107-109.)

There were other problems that he had not solved, and the greatest of these was slavery. Analysis of the attempts that other men made to do so belongs in the next volume.

Chronology: 1841 - 1849

1841

March 5-6. Whig Cabinet appointed by President William Henry Harrison consists largely of supporters of Henry Clay. Clay himself refuses to head the State Department, and post is given to Daniel Webster.

March 9. Supreme Court in Amistad Case sustains lower court decision that frees Negroes who had mutinied on a Spanish slaver, were subsequently captured by a U.S. warship off Long Island, and were taken to New London, Connecticut.

April 4. President Harrison dies of pneumonia and Vice-President John Tyler becomes tenth President of the U.S., the first Vice-President to succeed to the presidency. **April 9.** Address by Tyler, a Virginia states' rights Democrat opposed to the Jacksonians, threatens Whig program by advocating restrained fiscal policies.

April 10. Horace Greeley founds the *New York Tribune,* which becomes the most influential paper in the North and West until the Civil War. A liberal Whig until 1854, Greeley is afterward a founding and leading figure in the Republican Party.

July 7. Whig program is set forth by Clay in Senate resolutions that call for repeal of Independent Treasury Act, creation of a new national bank, higher tariffs, and distribution among the states of proceeds from sale of public lands.

Aug. 6. Bill to establish new bank is passed by Whig majorities in Congress. **Aug. 13.** As a necessary condition, Independent Treasury Act is repealed. **Aug. 16.** President Tyler accepts repeal but vetoes the bank bill as unconstitutional. **Sept. 9.** Second bank bill, incorporating changes supposed to be required by Tyler, is also vetoed for the same reasons. Since Whig majority is insufficient to pass bill over veto, stalemate lasting until 1846 develops, with Democrats determined to reestablish subtreasury system, but unable to, and with management of public funds meanwhile left to secretary of the treasury, who is obliged to use state banks for deposit.

Sept. 4. Distribution-Pre-emption Act ends long struggle between factions that disagree as to whether settlement or revenue should be the basic object of public land policy. Provisions of this act serve Western (pre-emption) interests by making permanent the allowance of squatters' rights granted temporarily and renewed at intervals since 1830. Proponents of distribution led by Henry Clay, who regard public lands as a national rather than a merely Western possession, are appeased by requirement that part of the proceeds of the sale of lands be apportioned among the states. At insistence of Southerners, who fear that depletion of the federal treasury will be used as an excuse to raise the tariff rates, distribution of proceeds is to be repealed if tariffs reach 20 percent. Rise in rates passed in 1842 results in repeal of distribution requirement.

Overland migration to California is begun when John Bidwell, New York schoolteacher, and John Bartleson, land speculator and wagon master, lead party through South Pass in the Rocky Mountains and across Nevada to settle near Stockton.

Brook Farm, Transcendentalist experiment in communal living, established in Massachusetts by Unitarian minister George Ripley. The most famous of many cooperative, anti-capitalist communities that flourish from Massachusetts to Wisconsin between 1840 and 1852, it includes Nathaniel Hawthorne, Charles A. Dana, and other intellectuals among its members; it is destroyed by fire in 1846 and abandoned.

Letters and Notes on the Manners, Customs, and Condition of the North American Indians is published in two volumes with more than 300 engravings by George Catlin, pioneer American ethnologist who devotes most of his life to "rescuing from oblivion the looks and customs of the vanishing races of native man in America."

The Mercantile Agency, first commercial credit-rating agency, is established by Lewis Tappan, New York merchant; agency becomes R. G. Dun & Company in 1859, Dun & Bradstreet in 1933.

1841 - 1842

Dorr's Rebellion in Rhode Island. Rhode Island royal charter of 1663, which is state's constitution, allows suffrage only to property owners and their eldest sons; since popu-

lation of state has grown increasingly urban, these obsolete requirements have disfranchised most city-dwellers — half the white male population. **Oct. 4, 1841.** Unauthorized convention led by Thomas W. Dorr meets at Providence to draw up new state constitution (the People's Constitution). **Dec.** It is ratified by large popular vote. **Feb. 1842.** Legislature, alarmed at prospect of people's rebellion, calls convention that draws up Freeman's Constitution that modifies charter. **March.** It is rejected in close vote. **April 18.** In separate elections, Dorr is chosen governor by People's Party and Governor Samuel W. King is reelected by Freeman's Party. State Supreme Court and federal government refuse to recognize People's Constitution, and Governor King calls out militia to put down Dorr's uprising. **May 18.** Dorr and followers fail in attempt to capture state arsenal, and rebellion collapses. **Nov. 21-23.** New Freeman's Constitution, modified in convention of September 12 to November 5, is adopted by popular vote; it allows for wider suffrage, but only for those born in United States.

Oct. 27, 1841. Slaveship *Creole* sails from Hampton Roads, Virginia, bound for New Orleans. During voyage, slaves mutiny and force officers to land at Nassau in the Bahamas, where British authorities free all except ringleaders. Secretary of State Daniel Webster attempts to recover the slaves as U.S. property, and is ignored by the British. **March 21-22, 1842.** Congressman Joshua R. Giddings of Ohio proposes resolutions against slavery and the coastal slave trade. **March 23.** He is censured by the Southern-dominated House and resigns. **April.** Giddings is reelected with a large majority by his district in a special election.

1841 - 1844

Sept. 11, 1841. Entire Cabinet except Daniel Webster resigns in protest against

President Tyler's second bank veto. **Sept. 13.** New Cabinet is appointed; replacements are followed by frequent shifts, leaving Webster, who remains in Cabinet until his resignation on May 8, 1843, the dominant figure in the administration. Webster's resignation paves way for eventual appointment a year later of John C. Calhoun as secretary of state. Calhoun's appointment indicates defeat of President Tyler's attempt to organize independent political backing and resurgence of the Democrats under Southern leadership.

1841 - 1850

Iron industry makes rapid progress as a result of improved production techniques, use of anthracite coal instead of charcoal; adoption of steam power and expansion of railroads creates demands for iron products. In addition, production of farm machinery, pistols, sewing machines, clocks, and stoves made with standard parts multiplies quantity and variety of iron production.

1842

Aug. 9. Lengthy negotiations culminate in Webster-Ashburton Treaty between U.S. and Britain, finally establishing Canadian boundary from Maine to Lake of the Woods. Settlement involves issues as old as the Revolution, and concessions are mutual, but American gains include area of northeastern Minnesota, the Mesabi Range, that later is found to be one of the great iron-ore regions of the world.

U.S. Supreme Court in *Prigg* v. *Pennsylvania* overturns Pennsylvania law that prohibits return of fugitive slaves, but also holds that no state has responsibility of enforcing federal Fugitive Slave Law. Decision leads to enactment of "personal liberty" laws in many Northern states, forbidding state authorities to assist federal agents seeking to return fugitive slaves.

In widely copied decision of *Commonwealth* v. *Hunt*, Chief Justice Lemuel Shaw for the Massachusetts Supreme Court rejects criminal conspiracy doctrine under which labor unions have been prosecuted since 1806. Doctrine had made social and economic pressure to persuade workmen to join unions a criminal offense; thus unions were unable to gain enough strength for effective strikes.

Phineas T. Barnum, former newspaper editor, opens Barnum's American Museum in New York, using collections from Scudder's American Museum and Peale's Museum, bought in previous year; he exhibits General Tom Thumb and other freaks as well as many hoaxes, drawing the public with extravagant advertising.

Rufus W. Griswold edits and publishes *Poets and Poetry of America,* unusually popular anthology.

1842 - 1843

"Oregon fever" starts migration to the Oregon Country, chiefly from the Ohio Valley states and Missouri. Main route is the Oregon Trail, from Independence, Missouri, to the mouth of the Columbia River.

1842 - 1846

Jan. 1842. Ether first used as an anesthetic by William E. Clarke, a medical student, in tooth extraction performed by Dr. Elijah Pope in Rochester, New York. **Oct. 16, 1846.** William T. G. Morton, another dentist, administers ether for the first time in general surgery during a public operation for a neck tumor performed by Dr. John C. Warren at Massachusetts General Hospital.

1843

January. *Memorial to the Legislature of Massachusetts,* indicting the treatment and care of the insane, is published by Dorothea Lynde Dix, pioneer in the reform of prisons, asylums, poorhouses, and hospitals; in previous two years she has visited hundreds of such institutions in Massachusetts and other states.

July 5. Settlers in Oregon Country, jurisdiction over part of which is disputed by Britain and the U.S., adopt constitution for a provisional government pending anticipated establishment of American authority. Disputed region is that between Columbia River and 49th parallel, claimed by both countries. **July.** Cincinnati convention on Oregon Country adopts resolution demanding land north to 54°40′ for the U.S. Anglo-U.S. friction precipitates Oregon issue into campaign of 1844.

Texas question, dormant since the establishment of Texan independence in 1836, is revived when Mexico invades Texas in 1842. Britain and France, both anxious to encourage an independent buffer state against American expansion, arrange a truce between Texas and Mexico, after which Texas minister to Washington, Isaac Van Zandt, withdraws latest of several offers of U.S. annexation. Move arouses concern in the South, which has hoped annexed territory will become new slave state and is alarmed at reports that Britain will press for abolition of slavery in Texas if its independence is maintained. **Aug. 23.** Mexican President Santa Anna declares that annexation will mean war between Mexico and the U.S. **Oct. 16.** Negotiations for annexation are reopened with Van Zandt by the Tyler administration in the face of Northern opposition that makes Senate acceptance doubtful. Fearful that Texas will lose support of Great Britain if annexation is defeated in Senate, President Houston refuses U.S. offer.

Beginning of substantial immigration to U.S. of Scandinavians, who settle chiefly in Wisconsin and Minnesota; an average of 2,100 arrive annually from 1843 to 1860.

Law of Cooling of Atmospheric Air, one of the most important American contributions to meteorology, is published by James P. Espy.

Oliver Wendell Holmes, author and physician, publishes "The Contagiousness of Puerperal Fever," a paper that shows by use of statistics that childbed fever, almost always fatal to mothers of newborn infants, is caused by contagion. Holmes is criticized for his opinion, but it is later confirmed by additional observations of other physicians.

Typewriter invented by Charles Thurber of Worcester, Massachusetts, but like other machines of the period, it is slower than writing by hand; first practical machine is not constructed until 1867.

Edgar Allan Poe, one of the originators of the detective story, wins $100 prize for his "The Gold Bug," published in the *Philadelphia Dollar Newspaper.* "The Murders in the Rue Morgue" has been published two years before.

History of the Conquest of Mexico published by William Hickling Prescott, known as first American scientific historian of U.S.; Prescott's dramatic writing style combined with untiring scholarship popularizes reading of history in the country.

Robert Sears, publisher and author, issues *The Wonders of the World, in Nature, Art, and Mind,* a best-selling illustrated volume that, with other heavily pictorial works, gains him a reputation as a patron of engraving.

1843 - 1845

Baptist church splits over slavery, with Southerners withdrawing to form Southern

Baptist Convention at Atlanta in 1845. Methodist Church, South, is established separately from main body for same reason the year before.

Preaching of William Miller launches Millerite movement, based on belief in Second Coming of Christ in 1843-1844 period. Adventist Church is formed in 1845; Seventh-Day Adventists establish separate body in 1863.

1843 - 1847

Appearance of the Great Comet in 1843 stimulates astronomical observation; mathematician Benjamin Peirce, of Harvard University, does work on undiscovered but suspected celestial body simultaneously with others in Europe; concerted effort results in identification of planet Neptune in 1846. Maria Mitchell of Nantucket Island, Massachusetts, discovers comet in 1847.

1844

April 12. Treaty of annexation is negotiated with Texas government by Secretary of State John C. Calhoun. **April 18.** Calhoun sends note to British minister strongly defending slavery. **April 22.** President Tyler submits annexation treaty to Senate with message urging Southern states to act to guard their security and warning of the abolition risk in case of British interference in Texas. **June 8.** Calhoun's note arouses Northern suspicion, with the result that treaty is rejected in the Senate as a slaveholders' conspiracy. Tyler, realizing that he cannot hope for two-thirds support necessary to ratify treaty, moves that annexation be brought about by joint congressional resolution, but measure is still not acted on by June, when Congress adjourns.

Since President Tyler is without party support for renomination, leading candidates for President are Democrat Martin Van Buren and Henry Clay, absent from the Senate since 1842 to seek Whig nomination. Crucial issue is Texas which places both men in a dilemma: neither can oppose annexation without alienating the South or support it without giving up Northern antislavery vote. **April 27.** Possibly after making an agreement, candidates publish letters expressing their opposition to immediate annexation; Clay's reason is that he cannot hope for Whig nomination without it; Van Buren's, that antislavery feeling is strong in key Democratic state of New York.

May 1. Henry Clay is unanimously nominated by Whig convention in Baltimore. **May 29.** At Democratic convention, James Knox Polk of Tennessee, an able but colorless congressional veteran, is nominated with Jackson's support after "two-thirds" rule proves insuperable obstacle to Van Buren, whose letter has offended not only the South but also Andrew Jackson, now an advocate of annexation. In effort to offset Polk's obscurity (Whigs in campaign ask "Who is James K. Polk?"), Democratic platform drawn up by Robert J. Walker of Mississippi takes an aggressive stand, demands acquisition of both Texas and all of Oregon Territory. From 1846 on demand is expressed by slogan "54°40' or Fight!"

May 6-July 8. Several armed conflicts between Protestants and Catholics in Philadelphia leave 20 persons dead and about 100 injured. Clashes result from agitation by nativists, who are anti-Catholic and who resent naturalization of foreign immigrants, especially those from Catholic countries.

May 24. First successful telegraph is demonstrated by Samuel F. B. Morse, its developer, and his partner, Alfred Vail, who invent telegraphic printer in same year. Message "What Hath God Wrought!" is transmitted in Morse code on line from Washington, D. C., to Baltimore. Though construction of line has been financed by the government, Morse fails to persuade it to buy rights to his invention and forms his own company instead.

July 1 and 27. Decisive turn in campaign occurs when Henry Clay tries to counter "patriotic" appeal of Democrats by changing his position on Texas, coming out with qualified support for annexation in "Alabama letters." **Dec. 4.** Clay's move proves fatal politically; Polk takes New York's 36 electoral votes with a bare 5,100 majority, made possible by 16,300 antislavery Whig votes that Clay has lost to James G. Birney of Liberty Party. Total electoral vote for Polk, who carries 15 states, is 170, with Clay having 105 and 11 states. Popular vote is Polk, 1,338,000; Clay, 1,300,000; Birney, 62,300. George M. Dallas of Pennsylvania is elected Vice-President.

American Journal of Psychiatry begins publication; it is first specialized medical journal. Association of Medical Superintendents of American Institutions for the Insane is founded; now known as American Psychiatric Association.

Springfield (Massachusetts) *Republican,* founded as a weekly in 1824, begins publication as a Whig daily under ownership of Samuel Bowles; it is noted for independent reporting.

1845

Jan. 23. Tuesday following first Monday in November established as national presidential election day by act of Congress.

March 2. Republic of Texas annexed by joint resolution of Congress as recommended by President Tyler in 1844; it is to become a state without first being a U.S. territory. Area thus acquired is arguably foreign territory, since Mexico has refused to recognize Texan independence; annexation

measure therefore empowers the President to negotiate a treaty, but Mexican consent is not mentioned in the act.

March 3. Florida is admitted to the Union as twenty-seventh state and fourteenth slave state. A U.S. territory since 1822, population is 85,000.

March 3. For first time Congress overrides a presidential veto. Measure, which withholds payment for naval vessels ordered by President Tyler, had been vetoed by him on February 20.

March 4. President Polk's inaugural address asserts "clear and unquestionable" U.S. title to Oregon, maintains that annexation is exclusively a question between the U.S. and Texas since they are both "independent powers," does not acknowledge that Mexico has failed to recognize Texan independence.

March 28. Mexico breaks off diplomatic relations with U.S. **June.** It begins military preparations to prevent annexation of Texas. Other Mexican grievances are American boundary claims along Southwest border and influx of American settlers into California contrary to Mexican law. **May 28.** President Polk responds by ordering General Zachary Taylor, American commander in the Southwest, to maintain his troops as an "Army of Observation" ready to advance from Louisiana into Texas if Mexico invades Texas. **June 15.** Taylor is ordered to place himself "on or near the Rio Grande" for this purpose, though position is south of any border recognized by Mexico. **July 31.** Taylor actually marches only as far as the Nueces River where he stations himself near Corpus Christi with 3,500 men — about half the U.S. Army.

Upon news of Congress' action, Texas breaks off independence negotiations with

Mexico, which is about to grant recognition on condition that Texas refuse annexation. **June 23.** Texas Congress votes in favor of U.S. proposal. **July 4.** A special Texas convention is called to accept the terms. **Oct. 13.** Annexation as a state is ratified by popular vote. **Dec. 29.** Texas is admitted to the union as twenty-eighth state and fifteenth slave state. This is first time since 1802 that balance of slave and free states has not been observed, and only time a state has been admitted by joint resolution of Congress; action provokes Northern protest.

August. U.S. receives secret information that Mexican government is again willing to discuss Texas boundary. **Nov. 7.** President Polk and Secretary of State James Buchanan decide to send John Slidell of Louisiana on confidential mission to negotiate not only boundary but also the sale of New Mexico and Upper California as well, authorizing payment of $15 to $20 million and canceling of unpaid Mexican debt to U.S. **Dec. 16.** By the time Slidell reaches Mexico City, his mission is public knowledge, and Mexican government, faced with hostile public opinion, refuses to receive him on the ground that he does not officially represent the U.S.

Oct. 10. "Naval School" opens at Fort Severn, Annapolis, Maryland; it is called U.S. Naval Academy after 1850.

Dec. 2. President Polk's first annual message sets forth "Polk Doctrine" — an elaboration of Monroe Doctrine with respect to Texas and Oregon that asserts exclusive right of the people on "this continent" to decide "their own destiny." Message is aimed at British claims in Oregon as well as possible British and French support of Mexico.

Postal Act authorizes subsidies for steamers carrying mail to and from Europe and reduces postage rate to five cents per half ounce for 300 miles.

Narrative of the Life of Frederick Douglass, an American Slave is published by Frederick Douglass, Negro Abolitionist, writer, orator, and escaped slave, just before he goes to Europe to avoid danger of recapture.

George Lippard, reporter, author, lecturer, publishes *The Monks of Monk Hall,* later called *Quaker City,* an exposé of Philadelphia vice; it has an enormous sale in the U.S. and Europe. Scheduled to be shown in dramatized form in Philadelphia, it is canceled by the mayor, who fears that mobs will destroy the theater.

Leonora by William H. Fry, first grand opera composed by a native of the U.S., is performed in Philadelphia.

1845 - 1846

July 1845. Phrase "manifest destiny" appears in the *United States Magazine and Democratic Review* in an article by its editor, John L. O'Sullivan, that asserts the divine right of the American people to cover the continent. **Dec. 27.** Phrase becomes current with repetition by O'Sullivan in *New York Morning News* in an editorial on the annexation of Texas. **Jan. 3, 1846.** First use in Congress is by Representative Robert C. Winthrop of Massachusetts, who argues during Oregon debate that it is by right "our manifest destiny to spread over this whole continent."

Aug. 1845. Deputy sheriff murdered in upstate New York during Antirent War that has continued since 1839. Farmers, resentful of perpetual leases that have been in effect since colonial days, have formed secret societies and attacked law-enforcement agents. As a result of war, New York Governor Silas Wright recommends reform legislation that leads to writing of more liberal New York constitution of 1846.

1846

Jan. 4. New president of Mexico takes office after revolution overthrows government willing to negotiate Texas boundary with John Slidell. New government, believing that U.S. will soon be occupied in war with Britain over Oregon dispute, reasserts Mexican claim to most of Texas. **Feb. 6.** Slidell reports to Washington that Mexicans need to be "chastised," then leaves for home after his final request for an interview is refused on March 12.

Jan. 13. President Polk, apparently wishing either to force negotiations or to provoke an incident, orders General Zachary Taylor to proceed southward from the Nueces River to the Rio Grande.

April 23. President Polk's demand for the whole of Oregon leads to resolution by Congress calling for an end to joint Anglo-American occupation established by convention of 1818. **May 21.** Polk gives Britain required year's notice of termination of the agreement, although British have in previous December requested renewal of American proposal of 1827 for settlement on basis of 49th parallel and have been refused. **June 10.** President Polk, having received (at his insistence) a British treaty offering same terms as 1827 American proposal, lays it before the Senate for advice. **June 15.** Senate ratifies treaty, which provides for free navigation of Juan de Fuca Strait and Columbia River by both parties, as well as fixing Oregon's boundary at present-day line.

April 25. Mexican forces attack American scouting party north of the Rio Grande near Matamoros. **April 26.** General Taylor sends report to Washington saying that "hostilities may now be regarded as com-

menced" and calls upon governors of Texas and Louisiana for 5,000 volunteers. **May 1.** Mexicans cross the Rio Grande in force.

May 8-9. Early battles at Palo Alto and Resaca de la Palma near the Rio Grande result in defeat of numerically superior Mexican forces by Taylor, who becomes popular here ("Old Rough and Ready") by daring tactics. These engagements set the military pattern of a war won easily despite the vast distances involved, the lack of American preparations, and the strong opposition of the northeastern states. War proceeds in three main areas: the Rio Grande frontier, California, and central Mexico, invaded by sea-borne forces.

May 11. President Polk sends war message to Congress two days after news of skirmish at Matamoros reaches Washington. Message claims American right in disputed territory between Nueces and Rio Grande, asserts that "Mexico has invaded our territory . . . shed American blood on American soil." War with Mexico is formally recognized by House on same day, 174 to 14. Strength of opposition is indicated by 67 Whig votes against call for 50,000 volunteers and $10 million. **May 12.** In the Senate, Calhoun balks at resolution that assumes existence of a war Congress has never formally considered, but war declaration passes, 40 to 2. War is declared the next day.

June 14-July 5. Bear Flag revolt occurs in California, and Captain John C. Frémont at the head of a party of mountain men supposed to be "exploring" for the U.S., on his own initiative (or with secret instructions), supports the establishment by a few American settlers of the Republic of California (the Bear Flag Republic) at Sonoma. This maneuver antagonizes Spanish-speaking Californians on the verge of revolt from Mexico. **July 7.** Authority over California is proclaimed at Monterey with landing of naval expedition under Commodore John Sloat, whose forces also take San Francisco and occupy Sonoma. Frémont is made military commandant in the north. **Sept. 22-30.** Uprising of Mexican Californians under José Flores quickly reestablishes Mexican control in most of southern California.

July 6. General Taylor begins ascent of the Rio Grande and with 6,000 men advances on Monterrey, Mexico. **Sept. 21.** Monterrey is captured after a four-day siege. Taylor then grants an eight-week armistice, promising that American forces will not advance during that time. This is disapproved by President Polk, but Taylor does not receive word until November 2. **Nov. 19.** Feeling that Taylor, a Whig, does not fully support his policies, President Polk consents to another expedition urged by General Winfield Scott, also a Whig, against Veracruz and Mexico City.

Aug. 6. Independent Treasury system is reenacted by Congress. Passed by Democratic majority elected in 1844, bill is similar to the act of 1840, establishes fiscal system for the federal government that endures without substantial change until the Federal Reserve Act of 1913.

Dec. 12. Fearing that Great Britain or another foreign country might seize the Isthmus of Panama, the U.S. and New Granada (present-day Colombia and Panama) sign commercial treaty. Treaty gives the U.S. right of way across the isthmus as a route between the Atlantic and Pacific oceans in return for guarantee of Granadian sovereignty and a further guarantee that isthmus will remain neutral ground. Treaty is approved by the Senate on June 3, 1848.

Dec. 28. Iowa, originally part of Louisiana Purchase and until 1821 unsettled Indian territory, is admitted to the Union as the twenty-ninth state and fourteenth free state; population is 102,300.

Maine enacts first state-wide prohibition law. Similar laws have been passed in 12 more states by 1855, but by 1863 all except Maine's have been repealed or held invalid by state courts.

Smithsonian Institution is founded by act of Congress with bequest of £100,000 from James Smithson, English chemist. Physicist Joseph Henry is named first secretary-director.

Sewing machine invented by Elias Howe, who has experimented with it during previous two years while working in instrument maker's shop in Cambridge, Massachusetts.

Rotary press that can print 8,000 newspapers per hour is invented by Richard M. Hoe. First used by *Philadelphia Public Ledger* in 1847, it revolutionizes newspaper printing and circulation.

Commercial Review of the South and Southwest (later *De Bow's Review*) founded in New Orleans by James D. B. De Bow; at first moderate as to questions dividing North and South, it becomes the most important organ of extreme Southern views in the pre-Civil War period.

1846 - 1847

Congressman David Wilmot, a Pennsylvania Democrat, accelerates congressional debate on the merits of the Mexican War when he offers motion to exclude slavery from any territory acquired from Mexico. Attached as an amendment to a bill authorizing appropriation for territorial purchase, the so-called Wilmot Proviso, though never enacted, becomes the focus of national controversy for the next four years. **Aug. 8,**

1846. Bill is passed by the House but defeated in the Senate two days later. **Feb. 15, 1847.** Amended bill, including Wilmot Proviso, is again passed in the House. **March 1.** Bill is passed in the Senate, but without Proviso. **March 3.** Senate bill is approved by House. By now, debate has hardened Whig opposition to the war as an unconstitutional thrust for territorial gain, while Democrats continue to defend it.

Oct. 1846-March 1847. Whig gains in state and congressional elections indicate unpopularity of Mexican War. Congressional attack on Polk unites Whigs and antislavery Democrats, but Congress continues to vote appropriations for war.

Dec. 6, 1846 - Jan. 13, 1847. Conquest of California is completed when General Stephen Watts Kearny, arriving with 120 dragoons after occupying Santa Fe, defeats Mexican forces at San Pasqual, then, with Commodore Robert F. Stockton's forces, proceeds to Los Angeles, which is captured on January 10. Frémont, having subdued remnants of Mexican resistance, signs Treaty of Cahuenga on January 13.

George Donner, elderly Illinois farmer, attempts to lead group of 87 settlers to California through pass in Sierra Nevada, now called Donner Pass. Ill-equipped and inexperienced group is caught by severe winter in the pass and 41 die of cold or starvation. Many of the survivors are sustained only by eating the bodies of their companions, including that of George Donner.

1847

Jan. 14. General Taylor learns that he has been ordered to remain in defensive position at Monterrey while 9,000 of his troops are assigned to attack on Veracruz; he decides that political intrigue inspired by

mention of himself as a presidential possibility is responsible. **Feb. 5.** Taylor disobeys orders and advances with 5,000 men, mostly untried volunteers, farther into Mexico. **Feb. 22-23.** At Buena Vista, Taylor defeats Santa Anna's equally untrained and also exhausted 20,000 troops in a bloody battle, which ends war in north of Mexico. Reprimand sent January 27 from Secretary of War William L. Marcy for publishing complaints of the treatment he has received reaches Taylor shortly after battle; he is thereafter forced into idleness as commander in northern Mexico. **Nov. 26.** At his own request, he leaves for the U.S. and a hero's welcome.

Jan. 16. Conflict of authority between Kearny and Stockton, successor to Commodore Sloat, over right to organize a California government comes to a head when Stockton, opposed by Kearny, appoints Frémont territorial governor at Los Angeles. **Feb. 13.** Kearny receives orders to set up a government and establishes one at Monterey, but Frémont defies this move and continues as governor in Los Angeles. **May 31.** Frémont and Kearny leave for Washington where Frémont is eventually courtmartialed and dismissed from the service.

Feb. 19. Southern attitude toward newly acquired territory is stated by Calhoun in four resolutions aimed at keeping area involved in Mexican War open to slavery. He asserts that territories belong to all states and that the Union may not enact laws (against slavery) that will deprive any state of its rights. Argument set forth in four resolutions establishes Southern position that eventually becomes the basis of secession.

April 8. Having taken Veracruz on March 27, General Winfield Scott sets out for the interior of Mexico with 9,000 men. **April 18-Aug. 20.** Santa Anna withdraws toward Mexico City with Scott's force engaging him several times until at Churubusco more than a third of Santa Anna's army is killed, wounded, or captured. With American troops only five miles from Mexico City, Santa Anna requests an armistice. **Aug. 24.** Armistice of Tacubaya is granted so that Mexico can consider peace proposals conveyed by President Polk through Nicholas Trist, chief clerk of the State Department. **Aug. 27-Sept. 6.** Terms discussed in negotiations include demand that Mexico cede area north of the Rio Grande. **Sept. 6.** Mexican government rejects peace offer, ending armistice.

July 21-24. Mormons under Brigham Young arrive in Great Salt Lake Valley after arduous journey from Kanesville (now Council Bluffs, Iowa). Salt Lake City (originally Great Salt Lake City) is founded as capital of the state of Deseret, of which Young is chosen governor.

Sept. 8 and 12. U.S. assault on Mexico City is begun as soon as armistice ends, with battles at gun foundry of Molino del Rey and at Chapultepec Hill. **Sept. 13-14.** City is finally captured by 6,000 American troops, who break through walls during the night. **Oct. 12.** Last effort at resistance by Santa Anna, who attempts to cut American supply line by besieging garrison at Puebla, fails when siege is raised by U.S. reinforcements. Santa Anna, having resigned the presidency and been dismissed as head of the army, flees. **Nov. 22.** New Mexican government proposes reopening of peace negotiations with Trist, who decides to ignore order of November 16 for his recall. **Dec. 4.** Trist consents to Mexican offer of negotiations.

Irish immigration of 105,500 is triple that of previous year because of potato famine of 1846. All-time peak year is 1851, when 221,200 arrive. Emigrants, who have arrived in substantial numbers since 1820, are mostly employed in canal and railroad construction.

Cyrus Hall McCormick begins manufacture of his reaper in Chicago factory after small-scale production in Virginia and elsewhere. Reaper revolutionizes not only U.S. but also European agriculture in following years.

Matthew Fontaine Maury, who has been appointed Superintendent of Depot of Charts and Instruments (later U.S. Naval Observatory and Hydrographical Office) in 1842, begins compiling his *Wind and Current Chart of the North Atlantic* that by 1855 materially reduces time of ocean travel.

Henry Wadsworth Longfellow's first long narrative poem, *Evangeline,* is published; it is a tragedy based on the 1755 exile of settlers from Acadia (Nova Scotia).

Ralph Waldo Emerson, essayist, publishes his first book of poems, including "Threnody," "Brahma," and "Concord Hymn"; *Poems* is dated 1847, but actually published in time for Christmas 1846.

Herman Melville's *Omoo,* novel based on his sea voyage to Tahiti, although largely comedy, contains opinions on the hypocrisy of missionaries and their degradation of native peoples that enrage reviewers when it is published.

Chicago Daily Tribune is founded; after struggle for existence, it is taken over by Joseph Medill and his partners in 1874.

1848

Jan. 24. James W. Marshall, a mechanic employed by John A. Sutter to supervise building of a sawmill on the American River, discovers a gold nugget in the millrace on Sutter's property in the Sacramento Valley, California. **Dec. 5.** News, which has already spread locally, becomes national when President Polk announces gold discovery in annual message. Gold Rush that results brings 80,000 miners to California during 1849, about one quarter of them from foreign countries.

Need for territorial government for Oregon again raises issue of slavery in far Western territories. **Jan.-Aug.** Long debate covers extension of the principles of the Northwest Ordinance of 1787, which prohibited slavery in territories north of the Ohio River or extension of Missouri Compromise line of 1820 (latitude 36°30′) to the Pacific. Provisional Oregon law excludes slavery; Mexican laws have forbidden slavery in California and New Mexico regions. Various proposals covering all these points pass one house or the other of Congress. **June 27.** Calhoun objects that Mexican laws have been superseded, and that constitutional right to own slaves cannot be altered by Congress or territorial governments. **Aug. 13.** Oregon Bill is finally passed; it retains prohibition of slavery in Oregon, but leaves other questions unresolved. **Aug. 14.** President Polk signs bill despite Calhoun's plea for a veto.

Feb. 2. Negotiations between Nicholas Trist and the Mexican government, though unauthorized because of previous order for Trist's recall, result in signing of Treaty of Guadalupe Hidalgo that ends Mexican War. By its terms an area that encompasses present-day California, Nevada, Utah, western Colorado, western New Mexico, and most of Arizona, together with Texas (as of 1848), is relinquished to the U.S. by Mexico for the sum of $15 million and U.S. payment of its citizens' claims of $3,250,000. The southwest Texas border is fixed at the Rio Grande.

Feb. 23. President Polk submits treaty to Senate, though hesitantly because Trist lacked authority to negotiate it. **March 10.** Senate ratifies treaty 38 to 14; opponents are expansionists who want the annexation of all of Mexico. A proposal to append the Wilmot Proviso is defeated 38 to 15. **May 25.** Mexican congress ratifies, and treaty is declared in effect on July 4.

May 22-26. Slavery issue is brought into election campaign of 1848 when two separate New York delegations, the "Barnburners" (antislavery, anti-Polk, and pro-Wilmot Proviso) and the "Hunkers" (party regulars pledged to support the party candidate), arrive at Democratic National Convention in Baltimore. Neither delegation is seated by the convention, which nominates General Lewis Cass of Michigan for President, Polk having refused a second term. General William O. Butler is nominated for Vice-President. Cass is an advocate of "squatter sovereignty" (local right to allow or prohibit slavery), but Democratic platform fails to include this principle; it denies the power of Congress to interfere with slavery in the states, and is silent on slavery in the territories.

May 29. Wisconsin, which as a territory has included a third of present-day Minnesota, is admitted to the Union as thirtieth state and fifteenth free state, restoring balance of slave and free states. Population is about 150,000.

May. Six New York City newspapers join to pay costs of relaying by telegraph foreign news from Boston, where transatlantic ships make first stop. Association eventually becomes the Associated Press, largest and oldest of U.S. agencies.

June 7. At Whig National Convention in Philadelphia, Whigs reject Henry Clay, nominate General Zachary Taylor for President and Millard Fillmore of New York for

Vice-President despite opposition of New England states and Ohio. Convention defeats attempt to affirm right of Congress to control slavery in the territories, confines Whig platform to a recitation of Taylor's military accomplishments.

June 22. New York Barnburners hold their own convention in Utica, New York, where they nominate Martin Van Buren for President. **Aug. 9.** Barnburners combine with other antislavery Democrats, Liberty Party adherents, and New England "Conscience Whigs," who are opposed to slavery, to form the Free-Soil Party at a national convention in Buffalo. Composed of delegates from 17 states, including 3 slave states (Maryland, Virginia, and Delaware), the Free-Soil Convention again chooses Van Buren for President and nominates Charles Francis Adams, son of John Quincy Adams of Massachusetts, for Vice-President. Antislavery platform supports Wilmot Proviso and free land for settlers; party adopts slogan "free soil, free speech, free labor, and free men."

July 19-20. Women's Rights Convention held in Wesleyan Methodist Church at Seneca Falls, New York, inaugurates modern feminist movement with resolutions on women's rights prepared under the leadership of Lucretia Mott and Elizabeth Cady Stanton.

Aug. 2. American forces evacuate Mexico. American casualties total 13,000 dead (11,000 from disease) and 4,000 wounded. Military and naval costs have been almost $100 million. Among young officers who have gained valuable experience are Lieutenants William T. Sherman, Ulysses S. Grant, John B. Sedgwick, George B. McClellan, Thomas J. Jackson, Pierre Beauregard, and Captain Robert E. Lee; except for Lee, they are all from 22 to 30 years old.

Although Oregon boundaries had been settled by treaty of 1846 with British, Congress fails to consider Oregon's requests for territorial organization until the massacre by Indians of Marcus Whitman and 13 members of his mission. **August.** Bill to organize Oregon Territory is finally signed by President Polk.

Nov. 7. Taylor is elected twelfth President of the U.S. with vote of 1,361,000 to 1,222,000 for Cass. Each candidate carries 15 states, with 8 slave and 7 free states for Taylor and 8 free and 7 slave for Cass. Van Buren, with 291,000 Free-Soil votes, carries no states, but prevents New York from going Democratic by outpolling Cass there, which gives New York with its decisive 36 electoral votes to Taylor. Total electoral vote for Taylor and Fillmore is 163; Cass and Butler receive 127.

Rabbi Isaac Mayer Wise, having emigrated from Bohemia two years earlier, writes at the age of 29 years his "To the Ministers and Other Israelites," a document that outlines his planned program for the next 25 years. Wise advocates a reform of Judaism, plans union of Jewish congregations throughout the U.S., and founds Hebrew Union College in 1875.

James Russell Lowell publishes first series of his *Biglow Papers* in book form; they satirize the Mexican War as an effort to extend slavery. He also publishes *The Vision of Sir Launfal* and his witty *Fable for Critics,* which urges Americans to forget European writers and appreciate their own.

1848 - 1854

European revolutions of 1848 increase immigration, notably of Germans, to the U.S. German communities are established in New York, Baltimore, Cincinnati, St. Louis, and especially Milwaukee, which becomes virtually a German city. Peak years are 1852 to 1854, when 357,000 Germans arrive. The German migration includes large numbers of well-educated liberals and many professional men.

1848 - 1862

"Oh! Susanna" by Stephen Foster is published and becomes popular in Gold Rush. Engaged to write songs for Christy's Minstrels, he writes over the next 15 years "Camptown Races," "Old Folks at Home" (also known as "Swanee River" and originally signed E. P. Christy), "Massa's in de Cold, Cold Ground," "My Old Kentucky Home," "Old Dog Tray," "Jeanie with the Light Brown Hair," "Old Black Joe," and "Beautiful Dreamer." Although most of Foster's songs are associated with the South, he visits the South only once, in 1852.

1849

Jan. 22. Sixty-nine Southern congressmen, having met on December 22, 1848, and again with a dozen more in January 1849, to consider ways of preventing legislation prohibiting slavery in the District of Columbia, present "Address" written by Calhoun listing Southern grievances against the North, but party discipline prevails over sectional alliances when Whig opposition induces all but two Southern Whigs to refuse their signatures.

March 3. Minnesota Territory is established by Congress. Population, which skyrockets within next 10 years, is about 4,000. At various times, parts of Minnesota have belonged to the territories of Wisconsin, Missouri, Iowa, Michigan, Indiana and Louisiana.

March 3. Department of the Interior (originally called Home Department) is created as sixth Cabinet post; it combines several departments, including Office of the Census, Office of Indian Affairs, General Land Office, and Pensions Office.

May 10. Astor Place riot in New York City takes place when partisans of American actor Edwin Forrest resent appearance of his competitor, British actor William Charles Macready, and angry mob stones Astor Place Opera House. When, in desperation, militia is called out, attacked by mob, and finally ordered to fire, 22 are killed and 36 injured.

Difficulty of resolving slavery question continues to prevent organization of New Mexico and California, with California particularly in need of a territorial government to control the waves of arriving goldseekers. **Sept. 1 - Oct. 13.** At Monterey convention, California decides to wait no longer for a congressional decision and adopts a constitution that prohibits slavery. **Dec. 4.** President Taylor, in his annual message, recommends that Congress admit California on that basis, but Southern senators and representatives declare their opposition, since with 15 free and 15 slave states the admission of California will tip the balance against the South.

Dec. 3. New House of Representatives has slight Democratic majority, with 13 Free-Soil representatives holding balance of power. Deepening sectional conflict, foreshadowing doom of the split Whig Party, is indicated by bitter struggle to elect a speaker of the House. Southern Whigs oppose Whig candidate Robert C. Winthrop of Massachusetts because Northern Whigs have refused to declare themselves against the Wilmot Proviso; but Free-Soilers are equally strong against him because as speaker of previous House he has not given antislavery factions sufficient recognition. **Dec. 22.** After 63 ballots, Howell Cobb of Georgia is elected speaker, following a three-week debate in which disunion is frequently threatened.

Pacific Railroad Company (later the Missouri Pacific Railroad) chartered; built during 1851 to 1856 from St. Louis to Kansas City, it becomes the first railroad west of the Mississippi River.

To satisfy a $15 debt owed to J. R. Chapin, Walter Hunt of New York spends three hours bending wire into various forms and designs first modern safety pin. He sells rights to it to Chapin for $400.

Elizabeth Blackwell receives her medical degree from medical school in Geneva, New York; she is first woman in the world to receive an M.D.

Henry David Thoreau, unable to find a publisher for his book of comments on life and literature, *A Week on the Concord and Merrimack Rivers,* publishes it at his own expense; it sells only 200 copies. Thoreau's essay, "Resistance to Civil Government" (later called "Civil Disobedience"), appears in *Aesthetic Papers;* it tells of his jailing for refusing to pay poll tax as a protest against slavery and the Mexican War.

Poems "Annabel Lee," "The Bells," and "Eldorado" by Edgar Allan Poe are published, "The Bells" a month after his death on October 7.

Roads, Canals, and Railroads

The movement of population across the continent after the Revolution necessitated effective surface transportation, in part to facilitate travel, but especially to haul freight. The development of the United States into a commercial-industrial nation prompted the growth of a transportation network unequalled anywhere in the world. Most public works such as canals and roads were undertaken by private companies or local governments. In the 19th century only the Cumberland Road was constructed by the national government. Not until the heavy increase in automotive traffic in the 20th century did the federal government undertake a program of highway construction. Ninety percent of the cost of the interstate highway system projected for 1975 would be paid for by federal funds.

The geography of the area between the Atlantic Coast and the Mississippi River made the use of natural inland waterways and canals ideal for transporting larger amounts of freight than could be hauled by road. By 1860 more than 3,000 miles of canals had been constructed, of which the most famous was the Erie, which is still in use in New York. The most ambitious and recent addition to the inland waterway system is the St. Lawrence Seaway. Opened in 1959, it made the Great Lakes port cities accessible to ocean-going vessels from all nations.

Canal-building was hardly under way when the railroad came on the scene. Between 1830 and 1865 more than 30,000 miles of track were laid, and in the decades following the Civil War railroad networks covered the United States and became the leading means of surface transportation. The railroads still maintain the advantage of being able to haul greater amounts of freight than any competing form of transportation, while individual travel becomes more and more the province of the airlines and of automobiles.

Maps prepared by Uni-Map Inc., Palatine, Ill.
for Encyclopaedia Britannica, Inc.

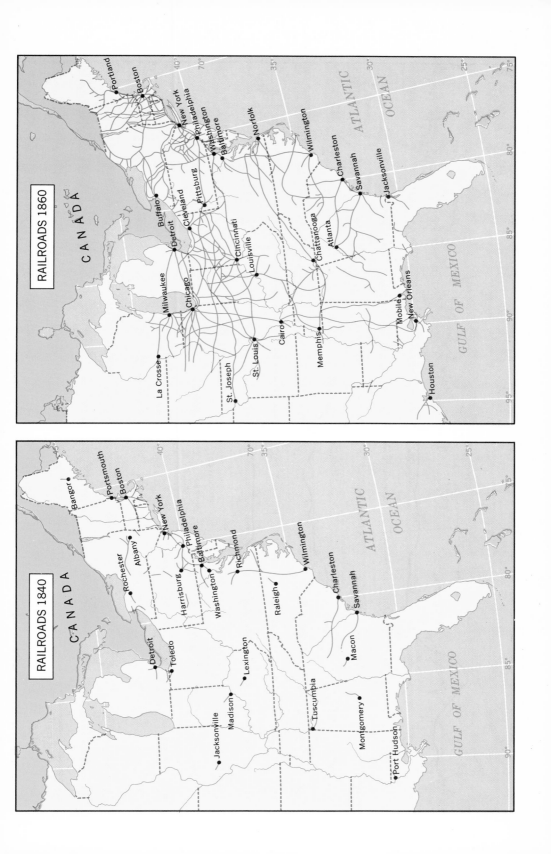

RAILROADS 1840

CANADA

Bangor
Portsmouth
Boston
New York
Philadelphia
Baltimore
Harrisburg
Washington
Rochester
Albany
Detroit
Toledo
Lexington
Madison
Jacksonville
Richmond
Raleigh
Wilmington
Charleston
Savannah
Macon
Tuscumbia
Montgomery
Port Hudson

ATLANTIC OCEAN

GULF OF MEXICO

RAILROADS 1860

CANADA

Portland
Boston
New York
Philadelphia
Washington
Baltimore
Norfolk
Wilmington
Charleston
Savannah
Jacksonville
Buffalo
Cleveland
Pittsburg
Detroit
Cincinnati
Louisville
Chattanooga
Atlanta
Milwaukee
Chicago
La Crosse
St. Joseph
St. Louis
Cairo
Memphis
Mobile
New Orleans
Houston

ATLANTIC OCEAN

GULF OF MEXICO

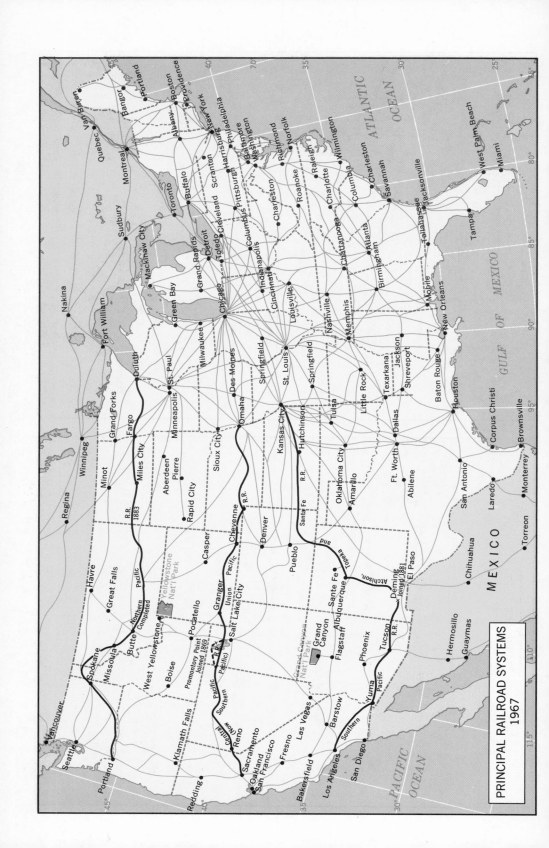

PRINCIPAL RAILROAD SYSTEMS
1967

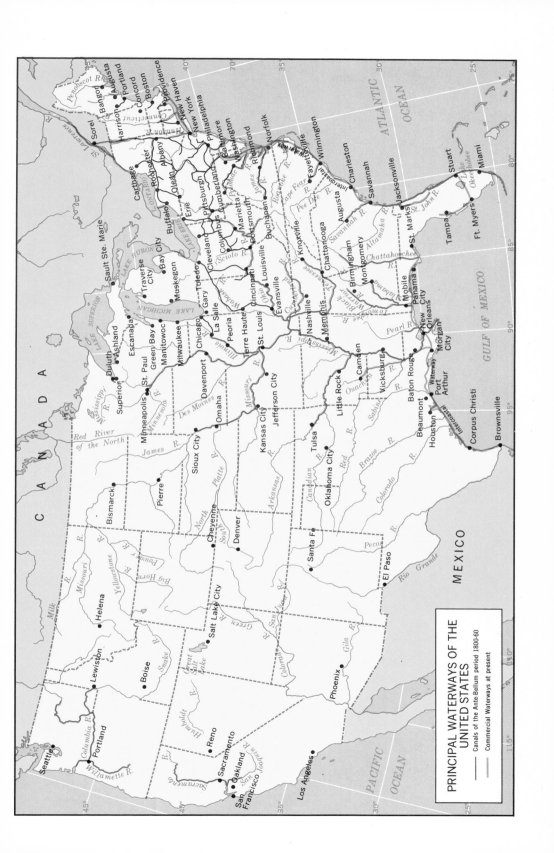

PRINCIPAL WATERWAYS OF THE
UNITED STATES

—— Canals of the Ante-Bellum period 1800-60

—— Commercial Waterways at present

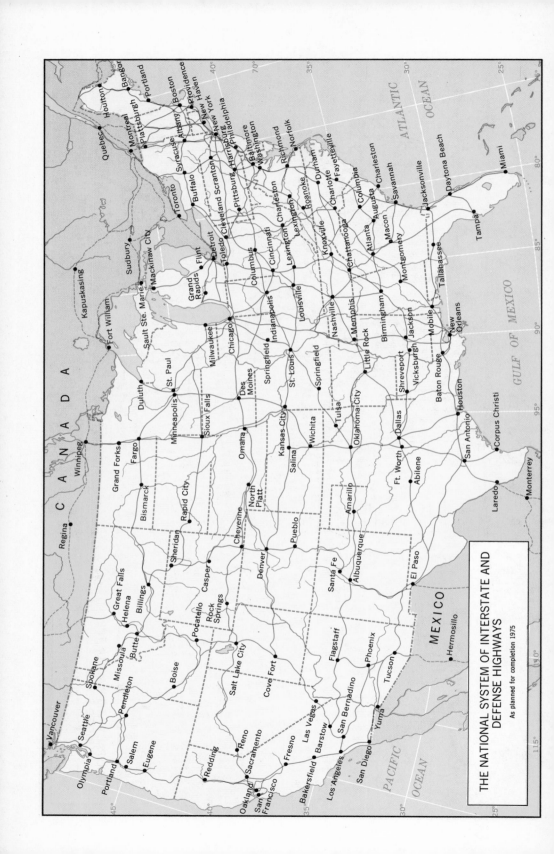

THE NATIONAL SYSTEM OF INTERSTATE AND
DEFENSE HIGHWAYS

As planned for completion 1975

1841

1.

WILLIAM H. SEWARD: Uprooting the Indians

Despite the Indian removal policies of the Jackson administration, a few tribes of the Iroquois League were left to dwell on reservations in New York State. In January 1838 a treaty was made with the Senecas, by the terms of which they were to be removed from their lands. The treaty was revised in April 1840, but not in favor of the Indians, most of whom neither desired to move nor consented to the treaty. Some white men felt that the Indians had been tricked into signing treaties whose provisions were unclear. In the following letter, written June 15, 1841, William H. Seward, governor of New York, discussed both the injustice to the Six Nations and his hope that the government would reconsider its treaties. In 1842 a new treaty was signed allowing these Indians who did not choose to leave to remain on their reservations.

Source: *The Works of William H. Seward*, George E. Baker, ed., New edition, Vol. III, Boston, 1887, pp. 484-487.

YOU ASK MY OPINION concerning the treaty which has been made by the United States with the Seneca Indians; and you observe that it is important for those Indians to show that their removal is against the decided wishes of fifteen-sixteenths of the nation, and that it is not called for by the executive of this state, by the legislature, or by the well-disposed and humane people of the western counties.

The history of the several nations which have dwelt within our borders shows many coincidents of painful interest. Each nation has in its turn been surrounded and crowded by white men. White men have always wanted more room while an Indian reservation remained; and the Indians have, therefore, been obliged to contract their hunting grounds. Indians have been ignorant and confiding, and white men shrewd and sagacious. Indians have been reckless of the value of property and have always found avaricious white men among their neighbors. White men have sold intoxicating liquors, and Indians have too often surrendered themselves to drunkenness. Indians have generally neglected, if they have not despised, agriculture, and white men have suffered inconvenience from the neglected condition of the Indian lands. White men have coveted those neglected lands, and the community has been benefited in consequence of their acquisition.

The effect is that we have now among us only some wasting remnants of half a dozen of the Indian nations. Yet each of these nations, for a time, resisted propositions for their removal strenuously and with apparent unanimity. Each has, in its turn, divided upon the question of removal. The weak and improvident have been wrought upon to increase the numbers of those disposed to sell their lands, while philanthropic efforts have not been wanting to fortify the domestic party in their resistance.

I do not know that the disproportion of the two parties among the Senecas is so great as you have stated. I must refer you on that head to other persons for information. Neither should I speak candidly if I said that the people of the western counties did not desire such a change in the condition of the Senecas as would bring their lands into cultivation, and render them tributary to the aggregate wealth and general improvement of the state. Such, I must add, is my own wish. The legislature has not spoken on the subject, but its concurrence in the same view might be inferred from the general policy which the state has pursued.

Nevertheless, there is nothing which would be more gratifying to the people of this state, and certainly there is, on my part, no desire affecting the Indians more sincere, than to see the remnants of the Indian tribes forsake entirely the manners and customs of their forefathers and adopt those of civilized life. The signal disappointment of such philanthropic hopes in regard to the other tribes of Indians has produced a great distrust of any better fate for the Senecas, while the contiguity of that people to a great city exposes them in an especial degree to the frauds and introduces among them the vices of depraved men of our own race. Very many who entertain this distrust and deplore the wretchedness and degradation of a portion of the Senecas are of opinion that it would be wise and prudent for them to relinquish their lands at a fair valuation, and seek a new home in the far West.

But no humane or enlightened citizen can wish to see the expulsion of the Senecas by force or fraud. It is a fearful thing to uproot a whole people and send them, regardless of their own rights, interests, and welfare, their feelings and affections, into a distant and desolate region. It is peculiarly so when a large portion, relying upon the protection of the laws and the justice of their white brethren, have become cultivators of the soil, and of the affections and habits of civilized life. Such is the condition of a large portion of the Senecas.

Injustice to the Indians is repugnant alike to the settled policy of this state, and the feelings and sentiments of its people. This state has endeavored steadily to pursue a benign policy toward them. We have suffered every tribe to remain unmolested and have ever discouraged the desire of small factions among them to effect the sale of their lands without the general consent of the tribe. We have left the Indians to debate and consider the subject without our interference. When a portion of a tribe have made arrangements to purchase lands elsewhere, and obtained the consent of the whole nation to a partition, we have bought that portion of the lands equitably belonging to those who had determined to emigrate, requiring, in all cases, the consent of the whole tribe to such partial sales.

During the last few years the state, instead of purchasing for its own advantage, has taken the title of the Indians, sold the lands as their trustee, and accounted to them for the whole proceeds of the subsequent sales in fee to actual settlers. We have paid interest upon the purchase moneys to the emigrating Indians in their new settlements, and have paid them the principal when they have provided a proper and safe investment. At the same time we have endeavored, through the agency of peacemakers and superintendents, to exercise a guardian care over those who preferred to remain among us.

No bribe, gratuity, or other improper appliance has been used, or with knowledge permitted, by the state, to obtain a relinquishment of Indian lands. We take, in all cases, a census of the tribe and of each family. We regard all their members with perfect equality. And we take care that the moneys paid to the nation are fairly and justly distributed among them.

Such is the course which it may be assumed the people of this state would desire to see prevail in regard to the Senecas. In this way we might hope to accomplish, if it be at all practicable, the civilization of a remnant of the Six Nations, once the proprietors of more than half the state. On the other hand, if the humane experiment must fail, we should enjoy, under such circumstances, the consoling reflection that the ef-

fort had failed because a higher than any human power had forbidden its success.

But, my dear sir, I cannot hesitate to declare my full conviction, derived from history now open to the world, that the treaty which has been made by the United States with the Senecas was made in open violation of the policy I have described. I am fully satisfied that the consent of the Senecas was obtained by fraud, corruption, and violence, and that it is therefore false, and ought to be held void. The removal of the Indians would, under such circumstances, be a great crime against an unoffending and injured people; and I earnestly hope that, before any further proceedings are taken to accomplish that object, the whole subject may be reconsidered by the United States.

2.

HANS BRANDT: Poor Prospects for Immigrants to America

Dr. Hans Brandt was not an average immigrant. He was a well-educated physician who came to serve his fellow Norwegians in the Midwest. His letter to friends back in Norway must be read against the background of the early Scandinavian immigration, when those who came had the difficult task of settling in a new land without fellow countrymen to ease the way for them. In an unpublished portion of the following letter Brandt criticizes much in American life: corrupt politics, materialism, lack of educational opportunities, and medical quackery. But his general advice as to who should emigrate is much the same as that sent to prospective immigrants even in colonial times.

Source: Blegen, pp. 79-83.

ON MAY 18, 1840, I EMBARKED in Hamburg to go to New York, where I arrived after a voyage of sixty-seven days. The crossing was difficult and unpleasant. The excessive gaiety of my fellow passengers . . . was not calculated to put me in a good mood, for I was constantly musing on what the future might bring. The conceptions my fellow travelers had formed about America surprised me not a little, as they

revealed a great deal of ignorance of the states to which they were going. It seemed to them that America had been discovered very recently: Columbus was still on St. Salvador, Cortés in Mexico, and so on.

The object of their journey was to get gold and silver, and they were always talking about this. They seemed to be under the impression that New York's roofs, streets, and alleys were covered with these precious and rare metals, and that they were even easily accessible in the rivers. The thing was simply to reach America. With bagsful of pure gold they would then return and in the Old World spend what the New World had so generously given them. They were artisans and mechanics and had just enough money to pay their passage across the ocean.

But soon, of course, they were disillusioned. Shortly after their arrival in New York, they met some of their countrymen whose truthful accounts completely destroyed their beautiful castles in the air. Hardly one of them got a job as a skilled worker in his occupation; and most of them had to get work at canal digging, the coal mines, the railroad, and so on.

Everything is here as it is in Europe, only with somewhat greater activity. In New York there are a great many foreigners, and many an educated youth of considerable promise there associates with drunkards and good-for-nothings. The prospects seemed somewhat dubious to me, but I was encouraged by an acquaintance I had made during the voyage. I had become the friend of Baron Mattilz, who had left his native country because of his republican views.

I spent twenty-five days with him in New York, and it was only chance that I did not make my home in this wonderful city. Mattilz had offered me a loan sufficient to establish a dispensary, which is almost a requisite for the practice of medicine. But first I had to learn the English language, and the time that was required for this I was to spend with Mattilz. In the meantime, Anchersen arrived with some Norwegian immigrants, among whom were farmer Heg and his brother-in-law from Lier. They asked me to go with them, for I might be of use to them as I knew German, and the area they were to travel through was full of Germans.

I accepted their offer and we went up the Hudson River, through a canal 300 miles long, and via lakes Ontario, Huron, and Michigan to Milwaukee, a city of 1,800 inhabitants in Wisconsin territory. On this trip I was lawyer, doctor, minister, mediator, everything. A child that was born on the Atlantic was overlain, and I had to function at the burial ceremony. Some of our travelers spent a great many "two-skillings" and other Norwegian coins as current money; they were arrested by the police, and I had to be mediator, interpreter, and lawyer, and was successful in my pleading on their behalf. A woman fell ill in Milwaukee and gave birth to a child in a cool night, out in the open; and here, too, I had to function as doctor, police officer, and clergyman, this last at the baptizing of the child.

Twenty miles from Milwaukee there is a Norwegian colony consisting of about twelve families from Numedal, Telemark, and Stavanger. They arrived in the autumn of 1839, bought land at once, and built good Norwegian timber houses. In the same place, Bache, Johansen, and Heg have settled and bought a considerable amount of land. It is all wooded, high, and with very good soil. The colonists that have settled here are satisfied and live a quiet, happy life in good understanding with one another. Farther up in Wisconsin there is another colony of immigrants from the autumn of 1839. I did not go there, but it is said that they do not get along too well.

After a stay of a day and a half among these Norwegian farmers, I took a small traveling bag on my back and set out on foot toward the Norwegian colony in Illinois, 150 miles away. On this trip I had to walk through uncleared forests and prairies at first, at times for seven or eight hours without seeing a single human being or a house. Finally, I found the main road and then everything was fine. I had seen little illness in Wisconsin, but as soon as I entered Illinois it was common; in almost every house people were suffering from the ague.

The Norwegian colony in Illinois, which

consists of some thirty or forty families, is located 150 miles southwest of Chicago, between the cities of Ottawa and Charleston, 14 miles from the Illinois River. A vast prairie here is crossed by the main roads from St. Louis and other cities, and there are Norwegians living on all the various roads. The settlers include earlier as well as more recent immigrants. They all have a good deal of land, some 200 or 300 acres, with horses, cows, and so on. They live well. For the most part they are ignorant, as unfamiliar with the institutions of their native country as with those of the United States, indifferent to the common good, and sometimes quarrelsome among themselves.

Religion means nothing to them whatsoever; they have abandoned its principles completely, and they even leave their children unbaptized and bring them up in deep ignorance. To make a living here as a clergyman would be out of the question. A couple of so-called holy men from Stavanger preach and interpret the Bible, but they do not have much of a following, for people know that they are undependable. For four months I practised as a doctor among these people, but I should have starved to death if I had stayed there, since they would not even pay for the medicine.

At Beaver Creek there is not one Norwegian left. Ole Rynning was practically the last one. He made many sacrifices for the Norwegians, paid the passages of several of them, and helped them in everything; and when he himself became destitute, he worked with all his might to get on his feet again. One month he worked at the canal, digging, which contributed considerably to the undermining of his health. In the middle of the winter he once walked over a prairie almost barefooted. He was close to his home but could not reach it without help. He was almost frozen to death when people found him and brought him home. He was then attacked by the ague and later by typhoid fever, which ended his life. Those who owed him money denied it after his death and his belongings were sold at a ridiculously low price.

This is the way the Norwegian farmers honor the memory of the man to whom they owe so much, the man who made so many sacrifices for them! The little book he published was based on the accounts of others rather than on his own experiences; and if he had lived, he would have changed many things in a new edition.

In Missouri there was a Norwegian colony which has now moved to Iowa territory. Here live the immigrants Hans Barlien and Hans Agger, who has married and is a competent quacksalver. I have seen an application from Hans Barlien to the Norwegian king for 100,000 specie dollars as compensation for his ill usage by Norwegian officials. He stayed a long time in St. Louis to devise an improvement in steam engines by which water, gas, and fuel might be saved. But poor Barlien! The engine would not run. . . .

I ADVISE THE STUDENT, whether of law, theology, or medicine, against going to America. I know that Danish, German, and even Norwegian students have had a hard time making a living, and even competent graduates have had to take undignified jobs as bartenders. Offices are crowded, and clerks are found in abundance. There are also many artisans, but perhaps tanners, shoemakers, tailors, or carpenters might find it easier to make a living here than in Norway, especially in the Western states. The seaport towns and the larger cities are everywhere so crowded that workers and artisans are often unemployed. . . .

The only one I advise to come here is the farmer, although not the one who is wealthy and making a good living in his native country, for he will have too great difficulties and wish that he were back home again. Everything goes against him: language difficulties bother him, he gets into wild forests or vast prairies where he often has three to seven miles to his nearest neighbor. There is no church, no divine service, no friends or acquaintances; in short, everything is unfamiliar. To hire laborers to work on the farm is very expensive, and because of this and the low prices on grain, it is often difficult to make a profit on the large farms. Besides, the well-to-do foreigner is in grave danger of being exploited in some way. I know many people who have come over here with capital and have suffered considerable losses, while those who had nothing have learned to work ahead to success through adversity and tribulations. This is true of the Norwegian farmers; several of those who had capital have suffered setbacks; others, on the other hand, who had nothing, now own homesteads.

Thus I advise only those to come here who have the funds necessary to pay for their passage and to buy forty acres of land, though twelve acres may be enough for a family, as the land is fertile. I advise people to select places that are elevated, half prairie and half forest. I prefer Wisconsin to Illinois; it is higher, has fewer swamps, is more healthful and on the whole more fertile. Besides, the water is bad in Illinois but good in Wisconsin, and the best areas in Illinois have been bought up by speculators.

3.

Public Lands and Squatters' Rights

The Pre-emption Act of September 4, 1841, part of which follows, was introduced by Senator Thomas Hart Benton of Missouri in December 1840. Before this time any settler who had cleared and improved a portion of public land could find that his effort had been in vain when the land was put up for sale at a public auction and someone outbid him. The Pre-emption Act of 1841 was unique in that it projected the right to claim land into the future. Any squatter who made limited improvements was guaranteed the right to buy as many as 160 acres by staking out a prior claim before they were put up for auction.

Source: *Statutes*, V, pp. 453-458.

An Act to appropriate the proceeds of the sales of the public lands, and to grant pre-emption rights. . . .

Section 8. *And be it further enacted,* that there shall be granted to each state specified in the 1st Section of this act 500,000 acres of land for purposes of internal improvement: *Provided,* that to each of the said states which has already received grants for said purposes, there is hereby granted no more than a quantity of land which shall, together with the amount such state has already received as aforesaid, make 500,000 acres, the selections in all of the said states to be made within their limits respectively in such manner as the legislatures thereof shall direct; and located in parcels conformably to sectional divisions and subdivisions of not less than 320 acres in any one location, on any public land except such as is or may be reserved from sale by any law of Congress or proclamation of the President of the United States, which said locations may be made at any time after the lands of the United States in said states respectively shall have been surveyed according to existing laws.

And there shall be and hereby is granted

to each new state that shall be hereafter admitted into the Union, upon such admission, so much land as, including such quantity as may have been granted to such state before its admission, and while under a territorial government, for purposes of internal improvement as aforesaid, as shall make 500,000 acres of land, to be selected and located as aforesaid.

Section 9. *And be it further enacted,* that the lands herein granted to the states above named shall not be disposed of at a price less than $1.25 per acre, until otherwise authorized by a law of the United States; and the net proceeds of the sales of said lands shall be faithfully applied to objects of internal improvement within the states aforesaid, respectively, namely: roads, railways, bridges, canals and improvement of watercourses, and draining of swamps; and such roads, railways, canals, bridges and watercourses, when made or improved, shall be free for the transportation of the United States mail, and munitions of war, and for the passage of their troops, without the payment of any toll whatever.

Section 10. *And be it further enacted,* that from and after the passage of this act, every person being the head of a family, or widow, or single man, over the age of twenty-one years, and being a citizen of the United States, or having filed his declaration of intention to become a citizen as required by the naturalization laws, who since the 1st day of June, A.D. 1840, has made or shall hereafter make a settlement in person on the public lands to which the Indian title had been at the time of such settlement extinguished, and which has been, or shall have been, surveyed prior thereto, and who shall inhabit and improve the same, and who has or shall erect a dwelling thereon, shall be, and is hereby, authorized to enter with the register of the Land Office for the district in which such land may lie, by legal subdivisions, any number of acres not exceeding 160, or a quarter section of land, to include the residence of such claimant, upon paying to the United States the minimum price of such land, subject, however, to the following limitations and exceptions:

No person shall be entitled to more than one pre-emptive right by virtue of this act; no person who is the proprietor of 320 acres of land in any state or territory of the United States, and no person who shall quit or abandon his residence on his own land to reside on the public land in the same state or territory, shall acquire any right of pre-emption under this act; no lands included in any reservation, by any treaty, law, or proclamation of the President of the United States, or reserved for salines, or for other purposes; no lands reserved for the support of schools, nor the lands acquired by either of the two last treaties with the Miami tribe of Indians in the state of Indiana, or which may be acquired of the Wyandot tribe of Indians in the state of Ohio, or other Indian reservation to which the title has been or may be extinguished by the United States at any time during the operation of this act; no sections of land reserved to the United States alternate to other sections granted to any of the states for the construction of any canal, railroad, or other public improvement; no sections or fractions of sections included within the limits of any incorporated town; no portions of the public lands which have been selected as the site for a city or town; no parcel or lot of land actually settled and occupied for the purposes of trade and not agriculture; and no lands on which are situated any known salines or mines, shall be liable to enter under and by virtue of the provisions of this act.

And so much of the proviso of the act of 22nd of June, 1838, or any order of the President of the United States as directs certain reservations to be made in favor of certain claims under the treaty of Dancing-rabbit Creek, be, and the same is hereby, repealed: *Provided,* that such repeal shall not affect any title to any tract of land secured in virtue of said treaty.

Section 11. *And be it further enacted,* that when two or more persons shall have settled on the same quarter section of land, the right of pre-emption shall be in him or her who made the first settlement, provided such persons shall conform to the other provisions of this act; and all questions as to the right of pre-emption arising between different settlers shall be settled by the register and receiver of the district within which the land is situated, subject to an appeal to and a revision by the secretary of the treasury of the United States.

Section 12. *And be it further enacted,* that prior to any entries being made under and by virtue of the provisions of this act, proof of the settlement and improvement thereby required shall be made to the satisfaction of the register and receiver of the land district in which such lands may lie. . . .

Section 13. *And be it further enacted,* that before any person claiming the benefit of this act shall be allowed to enter such lands, he or she shall make oath before the receiver or register of the land district in which the land is situated (who are hereby authorized to administer the same) that he or she has never had the benefit of any right of pre-emption under this act; that he or she is not the owner of 320 acres of land in any state or territory of the United States, nor has he or she settled upon and improved said land to sell the same on speculation, but in good faith to appropriate it to his or her own exclusive use or benefit; and that he or she has not, directly or indirectly, made any agreement or contract, in any way or manner, with any person or persons whatsoever, by which the title which he or she might acquire from the government of the United States, should enure in whole or in part, to the benefit of any person except himself or herself.

4.

Gustaf Unonius: Problems of Frontier Land Ownership

In 1841 a Swedish pastor, Gustaf Unonius, led a group of fellow countrymen to Pine Lake, Wisconsin, and there established the first nineteenth-century Swedish colony in the United States. In the following selection from his memoirs, Unonius describes the complexities of establishing land title. Extra-legal organizations, such as the one to which Unonius and his neighbors belonged, were frequently formed in the frontier areas to adjudicate boundary and title disputes and to force those who sought to violate the communal consensus to leave or conform. These organizations were variously called "settlers' clubs" and "claimants' unions."

Source: *A Pioneer in Northwest America 1841-1858, The Memoirs of Gustaf Unonius,* translated by Jonas Oscar Backlund, Nils W. Olsson, ed., Minneapolis, 1950, Vol. I, pp. 152-164, 323-329.

While we were waiting for Lange, Carl and I, guns on our shoulders, had the opportunity to take some excursions around the city of Milwaukee. To be armed with guns to take an excursion within a city sounds perhaps a little strange, but we must remember that Milwaukee, like most American cities, had been laid out on a rather large scale and that most of it was still nothing but an uninhabited wilderness; furthermore, a kind of watery wilderness. . . .

We were shown city lots, that is, puddles of mire or water fifty feet wide and a hundred feet long, offered for sale at from $50 to $200 each. In spite of the great faith we had in the speedy growth and development of American cities, we could not make ourselves believe that purchasing such a lot would not be literally throwing the money into the water or, rather, into the mire. It excited our ridicule and pity to see how some newcomers, whose expectations of the future growth of the city we thought too sanguine, had erected on posts in the swamp itself a sort of small portable wooden shack, connected to firm ground by means of several timbers and boards laid down in the mire, constituting what seemed to us very dangerous bridges to walk on. Time has shown, however, that those newcomers understood better than we the trend of the city's development.

But still one must accept things calmly. Though Providence did not will it that we should grow rich in America, it may nevertheless be pleasant enough to recall that we once just missed being so. An opportunity was really offered us at that time. On the very spot where we shot our ducks in 1841, one of the principal hotels of the city has since been built, and, in the neighborhood, city lots now sell at almost as much for four square yards as we were asked a few years earlier to pay for the entire lot. To be sure, the lots at that time were not firm ground, but a few loads of gravel for filling would not have cost very much.

Milwaukee, however, is not entirely built on a morass. Far from it. On both sides of the river the land rises in terraces from fifty to a hundred feet above the river. Part of the lakefront is steep, in some places almost completely perpendicular. On this height, as well as on the terraces mentioned above, several fine buildings had been erected, offering an excellent view of the river and the semicircular bay, which forms a natural, though rather exposed, harbor and anchorage. The city was platted in 1835, when the first settlers located there. The next year the population increased to 1,200 and has been growing ever since, although not so fast as one might expect considering the excellent location and the fertility of the surrounding country. Since 1841, however, the city has grown considerably and is without question one of the most attractive and well-built cities in the West. . . .

Our friend Lange finally informed us that he was ready to go with us. Early in the morning of Thursday, October 7, we started off on our exploration, duly equipped with guns and hunting bags. Although it was late in the fall and we already had had some nights of frost, the air was mild and summery. For the first ten miles we had to walk through a thick forest, where we saw only a single, little, new-built house, which also served as a kind of inn. The road, which at the time was one of the most frequently traveled in this part of the territory, was in miserable condition. It seemed incredible that anybody could travel over it with a load. Awaiting the laying of a plank road and later the building of railroads in every direction, people paid little attention to road improvements.

It is true that so-called pathmasters are appointed in every township, and everyone living in the township is required to give a certain number of days to road work. But that work is generally limited to chopping down a few trees, building bridges across rivers and creeks, and constructing corduroy bridges over the swampiest places, to make the road somewhere near passable. . . .

Finally, we arrived at the shores of the loveliest little lake we had seen in the course of our walk. In Indian language it was called *Chenequa*, or Pine Lake, since pines, which otherwise do not grow in this part of Wisconsin, are found here along with the red cedar in a couple of places along its shores. Most of these trees have been hewn down, probably by the Indians, who used their easily hollowed-out trunks for canoes. On a small isle we found one of these small boats, left unfinished and partly destroyed by fire.

This spot was one of the prettiest one could ever hope to see. The lake, about two miles long, and branching off into a number of bays and coves, was surrounded almost everywhere by dry, high shores. Only in a couple of places was the ground low and swampy. Close to the lake the ground was somewhat rough, but a short distance away the land was even, and on one side lay a big, perfectly level burr-oak field. Now, we insisted firmly, it was no use to go any farther, especially as the land, in addition to being incredibly beautiful, seemed also to be excellent in every other respect. According to Pearmain's statement, and as far as we ourselves were able to judge, the soil of the burr-oak plain appeared to be of the richest and best quality — a deep black loam with an admixture of clay. In the opening land next to that plain we found the soil to consist of sandy clay, growing stiffer as we approached the shore.

Since we did not want any of the thousands of prospective settlers roaming about the country looking for homesites to get ahead of us, we decided to return to Milwaukee at once and announce at the Land Office that we each wanted to take under preemption a quarter section of land. Pearmain informed us, however, that the section in question, as well as others in the same township, could not be purchased at the Land Office or be occupied under preemption right. The situation was that a company had been organized some years earlier for the purpose of constructing a canal from Milwaukee to the Mississippi. To this company Congress had ceded, on certain conditions, all odd-numbered sections along the proposed canal route, and to such a section the piece of land on which we wanted to settle belonged.

However, a certain time had been set in which the canal was to be completed, and of that time only two or three years still remained. The work, which had hardly been begun, had stopped long ago, and it seemed almost impossible that the company should ever be able to carry out its contract. Hence it was fairly certain that when the time specified in the contract had expired, these canal lands would revert to the United States and be offered for sale in the regular way. Nevertheless, until that time had expired, the land could not be purchased at the Land Office. As far as the canal company was concerned, no one ever bothered to make any payments to it for this land, since it was regarded as certain that the land would revert to the government and then be offered at half the price demanded by the canal company. We might, therefore, take it for granted that we should not have to pay for land thus occupied for a couple of years. Considering our financial status, this was welcome news, although we realized that there would be some uncertainty about our right of ownership, inasmuch as the canal company still had the legal right to sell these sections.

Suppose that we, without regarding the company, were to take possession of a piece of land, cultivate it, and build our home on it as though it were our own, what was to prevent some other person after a few months from purchasing it? In this case, would there be anything for us to do but leave our homestead without even being able to claim remuneration for the work we had put into it? Pearmain maintained, however, that we need not fear this eventuality. Many before us had taken possession of land in just this way. In their right of ownership they were protected by what he termed club law, the law, that is, which the people themselves in remote regions had established because of the peculiar conditions under which they were living. According to this law, Judge Lynch makes all judicial decisions. No one could prevent the canal company from selling the land, but it was quite possible effectively to prevent the land's being sold to anyone but its present occupant, who had spent time and money making it habitable.

All the settlers, whether on land held by Congress or by the canal company, had made a compact to stand by and protect one another against such trespassing. And woe betide anyone who sought to appropriate another man's land! He would do well before taking possession of his purchased ground to obtain the highest possible insurance on his house and life; otherwise neither would be worth much. I know of only one instance where such a thing was attempted. . . .

There may be divergent views on such a law of terror, but there is much that may be said in its defense. Nobody was the loser by it. Not the government, for when the privilege of the canal company expired, the land would have to be paid for, and then club law would not protect the settler from having to do his duty. Nor was the canal company the loser, for it had to all practical intents and purposes already lost its rights and would be compelled, when it found itself unable to carry out its agreements, to return to the government the property tentatively given to it. On the other hand, the rights of the poor settler were protected. He was saved from having to pay double the price of other land without getting any additional privileges. At the same time the community profited, for in this way the land was settled and tilled earlier than otherwise would have been the case.

Inasmuch as others did not fear to settle on this kind of land, we thought we might risk it, all the more because in this way we might count on two or three years of suspended payment, in our circumstances a great privilege. Our capital had been melting away so fast that the combined cash supply of Carl and me was reduced to about $400. From this amount we still had to purchase land, build our home, buy at least one team of oxen, a cow, a few pigs, and some essential household articles. In addition, we had to provide food for at least

the first winter. How this small amount was to see us through was hard for us or anybody else to see. Here there was no opportunity to borrow money. Notwithstanding all this, we were of good courage, though I cannot deny that with my poetic dreams of a "cottage and a hearth" were mingled in realistic moments some very doubtful intermezzos.

Under these conditions we were happy indeed to cross off from our calculation, at least for the time being, the $200 — exactly one-half of our present cash — that we had hitherto expected to pay for a quarter section of congressional land. For though we had planned to use our preemption rights, these would not have allowed us more than a year to pay, and it was not likely that we should find it any easier in twelve months than now. On the other hand, we might well hope to have improved our finances enough in two or three years to be able to pay for our land. We had at least during this time some harvests to expect, which naturally we could not look for the first year.

Without long deliberation, we decided, therefore, to settle on the shore of the little lake, where both the natural beauty and the good soil promised us a pleasant home, and where, among oak, beech, and hickory trees, the evergreen pines, untouched by the axe, would always stand as a pleasant reminder of the pine forest of our old homeland. We needed to take no steps to insure our claim except to inform our neighbors that we were planning to make our home here, and as a sign of our intention, start some improvement to indicate that this part of the section had been occupied. Pearmain, as an experienced settler prepared for any eventualities, had brought his axe. As Columbus on first landing in the New World had raised the Castilian flag inscribed with *F & I*, the initials of his sovereigns, so we chopped down a few trees, and into the bark of a couple of others cut a big *C*, signifying "Claimed," a sign that we in our

Rev. Gustaf Unonius

own name had taken possession of the W½ of Section 33, Township 8, Range 18, *in hac altera mundi parte* [in this other part of the world], with full and complete legal right of possession, to be inhabited, settled, and held by us and our descendants forever. . . .

Up to this time we had taken no part in current political activities, which nevertheless were discussed with the same earnestness at meetings in the small schoolhouses here as ever in Faneuil Hall in Boston or in a great public hall in New York. Often we had found notices nailed to some tree close to the public road announcing such meetings, and had had private invitations to attend them, especially from zealous partisans of the Democratic Party apparently eager to convert us to their political faith. Notwithstanding these solicitations, we had not as yet even applied for United States citizenship. This would not have prevented us, though, from taking part in various communal affairs and from voting in the local elections. But we did not consider ourselves well-enough informed in these matters to be willing to take active part in them. Who were to become justices of the peace, road inspectors, constables, tax collectors, and so forth, did not much concern us. We were protected as to person and property and felt fully satisfied with our government, or, rather, we hardly noticed that we had any.

Foreigners are generally inclined to engage in political disputes long before they know what things are all about, and the rashness with which they make use of a citizenship they have gained all too soon is without question harmful to the country. The American republic will no doubt sooner or later find it necessary to change its naturalization laws. The Germans and especially the Irish have hardly had time to get a roof over their heads before they begin to busy themselves with political affairs of all kinds, become eager partisans, get their hands into everything, and cause no end of trouble and disorder — all of which could be avoided if Americans were left to govern the country alone.

Accustomed perhaps to being of little or no importance before, in a more liberal social order they feel all-important, and the spirit of opposition that led them to political radicalism at home now induces them to oppose almost everything proposed by sane and wise Americans for the good of the country. Many a time I have heard Germans who hardly understood the simplest English sentences say, "We are not going to let the Americans rule over us." Their false conception of liberty and citizenship and that of the Irish gave me an absolute distaste for all politics, and neither then nor later did I meddle with it except in questions where my duty bade me appear quietly and calmly at the ballot box.

I love the democratic social order where the majesty of the people really is a majesty before which a man can stand with the same veneration, yes, with even more, than before a royal throne; and I believe that the American people, left to themselves, will one day reveal that majesty to the world. But when one sees European immigrants assume the democratic toga, which on their shoulders easily becomes the fool's motley; when one hears them speak of freedom and with an air of authority pronounce judgment on the most weighty social questions, of which they have not the least comprehension, being mere tools in the hands of selfish partisans, then one can hardly help smiling at the thought of the kind of republic most European countries would be blessed with were these modern apostles of freedom to have their way. A popular government in Europe would undoubtedly prove very different from what it is in America. Whereas the latter is developing more and more an innate power to construct and build, the former — to judge by signs here — would be excellent in tearing down and destroying things and in fighting the opposition but altogether useless, yes, even dangerous, when it was a question of construction.

As for my application for naturalization, I delayed a long time, I hardly know why. I had no thought then of returning to my native country, but with all my well-known radicalism when I was there, and with all my notions of liberty, I was still haunted by the oath of allegiance which once as a Swedish citizen I had given the ruler of Sweden, and it went a little against my feelings to file my application to become a naturalized citizen of the United States and according to the established formulation swear to "renounce all allegiance and loyalty to every foreign potentate, monarch, state or authority whatsoever, and especially Charles XIV John, King of Sweden and Norway."

Nevertheless one cannot completely ignore public affairs, especially when something is afoot in which one is personally interested. So we went one day to attend a town meeting, that is, a meeting of all the landowners within the township.

I have already described the kind of land

of which we, like many other new settlers, had taken possession; how Congress had ceded it as a subvention to a canal company for building a canal which was never constructed, and how all the settlers on it refused to pay for it while its ownership was so unsettled. As has also been mentioned, all the squatters on these lands had entered into an agreement to stand by one another until the manner of payment had been determined upon and to protect one another in their possession of the land. This compact provided, among other things, that we would prevent anyone else from buying the lands on which we had settled and made improvements. Such a protective compact had also been agreed to by those who had settled on ordinary Congress land, and though they had no interest in the matter except to get the land settled and cultivated as quickly as possible, they also considered it their duty to prevent anyone from jumping another man's claim, that is to say, from buying the piece of land another person had taken possession of though he had not yet paid for it.

Now it happened that an American, who apparently had more money than most newcomers, had moved here from one of the Eastern states and had bought a quarter section that had not up to that time been settled, and paid the price demanded by the canal company. To this no one had any objection since he was encroaching on nobody's rights. We merely laughed at him for wasting good money. But when he also after a time bought eighty acres adjoining his quarter on which a poor immigrant shortly before had settled under the protection of the club law and on which he was just building a cabin, that was quite another story.

Owing to this development and the dispute arising from it, a call went out to all the settlers in the township to meet in the schoolhouse. Almost all of us Swedes were there at the appointed time. The gathering was large, and in the weatherbeaten faces of some of the backwoodsmen there was an expression of wrath and determination that suggested they had already made up their minds in a way boding no good to the culprit. Others, apparently quite calm, had seated themselves close to the red-hot stove, and the low room was soon filled with stifling heat and the smell of burned leather.

Some Americans are accustomed, when it is cold, to putting their feet almost into the fire. Enter a hotel or some other public place in the wintertime and you will find them rocking in their chairs, as many as possible crowding around the stove, their feet resting upon it. The snow underneath the soles of their shoes will melt and sizzle on the hot sheet iron, and from the singed boots rises one pillar of smoke beside another, making a sweet smell at least for the cobbler, if not for anyone else.

As usual, the jackknives were busy, in the handling of which the men in the West have acquired considerable skill. The urge to whittle is apparently irresistible. An ordinary stick of wood in the hands of a skillful whittler goes through one transformation after another, taking the form of now a cone, now a cube, now a pyramid, now some other geometric figure, till the entire stick has been reduced to chips. Let us not imagine, though, that this is merely idle pastime. Oftentimes while a man's jackknife is busy, his head is full of deep thoughts, and just when one might fancy he has no thought for anything but his shining blade or his stick, he may be hatching a plan for a profitable deal.

While matters of business are being discussed, the whittling becomes merely a mutual byplay through which one party seeks to gain insight into the mind of the other. The way in which the stick and the knife are being used may serve as a thermometer for the experienced eye to discover the plus or minus degrees of the whittler's frame of mind. When a deal is in prospect between two parties and one of them stops whittling, closes his knife, and puts it in his

pocket, one may be certain that either his negotiations have brought the other party to the point where he wants him or he himself has made a decision from which it would be useless to try to budge him.

On this occasion the broad-bladed knives of various dimensions seemed to me bared less for whittling than for stabbing some opponent through the chest. The chips were flying from one bench to another with more than ordinary vigor; in the movements of the hands there was something ominous, and the gleaming knife blade as well as the face of each whittler appeared to reflect a judgment already pronounced in accordance with the lynch law's stern justice.

In a short while the meeting was called to order in the regular way. One man arose and moved, in a few words, that Mr. Skinner be made the chairman of the meeting. Mr. Skinner was a farmer, well-to-do, but, like most of those present, uneducated. He was one of the oldest settlers in the neighborhood, and a man of great influence and high reputation in the community. Recently he had been elected justice of the peace and still held that office. He accepted the chairmanship and took his place back of the schoolmaster's table at one end of the room, expressed his thanks for the honor bestowed on him, and asked the meeting to proceed to elect a secretary.

Another man arose and moved that Mr. Unonius be elected to fill that office. But Mr. Unonius asked to be excused from this position of trust because he was not accustomed to keeping the minutes of such meetings. Thereupon another man was elected and took his place by the side of the chairman. Everything was done in perfect parliamentary order. Next, the chairman declared the meeting duly organized, explained in a few words its purpose, and invited those in attendance to express themselves on the subject before them.

A tall, strong-built farmer, a perfect example of the genuine backwoodsman, arose.

In his dark face and sharply marked features could be read the record of an unremitting but freely chosen struggle with wild nature; of a strength hardened by many years of troubles and privations cheerfully and courageously borne; of a resoluteness and presence of mind attesting dangers undergone among the wild beasts and wild sons of the prairie and the forest. In a word, in his bearing and appearance was written the whole life history of a frontiersman.

His clothing was half that of a white, half that of a red man. A hunting shirt of red flannel girded by a broad leather belt was visible under the wide tunic that extended to his knees — a garment that had been made from a blue blanket and so constructed that its broad black borders formed a kind of hem or decoration at the bottom and at the lapels. On his feet he wore a pair of deerskin moccasins, and extending up to his knees a pair of tight leggings from the same material. In his hand he held a long rifle, which no doubt had often been put to use and had long been his faithful companion in a richly adventurous life.

After greeting the chairman with the customary "Mr. President and Gentlemen," he developed in a coherent, orderly address, presented with natural ease and fluency, the subject of the canal lands. He sought to show that the canal company had never done anything but cheat both Congress, which had voted public funds for performing work the company was evidently neither able nor willing to carry through, and the individual settlers, who in the hope of corresponding advantages had paid a higher price for that land than the law provided; that under these conditions it was nothing less than a fraud for the government to continue to demand a higher price for this land than for any other; that the people had a perfect right to oppose such a proceeding; but that the land in the meantime ought not to be left idle and unpopulated when daily new crowds of immigrants, "a respectable class of native citizens and foreigners,"

were arriving to build for themselves happy homes and in a few years lift this "glorious territory to one of the greatest and most important states in the Union."

He next developed each settler's legal and moral right to the claim he had chosen with intent and purpose to make on it his home, calling it "the greatest piece of rascality" that ever could be perpetrated that anybody should secretly proceed to buy the same; and he sincerely hoped that now that such an unjust deed had been done, they all might stick together as one man and establish an example of stern justice so that they might for the future be protected from such encroachments. . . .

He suggested that the accused be placed under a kind of interdict: that no one was to speak to him, have any intercourse with him, or visit him in his house, and if he came to the threshold of any other man's, he was not to be admitted. No one was to buy from him or sell anything to him. In short, he was to be regarded as an excommunicated man, avoided and shunned by all, till he had atoned for his error and deeded the land in question to the man to whom it really belonged. For this he was to be paid the legal price when the dispute concerning the canal lands finally had been settled.

His suggestion won the approval of the meeting. It contained an element of novelty; it could even be published in the papers as a warning to other claim jumpers; it would lend a kind of respectability to the entire community. Petterson was complimented as a clever, just, and wise judge under the lynch law. To be sure, the proposal did not please the Irishman and his friends. Fire and violence would have agreed far better with their volatile and fiery spirits, and tarring and feathering would to them have been as exciting a spectacle as a bullfight to a Spaniard. For once, though, they had to forgo the pleasure. Petterson's proposal was adopted and recorded in the minutes as unanimously approved, with the amendment that whosoever might be found breaking the agreement and entering into any kind of intercourse whatsoever with the interdicted man was to be regarded as guilty along with him and to be visited with the same punishment.

The decision of the meeting was carried out, with the result that the wrongdoer soon found it advisable to give the opposite party full restitution for the loss he had suffered.

5.

Anonymous: Banking and the Merchant-Capitalist

Complaints against banks and concentrated wealth did not cease with the demise of the Second Bank of the United States. The average man — farmer or laborer — continued to regard banks with hostility, believing that the merchant-capitalist used the banks to create a business monopoly and obtain for himself what should have been the rewards of labor. The following newspaper editorial of January 30, 1841, contrasts the industrious average worker with the specter of influence wielded by banks in partnership with the already wealthy merchant.

Source: *Philadelphia Public Ledger*, January 30, 1841 [Commons, VII, pp. 102-103].

WE WILL SUPPOSE the state of Pennsylvania without banks or manufacturing corporations, and yet with a population as intelligent, industrious, and enterprising as the present. A mechanic, without money, wishes to buy leather for making shoes. What are his resources? His intelligence, industry, and integrity, which will surely procure credit with the tanner and dealer in leather. A jobber or retailer wishes to commence business in Philadelphia. What is his capital? The same as that of the shoemaker, and which will certainly procure credit from the importer or jobber. A merchant or mechanic would establish a manufactory and has not sufficient means. What is his expedient? Union with others in a partnership combined with credit founded upon their intellectual and moral capital.

Does either of these beginners need a bank? Certainly not. The dealer in leather,

the importer, who represent the rich, will trust the shoemaker and the retailer, who represent the poor, upon no other security than intelligence, industry, and integrity; and the operation of the system enriches the poor without impoverishing the rich.

We will next suppose the establishment of a bank, which, upon a capital of $1 million of silver, issues $2 million in paper. Who are the borrowers? The wealthy importer, the extensive manufacturer, or jobber, or ship owner, and not the poor mechanic or retailer; the rich and not the poor; those who can dispense with credit, and not those who need it.

What is the consequence? These men with means already ample, thus augmented, drive all smaller competitors out of the market and monopolize its business. An importer with a capital of $100,000 can more easily borrow $50,000 of this bank than any one of ten importers, each having a capital of $10,000, can borrow $5,000; and thus his business is increased by one-half, and theirs diminished in the same ratio. And the system still proceeding, and the one growing richer and the ten poorer, the one finally monopolizes the importing and drives the ten into other business.

Such is the natural tendency of one bank, which can be counteracted only by a multiplication of banks, that will finally produce overtrading and revulsion. Thus the system, carried to a certain extent, produces monopoly; and this mischief can be counteracted only by pushing it to the greater mischief of revulsion.

6.

Gilbert Vale: Happiness for All Through the Diffusion of Wealth

In the 1830s and 1840s reformers sought a panacea to preserve the benefits and remove the iniquities of the Industrial Revolution. Gilbert Vale, in an article titled "Political Economy," discussed four of the major social remedies proposed at the time: Robert Owen's communal experiment; Thomas Skidmore's plan to redistribute the land; the utopian socialist community (which came under the influence of Associationism in the 1840s); and a plan that originated with Frances Wright and was promoted by Vale, the "state guardianship" scheme of education. Vale's article, a portion of which is reprinted below, appeared in The Diamond *in 1841 and was an expanded version of articles written originally in 1832.*

Source: *The Diamond*, Supplement to the 2nd Series, April, August 1841.

What is wealth? Fifty different answers may be given, notwithstanding the apparent simplicity of the question. The difficulty consists in being able to give one that is free from objections, and to this, we shall not pretend. The answer we select as subject to least objection is this — *Wealth is the produce of labor*. This is not true when the produce is of no utility, yielding neither pleasure nor profit, but such labor will always be discontinued. It is not strictly true of land yielding herbage and fruits spontaneously, but the difference between the product of cultivated and uncultivated land is so great as to render the small produce of the latter scarcely an exception, especially when we consider that some labor is necessary to gather the fruits and enclose the pasturage. . . .

PRODUCERS AND CONSUMERS OF WEALTH

All men are necessarily consumers of wealth, and most men producers. The object of this essay will be to point out the distinctions. The farmer and mechanic are direct producers of wealth, and the storekeeper, by rendering services to both, causes the production of wealth. We shall now examine the claims of the physician, the lawyer, and the parson, who have no existence in the patriarchal state of society. In order to get rid of a great deal of matter, not necessarily connected with political economy, we assume, and we think the assumption will be granted that the services of the above classes are *desired* by those who employ them; and then it will be found that they cause the production of wealth nearly in the same manner as the storekeeper.

Thus the prudent farmer grows enough to pay his family physician, his lawyer, and his parson, if he need them. The mechanic produces more, for the same purpose, than he otherwise would do. Thus these classes are the immediate cause of a production equal to their consumption: and if, in addition to their immediate services they make for and communicate to the public *useful* discoveries in physics, legislation, or divinity so that they add to the enjoyments of life or decrease its evils, they substantially and permanently cause an increase in national wealth, which consists in everything from which we derive enjoyments.

With the physician, the lawyer, and the clergy, as it regards political economy, we must place the musician, the dancing master, the actor, and indeed all whose services are *desired*, and for which the other classes are willing to pay. They are all the cause of production equal to their own consumption, and frequently far beyond it, as it is manifested by the fortunes which some of these individuals accumulate; and if the mechanics can be induced to work harder, that is, to produce more, for the pleasure of seeing a Kean, in all his favorite characters, both Kean and the public are benefited by the expenditure. If, however, the mechanic make the expenditure without producing more than his usual quantity, it is clear that he must forgo some other enjoyment, and then there is no increase of wealth, but a mere transfer.

We now come to speak of mere consumers. Among these may be classed an established clergy, a standing army, pensioners, unnecessary placemen, gamblers and cheats,

in fact, all whose services are *not desired*, but who, nevertheless, derive their support from the public; if these grow rich, others must grow poor, or work for their support, without receiving an equivalent. If, therefore, public money is paid for services desired by a part of the people only, the rest are robbed to the amount of their proportion. There is an error upon this subject which supposes that all who grow rich, who are not producers in the direct form, necessarily do so at the expense of others; the reverse is frequently true.

The merchant who buys of the manufacturer benefits him to the extent of his profits, especially if the merchant has discovered a new vent for that particular kind of goods. He benefits those to whom he sells, because they give him in exchange what they value less. A successful merchant will frequently make a large fortune with very small profits, merely by the extent of his business. The difference is that the laboring mechanic cannot add much to his income by mere increase of labor, but the merchant may increase his trade without a proportionate increase of personal labor. The merchant who collects skins from the Indians and gives them in exchange, manufactured goods, may very fairly get rich himself, upon small profits, and enrich those to whom he sells, and from whom he buys, merely by the extent of his transactions.

LABOR, THE DEMAND FOR IT, AND ITS PRICE

By LABOR we mean employment of every kind, from the most refined to the coarsest. We shall first consider its price, as it will be a natural introduction to its demand, and a subject not yet generally understood or there would not be attempts to regulate the price of labor by legislation, which always proves abortive. Riots would never have occurred upon that subject if the parties had been acquainted with the fact that wages will always be in proportion to the demand for labor, and that that demand is always in proportion to the progress of national wealth or general prosperity; for national wealth is the wealth of the individuals forming a nation. The price of labor will be high in times of prosperity; low, in times of adversity; and stationary, when the progress of wealth is stationary, in the spite of legislation to keep the prices low, or combinations to make it high, although these measures may effect a temporary change.

If the demand for labor is great, no power on earth will make men work for low wages, and the only inducement employers can offer to get men to produce largely is high wages; yet high wages generally reduce the profits of employers, and do not always increase the price of the manufactured articles, because as the employer chiefly lives upon profits, he can afford to lessen them with the increase of his sales. As high wages are the only inducement to increased exertion on the part of the laborer when labor is in great demand, it is clear that he will obtain them in times of prosperity, and that such increase of wages will not necessarily affect the price of the manufactured article but the profits of the employer.

If there is very little demand for labor, the competition among the laborers will necessarily reduce the price, as employers have a direct interest in employing those who will work for the least sum, their profits being in the inverse proportion to the price of labor; and taking human nature as it is, we find the mass of mankind governed by their interests. But if *some* are only influenced to employ cheap labor, these will gradually influence the rest, because, employing cheaper labor than others, they can, if they choose, forgo higher profits and undersell those who pay more than themselves for labor.

No combination of men will prevent a reduction of wages if labor is not in demand; for at that time employers are bent upon saving expenses, and they will employ more apprentices, women, or men drawn from other employments less profitable, or more disagreeable; or altogether suspend their work if necessary. By the concurrence of both employers and employed in the times of adversity, an intermediate state has been introduced with partial success. The whole of the men have been employed for a *part* of the time in each week, at the fair or usual wages.

If it be a fact that wages depend upon supply and demand of labor, it becomes an interesting inquiry, "What regulates that?" And if the answer is that the demand is in proportion to the increase of national wealth or a general prosperity, then "What regulates that?" The increase of wealth is the increase of produce, affording comfort and gratifications. If a shoemaker introduce his shoes for the first time, and they become an object of general desire, as affording increased comfort, all who desire to partake of them must produce something in exchange; for money is the mere medium of exchange or representative of produce; but this increased produce is wealth, and this produce is the reward of labor and the cause of its demand; and one man employs another when he has the means of exchange. A merchant imports some new and desirable article or commodity. It is clear, to enjoy this, the people must produce something more than usual for exchange; here again is an increase of produce or wealth, and this increase of produce gives employment, first in its own creation, and then as the wages for something else.

ON THE INCREASE OF WEALTH

A VOLUNTARY UNION of ten, a thousand, ten thousand, or as many millions of men, forms a nation. By this union they give up a portion of their natural rights for acquisitions which they deem more valuable, viz., protection of person and property; and this security operates upon production, because none would labor beyond his immediate necessities if he could not enjoy his produce in security. There is scarcely any end to consumption, either of quantity or variety, and consequently there is abundant encouragement to production. Man can do with very little; but his desires are boundless. To satisfy these desires he taxes both his invention and his exertions, and if he produces largely of what he cannot consume, he does it that he may obtain what he can consume, and this explains a maxim in political economy that "there cannot be a general glut of goods or productions," or in other words, too much of everything, because whenever a man wants to sell anything, he does it that he may purchase something else of the same value.

The value of an article is the cost of production; that is, the value of the raw material added to the price of the labor; and this value necessarily limits the use of the article. If, therefore, the cost of production can be reduced, an extensive use of that article will necessarily follow; or in other words, produce or wealth will be increased. This reduction is first effected by a division of labor; and, again, by improved implements or machinery; and these are assisted by commerce, which introduces the best materials at the lowest price; or it imports instruments to facilitate agriculture or manufactures.

The advantage gained by division of labor is chiefly in saving time lost in the change from one employment to another, and in the facility of performing any employment acquired by constant practice.

The advantage gained by improved instruments or machinery is only limited by the cost of such implements. Thus, a machine doing the work of ten men, which would be worn out in a year, would be no gain if it cost the wages of ten men for the same period. The gradual and general introduction of improved implements and machinery must be a general good, because a greater produce would be obtained for the community; and the cost of production be-

ing less, the price of the produce would be decreased, and its increased consumption insured.

But if the improvement in implements and machinery is rapid and partial in their application from their great cost, or any other cause, the public will be generally benefited and individuals greatly so, but at the expense of other individuals; for those who cannot procure the improved instruments or machinery will suffer the loss of their business, which will be gained by those who can employ the less expensive mode of production. A remedy for this inconvenience might be found in the combination of the poorer classes of workmen in order to procure implements or machinery for their own benefit; but as machinery increases production, that is, forms wealth, if it be not a national benefit the fault is in the government.

Commerce is necessarily connected with manufactures. It equalizes the produce of the world by transporting the surplus of one part to another, where it is wanted, and bringing back something useful in exchange. Commerce is in fact an extension of the principle of the division of labor, and the profits which it affords is the remuneration for the labor of transporting the objects of commerce to the consumers. The whole value of an article sometimes consists in this, as lumber transported from the waters of America to Italy, which has been frequently done by some of our friends down East.

It is evident that there may be a *general* increase of wealth if no obstructions are placed in the way of an industrious people, and that an individual may benefit the community and himself by introducing an improvement that shall lessen the cost of production, or by discovering a new source of commerce. . . .

In our own country those branches of industry, and we might almost say only those, have been steadily successful which have not been taken under the protection of the

American system. The protected occupations have been subject to great unsteadiness, and have been repeatedly overwhelmed by ruinous reverses. Witness the silk business on the one side and the woolen business on the other. . . .

EFFECTS OF MACHINERY UPON NATIONAL WEALTH

MACHINERY is never introduced into any manufacture but to effect work better, quicker, or cheaper, than by the labor of the hands only, but the produce of labor is wealth; the produce of machinery is, therefore, wealth too; for upon that supposition only is machinery used. Machinery can then be called contrivances to make property. The direct consequence of goods being made cheaper, better, or quicker is an increased consumption, but what is the meaning of an increased consumption, but either the same individuals use more of the same articles, or that the article upon which machinery has been employed, becomes common to a larger portion of the people; that is, property which machinery has made cheap comes within the use of a large and increasing number of persons. Where machinery is not used, the inhabitants want the comforts and elegancies of life, and the mass of them necessarily remain in an uncivilized or barbarous state; for nearly the whole of every individual's time must be occupied with procuring and preparing the most common necessaries of life.

Go back to the time when corn was ground between two small stones — the one a concave and the other convex — where one woman was engaged in putting corn into the concave, and another rubbing round the convex stone. What must be the state of society when time was thus employed, and when the other arts, which have properly been called the civilizing arts, were equally at a low ebb. History, but especially old tales, songs, law, and other records, informs us; huts without boarded floors or chimneys supplied the place of houses; and skins or coarse cloth, loosely hung about the body, were substitutes for beautiful broadcloth and a neat fit from a scientific tailor.

Or if we go into the boyhood of the arts, when machinery was used, as some people think it ought to be, a *little,* and which happened, almost within our memory, what do we find? Why men with leather breeches which would serve in duration father and son, *hung* upon the hips with upper garments of any shape, coarse worsted stockings knit at an immense loss of time, and heavy shoes, which gradually drew the calves of the legs within them; women clothed in woolen in one uniform garb, with house and household furniture equally plain, and intelligence on a par with their garb and furniture.

Then was the reign of witchcraft charms, ghosts, goblins, superstitions, all of which have fled before the civilizing arts, chiefly aided by machinery. Instead of which, what do we find? The actual laboring people decreased in number, and all better clothed, fed, and educated than before, excepting where other counteracting causes prevailed, to induce poverty, etc., as *excessive taxation* in England. The same with absenteeism and the support of *two* churches in Ireland, etc.

We are levelers, agrarians, or anything else that means the same thing, but then we are disposed to level *upward* not downward. We should be glad to see machinery do all the work which is not necessary for health of body and mind. We should be glad to see universal abundance, and the civilizing arts and every man a philosopher in mind, a gentleman in purpose, and a workingman in body, without his ill shape, rude habits, and limited information, generally the effect of bad education, bad habits, or bad government, and which the *civilizing* arts chiefly impelled by machinery are great means of correcting.

Objections to Machinery Considered. Machinery reduces wages, throws men out of em-

ploy, and buries children alive in factories. It does all this, some part unnecessarily, the rest a necessary evil, accompanying a greater good. Machinery reduces wages till the manual artisans have died off, or changed their employment. This is usually done gradually, while the machinery is arriving at perfection. Those employed in making the machine and in superintending its operation are as well paid at least as formerly, and much more rationally employed than in doing the work of a machine, by which the man is leveled with a mere brute, or inanimate piece of workmanship. We do not think the firemen of New York would be less useful if their engines were drawn or driven by horses or steam.

The same cause which reduces wages at first throws men out of employ, but when the machinery is fairly established, we believe in *every case,* it puts into employment a greater number of persons than it ever throws out. This we know to be the case in the manufacture of cotton, china, porcelain, silk, and many iron works, and printing (since stereotyping was introduced) etc.; indeed in *all* cases we have had an opportunity of examining, and of those also where we have been enabled to catechize others in relation to their particular trades.

As to the employment of children, we recommend industrial schools where they may spend pleasantly and profitably a few hours in work, a few in study, and a few in open-air juvenile sports. This subject is no longer one of theory; it has been tested by experiment, and proved that *four* hours judicious labor of a child is sufficient to support it. Were the government to erect industrial schools, the employment of children in future for thirteen hours a day would cease, or legislative measures should attempt the correction of so great an evil; we say attempt, for direct acts, which oppose the interests of manufacturers and the parents of the children would probably fail.

Objection the Second. Machinery will produce too much of everything. — Every politi-

cal economist will at once perceive that this is the objection of ignorance, that among men who understood the subject, the fact is indisputable, that *too much of everything will not and cannot exist.* The objection is, however, repeatedly urged, and that in public, with assurance, and therefore demands attention, though we deprecate the practice of those men who, through ignorance, oblige their opponents first to teach them a science before they can convince them of their errors. There cannot be too much of everything, because no man produces an article which he does not wish and is willing to exchange for something else produced by another of the same value, or whose cost of production is the same. Now, as this is universally the case, as everybody is willing to exchange what he has produced, it follows that there cannot be too much of everything. If too much of any one thing is produced, it will not exchange for its ordinary value, and then the producer will cease his operation, or produce something else. There will be some danger of producing too much when men have *enough.* We have never yet met with one man who had enough, indeed enough means as in the Scotchman's prayer, a little more than we have. It is clear that as there is *no limit* to expenditure, there can be no having enough; we might be content with a biscuit, a glass of water, homespun, and independence, but we could very well spend any amount.

Objection the Third. Expensive machinery requires large capitals; men of small capitals cannot therefore compete with men of large capitals; the little man is therefore crushed by the larger. We know that big fishes will eat little ones, but we know also that the big fish is sometimes caught in the meshes of a net which will allow the little ones to pass through. No arrangement will prevent all the advantages of capital over those who have none, or of great capitals over those who have small ones, though a combination of small capitals *might* (we say might for we are doubtful of the result, excepting for short periods) compete with a large one. The evil, however, will be remedied by the *improvement and simplification of machinery,* and subdivisions of manufactures. Thus in the business of printing, the invention of stereotyping has led to a new business, and therefore lessened the amount of capital required by the printer. In the same business, the introduction of power presses has led to a new business, and the printer can now do without a press, and get his work done cheaper and more expeditiously by those who keep a power press, and work for the public, than he could do it. In this way are nearly all the newspapers worked in cities; and thus the printer, and especially newspaper printers, employ less capital than formerly by the introduction of an expensive machine.

In the case of mills of every description, this is strikingly the case. The first man who possessed a flour mill must have an advantage over every other, and appear to impose the expense of a mill on every farmer, but the desire of everyone to have a mill suggested the advantage to some capitalists to build one for the public. So of a sawmill and perhaps of every other. The improvement of machinery, then, and the introduction of expensive machinery, too, in its course serves to subdivide business and consequently to divide capital. . . .

AN ERROR IN LEGISLATION

THERE IS SOMETHING very discouraging to the political philanthropist in the fact that generations have passed away, one after another, without establishing *truths* known to many in each generation. A man may leave his property to his successors, but he cannot his information, and the most valuable truths are suffered to die, and are again eternally brought forward as something *new* when they are really old and ought to have been acted upon, successively, since the first formation of society.

The truths we refer to are that political

society is, or ought to be, a *voluntary association for mutual protection,* for the good of the whole; and that all legislation should be upon those subjects in which they have a common interest. The object then of legislation should be the protection of the *natural rights* of a man, as far as those rights do not interfere with the *natural rights* of other men. These principles appear self-evident, and so we think they did to some of our forefathers several thousand years ago.

But are they established? Do the history of nations and the records of legislation show that these principles have been well understood and uniformly acted upon? Would not these principles lead generally to a *negative* rather than to a *positive* legislation? Would not laws be prohibitory of individuals invading the natural rights of others, and would they not impose penalties on such violations? Yet investigation upon this subject brings to light a long list of facts in direct opposition to these principles, and even other principles are set up in violation of these: both cannot be correct.

We find it gravely asserted, and almost uniformly acted upon, that the *majority should govern the minority;* and this is the key to all the miserable legislation in the world, and the foundation of most of the evils. This is the father of the religious and political persecutions, and the grand impediment to improvement. We have before published some such sentiments as these, and we may again do so; the subject is too important, and too much neglected to render repetition a fault.

What is this governing majority but a subversion of all justice; the uprooting of the very foundation of political society, and establishing *club law,* with the sanction of forms. What need of written laws at all if a majority is to rule, and questions affecting partial interest be decided by numbers? What matters it to the sufferer whether he is persecuted *according* to law or *contrary* to law? Look the monster full in the face, and we shall see the evil it inflicts on society.

Admit the right of legislators to legislate upon *any* subject, and to decide by a *majority,* then *any* religious body which could obtain a majority could and would oppress the rest and persecute *according to law.*

And this object has been attempted by a union of the self-styled orthodox parties. To a division of sects do we now evidently owe our religious liberty, and not to sound principles of politics or morals. To the curse of assuming the right of a majority to legislate for a minority do we owe the blundering upon the tariff question. To this doctrine do we owe the electioneering trickery, each party attempting to get a majority, in order to control or mold society to *its standard.* But what is to be done, will some ask, who have read too fast? Why, *deny the right of legislating at all* upon such subjects in which a common interest does not exist, or in which one party goes beyond the defense of their own *natural rights,* and invades the *natural rights* of another. Or, if necessary, let each individual systematically break or disregard laws thus oppressive. There is more *honor in the breach than the observance of such laws,* and an appeal to the Constitution will in these states generally support the resistance.

Agrarianism. It appears to us that the above reasoning applies to agrarianism in every form; that it requires legislation on subjects about which nobody on earth has a right to legislate. We are agrarians if by that is meant the removal of all partial laws which *bestow privileges* or *deny rights* to one man which another enjoys; but every kind of agrarianism which we have known goes beyond this, and we think invades the rights of others. The modified agrarianism was advocated in New York, and as set forth in Skidmore's "Rights of Man to Property," is not exempt from this charge.

First, it advocates an actual division of property.

Second, to avoid a recurrence to such violence, it recommends securing personal acquisitions. to the acquirer, but making the state the heir to all such acquired property. . . .

As to the notion of the state becoming the heir of every man's property, and doling out proportional parts to each individual as he becomes of age, we must say we have the same objection to it; it is giving to the state, to governors, or to legislators what never ought to belong to them. This scheme to which we know the author attached the greatest importance, we consider as one of the wildest schemes that ever entered the brain of man; and the only thing that can be said in its favor is that it has never been tried. The legitimate object of legislators and governors is to *protect* the natural rights of man, and not to take the control of the property of society. The scheme appears big with mischief in every way we can conceive of it and calculated to raise up a set of men to *dispense* the public property instead of *adding* to public wealth.

It would probably be abused, as all almoners of long standing that we ever heard of ever did abuse their trust. It would defeat itself, for many would not accumulate for the *public,* and others would dispose of their accumulation just before death, as is now done in England merely to avoid a tax. It would thus in one case prevent the growth of wealth, and in the other cause secret hoards; and then would come penalties, and these could be but partially enforced; and if vigorously enforced on one side, and resisted on the other, suffering and persecution, *according to law,* would be the consequence; and the whole arising from a *majority* assuming to rule a minority, instead of a government confining itself to its legitimate object — that of protecting the rights of every individual.

In point of experience it is found that individuals do that best and cheapest which they are capable of doing at all; but this scheme would take from man the principal excitement to well-being and well-doing. The scheme would require violence *according to law* to put it into order, and would be out of joint at the end of every week, after its commencement, and never in joint after a three-month trial, because it would have to contend against the nature of man in social life, which moves easier when left alone, and the best aid that can be given to it, is to remove obstructions of every kind. Society is harassed and vexed by too much legislation.

THE COMMUNITY SYSTEM *vs.* THE COMPETITION SYSTEM

THE COMMUNITY system combining common property, equal rights, and mutual labor, under the direction of elected officers, according to rules made or agreed to by the whole community, has never been tried, that we know of, on an extended scale. Someone has always appeared in the character of a *dictator,* which adds to the facility, harmony, and prosperity of such a society, but it violates equal rights, and is a foundation on which despotism, tyranny, and fraud will *necessarily* be built, and the community either destroyed or turned to private benefit. Such a community will have abundance of the physical comforts of life; such comforts have Rapp's community, and the Shaking Quakers, except in the case of matrimony, on which subject the rulers have imposed a painful and unnatural restraint. Abundance without such restraint would no doubt follow Mr. Owen's plan, but Mr. Owen is a dictator, and that will succeed under his immediate direction which might, nay, has failed, in other hands. Any plan which denies individual property and demands continued common services must restrain individual liberty, and fail to bring out talents, energies, and virtues peculiar to a competitive state.

A community of equal rights where officers are elected, and where no dictators exist, will necessarily be divided into factions, as other societies similarly governed are. And when employment is dictated, genius will frequently be overlooked and not prop-

erly estimated, for genius is not always observed on the surface, and generally brings itself out, in spite of family, friends, and early failures, as did Demosthenes, Patrick Henry, Kean, Arkwright, Belzoni, and all the eminent men in the American and French Revolutions.

A community system offers comfortable maintenance for moderate labor, care in sickness, a liberal education, equality (except from cliques, intrigue, etc.), and thus removes anxiety; and it offers a splendid public establishment, assembly rooms, public conveniences, etc. . . . .

The drawbacks are a temptation to apathy, divisions, intrigue, and supposed neglect, common to all societies, with a restraint on personal liberty, *unbearable* to thousands who always go straight when left alone, but are uneasy in harness, and who, following a feeling *natural* to sheep and some men, leap a barrier merely to indulge their love of liberty. And the wisest men are directed by their judgments and *feelings;* the latter, an instinct less liable to err than reason, subject to various influences.

Now, a *good* government will secure all the above advantages, encourage genius, and preserve individual liberty; for it will *comfortably* maintain its poor, the aged, and the sick in need; an ample provision will be made for education; and the children whose parents cannot, or will not, provide and educate them, will be made the children of the state — liberally educated and taught agriculture, mechanism, with the arts and sciences, including even the rudiments of the fine arts, so that to be a child of the state should be a recommendation.

A good government, by equal laws and favoring the distribution of wealth, will promote industry, and, by judicious laws, the harassing credit system might be destroyed; and the *one-price* cash system can at any time become popular, for it is safe for an individual, or for numbers, to try, as in Turkey; and then the worst feature in the competitive system is destroyed, and a liberal self-interest shown to be a social virtue; for "self-interest and social are the same."

A *good* government, having the authority of a dictator over the criminal, the idle, the unemployed, and the destitute children, could to *advantage* apply the community system to them; while individuals in a free government, who imagine they could live in peace under the restraints of a community, can at any time so associate to their fancy, and might be happy; but to bring out the energies of a whole nation requires the powerful motive of "self-interest," enlightened by a liberal education, which then becomes a national blessing, and a source of individual and social happiness.

7.

Constitution of the Brook-Farm Association

Because of its distinguished membership, which included William Ellery Channing, George Ripley, Nathaniel Hawthorne, Ralph Waldo Emerson, Orestes A. Brownson, Margaret Fuller, and Charles A. Dana, the Brook-Farm Institute of Agriculture and Education, established at West Roxbury, Massachusetts (about nine miles from Boston), in 1841, was the best known of the many utopian experiments set up in the twenty-five years before the Civil War. It was a self-supporting agricultural association organized as a joint-stock company in which the members, freed from the competitive pressures of a materialistic society, could associate among themselves on a high intellectual and spiritual plane. In 1846, a fire precipitated a decline of the society; however, signs of internal dissension were evident before the disaster occurred.

Source: Octavius B. Frothingham, *Transcendentalism in New England*, Boston, 1903, pp. 159-163.

IN ORDER MORE EFFECTUALLY to promote the great purposes of human culture; to establish the external relations of life on a basis of wisdom and purity; to apply the principles of justice and love to our social organization in accordance with the laws of Divine Providence; to substitute a system of brotherly cooperation for one of selfish competition; to secure to our children and those who may be entrusted to our care the benefits of the highest physical, intellectual, and moral education, which, in the progress of knowledge, the resources at our command will permit; to institute an attractive, efficient, and productive system of industry; to prevent the exercise of worldly anxiety by the competent supply of our necessary wants; to diminish the desire of excessive accumulation by making the acquisition of individual property subservient to upright and disinterested uses; to guarantee to each other forever the means of physical support and of spiritual progress; and thus to impart a greater freedom, simplicity, truthfulness, refinement, and moral dignity to our mode of life; we, the undersigned, do unite in a voluntary association, and adopt and ordain the following articles of agreement, to wit:

ARTICLE I.
NAME AND MEMBERSHIP

Section 1. The name of this Association shall be "The Brook-Farm Association for

Industry and Education." All persons who shall hold one or more shares in its stock, or whose labor and skill shall be considered an equivalent for capital, may be admitted by the vote of two-thirds of the Association, as members thereof.

Section 2. No member of the Association shall ever be subjected to any religious test; nor shall any authority be assumed over individual freedom of opinion by the Association, nor by one member over another; nor shall anyone be held accountable to the Association, except for such overt acts or omissions of duty as violate the principles of justice, purity, and love on which it is founded; and in such cases the relation of any member may be suspended or discontinued at the pleasure of the Association.

ARTICLE II. CAPITAL STOCK

Section 1. The members of this Association shall own and manage such real and personal estate in joint stock proprietorship, divided into shares of $100 each, as may from time to time be agreed on.

Section 2. No shareholder shall be liable to any assessment whatever on the shares held by him; nor shall he be held responsible individually in his private property on account of the Association; nor shall the trustees, or any officer or agent of the Association, have any authority to do anything which shall impose personal responsibility on any shareholder, by making any contracts or incurring any debts for which the shareholders shall be individually or personally responsible.

Section 3. The Association guarantees to each shareholder the interest of 5 percent annually on the amount of stock held by him in the Association, and this interest may be paid in certificates of stock and credited on the books of the Association; provided that each shareholder may draw on the funds of the Association for the amount of interest due at the third annual settlement from the time of investment.

Section 4. The shareholders on their part, for themselves, their heirs, and assigns, do renounce all claim on any profits accruing to the Association for the use of their capital invested in the stock of the Association, except 5 percent interest on the amount of stock held by them, payable in the manner described in the preceding section.

ARTICLE III. GUARANTIES

Section 1. The Association shall provide such employment for all its members as shall be adapted to their capacities, habits, and tastes; and each member shall select and perform such operations of labor, whether corporal or mental, as shall be deemed best suited to his own endowments and the benefit of the Association.

Section 2. The Association guarantees to all its members, their children, and family dependents, house rent, fuel, food, and clothing, and the other necessaries of life, without charge, not exceeding a certain fixed amount to be decided annually by the Association; no charge shall ever be made for support during inability to labor from sickness or old age, or for medical or nursing attendance, except in case of shareholders, who shall be charged therefor, and also for the food and clothing of children, to an amount not exceeding the interest due to them on settlement; but no charge shall be made to any members for education or the use of library and public rooms.

Section 3. Members may withdraw from labor, under the direction of the Association, and, in that case, they shall not be entitled to the benefit of the above guaranties.

Section 4. Children over ten years of age shall be provided with employment in suitable branches of industry; they shall be credited for such portions of each annual dividend as shall be decided by the Association. And, on the completion of their education in the Association at the age of twenty, shall be entitled to a certificate of stock to the amount of credits in their favor, and may be admitted as members of the Association.

ARTICLE IV.
DISTRIBUTION OF PROFITS

Section 1. The net profits of the Association, after the payment of all expenses, shall be divided into a number of shares corresponding to the number of days' labor; and every member shall be entitled to one share of every day's labor performed by him.

Section 2. A full settlement shall be made with every member once a year, and certificates of stock given for all balances due; but in case of need, to be decided by himself, every member may be permitted to draw on the funds in the treasury to an amount not exceeding the credits in his favor for labor performed.

ARTICLE V. GOVERNMENT

Section 1. The government of the Association shall be vested in a Board of Directors, divided into four departments, as follows: (1) General Direction; (2) Direction of Education; (3) Direction of Industry; (4) Direction of Finance; consisting of three persons each, provided that the same person may be elected member of each Direction.

Section 2. The General Direction and Direction of Education shall be chosen annually by the vote of a majority of the members of the Association. The Direction of Finance shall be chosen annually by the vote of a majority of the shareholders and members of the Association. The Direction of Industry shall consist of the chiefs of the three primary series.

Section 3. The chairman of the General Direction shall be the president of the Association, and, together with the Direction of Finance, shall constitute a Board of Trustees, by whom the property of the Association shall be held and managed.

Section 4. The General Direction shall oversee and manage the affairs of the Association, so that every department shall be carried on in an orderly and efficient manner.

Section 5. The departments of Education and Finance shall be under the control each of its own Direction, which shall select, and in concurrence with the General Direction, shall appoint such teachers, officers, and agents as shall be necessary to the complete and systematic organization of the department. No directors or other officers shall be deemed to possess any rank superior to the other members of the Association, nor shall they receive any extra remuneration for their official services.

Section 6. The Department of Industry shall be arranged in groups and series, as far as practicable, and shall consist of three primary series; to wit, Agricultural, Mechanical, and Domestic Industry. The chief of each series shall be elected every two months by the members thereof, subject to the approval of the General Direction. The chief of each group shall be chosen weekly by its members.

Whoso would be a man, must be a nonconformist. He who would gather immortal palms must not be hindered by the name of goodness, but must explore if it be goodness. Nothing is at last sacred but the integrity of your own mind.
RALPH WALDO EMERSON, "Self-Reliance"

George Eastman House

Tintype of two unidentified men by an unknown photographer

GROWING URBANIZATION

As the country recovered from the Panic of 1837 and the subsequent depression, cities increasingly dominated American life. They were the financial centers and the focus of the industrialization that was gradually transforming the country's economic and social perspectives. The vast majority of the population still lived outside the urban centers. The distribution of government land remained a major issue in the Midwest. Products of the land still dominated the economy. Railway connections to the East were still to be built and most goods made their way slowly to New Orleans on the inland waterways. But the trend to urbanization was evident throughout the country as towns on the Midwestern rivers or the Great Lakes grew into cities.

Washington, D.C., 1843; daguerreotype of Pennsylvania Ave. with White House at top center

Commerce Breeds Cities

During the 1840s railroads began reaching out into the Midwest and South, entering Chicago in 1852. As transportation improved so did commerce, and trading cities like St. Louis and Cincinnati grew rapidly. These cities served as depots and shipping centers for the agricultural lands around them. Slaughter houses, grain elevators, lumber yards, and cotton warehouses lined the riverbanks. But the rapidly built cities were ill-conceived and poorly protected. In the absence of adequate public safety standards, epidemics were common and fires were a constant danger.

Cincinnati, Ohio, in 1848, as seen from the Kentucky shore

"Oakland House and Race Course, Louisville, 1840"; painting by Robert Brammer and Augustus A. Von Smith, Sr.

(Right) Lithograph of Natchez, Miss., in 1847; by H. Lewis; (below) Nashville, Tenn., about 1850

(Above left) Hartford, Conn.; hand-colored aquatint by Robert Havell; (above right) view of the Arcade in Providence, R.I., designed by Russell Warren; (left) Buffalo, N.Y., as seen from Lake Erie in 1836; aquatint by W. J. Bennett

The Cincinnati panorama is composed of eight daguerreotypes by Fontayne and Porter taken on a Sunday morning when the usually bustling waterfront was still and deserted

(Above right) The great
fire at St. Louis, Mo., May
1849, in which over five
million dollars worth of
property was destroyed.
(Right) View of Pittsburgh
after the fire of 1845,
from Boyd's Hill; painting
by William Coventry Wall

North Carolina Museum of Art

Library of Congress

(Top) "Kitchen Ball, White Sulphur Springs";
Red Sulphur Springs, another Virginia resort

Resorts

Resort areas for the relaxation of the city dwellers were already well established by the end of the 1840s. Paid vacations were unknown and the resorts were reserved for the professional and upper classes. For those who could afford them, spas and mountain retreats were a welcome escape in the summer when the pestilential dangers of city life were at their height.

For the common man there were simpler diversions. Racing, a commonplace wherever men owned horses, became an organized entertainment with enormous prizes offered in special match races. Anything offering a chance to gamble was sure to draw a crowd.

The resort town of Legareville, on John's Island off the South Carolina coast, 1850

Colonial Williamsburg, Rockefeller Collection

Congress Spring at the popular resort town of Saratoga, N.Y., where the wealthy escaped the heat and crowds of New York City

(Above) Honeymooners photographed in about 1850 at Niagara Falls, already established as a mecca for newlyweds; (right) view of the Catskill Mountain House, engraved from a painting by Thomas Cole, whose paintings did much to popularize the region as a resort area

(Top) Daguerreotype of a brass ensemble taken about 1850; (center) an unidentified man shown with his butterfly collection, about 1850; (bottom) a game of cards, photographed about the same time by an unknown American daguerreotypist

"Great Fight Between Tom Hyer and Yankee Sullivan" held in Kent Co., Maryland, February 1849. Hyer won

An unidentified hunter photographed with his dog about 1850 (left)

A humorous view of the "dance craze" of the day

"Peytona and Fashion's Great Match" held over the Union Course, Long Island. The $20,000 purse was won by Peytona

"An Indian Summer View of the Farm and Stock of James Cornell, Bucks County" by Edward Hicks

Rural life during the 1840s saw the first beginnings of widespread change. The railroads had begun to reach the isolated communities in New England, accelerating the drift away from agriculture. In 1847, McCormick began manufacturing his reaper in Chicago. This machine, the coming of the railroads, and other improvements in farm tools revolutionized the farm economy in the Midwest. The reaper made large yields possible and improved transportation to markets made them feasible.

"The Pill Vendor" shows a traveling salesman, Dr. Brandeth, selling his remedies and pills to a rural housewife

View of the village of Buckland, Massachusetts, by an unknown artist

(Above) Trial in a country court; (below) Dixon's ferry over the Rock River, Illinois, 1842; (bottom) daguerreotype of a scene in an unknown town on a winter's day

In 1839 S. F. B. Morse, in Paris to obtain a French patent for his telegraph, visited the studio of Louis Daguerre to see his "daguerreotype" views. As a painter, Morse's interest was acute, but Daguerre kept his process secret while he negotiated with the French government for a lifetime annuity. A month after Daguerre released details of his method, accounts reached the American papers. Within a matter of days a dozen men, including Morse and Theodore Draper, were experimenting with cameras made of cigar boxes and spectacle lenses. By late 1840 improved equipment shortened Daguerre's original five-minute exposure to less than one minute, making portraits possible. Soon most towns had a daguerreotype artist at work. Morse himself taught many of these early photographers.

(Left) The first photograph from nature by the Frenchman, Nicephore Niepce, 1826; (above) Louis Daguerre; (below) Samuel F. B. Morse

Daguerreotype of the Philadelphia Arsenal and Old Central High School made by Joseph Saxton, October 16, 1839. It is the oldest American photograph still extant, though not the first

(Both) Smithsonian Institution

(Above) Self-portrait of Henry Fitz; (left) Baltimore street scene photographed by Fitz early in 1840

George Eastman House

(Above) King's Chapel, Boston, photographed by Samuel Bemis in April 1840, with a forty minute exposure; (right) post-mortem photographs, such as the one shown here had a brief popularity in the early 1840s with people who wanted to preserve a likeness of a relative who had never been photographed

Mrs. Ralph Mackay

Daguerreotype of an unidentified man taken about 1850

Daniel Webster at his country place, "Green Harbor," near Marshfield, Mass.

Dolly Madison, photographed by Brady at the age of 80, was still a major figure in Washington society

Daguerreotype portrait of a young and lovely woman taken by Southworth and Hawes about 1850

8.

Henry Wadsworth Longfellow: "The Village Blacksmith"

Longfellow was the best-loved poet of his time, and "The Village Blacksmith" was among his best-loved poems. The poem exhibits many of the features that recommended Longfellow to his readers: its diction is simple; its meter is regular; its moral is pleasing and easily grasped; it is romantic and sentimental and glorifies both the American ethos and the common life. "The Village Blacksmith" was published in 1841 in the collection Ballads and Other Poems.

Source: *Complete Poetical Works,* Cambridge Edition, Boston, 1893.

THE VILLAGE BLACKSMITH

Under a spreading chestnut tree
  The village smithy stands;
The smith, a mighty man is he,
  With large and sinewy hands;
And the muscles of his brawny arms
  Are strong as iron bands.

His hair is crisp, and black, and long,
  His face is like the tan;
His brow is wet with honest sweat,
  He earns whate'er he can,
And looks the whole world in the face,
  For he owes not any man.

Week in, week out, from morn till night,
  You can hear his bellows blow;
You can hear him swing his heavy sledge
  With measured beat and slow,
Like a sexton ringing the village bell,
  When the evening sun is low.

And children coming home from school
  Look in at the open door;
They love to see the flaming forge,
  And hear the bellows roar,
And catch the burning sparks that fly
  Like chaff from a threshing floor.

He goes on Sunday to the church,
  And sits among his boys;
He hears the parson pray and preach,
  He hears his daughter's voice
Singing in the village choir,
  And it makes his heart rejoice.

It sounds to him like her mother's voice,
  Singing in Paradise!
He needs must think of her once more,
  How in the grave she lies;
And with his hard, rough hand he wipes
  A tear out of his eyes.

Toiling — rejoicing — sorrowing,
  Onward through life he goes;
Each morning sees some task begun,
  Each evening sees its close;
Something attempted, something done,
  Has earned a night's repose.

Thanks, thanks to thee, my worthy friend,
  For the lesson thou hast taught!
Thus at the flaming forge of life
  Our fortunes must be wrought;
Thus on its sounding anvil shaped
  Each burning deed and thought!

1842

9.

Horace Mann: The Pecuniary Value of Education

In order to institute his massive program of educational reform, Horace Mann had to win public support. Each of the annual reports that he was obliged, as secretary to the Massachusetts Board of Education, to submit to the legislature was written with that goal in mind. The Fifth Annual Report was directed primarily at securing the support of the poor, who as a group tended to underrate the value of schools and to balk at the public expenditure for them. In this report, part of which appears below, Mann pointed out to this portion of the population the monetary advantages that an education could bring. The report was submitted to the legislature on January 1, 1842.

Source: *Annual Reports of the Secretary of the Board of Education of Massachusetts for the Years 1839-1844*, Boston, 1891, pp. 92-128.

I will occupy the short space which propriety allows to me . . . by showing the effect of education upon *the worldly fortunes and estates* of men — its influence upon property, upon human comfort and competence, upon the outward, visible, material interests or well-being of individuals and communities.

This view, so far from being the highest which can be taken of the beneficent influences of education, may, perhaps, be justly regarded as the lowest. But it is a palpable view. It presents an aspect of the subject susceptible of being made intelligible to all; and, therefore, it will meet the case of thousands who are now indifferent about the education of their offspring because they foresee no reimbursement in kind, no return in money, or in money's worth, for money expended. The cooperation of this numerous class is indispensable in order to carry out the system; and if they can be induced to educate their children, even from inferior motives, the children, when educated, will feel its higher and nobler affinities.

So, too, in regard to towns. If it can be proved that the aggregate wealth of a town will be increased just in proportion to the increase of its appropriations for schools, the opponents of such a measure will be silenced. The tax for this purpose, which they now look upon as a burden, they will then regard as a profitable investment. Let it be shown that the money which is now clung to by the parent, in the hope of increasing his children's legacies some 6 or 10 percent can be so invested as to double their patrimony, and the blind instinct of parental love, which now, by voice and vote, opposes such outlay, will become an advocate for the most generous endowments. When the money expended for education shall be viewed in its true character, as seed grain sown in a soil which is itself enriched by yielding, then the most parsimonious will not stint the sowing, lest the harvest also should be stinted, and thereby thirty, sixty, or a hundredfold should be lost to the garners.

I am the more induced to take this view of the subject because the advocates and eulogists of education have rarely, if ever, descended to so humble a duty as to demonstrate its pecuniary value both to individuals and to society. They have expended their strength in portraying its loftier attributes, its gladdening, refining, humanizing tendencies. They have not deigned to show how it can raise more abundant harvests and multiply the conveniences of domestic life; how it can build, transport, manufacture, mine, navigate, fortify; how, in fine, a single new idea is often worth more to an individual than a hundred workmen and to a nation than the addition of provinces to its territory. I have novel and striking evidence to prove that education is convertible into houses and lands, as well as into power and virtue. . . .

Now, many of the most intelligent and valuable men in our community, in compliance with my request, for which I tender them my public and grateful acknowledgements, have examined their books for a series of years and have ascertained both the quality and the amount of work performed by persons in their employment; and the result of the investigation is a most astonishing superiority, in productive power, on the part of the educated over the uneducated laborer. The hand is found to be another hand when guided by an intelligent mind. Processes are performed, not only more rapidly but better, when faculties which have been exercised in early life furnish their assistance.

Individuals who, without the aid of knowledge, would have been condemned to perpetual inferiority of condition and subjected to all the evils of want and poverty, rise to competence and independence by the uplifting power of education. In great establishments, and among large bodies of laboring men, where all services are rated according to their pecuniary value; where there are no extrinsic circumstances to bind a man down to a fixed position after he has shown a capacity to rise above it; where, indeed, men pass by each other, ascending or descending in their grades of labor, just as easily and certainly as particles of water of different degrees of temperature glide by each other — there it is found as an almost invariable fact, other things being equal, that those who have been blessed with a good common-school education rise to a higher and a higher point in the kinds of labor performed and also in the rate of wages paid, while the ignorant sink like dregs and are always found at the bottom. . . .

Education is not only a moral renovator and a multiplier of intellectual power but . . . it is also the most prolific parent of material riches. It has a right, therefore, not only to be included in the grand inventory of a nation's resources but to be placed at the very head of that inventory. It is not only the most honest and honorable but the surest means of amassing property. A trespasser or a knave may forcibly or fraudulently appropriate the earnings of others to himself; but education has the prerogative of originating or generating property more certainly and more rapidly than it was ever accumulated by force or fraud. It has more than the quality of an ordinary mercantile commodity, from which the possessor realizes but a single profit as it passes through his hands; it rather resembles fixed capital, yielding constant and high revenues.

As it enjoys an immunity from common casualties, it incurs no cost for insurance or defense. It is above the reach of changes in administration or in administrational policy; and it is free from those fluctuations of trade which agitate the market and make it so frequent an occurrence that a merchant who goes to bed a man of wealth at night rises a pauper in the morning. Possessing these qualities, it has the highest economical value; and although statesmen who assail or defend, who raise up or put down, systems of commercial, manufacturing, or agricultural policy, have seldom or never deigned to look at education as the grand agent for the development or augmentation of national resources, yet it measures the efficacy of every other means of aggrandizement and is more powerful in the production and gainful employment of the total wealth of a country than all other things mentioned in the books of the political economist.

Education is an antecedent agency; for it must enlighten mankind in the choice of pursuits, it must guide them in the selection and use of the most appropriate means, it must impart that confidence and steadiness of purpose which results from comprehending the connections of a long train of events and seeing the end from the beginning, or all enterprises will terminate in ruin.

Considering education, then, as a producer of wealth, it follows that the more educated a people are, the more will they abound in all those conveniences, comforts, and satisfactions which money will buy; and, other things being equal, the increase of competency and the decline of pauperism will be measurable on this scale. . . .

Among a people, then, who must gain their subsistence by their labor, what can be so economical, so provident and farsighted, and even so wise — in a lawful and laudable, though not in the highest sense of that word — as to establish and, with open heart and hand, to endow and sustain, the most efficient system of universal education for their children; and, where the material bounties of nature are comparatively narrow and stinted, to explore, in their stead, those exhaustless and illimitable resources of comfort and competency and independence which lie hidden in the yet dormant powers of the human intellect?

But, notwithstanding all I have said of the value of education in a pecuniary sense and of its power to improve and elevate the outward domestic and social condition of all men, yet . . . I should do injustice to my feelings did I abstain from declaring that, to my own mind, this tribute to its worth, however well deserved, is still the faintest note of praise which can be uttered in honor of so noble a theme; and that, however deserving of attention may be the *economical* view of the subject which I have endeavored to present, yet it is one that dwindles into insignificance when compared with those loftier and more sacred attributes of the cause which have the power of converting material wealth into spiritual well-being, and of giving to its possessor lordship and sovereignty alike over the temptations of adversity and the still more dangerous seducements of prosperity, and which, so far as human agency is concerned, must be looked to for the establishment of peace and righteousness upon earth, and for the enjoyment of glory and happiness in Heaven.

Lost, yesterday, somewhere between sunrise and sunset, two golden hours, each set with sixty diamond minutes. No reward is offered for they are gone forever.

HORACE MANN

10.

Francis Wayland: Our Present System of Colleges

Francis Wayland, the president of Brown University in Rhode Island from 1827 to 1855, believed that the school should draw its students from every segment of society and should train them for every walk of life. To this end, tuition should be kept low, and the curriculum should be broad and useful. His concept of the democratic function of the college reflected the influence of Swiss and German educational philosophy which, beginning in the 1830s, profoundly affected the philosophy of education in America. In Thoughts on the Present Collegiate System in the United States, *published in 1842, Wayland pointed out the shortcomings of higher education and stressed the need for radical changes. Wayland's ideas were shared by other influential educators, and in the state universities established in the Midwest those ideas were effectively and fully tested. The concluding summary chapter of Wayland's book is reprinted below.*

Source: *Thoughts on the Present Collegiate System in the United States*, Boston, 1842, Ch. 5.

I HAVE CONSIDERED at considerable length some of the most important points of our present collegiate system. Unless I have been greatly deceived, I have shown that this system calls for serious revision if we desire that it should be adapted to the existing wants of the community.

I propose in these few concluding remarks to review briefly the points which I suppose to call most loudly for attentive consideration. I beg leave, however, to repeat what I have often stated before, that I only present these topics as matters for consideration. I by no means suppose it practicable, or even wise were it practicable, to transform all our colleges at once in order to conform them to the plans which I have indicated. There is a demand for a change in our collegiate system. Changes are from time to time effected, without, as it would seem, any great practical improvement.

My object is simply to point out the objects at which we should aim in our attempts at change. If it should seem that in any respects I have indicated the direction in which we should move, let us move in that direction. If I have illustrated the evils under which we labor, let us strive to remove them. If I have totally failed in this attempt let someone better qualified accomplish the task more successfully. But at any rate, let us have the object which we desire to attain placed full in our own view and in the view of the whole community; and let us all labor for its accomplishment, sincerely, earnestly, and harmoniously. In this manner alone can we hope to improve the condition of higher education throughout our country.

1. *I begin, then, with the corporations, or boards of visitors, in our colleges.* On them devolves, in truth, the incipient action which shall effect this whole subject. They are the appointed guardians of education. In

them is vested the whole power of ordering, directing, and governing the institutions of higher learning. They hold all the funds appropriated, either by private or public munificence, to the purpose of elevating the standard of knowledge in the youth of our country. They appoint and remove officers, fix the rate and manner of their compensation, ordain the studies to be pursued, and on them it is devolved to see that the designs of the public or the founder are carried into effect. This power can be exercised by no other person whatever. So long as they hold their office, no one else can act in the premises without usurpation. If they do not act according to their solemn promises, no action can be had.

Such being their power and their responsibility, I beg leave most respectfully to remind them of their duty. Unless they make themselves acquainted with the subject of education, unless they will devote to the proper duties of their office a portion of their time, unless they will assume the responsibility which must be incurred by efficient action, unless, in a word, they will make an earnest effort to improve the present system of education, on them a charge of grave dereliction of duty will rest. If, as is doubtless in many instances the case, their organization is imperfect, it may be modified. If the duties to be discharged are onerous, they may be divided among them. In the officers of colleges they will, I am convinced, find ready and active coadjutors.

If these two principal agents in the collegiate system seriously undertake a revision of its fundamental principles, I am convinced that they will confer a most important benefit on the community. It is in their power to extend the blessings of higher education very widely among all classes of our fellow citizens, and also render education incomparably more valuable than it has ever been in this country. But the work must commence with the visitors. To them it

properly appertains. They owe it to the public to whom they are responsible. They owe it to the rising youth of our country, who in this respect are placed specially under their pupilage. They owe it to their God who has committed to their charge so solemn a responsibility, and placed in their hands in no small degree the destinies of this great republic. I cannot believe for a moment that they will be recreant to so grave and important a trust.

2. *Of the organization of our colleges.* Our colleges, as I have already remarked, are at present scarcely anything more than schools for the education of young men for the professions. So long as we continue the present organization they can be no other. While we construct our system for this purpose and adhere to a regular gradation of classes and prescribed studies for each, we may make what changes we please, but the regular course will control every other. But while we have made our college course a mere preparation for professional education, we have so crowded it with studies as to render it superficial and probably less valuable for its particular purpose than it was originally. I am not sure that we are not already suffering from the effect of the course which we have pursued.

I rather fear that the impression is gaining ground that this preparation is not essential to success in professional study. A large proportion of our medical students are not graduates. The proportion of law students of the same class is, I rather think, increasing. The proportion of students for the ministry who resort to college is much larger than formerly. This is owing in no small degree to the aid of education societies. What would be the case if this aid were out of the question, I am unable to determine. If these things be so, it would seem that while we have been restricting our collegiate education to one class, its value by that class is less and less appreciated.

But while this is the case, in consequence

of this unintentional restriction, a very large class of our people have been deprived of all participation in the benefits of higher education. It has been almost impossible in this country for the merchant, the mechanic, the manufacturer to educate his son beyond the course of a common academy unless he gave him the education preparatory for a profession. This was not the education which he wanted, and, of course, his son has been deprived of the cultivation which the parent was able and willing to bestow.

Now the class of society that is thus left unprovided for constitutes the bone and sinew, the very choicest portion of this or of any community. They are the great agents of a production, they are the safest depositories of political power. It is their will that, in the end, sways the destinies of the nation. It is of the very highest importance, on every account, that this portion of a people should possess every facility for the acquisition of knowledge and intellectual discipline. Nothing would tend so much to the progress of wealth among us as the diffusion throughout the whole people of a knowledge of the principles of science and the application of science to the arts.

And besides, a knowledge of moral and intellectual philosophy, of the fundamental principles of law, of our own constitution, of history, of vegetable and animal physiology, and of many other sciences is just as necessary and just as appropriate to the merchant, the manufacturer, the mechanic, and the farmer, as to the lawyer, the clergyman, or the physician. Why should it be supposed that all higher knowledge should be engrossed exclusively by the professions? If a man wishes to give his son a good education, why should he be obliged to make him a lawyer, a physician, or a clergyman? Why should not the highest intellectual endowment, cultivated by the best preparatory discipline, be found in every mode of occupation? And if this be so, why has this whole subject been so long neglected

Francis Wayland, president of Brown University

among us? Is it not time that our system should in this matter undergo a complete and radical revision?

What I would propose on this subject, then, is briefly as follows. In the first place, let the course preparatory to a profession be distinctly marked out and let it be generous and thorough. Let it embrace such branches of study as are particularly necessary for fitting men for the professions, and let it be carried on to such an extent as shall communicate enlarged and generous knowledge and vigorous mental discipline. But while this is done, let our system be so enlarged in its provisions that the means of education in other branches may be open to all who choose to avail themselves of them. Let there be established courses of lectures on all the subjects which I have specified, and as many more as may be necessary to which men of all classes may resort. Let there be no compulsory residence, let every man come by ticket, and let him be admitted to every privilege which the nature of the case demands.

In a word, let the college be the grand center of intelligence to all classes and conditions of men, diffusing among all the light of every kind of knowledge and approving itself to the best feelings of every class of the community. Let it, besides being a preparatory school to the professions, be a Lowell Institute to the region in which it is placed. I know of nothing that would tend so strongly to promote the growth of wealth and civilization and refinement among us. Nothing would so surely annihilate that division of the community into classes, which already, in spite of our democratic institutions, threatens the direst evils to our republic.

3. *Of the officers of colleges.* I have . . . endeavored to set forth the evils of our present organization in this respect. I would suggest the importance of opening our professorships to a freer competition so that the college may have the benefit of a choice from all the talent that is willing to employ itself in the profession of instruction. Besides this I would have the emolument of every professor so adjusted that he shall feel directly the results of his diligence and ability, or of his indolence and inefficiency. There can be no reason why a teacher in college should not be placed under the same inducements to labor as any other man. In no other way can we expect him to devote his whole talent with earnestness to his profession. On no other principles can we expect the cause of education to be sustained with the vigor and efficiency which its importance so clearly demands.

If it be said that this is impracticable then there are other means which must be resorted to. The college must be placed under close and active supervision. The board of visitors must annually examine its condition, and, without fear, favor, or affection, remove from time to time every unsuitable incumbent. This would accomplish the same result in another way, but it would be an onerous, an unpleasant, and an odious duty. It is better to construct the system in such manner that an inefficient officer would have no desire to remain than to make the place desirable for him and then displace him by an arbitrary act.

4. *Of the discipline of our colleges.* I have endeavored to show that our discipline is too lax for the young and unnecessarily strict for the older students. Two methods would present themselves for relieving this embarrassment. The one is to admit no student until he had attained to the age of self-government, and then leave him to his own responsibility. The other would be to admit the young, but place them under stricter supervision. I think that either plan would have advantages over our present system. How far such a change could be carried into effect, I must leave to the judgment of the officers of each particular institution. I am, however, well convinced that our colleges would be greatly improved by raising the requirements of admission to the regular or professional course so high that the student might be obliged to spend a year or two years longer in the grammar school. The studies of most of our colleges during the first year might be more successfully pursued in school under the eye of the instructor than within the walls of a university. A change of this kind would be greatly for the advantage both of the college and of the grammar school.

And if the plan which I have suggested were carried into effect, that is, if the advantages of the institution were thrown open to every class of society, this extension of the requirements might the more easily be enforced. There would be no crowding into the regular course of those who enter merely for the sake of the benefit of particular studies and who wish to graduate at the earliest practicable age. Their object could be accomplished more successfully in another way. Each course of instruction would stand on its own merits, and the object of the institution would be to render each one as perfect as the nature of the case would permit.

On the subject of residence in college, I have already suggested an opinion. It seems to me that in investing so large a portion of our funds in erecting dormitories, we have committed an error. The funds have, however, been thus appropriated, and they cannot be recalled. Were the system of residence abandoned, these buildings could be of no use except for the residence of professors. If this part of our plan be injudicious, we can, however, cease to repeat our error. We can refrain from spending any more of our money in this manner. And we can, as opportunity occurs, try the experiment of allowing residence out of college. If it be found on a fair trial to succeed, it will at least demonstrate the important fact that a college or university can be established, with all the means of instruction which we now possess, at half or one-third of the expense which it now involves. This will certainly be an important addition to our knowledge on the subject.

5. *Of premiums.* I have alluded to the importance of this mode of stimulants in a course of education. I will only add that I would extend the benefit of this incentive to every branch of knowledge taught by a college, not merely to the regular preparatory course but to every other. Were this done, I am persuaded that a keen and honorable emulation would be excited among all classes of students. Prizes would be borne away by young men in every occupation. Mechanics, farmers, merchants, and manufacturers would vie with their fellows preparing for the professions, and would as often be entitled to the distinction conferred upon merit. The effect of this upon all classes of the community would be incalculable, and I can conceive of no case in which it would not be beneficial.

In this manner, also, deserving young men of narrow means might be most advantageously assisted. The prize, if in money, would materially relieve their wants, while instead of being bestowed as an alms, it would be conferred as a reward of merits; instead of depressing the recipient by proclaiming his poverty, it would distinguish him in the eyes of the community as one who had deserved well. I believe that if a large part of the funds appropriated in our colleges for the support of the indigent were distributed in this manner, it would have the most beneficial effect upon the cause of education.

Here I close these remarks which have, I fear, been already too far extended. It has been my lot to speak chiefly of the defects of our system of education. It would have been much more agreeable to treat of its excellencies, which I believe to be great and manifold. To speak of these, however, did not come within the scope of my design, which was merely to take notice of those things which need to be improved. The motive with which I have written, so far as I am conscious of it, has been to contribute my mite toward the improvement of higher education in our country. I offer it to the consideration of the public with unfeigned diffidence, in the humble hope that it may in a small degree contribute to the wider diffusion of intellectual cultivation among all classes of the community.

The years teach much which the days never know.
RALPH WALDO EMERSON, "Experience"

11.

PHILIP HONE: Rebellion in Rhode Island

In early 1842 Rhode Island had two governors: one, Sam King, had been elected under the charter constitution, unrevised since 1663; the other, Thomas Dorr, had been elected under a new constitution adopted by a majority of Rhode Island voters in defiance of the state government. The situation was tense. Both King and Dorr looked outside the state for military aid. President Tyler backed King, while Dorr was promised aid from New York City's Radical Democrats. On May 17 Dorr staged an insurrection. After that failed, he gathered together the proffered forces from New York and Connecticut at Chepachet, Rhode Island. When these were dispersed in June, Dorr disbanded his movement. Philip Hone, a conservative New Yorker, had no sympathy for Dorr, but he realized that the legality of Dorr's action was being seriously debated throughout the nation. Hone's comments on the Dorr Rebellion are from diary entries of April and May 1842.

Source: *The Diary of Philip Hone 1828-1851*, Bayard Tuckerman, ed., New York, 1889, Vol. II, pp. 123-131.

April 4. The anniversary of the death of William Henry Harrison, the good President. The flags are suspended at half-mast from the Whig public houses and some other conspicuous places, and well may they be! The bells should be tolled, and if the people were to put on sackcloth and ashes, such manifestations of grief would not transcend the cause. The decease of the good old man, much to be lamented by his personal and political friends, was to him of small importance. He had arrived at the summit of a man's ambition in this country and could not have died at a better time for himself. But how little did the American people comprehend the extent of their bereavement! One year of the rule of imbecility, arrogance, and prejudice has taught them the folly of selecting for vice-president a man of whose fitness for the office of President they had no reasonable assurance.

The *New York Herald*, which is said to be high in favor with Mr. Tyler and considered a sort of semi-official, says that he is about to resign. God grant it may be true! But if he does, he will gain no credit for it. He would undoubtedly serve his country more effectually by such a step than by all the actions of his previous life, and would for once be entitled to the gratitude of his fellow citizens; but he would not receive it. No credit would be given to him for a motive so patriotic; it would rather be attributed to that sort of patriotism which caused Hull to desert his post and surrender Detroit when he spied out in the cloud which darkened the horizon a hostile force approaching.

But the report can have no foundation. It is only raised to keep Bennett's hand in, who lives by lying. John Tyler resign! Why, he is just *weak* enough to believe himself the *strongest* man in the United States! He has all the self-conceit of him who announced in the plenitude of his arrogance that "he would administer the laws as *he*" (not the Supreme Court) "understood them"; while at the same time he does not possess a tithe of his force of mind and strength of intellect. . . .

April 21. A terrible hubbub has been going on in the redoubtable little state of Rhode Island for some time past. A party of disorganizing, radical demagogues, unable to accomplish their object of changing the politics of this steady state and bringing themselves into office by fair means, have set about defeating the will of the people (of which, when it suits them, they pretend to be the champions and supporters) and, having made a constitution of their own, have elected a governor (one Mr. Dorr) and state officers; while the sober part of the community, proceeding according to law and the constitution, have reelected the present governor (King) and the state officers as at present constituted. So the smallest state in the Union is the only one which can boast of *two* governors, and the sword of civil commotion is likely to be drawn in a quarter hitherto distinguished for good order and obedience to the laws.

The incendiaries, headed by Dutee J. Pierce, and other such warriors, many of whom are auxiliaries from other states, impelled solely by a love of liberty and reverence for other men's rights, swear that the state belongs to them, and that they will govern it; while the other party swear that it does not, and that they shall not, and so they are preparing to go to blows about the matter. President Tyler, on being applied to by the regulars, has written a letter, which is published, in which he avows his intention, in a manly, frank manner, to carry out

the duty prescribed to him in the Constitution of the United States, by supporting the constitution of the state and standing by the right. And, if more gentle means are unavailable, United States troops will be sent to settle the hash.

What acts of tyranny are committed nowadays under the name of *liberty,* and how the people's will is defeated by those who profess to be their best friends. The Rhode Island rebels, as well as the New York Locofocos, have no notion of heeding the *vox populi,* when that *vox* fails to raise the one to power in the state or to secure to the other the patronage and emoluments of municipal supremacy. . . .

April 26. When I returned home, I found that Dr. Wainwright had called in the course of the morning to invite me to a family dinner to meet Mr. William H. Prescott, of Boston, the accomplished author of the *History of the Reign of Ferdinand and Isabella,* who had just arrived in town on a very short visit. I joined the pleasant little party after they had dined and enjoyed a highly intellectual treat. The party consisted of the doctor, Mr. Prescott, Henry Brevoort, George Griffin, John C. Hamilton, Henry Cary, and myself. Mr. Prescott is rather a handsome man of about six-and-forty, of intellectual appearance, good manners, agreeable conversation, and much vivacity. Mr. Prescott reminded me that we had met before, at dinner at General Lyman's in Boston.

April 28. Our city was disgraced by a meeting, last evening, at Tammany Hall, called by Alderman Purdy, Messrs. Slamm, Vanderpoel, and such persons to approve the proceedings of the insurrectionists in Rhode Island, who are in arms against the constitution and laws of the state, and to encourage them in their factious opposition to the constituted authorities and their con-

Philip Hone, Whig mayor of New York, 1825

tempt for the expressed opinion of the general government. Aaron Vanderpoel (the "Kinderhook roarer," as he is familiarly called by those who have listened to the dulcet tones of his voice in the House of Representatives) was most appropriately chosen chairman of the meeting, and addresses were made by Mr. Parmenter, a Rhode Island Jacobin, and Mr. Davezac, Mr. Edmunds, and other New York patriots, and resolutions were passed suited to the occasion.

What would these fellows have said if the people of Providence had held a meeting to denounce the law of the last legislature of New York, repealing the late salutary Registry Act, or that which destroyed the beneficial influence of the public schools to propitiate the Irish Catholics and secure their votes at the expense of the rights of native Americans? That would have been stigmatized as an impertinent interference in other people's affairs, while their meeting last night was a generous ebullition of patriotic sympathy in favor of the oppressed victims of official tyranny. . . .

May 3. Tomorrow is the day appointed by the Rhode Island insurgents for the organization of their pretended government under the officers illegally elected by what is called the "Free Suffrage Party." In expectation of the violence which it is feared will attend these insurrectionary proceedings, United States troops have been sent on to Providence from the different stations; two companies went from Governor's Island a day or two since, and yesterday a detachment from Norfolk passed through this city. General Wood is on the spot prepared for *business,* and it is hoped that the prompt interference of the general government to "keep the peace" will prevent bloodshed for the present; but finally it will result, as it always does, in the "fierce democracy" getting the better of law and good order. Downward, downward is the tendency of all political affairs in this country! If old King George III, who so reluctantly released us from colonial bondage, could raise his obstinate head and take a look at us, how would he rejoice to contemplate the probable failure of our experiment of self-government.

May 19. The face of affairs has changed in Rhode Island. Governor Dorr, the supernumerary governor of that redoubtable little state, who came to New York a lamb and was sent on to Providence a lion by the Tammany sympathizers, drew his sword, planted his cannon, fortified his castle, issued his proclamation, and doomed to death, without "benefit of clergy," every man opposed to him. But finding that his friends fell from him, and his enemies gathered strength and courage, he sheathed his Durandina [Durandal, sword of Roland], withdrew his bloody sentence, as he did his own person, and, his cannon refusing to *go off*, went off himself in the middle of the night. And when Governor King, accompanied by the sheriff, went to arrest him yesterday morning, he had "absquatulated," "mizzled," "made tracks" (either of which terms may be used, each being considered equally classical in the slang nomenclature of the day, and particularly appropriate and expressive in the present case) —

> And Governor Dorr
> Was seen no more.

The first accounts from Providence led us to suppose that, with the retreat of the leader, the opposition to the laws and the constituted authorities had ceased; but it appears that a body of his followers still retained possession of the cannon and had thrown up a sort of redoubt for their defense. But this was probably intended as a means of securing a favorable capitulation, and the steamboat tomorrow will, it is hoped, bring us the agreeable tidings that the civil war is at an end.

Now, what a pretty figure do the men cut who encouraged the Rhode Island rebels and denounced the general government for the interference to which it was enjoined by the Constitution! Some of them begin already to back out. Stephen Allen has published a sort of halfway disavowal. He only meant "to *advise* the President, not to interfere." "He did not mean to take sides with the insurgents" — not he, good, easy man! "He was engaged and did not attend the meeting." Most virtuous citizen! But he *did* allow his name to be used by a set of fellows, of whose companionship he was ashamed, for a purpose which he knew could come to no good; and so he will again, whenever his tools say he must; and so will Walter Browne, and John J. Morgan, and Churchill C. Cambreling, and Campbell P. White; but they have done a deed, the bad odor of which they will never be able to shake from their garments.

If, hereafter, any of them shall go to Newport or Providence, the finger of scorn will be pointed at them, as incendiaries who threw from a distance a brand to light the flames of civil discord in a sister state and put weapons in the hands of misguided men to shed the blood of their brethren and neighbors. I record with pleasure the fact that some of the leading men of the Locofoco Party refused to be made parties to this nefarious proceeding. My old acquaintance John Targee (whose orthodoxy nobody can doubt) told me today that he refused to sign the call for the meeting as an affair which he did not understand, and an interference which he could not justify; and, furthermore, if they used his name he would come out publicly and disavow it.

12.

Thomas Dorr: The People's Right to Remake Their Constitution

The government of Rhode Island operated under the colonial charter of 1663, which severely restricted the franchise and made no provisions for constitutional change. In 1841, after the government proved unwilling to liberalize itself, Thomas Dorr called a people's convention. It framed a new constitution that was submitted to and endorsed by the citizens in December. To establish his government, which the charter government refused to recognize, Dorr led two armed revolts, in mid-May and June of 1842. When the second failed, Dorr fled the state. The charter government then succumbed to public sentiment and promulgated a new and acceptable constitution. After its adoption in November 1842, Dorr returned to Rhode Island. He was arrested, convicted of high treason, and sentenced to prison for life. However, in 1845 he was liberated and in 1854 the charges against him were annulled. Dorr delivered the speech from which the following selection is reprinted on May 3, 1842, to the Constitutional (Dorrite) Assembly.

Source: 28 Congress, 1 Session, House Report No. 546.

Two QUESTIONS . . . arise to which it is our duty to reply — a question of right, and a question of fact. Had the people of this state a right to adopt a constitution of government in the mode they have pursued? And, if so, have they adopted this constitution by a majority of their whole number?

That the sovereignty of this country resides in the people is an axiom in the American system of government which it is too late to call in question. By the theory of other governments, the sovereign power is vested in the head of the state or shared with him by the legislature. The sovereignty of the country from which we derive our origin and, I may add, many of our opinions upon political subjects, inconsistent with our present condition, is in the King and Parliament; and any attempt on the part of the people to change the govern-

ment of that country, would be deemed an insurrection.

There, all reform must proceed from the government itself, which calls no conventions of the people and recognizes no such remedy for political grievances. In this country, the case is totally the reverse. When the Revolution severed the ties of allegiance which bound the colonies to the parent country, the sovereign power passed from its former possessors, not to the general government, which was the creation of the states; nor to the state governments; nor to a portion of the people; but to the whole people of the states, in whom it has ever since remained. This is the doctrine of our fathers and of the early days of the republic, and should be sacredly guarded as the only safe foundation of our political fabric.

The idea that government is in any proper sense the source of power in this country is of foreign origin, and at war with the letter and spirit of our institutions. The moment we admit the principle that no change in government can take place without permission of the existing authorities, we revert to the worn-out theory of the monarchies of Europe; and whether we are the subjects of the czar of Russia, or of the monarch of Great Britain, or of a landed oligarchy, the difference to us is only in degree; and we have lost the reality, though we may retain the forms, of a democratic republic.

If the people of Rhode Island are wrong in the course they have pursued, they will nevertheless have conferred one benefit upon their countrymen by the agitation of this question, in dissipating the notion that the people are the sovereigns of the country, and in consigning to the department of rhetorical declamation those solemn declarations of 1776, which are repeated in so many of the state constitutions, and which are so clearly and confidently asserted by the most eminent jurists and statesmen of our country.

By sovereign power, we understand that ultimate power which must be vested somewhere and which prescribes the form and functions of government. It is, of course, superior to the legislative power, which can be properly exerted only according to rules laid down for its action, in that expression of the sovereign will called a constitution. This sovereignty is a personal attribute and belongs to the man himself, and not to the soil or property with which he may be endowed. It is a power seldom visible, which ought to be, and can be, but rarely exerted. The making and altering of laws, which lie at the foundations of society, should be a work of great care and caution; and when done, ought to be well done, that it may be effectual and permanent.

It is our misfortune in this state that, as no expression of the sovereign will has been, until recently, made in the adoption of a constitution, and no index of this will

Thomas Dorr, engraving from a daguerreotype, 1845

constantly before the public eye, the distinction between the two powers has become obliterated among us; and the legislature has been regarded not only as the immediate acting power but as the sole power of the state; and all who maintain the right of the people in their original, sovereign capacity, to alter the present government and render it conformable to their just rights, have been represented as hostile to law and order and as putting in jeopardy the stability of government.

On the other hand, we contend that the people have a right to change the government when necessary to their welfare; that they are the judges of that necessity; that "time does not run against the people, any more than against the king," and that they have not forfeited this right by any acquiescence; that a power to assent, involves another to dissent; that even if a past generation had surrendered to a minority their political rights (which they never have done), they did not, and could not, bind their successors or prevent them from reassuming their sovereignty.

If time permitted, I should take great sat-

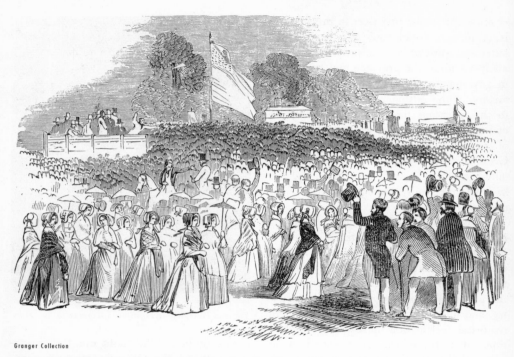

Granger Collection

"Great Mass Meeting for Democracy and Dorr," at Providence, R.I., September 4, 1844

isfaction in laying before you the most abundant evidence that these are the well-recognized principles of our republican system and are not to be regarded as revolutionary.

The Declaration of American Independence asserts that governments derive their just powers from the consent of the governed; and that it is the right of the people (meaning the whole people, the governed) to alter or abolish their government whenever they deem it expedient, and to institute new government, laying its foundations on such principles and organizing its powers in such form as to them shall seem most likely to effect their safety and happiness. This declaration was expressly adopted by the General Assembly of this state in July 1776.

The constitutions of many of the states, while they contain specific provisions for the mode of their amendment, set forth, in the strongest terms, the right of the people to change them as they may deem expedient. Any other construction would render a portion of the declarations of rights in these constitutions entirely nugatory.

The Convention which framed the Constitution of the United States acted as the representatives of the sovereignty of the people of the states, without regard to the limitation attempted to be imposed by the Congress of the Confederation. That the whole people, by an explicit and authentic act — the great body of society — have a right to make and alter their constitutions of government is a principle which has been laid down by the fathers of the Constitution, and the ablest expounders of our political institutions, by Washington, Hamilton, and Madison. The strong opinions of Jefferson on this point are too well known to need a particular repetition. . . .

But, whatever opinions may be entertained respecting the right of the whole people to change a constitution in any other than the prescribed mode, where such a mode exists, there is a point in our case to which the attention of everyone should be closely invited. Until the adoption of the present constitution, there has been no mode prescribed in this state, either by the charter or by any law or usage, for amending our form of government. The charter contains no such direction; being a royal grant, the power to amend by a supplemental charter remained in the grantor and needed no specification. The charter contains a very general authority to make all necessary laws; but they must be consistent with the royal prerogative and with the rights of Parliament. The power of amending the charter passed over to the people of the state as an incident to their sovereignty at the Revolution.

In the absence of any such provision, it is a totally unfounded assumption in the charter Assembly to pretend that the proceedings of the people are null and void for want of a compliance with law, when no legal or other provision exists upon the subject. All that the General Assembly have ever done has been to request, in their own form, the freemen to assemble and elect delegates to form a constitution.

The freemen, if they saw fit, might at any time have chosen such delegates, without such a request, in their own form and with an equally valid effect. Is it not apparent that the people at large have a still greater right to do the same thing in this state? They have demanded in vain that any valid legal objections to their proceedings should be produced. It is to the last degree ungenerous and unjust that the freemen should set up their own neglect in years past to provide a constitutional mode of amendments as a bar to the action of the people, in the only mode in which they can act at all. When any disposition is manifested to amend our constitution in a different mode from that prescribed in it, it will be time for alarmists to suggest the danger and instability that may possibly occur from any irregular action of the people. . . .

When the constitution of the people is examined, without reference to its origin, it is found that there are few objections made against it. It guards with great care all civil and political rights; it establishes as equal a representation as the circumstances of the state will permit, and a Senate to be chosen in districts under such an apportionment as to secure to a majority of the population a majority of its members. The freeholders' constitution, on the other hand, was rejected for many reasons — one of which was its defective provisions relating to suffrage and its exclusion of the vote by ballot. The main objection was that it entirely abolished the majority principle in our government. Under it, both the House of Representatives and the Senate were to be elected by towns and districts containing less than one-third of the inhabitants of the state. The senators were also assigned to the districts, without scarcely any reference to their population.

By the nature of the provisions relative to amendment, any subsequent improvement of this instrument was rendered nearly impracticable.

At the session of the Assembly in March 1842, the people's constitution came under the consideration of that body, twice ratified — directly by the votes of the people in its favor, and indirectly by the rejection of another instrument. But these repeated manifestations of the popular will were totally disregarded. A bill to conform the general election to the provisions of this constitution, and another to submit it to those who were qualified to vote under the constitution of the freeholders, were promptly rejected. A proposition was made to extend suffrage; and a second proposition was offered at the adjourned session in April for the call of another convention to form a constitution — the delegates to which convention were to be voted for by a constituency not much extended beyond the present freeholder. Both propositions shared the fate of the preceding.

Your attention will be required to the Force Law and resolutions recently adopted by the General Assembly for the suppression of the constitution. Laws like these, which violate in some of their provisions the well-known privileges enjoyed by the subjects of the British monarchy, could hardly find favor in the land of Roger Williams. These enactments have been regarded by the considerate men among our opponents as most impolitic and unjust, and by the people as null and void, because conflicting with the paramount provisions of the constitution.

Military preparations have been made by direction of the Assembly; and the people have been consequently put upon the defensive. But this is not the age nor the country in which the will of the people can be overawed or defeated by measures like these. There is reason to believe that a letter addressed to Governor King by the President of the United States was written under a mistake of the facts, occasioned by the misrepresentation of the character, motives, and objects of the constitutionalists of this state.

Our fellow citizens in other states will perceive, from the exposition which has been made, without further comment, that the people of this state are engaged in a just and honorable cause; and that they have taken the only course for the attainment and security of their just rights.

We are assembled in pursuance of the constitution, and under a sacred obligation to carry its provisions into effect. Knowing the spirit which you have manifested throughout this exciting controversy; the moderate but determined course which you have pursued; your love of order and re-

spect for all constitutional laws and for the rights of all other persons while engaged in the acquisition of your own; I hardly need to remind you of your duty to cast behind you all injuries or provocations, and to leave them to the retributive justice of public opinion, which will ultimately appreciate every sincere sacrifice to the cause of truth, of freedom, and humanity.

Entertaining the deep and earnest conviction that we are engaged in such a cause, and conscious of our own imperfections, let us implore the favor of that gracious Providence which guided the steps of our ancestors, upon this our attempt to restore and permanently secure the blessings of that well-ordered and rational freedom here established by the patriotic founders of our state.

The provisions in the constitution, relating to the security of the right of suffrage against fraud and to the registration of voters, will require your immediate action. The state demands of its government an economical administration of affairs and will justly complain of any increase of its ordinary expenses at the present period.

I cannot more appropriately conclude this communication than in the words of the constitution, which declares that "No favor or disfavor ought to be shown in legislation toward any man, or party, or society, or religious denomination. The laws should be made, not for the good of the few but of the many; and the burdens of the state ought to be fairly distributed among its citizens."

———◆———

Any man more right than his neighbors constitutes a majority of one already.
HENRY DAVID THOREAU, *Resistance to Civil Government*, 1849

13.

LEMUEL SHAW: *Commonwealth of Massachusetts v. Hunt*

The opinion handed down by Chief Justice Lemuel Shaw of the Massachusetts Supreme Court in Commonwealth v. Hunt *was the first judicial decision in the United States that labor unions were not illegal criminal conspiracies. The defendants, seven journeymen bootmakers, had been found guilty by a lower court, on the basis of the decision in the New York case of* People v. Fisher *(1835). Justice Shaw's decision recognized the right of workmen both to strike and to maintain a closed shop. The idea that workingmen might lawfully organize unions was generally accepted in the United States after 1842, but the right to strike continued to be opposed for many years.*

Source: *Reports of Cases Argued and Determined in the Supreme Judicial Court of Massachusetts,* Theron Metcalf, ed., Boston, 1864, Vol. IV, pp. 111-137.

WHEN THE CRIMINALITY of a conspiracy consists in an unlawful agreement of two or more persons to compass or promote some criminal or illegal purpose, that purpose must be fully and clearly stated in the indictment; and if the criminality of the offense which is intended to be charged consists in the agreement to compass or promote some purpose, not of itself criminal or unlawful, by the use of fraud, force, falsehood, or other criminal or unlawful means, such intended use of fraud, force, falsehood, or other criminal or unlawful means must be set out in the indictment. . . .

The counsel for the defendants contended, and requested the court to instruct the jury, that the indictment did not set forth any agreement to do a criminal act, or to do any lawful act by any specified criminal means, and that the agreements therein set forth did not constitute a conspiracy indictable by any law of this commonwealth. But the judge refused so to do, and instructed the jury that the indictment did, in his opinion, describe a confederacy among the defendants to do an unlawful act and to effect the same by unlawful means; that the

society, organized and associated for the purposes described in the indictment was an unlawful conspiracy against the laws of this commonwealth; and that if the jury believed from the evidence in the case, that the defendants, or any of them, had engaged in such a confederacy, they were bound to find such of them guilty.

We are here carefully to distinguish between the confederacy set forth in the indictment and the confederacy or association contained in the constitution of the Boston Journeymen Bootmakers' Society, as stated in the little printed book which was admitted as evidence on the trial. Because, though it was thus admitted as evidence, it would not warrant a conviction for anything not stated in the indictment. It was proof, as far as it went, to support the averments in the indictment. If it contained any criminal matter not set forth in the indictment, it is of no avail. The question then presents itself in the same form as on a motion in arrest of judgment.

The first count set forth that the defendants, with diverse others unknown, on the day and at the place named, being workmen and journeymen in the art and occupation of bootmakers, unlawfully, perniciously, and deceitfully designing and intending to continue, keep up, form, and unite themselves into an unlawful club, society, and combination, and make unlawful bylaws, rules, and orders among themselves, and thereby govern themselves and other workmen in the said art, and unlawfully and unjustly to extort great sums of money by means thereof, did unlawfully assemble and meet together, and, being so assembled, did unjustly and corruptly conspire, combine, confederate, and agree together that none of them should thereafter, and that none of them would, work for any master or person whatsoever in the said art, mystery, and occupation, who should employ any workman or journeyman, or other person, in the said art who was not a member of said club, society, or combination, after notice given him to discharge such workman, from the employ of such master; to the great damage and oppression, etc.

Now it is to be considered that the preamble and introductory matter in the indictment — such as unlawfully and deceitfully designing and intending unjustly to extort great sums, etc. — is mere recital and not traversable, and therefore cannot aid an imperfect averment of the facts constituting the description of the offense. The same may be said of the concluding matter, which follows the averment, as to the great damage and oppression not only of their said masters employing them in said art and occupation but also of diverse other workmen in the same art, mystery, and occupation, to the evil example, etc. If the facts averred constitute the crime, these are properly stated as the legal inferences to be drawn from them. If they do not constitute the charge of such an offense, they cannot be aided by these alleged consequences.

Stripped then of these introductory recitals and alleged injurious consequences, and of the qualifying epithets attached to the facts, the averment is this: that the defendants and others formed themselves into a society and agreed not to work for any person who should employ any journeyman or other person not a member of such society, after notice given him to discharge such workman.

The manifest intent of the association is to induce all those engaged in the same occupation to become members of it. Such a purpose is not unlawful. It would give them a power which might be exerted for useful and honorable purposes, or for dangerous and pernicious ones. If the latter were the real and actual object, and susceptible of proof, it should have been specially charged. Such an association might be used to afford each other assistance in times of poverty, sickness, and distress; or to raise their intellectual, moral, and social condition; or to make improvement in their art; or for other proper purposes. Or the association might be designed for purposes of oppression and injustice. But in order to charge all those who become members of an association with the guilt of a criminal conspiracy, it must be averred and proved that the actual if not the avowed object of the association was criminal.

An association may be formed, the declared objects of which are innocent and laudable, and yet they may have secret articles, or an agreement communicated only to the members, by which they are banded together for purposes injurious to the peace of society or the rights of its members. Such would undoubtedly be a criminal conspiracy, on proof of the fact, however meritorious and praiseworthy the declared objects might be. The law is not to be hoodwinked by colorable pretenses. It looks at truth and reality, through whatever disguise it may assume. But to make such an association, ostensibly innocent, the subject of prosecution as a criminal conspiracy, the secret agreement which makes it so is to be averred and proved as the gist of the offense.

But when an association is formed for purposes actually innocent, and afterward its powers are abused by those who have the control and management of it to purposes of oppression and injustice, it will be criminal in those who thus misuse it, or give consent thereto, but not in the other members of the association. In this case, no such secret agreement, varying the objects of the association from those avowed, is set forth in this count of the indictment.

Nor can we perceive that the objects of this association, whatever they may have been, were to be attained by criminal means. The means which they proposed to employ, as averred in this count, and which, as we are now to presume, were established by the proof, were that they would not work for a person who, after due notice, should employ a journeyman not a member of their society. Supposing the object of the association to be laudable and lawful, or at least not unlawful; are these means criminal? The case supposes that these persons are not bound by contract but free to work for whom they please, or not to work, if they so prefer. In this state of things, we cannot perceive that it is criminal for men to agree together to exercise their own acknowledged rights in such a manner as best to subserve their own interests.

One way to test this is to consider the effect of such an agreement, where the object of the association is acknowledged on all hands to be a laudable one. Suppose a class of workmen, impressed with the manifold evils of intemperance, should agree with each other not to work in a shop in which ardent spirit was furnished, or not to work in a shop with anyone who used it, or not to work for an employer who should, after notice, employ a journeyman who habitually used it. The consequences might be the same. A workman who should still persist in the use of ardent spirit would find it more difficult to get employment; a master employing such a one might, at times, experience inconvenience in his work in losing the services of a skillful but intemperate workman. Still it seems to us that as the

object would be lawful, and the means not unlawful, such an agreement could not be pronounced a criminal conspiracy.

From this count in the indictment, we do not understand that the agreement was that the defendants would refuse to work for an employer to whom they were bound by contract for a certain time in violation of that contract; nor that they would insist that an employer should discharge a workman engaged by contract for a certain time in violation of such contract. It is perfectly consistent with everything stated in this count that the effect of the agreement was that when they were free to act they would not engage with an employer, or continue in his employment, if such employer, when free to act, should engage with a workman, or continue a workman in his employment, not a member of the association.

If a large number of men, engaged for a certain time, should combine together to violate their contract and quit their employment together, it would present a very different question. Suppose a farmer, employing a large number of men, engaged for the year, at fair monthly wages, and suppose that just at the moment that his crops were ready to harvest, they should all combine to quit his service, unless he would advance their wages, at a time when other laborers could not be obtained. It would surely be a conspiracy to do an unlawful act, though of such a character that, if done by an individual, it would lay the foundation of a civil action only and not of a criminal prosecution. It would be a case very different from that stated in this count.

The second count, omitting the recital of unlawful intent and evil disposition, and omitting the direct averment of an unlawful club or society, alleges that the defendants, with others unknown, did assemble, conspire, confederate, and agree together not to work for any master or person who should employ any workman not being a member of a certain club, society, or combination, called the Boston Journeymen Bootmaker's

Society, or who should break any of their bylaws, unless such workmen should pay to said club such sum as should be agreed upon as a penalty for the breach of such unlawful rules, etc.; and that by means of said conspiracy they did compel one Isaac B. Wait, a master cordwainer, to turn out of his employ one Jeremiah Horne, a journeyman bootmaker, etc., in evil example, etc. So far as the averment of a conspiracy is concerned, all the remarks made in reference to the first count are equally applicable to this.

It is simply an averment of an agreement among themselves not to work for a person who should employ any person not a member of a certain association. It sets forth no illegal or criminal purpose to be accomplished, nor any illegal or criminal means to be adopted for the accomplishment of any purpose. It was an agreement as to the manner in which they would exercise an acknowledged right to contract with others for their labor. It does not aver a conspiracy or even an intention to raise their wages; and it appears by the bill of exceptions that the case was not put upon the footing of a conspiracy to raise their wages. . . .

As to the latter part of this count, which avers that by means of said conspiracy the defendants did compel one Wait to turn out of his employ one Jeremiah Horne, we remark, in the first place, that as the acts done in pursuance of a conspiracy, as we have before seen, are stated by way of aggravation and not as a substantive charge; if no criminal or unlawful conspiracy is stated, it cannot be aided and made good by mere matter of aggravation. If the principal charge falls, the aggravation falls with it. . . .

But, further, if this is to be considered as a substantive charge, it would depend altogether upon the force of the word "compel," which may be used in the sense of coercion, or duress, by force or fraud. It would therefore depend upon the context and the connection with other words to de-termine the sense in which it was used in the indictment. If, for instance, the indictment had averred a conspiracy, by the defendants, to compel Wait to turn Horne out of his employment, and to accomplish that object by the use of force or fraud, it would have been a very different case; especially if it might be fairly construed, as perhaps in that case it might have been, that Wait was under obligation, by contract, for an unexpired term of time, to employ and pay Horne. As before remarked, it would have been a conspiracy to do an unlawful though not a criminal act to induce Wait to violate his engagement, to the actual injury of Horne.

To mark the difference between the case of a journeyman, or a servant, and master, mutually bound by contract, and the same parties when free to engage anew, I should have before cited the case of the *Boston Glass Co.* v. *Binney.* . . . In that case, it was held actionable to entice another person's hired servant to quit his employment during the time for which he was engaged; but not actionable to treat with such hired servant while actually hired and employed by another to leave his service and engage in the employment of the person making the proposal when the term for which he is engaged shall expire. It acknowledges the established principle that every freeman, whether skilled laborer, mechanic, farmer, or domestic servant, may work or not work, or work or refuse to work with any company or individual, at his own option, except so far as he is bound by contract.

But whatever might be the force of the word "compel," unexplained by its connection, it is disarmed and rendered harmless by the precise statement of the means by which such compulsion was to be effected. It was the agreement not to work for him by which they compelled Wait to decline employing Horne longer. On both of these grounds, we are of opinion that the statement made in this second count, that the unlawful agreement was carried into execution, makes no essential difference between this and the first count.

The third count, reciting a wicked and unlawful intent to impoverish one Jeremiah Horne and hinder him from following his trade as a bootmaker, charges the defendants, with others unknown, with an unlawful conspiracy, by wrongful and indirect means, to impoverish said Horne and to deprive and hinder him from his said art and trade and getting his support thereby; and that, in pursuance of said unlawful combination, they did unlawfully and indirectly hinder and prevent, etc., and greatly impoverish him.

If the fact of depriving Jeremiah Horne of the profits of his business, by whatever means it might be done, would be unlawful and criminal, a combination to compass that object would be an unlawful conspiracy and it would be unnecessary to state the means. Such seems to have been the view of the court in *The King* v. *Eccles* . . . though the case is so briefly reported that the reasons on which it rests are not very obvious. The case seems to have gone on the ground that the means were matter of evidence and not of averment; and that after verdict, it was to be presumed that the means contemplated and used were such as to render the combination unlawful. . . .

Suppose a baker in a small village had the exclusive custom of his neighborhood and was making large profits by the sale of his bread. Supposing a number of those neighbors, believing the price of his bread too high, should propose to him to reduce his prices, or, if he did not, that they would introduce another baker; and on his refusal, such other baker should, under their encouragement, set up a rival establishment and sell his bread at lower prices. The effect would be to diminish the profit of the former baker and to the same extent to impoverish him. And it might be said and proved that the purpose of the associates was to diminish his profits and thus impoverish him, though the ultimate and laudable object of the combination was to reduce the cost of bread to themselves and their neighbors.

The same thing may be said of all competition in every branch of trade and industry; and yet it is through that competition that the best interests of trade and industry are promoted. It is scarcely necessary to allude to the familiar instances of opposition lines of conveyance, rival hotels, and the thousand other instances, where each strives to gain custom to himself by ingenious improvements, by increased industry, and by all the means by which he may lessen the price of commodities and thereby diminish the profits of others.

We think, therefore, that associations may be entered into, the object of which is to adopt measures that may have a tendency to impoverish another, that is, to diminish his gains and profits, and yet so far from being criminal or unlawful, the object may be highly meritorious and public spirited. The legality of such an association will therefore depend upon the means to be used for its accomplishment. If it is to be carried into effect by fair or honorable and lawful means, it is, to say the least, innocent; if by falsehood or force, it may be stamped with the character of conspiracy.

It follows as a necessary consequence that if criminal and indictable, it is so by reason of the criminal means intended to be employed for its accomplishment; and as a further legal consequence, that as the criminality will depend on the means, those means must be stated in the indictment. If the same rule were to prevail in criminal which holds in civil proceedings — that a case defectively stated may be aided by a verdict — then a court might presume, after verdict, that the indictment was supported by proof of criminal or unlawful means to effect the object. But it is an established rule in criminal cases that the indictment must state a complete indictable offense and cannot be aided by the proof offered at the trial.

14.

Lydia M. Child: Against Capital Punishment

Lydia Child was an active humanitarian and a prolific writer. Her Letters from
New-York *were written during the eight years she resided in New York City helping
her husband edit the* Anti-Slavery Standard, *and were published in two volumes
in 1843 and 1845. Letter XXXI, on capital punishment, dated November 19, 1842, is
reproduced below. A bill to abolish capital punishment had been recommended by a
select committee of New York state legislators in 1841. The bill was reputedly popular
among both citizens and lawmakers, but it was defeated by a narrow margin.*

Source: *Letters from New-York,* New York, 1846, pp. 220-230.

TODAY, I CANNOT WRITE of beauty, for I am sad and troubled. Heart, head, and conscience are all in battle array against the savage customs of my time. By and by, the law of love, like oil upon the waters, will calm my surging sympathies and make the current flow more calmly, though nonetheless deep or strong. But, today, do not ask me to love governor, sheriff, or constable, or any man who defends capital punishment. I ought to do it; for genuine love enfolds even murderers with its blessing. By tomorrow, I think I can remember them without bitterness; but, today, I cannot love them; on my soul, I cannot.

We were to have had an execution yesterday; but the wretched prisoner avoided it by suicide. The gallows had been erected for several hours, and with a cool refinement of cruelty was hoisted before the window of the condemned. The hangman was all ready to cut the cord; marshals paced back and forth, smoking and whistling; spectators were waiting impatiently to see whether he would "die game." Printed circulars had been handed abroad to summon the number of witnesses required by law: "You are respectfully invited to witness the execution of John C. Colt." I trust some of them are preserved for museums. Specimens should be kept, as relics of a barbarous age, for succeeding generations to wonder at. They might be hung up in a frame; and the portrait of a New Zealand chief, picking the bones of an enemy of his tribe, would be an appropriate pendant.

This bloody insult was thrust into the hands of *some* citizens, who carried hearts under their vests, and they threw it in tattered fragments to the dogs and swine, as more fitting witnesses than human beings. It was cheering to those who have faith in human progress to see how many viewed the subject in this light. But as a general thing, the very spirit of murder was rife among the dense crowd, which thronged the place of execution. They were swelling with revenge and eager for blood. One man came all the way from New Hampshire, on purpose, to witness the entertainment; thereby showing himself a likely subject for the gallows, whoever he may be.

Women deemed themselves not treated with becoming gallantry, because tickets of admittance were denied them; and I think it showed injudicious partiality; for many of them can be taught murder by as short a lesson as any man, and sustain it by arguments from Scripture as ably as any theologian. However, they were not admitted to this edifying exhibition in the great school of public morals; and had only the slim comfort of standing outside, in a keen November wind, to catch the first toll of the bell which would announce that a human brother had been sent struggling into eternity by the hand of violence.

But while the multitude stood with open watches and strained ears to catch the sound, and the marshals smoked and whistled, and the hangman walked up and down, waiting for his prey, lo! word was brought that the criminal was found dead in his bed! He had asked one half hour alone to prepare his mind for departure; and at the end of that brief interval, he was found with a dagger thrust into his heart. The tidings were received with fierce mutterings of disappointed rage. The throng beyond the walls were furious to see him with their own eyes, to be sure that he was dead. But when the welcome news met *my* ear, a tremendous load was taken from my heart. I had no chance to analyze right and wrong; for over all thought and feeling flowed impulsive joy that this "Christian" community were cheated of a hanging.

They who had assembled to commit legalized murder in cold blood, with strange confusion of ideas, were unmindful of their own guilt, while they talked of his suicide as a crime equal to that for which he was condemned. I am willing to leave it between him and his God. For myself, I would rather have the burden of it on my own soul than take the guilt of those who would have executed a fellow creature. *He* was driven to a fearful extremity of agony and desperation. He was precisely in the situation of a man on board a burning ship, who being *compelled* to face death, jumps into the waves as the least painful mode of the two. But they, who thus drove him "to walk the plank," made cool, deliberate preparations to take life, and with inventive

cruelty sought to add every bitter drop that *could* be added to the dreadful cup of vengeance.

To me, human life seems so sacred a thing that its violent termination always fills me with horror, whether perpetrated by an individual or a crowd; whether done contrary to law and custom, or according to law and custom. Why John C. Colt should be condemned to an ignominious death for an act of resentment altogether unpremeditated, while men who deliberately, and with malice aforethought, go out to murder another for some insulting word are judges and senators in the land, and favorite candidates for the President's chair, is more than I can comprehend. There is, to say the least, a strange inconsistency in our customs.

At the same moment that I was informed of the death of the prisoner, I heard that the prison was on fire. It was soon extinguished, but the remarkable coincidence added not a little to the convulsive excitement of the hour. I went with a friend to look at the beautiful spectacle; for it was exceedingly beautiful. The fire had kindled at the very top of the cupola, the wind was high, and the flames rushed upward, as if the angry spirits below had escaped on fiery wings. Heaven forgive the feelings that for a moment mingled with my admiration of that beautiful conflagration! Society had kindled all around me a bad excitement, and one of the infernal sparks fell into my own heart. If this was the effect produced on me, who am by nature tender-hearted, by principle opposed to all retaliation, and by social position secluded from contact with evil, what must it have been on the minds of rowdies and desperadoes? The effect of executions on *all* brought within their influence is evil, and nothing but evil.

For a fortnight past, this whole city has been kept in a state of corroding excitement, either of hope or fear. The stern pride of the prisoner left little in his peculiar case to appeal to the sympathies of society; yet the instincts of our common nature rose up against the sanguinary spirit manifested toward him. The public were, moreover, divided in opinion with regard to the legal construction of his crime; and in the keen discussion of *legal* distinctions, *moral* distinctions became woefully confused. Each day hope and fear alternated; the natural effect of all this was to have the whole thing regarded as a game in which the criminal might or might not become the winner; and every experiment of this kind shakes public respect for the laws, from center to circumference.

Worse than all this was the horrible amount of diabolical passion excited. The hearts of men were filled with murder; they gloated over the thoughts of vengeance, and were rabid to witness a fellow creature's agony. They complained loudly that he was not to be hung high enough for the crowd to see him. "What a pity!" exclaimed a woman, who stood near me, gazing at the burning tower; "they will have to give him two hours more to live." "Would you feel so, if he were your *son?*" said I. Her countenance changed instantly. She had not before realized that every criminal was *somebody's* son.

As we walked homeward, we encountered a deputy sheriff; not the most promising material, certainly, for lessons on humanity; but to him we spoke of the crowd of savage faces and the tones of hatred as obvious proofs of the bad influence of capital punishment. "I know that," said he; "but I don't see how we could dispense with it. Now suppose we had fifty murderers shut up in prison for life, instead of hanging 'em; and suppose there should come a revolution; what an awful thing it would be to have fifty murderers inside the prison to be let loose upon the community!" "There is another side to that proposition," we answered; "for every criminal you execute, you make a hundred murderers

outside the prison, each as dangerous as would be the one inside." He said perhaps it was so, and went his way.

As for the punishment and the terror of such doings, they fall most keenly on the best hearts in the community. Thousands of men, as well as women, had broken and startled sleep for several nights preceding that dreadful day. Executions always excite a universal shudder among the innocent, the humane, and the wise-hearted. It is the voice of God, crying aloud within us against the wickedness of this savage custom. Else why is it that the instinct is so universal?

The last conversation I had with the late William Ladd made a strong impression upon my mind. While he was a sea captain, he occasionally visited Spain, and once witnessed an execution there. He said that no man, however low and despicable, would consent to perform the office of hangman; and whoever should dare to suggest such a thing to a decent man would be likely to have his brains blown out. This feeling was so strong and so universal that the only way they could procure an executioner was to offer a condemned criminal his own life if he would consent to perform the vile and hateful office on another. Sometimes executions were postponed for months because there was no condemned criminal to perform the office of hangman. A fee was allotted by law to the wretch who did perform it, but no one would run the risk of touching his polluted hand by giving it to him; therefore, the priest threw the purse as far as possible; the odious being ran to pick it up, and hastened to escape from the shuddering execrations of all who had known him as a hangman.

Even the poor animal that carried the criminal and his coffin in a cart to the foot of the gallows was an object of universal loathing. He was cropped and marked that he might be known as the "Hangman's Donkey." No man, however great his needs, would use this beast, either for pleasure or labor; and the peasants were so averse to having him pollute their fields with his footsteps that, when he was seen approaching, the boys hastened to open the gates and drive him off with hisses, sticks, and stones. Thus does the human heart cry out aloud against this wicked practice!

A tacit acknowledgment of the demoralizing influence of executions is generally made in the fact that they are forbidden to be public, as formerly. The scene is now in a prison yard instead of open fields, and no spectators are admitted but officers of the law and those especially invited. Yet a favorite argument in favor of capital punishment has been the terror that the spectacle inspires in the breast of evildoers. I trust the 200 or 300 singled out from the mass of New York population by particular invitation, especially the judges and civil officers, will feel the full weight of the compliment. During the French Revolution, public executions seemed too slow, and Fouquier proposed to put the guillotine under cover, where batches of a hundred might be dispatched with few spectators. "Wilt thou *demoralize the guillotine?*"asked Callot reproachfully.

That bloody guillotine was an instrument of *law* as well as our gallows; and what, in the name of all that is villainous, has *not* been established by law? Nations, clans, and classes, engaged in fierce struggles of selfishness and hatred, made laws to strengthen each other's power and revenge each other's aggressions. By slow degrees, always timidly and reluctantly, society emerges out of the barbarisms with which it thus became entangled. It is but a short time ago that men were hung in this country for stealing. The last human brother who suffered under this law, in Massachusetts, was so wretchedly poor that when he hung on the gallows his rags fluttered in the wind. What think you was the comparative guilt, in the eye of God, between him and those who

hung him? Yet, it was *according to law;* and men cried out as vociferously then as they now do, that it was not *safe* to have the law changed.

Judge McKean, governor of Pennsylvania, was strongly opposed to the abolition of death for stealing, and the disuse of the pillory and whipping post. He was a very humane man, but had the common fear of changing old customs. "It will not do to abolish these salutary restraints," said the old gentleman; "it will break up the foundations of society." Those relics of barbarism were banished long ago; but the foundations of society are in nowise injured thereby.

The testimony from all parts of the world is invariable and conclusive: that crime diminishes in proportion to the mildness of the laws. The *real* danger is in having laws on the statute book at variance with universal instincts of the human heart, and thus tempting men to continual evasion. The *evasion*, even of a bad law, is attended with many mischievous results; its *abolition* is always safe.

In looking at capital punishment in its practical bearings on the operation of justice, an observing mind is at once struck with the extreme uncertainty attending it. The balance swings hither and thither, and settles, as it were, by chance. The strong instincts of the heart teach juries extreme reluctance to convict for capital offenses. They will avail themselves of every loophole in the evidence to avoid the bloody responsibility imposed upon them. In this way, undoubted criminals escape all punishment, until society becomes alarmed for its own safety and insists that the next victim *shall* be sacrificed. It was the misfortune of John C. Colt to be arrested at the time when the popular wave of indignation had been swelling higher and higher, in consequence of the impunity with which Robinson, White, and Jewell had escaped. The wrath and jealousy which they had excited was visited upon him, and his chance for a merciful verdict was greatly diminished. The scale now turns the other way; and the next offender will probably receive very lenient treatment, though he should not have half so many extenuating circumstances in his favor.

Another thought which forces itself upon the mind in consideration of this subject is the danger of convicting the innocent. Murder is a crime which must of course be committed in secret, and therefore the proof must be mainly circumstantial. This kind of evidence is in its nature so precarious that men have learned great timidity in trusting to it. In Scotland, it led to so many terrible mistakes that they long ago refused to convict any man of a capital offense upon circumstantial evidence.

A few years ago, a poor German came to New York and took lodgings where he was allowed to do his cooking in the same room with the family. The husband and wife lived in a perpetual quarrel. One day the German came into the kitchen with a clasp knife and a pan of potatoes, and began to pare them for his dinner. The quarrelsome couple were in a more violent altercation than usual; but he sat with his back toward them, and, being ignorant of their language, felt in no danger of being involved in their disputes. But the woman, with a sudden and unexpected movement, snatched the knife from his hand, and plunged it in her husband's heart. She had sufficient presence of mind to rush into the street and scream murder. The poor foreigner, in the meanwhile, seeing the wounded man reel, sprang forward to catch him in his arms and drew out the knife. People from the street crowded in and found him with the dying man in his arms, the knife in his hand, and blood upon his clothes. The wicked woman swore, in the most positive terms, that he had been fighting with her husband and had stabbed him with a knife he always carried.

The unfortunate German knew too little English to understand her accusation or to tell his own story. He was dragged off to prison, and the true state of the case was made known through an interpreter; but it was not believed. Circumstantial evidence was exceedingly strong against the accused, and the real criminal swore unhesitatingly that she saw him commit the murder. He was executed, notwithstanding the most persevering efforts of his lawyer, John Anthon, Esq., whose convictions of the man's innocence were so painfully strong that from that day to this he has refused to have any connection with a capital case. Some years after this tragic event, the woman died, and on her deathbed confessed her agency in the diabolical transaction; but her poor victim could receive no benefit from this tardy repentance; society had wantonly thrown away its power to atone for the grievous wrong.

Many of my readers will doubtless recollect the tragical fate of Burton, in Missouri, on which a novel was founded, which still circulates in the libraries. A young lady, belonging to a genteel and very proud family in Missouri, was beloved by a young man named Burton; but, unfortunately, her affections were fixed on another less worthy. He left her with a tarnished reputation. She was by nature energetic and high-spirited, her family were proud, and she lived in the midst of a society which considered revenge a virtue, and named it honor. Misled by this false popular sentiment and her own excited feelings, she resolved to repay her lover's treachery with death. But she kept her secret so well that no one suspected her purpose, though she purchased pistols and practised with them daily. Mr. Burton gave evidence of his strong attachment by renewing his attentions when the world looked most coldly upon her. His generous kindness won her bleeding heart, but the softening influence of love did not lead her to forgo the dreadful purpose she had formed.

She watched for a favorable opportunity and shot her betrayer when no one was near to witness the horrible deed. Some little incident excited the suspicion of Burton, and he induced her to confess to him the whole transaction. It was obvious enough that suspicion would naturally fasten upon him, the well-known lover of her who had been so deeply injured. He was arrested, but succeeded in persuading her that he was in no danger. Circumstantial evidence was fearfully against him, and he soon saw that his chance was doubtful; but with affectionate magnanimity, he concealed this from her. He was convicted and condemned. A short time before the execution, he endeavored to cut his throat; but his life was saved for the cruel purpose of taking it away according to the cold-blooded barbarism of the law. Pale and wounded, he was hoisted to the gallows before the gaze of a *Christian* community.

The guilty cause of all this was almost frantic when she found that he had thus sacrificed himself to save her. She immediately published the whole history of her wrongs and her revenge. Her keen sense of wounded honor was in accordance with public sentiment, her wrongs excited indignation and compassion, and the knowledge that an innocent and magnanimous man had been so brutally treated excited a general revulsion of popular feeling. No one wished for another victim, and she was left unpunished, save by the dreadful records of her memory.

Few know how numerous are the cases where it has subsequently been discovered that the innocent suffered instead of the guilty. Yet one such case in an age is surely enough to make legislators pause before they cast a vote against the abolition of capital punishment.

But many say, "The Old Testament requires blood for blood." So it requires that a woman should be put to death for adultery; and men for doing work on the Sabbath; and children for cursing their parents; and "If an ox were to push with his horn, in time past, and it hath been testified to his owner and he hath not kept him in, but that he hath killed a man or a woman, the ox shall be stoned, and his owner also shall be put to death." The commands given to the Jews in the old dispensation do not form the basis of any legal code in Christendom. They could not form the basis of any civilized code. If one command is binding on our consciences, all are binding; for they all rest on the same authority. They who feel bound to advocate capital punishment for murder on account of the law given to Moses ought, for the same reason, to insist that children should be executed for striking or cursing their parents.

"It was said by them of old time, an eye for an eye, and a tooth for a tooth; but *I* say unto you, resist not evil." If our "eyes were lifted up," we should see not Moses and Elias but Jesus only.

15.

ISIDORE LÖWENSTERN: The Philadelphia Penitentiary

The Eastern State Penitentiary near Philadelphia was a tourist attraction. It was built in 1829, at the insistence of the Philadelphia Society for Alleviating the Miseries of Public Prisons, and cost more than $700,000. Each of the fewer than 300 prisoners maintained by the institution was confined in a well-furnished cell with a private courtyard, and except for occasional visits from the chaplain, had only his work and his Bible for mental and spiritual sustenance. Those who admired the so-called Pennsylvania system said it made men honest, and those who criticized the system said it made them insane. Nevertheless, many prisons in Europe were patterned after it. The following description of the prison appeared in a book entitled Les États-Unis et la Havane souvenirs d'un voyage. *It was written by Isidore Löwenstern, a Viennese scholar who toured the States in 1837, and was published in 1842.*

Source: TWA, pp. 184-185.

THE PENITENTIARY, one of the most important institutions in Philadelphia, is distinguished by a special character derived from the healthy and unprejudiced conceptions of a new people. Here they have rejected the idea, relic of a barbarous past, that punishment is the only reward for crime. They have replaced it with the civilized objective of reforming the guilty, of making them safe for society, without the permanent loss involved in being branded as a criminal. I did not fail to visit an establishment which has given rise to so many controversies. The justification of the system lies in the fact that the criminal is actually reformed. There is not a single example of a discharged convict who was ever brought back for a new crime.

The basic principle of this prison is solitary confinement. Each prisoner is separated from all the others and is alone in a cell, which he never leaves until the day his sentence expires, a period which may last from one to twelve years. Until his release he is strictly forbidden to communicate with anyone, even with strangers who visit the place, unless the latter secure from the director a special permit, very difficult to obtain. The prisoner is thus entirely isolated; he has no distraction but his work, which alone can relieve his terrible solitude. He becomes industrious by despair, by necessity to forget the torments of his isolation. From that necessity comes a habit, a need for work, which is so powerful that there is no punishment in the prison more severe than depriving the criminal of the consolation of his labor for a few days.

The prison building lies in a court surrounded by a very high wall. From a central rotunda seven long corridors stretch out like the spokes of a wheel. The cells open onto each of the corridors in such a manner that a guard in the hall can survey all the corridors in a few seconds. Each cell is about eight feet long and twelve high, and receives the light of day only through a very narrow and high window.

An enclosure twice as long as the cell leads off each cell so that the prisoner may get some fresh air for an hour every day. He enters and leaves directly from his cubicle through a little trapdoor raised and lowered by a mechanism from outside. Each enclosure is surrounded by a high wall, so that the prisoners can no more be seen there than inside, except by the guard on top of the rotunda. The latter watches all the inmates who go in and out at the same time, but all remain isolated.

The convicts are fed three times a day through a locked opening in the door of their cells. In this manner 12 unarmed guards can take care of 586 criminals. The prisoners work at weaving and cobbling. They are taught at the beginning by the guards, who thereafter are chiefly concerned with preventing conversation. The revenue from this work is enough to pay the expenses of the prison, for the inmates themselves receive absolutely nothing, even when they are dismissed.

On Sundays and holidays the doors of the cells are opened for morning and afternoon prayers. The prisoners remain behind their open doors so that they can hear the minister at the end of the corridor, but cannot see or be seen by him. Everything is thus arranged so that the convict cannot be recognized by anyone. As soon as he is sentenced he is taken to the penitentiary in a completely closed carriage. Before getting out he is blindfolded with a black handkerchief, and two men, holding him under the arms, lead him to his cell, so that no one can know him and he himself has no idea of the place in which he is. When he is released he is taken out in the same way, and leaves prison confident that no one but the director is aware of his name, for he himself knows the name of no one else.

New County Prison and Debtors Apartment, Philadelphia, Pa.; talbotype by Langenheim, 1850
Missouri Historical Society; photo, Library of Congress

16.

CHARLES LENOX REMOND: A Negro Protest Against Segregation in Travel

In 1840 the American Anti-Slavery Society sent the distinguished Negro, Charles Remond, to the London World Anti-Slavery Conference. Remond remained abroad for nearly two years, lecturing in England and Ireland and enjoying the absence of Negro prejudice there. Immediately after he returned to Massachusetts he was compelled to take a seat in a special railroad car for Negroes, and his friends prevailed on him to testify about the situation at the hearings then being conducted by a committee of the Massachusetts House of Representatives. Remond addressed the committee in late February 1842; portions of his remarks are reprinted below. In April 1848 the Massachusetts railroads were desegregated.

Source: *Liberator*, February 25, 1842.

Mr. Chairman, and Gentlemen of the Committee:

In rising at this time and on this occasion, being the first person of color who has ever addressed either of the bodies assembling in this building, I should, perhaps, in the first place, observe that, in consequence of the many misconstructions of the principles and measures of which I am the humble advocate, I may in like manner be subject to similar misconceptions from the moment I open my lips in behalf of the prayer of the petitioners for whom I appear, and therefore feel I have the right at least to ask, at the hands of this intelligent Committee, an impartial hearing; and that whatever prejudices they may have imbibed be eradicated from their minds, if such exist. I have, however, too much confidence in their intelligence and too much faith in their determination to do their duty as the representatives of this Commonwealth to presume they can be actuated by partial motives.

Trusting, as I do, that the day is not distant when, on all questions touching the rights of the citizens of this state, men shall be considered *great* only as they are *good*, and not that it shall be told and painfully experienced, that, in this country, this state, aye, this city, the Athens of America, the rights, privileges, and immunities of its citizens are measured by complexion, or any other physical peculiarity or conformation, especially such as over which no man has any control. Complexion can in no sense be construed into crime, much less be rightfully made the criterion of rights. Should the people of color, through a revolution of Providence, become a majority, to the last I would oppose it upon the same principle; for, in either case, it would be equally reprehensible and unjustifiable — alike to be condemned and repudiated. It is JUSTICE I stand here to claim and not FAVOR for either complexion. . . .

Our right to citizenship in this state has been acknowledged and secured by the allowance of the elective franchise and consequent taxation; and I know of no good reason, if admitted in this instance, why it should be denied in any other.

With reference to the wrongs inflicted

and injuries received on railroads by persons of color, I need not say they do not end with the termination of the route, but, in effect, tend to discourage, disparage, and depress this class of citizens. All hope of reward for upright conduct is cut off. Vice in them becomes a virtue. No distinction is made by the community in which we live. The most vicious is treated as well as the most respectable, both in public and private.

But it is said we all look alike. If this is true, it is not true that we all behave alike. There is a marked difference; and we claim a recognition of this difference.

In the present state of things, they find God's provisions interfered with in such a way, by these and kindred regulations, that virtue may not claim her divinely appointed rewards. Color is made to obscure the brightest endowments, to degrade the fairest character, and to check the highest and most praiseworthy aspirations. If the colored man is vicious, it makes but little difference; if besotted, it matters not; if vulgar, it is quite as well; and he finds himself as well treated and received as readily into society as those of an opposite character. . . .

Nay, the higher our aspirations, the loftier our purposes and pursuits, does this iniquitous principle of prejudice fasten upon us; and especial pains are taken to irritate, obstruct, and injure. No reward of merit, no remuneration for services, no equivalent is rendered the deserving. And I submit whether this unkind and unchristian policy is not well calculated to make every man disregardful of his conduct, and every woman unmindful of her reputation.

The grievances of which we complain, be assured, sir, are not imaginary but real; not local but universal; not occasional but continual, every-day, matter-of-fact things, and have become, to the disgrace of our common country, matter of history.

Mr. Chairman, the treatment to which colored Americans are exposed in their own country finds a counterpart in no other; and I am free to declare that, in the course of nineteen months' traveling in England, Ireland, and Scotland, I was received, treated, and recognized in public and private society without any regard to my complexion. . . . In no instance was I insulted or treated in any way distinct or dissimilar from other passengers or travelers, either in coaches, railroads, steampackets, or hotels; and if the feeling was entertained, in no case did I discover its existence. . . .

There is a marked difference between social and civil rights. It has been well and justly remarked by my friend Mr. Phillips that we all claim the privilege of selecting our society and associations; but, in civil rights, one man has not the prerogative to define rights for another. For instance, sir, in public conveyances, for the rich man to usurp the privileges to himself, to the injury of the poor man, would be submitted to in no well-regulated society. And such is the position suffered by persons of color.

On my arrival home from England, I went to the railway station to go to Salem, being anxious to see my parents and sisters as soon as possible; asked for a ticket; paid 50 cents for it; and was pointed to the American designation car. Having previously received information of the regulations, I took my seat peaceably, believing it better to suffer wrong than do wrong. I felt then, as I felt on many occasions prior to leaving home, unwilling to descend so low as to bandy words with the superintendents or contest my rights with conductors, or any others in the capacity of servants of any stage or steamboat company or railroad corporation; although I never, by any means, gave evidence that, by my submission, I intended to sanction usages which would derogate from uncivilized, much less long and loud professing and high pretending America.

Bear with me while I relate an additional occurrence. On the morning after my return home, I was obliged to go to Boston again, and, on going to the Salem station, I met two friends, who inquired if I had any objection to their taking seats with me. I answered I should be most happy. They took their seats accordingly, and soon afterward one of them remarked to me; "Charles, I don't know if they will allow us to ride with you." It was some time before I could understand what they meant, and, on doing so, I laughed, feeling it to be a climax to every absurdity I had heard attributed to Americans. To say nothing of the wrong done those friends, and the insult and indignity offered me by the appearance of the conductor, who ordered the friends from the car in a somewhat harsh manner, they immediately left the carriage.

On returning to Salem some few evenings afterward, Mr. Chase, the superintendent on this road, made himself known to me by recalling bygone days and scenes; and then inquired if I was not glad to get home after so long an absence in Europe. I told him I was glad to see my parents and family again, and this was the only object I could have, unless he thought I should be glad to take a hermit's life in the great pasture, inasmuch as I never felt to loathe my American name so much as since my arrival. He wished to know my reasons for the remark. I immediately gave them and wished to know of him if, in the event of his having a brother with red hair, he should find himself separated while traveling because of this difference he should deem it just. He could make no reply. I then wished to know if the principle was not the same; and if so, there was an insult implied by his question.

In conclusion, I challenged him as the instrument inflicting the manifold injuries upon all not colored like himself to the presentation of an instance in any other Christian or unchristian country, tolerating usages at once so disgraceful, unjust, and inhuman. What if some few of the West or East India planters and merchants should visit our liberty-loving country with their colored wives; how would he manage? Or, if R. M. Johnson, the gentleman who has been ele-

vated to the second office in the gift of the people, should be traveling from Boston to Salem, if he was prepared to separate him from his wife or daughters. [*Involuntary burst of applause, instantly restrained.*]

Sir, it happens to be my lot to have a sister a few shades lighter than myself; and who knows, if this state of things is encouraged, whether I may not on some future occasion be mobbed in Washington Street on the supposition of walking with a white young lady! [*Suppressed indications of sympathy and applause.*]

Gentlemen of the Committee, these distinctions react in all their wickedness, to say nothing of their concocted and systematized odiousness and absurdity, upon those who instituted them; and particularly so upon those who are illiberal and mean enough to practise them.

Mr. Chairman, if colored people have abused any rights granted them, or failed to exhibit due appreciation of favors bestowed, or shrunk from dangers or responsibility, let it be made to appear. Or if our country contains a population to compare with them in loyalty and patriotism, circumstances duly considered, I have it yet to learn. The history of our country must ever testify in their behalf. In view of these and many additional considerations, I unhesitatingly assert their claim, on the naked principle of merit, to every advantage set forth in the constitution of this Commonwealth.

Finally, Mr. Chairman, there is in this and other states a large and growing colored population, whose residence in your midst has not been from choice (let this be understood and reflected upon), but by the force of circumstances over which they never had control. Upon the heads of their oppressors and calumniators be the censure and responsibility. If to ask at your hands redress for injuries, and protection in our rights and immunities, as citizens is reasonable, and dictated alike by justice, humanity, and religion, you will not reject, I trust, the prayer of your petitioners.

1842 - 1843

17.

Pro-Slavery Churches

Both of the following selections attacking pro-slavery churches were written by staunch Abolitionists. The first is taken from a pamphlet entitled The American Churches, the Bulwarks of American Slavery, *by Southerner James G. Birney. It was originally published in England in 1840 on the occasion of the London World Anti-Slavery Conference, which Birney attended, and was addressed to the English reader. It was issued in the United States in 1842 and reissued in an enlarged edition in 1885. The second selection is from a letter in Stephen S. Foster's book,* The Brotherhood of Thieves; or A True Picture of the American Church and Clergy. *The letter was written in July 1843 to Nathaniel Barney, who had requested that Foster vindicate the strong anticlerical language employed at an antislavery convention in Massachusetts.*

Source: James G. Birney, *The American Churches, the Bulwarks of American Slavery*, 3rd edition, Concord, N.H., 1885, pp. 7-11, 48.
Stephen S. Foster, *The Brotherhood of Thieves*, New London, 1843, pp. 5-14.

I.

JAMES G. BIRNEY: The Guilt of the Churches Supporting Slavery

THE EXTENT to which most of the churches in America are involved in the guilt of supporting the slave system is known to but few in this country [England]. So far from being even suspected by the great mass of the religious community here, it would not be believed but on the most indisputable evidence. Evidence of this character it is proposed now to present — applying to the Methodist Episcopal, the Baptist, the Presbyterian, and the Protestant Episcopal churches. It is done with a single view to make the British Christian public acquainted with the real state of the case, in order that it may in the most intelligent and effective manner exert the influence it possesses with the American churches to persuade them to purify themselves from a sin that has greatly debased them and that threatens in the end wholly to destroy them.

The following memoranda will assist English readers in more readily apprehending the force and scope of the evidence.

1. Of the twenty-six American states, thirteen are slave states. Of the latter,

Maryland, Virginia, Kentucky, Missouri, and Tennessee (in part), are slave-*selling* states; the states south of them are slave-*buying* and slave-*consuming* states.

2. Between the slave-selling and slave-buying states the slave trade is carried on extensively and systematically. The slave trader, on completing his purchases for a single adventure, brings the gang together at a convenient point; confines the men in double rows to a large chain running between the rows, by means of smaller lateral chains tightly riveted around the wrists of the slaves and connected with the principal chain. They are in this way driven along the highways (the small boys, the women, and girls following), without any release from their chains till they arrive at the ultimate place of sale. Here they occupy barracoons [temporary barracks] till they are disposed of, one by one or in lots, to those who will give most for them.

3. Ministers and office-bearers and members of churches are slaveholders — buying and selling slaves (not as the regular slave trader but as their convenience or interest may from time to time require). As a general rule, the itinerant preachers in the Methodist Church are not permitted to hold slaves, but there are frequent exceptions to the rule, especially of late.

4. There are in the United States, about 2,487,113 slaves and 386,069 *free people of color*. Of the slaves, 80,000 are members of the Methodist Church; 80,000 of the Baptist; and about 40,000 of the other churches. These church members have no exemption from being sold by their owners as other slaves are. Instances are not rare of slaveholding members of churches selling slaves who are members of the same church with themselves. And members of churches have followed the business of slave auctioneers.

5. In most of the slave states, the master is not permitted formally to emancipate, unless the emancipated person be removed

Library of Congress

James G. Birney

from the state (which makes the formal act unnecessary), or, unless by a special act of the legislature. If, however, he disregards the law and permits the slave to go at liberty and "do" for himself, the law — on the theory that every slave ought to have a master to *see to him* — directs him to be sold for the benefit of the state. Instances of this, however, must be very rare. The people are better than their laws, for the writer, during a residence of more than thirty years in the slave states, never knew an instance of such a sale nor has he ever heard of one that was fully proved to have taken place.

6. There is no law in any of the slave states forbidding the slaveholder to remove his slaves to a free state; nor against his giving the slaves themselves a "pass" for that purpose. The laws of some of the *free* states present obstructions to the settlement of colored persons within their limits — but these obstructions are not insurmountable, and if the validity of the laws should be tried in the tribunals, it would be found they are unconstitutional.

7. In the slave states a slave cannot be a witness in any case, civil or criminal, in which a white is a party; neither can a free colored person, except in Louisiana. Ohio, Indiana, and Illinois (free states) make colored persons incompetent as witnesses in any case in which a white is a party. In Ohio, a white person can prove his own ("book") account, not exceeding a certain sum, by his own oath or affirmation; a colored person cannot, as against a white. In Ohio, the laws regard all who are mulattoes or above the grade of mulattoes, as *white*.

8. There is no law in the slave states forbidding the several church authorities making slaveholding an offense, for which those guilty of it might be excluded from membership.

The Society of Friends exists in the slave states — it excludes slaveholders.

The United Brethren exist as a church in Maryland and Virginia, slave states. Their annual conference for these two states (in which are thirty preachers) met in February [1840]. The following is an extract from its minutes: —

No charge is preferred against any (preachers) except Franklin Echard and Moses Michael.

It appeared in evidence that Moses Michael was the owner of a female slave, which is contrary to the discipline of our church. Conference therefore resolved that unless brother Michael manumit or set free such slave in six months, he no longer be considered a member of our church.

9. When ecclesiastical councils excuse themselves from acting for the removal of slavery from their respective communions by saying they cannot *legislate* for the abolition of slavery; that slavery is a *civil* or *political* institution; that it "belongs to Caesar" and not to the church to put an end to it, they shun the point at issue. To the church member who is a debauchee, a drunkard, a seducer, a murderer, they find no difficulty in saying, "We cannot indeed proceed against your person, or your property — *this* belongs to Caesar, to the *tribunals* of the country, to the *legislature*; but we can suspend or wholly cut you off from the communion of the church, with a view to your repentance and its purification." If a white member should by force or intimidation, day after day, deprive another white member of his property, the authorities of the churches would expel him from their body should he refuse to make restitution or reparation, although it could not be *enforced* except through the tribunals, over which they have no control. There is, then, nothing to prevent these authorities from saying to the slaveholder, "Cease being a slaveholder and remain in the church, or continue a slaveholder and go out of it. You have your choice."

10. The slave states make it penal to teach the slaves to read. So also some of them to teach the *free colored people* to read. Thus a free colored parent may suffer the penalty for teaching his own children to read even the Scriptures. None of the slaveholding churches or religious bodies, so far as is known, have, at any time, remonstrated with the legislatures against this iniquitous legislation or petitioned for its repeal or modification. Nor have they reproved or questioned such of their members, as, being also members of the legislatures, sanctioned such legislation by their votes.

11. There is no systematic instruction of the slave members of churches, either orally or in any other way.

12. Uniting with a church makes no change in the condition of slaves *at home*. They are thrown back just as before, among their old associates, and subjected to their corrupting influences.

13. But little pains are taken to secure their attendance at public worship on Sundays.

14. The "house servants" are rarely present at family worship; the "field hands," never.

15. It is only one here and there who seems to have any intelligent views of the nature of Christianity or of a future life.

16. In the Methodist, Baptist, Presbyterian, and Episcopal churches, the colored people, during service, sit in a particular part of the house, now generally known as the "Negro pew." They are not permitted to sit in any other, nor to hire or purchase pews as other people, nor would they be permitted to sit, even if invited, in the pews of white persons. This applies to all colored persons, whether *members* or not, and even to *licensed ministers* of their respective connections. The "Negro pew" is almost as rigidly kept up in the free states as in the slave.

17. In some of the older slave states, as Virginia and South Carolina, churches, in their *corporate* character, hold slaves, who are generally hired out for the support of the minister. The following is taken from the *Charleston Courier* of February 12, 1835.

Field Negroes
by Thomas Gadsden

On Tuesday, the 17th instant, will be sold, at the north of the exchange, at ten o'clock, a prime gang of ten Negroes, accustomed to the culture of cotton and provisions, belonging to the Independent Church, in *Christ's Church Parish.* . . .

18. Nor are instances wanting in which Negroes are *bequeathed* for the benefit of the Indians, as the following Chancery notice, taken from a Savannah (Ga.) paper will show.

Bryan Superior Court
Between John J. Maxwell and others, executors of Ann Pray, complainants, and Mary Sleigh and others, devisees and legatees, under the will of Ann Pray, defendants, IN EQUITY.

A bill having been filed for the distribution of the estate of the Testatrix, Ann Pray, and it appearing that among other legacies in her will, is the following, viz., a legacy of one-fourth of certain Negro slaves to the American Board of Commissioners for domestic [foreign it probably should have been] missions, for the purpose of sending the gospel to the heathen, and particularly to the Indians of this continent. It is on motion of the solicitors of the complainants ordered, that all persons claiming the said legacy, do appear and answer the bill of the complainants, within four months from this day. And it is ordered that this order be published in a public gazette of the city of Savannah and in one of the gazettes of Philadelphia, once a month for four months.

Extract from the minutes, Dec. 2, 1832. . . . The bequest was not accepted. . . .

We would have the reader bear in mind that the foregoing presents but one side of the antislavery cause in the several churches whose proceedings have been considered; and that in them all, there are Abolitionists earnestly laboring to purify them from the defilements of slavery; and that they have strong encouragement to proceed, not only in view of what they have already effected toward that end, but in the steady increase of their numbers, and in other omens of success.

We wish him also to bear in mind that the churches which have been brought before him are not the only American churches which are guilty in giving their countenance and support to slavery. Of others we have said nothing, simply because, to examine their cases, would be to make this work too long for the object we have in view — and because enough has been said to show substantially the state of the slavery question in America, so far as the *church* in that country is connected with it.

Last, we take pleasure in assuring him

that there are considerable portions of the Methodist, Baptist, and Presbyterian churches, as well as the entire of some of the smaller religious bodies in America, that maintain a commendable testimony against slavery and its abominations.

II.

STEPHEN S. FOSTER:
A Brotherhood of Thieves

THE REMARKS WHICH I MADE at your convention were of a most grave and startling character. They strike at the very foundation of all our popular ecclesiastical institutions and exhibit them to the world as the apologists and supporters of the most atrocious system of oppression and wrong beneath which humanity has ever groaned. They reflect on the church the deepest possible odium, by disclosing to public view the chains and handcuffs, the whips and branding irons, the rifles and bloodhounds, with which her ministers and deacons bind the limbs, and lacerate the flesh of innocent men and defenseless women. They cast upon the clergy the same dark shade which Jesus threw over the ministers of his day, when he tore away the veil beneath which they had successfully concealed their diabolical schemes of personal aggrandizement and power, and denounced them before all the people, as a "den of thieves," as "fools and blind," "whited sepulchers," "blind guides, which strain at a gnat and swallow a camel," "hypocrites, who devour widow's houses, and for a pretense make long prayers," "liars," "adulterers," "serpents," "a generation of vipers" who could not "escape the damnation of hell."

But appalling and ominous as they were, I am not aware that I gave the parties accused, or their mobocratic friends, any just cause of complaint. They were all spoken in public, in a free meeting, where all who dissented from me were not only invited but warmly urged to reply. I was an entire stranger among you, with nothing but the naked truth and a few sympathizing friends to sustain me, while the whole weight of popular sentiment was in their favor. Was the controversy unequal, on their part? Were they afraid to meet me with the same honorable weapons which I had chosen? Conscious innocence seldom consents to tarnish its character by a dishonorable defense.

Had my charges been unfounded, a refutation of them, under the circumstances, would have been most easy and triumphant. My opponents, had they been innocent, could have acquitted themselves honorably, and overwhelmed their accuser in deep disgrace, without the necessity of resorting to those arguments which appeal only to one's fears of personal harm and which are certain to react upon their authors when the threatened danger subsides.

But if all that I have alleged against them be true, it was, obviously, my right, nay, my imperative duty, to make the disclosures which I did, even though it might be, as you well know it was, at the peril of my life and the lives of my associates.

In exposing the deep and fathomless abominations of those *pious* thieves who gain their livelihood by preaching sermons and stealing babies, I am not at liberty to yield to any intimidations, however imposing the source from which they come. The right of speech — the liberty to utter our own convictions *freely,* at all times, and in all places, at discretion, unawed by fear, unembarrassed by force — is the gift of God to every member of the family of man and should be preserved inviolate. And for one, I can consent to surrender it to no power on earth, but with the loss of life itself. Let not the petty tyrants of our land, in church or state, think to escape the censures which their crimes deserve by hedging themselves about with the frightful penalties of human law or the more frightful violence of a drunken and murderous mob.

There live the men who are not afraid to die, even though called to meet their fate within the gloomy walls of a dismal prison, with no kind hand to wipe the cold death-sweat from their sinking brow; and they scorn a fetter on limb or spirit. They know their rights and know how to defend them or to obtain more than an equivalent for their loss, in the rewards of a martyr to the right. While life remains, they will speak, and speak *freely*, though it be in "A voice from the jail." Nor will they treat the crimes and vices of slave-breeding priests and their *consecrated* abettors of the North with less severity than they do the crimes and vices of other *marauders* on their neighbor's property and rights. Nor should the friends of freedom be alarmed at the consequences of this faithful dealing with "spiritual wickedness in high places." The *mobs* which it creates are but the violent contortions of the patient, as the deep gashes of the operator's knife severs the infected limb from his sickly and emaciated body.

The fact that my charges against the religious sects of our country were met with violence and outrage, instead of sound arguments and invalidating testimony, is strong presumptive evidence of their truth. The innocent never find occasion to resort to this disgraceful mode of defense. If our clergy and church were the ministers and church of Christ, would their reputation be defended by drunken and murderous mobs? Are brickbats and rotten eggs the weapons of truth and Christianity? Did Jesus say to his disciples, "Blessed are ye when the *mob* shall speak well of you and shall defend you"?

The church, slavery, and the mob are a queer trinity! And yet that they are a trinity — that they all "agree in one" — cannot be denied. Every assault which we have made upon the bloody slave system . . . has been promptly met and repelled by the church, which is herself the claimant of several hundred thousand slaves; and whenever we have attempted to expose the guilt and hypocrisy of the church, the *mob* has uniformly been first and foremost in her defense. But I rest not on presumptive evidence, however strong and conclusive, to sustain my allegations against the American church and clergy. The proof of their identity with slavery and of their consequent deep and unparalleled criminality is positive and overwhelming; and is fully adequate to sustain the gravest charges and to justify the most denunciatory language that have ever fallen from the lips of their most inveterate opponents.

I said at your meeting, among other things, that the American church and clergy, as a body, were thieves, adulterers, man-stealers, pirates, and murderers — that the Methodist Episcopal Church was more corrupt and profligate than any house of ill fame in the city of New York — that the Southern ministers of that body were desirous of perpetuating slavery for the purpose of supplying themselves with concubines from among its hapless victims — and that many of our clergymen were guilty of enormities that would disgrace an Algerine pirate!! These sentiments called forth a burst of holy indignation from the *pious* and *dutiful* advocates of the church and clergy, which overwhelmed the meeting with repeated showers of stones and rotten eggs and eventually compelled me to leave your island, to prevent the shedding of human blood.

But whence this violence and personal abuse, not only of the author of the obnoxious sentiments but also of your own unoffending wives and daughters whose faces and dresses, you will recollect, were covered with the most loathsome filth? It is reported of the ancient Pharisees and their adherents that they stoned Stephen to death for preaching doctrines at war with the popular religion of their times, and charging them with the murder of the Son of God; but their successors of the modern church, it would seem, have discovered some new principle in theology, by which it is made their duty not only to stone the heretic himself but all those also who may at any time be found listening to his discourse without a *permit* from their *priest.* Truly, the church is becoming "Terrible as an army with banners."

This violence and outrage on the part of the church were, no doubt, committed to the glory of God and the honor of religion, although the connection between rotten eggs and holiness of heart is not very obvious. It is, I suppose, one of the mysteries of religion which laymen cannot understand without the aid of the clergy; and I therefore suggest that the pulpit make it a subject of Sunday discourse. But are not the charges here alleged against the clergy strictly and literally true? I maintain that they are true to the letter — that the clergy and their adherents are literally, and beyond all controversy, a "brotherhood of thieves" — and in support of this opinion I submit the following considerations.

You will agree with me, I think, that slaveholding involves the commission of all the crimes specified in my first charge, viz., theft, adultery, manstealing, piracy, and murder. But should you have any doubts on this subject, they will be easily removed by analyzing this atrocious outrage on the laws of God and the rights and happiness of man and examining separately the elements of which it is composed. Wesley, the celebrated founder of the Methodists, once denounced it as the "sum of all villainies." Whether it be the sum of *all* villainies or not, I will not here express an opinion, but that it is the sum of at least *five,* and those by no means the least atrocious in the catalog of human aberrations, will require but a small tax on your patience to prove.

1. *Theft.* To steal is to take that which belongs to another without his consent. Theft and robbery are, *morally,* the same act, differing only in form. Both are included under the command, "Thou shalt not steal" — that is, thou shalt not take thy neighbor's property. Whoever, therefore, either secretly or by force, possesses himself of the property of another is a thief. Now, no proposition is plainer than that every man owns his own industry. He who tills the soil has a right to its products and cannot be deprived of them but by an act of felony. This principle furnishes the only solid basis for the right of private or individual property, and he who denies it, either in theory or practice, denies that right also. But every slaveholder takes the entire industry of his slaves from infancy to gray hairs. They dig the soil, but he receives its products. No matter how kind or humane the master may be, he lives by plunder. He is emphatically a freebooter, and, as such, he is as much more despicable a character than the common horse thief, as his depredations are more extensive.

2. *Adultery.* This crime is disregard for the requisitions of marriage. The conjugal relation has its foundation deeply laid in man's nature, and its observance is essential to his happiness. Hence, Jesus Christ has thrown around it the sacred sanction of his written law and expressly declared that the man who violates it, even by a lustful eye, is an adulterer. But does the slaveholder respect this sacred relation? Is he cautious never to tread upon forbidden ground? No! His very position makes him the minister of unbridled lust. By converting woman into a commodity, to be bought and sold and used by her claimant as his avarice or lust may dictate, he totally annihilates the marriage institution; and transforms the wife into what he very significantly terms a *"breeder,"* and her children into *"stock."*

This change in woman's condition from a free moral agent to a chattel places her domestic relations entirely beyond her own control and makes her a mere instrument for the gratification of another's desires. The master claims her body as his property and of course employs it for such purposes as best suit his inclinations, demanding free access to her bed; nor can she resist his demands, but at the peril of her life. Thus is her chastity left entirely unprotected, and she is made the lawful prey of every pale-faced libertine who may choose to prostitute her!! To place woman in this situation, or to retain her in it, when placed there by another, is the highest insult that one could possibly offer to the dignity and purity of her nature; and the wretch who is guilty of it deserves an epithet, compared with which adultery is spotless innocence. *Rape* is his crime! — death his desert, if death be ever due to criminals!

Am I too severe? Let the offense be done to a sister or a daughter of yours; nay, let the Rev. Dr. Witherspoon, or some other *ordained* miscreant from the South, lay his vile hands on your own bosom companion and do to her what he has done to the companion of another and what Prof. Stuart and Dr. Fisk say he may do, "without violating the Christian faith," and I fear not your reply. None but a moral monster ever consented to the enslavement of his own daughter, and none but fiends incarnate ever enslaved the daughter of another. Indeed, I think the demons in hell would be ashamed to do to their fellow demons what many of our clergy do to their own church members.

3. *Manstealing.* What is it to steal a man? Is it not to claim him as your property? To call him yours? God has given to every man an inalienable right to himself — a right of which no conceivable circumstance of birth or forms of law can divest him; and he who interferes with the free and unrestricted exercise of that right; who, not content with the proprietorship of his own body, claims the body of his neighbor

is a manstealer. This truth is self-evident. Every man, idiots and the insane only excepted, knows that he has no possible right to another's body; and he who persists, for a moment, in claiming it incurs the guilt of manstealing. The plea of the slave claimant, that he has bought or inherited his slaves, is of no avail. What right had he, I ask, to purchase or to inherit his neighbors? The purchase, or the inheritance of them as a legacy, was itself a crime of no less enormity than the original act of kidnapping. But every slaveholder, whatever his profession or standing in society may be, lays his felonious hands on the body and soul of his equal brother, robs him of himself, converts him into an article of merchandise, and leaves him a mere chattel personal in the hands of his claimant. Hence, he is a kidnapper or man-thief.

4. *Piracy.* The American people, by an act of solemn legislation, have declared the enslaving of human beings, on the coast of Africa, to be piracy and have affixed to this crime the penalty of death. And can the same act be piracy in Africa and not be piracy in America? Does crime change its character by changing longitude? Is killing with malice aforethought no murder where there is no human enactment against it? Or can it be less piratical and heaven-daring to enslave our own native countrymen than to enslave the heathen sons of a foreign and barbarous realm? If there be any difference in the two crimes, the odds [are] in favor of the foreign enslaver.

Slaveholding loses none of its enormity by a voyage across the Atlantic nor by baptism into the Christian name. It is piracy in Africa — it is piracy in America — it is piracy the wide world over. And the American slaveholder, though he possess all the sanctity of the ancient Pharisees, and make prayers as numerous and long, is a *pirate* still, a base, profligate adulterer, and wicked contemner of the holy institution of marriage, identical in moral character with the

African slave trader, and guilty of a crime which, if committed on a foreign coast, he must expiate on the gallows.

5. Murder. Murder is an act of the mind and not of the hand. "Whosoever hateth his brother is a murderer." A man may kill — that is, his hand may inflict a mortal blow — without committing murder. On the other hand, he may commit murder without actually taking life. The intention constitutes the crime. He who, with a pistol at my breast, demands my pocketbook or my life is a murderer, whichever I may choose to part with. And is not he a murderer who, with the same deadly weapon, demands the surrender of what to me is of infinitely more value than my pocketbook, nay, than life itself — my liberty — myself — my wife and children — all that I possess on earth or can hope for in heaven?

But this is the crime of which every slaveholder is guilty. He maintains his ascendancy over his victims, extorting their unrequited labor and sundering the dearest ties of kindred, only by the threat of extermination. With the slave, as every intelligent person knows, there is no alternative. It is submission or death, or, more frequently, protracted torture more horrible than death. Indeed, the South never sleeps, but on dirks and pistols and bowie knives, with a troop of bloodhounds standing sentry at every door!

What, I ask, means this splendid enginery of death, which gilds the palace of the tyrant master? It tells the story of his guilt. The burnished steel which waits beneath his slumbering pillow, to drink the blood of outraged innocence, brands him as a murderer. It proves, beyond dispute, that the submission of his victims is the only reason why he has not already shed their blood.

By this brief analysis of slavery, we stamp upon the forehead of the slaveholder with a brand deeper than that which marks the victim of his wrongs, the infamy of theft, adultery, manstealing, piracy, and murder.

We demonstrate beyond the possibility of doubt that he who enslaves another, that is, robs him of his right to himself, to his own hands and head and feet, and transforms him from a free moral agent into a mere *brute,* to obey, not the commands of God but his claimant, is guilty of every one of these atrocious crimes. And in doing this, we have only demonstrated what, to every reflecting mind, is self-evident. Every man, if he would but make the case of the slave his own, would feel in his inmost soul the truth and justice of this charge.

But these are the crimes which I have alleged against the American church and clergy. Hence, to sustain my charge against them, it only remains for me to show that they are slaveholders. That they are slaveholders — party to a conspiracy against the liberty of more than 2 million of our countrymen, and, as such, are guilty of the crimes of which they stand accused — I affirm, and will now proceed to prove.

It may be necessary for me first, however, to show what constitutes slaveholding, as there seems to be no little confusion in the minds of many on this point. And here let me say, the word itself, if analyzed, will give an accurate description of the act. It is to *hold* one in slavery — to keep him in the condition of a chattel. But slaveholding, in all cases, is necessarily a social crime. A man may commit theft or murder alone, but no *solitary* individual can ever *enslave* another. It is only when several persons associate together and combine their influence against the liberty of an individual, that he can be deprived of his freedom and reduced to slavery. Hence, connection with an association, any part of whose object is to hold men in slavery, constitutes one a slaveholder.

Nor is the nature or criminality of his offense altered or affected by the number of persons connected with him in such an association. If a million of people conspire together to enslave a solitary individual, each of them is a slaveholder, and no less guilty than if he were alone in the crime. It is no palliation of his offense to say that he is opposed to slavery. The better feelings of every slaveholder are opposed to slavery. But if he be opposed to it, why, I ask, is he concerned in it? Why does he countenance, aid, or abet the infernal system? The fact of his opposition to it, in feeling instead of mitigating his guilt only enhances it, since it proves, conclusively, that he is not unconscious of the wrong he is doing.

It is a common but mistaken opinion that to constitute one a slaveholder he must be the claimant of slaves. That title belongs alike to the slave claimant and all those who, by their countenance or otherwise, lend their influence to support the slave system. If I aid or countenance another in stealing, I am a thief, though he receive all the booty. The Knapps, it will be recollected, were hung as the murderers of Mr. White, though Crowninshield gave the fatal blow, and that, too, while they were at a distance from the bloody scene. It matters little who does the mastery and puts on the drag chain and handcuffs, whether it be James B. Gray, or the Boston Police, Judge Story, or some distinguished doctor of divinity of the South; the guilt of the transaction consists in authorizing or allowing it to be done. Hence, all who, through their political or ecclesiastical connections, aid or countenance the master in his work of death, are slaveholders, and as such, are stained with all the moral turpitude which attaches to the man, who, by their sanction, wields the bloody lash over the heads of his trembling victims and buries it deep in their quivering flesh. Nay, the human hounds which guard the plantation, ever eager to bark on the track of the flying fugitive, are objects of deeper indignation and abhorrence than even its lordly proprietor.

How stands this matter, then, in regard to the American church and clergy? Is it true of them, that they are either claimants of slaves, or *watchdogs* of the plantation? Such, I regret to say, is the shameful and humiliating fact. It is undeniably true that, with comparatively few exceptions, they occupy one of these two positions in relation to the "peculiar institution." Thousands of the ministers and tens of thousands of the members of the different sects are actual claimants of slaves. They buy and sell, mortgage and lease their own "brethren in the Lord," not infrequently breaking up families and scattering their bleeding fragments over all the land, never to be gathered again, till the archangel's trumpet shall wake their slumbering ashes into life.

———◆———

The compact which exists between the North and the South is a covenant with death and an agreement with hell.
    WILLIAM LLOYD GARRISON, "Resolution" adopted by the Anti-Slavery Society, Jan. 27, 1843

1843

18.

John C. Calhoun: On Territorial Expansion

Great Britain and the United States were unable to agree on the northern boundary of the Oregon Territory. In order to sidestep the issue, a treaty was concluded between the two nations in 1818 (and renewed in 1827) that provided that both would jointly occupy the territory and that either could terminate the arrangement by giving the other a year's prior notice. In December 1841, a bill providing for the erection of fortifications in the Oregon Territory was introduced into Congress. On January 24, 1843, John C. Calhoun opposed the bill as a direct and needless violation of the pact with Great Britain. The bill passed the Senate in February but was defeated in the House. Part of Calhoun's speech is reprinted below.

Source: *A Digest of International Law*, John B. Moore, ed., Washington, 1906, Vol. I, pp. 429-431.

TIME IS ACTING FOR US; and if we shall have the wisdom to trust its operation, it will assert and maintain our right with restless force, without costing a cent of money or a drop of blood. There is, often, in the affairs of government, more efficiency and wisdom in nonaction than in action. All we want to effect our object in this case is "a wise and masterly inactivity."

Our population is rolling toward the shores of the Pacific with an impetus greater than what we realize. It is one of those forward movements which leaves anticipation behind. In the period of thirty-two years which have elapsed since I took my seat in the other house, the Indian frontier has receded 1,000 miles to the west. At that time our population was much less than half what it is now. It was then increasing at the rate of about 250,000 annually; it is now not less than 600,000, and still increasing at the rate of something more than 3 percent compound annually. At that rate it will soon reach the yearly increase of 1 million.

If to this be added that the region west of Arkansas and the state of Missouri, and south of the Missouri River, is occupied by half civilized tribes, who have their lands secured to them by treaty (and which will prevent the spread of population in that direction), and that this great and increasing tide will be forced to take the comparatively narrow channel to the north of that river and south of our northern boundary, some conception may be formed of the strength with which the current will run in that direction and how soon it will reach the eastern gorges of the Rocky Mountains. I say some conception, for I feel assured that the reality will outrun the anticipation.

In illustration, I will repeat what I stated when I first addressed the Senate on this subject. As wise and experienced as was President Monroe, as much as he had witnessed of the growth of our country in his time, so inadequate was his conception of its rapidity, that near the close of his administration, in the year 1824, he proposed to colonize the Indians of New York and those north of the Ohio River and east of the Mississippi, in what is now called the Wisconsin territory, under the impression that it was a portion of our territory so remote that they would not be disturbed by our increasing population for a long time to come. It is now but eighteen years since, and already, in that short period, it is a great and flourishing territory, ready to knock at our door for admission as one of the sovereign members of the Union. But what is still more striking, what is really wonderful and almost miraculous is that another territory (Iowa), still farther west, (beyond the Mississippi) has sprung up as if by magic, and has already outstripped Wisconsin, and may knock for entrance before she is prepared to do so.

Such is the wonderful growth of a population which has attained the number ours has, yearly increasing at a compound rate and such the impetus with which it is forcing its way, resistlessly, westward. It will soon, far sooner than anticipated, reach the Rocky Mountains and be ready to pour into the Oregon territory, when it will come into our possession without resistance or struggle; or, if there should be resistance it would be feeble and ineffectual.

We should then be as much stronger there, comparatively, than Great Britain, as she is now stronger than we are; and it would then be as idle for her to attempt to assert and maintain her exclusive claim to the territory against us as it would now be in us to attempt it against her. Let us be wise and abide our time; and it will accomplish all that we desire with more certainty and with infinitely less sacrifice than we can without it.

19.

Jesse Applegate: A Day on the Oregon Trail

The status of the Oregon Territory was left unsettled by the British-American Convention of 1818. In 1842 the Webster-Ashburton Treaty also failed to settle the boundary question, which went undecided until 1846. But interest in this remote region grew as reports came back from those who had traveled in the Northwest. Literature designed to lure settlers to Oregon was circulated in the Midwest, which was still feeling the effects of the depression of 1837. In the spring of 1843 a party of more than 1,000 people converged on Independence, Missouri, with all they could carry and with 5,000 cattle, to make the overland journey to Oregon. Those who owned herds of cattle traveled in a "cow column" under the leadership of Jesse Applegate, who wrote up the journey in "A Day with the Cow Column," from which the following selection is taken. This first of the large migrations to Oregon reachèd the Willamette Valley in November. Subsequent migrations followed rapidly.

Source: *Transactions of the Fourth Annual Re-Union of the Oregon Pioneer Association; for 1876,* Salem, Ore., 1877, pp. 57-65.

THE MIGRATING BODY numbered over 1,000 souls, with about 120 wagons, drawn by six ox teams, averaging about six yokes to the team, and several thousand loose horses and cattle.

The emigrants first organized and attempted to travel in one body, but it was soon found that no progress could be made with a body so cumbrous, and as yet so averse to all discipline. And at the crossing of the "Big Blue" it divided into two columns, which traveled in supporting distance of each other as far as Independence Rock, on the Sweet Water.

From this point, all danger from Indians being over, the emigrants separated into small parties better suited to the narrow mountain paths and small pastures in their front. Before the division on the Blue River there was some just cause for discontent in respect to loose cattle. Some of the emigrants had only their teams, while others had large herds in addition which must share the pastures and be guarded and driven by the whole body.

This discontent had its effect in the division on the Blue, those not encumbered with or having but few loose cattle attached themselves to the light column; those having more than four or five cows had of necessity to join the heavy, or cow, column. Hence the cow column, being much larger than the other and encumbered with its large herds, had to use greater exertion and observe a more rigid discipline to keep pace with the more agile consort. It is with the cow, or more clumsy, column that I propose to journey with the reader for a single day.

It is 4 A.M.; the sentinels on duty have discharged their rifles — the signal that the hours of sleep are over; and every wagon and tent is pouring forth its night tenants, and slow-kindling smokes begin largely to rise and float away on the morning air. Sixty men start from the corral, spreading as they make through the vast herd of cattle and horses that form a semicircle around the encampment, the most distant perhaps two miles away.

The herders pass to the extreme verge and carefully examine for trails beyond, to see that none of the animals have strayed or been stolen during the night. This morning no trails lead beyond the outside animals in sight, and by 5 o'clock the herders begin to contract the great moving circle and the well-trained animals move slowly toward camp, clipping here and there a thistle or tempting bunch of grass on the way. In about an hour, 5,000 animals are close up to the encampment, and the teamsters are busy selecting their teams and driving them inside the "corral" to be yoked. The corral is a circle 100 yards deep, formed with wagons connected strongly with each other, the wagon in the rear being connected with the wagon in front by its tongue and ox chains. It is a strong barrier that the most vicious ox cannot break, and in case of an attack of the Sioux would be no contempt-ible entrenchment.

From 6 to 7 o'clock is a busy time; breakfast is to be eaten, the tents struck, the wagons loaded, and the teams yoked and brought up in readiness to be attached to their respective wagons. All know when, at 7 o'clock, the signal to march sounds that those not ready to take their proper places in the line of march must fall into the dusty rear for the day.

There are sixty wagons. They have been divided into fifteen divisions, or platoons, of four wagons each, and each platoon is enti-tled to lead in its turn. The leading platoon of today will be the rear one tomorrow and will bring up the rear unless some teamster, through indolence or negligence, has lost his place in the line and is condemned to that uncomfortable post. It is within ten minutes of 7; the corral but now a strong barricade is everywhere broken, the teams being at-tached to the wagons. The women and chil-dren have taken their places in them. The

pilot (a borderer who has passed his life on the verge of civilization and has been cho-sen to the post of leader from his knowl-edge of the savage and his experience in travel through roadless wastes) stands ready, in the midst of his pioneers and aids, to mount and lead the way. Ten or fifteen young men, not today on duty, form anoth-er cluster. They are ready to start on a buf-falo hunt, are well mounted, and well armed as they need be, for the unfriendly Sioux have driven the buffalo out of the Platte, and the hunters must ride fifteen or twenty miles to reach them. The cow driv-ers are hastening, as they get ready, to the rear of their charge to collect and prepare them for the day's march.

It is on the stroke of 7; the rushing to and fro, the cracking of the whips, the loud command to oxen, and what seems to be the inextricable confusion of the last ten minutes has ceased. Fortunately everyone has been found, and every teamster is at his post. The clear notes of the trumpet sound in the front; the pilot and his guards mount their horses, the leading division of wagons moves out of the encampment, and takes up the line of march, the rest fall into their places with the precision of clockwork, until the spot so lately full of life sinks back into that solitude that seems to reign over the broad plain and rushing river as the caravan draws its lazy length toward the distant El Dorado.

It is with the hunters we will briskly canter toward the bold but smooth and grassy bluffs that bound the broad valley, for we are not yet in sight of the grander but less beautiful scenery (of the Chimney Rock, Courthouse, and other bluffs, so near-ly resembling giant castles and palaces) made by the passage of the Platte through the Highlands near Laramie. We have been traveling briskly for more than an hour. We have reached the top of the bluff and now have turned to view the wonderful panora-ma spread before us. To those who have not been on the Platte, my powers of description are wholly inadequate to convey an idea of the vast extent and grandeur of the picture and the rare beauty and distinctness of its detail. No haze or fog obscures objects in the pure transparent atmosphere of this lofty region.

To those accustomed only to the murky air of the seaboard, no correct judgment of distance can be formed by sight, and objects which they think they can reach in a two hours' walk may be a day's travel away; and though the evening air is a better conductor of sound, on the high plain during the day the report of the loudest rifle sounds little louder than the bursting of a cap; and while the report can be heard but a few hundred yards, the smoke of the discharge may be seen for miles. So extended is the view from the bluff on which the hunters stand that the broad river glowing under the morning sun like a sheet of silver and the broader emerald valley that borders it stretch away in the distance until they narrow at almost two points in the horizon, and when first seen, the vast pile of the Wind River Mountain, though hundreds of miles away, looks clear and distinct as a white cottage on the plain.

We are full six miles away from the line of march; though everything is dwarfed by distance, it is seen distinctly. The caravan has been about two hours in motion and is now extended as widely as a prudent regard for safety will permit. First, near the bank of the shining river, is a company of horsemen; they seem to have found an obstruction, for the main body has halted while three or four ride rapidly along the bank of the creek or slough. They are hunting a favorable crossing for the wagons; while we look they have succeeded; it has apparently required no work to make it passable, for all but one of the party have passed on and he has raised a flag, no doubt a signal to the wagons to steer their course to where he stands.

The leading teamster sees him though he is yet two miles off and steers his course

directly toward him, all the wagons following in his track. They (the wagons) form a line three quarters of a mile in length; some of the teamsters ride upon the front of their wagons, some walk beside their teams; scattered along the line companies of women and children are taking exercise on foot; they gather bouquets of rare and beautiful flowers that line the way; near them stalks a stately greyhound or an Irish wolf dog, apparently proud of keeping watch and ward over his master's wife and children.

Next comes a band of horses; two or three men or boys follow them, the docile and sagacious animals scarce needing this attention, for they have learned to follow in the rear of the wagons and know that at noon they will be allowed to graze and rest. Their knowledge of time seems as accurate as of the place they are to occupy in the line, and even a full-blown thistle will scarcely tempt them to straggle or halt until the dinner hour has arrived. Not so with the large herd of horned beasts that bring up the rear; lazy, selfish and unsocial, it has been a task to get them in motion, the strong, always ready to domineer over the weak, halt in the front and forbid the weaker to pass them. They seem to move only in fear of the driver's whip; though in the morning, full to repletion, they have not been driven an hour before their hunger and thirst seem to indicate a fast of days' duration. Through all the long day their greed is never sated nor their thirst quenched, nor is there a moment of relaxation of the tedious and vexatious labors of their drivers, although to all others the march furnishes some season of relaxation or enjoyment. For the cow drivers there is none.

But from the standpoint of the hunters the vexations are not apparent; the crack of the whips and loud objurgations are lost in the distance. Nothing of the moving panorama, smooth and orderly as it appears, has more attractions for the eye than that vast square column in which all colors are mingled, moving here slowly and there briskly, as impelled by horsemen riding furiously in front and rear.

But the picture, in its grandeur, its wonderful mingling of colors and distinctness of detail, is forgotten in contemplation of the singular people who give it life and animation. No other race of men with the means at their command would undertake so great a journey; none save these could successfully perform it with no previous preparation, relying only on the fertility of their invention to devise the means to overcome each danger and difficulty as it arose. They have undertaken to perform, with slow-moving oxen, a journey of 2,000 miles.

The way lies over trackless wastes, wide and deep rivers, rugged and lofty mountains, and is beset with hostile savages. Yet, whether it were a deep river with no tree upon its banks, a rugged defile where even a loose horse could not pass, a hill too steep for him to climb, or a threatened attack of an enemy, they are always found ready and equal to the occasion and always conquerors. May we not call them men of destiny? They are people changed in no essential particulars from their ancestors, who have followed closely on the footsteps of the receding savage, from the Atlantic seaboard to the valley of the Mississippi.

But while we have been gazing at the picture in the valley, the hunters have been examining the high plain in the other direction. Some dark moving objects have been discovered in the distance, and all are closely watching them to discover what they are, for in the atmosphere of the plains a flock of crows marching miles away or a band of buffaloes or Indians at ten times the distance, look alike, and many ludicrous mistakes occur. But these are buffaloes, for two have stuck their heads together and are alternately pushing each other back. The hunters mount and away in pursuit, and I, a poor cow driver, must hurry back to my daily toil and take a scolding from my fellow herders for so long playing truant.

The pilot, by measuring the ground and timing the speed of the wagons and the walk of his horses, has determined the rate of each so as to enable him to select the nooning place, as nearly as the requisite grass and water can be had at the end of five hours' travel of the wagons. Today, the ground being favorable, little time has been lost in preparing the road, so that he and his pioneers are at the nooning place an hour in advance of the wagons, which time is spent in preparing convenient watering places for the animals and digging little wells near the bank of the Platte. As the teams are not unyoked but simply turned loose from the wagons, a corral is not formed at noon, but the wagons are drawn up in columns, four abreast, the leading wagon of each platoon on the left — the platoons being formed with that view. This brings friends together at noon as well as at night.

Today an extra session of the council is being held to settle a dispute, that does not admit of delay, between a proprietor and a young man who has undertaken to do a man's service on the journey for bed and board. Many such engagements exist and much interest is taken in the manner this high court, from which there is no appeal, will define the rights of each party in such engagements. The council was a high court in the most exalted sense. It was a senate composed of the ablest and most respected fathers of the emigration. It exercised both legislative and judicial powers, and its laws and decisions proved it equal [to] and worthy of the high trust reposed in it.

Its sessions were usually held on days when the caravan was not moving. It first took the state of the little commonwealth into consideration; revised or repealed rules defective or obsolete and exacted such others as the exigencies seemed to require. The commonwealth being cared for, it next resolved itself into a court, to hear and settle private disputes and grievances. The offender and aggrieved appeared before it, witnesses were examined, and the parties were heard by themselves and sometimes by counsel. The judges thus being made fully acquainted with the case, and being in no way influenced or cramped by technicalities, decided all cases according to their merits. There was but little use for lawyers before this court, for no plea was entertained which was calculated to defeat the ends of justice.

Many of these judges have since won honors in higher spheres. They have aided to establish on the broad basis of right and universal liberty two of the pillars of our great republic in the Occident. Some of the young men who appeared before them as advocates have themselves sat upon the highest judicial tribunals, commanded armies, been governors of states, and taken high positions in the Senate of the nation.

It is now 1 o'clock; the bugle has sounded, and the caravan has resumed its westward journey. It is in the same order, but the evening is far less animated than the morning march; a drowsiness has fallen apparently on man and beast; teamsters drop asleep on their perches and even when walking by their teams, and the words of command are now addressed to the slowly creeping oxen in the softened tenor of women or the piping treble of children, while the snores of teamsters make a droning accompaniment.

But a little incident breaks the monotony of the march. An emigrant's wife, whose state of health has caused Dr. Whitman to travel near the wagon for the day, is now taken with violent illness. The doctor has had the wagon driven out of the line, a tent pitched, and a fire kindled. Many conjectures are hazarded in regard to this mysterious proceeding and as to why this lone wagon is to be left behind.

And we too must leave it, hasten to the front and note the proceedings, for the sun is now getting low in the west, and at length the painstaking pilot is standing ready to conduct the train in the circle which he has previously measured and marked out, which is to form the invariable fortification for the night. The leading wagons follow him so nearly round the circle that but a wagon length separates them. Each wagon follows in its track, the rear closing on the front, until its tongue and ox chains will perfectly reach from one to the other, and so accurate the measurement and perfect the practice, that the hindmost wagon of the train always precisely closes the gateway. As each wagon is brought into position, it is dropped from its team (the teams being inside the circle), the team unyoked, and the yokes and chains are used to connect the wagon strongly with that in its front. Within ten minutes from the time the leading wagon halted, the barricade is formed, the teams unyoked and driven out to pasture.

Everyone is busy preparing fires of buffalo chips to cook the evening meal, pitching tents, and otherwise preparing for the night. There are anxious watchers for the absent wagon, for there are many matrons who may be afflicted like its inmate before the journey is over; and they fear the strange and startling practice of this Oregon doctor will be dangerous. But as the sun goes down, the absent wagon rolls into camp, the bright, speaking face and cheery look of the doctor, who rides in advance, declares without words that all is well, and both mother and child are comfortable.

I would fain now and here pay a passing tribute to that noble, devoted man, Dr. Whitman. I will obtrude no other name upon the reader, nor would I his, were he of our party or even living, but his stay with us was transient, though the good he did us permanent, and he has long since died at his post.

From the time he joined us on the Platte until he left us at Fort Hall, his great experience and indomitable energy were of priceless value to the migrating column. His constant advice, which we knew was based upon a knowledge of the road before us, was — "travel, *travel*, TRAVEL — nothing else will take you to the end of your journey; nothing is wise that does not help you along, nothing is good for you that causes a moment's delay." His great authority as a physician and complete success in the case above referred to saved us many prolonged and perhaps ruinous delays from similar causes, and it is no disparagement to others to say that to no other individual are the emigrants of 1843 so much indebted for the successful conclusion of their journey as to Dr. Marcus Whitman.

All able to bear arms in the party have been formed into three companies, and each of these into four watches. Every third night it is the duty of one of these companies to keep watch and ward over the camp, and it is so arranged that each watch takes its turn of guard duty through the different watches of the night. Those forming the first watch tonight will be second on duty, then third and fourth, which brings them through all the watches of the night. They begin at 8 P.M. and end at 4 A.M.

It is not yet 8 o'clock when the first watch is to be set; the evening meal is just over, and the corral now free from the intrusion of the cattle or horses, groups of children are scattered over it. The larger are taking a game of romps, "the wee toddling things" are being taught that great achievement that distinguishes man from the lower animals. Before a tent near the river a violin makes lively music, and some youths and maidens have improvised a dance upon the green; in another quarter a flute gives its mellow and melancholy notes to the still air, which as they float away over the quiet river seem a lament for the past rather than a hope for the future.

It has been a prosperous day; more than twenty miles have been accomplished of the great journey. The encampment is a good one; one of the causes that threatened much future delay has just been removed by the skill and energy of "that good angel," Dr. Whitman, and it has lifted a load from the hearts of the elders. Many of these are assembled around the good doctor at the tent of the pilot (which is his home for the time being) and are giving grave attention to his wise and energetic counsel. The careworn pilot sits aloof, quietly smoking his pipe, for he knows the brave doctor is "strengthening his hands."

But time passes; the watch is set for the night; the council of old men has broken up and each has returned to his own quarter. The flute has whispered its last lament to the deepening night, the violin is silent, and the dancers have dispersed. Enamored youth have whispered a tender "good night" in the ears of blushing maidens or stolen a kiss from the lips of some future bride — for Cupid here as elsewhere has been busy bringing together congenial hearts, and among those simple people he alone is consulted in forming the marriage tie. Even the doctor and the pilot have finished their confidential interview and have separated for the night. All is hushed and repose from the fatigue of the day, save the vigilant guard and the wakeful leader who still has care upon his mind that forbid sleep.

He hears the 10 o'clock relief taking post and the "all well" report of the returned guard; the night deepens, yet he seeks not the needed repose. At length a sentinel hurries to him with the welcome report that a party is approaching — as yet too far away for its character to be determined, and he instantly hurries out in the direction seen. This he does both from inclination and duty, for in times past the camp had been unnecessarily alarmed by timid or inexperienced sentinels, causing much confusion and fright among women and children, and it had been made a rule that all extraordinary incidents of the night should be reported directly to the pilot, who alone had the authority to call out the military strength of the column or so much of it as was in his judgment necessary to prevent a stampede or repel an enemy.

Tonight he is at no loss to determine that

he approaching party are our missing hunt-
rs, and that they have met with success,
nd he only waits until by some further sig-
al he can know that no ill has happened to
nem. This is not long wanting. He does
ot even await their arrival, but the last
care of the day being removed, and the last
duty performed, he too seeks the rest that
will enable him to go through the same
routine tomorrow. But here I leave him, for
my task is also done, and unlike his, it is to
be repeated no more.

20.

Andrew Jackson: The Annexation of Texas as Essential to the United States

*One of the first attempts in the 1840s to revive the issue of the annexation of Texas
was a letter written by Thomas Gilmer and published in the* Madisonian *on
January 23, 1843. Gilmer argued that unless the United States acquired Texas, it
would come under the political and economic influence of Great Britain and the abolition
of slavery would be effected there. Gilmer's letter was sent by Congressman
Aaron V. Brown of Tennessee to ex-President Andrew Jackson for comment. Jackson's
reply of February 12, 1843, which is reprinted here, was first published a year
later without his consent to enlist Democratic support for the annexation of Texas and
to dissuade the Democrats from choosing Martin Van Buren, who opposed immediate
annexation, as their presidential nominee.*

Source: James Parton, *Life of Andrew Jackson*, Boston, 1888, Vol. III, pp. 658-660.

OURS OF THE 23RD ULTIMO has been re-
•ived, and with it the *Madisonian* contain-
1g Governor Gilmer's letter on the subject
f the annexation of Texas to the United
•tates.

You are not mistaken in supposing that I
ave formed an opinion on this interesting
ibject. It occupied much of my attention
uring my presidency, and, I am sure, has
•st none of its importance by what has
nce transpired.

Soon after my election, in 1829, it was
iade known to me by Mr. Erwin, formerly
ur minister at the court of Madrid, that
·hile at that court he had laid the founda-
on of a treaty with Spain for the cession
f the Floridas and the settlement of the
oundary of Louisiana, fixing the western
limit of the latter at the Rio Grande, agree-
ably to the understanding of France; that he
had written home to our government for
powers to complete and sign this negotiation; but that, instead of receiving such authority, the negotiation was taken out of his
hands and transferred to Washington, and a
new treaty was there concluded, by which
the Sabine, and not the Rio Grande, was
recognized and established as the boundary
of Louisiana.

Finding that these statements were true,
and that our government did really give up
that important territory when it was at its
option to retain it, I was filled with astonishment. The right of the territory was obtained from France. Spain stood ready to
acknowledge it to the Rio Grande, and yet

Daguerreotype of Andrew Jackson by Dan Adams, c.
1845

the authority asked by our minister to insert
the true boundary was not only withheld
but, in lieu of it, a limit was adopted which
stripped us of the whole of the vast country
lying between the two rivers.

On such a subject, I thought with the ancient Romans, that it was right never to
cede any land or boundary of the republic,
but always to add to it by honorable treaty,
thus extending the area of freedom; and it
was in accordance with this feeling that I
gave our minister to Mexico instructions to
enter upon a negotiation for the retroces-
sion of Texas to the United States. This negotiation failed, and I shall ever regret it as
a misfortune to both Mexico and the United States.

Mr. Gilmer's letter presents many of the
considerations which, in my judgment, rendered the step necessary to the peace and
harmony of the two countries; but the
point in it, at that time, which most strongly impelled me to the course I pursued was
the injustice done to us by the surrender of
the territory, when it was obvious that it
could have been retained without increasing
the consideration afterward given for the
Floridas. I could not but feel that the sur-

render of so vast and important a territor
was attributable to an erroneous estimate
the tendency of our institutions, in whic
there was mingled somewhat of jealousy t
the rising greatness of the South and West

But I forbear to dwell on this part of th
history of this question. It is past an
cannot now be undone. We can now onl
look at it as one of annexation, if Texa
presents it to us; and if she does, I do nd
hesitate to say that the welfare and happ
ness of our Union require that it should b
accepted.

If, in a military point of view alone, th
question be examined, it will be found t
be most important to the United States t
be in possession of that territory.

Great Britain has already made treatie
with Texas, and we know that farseeing na
tion never omits a circumstance, in her ex
tensive intercourse with the world whic
can be turned to account in increasing he
military resources. May she not enter int
an alliance with Texas? And reserving,
she doubtless will, the northwestern boun
ary question as the cause of war with
whenever she chooses to declare it, let t
suppose that, as an ally with Texas, we a
to fight her! Preparatory to such a mov
ment, she sends her 20,000 or 30,000 me
to Texas; organizes them on the Sabin
where her supplies and arms can be concer
trated before we have even notice of he
intentions; makes a lodgment on the Mi
sissippi; excites the Negroes to insurrectio
the lower country falls, and, with it, Ne
Orleans; and a servile war rages throug
the whole South and West.

In the meanwhile, she is also moving a
army along the western frontier from Cana
da, which, in cooperation with the arm
from Texas, spreads ruin and havoc fro
the Lakes to the Gulf of Mexico.

Who can estimate the national loss w
may sustain before such a movement coul
be repelled with such forces as we could o
ganize on short notice?

Remember that Texas borders upon u

on our west, to 42° of north latitude, and is our southern boundary to the Pacific. Remember, also, that if annexed to the United States, our western boundary would be the Rio Grande, which is of itself a fortification on account of its extensive, barren, and uninhabitable plains. With such a barrier on our west we are invincible. The whole European world could not, in combination against us, make an impression on our Union. Our population on the Pacific would rapidly increase and soon be strong enough for the protection of our Eastern whalers, and, in the worst event, could always be sustained by timely aids from the intermediate country.

From the Rio Grande, over land, a large army could not march or be supplied, unless from the Gulf by water, which, by vigilance, could always be intercepted; and to march an army near the Gulf, they could be harassed by militia and detained until an organized force could be raised to meet them.

But I am in danger of running into unnecessary details, which my debility will not enable me to close. The question is full of interest, also, as it affects our domestic relations and as it may bear upon those of Mexico to us. I will not undertake to follow it out to its consequences in those respects, though I must say that, in all aspects, the annexation of Texas to the United States promises to enlarge the circle of free institutions, and is essential to the United States, particularly as lessening the probabilities of future collision with foreign powers, and giving them greater efficiency in spreading the blessings of peace.

21.

DOROTHEA DIX: Plea for Humane Treatment of the Insane

Dorothea Dix, novelist and school teacher, visited a jail in East Cambridge, Massachusetts, in March 1841 and there found insane persons neglected in unheated rooms. The discovery prompted her to investigate the condition of the insane throughout the state, and she found it everywhere the same. In 1843 she composed a memorial to the legislature of Massachusetts, portions of which are reprinted here. It was written in the home of William Ellery Channing and delivered to the legislature by influential friends. The committee reviewing the memorial recommended reforms that were soon enacted into law. In the years that followed, Miss Dix continued her reform work throughout the United States and Europe.

Source: OSL 148.

I RESPECTFULLY ASK to present this memorial, believing that the *cause*, which actuates to and sanctions so unusual a movement, presents no equivocal claim to public consideration and sympathy. Surrendering to calm and deep convictions of duty my habitual views of what is womanly and becoming, I proceed briefly to explain what has conducted me before you unsolicited and unsustained, trusting, while I do so, that the memorialist will be speedily forgotten in the memorial.

About two years since leisure afforded opportunity and duty prompted me to visit several prisons and almshouses in the vicinity of this metropolis. I found, near Boston, in the jails and asylums for the poor, a numerous class brought into unsuitable connection with criminals and the general mass of paupers. I refer to idiots and insane persons, dwelling in circumstances not only adverse to their own physical and moral improvement, but productive of extreme disadvantages to all other persons brought into association with them.

I applied myself diligently to trace the causes of these evils, and sought to supply remedies. As one obstacle was surmounted, fresh difficulties appeared. Every new investigation has given depth to the conviction that it is only by decided, prompt, and vigorous legislation the evils to which I refer, and which I shall proceed more fully to illustrate, can be remedied. I shall be obliged to speak with great plainness, and to reveal many things revolting to the taste, and from which my woman's nature shrinks with peculiar sensitiveness.

But truth is the highest consideration. *I tell what I have seen* — painful and shocking as the details often are — that from them you may feel more deeply the imperative obligation which lies upon you to prevent the possibility of a repetition or continuance of such outrages upon humanity. If I inflict pain upon you, and move you to horror, it is to acquaint you with sufferings which you have the power to alleviate, and make you hasten to the relief of the victims of legalized barbarity.

I come to present the strong claims of suffering humanity. I come to place before the legislature of Massachusetts the condition of the miserable, the desolate, the outcast. I come as the advocate of helpless, forgotten, insane, and idiotic men and women; of beings sunk to a condition from which the most unconcerned would start with real horror; of beings wretched in our prisons, and more wretched in our almshouses. And I cannot suppose it needful to employ earnest persuasion, or stubborn argument, in order to arrest and fix attention upon a subject only the more strongly pressing in its claims because it is revolting and disgusting in its details.

I must confine myself to few examples, but am ready to furnish other and more complete details, if required. If my pictures are displeasing, coarse, and severe, my subjects, it must be recollected, offer no tranquil, refined, or composing features. The condition of human beings, reduced to the extremest states of degradation and misery, cannot be exhibited in softened language, or adorn a polished page.

I proceed, gentlemen, briefly to call your attention to the *present* state of insane persons confined within this Commonwealth, in *cages, closets, cellars, stalls, pens! Chained, naked, beaten with rods,* and *lashed* into obedience.

As I state cold, severe *facts,* I feel obliged to refer to persons, and definitely to indicate localities. But it is upon my subject, not upon localities or individuals, I desire to fix attention; and I would speak as kindly as possible of all wardens, keepers, and other responsible officers, believing that *most* of these have erred not through hardness of heart and willful cruelty so much as want of skill and knowledge, and want of consideration. Familiarity with suffering, it is said, blunts the sensibilities, and where neglect once finds a footing other injuries are multiplied. This is not all, for it may justly and strongly be added that, from the deficiency of adequate means to meet the wants of these cases, it has been an absolute impossibility to do justice in this matter. Prisons are not constructed in view of being converted into county hospitals, and almshouses are not founded as receptacles for the insane. And yet, in the face of justice and common sense, wardens are by law compelled to receive, and the masters of almshouses not to refuse, insane and idiotic subjects in all stages of mental disease and privation.

It is the Commonwealth, not its integral parts, that is accountable for most of the abuses which have lately and do still exist.

repeat it, it is defective legislation which perpetuates and multiplies these abuses. In illustration of my subject, I offer the following extracts from my Notebook and Journal:

Springfield. In the jail one lunatic woman, furiously mad, a state pauper, improperly situated, both in regard to the prisoners, the keepers, and herself. It is a case of extreme self-forgetfulness and oblivion to all the decencies of life, to describe which would be to repeat only the grossest scenes. She is much worse since leaving Worcester. In the almshouse of the same town is a woman apparently only needing judicious care, and some well-chosen employment, to make it unnecessary to confine her in solitude, in a dreary unfurnished room. Her appeals for employment and companionship are most touching, but the mistress replied "she had no time to attend to her."

Northampton. In the jail, quite lately, was a young man violently mad, who had not, as I was informed at the prison, come under medical care, and not been returned from any hospital. In the almshouse the cases of insanity are now unmarked by abuse, and afford evidence of judicious care by the keepers.

Williamsburg. The almshouse has several insane, not under suitable treatment. No apparent intentional abuse. *Rutland.* Appearance and report of the insane in the almshouse not satisfactory.

Sterling. A terrible case; manageable in a hospital; at present as well controlled perhaps as circumstances in a case so extreme allow. An almshouse, but wholly wrong in relation to the poor crazy woman, to the paupers generally, and to her keepers.

Burlington. A woman, declared to be very insane; decent room and bed; but not allowed to rise oftener, the mistress said, "than every other day: it is too much trouble."

Concord. A woman from the hospital in a cage in the almshouse. In the jail several, decently cared for in general, but not properly placed in a prison. Violent, noisy, unmanageable most of the time.

Lincoln. A woman in a cage. *Medford.* One idiotic subject chained, and one in a closed stall for seventeen years. *Pepperell.* One often doubly chained, hand and foot; another violent; several peaceable now. *Brookfield.* One man caged, comfortable. *Granville.* One often closely confined; now losing the use of his limbs from want of exercise. *Charlemont.* One man caged. *Savoy.* One man caged. *Lenox.* Two in the jail, against whose unfit condition there the jailer protests.

Dedham. The insane disadvantageously placed in the jail. In the almshouse, two females in stalls, situated in the main building; lie in wooden bunks filled with straw; always shut up. One of these subjects is supposed curable. The overseers of the poor have declined giving her a trial at the hospital, as I was informed, on account of expense.

Franklin. One man chained; decent. *Taunton.* One woman caged. *Plymouth.* One man stall-caged, from Worcester Hospital. *Scituate.* One man and one woman stall caged. *West Bridgewater.* Three idiots. Never removed from one room. *Barnstable.* Four females in pens and stalls. Two chained certainly. I think all. Jail, one idiot. *Wellfleet.* Three insane. One man and one woman chained, the latter in a bad condition. *Brewster.* One woman violently mad, solitary. Could not see her, the master and mistress being absent, and the paupers in charge having strict orders to admit no one. *Rochester.* Seven insane; at present none caged. *Milford.* Two insane, not now caged. *Cohasset.* One idiot, one insane; most miserable condition. *Plympton.* One insane, three idiots; condition wretched.

Besides the above, I have seen many who, part of the year, are chained or caged. The use of cages all but universal. Hardly a town but can refer to some not distant period of using them; chains are less common; negligences frequent; willful abuse less frequent than sufferings proceeding from ignorance, or want of consideration. I encountered during the last three months many poor creatures wandering reckless and unprotected through the country. Innumerable accounts have been sent me of persons who had roved away unwatched and unsearched after; and I have heard that responsible persons, controlling the almshouses, have not thought themselves culpable in sending away from their shelter, to cast upon the chances of remote relief, insane men and women. These, left on the highways, unfriended and incompetent to control or direct their own movements, sometimes have found refuge in the hospital, and others have not been traced.

But I cannot particularize. In traversing the state, I have found hundreds of insane persons in every variety of circumstance and condition, many whose situation could not and need not be improved; a less number, but that very large whose lives are the saddest pictures of human suffering and degradation. I give a few illustrations; but description fades before reality.

Danvers. November. Visited the almshouse. A large building, much out of repair. Understand a new one is in contemplation. Here are from fifty-six to sixty inmates, one idiotic, three insane; one of the latter in close confinement at all times.

Long before reaching the house, wild shouts, snatches of rude songs, imprecations and obscene language, fell upon the ear, proceeding from the occupant of a low building, rather remote from the principal building to which my course was directed. Found the mistress, and was conducted to the place which was called "the home" of the forlorn maniac, a young woman, exhibiting a condition of neglect and misery blotting out the faintest idea of comfort, and outraging every sentiment of decency. She had been, I learned, "a respectable person, industrious and worthy. Disappointments

and trials shook her mind, and finally, lai prostrate reason and self-control. She be came a maniac for life. She had been a Worcester Hospital for a considerable time and had been returned as incurable." Th mistress told me she understood tha "while there, she was comfortable and de cent."

Alas, what a change was here exhibited She had passed from one degree of violenc to another, in swift progress. There sh stood, clinging to or beating upon the bar of her caged apartment, the contracted siz of which afforded space only for increasin accumulations of filth, a foul spectacle There she stood with naked arms and di sheveled hair, the unwashed frame investe with fragments of unclean garments, the ai so extremely offensive, though ventilatio was afforded on all sides save one, that i was not possible to remain beyond a fev moments without retreating for recovery t the outward air. Irritation of body, pro duced by utter filth and exposure, incite her to the horrid process of tearing off he skin by inches. Her face, neck, and perso were thus disfigured to hideousness. Sh held up a fragment just rent off. To my ex clamation of horror, the mistress replied "Oh, we can't help it. Half the skin is o sometimes. We can do nothing with her and it makes no difference what she eat for she consumes her own filth as readily a the food which is brought her."

It is now January. A fortnight since tw visitors reported that most wretched outca as "wallowing in dirty straw, in a place ye more dirty, and without clothing, withou fire. Worse cared for than the brutes, an wholly lost to consciousness of decency." I the whole story told? What was seen is what is reported is not. These gross expo sures are not for the pained sight of on alone. All, all, coarse, brutal men, wonder ing, neglected children, old and young, eacl and all, witness this lowest, foulest state o miserable humanity. And who protects her that worse than pariah outcast, from other wrongs and blacker outrages? I do not *know* that such *have been*. I do know that they are to be dreaded, and that they are not guarded against.

Some may say these things cannot be remedied, these furious maniacs are not to be raised from these base conditions. I *know* they are. Could give many examples. Let one suffice. A young woman, a pauper, in a distant town, Sandisfield, was for years a raging maniac. A cage, chains, and *the whip* were the agents for controlling her, united with harsh tones and profane language. Annually, with others (the town's poor), she was put up at auction, and bid off at the lowest price which was declared for her. One year, not long past, an old man came forward in the number of applicants for the poor wretch. He was taunted and ridiculed. "What would he and his old wife do with such a mere beast?" "My wife says yes," replied he, "and I shall take her."

She was given to his charge. He conveyed her home. She was washed, neatly dressed, and placed in a decent bedroom, furnished for comfort and opening into the kitchen. How altered her condition! As yet *the chains* were not off. The first week she was somewhat restless, at times violent, but the quiet, kind ways of the old people wrought a change. She received her food decently, forsook acts of violence, and no longer uttered blasphemies or indecent language. After a week the chain was lengthened, and she was received as a companion into the kitchen. Soon she engaged in trivial employments. "After a fortnight," said the old man, "I knocked off the chains and made her a free woman."

She is at times excited, but not violently. They are careful of her diet. They keep her very clean. She calls them "father" and "mother." Go there now, and you will find her "clothed," and, though not perfectly in her "right mind," so far restored as to be a safe and comfortable inmate.

Newburyport. Visited the almshouse in June last. Eighty inmates. Seven insane, one idiotic. Commodious and neat house. Several of the partially insane apparently very comfortable. Two very improperly situated; namely, an insane man, not considered incurable, in an out building, whose room opened upon what was called "the dead room," affording, in lieu of companionship with the living, a contemplation of corpses. The other subject was a woman in a cellar. I desired to see her. Much reluctance was shown. I pressed the request. The master of the house stated that she was in the cellar; that she was dangerous to be approached; that she had lately attacked his wife, and was often naked.

I persisted, "If you will not go with me, give me the keys and I will go alone." Thus importuned, the outer doors were opened. I descended the stairs from within. A strange, unnatural noise seemed to proceed from beneath our feet. At the moment I did not much regard it. My conductor proceeded to remove a padlock, while my eye explored the wide space in quest of the poor woman. All for a moment was still. But judge my horror and amazement, when a door to a closet beneath the staircase was opened, revealing in the imperfect light a female apparently wasted to a skeleton, partially wrapped in blankets, furnished for the narrow bed on which she was sitting. Her countenance furrowed, not by age, but suffering, was the image of distress.

In that contracted space, unlighted, unventilated, she poured forth the wailings of despair. Mournfully she extended her arms and appealed to me: "Why am I consigned to hell? dark — dark — I used to pray, I used to read the Bible — I have done no crime in my heart. I had friends. Why have all forsaken me! — my God, my God, why hast Thou forsaken me!" Those groans, those wailings, come up daily, mingling with how many others, a perpetual and sad memorial. When the good Lord shall require an account of our stewardship, what shall all and each answer?

Perhaps it will be inquired how long, how many days or hours, was she imprisoned in these confined limits? *For years!* In another part of the cellar were other small closets, only better, because higher through the entire length, into one of which she by turns was transferred, so as to afford opportunity for fresh whitewashing, etc.

Saugus. December 24. Thermometer below zero; drove to the poorhouse; was conducted to the master's family room by himself; walls garnished with handcuffs and chains, not less than five pairs of the former; did not inquire how or on whom applied; thirteen pauper inmates; one insane man; one woman insane; one idiotic man; asked to see them; the two men were shortly led in; appeared pretty decent and comfortable. Requested to see the other insane subject; was denied decidedly; urged the request, and finally secured a reluctant assent. Was led through an outer passage into a lower room, occupied by the paupers; crowded; not neat; ascended a rather low flight of stairs upon an open entry, through the floor of which was introduced a stovepipe, carried along a *few feet*, about six inches above the floor, through which it was reconveyed below. From this entry opens a room of moderate size, having a sashed window; floor, I think, painted; apartment entirely unfurnished; no chair, table, nor bed; neither, what is seldom missing, a bundle of straw or lock of hay; cold, very cold; the first movement of my conductor was to throw open a window, a measure imperatively necessary for those who entered.

On the floor sat a woman, her limbs immovably contracted, so that the knees were brought upward to the chin; the face was concealed; the head rested on the folded arms. For clothing she appeared to have been furnished with fragments of many discharged garments. These were folded about

her, yet they little benefited her, if one might judge by the constant shuddering which almost convulsed her poor crippled frame. Woeful was this scene. Language feeble to record the misery she was suffering and had suffered.

In reply to my inquiry if she could not change her position, I was answered by the master in the negative, and told that the contraction of limbs was occasioned by "neglect and exposure in former years," but since she had been crazy, and before she fell under the charge, as I inferred, of her present guardians. Poor wretch! she, like many others, was an example of what humanity becomes when the temple of reason falls in ruins, leaving the mortal part to injury and neglect, and showing how much can be endured of privation, exposure, and disease without extinguishing the lamp of life.

Passing out, the man pointed to a something, revealed to more than one sense, which he called "her bed; and we throw some blankets over her at night." Possibly this is done; others, like myself, might be pardoned a doubt if they could have seen all I saw and heard abroad all I heard. The bed, so called, was about three feet long, and from a half to three-quarters of a yard wide; of old ticking or tow cloth was the case; the contents might have been a full handful of hay or straw. My attendant's exclamations on my leaving the house were emphatic, and can hardly be repeated.

The above case recalls another of equal neglect or abuse. Asking my way to the almshouse in Berkeley, which had been repeatedly spoken of as greatly neglected, I was answered as to the direction and informed that there were "plenty of insane people and idiots there." "Well taken care of?" "Oh, well enough for such sort of creatures!" "Any violently insane?" "Yes, my sister's son is there, — a real tiger. I kept him here at my house awhile, but it was too much trouble to go on: so I carried

im there." "Is he comfortably provided
or?" "Well enough." "Has he decent
clothes?" "Good enough; wouldn't wear
them if he had more." "Food?" "Good
enough; good enough for him." "One more
question, — has he the comfort of a fire?"
Fire! fire, indeed! what does a crazy man
need of fire? Red-hot iron wants fire as
much as he!" And such are sincerely the
ideas of not a few persons in regard to the
actual wants of the insane. Less regarded
than the lowest brutes. No wonder they
sink even lower. . . .

Violence and severity do but exasperate
the insane: the only availing influence is
kindness and firmness. It is amazing what
these will produce. How many examples
might illustrate this position! I refer to one
recently exhibited in Barre. The town paupers are disposed of annually to some family who, for a stipulated sum, agree to take
charge of them. One of them, a young
woman, was shown to me well clothed,
neat, quiet, and employed at needlework. Is
it possible that this is the same being who,
but last year, was a raving mad woman, exhibiting every degree of violence in action
and speech; a very tigress wrought to fury;
raged, chained, beaten, loaded with injuries,
and exhibiting the passions which an iron
rule might be expected to stimulate and sustain. It is the same person. Another family
hold her in charge who better understand
human nature and human influences. She is
no longer chained, caged, and beaten; but,
if excited, a pair of mittens drawn over the
hands secures from mischief. Where will she
be next year after the annual sale? . . .

Could we in fancy place ourselves in the
situation of some of these poor wretches,
bereft of reason, deserted of friends, hopeless, troubles without, and more dreary
troubles within, overwhelming the wreck of
the mind as "a wide breaking in of the waters," — how should we, as the terrible il-
lusion was cast off, not only offer the thank
offering of prayer, that so mighty a destruc-

Library of Congress
Dorothea Dix

tion had not overwhelmed our mental nature, but as an offering more acceptable devote ourselves to alleviate that state from
which we are so mercifully spared?

It may not appear much more credible
than the fact above stated, that a few
months since a young woman in a state of
complete insanity was confined entirely naked in a pen or stall in a barn. There, unfurnished with clothes, without bed and
without fire, she was left — but not alone.
Profligate men and idle boys had access to
the den, whenever curiosity or vulgarity
prompted. She is now removed into the
house with other paupers; and for this humanizing benefit she was indebted to the
remonstrances, in the first instance, *of an insane man.*

Another town now owns a poorhouse,
which I visited, and am glad to testify to
the present comfortable state of the inmates; but there the only provision the
house affords for an insane person, should
one, as is not improbable, be conveyed
there, is a closet in the cellar, formed by the
arch upon which the chimney rests. This

has a closed door, not only securing the prisoners, but excluding what of light and pure air might else find admission.

Abuses assuredly cannot always or altogether be guarded against; but, if in the civil and social relations all shall have "done what they could," no ampler justification will be demanded at the great tribunal.

Of the dangers and mischiefs sometimes following the location of insane persons in our almshouses, I will record but one more example. In Worcester has for several years resided a young woman, a lunatic pauper of decent life and respectable family. I have seen her as she usually appeared, listless and silent, almost or quite sunk into a state of dementia, sitting one amidst the family, "but not of them." A few weeks since, revisiting that almshouse, judge my horror and amazement to see her negligently bearing in her arms a young infant, of which I was told she was the unconscious parent. Who was the father, none could or would declare.

Disqualified for the performance of maternal cares and duties, regarding the helpless little creature with a perplexed or indifferent gaze, she sat a silent, but, oh, how eloquent, a pleader for the protection of others of her neglected and outraged sex! Details of that black story would not strengthen the cause. Needs it a mightier plea than the sight of that forlorn creature and her wailing infant? Poor little child, more than orphan from birth, in this unfriendly world! A demented mother, a father on whom the sun might blush or refuse to shine!

Men of Massachusetts, I beg, I implore, I demand pity and protection for these of my suffering, outraged sex. Fathers, husbands, brothers, I would supplicate you for this boon; but what do I say? I dishonor you, divest you at once of Christianity and humanity, does this appeal imply distrust. If it comes burdened with a doubt of your righteousness in this legislation, then blot i out; while I declare confidence in your honor, not less than your humanity. Here you will put away the cold, calculating spirit o selfishness and self-seeking; lay off the ar mor of local strife and political opposition here and now, for once, forgetful of th earthly and perishable, come up to thes halls and consecrate them with one hear and one mind to works of righteousnes and just judgment. Become the benefactor of your race, the just guardians of the sol emn rights you hold in trust. Raise up th fallen, succor the desolate, restore the out cast, defend the helpless, and for your eter nal and great reward receive the benedic tion, "Well done, good and faithful ser vants, become rulers over many things!"

But, gentlemen, I do not come to quick en your sensibilities into short-lived action to pour forth passionate exclamation, no yet to move your indignation against thos whose misfortune, not fault, it surely is t hold in charge these poor demented crea tures, and whose whole of domestic econo my or prison discipline is absolutely over thrown by such proximity of conflicting cir cumstances and opposite conditions of min and character. Allow me to illustrate thi position by a few examples: it were easy t produce hundreds.

The master of one of the best-regulate almshouses, namely, that of Plymouth where every arrangement shows that th comfort of the sick, the aged, and the in firm, is suitably cared for, and the amend ment of the unworthy is studied and ad vanced, said, as we stood opposite a lattice stall where was confined a madman, tha the hours of the day were few when th whole household was not distracted from employment by screams and turbulen stampings, and every form of violence which the voice or muscular force coul produce. This unfortunate being was one o the "returned incurables," since whose las admission to the almshouse they were no longer secure of peace for the aged or decency for the young.

It was morally impossible to do justice to the sane and insane in such improper vicinity to each other. The conviction is continually deepened that hospitals are the only places where insane persons can be at once humanely and properly controlled. Poorhouses converted into madhouses cease to effect the purposes for which they were established, and instead of being asylums for the aged, the homeless, and the friendless, and places of refuge for orphaned or neglected childhood, are transformed into perpetual bedlams.

This crying evil and abuse of institutions is not confined to our almshouses. The warden of a populous prison near this metropolis, populous not with criminals only, but with the insane in almost every stage of insanity, and the idiotic in descending states from silly and simple, to helpless and speechless, has declared that, since their admission under the Revised Statutes of 1835, page 382, "the prison has often more resembled the infernal regions than any place on earth!"

And, what with the excitement inevitably produced by the crowded state of the prisons and multiplying causes, not subject to much modification, there has been neither peace nor order one hour of the twenty-four. If ten were quiet, the residue were probably raving. Almost without interval might, and *must,* these be heard, blaspheming and furious, and to the last degree impure and indecent, uttering language from which the base and the profligate have turned shuddering aside and the abandoned have shrunk abashed. I myself, with many beside, can bear sad witness to these things.

Such cases of transcendent madness have not been few in this prison. Admission for a portion of them, not already having been discharged as incurable from the state hospital, has been sought with importunity and pressed with obstinate perseverance, often without success or advantage; and it has not been till application has followed application, and petition succeeded petition, that the judge of probate, absolutely wearied by the "continual coming," has sometimes granted warrants for removal. It cannot be overlooked that in this delay or refusal was more of just deliberation than hardness; for it is well known that, in the present crowded state of the hospital, every new patient displaces one who has for a longer or a shorter time received the benefit of that noble institution. . . .

The greatest evils in regard to the insane and idiots in the prisons of this Commonwealth are found at Ipswich and Cambridge, and distinguish these places only, as I believe, because the numbers are larger, being more than twenty in each. Ipswich has the advantage over Cambridge in having fewer furious subjects, and in the construction of the buildings, though these are so bad as to have afforded cause for presentment by the grand jury some time since. It is said that the new county house, in progress of building, will meet the exigencies of the case.

If it is meant that the wing in the new prison, to be appropriated to the insane, will provide accommodation for all the insane and idiotic paupers in the county, I can only say that it could receive no more than can be gathered in the three towns of Salem, Newburyport, and Ipswich, supposing these are to be removed, there being in Ipswich twenty-two in the prison and eight in the almshouse; in Salem almshouse, seventeen uniformly crazy, and two part of the time deranged; and in that of Newburyport eleven, including idiots. Here at once are sixty. The returns of 1842 exhibit an aggregate of one hundred and thirty-five. Provision is made in the new prison for fifty-seven of this class, leaving seventy-eight unprovided for, except in the almshouses. From such a fate, so far as Danvers, Saugus, East Bradford, and some other towns in the county reveal conditions of insane subjects, we pray they may be exempt.

I have the verbal and written testimony of many officers of this Commonwealth, who are respectable alike for their integrity and the fidelity with which they discharge their official duties, and whose opinions, based on experience, are entitled to consideration, that the occupation of prisons for the detention of lunatics and of idiots is, under all circumstances, an evil, subversive alike of good order, strict discipline, and good morals. I transcribe a few passages which will place this mischief in its true light.

The sheriff of Plymouth County writes as follows:

I am decidedly of the opinion that the county jail is a very improper place for lunatics and idiots. The last summer its bad effects were fully realized here, not only by the prisoners in jail, but the disturbance extended to the inhabitants dwelling in the neighborhood. A foreigner was sentenced by a justice of the peace to thirty days' confinement in the house of correction. He was to all appearance a lunatic or madman. He destroyed every article in his room, even to his wearing apparel, his noise and disturbance was incessant for hours, day and night. I consider prisons places for the safekeeping of prisoners, and all these are equally entitled to humane treatment from their keepers, without regard to the cause of commitment. We have in jails no conveniences to make the situation of lunatics and idiots much more decent than would be necessary for the brute creation, and impossible to prevent the disturbance of the inmates under the same roof. . . .

A letter from the surgeon and physician of the prison hospital at Cambridge, whose observation and experience have laid the foundation of his opinions, and who hence has a title to speak with authority, affords the following views:

On this subject, it seems to me, there can be but one opinion. No one can be more impressed than I am with the great injustice done to the insane by confining them in jails and houses of correction. It must be revolting to the better feelings of everyone to see the innocent and unfortunate insane occupying apartments with or consigned to those occupied by the criminal. Some of the insane are conscious of the circumstances in which they are placed, and feel the degradation. They exclaim sometimes in their ravings, and sometimes in their lucid intervals, "What have *I* done that I must be shut up in jail?" and "Why do you not let me out?" This state of things unquestionably retards the recovery of the few who do recover their reason under such circumstances, and may render those permanently insane who under other circumstances might have been restored to their right mind. There is also in our jails very little opportunity for the classification of the insane. The quiet and orderly must in many cases occupy the same rooms with the restless and noisy — another great hindrance to recovery. . . .

It is not few, but many, it is not a part, but the whole, who bear unqualified testimony to this evil. A voice strong and deep comes up from every almshouse and prison in Massachusetts where the insane are or have been protesting against such evils as have been illustrated in the preceding pages.

Gentlemen, I commit to you this sacred cause. Your action upon this subject will affect the present and future condition of hundreds and of thousands.

In this legislation, as in all things, may you exercise that "wisdom which is the breath of the power of God."

22.

The Sylvania Association

The ideas of the French socialist Charles Fourier were initially popularized in the United States by Albert Brisbane. Basic to Fourierism was the conception of self-sufficient communities, limited in size, in which the welfare of individuals would be better served than in society at large. One of the several experimental communities that flourished in the 1840s was the Sylvania Association in New York. One of the men who helped organize it in 1843 was Horace Greeley, who acted as its treasurer. The principles and early history of the Sylvania Association were described in a pamphlet, part of which appears here, issued by the community's executive officers in 1843. The failure of the association a few years later was attributed to the poorness of the land on which it had been established.

Source: John Humphrey Noyes, *History of American Socialisms*, Philadelphia, 1870, pp. 235-238.

THIS ASSOCIATION was formed early in 1843 by a few citizens of New York, mainly mechanics, who, deeply impressed with the present defective, vice-engendering, and ruinous system of society, with the wasteful complication of its isolated households, its destructive competition and anarchy in industry, its constraint of millions to idleness and consequent dependence or famine for want of employment, and its failure to secure education and development to the children growing up all around and among us in ignorance and vice, were impelled to immediate and energetic action in resistance to these manifold and mighty evils. Having earnestly studied the system of industrial organization and social reform propounded by Charles Fourier, and been led to recognize in it a beneficent, expansive, and practical plan for the melioration of the condition of man and his moral and intellectual elevation, they most heartily adopted that system as the basis and guide of their operations.

Holding meetings from time to time, and through the press informing the public of their enterprise and its objects, their numbers steadily increased; their organization

was perfected; explorations with a view to the selection of a domain were directed and made; and in the last week of April a location was finally determined on and its purchase effected. During the first week in May, a pioneer division of some forty persons entered upon the possession and improvement of the land. Their number has since been increased to nearly sixty, of whom over forty are men, generally young or in the prime of life, and all recognizing labor as the true and noble destiny of man on earth. The Sylvania Association is the first attempt in North America to realize in practice the vast economies, intellectual advantages, and social enjoyments resulting from Fourier's system.

Any person may become a stockholder by subscribing for not less than one share ($25); but the council, having as yet its headquarters in New York, is necessarily entrusted with power to determine at what time and in what order subscribers and their families can be admitted to resident membership on the domain. Those who are judged best calculated to facilitate the progress of the enterprise must be preferred;

those with large families unable to labor must await the construction of buildings for their proper accommodation; while such as shall, on critical inquiry, be found of unfit moral character or debasing habits, cannot be admitted at all. This, however, will nowise interfere with their ownership in the domain; they will be promptly paid the dividends on their stock, whenever declared, the same as resident members.

The enterprise here undertaken, however humble in its origin, commends itself to the respect of the skeptical and the generous cooperation of the philanthropic. Its consequences, should success (as we cannot doubt it will) crown our exertions, must be far-reaching, beneficent, unbounded. It aims at no aggrandizement of individuals, no upbuilding or overthrow of sect or party, but at the founding of a new, more trustful, more benignant relationship between capital and labor, removing discord, jealousy, and hatred, and replacing them by concord, confidence, and mutual advantage. The end aimed at is the emancipation of the mass; of the depressed toiling millions, the slaves of necessity and wretchedness, of hunger and constrained idleness, of ignorance, drunkenness, and vice; and their elevation to independence, moral and intellectual development — in short, to a true and hopeful manhood.

23.

WILLIAM HENRY CHANNING: The Christian Destiny of America

William Henry Channing, nephew of the more famous William Ellery Channing, was a Unitarian minister with a strong belief in the progress of mankind that led him to participate in several reform movements of the day. For several months, from September 1843 to April 1844, he was editor of a monthly paper called The Present, *whose goal, as Channing defined it in the first issue, was "to show the grounds of reconciliation between the sects and parties, native and foreign, the controversies, theological and political, the social reformers and prudent conservatives, the philosophers and poets, prophets and doubters, which divide these United States."*
He was convinced that America "has a plain and urgent duty . . . to advance the Reign of Heaven on Earth." In the creed that was published in the same issue, Channing expressed his beliefs about the destiny of the nation. That portion of the creed appears below.

Source: *The Present*, September 1843.

I BELIEVE:

1. That, as a member of the confederacy of Christendom, these United States have peculiar opportunities and duties; that consecrated by the devout faithfulness of forefathers, whom Providence led to this newfound land — planted at the very season when the vital elements of Europe, Christian love, and German freedom were casting off the oppressions of outgrown usages and prompting men to seek a more earnest piety and a purer virtue; guided onward through a discipline of toil and poverty and simple habits, through unexampled experi-

ences in social government and the gradual growth of untried institutions; forced by necessities of condition, by slow-formed convictions and the tendencies of a whole age, to a declaration of principles, which is the clearest announcement of universal rights, though, unfortunately, not of universal duties, ever made by any people; permitted to expand through an unobstructed, unexhausted, healthful, fertile, and most beautiful country; wondrously composed of representatives from every European state, who bring hither the varied experiences, convictions, manners, tastes of the whole civilized world, to fuse and blend anew — this nation is manifestly summoned to prove the reality of human brotherhood and of a worship of the heavenly Father, varied as the relations, grand as the destinies of present existence;

2. That, acknowledging as we do our providential mission to fulfill the law of love, and professing as we do to encourage each and every member of our communities in the exercise of their inalienable rights, we stand before the face of God and fellow nations as guilty of hypocrisy and of a breach of trust;

3. That we deserve the retributions, losses, disgraces which our savage robberies of the Indians, our cruel and wanton oppressions of the Africans, our unjust habits of white serfdom, our grasping national ambition, our eagerness for wealth, our deceitful modes of external and internal trade, our jealous competitions between different professions and callings, our aping of aristocratic distinctions, our licentiousness and sensuality, our profligate expenditures, public and private, have brought, and will continue to bring upon us;

4. That it behooves our religious bodies, our political parties, our statesmen and philosophers, our scholars and patriots, and all who desire a growing life for themselves or their race, to put aside questions of minor importance and concentrate their energies upon measures which may remove inhumanity utterly from our land;

5. That our duties will not be done, our ideal will not be fulfilled till we solve the problem of UNITED INTERESTS now pressing upon all Christendom; till, within our own borders, we secure for every individual man, woman, child, full culture, under healthy, pure, and holy influences; free exercise of their faculties, for the glory of God and the good of man; recompense for all services that shall be just; such stations of honorable usefulness as their virtues merit, and access to all sources of refinement and happiness which our communities can command — till, in intercourse with other lands, we strive honestly and bountifully to share the blessings which the universal Father gives, and so aid to reunite all nations in one family of the children of God, where His will shall be done on earth as it is in heaven.

————◆————

Thank God! I — I also — am an American.
DANIEL WEBSTER, address on completion of Bunker Hill Monument, June 17, 1843

24.

JAMES RUSSELL LOWELL: Opposition to Nationalism in Literature

As a critic, Lowell encouraged the growth of a native literature, but he demanded that such American writing satisfy standards of literary excellence rather than national pride. In 1843 he started a monthly literary and critical journal, The Pioneer, *dedicated to the publication of good literature and criticism. The salutatory in the first issue of this short-lived endeavor (it survived only three issues) is reprinted below.*

Source: *The Pioneer*, January 1843.

DR. JOHN NORTH, a man of some mark in his day, wrote on the first leaf of his notebook these significant words: "I beshrew his heart that gathers my opinion from anything wrote here!"

As we seated ourselves to the hard task of writing an introduction for our new literary journal, this sentence arose to our minds. It seemed to us to point clearly at the arch-want of our periodical literature. We find opinions enough and to spare, but scarce any of the healthy, natural growth of our soil. If native, they are seldom more than scions of a public opinion, too often planted and watered by the prejudices or ignorant judgments of individuals, to be better than a upas tree shedding a poisonous blight on any literature that may chance to grow up under it. Or, if foreign, they are, to borrow a musical term, "recollections" of Blackwood or the quarterlies of Wilson, Macaulay, or Carlyle — not direct imitations but endeavors, as it were, to write with their cast-off pens, fresh-nibbed for cisatlantic service. The whole regiment comes one by one to our feast of letters in the same yellow domino.

Criticism, instead of being governed as it should be by the eternal and unchanging laws of beauty, which are a part of the soul's divine nature, seems rather to be a striving to reduce art to one dead level of conventional mediocrity — which only does not offend taste because it lacks even the life and strength to produce any decided impression whatever.

We are the farthest from wishing to see what many so ardently pray for; namely, a *national* literature; for the same mighty lyre of the human heart answers the touch of the master in all ages and in every clime; and any literature, as far as it is national, is diseased, inasmuch as it appeals to some climatic peculiarity rather than to the universal nature. Moreover, everything that tends to encourage the sentiment of *caste,* to widen the boundary between races and so to put farther off the hope of one great brotherhood, should be steadily resisted by all good men.

But we do long for a *natural* literature. One green leaf, though of the veriest weed, is worth all the crape and wire flowers of the daintiest Paris milliners. For it is the glory of nature that in her least part she gives us all, and in that simple love token of hers we may behold the type of all her sublime mysteries; as in the least fragment of the true artist we discern the working of the same forces which culminate gloriously in a Hamlet or a Faust. We would no longer see the spirit of our people held up as a mirror to the Old World; but rather lying like one of our own inland oceans, reflecting not only the mountain and the rock, the forest and the red man, but also the steamboat and the railcar, the cornfield and the factory.

Let us learn that romance is not married to the past, that it is not the birthright of ferocious ignorance and chivalric barbarity, but that it ever was and is an inward quality, the darling child of the sweetest refinements and most gracious amenities of peaceful gentleness; and that it can never die till only water runs in these red rivers of the heart, that cunning adept which can make vague cathedrals with blazing oriels and streaming spires out of our square meeting boxes

James Russell Lowell, photographed by Mathew Brady

Whose rafters sprout upon the shady side.

We do not mean to say that our writers should not profit by the results of those who have gone before them, nor gather from all countries those excellencies which are the effects of detached portions of that universal tendency to the beautiful which must be centered in the Great Artist. But let us not go forth to them; rather let us draw them by sympathy of nature to our own heart, which is the only living principle of every true work. The artist must use the tools of others and understand their use, else were their lives fruitless to him, and his, in turn, vain to all who came after; but the skill must be of his own toilsome winning, and he must not, like Goethe's magician's apprentice, let the tools become his masters.

But it seems the law of our literature to receive its impulses from without rather than from within. We ask oftener than the wise king of Ashantee, "What is thought of us in England?" We write with the fear of the newspapers before our eyes, every one of which has its critic, the Choragus of his little circle, self-elected expounder of the laws of nature — which he at first blush understands more thoroughly than they whom nature herself has chosen — and who have studied them lifelong and who unites at pleasure the executive with the judiciary to crush some offender mad enough to think for himself. Men seem endowed with an insane alacrity to believe that wisdom elects the dullest heads for her confidants, and crowd to burn incense to the hooting owl, while the thoughtful silence of the goddess makes them to mistake her for her bird.

We boast much of our freedom, but they who boast thereof the loudest have mostly a secret sense of fetters.

License they mean when they cry liberty,

and there is among us too much freedom to speak and think ill — a freedom matched with which the lowest of all other slaveries were as the blue tent of heaven to a dungeon — and too little freedom to think, and speak, and act the highest and holiest promptings of the eternal soul. We cheat tomorrow to satisfy the petty dunning of today; we bribe ourselves with a bubble reputation, whose empty lightness alone lends it a momentary elevation, and show men our meanest part, as if we could make ourselves base enough to believe that we should offend their vanity by showing our noblest and highest.

Are prejudices to be overcome by groveling to them? Is truth any longer worthy of the name, when she stoops to take falsehood by the hand, and caresses her, and would fain wheedle her to forgo her proper nature? Can we make men noble, the aim and end of every literature worthy of the name, by showing them our own want of nobleness? In the name of all holy and beautiful things at once, no! We want a manly, straightforward, *true* literature, a criticism which shall give more grace to beauty and more depth to truth, by lovingly embracing them wherever they may lie hidden, and a creed whose truth and nobleness shall be ensured by its being a freedom from all creeds.

The young heart of every generation looks forth upon the world with restless and bitter longing. To it the earth still glitters with the dews of a yet unforfeited Eden, and in the midst stands the untasted tree of knowledge of good and evil. We hear men speak of the restless spirit of the age, as if our day were peculiar in this regard. But it has always been the same. The young is radical, the old, conservative; they who have not, struggle to get, and they who have gotten, clench their fingers to keep. The young, exulting in its tight and springy muscles, stretches out its arms to clasp the world as its plaything; and the old bids it be a good boy and mind its papa, and it shall have sugar plums.

But still the new spirit yearns and struggles, and expects great things; still the old shakes its head, ominous of universal anarchy; still the world rolls calmly on, and the youth grown old shakes its wise head at the next era. Is there any more danger to be looked for in the radicalism of youth than in the conservatism of age? Both gases must be mixed ere the cooling rain will fall on our seedfield.

The true reason for the fear which we often see expressed of a freedom which shall be debased into destructiveness and license is to be found in a false judgment of the natural progress of things. Cheerfully will men reverence all that is *true*, whether in the new or the old. It is only when you would force them to revere falsehoods that they will reluctantly throw off all reverence, without which the spirit of man must languish and at last utterly die. Truth, in her natural and infinitely various exponents of beauty and love, is all that the soul reverences long; and, as truth is universal and absolute, there can never be any balance in the progress of the soul till one law is acknowledged in all her departments.

Radicalism has only gone too far when it has *hated* conservatism, and has despised all reverence because conservatism is based upon it, forgetting that it is only so inasmuch as it is a needful part of nature. To have claimed that reverence should not play at blind-man's-buff had been enough.

In this country, where freedom of thought does not shiver at the cold shadow of Spielberg (unless we name this prison of "public opinion" so), there is no danger to be apprehended from an excess of it. It is only where there is no freedom that anarchy is to be dreaded. The mere sense of freedom is of too pure and holy a nature to consist with injustice and wrong. We would fain have our journal, in some sort at least, a journal of progress, one that shall keep pace with the spirit of the age, and sometimes go near its deeper heart. Yet, while we shall aim at the gravity which is becoming of a manly literature, we shall hope also to satisfy that lighter and sprightlier element of the soul, without whose due culture the character is liable to degenerate into a morose bigotry and selfish precisianism.

To be one exponent of a young spirit which shall aim at power through gentleness, the only mean for its secure attainment, and in which freedom shall be attempered to love by a reverence for all beauty wherever it may exist, is our humble hope. And to this end we ask the help of all who feel any sympathy in such an undertaking. We are too well aware of the thousand difficulties which lie in the way of such an attempt, and of the universal failure to make what is written come near the standard of what is thought and hoped, to think that we shall not at first disappoint the expectations of our friends.

But we shall do our best, and they must bear with us, knowing that what is written from month to month can hardly have that care and study which is needful to the highest excellence, and believing that

We shall be willing, if not apt to learn;
Age and experience will adorn our mind
With larger knowledge: and, if we have done
A wilful fault, think us not past all hope,
For once.

25.

Horatio Greenough: Remarks on the Training of American Artists

Horatio Greenough is better known today by his few brief essays on art than by his sculptures. However, critics have been unable to reconcile Greenough's theories with his actual practice. He held up functionalism as an ideal and derided the American predilection for indiscriminate borrowing of artistic elements, yet such eclecticism marked his most famous statue — that of George Washington, whom he sculpted in the guise of a noble Roman. Greenough proclaimed his faith in America's artistic future and commended his native land as conducive to artistic excellence, yet he spent the greater part of his own life in Italy, the traditional home of artists and especially of sculptors. The following essay was written in 1843 and published, with other works of the same kind, in 1852 in a book called Travels, Observations and Experiences of a Yankee Stonecutter.

Source: *A Memorial of Horatio Greenough*, Henry T. Tuckerman, ed., New York, 1853: "American Art."

THE SUSCEPTIBILITY, the tastes, and the genius which enable a people to enjoy the fine arts and to excel in them have been denied to the Anglo-Americans, not only by European talkers but by European thinkers. The assertion of our obtuseness and inefficiency in this respect has been ignorantly and presumptuously set forth by some persons, merely to fill up the measure of our condemnation. Others have arrived at the same conclusion after examining our political and social character, after investigating our exploits and testing our capacities.

They admit that we trade with enterprise

and skill; that we build ships cunningly and sail them well; that we have a quick and farsighted apprehension of the value of a territory; that we make wholesome homespun laws for its government; and that we fight hard when molested in any of these homely exercises of our ability. But they assert that there is a stubborn, antipoetical tendency in all that we do or say or think; they attribute our very excellence in the ordinary business of life to causes which must prevent our development as artists.

Enjoying the accumulated result of the thought and labor of centuries, Europe has witnessed our struggles with the hardships of an untamed continent and the disadvantages of colonial relations, with but a partial appreciation of what we aim at, with but an imperfect knowledge of what we have done. Seeing us intently occupied during several generations in felling forests, in building towns, and constructing roads, she thence formed a theory that we are good for nothing except these pioneer efforts.

She taunted us because there were no statues or frescoes in our log cabins; she pronounced us unmusical because we did not sit down in the swamp with an Indian on one side and a rattlesnake on the other to play the violin. That she should triumph over the deficiencies of a people who had set the example of revolt and republicanism was natural; but the reason which she assigned for those deficiencies was not the true reason. She argued with the depth and the sagacity of a philosopher who should conclude, from seeing an infant imbibe with eagerness its first aliment, that its whole life would be occupied in similar absorption.

Sir Walter Scott, rank Tory as he was, showed more good sense when, in recommending an American book to Miss Edgeworth, he accounted for such a phenomenon by saying that "people once possessed of a three-legged stool soon contrive to make an easy chair." Humble as the phrase is, we here perceive an expectation on his part that the energies now exercised in laying the foundations of a mighty empire would in due time rear the stately columns of civilization and crown the edifice with the entablature of letters and of arts. Remembering that one leg of the American stool was planted in Maine, a second in Florida, and the third at the base of the Rocky Mountains, he could scarce expect that the chair would become an easy one in a half century.

It is true that before the Declaration of Independence, Copley had in Boston formed a style of portrait which filled Sir Joshua Reynolds with astonishment; and that West, breaking through the bar of Quaker prohibition and conquering the prejudice against a provincial aspirant, had taken a high rank in the highest walk of art in London. Stuart, Trumbull, Allston, Morse, Leslie, Newton followed in quick succession, while Vanderlyn won golden opinions at Rome and bore away high honors at Paris. So far were the citizens of the republic from showing a want of capacity for art that we may safely affirm that the bent of their genius was rather peculiarly in that direction, since the first burins of Europe were employed in the service of the American pencil before Irving had written and while Cooper was yet a child. That England, with these facts before her, should have accused us of obtuseness in regard to art and that we should have pleaded guilty to the charge, furnishes the strongest proof of her disposition to underrate our intellectual powers, and of our own ultra docility and want of self-reliance.

Not many years since, one of the illustrious and good men of America exclaimed in addressing the nation:

Excudent alii mollius spirantia aera,
Credo equidem; vivos ducent de
marmore voltus!

[Others gracefully forge bronze statues which I consider truly lifelike representations; they draw from marble sculpture alive with expression or, as we say, speaking.]

Since that period art has received a new impulse among us. Artists have arisen in numbers; the public gives its attention to their productions; their labors are liberally rewarded. It seems now admitted that wealth and cultivation are destined to yield in America the same fruits that they have given in Italy, in Spain, in France, Germany, and England. It seems now admitted that there is no anomalous defect in our mental endowments; that the same powers displayed in clearing the forest and tilling the farm will trim the garden.

It seems clear that we are destined to have a school of art. It becomes a matter of importance to decide how the youth who devote themselves to these studies are to acquire the rudiments of imitation, and what influences are to be made to act upon them. This question seemed at one time to have been decided. The friends of art in America looked to Europe for an example and, with the natural assumption that experience had made the Old World wise in what relates to the fine arts, determined upon forming academies as the more refined nations of the continent have ended by doing. We might as well have proposed a national church establishment. That the youth must be taught is clear; but in framing an institution for that object, if we look to countries grown old in European systems, it must be for warning rather than example. We speak from long experience and much observation of European academies. We entertain the highest respect for the professional ability and for the personal character of the gentlemen who preside over those institutions. Nay, it is our conviction of their capacity and of their individual willingness to impart knowledge, which forces upon us the opinion of the rottenness of the systems of which they are the instruments.

De Tocqueville remarks upon the British aristocracy that, notwithstanding their sagacity as a body and their integrity and high-toned character as individuals, they have gradually absorbed everything and left the people nothing; while he declares the American *employés*, though they are sometimes defaulters and dishonest, yet, after all, get little beyond their dues and are obliged to sacrifice both reputation and self-respect in order to obtain that little. Those who direct the academies of fine arts in Europe are prone to take an advantage of their position analogous to that enjoyed by the aforesaid aristocracy. As the latter come to regard the mass as a flock to be fed and defended and cherished for the sake of their wool and mutton, so the former are not slow to make a band of educandi the basis of a hierarchy. Systems and manner soon usurp the place of sound precept. Faith is insisted on rather than works. The pupils are required to be not only docile but submissive. They are not free.

To minds once opened to the light of knowledge, an adept may speak in masses, and the seed will fall on good ground; but to awaken a dormant soul, to impart first principles, to watch the budding of the germ of rare talent, requires a contact and relations such as no professor can have with a class, such as few men can have with any boy. If Europe must furnish a model of artistical tuition, let us go at once to the records of the great age of art in Italy, and we shall there learn that Michelangelo and Raphael, and their teachers also, were formed without any of the cumbrous machinery and mill-horse discipline of a modern academy. They were instructed, it is true; they were apprenticed to painters. Instead of passively listening to an experienced proficient merely, they discussed with their fellow students the merits of different works, the advantages of rival methods, the choice between contradictory authorities. They formed one another. Sympathy warmed them, opposition strengthened, and emulation spurred them on. In these latter days, classes of boys toil through the rudiments under the eye of men who are themselves aspirants for the public favor, and who, deriving no benefit, as masters from their apprentices, from the proficiency of the lads, look upon every clever graduate as a stumbling block in their own way. Hence their system of stupefying discipline, their tying down the pupil to mere manual execution, their silence in regard to principles, their cold reception of all attempts to invent. To chill in others the effort to acquire is in them the instinctive action of a wish to retain. Well do we remember the expression of face and the tone of voice with which one of these bashaws of a European academy once received our praise of the labors of a man grown gray in the practice of his art, but who, though his works were known and admired at Naples and Petersburg, at London and Vienna, had not yet won from the powers that were his *exequatur:* "Yes, sir, yes! Clever boy, sir! *Promises well!*"

The president and the professors of an academy are regarded by the public as, of course, at the. head of their respective professions. Their works are models, their opinions give the law. The youth are awed and dazzled by their titles and their fame; the man of genius finds them arrayed in solid phalanx to combat his claim. In those countries where a court bestows all encouragement, it is found easy to keep from those in power all knowledge of a dangerous upstart talent. How far this mischievous influence can be carried may be gathered from the position in which Sir Joshua Reynolds and *his court* managed to keep men like Wilson and Gainsborough. He who sees the productions of these men in company with those of their contemporaries and who remembers the impression which Sir Joshua's writings had conveyed of their standing as artists will perceive with surprise that they were not the victims of any overt act of misrepresentation, but that they were quietly and gently praised out of the rank due to them into an inferior one by a union of real talent, constituted influence, and a sly, cool, consistent management.

Many of the ablest painters and sculptors of Europe have expressed to us directly and frankly the opinion that academies, furnished though they be with all the means to form the eye, the hand, and the mind of the pupil are positively hindrances instead of helps to art.

The great element of execution, whether in painting or in sculpture, is imitation. This is the language of art. Almost all clever boys can learn this to a degree far beyond what is supposed. That objects be placed before them calculated to attract their attention and teach them the rules of proportion, while they educate the eye to form and color, no one will dispute; but the insisting upon a routine, the depriving them of all choice or volition, the giving a false preference to readiness of hand over power of thought, all these are great evils, and we fully believe that they fall with a withering force on those minds especially whose nourishment and guidance they were intended to secure; we mean on those minds which are filled with a strong yearning after excellence; warm sympathies, quick, delicate, and nice perceptions, strong will and a proud consciousness of creative power of mind, joined to diffidence of their capacity to bring into action the energies they feel within them. The paltry prizes offered for the best performances seldom rouse men of this order; they may create in such souls an unamiable contempt for their unsuccessful competitors; they may give to successful mediocrity inflated hopes, a false estimate of its own powers. As a substantial help they are worthless even to the tyro [amateur] who wins them.

Leonardo da Vinci coiled a rope in his studio and drew from it, with the subtlest outline and the most elaborate study of light and shade. "Behold!" said he, "my academy!" He meant to show that the elements of art can be learned without the pompous array of the antique school or the lectures of the professor. Few will be tempted to follow his example; but even that were far better than a routine of instruction which, after years of drudgery and labor, sends forth the genius and the blockhead so nearly on a level with each other, the one manacled with precepts, the other armed with them at all points.

The above reflections have been drawn from us by the oft-repeated expressions of regret which we have listened to, "that from the constitution of our society and the nature of our institutions, no influences can be brought to bear upon art with the vivifying power of court patronage." We fully and firmly believe that these institutions are more favorable to a natural, healthful growth of art than any hotbed culture whatever. We cannot (as did Napoleon) make, by a few imperial edicts, an army of battle painters, a hierarchy of drum and fife glorifiers. Nor can we, in the lifetime of an individual, so stimulate this branch of culture, so unduly and disproportionately endow it, as to make a Valhalla start from a republican soil. The monuments, the pictures, the statues of the republic will represent what the people love and wish for, not what they can be made to accept, not how much taxation they will bear. We hope by such slow growth to avoid the reaction resulting from a morbid development; a reaction like that which attended the building of St. Peter's; a reaction like that consequent upon the outlay which gave birth to the royal mushroom at Versailles; a reaction like that which we anticipate in Bavaria, unless the people of that country are constituted differently from the rest of mankind.

If there be any youth toiling through the rudiments of art at the forms of the simple and efficient school at New York (whose title is the only pompous thing about it), with a chilling belief that elsewhere the difficulties he struggles with are removed or modified, we call upon him to be of good cheer, and to believe what from our hearts we are convinced of: that there is at present no country where the development and growth of an artist is more free, healthful, and happy than it is in these United States. It is not until the tyro becomes a proficient — nay, an adept — that his fortitude and his temper are put to tests more severe than elsewhere, tests of which we propose to speak more at large on a future occasion.

26.

John Neal: The Power of the Press

Social and technical factors combined to produce an extraordinary proliferation of newspapers and periodicals in the 1830s and 1840s. Among the technical factors were the introduction of the steam press, the improved transportation facilities that aided the rapid diffusion of news, and, in the early 1840s, the use of the telegraph. Among the social factors were the increase of popular participation in government, the organization of numerous reform societies and labor unions, many of which established their own publications, and the movement of people westward. John Neal, author of the article reprinted below, edited several New England magazines and wrote popular novels.

Source: *The Pioneer*, February 1843.

THE MIGHTIEST ENGINE OF OUR DAY is a newspaper. What are armies and treasuries, navies and forts, and magazines and foundries, or senate chambers and laws in comparison with newspapers, where newspapers are free? Of what avail are public meetings or combinations, or conspiracies, or revolutions, indeed, where newspapers are not free?

They are not so much the organs, or the expounders, or reservoirs, as they are the generators of public opinion.

We are a newspaper people. With us, newspapers are the fourth power of the state — or rather the *first* power, swallowing up all other powers. They are the president-makers, the lawgivers, the judiciary, the supreme executive, with a pardoning power beyond all that was ever claimed for any earthly sovereign.

What the newspapers of a land like ours agree to uphold becomes thereby established. What they combine to denounce, whether in morals or in manners, in litera-

ture or in science, in law, physic, or divinity, cannot live. To be troubled with a bad epitaph *after* your death is bad enough; but to be haunted by a bad epitaph while you are yet alive and breathing, to have it burned into your forehead, branded upon your very doorposts, and literally hawked about the streets, and cried by the newspaper boys — that, we take it, is a little too bad. Yet newspapers do this continually; and one might as well be buried alive as offend them, unless, like Mr. Cooper, he chooses to make a fool of himself by punishing them as they deserve.

Show us a man — or an action — or a law, good, bad, or indifferent, which the newspapers, banding together, may not make hateful or praiseworthy, according to their own good pleasure, in the estimation of the great multitude who read nothing but newspapers, and we will undertake to show you a race of "anthropophagi, or men whose heads do grow beneath their shoulders," just back of the hill yonder.

People so love to see themselves in print!

"A book's a book although there's
    nothing in 't."

Hence everybody rushes into print
through the newspapers; and what is still
more alarming, although everybody knows
this, nobody's faith in newspapers would
ever appear to be shaken — except in matters of fact. A man whose opinions upon
any subject, even upon the times, or the
weather, or upon matters and things in general, would neither be listened to nor tolerated, much less repeated, if uttered by the
mouth, has only to whip into the nearest
newspaper office and write down what he
dares not say aloud for his life lest he
should make himself ridiculous forever; under a fictitious name, or editorially, to find
himself quoted on 'Change, or perhaps in
the halls of legislation, before the sun goes
down; to the unspeakable amusement, not
only of the man himself, but of all who
knew him best. These things are of daily
occurrence. We could mention a score of
prodigies who have become terrible, in spite
of themselves, by writing anonymously for
the newspapers.

Again, forty-nine fiftieths of all the papers
in our country belong to a party. Even
those which pretend to be neutral are always changing with the subscription list,
and speaking more or less plainly — now
on this side, now on that, and now on
both, according to the "books." And all papers belonging to a party are either advocates or partisans; else the party would not
acknowledge them, nor even trust them
within their houses. As advocates or partisans, they are of course one-sided, so that
no man expects the truth of them. And,
when by chance, a newspaper, supposed to
belong to a party, ventures to speak above
its breath of anything questionable in the
doings thereof, or the simple truth of any

man, or of any measure not of its party, it
is always believed to be turning; and from
that hour is looked upon with distrust and
narrowly watched.

And what is the consequence? A man
who loves a newspaper for itself, who understands its capabilities, who knows that,
by the help of newspapers alone, if they are
honestly and ably carried on, he may educate a family, gets afraid of them, and is
obliged either to give them up altogether or
to confine himself to business papers, which
he must have and cannot do without —
mere catalogues, shipping lists, advertisements, and prices current — or to double
and triple the dose and take newspapers on
both sides and on all sides — at a prodi-
gious waste of time and patience, and money — before he can make up his mind
whether the chief magistrate of the Union,
with all the heads of departments, are so
many demigods or idiots, knaves, block-
heads, or madmen — worthy of a treadmill
or a lunatic asylum, or of temples and altars; whether they are statesmen or blundering schemers, philosophers or visionaries,
orators and reasoners, or clamorous fools
who have been qualified for lawgivers by
the whims of a people 10,000 times their
superiors in wisdom, understanding, and experience.

For, to the people, mark you, to the very
people who have chosen these wretched
dolts — and garrulous, wheezing, superan-
nuated zanies — both sides appeal for confirmation of what they say; affecting the
profoundest veneration for the wisdom and
honesty of those, the very best of whom,
when called apart and consecrated to the
service of their country in her halls of legislation, they set down for addle-headed nin-
compoops.

Luckily for mankind, however, these
combinations among the newspapers rarely
happen, to any great extent, except for political purposes — and *then!* — lo, the

changes that have taken place in the opinions and policy of our general government, upon all the great questions of the age within the last five-and-twenty years; upon commerce, manufactures, taxation, banking, Negro slavery, states' rights, and executive power; what are they, after all, but a record of newspaper adjudications for the same period?

On other occasions, where they combine to cry up a new actor, or to cry down a new author; to bring about a war; to drive a man into a duel by questioning his courage, and then, by making mouths at him to get him indicted; to disturb John Quincy Adams or Mr. Cooper, the novelist, in their glorious self-complacency; to establish a reputation for Brandreth, or Swaim, or Mrs. Restall, or Dr. Williams, the oculist, or a new razor strop; our only safety, as a people, thinking or unthinking, lies in the fact that they never pull together for a long time, and that there are, upon the average, about as many papers of established reputation upon the one side as upon the other of every possible question.

But, the *Quarterly Review,* Captain Trollope, and our amiable friend Boz to the contrary notwithstanding, these newspaper comforts are by no means peculiar to our country; although newspapers here, as everywhere else on earth, are essentially characteristic of the people, and are no more capable of being interchanged than are their laws and customs. Our worst papers are no worse than scores to be found in England; our best, quite equal to the ablest in Great Britain; though, in two or three particulars, inferior, while in others they are greatly superior to those of France and Germany.

The great body of them, constituting as they do the *People's Library,* are so essentially American that they belong to our institutions just as much as our system of equal rights or representation. They are part and parcel of *ourselves,* and with all their faults, have a strong and healthy influence upon the public mind. Not that our newspapers are what they ought to be — or what they will be after a few years have gone by; but, then, they are suited to our present wants, they correspond with the present condition of our people, and are, in fact, so many maps and charts of the public mind, of its ever shifting currents of opinion, of its ever changing purposes and character, of our hopes and our wishes.

Would you have advertisements of new goods continued for a twelvemonth? A list of shipping intelligence, or of deaths and marriages, or of auction sales stereotyped? Then why ask of a newspaper in this country that it should retain its shape, title, editor, politics or opinions for a single twelvemonth? Where all the elements of society are in everlasting commotion, would you make a landmark of a newspaper? Where the people are the sovereigns and the newspapers their unquestioned ministers, would you have them follow the fashions or arrangements common among a people overseas — our elder brethren, if you please; where newspapers, though powerful for some purposes, are powerless for all others; where the more vigorous and sprightly are forever shaking in their shoes if Her Majesty's attorney general but looks hard at them; while the average humdrums of the day never turn to the right nor left for a dozen years upon the stretch?

Here, no prosecution could be maintained for a slander upon the government or the heads of the government; here, it never enters our heads to believe that a newspaper could sow sedition or bring the powers that be into contempt, or that it is ever worth the while of a great man to appeal to the courts for redress against any, even the most wicked and slanderous falsehood, circulated to his prejudice. A few months, and all these lies are forgotten and laughed at for capital jokes; and even while most active, appearing as they always do in political papers, they are sure to be disbelieved, whether true or false, probable or improbable, by at least one-half of the whole reading population of the country, and to be credited by the other half, conditionally, as it were, until the election is over, or the party slandered has been chafed or bullied into "defining his position."

Overseas, on the contrary, in that land which we are supposed by the newpaper storytellers, and police reporters of the day, who may happen to find themselves here with their passages paid, to have always in our eye; and whose fashions in everything — even in newspapers — these gentry hold it to be little better than high treason for us not to follow blindfold; although a newspaper may now and then venture to charge its anointed sovereign with murdering his daughter and poisoning his wife, as in the case of George the Fourth, the Princess Charlotte, and Caroline of Brunswick; and although at another time, it may go so far as to charge one of the blood royal, the Duke of Cambridge, for instance, with ever so many horrible crimes, murder, among the rest; and half the noble houses of the land with bastardy; and although hundreds of the most respectable newspapers of the Empire may give the loathsome details of such a case as that of Queen Caroline, at full length, day after day and week after week; with all the minute particulars of Colonel Berkley's cohabitation with Miss Foote before he married her off to a nobleman of high rank; or of Edmund Kean's beastly licentiousness and more beastly love letters; of Harriet Wilson's amours; and of other cases never heard of nor alluded to in an American newspaper; for since the foundation of this republic, we have not had so many as a dozen trials for [criminal conversation — adultery] among people of any consideration or standing in society, and no case whatever corresponding with those which happen daily in and about London and are repeated in all the London newspapers.

Although these things may happen, have happened, and do happen daily, as things of course in England, and sometimes without being followed by prosecution; still the law has its terrors there, and, on the whole, may be regarded as a wholesome and proper restraint upon the newspapers. Set them above the law there, as they are here; enable them to cast off all fear, as they do sometimes, finding prosecutions profitable, and penalties only a cheaper way of advertising; and in no one particular are they a single whit more generous, or truthful, or dignified, or courteous, than the basest of ours. Unprincipled blackguards at the best, their cowardice and treachery, their filthiness and their falsehood are all of a piece.

Time was when, like the French, we had but few newspapers; and they were written for by the ablest men of the country, without pay. At the outbreak of the Revolutionary War, and after the treaty of 1783, up to the consummation of their great work, our whole literature was a newspaper literature, and the strongest minds and best hearts alive were engaged in wholesome newspaper controversies that shook the world. The Adamses, the Otises, the Franklins, the Hamiltons, the Jeffersons, the Madisons, the Jays were always at work upon the public mind through the newspapers.

And then, after this, up to about the year 1812, when there were not in the whole of these United States, peradventure, so many as half a dozen editors employed — proprietors being their own editors and almost always printers, depending upon gratuitous, and in ninety-nine cases out of a hundred, upon anonymous contributions, and extracts from one another to make up their sheets — papers went on multiplying over the land, as a mere experiment in business, a new branch in the book trade or job printing, till every village in the country had its one, two, or three, and sometimes its half a score of newspapers; most of which were never heard of at the end of a twelvemonth, when the subscription fell due, and patrons were asked for something more than their names.

About this time, editors began to be thought of at a regular salary. Proprietors were common enough, who were called editors, and occasionally wrote a paragraph or a stickful — or perhaps an essay; there was Duane, for example, and Alexander Hanson, and Colman, and Major Russell, but there were no editors, properly speaking, till about the time of Paul Allen's appearance in Bronson's *United States Gazette*.

Since then, although newspapers have multiplied like the frogs of Egypt — in worth as well as in quantity — they have been gradually and steadily growing better. Hardly one of the whole 2,000 now flourishing — after a fashion peculiar to newspapers — within our boundaries would permit such poetry, or such prose indeed, to appear in their columns (always excepting political papers and quack advertisements) as made up the larger part of our best magazines and book literature forty years ago.

Two thousand newspapers! Let us see what they cost our people, and how good a pennyworth they get for their money.

Suppose each paper to have upon the average 1,000 subscribers — an estimate below the truth, if we consider the present price of the most popular; hardly a fourth part of what they were a dozen years ago. Let us take for their average cost to the reader, $3 a year, including postage — a moderate computation, certainly, when we take into view the dailies and high-priced weeklies. Then have we for the yearly cost of each newspaper, which somebody must pay for, the wronged printer, the wronged typefounder, or the wronged papermaker, no less a sum than $3,000. This, multiplied by 2,000, the total number of newspapers published in our country (Vattemar collected specimens of more than that number), gives a grand total of $6 million yearly cost of this fourth estate to the American

people! Add the time wasted with newspapers, and the tax would be trebled. And then, what becomes of these newspapers? Of the 500 million copies, at least, circulating over the whole length and breadth of the land, at the rate of more than 1,500,000 per day, forty-nine fiftieths perish with the going down of the sun. Not one in 1,000 or perhaps in 10,000, is to be found alive at the end of a week; and before a month is over the only copy on earth must be looked for on the proprietor's file, or in the hands of a collector.

And yet, with all this worthlessness and waste, who that knows their true value would venture to say that newspapers cost this country more than they are worth? People read newspapers who read nothing else. People read newspapers *when* and *where* they read nothing else. To the great body of our men, women and children, a newspaper is a drama of the universe. To call it the *World*, or the *Times*, or the *Globe* or the *Sun* is by no means to overstate its value in their eyes. To them it is the only world they are acquainted with; a sun without which they and their families would grope in darkness forever. Of the times, either in the Old World or the New what know they but by the help of the newspapers? They have no books beyond the Bible, an almanac, or a stray Thomas-à-Kempis, or Josephus, or a tattered copy of Noah Webster's *Third Part*. And how would they be able to guess at the doings of the rest of the world; at the rise and fall of empire; the condition of Europe; or the progress of knowledge — ay, or of what their own rulers were doing for them — but for the newspapers?

There are 10 million people in these United States who never heard of the invasion of Russia, nor the overthrow of Napoleon, nor of Napoleon himself, except through the newspapers; and who, at this hour, but for the newspapers, would not know that such a man ever existed, to say nothing of the 10,000 sceptered shadows that have appeared and disappeared upon the thrones of the world within the last half century.

Do our newspapers cost us too much, then, even at this price?

But perhaps it may be said: the reason why your people have no books is because they have so many newspapers; and newspapers won't keep.

Worthy of profound consideration. But for our newspapers, it may be that our people would have libraries of their own — family libraries — bequeathable from sire to son. The merchant of New York, or Philadelphia, or New Orleans, where they are still more extravagant, who takes half a dozen daily papers — and multitudes are they who take a dozen or twenty — pays at least $60 a year, and, with postage, about $75. Let him continue this for twenty years and he will have expended $1,500, which, with the accumulated interest, will amount at the end of that time to about $2,000 — sufficient to purchase a library large enough and good enough for any household purposes. And what has he to show for this? Nothing.

Yet more; newspaper reading, to the busy man whose time is money and to whom good books and maps and large libraries are accessible, is the idlest of all reading. It is, in fact, such an undeniable waste of time that men of business in our large cities — like editors — never think of reading a newspaper; or if they do, are never to be caught in the act. You might as well hope to catch a physician taking his own medicines, or a vintner drinking his own wines, or a lawyer pleading his own cause.

After all, therefore, what is to be done? That newspapers in this country are not what they ought to be is true. That they are altogether too numerous and too worthless, taking them together, in the lump, notwithstanding a hundred exceptions, that in most cases they are alike ruinous to the proprietors and the papermaker, wearisome to the reader and exhausting to the hearer, is also true. That a much wiser application of money and time might be made, by men of business and of leisure, in the neighborhood of books and libraries than they now make under pretense of informing themselves and their families, is also true. But what of that; what of all this?

If the question to be decided is whether we shall have our 2,000 newspapers, with all their faults, at the expense of $20 million a year, if you please, instead of $6 million; or no newspapers, or even a system of newspapers like that of any other people upon earth, even of that people who are held up to us so modestly by one of themselves for a pattern beyond which and above which it were vain to think of going, then say we, give us our American newspapers! For the same reason that we would cry give us our equal distribution of wealth, of learning, or of intelligence, of political power, of rights and duties, of air and water, with no overgrown capitalists in either.

But is there no help for the evils that are acknowledged to exist in our newspaper system? Must the whole be torn up by the roots, or must we leave it untouched, unprofaned, till it overspreads the whole land with its rank and frightful luxuriance? For ourselves, we hope much in this matter. Our newspapers are wonderfully improved within the last dozen years. Still greater changes are in progress. Magazines are still to do the work of newspapers, in a department which, on account of their convenience and cheapness, they have hitherto monopolized; and newspapers are to extend themselves into new departments of science and the arts, and to become profitable and respectable; fewer in number, but ten thousand times worthier to be held in remembrance, and to be found in the workshops and about the firesides of the people, where they have heretofore held undisturbed possession.

27.

JOHN W. PITTS: Opposition to Fees for Lawyers

*The following indictment of the legal profession by John Pitts expressed the view
of many citizens. As a group, lawyers were conspicuous for their wealth and
success and for their importance in politics. To raise professional standards,
lawyers organized societies that only those considered qualified could join; but
such societies seemed to those who distrusted the profession to confirm their fear
that there was a conspiracy of lawyers dedicated to maintaining the unintelligibility
of the law and the consequent need for lawyers. Pitts's original intention was to
communicate his views without charge to the public, to which end he wrote six
essays and published them in the* Southern Recorder. *Two subsequent numbers
were refused by the* Recorder, *and Pitts printed and sold them as a pamphlet in
1843. Numbers One and Two are reprinted here.*

Source: *Eleven Numbers Against Lawyer Legislation and Fees at the Bar, Written and Printed
Expressly for the Benefit of the People*, n.p., January 1843.

Gentlemen:

In a country like this, a country which is
professed to be a country of freedom, it becomes every patriot to watch with jealousy
over its liberties, and to report forthwith every evil principle or practice in vogue, that
tends in the least to bring it into bondage.
Under a sense of this duty, I feel it incumbent on me to notify the public, through
the medium of your very valuable and
widely circulating paper, of a practice in our
country which, if it has not already absorbed the current of our liberties, is tending rapidly to it; and as this communication
is intended expressly for the public good, I
desire that you and all the editors in the
state will weigh well the matter couched in
it, and use all laudable means to arrest the
evil, and to put a stop to that stone which
is rolling recklessly through the land, deso-
lating city and hamlet, people and liberty,
and casting all indiscriminately and relent-
lessly into an unfathomable grave.

The time has arrived, and now is, when
silence becomes criminal, and when every
one who can speak a word, or perform a
deed, for the relief of his country, is called
to action. Let not timidity deter, nor selfishness neutralize our energies, but let all be
awake and all zealous in his country's good
and determined in the suppression of evil.

The sin to which I allude is the exceeding
lameness of our laws. We profess to live in
a free country, and to be heirs of liberty,
when in reality there is nothing more false,
nothing more untrue: indeed, it is a libel
upon the terms. But while we have to gaze
upon and mourn over the visage of our almost deceased freedom, and to listen with
horror to the knell of departed liberty, the
consoling thought arises, a remedy is at
hand: and may the God of Heaven help us
to apply it.

If I understand the term correctly, *Liberty
is the power of enjoying rights without paying
for them.* After the indispensable claims of a
government are satisfied, if impartial justice
awards $100 to me, for property, damage,

or anything else, that $100 are mine to all intents and purposes; and for the same reason that any other property is mine. And if I have to pay a portion of that $100 in order to get the remainder, I certainly pay tribute; and yet such is unfortunately the case in all the laws of Georgia.

I burn a man's corn house, and thereby, according to the verdict of an impartial and sworn jury, damage the man $500; he cannot, by the laws of Georgia, realize the verdict. He must pay a tribute of $150 to a lawyer for pleading for him. Again, you hold my note for $1,000 for value received. I confess the claim to be just; yet you cannot collect it by the laws of Georgia without paying a tribute of $50 to a lawyer. Again, I defraud you out of property to the amount of $1,000; it is well known by some, verily believed by others, and sworn to by yourself, to have been obtained by fraud; yet by the laws of Georgia you cannot receive the amount of me without paying $200 to a lawyer. Again, a man wills his property in truth and verity according to justice; but someone of the heirs imagines it ought to have been dealt out differently, and institutes a suit for a change of the dividends; the innocent as well as the guilty must fee a lawyer, and thus the estate is consumed by the lawyers.

These are a few of the thousands of parallel cases that happen every year in Georgia. Now let us examine the matter. In the first three examples given, we suppose the cases to have been decided according to equity, and for the claimants to have received from the defendants the amount of their claims; consequently they have received $1,600. Out of this sum, they pay the lawyers $400; $1,600 − 400 = $1,200 to the claimants, when justice had awarded them the full $1,600. Now in order for the claimants to realize the just claims of $1,600, they must receive $2,000 from the defendants: $2,000 − 400 = $1,600. But justice says defendants owe only $1,600, and cost

of suit; and to exact $2,000 from them will be $400 too much; and you had as well exact that amount from any other person or persons; for when defendant shall have satisfied the demands of justice, he becomes an innocent person. He has atoned to the law for violating its sacred ties, in paying the cost of the suit; he has satisfied the demand of the claimant; and who has any right to demand anything more?

Yet the $400 must be paid; and who has it to pay? The claimant out of his rightful demands and rightful property has it to pay; and to whom? To the lawyer. Why, what has the lawyer done to entitle him to any part of the claimant's property? Why, he read the law, and made that profession his study; and it was taken for granted by the people, that he was better qualified to make laws for the good of community than a man of any other profession; consequently, the people sent him to the legislature to enact laws for them; and what is the result? He leaves the interest of his confiding constituents out of mind; consults his own individual interest; makes the laws as complicated as his ingenuity can devise; come home and declares he has done the best he could for the land; and yet the laws are so complicated that no conjuror can ferret them, nor any two lawyers agree upon one point.

With this much fair speech he approaches the gentleman, and observes: "Mr. Claimant, your cases require much mental labor and talk, but I will nevertheless attend to them for $400. The sum is small for cases so complicated, but I think I can gain them; at all events I will do my best." The claimant admits the laws to be complicated, and sees himself placed between two losses, $1,600 and $400; and as a wise man he chooses the least.

We learn from this how it is that the lawyer becomes entitled to the $400 of the claimant's money. In short it is claimed on the ground of his infidelity, his ingenuity in framing laws without meaning, his little anecdotes to the jurors, and his palavering upon points that have no bearing upon the case under debate.

Thus *millions of dollars* are annually thrown away upon a class in community, who, if they were awarded according to their savings and doings, would live in a fine brick house with a fine brick wall around it. Many a poor vagrant lives on bread and water, and sleeps in the penitentiary, that never did half the mischief to society that many of these honorable esquires have done. And if the flood of evil is not stayed, every other class in community will be consumed with utter destruction.

A poor tailor saves a few dollars together over the midnight lamp; and the next morning it is demanded of him by a lawyer to defend him in a case that he is a perfect stranger to. The farmer may delve in brier beds and swamps until the last drop of sweat exudes from his melting frame, in order to support his family, or to provide for himself in his grey hairs; and the whole of it is demanded the next hour by a lawyer to rescue it from a robber who was detected in stealing it the night before. The pathetic cry of the perishing orphan for bread restrains not the avaricious hand of the attorney; but his ears to the mournful tale are deaf as to the zephyr of a distant clime, that passes unheeded and unknown. Known assassins, highway robbers, and midnight thieves, are all sustained against justice, with all the eloquence and zeal worthy of a better cause; and all right, nothing wrong! when if the same doings and sayings had been done and expressed by a saint, he would be considered accessory!

Messrs. Editors:

In my first number I endeavored to show the people that there is an evil in the land which, from its numerous and impressive tracks, has well nigh obliterated the features of liberty from our country; and if it is not soon arrested in its vagaries, we shall have reason to mourn over our supineness with the mourning of Haddadrimmon in the valley of Megeddo. I endeavored also, to show that this evil originated from the circumstance of entrusting our lawmaking business to the hands of lawyers. In this number shall prescribe a remedy for the evil; and which, if applied according to prescription will effectually remove the evil in future and restore the current of liberty to its native channel.

The subject under consideration in these numbers, is in my estimation one of the first magnitude; and it should elicit in its cause not only the heart, but the pen and lips of every freeman. Indeed, when I consider the ravages done by it, the desolation wrought by its angry foot, eloquence plays around my pen, impatient to be loosed from its confines, that it may lay hold upon the monster and quell him in his lair. But suppress its anxiety, and bid it hush and be still, and let reason do the work of reason We want no show, no display of words in this matter, no rules of rhetoric observed no halo of eloquence to dazzle the observer

The remedy is simply this: Let the people of each county in the state assemble at convenient time in their respective districts and elect delegates to meet in general convention at the courthouse in the county in which they live, for the purpose of nominating candidates for the legislature; let these delegates be instructed by their constituents not to nominate a lawyer under any circumstances; and if one should be nominated, not to vote for him. When these delegates shall have assembled in general convention at the courthouse, let these salutary injunctions be repeated by some competent member of the body, or by some other person selected by them, or by their constituents for that purpose; and let this individual state also his reasons for thus acting. Make it also his province and duty to lay before the convention a synopsis of the laws of the land, and the burdens under which we, our fathers, and our father's fa hers, have groaned from time immemorial up to this hour. Let him also show that these evils are founded in the influence which the lawyers wield in the legislature; and if their wily sports are not checked, we shall soon be hostages to destruction and the joint heirs of ruin.

With this picture before them, the will of their constituents, their own interests, the interests of their children and of their children's children, of their country and of millions unborn, will prompt them to do right; and in so doing, they will leave the names of lawyers off their tickets; and whomsoever the delegates nominate let the people support.

In their nomination I would recommend them to nominate farmers, mainly for the following reasons, and for many others of a like kind, which I have not time now to state: In the first place, they constitute a large majority of the population; and in representing them a majority of the people will be represented; secondly, they are the most important class in community, because all other classes, from the king upon his throne to the shoeblack upon his stool, are dependent upon them; thirdly, their numbers and occupation ensure the most talent; and in representing them you represent the wisdom of the land; and for the same reasons you represent the physical strength, the beauty, the merits, and the virtue of the country. Not with them as with other classes in society, virtue is the natural consequence of farming.

The farmer's baser thoughts and passions are paralyzed by his attention to his stock, his furrowed fields, his waving corn and stately ear. He listens with pleasure to the murmuring stream, the chirping songster as he bounds along the green; he views with delight the flowery mead, the clouds gliding in successive flakes along the high and holy heavens; the lightning streaming down the azure vault; and listening to the distant thunders, his soul rises aloft to the skies to kiss the hand that bid it roll. The tulip and the daisy are his, and "the cattle upon a thousand hills." With these associates and comforts around him, he has no need nor time to conjure harm to his fellow, or to plan schemes of self-aggrandizement. He stands already on the pinnacle of enjoyment and of glory, and envies not the king upon his throne. These are the hands in which the destinies of a nation may be committed with safety, and the result prove beneficial to all. And shall these ecstasies in a holy calling, and these depositories of virtue and fidelity, be unrepresented in our laws? Forbid! ye powers that be, forbid!

I repeat it, the farmers are the bone and sinew of the world. When they prosper all other classes prosper with them, and when they decline, 'tis felt by all the people through all the land. Suppose them all to die, or to cease their calling, want and nakedness would stride from sea to sea, and from shore to shore; the great earth herself would begirt her in mourning, and the winds that now bear in their bosoms the seeds of joy and sustenance to the disconsolate and perishing orphan would howl in despair.

But perhaps it will be urged by some that the farmers, have never made political matters and law their study, and therefore they cannot legislate upon matters so intricate. To this I reply, that laws and politics, when drifting along their natural channel, are as easily understood as the ordinary transactions of neighbor with neighbor; and if on inspection they are found to be otherwise, it is because they have been perverted from their ancient course, and rendered intricate for speculation. In proof of this I refer you to Washington, Franklin, Wm. Henry Harrison, and a host of others, who never saw a law book; yet whose sayings and doings have immortality won, and established them a character for ability in all departments of state, that shall stand plumed in perpetual day, while thousands of jurists shall lie "covered in shameful spewing."

28.

JOB DURFEE: Science and Political Progress

Dramatic new inventions like the steam engine, which promised to influence profoundly the life of a man, promoted an on-going discussion about the role of technology in society. Job Durfee, chief justice of the Supreme Court of Rhode Island, maintained that science and technology determined the progress of history, and he drew from that "eternal law" a conservative and deterministic philosophy of social change. His argument was advanced in an address to the Phi Beta Kappa society of Brown University on September 6, 1843. Durfee called his address "The Influence of Scientific Discovery and Invention on Social and Political Progress."

Source: *Oration Delivered Before the Phi Beta Kappa Society of Brown University*, Providence, 1843.

IF IT BE TRUE that knowledge is power, then, it would seem to follow, that any change in the arts and sciences, favorable or unfavorable, must be followed by corresponding changes in society. And such, in fact, we find to be the result. When the arts and sciences become stationary, all social and political institutions become stationary; when the arts and sciences become progressive, all social and political institutions become progressive. The universality of this fact, clearly demonstrates the necessary connection of cause and effect between scientific and social progress. And if the form in which this statement is made be correct, it does as clearly show which is the cause, and which the effect, and that we are not to seek for the causative energy of human progress in the wisdom of the political, but in that of the scientific and inventive mind. Let it moreover be recollected, that, at least in these our times, the scientific and inventive genius has a universality which elevates it above all human jurisdictions; that it belongs to the whole humanity; can be monopolized by no government; and that its discoveries and inventions walk the earth with the freedom of God's own messengers. . . .

In the realm of science and art, the most exalted geniuses and the brightest intellects that it contains, are ever at the head of affairs. They are there, not by the appointment of government, nor by the election of the masses, but by a decree of the Supreme Intelligence. And, if it be true . . . that their discoveries and inventions rule in the grand course of events, it will afford some consolation to reflect, that, whether government falls into the hands of demagogue or despot, (and it suffers equally from either) this high order of intellect does, after all, by setting limits to their follies, guide and govern in the main. To it we bow with deferential awe; to it we willingly own allegiance, and are proud to confess ourselves its subjects. . . .

But where and what is this point on which the scientific intellect takes this commanding stand? It is not to be found in that space which can be measured by a glance of the eye, or a movement of the hand. It is to be found only in the world of mind; and even there, only in that perfect reason, which is at once a law to humanity and the revealer of all truth. . . .

Now the sciences and arts, comprehending not merely the liberal and fine, but the physical and useful, consist of a logical series of discoveries and inventions, commenced at the earliest date of human progress, and continued down to the present time, the last grand result being the sum of all the labors that have gone before it; nay, not unfrequently the sum of the blood and sufferings of the ignoble masses, as well as of the labors of the exalted philosophic mind. I mean not to say that this law of reason, which impels man to discover and invent, conducts him from step to step, from truth to truth, in a direct line to the far result; for he has his liberty, and he often deviates, not for a day merely, but for a generation; nay, sometimes for a whole epoch. But, however widely he may err, he at last discovers the error of the first false step that he has made; his false premise is brought to its *reductio ad absurdum;* and, with the benefit of all the experience, discipline, and knowledge that he has acquired by pursuing it to this result, he returns to the point of departure, and, with redoubled energy, follows out the demonstration direct, to its *quod erat demonstrandum.*

Gentlemen, excuse me, while on an occasion so purely literary, I draw an illustration of this idea from a thought suggested by an invention in a branch of mechanic art.

I lately visited an establishment, perhaps in some respects the first of the kind in our country, for the manufacture of iron into bars, I stood by, and for the time, witnessed the operation of its enginery. I saw the large misshapen mass of crude metal taken blazing from the furnace, and passed through the illumined air to the appropriate machine. I saw it there undergo the designed transformation. It was made to pass repeatedly between two grooved, revolving cylinders, of immense weight. At every turn of the wheel it took new form; it lengthened, stretched, approximating still its intended shape, till at the end of the operation it came forth a well-fashioned fifteen or twenty foot bar of iron, ready for the hand of the artisan, or the machine that was

to resolve it into forms for ultimate use. . . .

I thought I saw . . . not only the reality of a progress in the race, but the unquestionable proof of the existence of a law of progress, carrying on its grand process through the whole humanity by a logical series of causes and effects, from its earliest premises, in far distant antiquity, to its latest result; and that the law, which rules in discovery and invention, is one and identical with that which governs in the progress of the race.

I speak not here of particular communities or nations, for nations, like men, decay and die — but of the whole humanity, which is as immortal as the spirit of man, or, perhaps, as the divinity that rules it; which feeds and grows in one branch of its existence upon the decaying energies of another, and which is thus ever renovating its vital and intellectual energies out of the past, and, amid unceasing decay, enjoying a perpetual rejuvenescence. On such an existence does this law of progress ever act; constantly forming and energizing the individual intellect by the unceasingly accumulating wisdom of the past, and by appropriating the forces of nature to the uses of social man, it is, at this day, carrying on in the world of mind that work of creation, which the Divine Author of humanity did but commence in the Garden of Eden.

There may be limits to man's capacities, but to the energies of nature which those capacities, acting under this law, may put in requisition, there are no limits. Each new discovery in science suggests the existence of something yet undiscovered; each new combination in art, on trial, suggests combinations yet untried; thus revealing, on the one hand, a law of suggestion, which, from the nature of mind, must ever act; and, on the other, objects and subjects of action which are as boundless, and as inexhaustible as the universe. . . .

The great truth that human progress is the result of an ever active law, manifesting itself chiefly in scientific discovery and invention, and thereby controlling legislation, and giving enduring improvement to all social and political institutions, cannot be a subject of historical question or doubt. It is a law as palpable in the history of the social mind, as the law of gravitation in the movement of matter. Indeed, I should feel that I owed a serious apology to my hearers for having detained them so long on this point, were it not for certain extravagant ideas which seem to be rife in the land.

The advocates of those ideas would teach us that there is an absolute, undefinable popular sovereignty, which can, in a manner its own, and at any moment, carry a certain supposed natural equality into social and political life, and *thereby* elevate poor human nature, however rude and degraded its condition, at once, as by a sort of magic, into a state of supreme and absolute perfection. When this sovereignty does not itself act to this end, it invokes the legislature, which is supposed to be competent to do nearly as much.

No doubt government can do much; it can suppress insurrection, it can repel invasion, it can enforce contracts, preserve the peace, concentrate and protect the existing arts; but all this is to organize, and sustain organization, and not to establish the *natural* equality. Yet this is all that government can do to promote human improvement; but in doing this, it does but act in obedience to that law, by which God governs in the progress of the race.

The idea that legislation necessarily acts an inferior part in human progress, that this progress is governed by a law that overrules and controls political sovereignty, may be humbling indeed to the demagogue, who would make everything bend to the popular will. But there this law is, an undoubted and incontrovertible reality, which will bear with no paltering, but demands the obedience of all, on the penalty of degradation or ruin. The true statesman, the real promoter of human progress, at once recognizes, and

feels proud to obey it. He feels that in so doing, he is performing the most elevated and dignified of duties. For though by legislation he cannot advance the entire humanity a single step, yet he may, by legislation, materially advance the nation for which he legislates.

You may be able to add nothing to the light of the sun, yet you may concentrate [its] rays in a focus, and thus make a particular point, as bright as the source from which they emanate. The statesman can concentrate the scattered arts; he may carry out each discovery and invention to all its available uses, and thus elevate the nation which he serves, to the head of the progressive humanity. Yet if he would do this, he must not wait to be driven to the task, like a galley slave, by the rival and threatening policy of foreign governments. For the very fact that they coerce him, shows that they are already in his advance.

Supposing that a people has already adopted the common arts and sciences, as far as they are available, there will still remain certain discoveries and inventions of more recent date, which are not fully applied, or carried to their necessary consequences. Among these, in modern times, there has always been someone susceptible of such universality of application, as would seem to merit the particular consideration of statesmen. Take for instance, at the present time, the steam engine. What is susceptible of more universal application? What, bringing out all its powers, can add greater energy and vigor to the arm of government? What has, or can perform greater wonders? Not gunpowder, not the compass, nay, not even the press. It may be made to toil in the field, and supplant the labor of the slave. It already works at the spindle and the loom, and the forge, and the mine. It is even now, while I am speaking, moving over earth with the speed of wings, walking up the downward torrent, and triumphantly striding over the roaring billows of the Atlantic. Already, where in use, has it reduced the distance one half between man and man, nation and nation, of extreme islands and continents of the habitable globe. It has brought civilization into immediate contact with barbarism, and Christianity with heathenism.

Unless all history be false, and the eternal laws of matter and mind nothing but a dream, there can be little danger in predicting too much for the progress of this invention. Indeed, the danger is, that the most extravagant predictions will fall short of the reality. No matter what government first applies this invention to all its practical naval and military uses; other governments must follow, however reluctantly, or cease to exist. Nay, should an unwonted apathy seize on all civilized governments, society would, at length, do the work to a great extent at their hands. The progress of this invention is ever onward, and will not cease until it has filled the world with its consequences. . . .

Think ye, that the military progress of this invention in the Old World, is to produce no effect on the New; that the breadth of the Atlantic is to set bounds to its effects? The breadth of the Atlantic! Why, it has become a narrow frith, over which armies may be ferried in twelve or fifteen days, to land in slave or nonslave-holding states at option; and that power, "whose home is in the deep," already transports, over her watery empire, on the wings of this invention, her victorious cannon. Other governments are little behind her in the application of this power. Thus menaced, have we strength to do our duty with dignity? Can we much longer be governed by factions?

I am not suggesting a course of policy; I am simply carrying our premises to their necessary consequences; and to *that* end I ask: If we continue a free and independent people, must we not organize ourselves on the basis which this invention affords? Can we avoid it? Have we any choice but to radiate our country with communications

for its defense, that the whole war force of the nation may be thrown with railroad speed on any point of danger? This system of defense may not be adopted till the shock of some foreign invasion, or some terrible internal convulsion, forces upon the government the necessity of adopting it; and then, if it be the will of God that we continue one people, it will, and must be adopted. When it is done, this Union will be complete; its duration will depend on no written scroll of parchment; on no variable popular breath; its strength on no constitutional constructions changing to suit the temper of the times, but the Constitution itself, resolved by the law of progress, shall take form, over the whole face of the land, in bands of iron.

Such must be the political progress of this invention. Government, in this country, has as yet done nothing, but society has done much. True to itself and its highest interests, it has been prompt in obedience to the law of progress. It has already extended, and still continues to extend the application of this sovereign invention. It has contracted, as it were, this country within half its former space. It has made a sparse population dense, and if a dense population has its evils, as in large cities it certainly has, the same invention offers an antidote. It can, without disadvantage, render those populations sparse. It can combine the morality and the occupation of a rural, with the intellectual activity of an urban population. It will and must proceed on its mission, by force of the very law which gave it existence, till the civilization of Christendom, on the basis which it affords, has been fully accomplished, and then, by force of the same law, will it bear that civilization into the bosom of barbarism, Christianize the nations, and establish the dominion of the arts over the broad face of earth and ocean. . . .

And now, gentlemen, if such be the law of human progress, if it must thus ever operate from the past into the present, and through the present to the future, and as by a sort of logical process, what becomes of those doctrines of social and political reform, with which our land is now so rife, and with which the public ear is so incessantly abused? What becomes of those ideas of a natural, absolute, unlimited and uncontrollable popular sovereignty which is at once to bring humanity to perfection, by establishing a *natural* liberty and a *natural* equality in *social* and *political* life?

There may be a dire clashing among some of the ideas that are thus brought forcibly together; but the wise advocates of these doctrines see it not, feel it not. They have sundry naked abstractions, which they have created for themselves, or others for them, upon which, by their own unassisted wisdom, they hope to build up society anew, on an improved plan. They would cut clear from the past; they would establish a new theory of human nature, and base a human progress upon ideas and laws their own.

Well! let them do it; but let them do it — as they must — with material their own. Let them create their world, and their man and woman, after their own image, and then, on their principles, run their course of events in rivalry with that of Divine Providence. But let them not lay their hands on those whom God has created after His image, and who are moving on to their high destiny under His divine guidance. Let them not undertake to substitute their will for His, their laws for His, over any except their own, and we shall then know what that progress is about which they are now so abundantly eloquent.

In their estimation, all social and political institutions can be removed, by their sovereign wills, with the same ease that you take the glove from your hand, and any of their own imaginings substituted in their place. Their abstractions have no reference to the influence of the past on the present; no reference to the existing social or political organizations which have grown out of bygone centuries; and it is not strange that they are utterly astonished to find, when they attempt to carry them into effect, that they are entering into conflict with all that the past has done for us. And then it is very natural for them to proceed, from lauding their own principles, to the abuse of the past; to the abuse of all our ancestral institutions and social and political ideas, as antiquated, and as obstructions to human progress.

Gentlemen, the present state of human progress is a child, of which the hoary past is the venerable father. . . . O! let us build monuments to the past. Let them tower on mound and mountain; let them rise from the corners of our streets, and in our public squares, that childhood may sport its marbles at their basements, and lisp the names of the commemorated dead, as it lisps the letters of its alphabet. Thus shall the past be made to stand out in a monumental history that may be seen by the eye, and touched by the hand. Thus shall it be made to subsist to the senses, as it still lives in the organization of the social mind; an organization from which its errors have died out, or are dying, and in which nothing but its Herculean labors do, or are to endure. Yes, let us sanctify the past, and let no hand, with sacrilegious violence dare mar its venerable aspect.

Change indeed must come, but then let it come by force of the necessary law of progress. So shall the present still ever build and improve on a patrimony formed by the deeds of heroic virtue, and the labors of exalted intellect. So shall the great and glorious be added to the great and glorious, and the labors of the illustrious dead still be made fruitful by the labors of the illustrious living, time without end.

Samuel F. B. Morse with the telegraph he developed in the 1830s; photo by Mathew Brady

PATENTS AND INDUSTRY

In 1791 Alexander Hamilton, in his "Report on Manufactures," had proposed a system of protective tariffs and federally-sponsored internal improvements to encourage manufacturing. The program was not adopted, but by the 1840s the country had reached a level of industrial development beyond anything Hamilton had foreseen. Many factors contributed to this growth, not the least of which were huge investments of foreign, particularly British, capital, but much of the progress is attributable to the inventiveness popularized as "Yankee ingenuity." The Patent Office was continually deluged with "new and improved" devices for this and that. The tremendous rewards flowing from a commercially successful patent filled the courts with patent litigation. Many of the fortunes made during the period were preceded by battles over rights. The inventor or scientist who failed to patent his discoveries and to capitalize on them was rare. One such man was Joseph Henry, who pioneered the principles of the telegraph but left its perfection and commercial application to Samuel F. B. Morse. Morse succeeded in prying money from Congress for a demonstration of his system in 1844. Within four years most cities were connected by telegraph.

Warshaw Collection

National Archives

Two of Hoe's many inventions which gave new dimension to the printing trade: (left) an eight-cylinder type-revolving printing machine in operation. This early version of the "lightning press" grew out of the printing press (right) shown in a detail from Hoe's 1845 patent drawing

In 1846 Robert Hoe and his son Richard patented their "lightning press." This machine was an improvement on the revolving cylinder principle that Hoe had been experimenting with for years. In 1844 they had patented a rotary press, employing a single flatbed of type that was a vast improvement over earlier single impression methods. But growing newspaper rivalries and circulation competition in the cities required ever faster presses. The "lightning press" met this demand by adding a revolving type cylinder that could carry more than one page of type. By making possible the rapid printing of large numbers of papers the "lightning press" stimulated the growth of mass-circulation newspapers and the popular journalism that characterized them.

Richard Hoe's patent drawing for an improved version of his cylinder printing press, 1844
National Archives

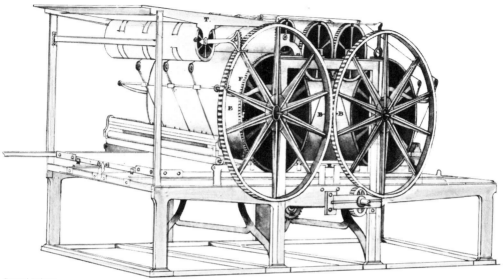

Two-cylinder printing press patented by Sereno Newton and then sold to Hoe and his partner

The Hoe factory in which the printing presses were manufactured

Elias Howe; daguerreotype by Southworth and Hawes

Drawing of the first sewing machine developed by Elias Howe in the 1840s

The Sewing Machine

The invention of the sewing machine brought immediate advantages for the cotton and woolen goods industries by allowing large-scale manufacture of ready-made clothing. The production of "store-bought" clothing doubled during the decade from 1850 to 1860. The machine was practicable for domestic use and also stimulated the shoemaking industry.

Elias Howe, who patented his invention in 1846, did not profit immediately from his discovery because he was unable to find financial backing in the U.S. and in England. Isaac M. Singer independently developed a superior machine in 1851 that sold very well, but he and several other companies were forced to pay royalties to Howe when the courts decided that they were infringing upon his patent.

The first contest between hand and machine sewing which was staged in Quincy Hall, Boston. Howe and his machine were victorious

Howe before the Supreme Court of Massachusetts in a suit to protect his patent rights as the original inventor of the sewing machine

Advertisement for a Singer sewing machine, 1853

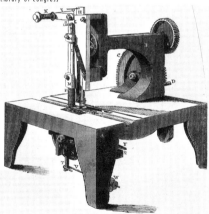

Drawing of Isaac Singer's improved sewing machine; from "Scientific American," 1851

Gathering rubber on a plantation in Africa (above); rubber boats and pontoons in the Goodyear display at the Crystal Palace Exposition, 1851, in London

FIREMAN'S COATS.

Double-breasted, with a standing collar and strap, close fitting, medium length, full skirt, with pockets; the sleeve buttons tightly at the wrist. Being proof against the action of extreme heat, where woollen fabrics would consume, they are peculiarly adapted for the use of firemen. Companies supplied at special rates, after furnished patterns.

Sizes — 1, 2, 3, 4, 5.

EACH.

Black, - - - Vulcanized, $5 50

CAPES OR CLOAKS.

Made of various lengths, from half to three-quarters circle, on light materials, silicia, &c.; buttoned down the front. An excellent article for ladies' or gentlemen's wear, and for the protection of uniforms, &c. &c.

Sizes — 1, 2, 3, 4.

EACH.

Black, - - -	Vulcanized,	$4 00
White, - - -	do. -	5 00
Black, - - -	Solarized,	3 00
White, - - -	do. -	4 00

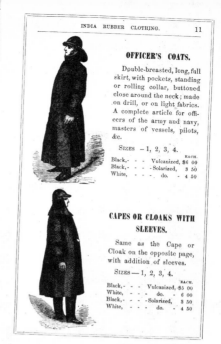

OFFICER'S COATS.

Double-breasted, long, full skirt, with pockets, standing or rolling collar, buttoned close around the neck; made on drill, or on light fabrics. A complete article for officers of the army and navy, masters of vessels, pilots, &c.

Sizes — 1, 2, 3, 4.

Black, - - -	Vulcanized,	$6 00
Black, - - -	Solarized,	3 50
White, - - -	do. -	4 50

CAPES OR CLOAKS WITH SLEEVES.

Same as the Cape or Cloak on the opposite page, with addition of sleeves.

Sizes — 1, 2, 3, 4.

EACH.

Black, - - -	Vulcanized,	$5 00
White, - - -	do. -	6 00
Black, - - -	Solarized,	3 50
White, - - -	do. -	4 50

Two pages from a catalog of the rubber products manufactured by Goodyear's company

Goodyear

Charles Goodyear began experimenting with Brazilian gum elastic in 1836 to produce a durable substance that would not become gummy in warm weather or brittle in cold. After a series of failures, he discovered the vulcanization process in 1839. In this method the rubber was heated with sulfur to produce the familiar elastic, stick-free substance. In 1844 he secured his patent.

Goodyear, like so many other inventors, was subjected to widespread infringements upon his patent. After years of litigation (Daniel Webster was his counsel at one time), he received a favorable court decision in 1852, but this did not provide sufficient protection of his interests. He fared no better with his patents in England and France.

Four styles of rubber boots, 1856

BOOTS.

LONG ELASTIC TOP BOOT. This style is superior to any other long top boot for gentlemen, as it has a light, elastic close-fitting leg, not requiring the aid of straps to hold it up. Price, per pair, $5.50.

Men's Long Top Boots, $5.50.   Men's Knee Boots, $5.00.

Boys' Boots, Sizes 1 to 6, - - - - - - - - - - -	$3 00
Youths' Boots, Sizes 13 and under, - - - - - -	2 00
Ladies' Boots, Felt or Wool Lined, - - - - - -	2 50
Misses' Long Boots, Felt or Wool Lined, - - - -	1 75
Misses' Long Boots, Net Lined, - - - - - - -	1 63

Men's Short Boots, 16 inches, $4.50.   Ladies' Boots, Net Lined, $2.00.

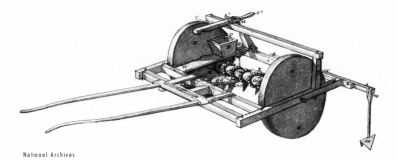

Patent drawings for some of the agricultural equipment invented around 1840: (Top) lever drill for planting designed by M. and L. Fennock; (right) horse-drawn thrasher created by Briggs and Carpenter; (below) machine designed by Levi Rice for planting and digging potatoes

Advertisement for reaper manufactured by McDonald Co., a competitor of McCormick

Testing the first reaping machine near Steeles Tavern, Va., 1831

McCormick

When Cyrus McCormick began marketing his reaper in the Midwest his success was assured. He had earlier demonstrated his invention to the farmers near his Virginia home, and they had bought some, but the machines were best suited to the great expanses of wheat grown in Ohio, Indiana, and Illinois. By 1851 a factory that he had established in Chicago four years earlier was producing 1,000 reapers a year, and by 1857 production had increased to 23,000.

CHICAGO, 1851.

(Above) Cyrus McCormick; unfinished painting by C. L. Elliott; (left) drawing of McCormick's reaper in operation; from an advertisement, 1851

The Crystal Palace and grounds at the London Exhibition of 1851

The London Exhibition of 1851, organized to celebrate the scientific and industrial progress of Victoria's Britain, marked, as well, the entrance of American manufacturing into world competition. Although American participation was limited, the entries were well received. McCormick's reaper was awarded the Grand Medal and the Council Medal after a public demonstration of its capacity. Goodyear received a medal for some of his applications of rubber and several other U.S. entries were given awards. But the principal reward was orders from European businessmen and a new international respect for "American ingenuity."

(Above) Agricultural equipment at the London exhibit; (below) interior view of the exhibit

29.

Henry David Thoreau: An Attack on Technology

Thoreau's essay, Paradise (To Be) Regained, *was a review of the first part of a proposed two-volume work by one J. A. Etzler, called* The Paradise Within the Reach of All Men, Without Labor, by Powers of Nature and Machinery: An Address to All Intelligent Men, *published in 1842. Etzler was the perfect target for the arch-individualist Thoreau; in glorifying the machine and in proposing the establishment of a Fourier-type community to put his mechanized paradise into effect, Etzler transgressed on everything Thoreau held dear. The humor in the piece belies Thoreau's austere image.*

Source: *United States Magazine and Democratic Review,* November 1843.

We learn that Mr. Etzler is a native of Germany, and originally published his book in Pennsylvania, ten or twelve years ago; and now a second English edition, from the original American one, is demanded by his readers across the water, owing, we suppose, to the recent spread of Fourier's doctrines. It is one of the signs of the times. We confess that we have risen from reading this book with enlarged ideas and grander conceptions of our duties in this world. It did expand us a little. It is worth attending to, if only that it entertains large questions. Consider what Mr. Etzler proposes:

Fellowmen! I promise to show the means of creating a paradise within ten years, where everything desirable for human life may be had by every man in superabundance, without labor and without pay; where the whole face of nature shall be changed into the most beautiful forms, and man may live in the most magnificent palaces, in all imaginable refinements of luxury, and in the most delightful gardens; where he may accomplish, without labor, in one year, more than hitherto could be done in thousands of years; may level mountains, sink valleys, create lakes, drain lakes and swamps, and intersect the land everywhere with beautiful canals and roads for transporting heavy loads of many thousand tons, and for traveling 1,000 miles in twenty-four hours; may cover the ocean with floating islands movable in any desired direction with immense power and celerity, in perfect security, and with all comforts and luxuries, bearing gardens and palaces, with thousands of families, and provided with rivulets of sweet water; may explore the interior of the globe, and travel from pole to pole in a fortnight; provide himself with means, unheard of yet, for increasing his knowledge of the world, and so his intelligence; lead a life of continual happiness, of enjoyments yet unknown; free himself from almost all the evils that afflict mankind, except death, and even put death far beyond the common period of human life, and finally render it less afflicting. Mankind may thus live in and enjoy a new world, far superior to the present, and raise themselves far higher in the scale of being.

It would seem from this and various indications beside that there is a transcendentalism in mechanics as well as in ethics. While the whole field of the one reformer lies beyond the boundaries of space, the other is pushing his schemes for the elevation of the race to its utmost limits. While one scours the heavens, the other sweeps the earth. One says he will reform himself, and then nature and circumstances will be right. Let us not obstruct ourselves, for that is the greatest friction. It is of little importance though a cloud obstruct the view of the astronomer compared with his own blindness. The other will reform nature and circumstances, and then man will be right. Talk no more vaguely, says he, of reforming the world — I will reform the globe itself.

What matters it whether I remove this humor out of my flesh, or this pestilent humor from the fleshy part of the globe? Nay, is not the latter the more generous course? At present the globe goes with a shattered constitution in its orbit. Has it not asthma, ague, and fever, and dropsy, and flatulence, and pleurisy, and is it not afflicted with vermin? Has it not its healthful laws counteracted, and its vital energy which will yet redeem it?

No doubt the simple powers of nature, properly directed by man, would make it healthy and paradise; as the laws of man's own constitution but wait to be obeyed to restore him to health and happiness. Our panaceas cure but few ails; our general hospitals are private and exclusive. We must set up another Hygeian than is now worshiped. Do not the quacks even direct small doses for children, larger for adults, and larger still for oxen and horses? Let us remember that we are to prescribe for the globe itself.

This fair homestead has fallen to us, and how little have we done to improve it, how little have we cleared and hedged and ditched! We are too inclined to go hence to a "better land," without lifting a finger, as our farmers are moving to the Ohio soil; but would it not be more heroic and faithful to till and redeem this New England soil of the world? The still youthful energies of the globe have only to be directed in their proper channel. Every gazette brings accounts of the untutored freaks of the wind — shipwrecks and hurricanes which the mariner and planter accept as special or general providences; but they touch our consciences, they remind us of our sins. Another deluge would disgrace mankind. We confess we never had much respect for that antediluvian race. A thoroughbred businessman cannot enter heartily upon the business of life without first looking into his accounts.

How many things are now at loose ends! Who knows which way the wind will blow tomorrow? Let us not succumb to nature. We will marshal the clouds and restrain the tempests; we will bottle up pestilent exhalations; we will probe for earthquakes, grub them up, and give vent to the dangerous gases; we will disembowel the volcano, and extract its poison, take its seed out. We will wash water, and warm fire, and cool ice, and underprop the earth. We will teach birds to fly, and fishes to swim, and ruminants to chew the cud. It is time we had looked into these things.

And it becomes the moralist, too, to inquire what man might do to improve and beautify the system; what to make the stars shine more brightly, the sun more cheery and joyous, the moon more placid and content. Could he not heighten the tints of flowers and the melody of birds? Does he perform his duty to the inferior races? Should he not be a god to them? What is the part of magnanimity to the whale and the beaver? Should we not fear to exchange places with them for a day lest by their behavior they should shame us? Might we not treat with magnanimity the shark and the tiger, not descend to meet them on their own level, with spears of shark's teeth and bucklers of tiger's skin? We slander the hyena; man is the fiercest and cruelest animal. Ah! he is of little faith; even the erring comets and meteors would thank him and return his kindness in their kind.

How meanly and grossly do we deal

with nature! Could we not have a less gross labor? What else do these fine inventions suggest — magnetism, the daguerreotype, electricity? Can we not do more than cut and trim the forest? — can we not assist in its interior economy, in the circulation of the sap? Now we work superficially and violently. We do not suspect how much might be done to improve our relation with animated nature; what kindness and refined courtesy there might be.

There are certain pursuits which, if not wholly poetic and true, do at least suggest a nobler and finer relation to nature than we know. The keeping of bees, for instance, is a very slight interference. It is like directing the sunbeams. All nations, from the remotest antiquity, have thus fingered nature. There are Hymettus and Hybla, and how many bee-renowned spots beside! There is nothing gross in the idea of these little herds — their hum like the faintest low of kine in the meads.

A pleasant reviewer has lately reminded us that in some places they are led out to pasture where the flowers are most abundant. "Columella tells us," says he, "that the inhabitants of Arabia sent their hives into Attica to benefit by the later-blowing flowers." Annually are the hives, in immense pyramids, carried up the Nile in boats, and suffered to float slowly down the stream by night, resting by day, as the flowers put forth along the banks; and they determine the richness of any locality, and so the profitableness of delay, by the sinking of the boat in the water. We are told, by the same reviewer, of a man in Germany whose bees yielded more honey than those of his neighbors, with no apparent advantage; but at length he informed them that he had turned his hives one degree more to the east, and so his bees, having two hours the start in the morning, got the first sip of honey. Here, there is treachery and selfishness behind all this, but these things suggest to the poetic mind what might be done.

Many examples there are of a grosser interference, yet not without their apology. We saw last summer, on the side of a mountain, a dog employed to churn for a farmer's family, traveling upon a horizontal wheel, and though he had sore eyes, an alarming cough, and withal a demure aspect, yet their bread did get buttered for all that. Undoubtedly, in the most brilliant success, the first rank is always sacrificed. Much useless traveling of horses, *in extenso,* has of late years been improved for man's behoof, only two forces being taken advantage of — the gravity of the horse, which is the centripetal, and his centrifugal inclination to go ahead. Only these two elements in the calculation. And is not the creature's whole economy better economized thus? Are not all finite beings better pleased with motions relative than absolute?

And what is the great globe itself but such a wheel — a larger treadmill — so that our horse's freest steps over prairies are oftentimes balked and rendered of no avail by the earth's motion on its axis? But here he is the central agent and motive power; and, for variety of scenery, being provided with a window in front, do not the ever varying activity and fluctuating energy of the creature himself work the effect of the most varied scenery on a country road? It must be confessed that horses, at present, work too exclusively for men, rarely men for horses; and the brute degenerates in man's society.

It will be seen that we contemplate a time when man's will shall be law to the physical world, and he shall no longer be deterred by such abstractions as time and space, height and depth, weight and hardness, but shall indeed be the lord of creation. "Well," says the faithless reader, "life is short, but art is long; where is the power that will effect all these changes?"

This it is the very object of Mr. Etzler's volume to show. At present, he would merely remind us that there are innumerable and immeasurable powers already existing in nature, unimproved on a large scale, or for generous and universal ends, amply sufficient for these purposes. He would only indicate their existence, as a surveyor makes known the existence of a waterpower on any stream; but for their application he refers us to a sequel to this book, called the *Mechanical System*. A few of the most obvious and familiar of these powers are the wind, the tide, the waves, the sunshine. Let us consider their value.

First, there is the power of the wind, constantly exerted over the globe. It appears from observation of a sailing vessel, and from scientific tables, that the average power of the wind is equal to that of one horse for every one hundred square feet. We do not attach much value to this statement of the comparative power of the wind and horse, for no common ground is mentioned on which they can be compared. Undoubtedly, each is incomparably excellent in its way, and every general comparison made for such practical purposes as are contemplated, which gives a preference to the one, must be made with some unfairness to the other. The scientific tables are, for the most part, true only in a tabular sense.

We suspect that a loaded wagon, with a light sail, ten feet square, would not have been blown so far by the end of the year, under equal circumstances, as a common racer or dray horse would have drawn it. And how many crazy structures on our globe's surface, of the same dimensions, would wait for dry rot if the traces of one horse were hitched to them, even to their windward side? Plainly this is not the principle of comparison. But even the steady and constant force of the horse may be rated as equal to his weight at least. Yet we should prefer to let the zephyrs and gales bear with all their weight upon our fences than that Dobbin, with feet braced, should lean ominously against them for a season. Nevertheless, here is an almost incalcula-

ble power at our disposal, yet how trifling the use we make of it! It only serves to turn a few mills, blow a few vessels across the ocean, and a few trivial ends besides. What a poor compliment do we pay to our indefatigable and energetic servant!

If you ask, perhaps, why this power is not used, if the statement be true, I have to ask in return, why is the power of steam so lately come to application? So many millions of men boiled water every day for many thousand years; they must have frequently seen that boiling water, in tightly closed pots or kettles, would lift the cover or burst the vessel with great violence. The power of steam was, therefore, as commonly known down to the least kitchen or washwoman as the power of wind; but close observation and reflection were bestowed neither on the one nor the other.

Men having discovered the power of falling water, which, after all, is comparatively slight, how eagerly do they seek out and improve these *privileges!* Let a difference of but a few feet in level be discovered on some stream near a populous town, some slight occasion for gravity to act, and the whole economy of the neighborhood is changed at once. Men do indeed speculate about and with this power as if it were the only privilege. But meanwhile this aerial stream is falling from far greater heights with more constant flow, never shrunk by drought, offering millsites wherever the wind blows; a Niagara in the air, with no Canada side — only the application is hard.

There are the powers, too, of the tide and waves, constantly ebbing and flowing, lapsing and relapsing, but they serve man in but few ways. They turn a few tide mills and perform a few other insignificant and accidental services only. We all perceive the effect of the tide; how imperceptibly it creeps up into our harbors and rivers and raises the heaviest navies as easily as the lightest ship. Everything that floats must yield to it. But man, slow to take nature's constant hint of assistance, makes slight and irregular use of this power in careening ships and getting them afloat when aground.

The following is Mr. Etzler's calculation on this head: To form a conception of the power which the tide affords, let us imagine a surface of 100 miles square, or 10,000 square miles, where the tide rises and sinks, on an average, 10 feet; how many men would it require to empty a basin of 10,000 square miles area, and 10 feet deep, filled with seawater, in 6¼ hours and fill it again in the same time? As one man can raise 8 cubic feet of seawater per minute, and in 6¼ hours 3,000, it would take 1,200,000,000 men, or as they could work only half the time, 2,400,000,000, to raise 3,000,000,000,000 cubic feet, or the whole quantity required in the given time.

This power may be applied in various ways. A large body, of the heaviest materials that will float, may first be raised by it, and being attached to the end of a balance reaching from the land, or from a stationary support fastened to the bottom, when the tide falls the whole weight will be brought to bear upon the end of the balance. Also, when the tide rises, it may be made to exert a nearly equal force in the opposite direction. It can be employed wherever a *point d'appui* can be obtained.

However, the application of the tide being by establishments fixed on the ground, it is natural to begin with them near the shores in shallow water, and upon sands, which may be extended gradually further into the sea. The shores of the continent, islands, and sands, being generally surrounded by shallow water, not exceeding from 50 to 100 fathoms in depth for 20, 50, or 100 miles and upward. The coasts of North America, with their extensive sandbanks, islands, and rocks, may easily afford, for this purpose, a ground about 3,000 miles long, and, on an average, 100 miles broad, or 300,000 square miles, which, with a power of 240,000 men per square

mile, as stated, at 10-feet tide, will be equal to 72,000 millions of men, or for every mile of coast, a power of 24 million men.

Rafts, of any extent, fastened on the ground of the sea, along the shore, and stretching far into the sea, may be covered with fertile soil, bearing vegetables and trees of every description, the finest gardens equal to those the firm land may admit of, and buildings and machineries which may operate, not only on the sea, where they are, but which also, by means of mechanical connections, may extend their operations for many miles into the continent. Thus this power may cultivate the artificial soil for many miles upon the surface of the sea, near the shores, and, for several miles, the dry land, along the shore, in the most superior manner imaginable; it may build cities along the shore, consisting of the most magnificent palaces, every one surrounded by gardens and the most delightful sceneries; it may level the hills and unevennesses, or raise eminences for enjoying open prospect into the country and upon the sea; it may cover the barren shore with fertile soil, and beautify the same in various ways; it may clear the sea of shallows, and make easy the approach to the land, not merely of vessels but of large floating islands, which may come from, and go to distant parts of the world, islands that have every commodity and security for their inhabitants which the firm land affords.

Thus may a power, derived from the gravity of the moon and the ocean, hitherto but the objects of idle curiosity to the studious man, be made eminently subservient for creating the most delightful abodes along the coasts, where men may enjoy at the same time all the advantages of sea and dry land; the coasts may hereafter be continuous paradisiacal skirts between land and sea, everywhere crowded with the densest population. The shores and the sea along them will be no more as raw nature presents them now but everywhere of easy and charming access, not even molested by the roar of waves, shaped as it may suit the purposes of their inhabitants; the sea will be cleared of every obstruction to free passage everywhere, and its productions in fishes, etc., will be gathered in large, appropriate receptacles, to present them to the inhabitants of the shores and of the sea.

Verily, the land would wear a busy aspect at the spring and neap tide, and these island ships, these *terrae infirmae*, which realize the fables of antiquity, affect our imagination. We have often thought that the fittest locality for a human dwelling was on the edge of the land, that there the constant lesson and impression of the sea might sink deep into the life and character of the landsman, and perhaps impart a marine tint to his imagination. It is a noble word, that "mariner" — one who is conversant with the sea. There should be more of what it signifies in each of us. It is a worthy country to belong to — we look to see him not disgrace it. Perhaps we should be equally mariners and terreners, and even our Green Mountains need some of that sea green to be mixed with them.

The computation of the power of the waves is less satisfactory. While only the average power of the wind and the average height of the tide were taken before, now the extreme height of the waves is used, for they are made to rise ten feet above the level of the sea, to which, adding ten more for depression, we have twenty feet, or the extreme height of a wave. Indeed, the power of the waves, which is produced by the wind blowing obliquely and at disadvantage upon the water, is made to be not only 3,000 times greater than that of the tide but 100 times greater than that of the wind itself, meeting its object at right angles. Moreover, this power is measured by the area of the vessel and not by its length mainly, and it seems to be forgotten that the motion of the waves is chiefly undulatory, and exerts a power only within the limits of a vibration, else the very continents, with their extensive coasts, would soon be set adrift.

Finally, there is the power to be derived from sunshine by the principle on which Archimedes contrived his burning mirrors, a multiplication of mirrors reflecting the rays of the sun upon the same spot till the requisite degree of heat is obtained. The principal application of this power will be to the boiling of water and production of steam.

How to create rivulets of sweet and wholesome water, on floating islands, in the midst of the ocean, will be no riddle now. Seawater changed into steam will distill into sweet water, leaving the salt on the bottom. Thus the steam engines on floating islands, for their propulsion and other mechanical purposes, will serve, at the same time, for the distillery of sweet water, which, collected in basins, may be led through channels over the island, while, where required, it may be refrigerated by artificial means, and changed into cool water, surpassing, in salubrity, the best spring water, because nature hardly ever distills water so purely, and without admixture of less wholesome matter.

So much for these few and more obvious powers already used to a trifling extent. But there are innumerable others in nature, not described nor discovered. These, however, will do for the present. This would be to make the sun and the moon equally our satellites. For, as the moon is the cause of the tides and the sun the cause of the wind, which, in turn, is the cause of the waves, all the work of this planet would be performed by these far influences.

But as these powers are very irregular and subject to interruptions, the next object is to show how they may be converted into powers that operate continually and uniformly forever, until the machinery be worn out, or, in other words, into perpetual motions. . . . Hitherto the power of the wind has been applied immediately upon the machinery for use, and we have had to wait the chances of the wind's blowing; while the operation was stopped as soon as the wind ceased to blow. But the manner . . . of applying this power is to make it operate only for collecting or storing up power, and then to take out of this store, at any time, as much as may be wanted for final operation upon the machines. The power stored up is to react as required, and may do so long after the original power of the wind has ceased. And though the wind should cease for intervals of many months, we may have by the same power a uniform perpetual motion in a very simple way.

The weight of a clock being wound up gives us an image of reaction. The sinking of this weight is the reaction of winding it up. It is not necessary to wait till it has run down before we wind up the weight, but it may be wound up at any time, partly or totally; and if done always before the weight reaches the bottom, the clock will be going perpetually. In a similar, though not in the same way, we may cause a reaction on a larger scale. We may raise, for instance, water by the immediate application of wind or steam to a pond upon some eminence, out of which, through an outlet, it may fall upon some wheel or other contrivance for setting machinery a-going. Thus we may store up water in some eminent pond, and take out of this store, at any time, as much water through the outlet as we want to employ, by which means the original power may react for many days after it has ceased. . . . Such reservoirs of moderate elevation or size need not be made artificially but will be found made by nature very frequently, requiring but little aid for their completion. They require no regularity of form. Any valley with lower grounds in its vicinity would answer the purpose. Small crevices may be filled up. Such places may be eligible for the beginning of enterprises of this kind.

The greater the height, of course, the less water required. But suppose a level and dry country; then hill and valley and "eminent pond" are to be constructed by main force; or, if the springs are unusually low, then dirt and stones may be used, and the disadvantage arising from friction will be coun-

terbalanced by their greater gravity. Nor shall a single rood of dry land be sunk in such artificial ponds as may be wasted, but their surfaces "may be covered with rafts decked with fertile earth, and all kinds of vegetables which may grow there as well as anywhere else."

And, finally, by the use of thick envelopes retaining the heat and other contrivances, "the power of steam caused by sunshine may react at will, and thus be rendered perpetual, no matter how often or how long the sunshine may be interrupted."

Here is power enough, one would think, to accomplish somewhat. These are the powers below. O ye millwrights, ye engineers, ye operatives and speculators of every class, never again complain of a want of power: it is the grossest form of infidelity. The question is, not how we shall execute but what. Let us not use in a niggardly manner what is thus generously offered.

Consider what revolutions are to be effected in agriculture. First, in the new country, a machine is to move along, taking out trees and stones to any required depth, and piling them up in convenient heaps; then the same machine, "with a little alteration," is to plane the ground perfectly, till there shall be no hills nor valleys, making the requisite canals, ditches, and roads as it goes along. The same machine, "with some other little alterations," is then to sift the ground thoroughly, supply fertile soil from other places if wanted, and plant it; and, finally, the same machine, "with a little addition," is to reap and gather in the crop, thresh and grind it, or press it to oil, or prepare it any way for final use. For the description of these machines we are referred to Etzler's *Mechanical System*. . . . We should be pleased to see that *Mechanical System*, though we have not been able to ascertain whether it has been published or only exists as yet in the design of the author. We have great faith in it. But we cannot stop for applications now.

Any wilderness, even the most hideous and sterile, may be converted into the most fertile and delightful gardens. The most dismal swamps may be cleared of all their spontaneous growth, filled up and leveled, and intersected by canals, ditches, and aqueducts for draining them entirely. The soil, if required, may be meliorated by covering or mixing it with rich soil taken from distant places, and the same be moldered to fine dust, leveled, sifted from all roots, weeds, and stones, and sowed and planted in the most beautiful order and symmetry, with fruit trees and vegetables of every kind that may stand the climate.

New facilities for transportation and locomotion are to be adopted:

Large and commodious vehicles for carrying many thousand tons, running over peculiarly adapted level roads, at the rate of 40 miles per hour, or 1,000 miles per day, may transport men and things, small houses, and whatever may serve for comfort and ease, by land. Floating islands, constructed of logs, or of wooden stuff prepared in a similar manner as is to be done with stone, and of live trees, which may be reared so as to interlace one another and strengthen the whole, may be covered with gardens and palaces, and propelled by powerful engines, so as to run at an equal rate through seas and oceans. Thus, man may move, with the celerity of a bird's flight, in terrestrial paradises, from one climate to another, and see the world in all its variety, exchanging, with distant nations, the surplus of productions. The journey from one pole to another may be performed in a fortnight; the visit to a transmarine country in a week or two; or a journey round the world in one or two months by land and water. And why pass a dreary winter every year while there is yet room enough on the globe where nature is blessed with a perpetual summer, and with a far greater variety and luxuriance of vegetation? More than one-half the surface of the globe has no winter. Men will have it in their power to remove and prevent all

bad influences of climate, and to enjoy, perpetually, only that temperature which suits their constitution and feeling best.

Who knows but by accumulating the power until the end of the present century, using, meanwhile, only the smallest allowance, reserving all that blows, all that shines, all that ebbs and flows, all that dashes, we may have got such a reserved accumulated power as to run the earth off its track into a new orbit some summer, and so change the tedious vicissitude of the seasons?

Or, perchance, coming generations will not abide the dissolution of the globe, but availing themselves of future inventions in aerial locomotion and the navigation of space, the entire race may migrate from the earth, to settle some vacant and more western planet, it may be still healthy, perchance unearthy, not composed of dirt and stones whose primary strata only are strewn, and where no weeds are sown. It took but little art, a simple application of natural laws, a canoe, a paddle, and a sail of matting to people the isles of the Pacific, and a little more will people the shining isles of space. Do we not see in the firmament the light carried along the shore by night, as Columbus did? Let us not despair nor mutiny.

The dwellings also ought to be very different from what is known, if the full benefit of our means is to be enjoyed. They are to be of a structure for which we have no name yet. They are to be neither palaces, nor temples, nor cities but a combination of all, superior to whatever is known.

Earth may be baked into bricks, or even vitrified stone by heat — we may bake large masses of any size and form into stone and vitrified substance of the greatest durability, lasting even thousands of years, out of clayey earth, or of stone ground to dust, by the application of burning mirrors. This is to be done in the open air without other preparation than gathering the substance, grinding and mixing it with water and cement, molding or casting it, and bringing the focus of the burning mirrors of proper size upon the same.

The character of the architecture is to be quite different from what it ever has been hitherto; large solid masses are to be baked or cast in one piece, ready shaped in any form that may be desired. The building may, therefore, consist of columns 200 feet high and upward, of proportionate thickness, and of one entire piece of vitrified substance; huge pieces are to be molded so as to join and hook on to each other firmly, by proper joints and folds, and not to yield in any way without breaking.

Foundries, of any description, are to be heated by burning mirrors, and will require no labor, except the making of the first molds and the superintendence for gathering the metal and taking the finished articles away.

Alas! in the present state of science, we must take the finished articles away; but think not that man will always be the victim of circumstances.

The countryman who visited the city and found the streets cluttered with bricks and lumber reported that it was not yet finished; and one who considers the endless repairs and reforming of our houses might well wonder when they will be done. But why may not the dwellings of men on this earth be built, once for all, of some durable material, some Roman or Etruscan masonry, which will stand so that time shall only adorn and beautify them? Why may we not finish the outward world for posterity and leave them leisure to attend to the inner?

Surely, all the gross necessities and economies might be cared for in a few years. All might be built and baked and stored up during this, the termtime of the world, against the vacant eternity, and the globe go provisioned and furnished, like our public vessels, for its voyage through space, as through some Pacific Ocean, while we would "tie up the rudder and sleep before the wind," as those who sail from Lima to Manila.

But, to go back a few years in imagination, think not that life in these crystal palaces is to bear any analogy to life in our present humble cottages. Far from it. Clothed, once for all, in some "flexible stuff," more durable than George Fox's suit of leather, composed of "fibers of vegetables," "glutinated" together by some "cohesive substances," and made into sheets, like paper, of any size or form, man will put far from him corroding care and the whole host of ills.

The 25 halls in the inside of the square are to be each 200 feet square and high; the 40 corridors, each 100 feet long and 20 wide; the 80 galleries, each from 1,000 to 1,250 feet long; about 7,000 private rooms, the whole surrounded and intersected by the grandest and most splendid colonnades imaginable; floors, ceilings, columns, with their various beautiful and fanciful intervals, all shining and reflecting to infinity all objects and persons, with splendid luster of all beautiful colors, and fanciful shapes and pictures.

All galleries, outside and within the halls, are to be provided with many thousand commodious and most elegant vehicles in which persons may move up and down like birds, in perfect security and without exertion. Any member may procure himself all the common articles of his daily wants by a short turn of some crank, without leaving his apartment.

He may, at any time, bathe himself in cold or warm water, or in steam, or in some artificially prepared liquor for invigorating health. He may, at any time, give to the air in his apartment that temperature that suits his feeling best. He may cause, at any time, an agreeable scent of various kinds. He may, at any time, meliorate his breathing air — that main vehicle of vital power. Thus, by a proper application of the physical knowledge of our days, man may be kept in a perpetual serenity of mind, and if there is no incurable disease or defect in his organism, in constant vigor of health, and his life be prolonged beyond any parallel which present times afford.

One or two persons are sufficient to direct the kitchen business. They have nothing else to do but to superintend the cookery and to watch the time of the victuals being done, and then to remove them, with the table and vessels, into the dining hall, or to the respective private apartments, by a slight motion of the hand at some crank. Any extraordinary desire of any person may be satisfied by going to the place where the thing is to be had; and anything that requires a particular preparation in cooking or baking may be done by the person who desires it.

This is one of those instances in which the individual genius is found to consent, as indeed it always does, at last, with the universal. These last sentences have a certain sad and sober truth, which reminds us of the scripture of all nations. All expression of truth does at length take the deep ethical form. Here is hint of a place the most eligible of any in space, and of a servitor in comparison with whom all other helps dwindle into insignificance. We hope to hear more of him anon, for even a Crystal Palace would be deficient without his invaluable services.

And as for the environs of the establishment:

> There will be afforded the most enrapturing views to be fancied, out of the private apartments, from the galleries, from the roof, from its turrets and cupolas — gardens as far as the eye can see, full of fruits and flowers, arranged in the most beautiful order, with walks, colonnades, aqueducts, canals, ponds, plains, amphitheaters, terraces, fountains, sculptural works, pavilions, gondolas, places for public amusement, etc., to delight the eye and fancy, the taste and smell. . . .
>
> The walks and roads are to be paved with hard, vitrified large plates, so as to be always clean from all dirt in any weather or season. . . .
>
> The channels being of vitrified substance, and the water perfectly clear, and filtrated or distilled if required, may afford the most beautiful scenes imaginable, while a variety of fishes is seen clear down to the bottom playing about, and the canals may afford at the same time, the means of gliding smoothly along between various sceneries of art

and nature, in beautiful gondolas, while their surface and borders may be covered with fine land and aquatic birds. The walks may be covered with porticos adorned with magnificent columns, statues, and sculptural works; all of vitrified substance, and lasting forever, while the beauties of nature around heighten the magnificence and deliciousness.

> The night affords no less delight to fancy and feelings. An infinite variety of grand, beautiful, and fanciful objects and sceneries, radiating with crystalline brilliancy, by the illumination of gaslight; the human figures themselves, arrayed in the most beautiful pomp fancy may suggest, or the eye desire, shining even with brilliancy of stuffs and diamonds, like stones of various colors, elegantly shaped and arranged around the body; all reflected a thousandfold in huge mirrors and reflectors of various forms; theatrical scenes of a grandeur and magnificence and enrapturing illusions, unknown yet, in which any person may be either a spectator or actor; the speech and the songs reverberating with increased sound, rendered more sonorous and harmonious than by nature, by vaultings that are movable into any shape at any time; the sweetest and most impressive harmony of music produced by song and instruments partly not known yet, may thrill through the nerves and vary with other amusements and delights.
>
> At night the roof and the inside and outside of the whole square are illuminated by gaslight, which in the mazes of many-colored crystal-like colonnades and vaultings, is reflected with a brilliancy that gives to the whole a luster of precious stones, as far as the eye can see — such are the future abodes of men. . . .

Such is the life reserved to true intelligence but withheld from ignorance, prejudice, and stupid adherence to custom. . . .

Such is the domestic life to be enjoyed by every human individual that will partake of it. Love and affection may there be fostered and enjoyed without any of the obstructions that oppose, diminish, and destroy them in the present state of men. . . . It would be as ridiculous, then, to dispute and quarrel about the means of life as it would be now about water to drink along mighty rivers, or about the permission to breathe air in the atmosphere, or about sticks in our extensive woods.

Thus is Paradise to be Regained, and that old and stern decree at length reversed. Man shall no more earn his living by the sweat of his brow. All labor shall be reduced to "a short turn of some crank," and "taking the finished article away." But here is a crank — oh, how hard to be turned! Could there not be a crank upon a crank — an infinitely small crank? — we would fain inquire. No — alas! not. But here is a certain divine energy in every man, but sparingly employed as yet, which may be called the crank within — the crank after all — the prime mover in all machinery — quite indispensable to all work. Would that we might get our hands on its handle!

In fact, no work can be shirked. It may be postponed indefinitely, but not infinitely. Nor can any really important work be made easier by cooperation or machinery. Not one particle of labor now threatening any man can be routed without being performed. It cannot be hunted out of the vicinity like jackals and hyenas. It will not run. You may begin by sawing the little sticks, or you may saw the great sticks first, but sooner or later you must saw them both.

We will not be imposed upon by this vast application of forces. We believe that most things will have to be accomplished still by the application called "Industry." We are rather pleased, after all, to consider the small private, but both constant and accumulated, force which stands behind every spade in the field. This it is that makes the valleys shine and the deserts really bloom. Sometimes, we confess, we are so degenerate as to reflect with pleasure on the days when men were yoked like cattle and drew a crooked stick for a plow. After all, the great interests and methods were the same.

It is a rather serious objection to Mr. Etzler's schemes that they require time, men, and money, three very superfluous and inconvenient things for an honest and well-disposed man to deal with. "The whole world," he tells us, "might therefore be really changed into a paradise, within less than ten years, commencing from the first year of an association for the purpose of constructing and applying the machinery." We are sensible of a startling incongruity when time and money are mentioned in this connection. The ten years which are proposed would be a tedious while to wait if every man were at his post and did his duty, but quite too short a period if we are to take time for it. But this fault is by no means peculiar to Mr. Etzler's schemes.

There is far too much hurry and bustle, and too little patience and privacy, in all our methods, as if something were to be accomplished in centuries. The true reformer does not want time, nor money, nor cooperation, nor advice. What is time but the stuff delay is made of? And depend upon it, our virtue will not live on the interest of our money. He expects no income, but outgoes; so soon as we begin to count the cost, the cost begins. And as for advice, the information floating in the atmosphere of society is as evanescent and unserviceable to him as gossamer for clubs of Hercules.

There is absolutely no common sense; it is common nonsense. If we are to risk a cent or a drop of our blood, who then shall advise us? For ourselves, we are too young for experience. Who is old enough? We are older by faith than by experience. In the unbending of the arm to do the deed there is experience worth all the maxims in the world.

It will now be plainly seen that the execution of the proposals is not proper for individuals. Whether it be proper for government at this time, before the subject has become popular, is a question to be decided; all that is to be done is to step forth, after mature reflection, to confess loudly one's conviction, and to constitute societies. Man is powerful but in union with many. Nothing great, for the improvement of his own condition, or that of his fellowmen, can ever be effected by individual enterprise.

Alas! this is the crying sin of the age, this want of faith in the prevalence of a man. Nothing can be effected but by one man. He who wants help wants everything. True, this is the condition of our weakness, but it can never be the means of our recovery. We must first succeed alone, that we may enjoy our success together. We trust that the social movements which we witness indicate an aspiration not to be thus cheaply satisfied. In this matter of reforming the world, we have little faith in corporations; not thus was it first formed.

But our author is wise enough to say that the raw materials for the accomplishment of his purposes are "iron, copper, wood, earth chiefly, and a union of men whose eyes and understanding are not shut up by preconceptions." Aye, this last may be what we want mainly — a company of "odd fellows" indeed.

"Small shares of $20 will be sufficient" — in all, from "200,000 to 300,000" — "to create the first establishment for a whole community of from 3,000 to 4,000 individuals"; at the end of five years we shall have a principal of $200 million and so paradise will be wholly regained at the end of the tenth year. But, alas! the ten years have already elapsed, and there are no signs of Eden yet, for want of the requisite funds to begin the enterprise in a hopeful manner. Yet it seems a safe investment. Perchance they could be hired at a low rate, the property being mortgaged for security, and, if necessary, it could be given up in any stage of the enterprise, without loss, with the fixtures.

Mr. Etzler considers this "Address as a touchstone, to try whether our nation is in any way accessible to these great truths, for raising the human creature to a superior state of existence, in accordance with the knowledge and the spirit of the most culti-

vated minds of the present time." He has prepared a constitution, short and concise, consisting of twenty-one articles, so that wherever an association may spring up, it may go into operation without delay. . . .

But we see two main difficulties in the way: first, the successful application of the powers by machinery (we have not yet seen the *Mechanical System*); and, second, which is infinitely harder, the application of man to the work by faith. This it is, we fear, which will prolong the 10 years to 10,000 at least. It will take a power more than "80,000 times greater than all the men on earth could effect with their nerves" to persuade men to use that which is already offered them.

Even a greater than this physical power must be brought to bear upon that moral power. Faith, indeed, is all the reform that is needed; it is itself a reform. Doubtless, we are as slow to conceive of Paradise as of Heaven, of a perfect natural as of a perfect spiritual world. We see how past ages have loitered and erred. "Is perhaps our generation free from irrationality and error? Have we perhaps reached now the summit of human wisdom, and need no more to look out for mental or physical improvement?" Undoubtedly, we are never so visionary as to be prepared for what the next hour may bring forth. . . .

The Divine is about to be, and such is its nature. In our wisest moments we are secreting a matter which, like the lime of the shellfish, encrusts us quite over, and well for us if, like it, we cast our shells from time to time, though they be pearl and of fairest tint. Let us consider under what disadvantages science has hitherto labored before we pronounce thus confidently on her progress.

There was never any system in the productions of human labor, but they came into existence and fashion a chance directed men. Only a few professional men of learning occupy themselve with teaching natural philosophy, chem istry, and the other branches of the sciences of nature, to a very limited extent, for very limited purposes, with very limited means. The science of mechanics is but in a state of infancy. It is true, improvements are made upon improvements, instigated by patents of government; but they are made accidentally or at haphazard. There is no general system of this science, mathematical as it is, which develops its principles in their full extent, and the outlines of the application to which they lead. There is no idea of comparison between what is explored and what is yet to be explored in this science. The ancient Greeks placed mathematics at the head of their education. But we are glad to have filled our memory with notions, without troubling ourselves much with reasoning about them.

Mr. Etzler is not one of the enlightened practical men, the pioneers of the actual, who move with the slow, deliberate tread of science, conserving the world; who execute the dreams of the last century, though they have no dreams of their own; yet he deals in the very raw but still solid material of all inventions. He has more of the practical than usually belongs to so bold a schemer, so resolute a dreamer. Yet his success is in theory and not in practice, and he feeds our faith rather than contents our understanding. His book wants order, serenity, dignity, everything, but it does not fail to impart what only man can impart to man of much importance, his own faith. It is true his dreams are not thrilling nor bright enough, and he leaves off to dream where he who dreams just before the dawn begins. His castles in the air fall to the ground because they are not built lofty enough; they should be secured to heaven's roof.

After all, the theories and speculations of men concern us more than their puny execution. It is with a certain coldness and languor that we loiter about the actual and so-called practical. How little do the most wonderful inventions of modern times detain us. They insult nature. Every machine or particular application seems a slight outrage against universal laws. How many fine inventions are there which do not clutter the ground? We think that those only succeed which minister to our sensible and animal wants, which bake or brew, wash or warm, or the like. But are those of no account which are patented by fancy and imagination and succeed so admirably in our dreams that they give the tone still to our waking thoughts?

Already nature is serving all those uses which science slowly derives on a much higher and grander scale to him that will be served by her. When the sunshine falls on the path of the poet, he enjoys all those pure benefits and pleasures which the arts slowly and partially realize from age to age. The winds which fan his cheek waft him the sum of that profit and happiness which their lagging inventions supply.

The chief fault of this book is that it aims to secure the greatest degree of gross comfort and pleasure merely. It paints a Mahometan's heaven, and stops short with singular abruptness when we think it is drawing near to the precincts of the Christian's — and we trust we have not made here a distinction without a difference. Undoubtedly if we were to reform this outward life truly and thoroughly, we should find no duty of the inner omitted. It would be employment for our whole nature; and what we should do thereafter would be as vain a question as to ask the bird what it will do when its nest is built and its brood reared. But a moral reform must take place first, and then the necessity of the other will be superseded, and we shall sail and plow by its force alone.

There is a speedier way than the *Mechanical System* can show to fill up marshes, to drown the roar of the waves, to tame hyenas, secure agreeable environs, diversify the land, and refresh it with "rivulets of sweet water," and that is by the power of rectitude and true behavior. It is only for a little while, only occasionally, methinks, that we want a garden. Surely a good man need not be at the labor to level a hill for the sake of a prospect, or raise fruits and flowers, and construct floating islands for the sake of a paradise. He enjoys better prospects than lie behind any hill. Where an angel travels it will be paradise all the way, but where Satan travels it will be burning marl and cinders. What says Veeshnoo Sunma? "He whose mind is at ease is possessed of all riches. Is it not the same to one whose foot is enclosed in a shoe, as if the whole surface of the earth were covered with leather?"

He who is conversant with the supernal powers will not worship these inferior deities of the wind, the waves, tide, and sunshine. But we would not disparage the importance of such calculations as we have described. They are truths in physics, because they are true in ethics. The moral powers no one would presume to calculate. Suppose we could compare the moral with the physical, and say how many horsepower the force of love, for instance, blowing on every square foot of a man's soul, would equal. No doubt we are well aware of this force; figures would not increase our respect for it; the sunshine is equal to but one ray of its heat. The light of the sun is but the shadow of love.

"The souls of men loving and fearing God," says Raleigh, "receive influence from that divine light itself, whereof the sun's clarity, and that of the stars, is by Plato called but a shadow. *Lumen est umbra Dei, Deus est Lumen Luminis.* Light is the shadow of God's brightness, who is the light of light," and, we may add, the heat of heat. Love is the wind, the tide, the waves, the sunshine. Its power is incalculable; it is many horsepower. It never ceases, it never slacks; it can move the globe without a resting place; it can warm without fire; it can feed without meat; it can clothe without garments; it can shelter without roof; it can make a paradise within, which will dispense with a paradise without.

But though the wisest men in all ages have labored to publish this force, and every human heart is, sooner or later, more or less, made to feel it, yet how little is actually applied to social ends. True, it is the motive power of all successful social machinery; but, as in physics, we have made the elements do only a little drudgery for us — steam to take the place of a few horses, wind of a few oars, water of a few cranks and handmills — as the mechanical forces have not yet been generously and largely applied to make the physical world answer to the ideal, so the power of love has been but meanly and sparingly applied, as yet. It has patented only such machines as the almshouses, the hospital, and the Bible Society, while its infinite wind is still blowing and blowing down these very structures too, from time to time. Still less are we accumulating its power, and preparing to act with greater energy at a future time. Shall we not contribute our shares to this enterprise, then?

30.

Daniel Webster: On Securing Trade with China

Commercial relations with China began following the American Revolution and increased steadily during the first four decades of the nineteenth century. But because China desired no other involvements with the outside world, diplomatic relations had never been established. The Opium War between Britain and China led in 1842 to an end of China's policy of exclusion, and the Nanking Treaty ending that conflict was the first ever signed by China with any European power. In 1843 President Tyler's secretary of state, Daniel Webster, sent Caleb Cushing, a Massachusetts Whig, to China to secure by treaty trading privileges similar to those acquired by Britain. A portion of Webster's instructions of May 8, 1843, is reprinted below. The main objectives of the United States were attained in the Treaty of Wanghia, signed on July 3, 1844.

Source: 28 Congress, 2 Session, Senate Executive Document No. 138, pp. 1-5.

Occurrences happening in China within the last two years have resulted in events which are likely to be of much importance, as well to the United States as to the rest of the civilized world. Of their still more important consequences to China herself, it is not necessary here to speak. The hostilities which have been carried on between that empire and England have resulted, among other consequences, in opening four important ports to English commerce, viz.: Amoy, Ning-po, Shang-hai, and Fu-chow.

These ports belong to some of the richest, most productive, and most populous provinces of the empire, and are likely to become very important marts of commerce. A leading object of the mission in which you are now to be engaged is, to secure the entry of American ships and cargoes into these ports on terms as favorable as those which are enjoyed by English merchants. It is not necessary to dwell here on the great and well-known amount of imports of the productions of China into the United States. These imports, especially in the great article of tea, are not likely to be diminished.

Heretofore they have been paid for in the precious metals, or, more recently, by bills drawn on London. At one time, indeed, American paper, of certain descriptions, was found to be an available remittance. Latterly, a considerable trade has sprung up in the export of certain American manufactures to China. To augment these exports, by obtaining the most favorable commercial facilities, and cultivating, to the greatest extent practicable, friendly commercial intercourse with China, in all its accessible ports, is matter of moment to the commercial and manufacturing as well as the agricultural and mining interests of the United States. . . .

As your mission has in view only friendly and commercial objects — objects, it is supposed, equally useful to both countries — the natural jealousy of the Chinese, and their repulsive feeling toward foreigners, it is hoped, may be in some degree removed or mitigated by prudence and address on your part. Your constant aim must be to produce a full conviction on the minds of the government and the people, that your mission is entirely pacific; that you come with no purposes of hostility or annoyance; that you are a messenger of peace, sent from the greatest power in America to the greatest empire in Asia, to offer respect and goodwill, and to establish the means of friendly intercourse.

It will be expedient, on all occasions, to cultivate the friendly dispositions of the government and people, by manifesting a proper respect for their institutions and manners, and avoiding, as far as possible, the giving of offense either to their pride or their prejudices. You will use the earliest and all succeeding occasions to signify that the government which sends you has no disposition to encourage, and will not encourage, any violation of the commercial regulations of China, by citizens of the United States. . . .

A letter, signed by the President as above intimated, and addressed to the Emperor, will be placed in your hands. As has been already stated, you will say that this letter can only be delivered to the Emperor, or to some one of the great officers of state, in his presence. Nevertheless, if this cannot be done, and the Emperor should still manifest a desire to receive the letter, you may consider the propriety of sending it to him upon an assurance that a friendly answer to it shall be sent, signed by the hand of the Emperor himself.

It will be no part of your duty to enter into controversies which may exist between China and any European state; nor will you, in your communications, fail to abstain altogether from any sentiment or any expression which might give to other governments just cause of offense. It will be quite proper, however, that you should, in a proper manner, always keep before the eyes of the Chinese the high character, importance, and power, of the United States. You may speak of the extent of their territory, their great commerce spread over all seas, their powerful navy everywhere giving protection to that commerce, and the numerous schools and institutions established in them, to teach men knowledge and wisdom.

It cannot be wrong for you to make known, where not known, that the United States, once a country subject to England, threw off that subjection years ago, asserted its independence, sword in hand, established that independence after a seven years' war, and now meets England upon equal terms upon the ocean and upon the land. The remoteness of the United States from China, and still more the fact that they have no colonial possessions in her neighborhood, will naturally lead to the indulgence of a less suspicious and more friendly feeling than may have been entertained toward England, even before the late war between England and China.

It cannot be doubted that the immense power of England in India must be regarded by the Chinese government with dissatisfaction, if not with some degree of alarm. You will take care to show strongly how free the Chinese government may well be from all jealousy arising from such causes toward the United States. Finally, you will signify, in decided terms and a positive manner, that the government of the United States would find it impossible to remain on terms of friendship and regard with the Emperor, if greater privileges or commercial facilities should be allowed to the subjects of any other government than should be granted to citizens of the United States.

It is hoped and trusted that you will succeed in making a treaty such as has been concluded between England and China; and if one containing fuller and more regular stipulations could be entered into, it would be conducting Chinese intercourse one step further toward the principles which regulate the public relations of the European and American states.

31.

John Greenleaf Whittier: "Massachusetts to Virginia"

Whittier's own note tells the occasion of this, one of his best-known poems: "Written on reading an account of the proceedings of the citizens of Norfolk, Va., in reference to George Latimer, the alleged fugitive slave, who was seized in Boston without warrant at the request of James B. Grey, of Norfolk, claiming to be his master. The case caused great excitement North and South, and led to the presentation of a petition to Congress, signed by more than fifty thousand citizens of Massachusetts, calling for such laws and proposed amendments to the Constitution as should relieve the Commonwealth from all further participation in the crime of oppression. George Latimer himself was finally given free papers for the sum of four hundred dollars."

Source: *Complete Poetical Works*, Cambridge Edition, Boston, 1894.

MASSACHUSETTS TO VIRGINIA

The blast from Freedom's Northern hills, upon its Southern way,
Bears greeting to Virginia from Massachusetts Bay:
No word of haughty challenging, nor battle bugle's peal,
Nor steady tread of marching files, nor clang of horsemen's steel.

No trains of deep-mouthed cannon along our highways go;
Around our silent arsenals untrodden lies the snow;
And to the land-breeze of our ports, upon their errands far,
A thousand sails of commerce swell, but none are spread for war.

We hear thy threats, Virginia! thy stormy words and high
Swell harshly on the Southern winds which melt along our sky;
Yet, not one brown, hard hand forgoes its honest labor here,
No hewer of our mountain oaks suspends his axe in fear.

Wild are the waves which lash the reefs along St. George's bank;
Cold on the shores of Labrador the fog lies white and dank;
Through storm, and wave, and blinding mist, stout are the hearts which man
The fishing-smacks of Marblehead, the seaboats of Cape Ann.

The cold north light and wintry sun glare on their icy forms,
Bent grimly o'er their straining lines or wrestling with the storms;
Free as the winds they drive before, rough as the waves they roam,
They laugh to scorn the slaver's threat against their rocky home.

What means the Old Dominion? Hath she forgot the day
When o'er her conquered valleys swept the Briton's steel array?
How, side by side with sons of hers, the Massachusetts men
Encountered Tarleton's charge of fire and stout Cornwallis, then?

Forgets she how the Bay State, in answer to the call
Of her old House of Burgesses, spoke out from Faneuil Hall?
When, echoing back her Henry's cry, came pulsing on each breath
Of Northern winds, the thrilling sounds of "Liberty or Death!"

What asks the Old Dominion? If now her sons have proved
False to their fathers' memory, false to the faith they loved;
If she can scoff at Freedom, and its great charter spurn,
Must we of Massachusetts from truth and duty turn?

We hunt your bondmen, flying from Slavery's hateful hell;
Our voices, at your bidding, take up the bloodhound's yell;
We gather, at your summons, above our fathers' graves,
From Freedom's holy altar-horns to tear your wretched slaves!

Thank God! not yet so vilely can Massachusetts bow;
The spirit of her early time is with her even now;
Dream not because her Pilgrim blood moves slow and calm and cool,
She thus can stoop her chainless neck, a sister's slave and tool!

All that a sister State should do, all that a free State may,
Heart, hand, and purse we proffer, as in our early day;
But that one dark loathsome burden ye must stagger with alone,
And reap the bitter harvest which ye yourselves have sown!

Hold, while ye may, your struggling slaves, and burden God's free air
With woman's shriek beneath the lash, and manhood's wild despair;
Cling closer to the "cleaving curse" that writes upon your plains
The blasting of Almighty wrath against a land of chains.

Still shame your gallant ancestry, the cavaliers of old,
By watching round the shambles where human flesh is sold;
Gloat o'er the new-born child, and count his market value, when
The maddened mother's cry of woe shall pierce the slaver's den!

Lower than plummet soundeth, sink the Virginia name;
Plant, if ye will, your fathers' graves with rankest weeds of shame;
Be, if ye will, the scandal of God's fair universe;
We wash our hands forever of your sin and shame and curse.

A voice from lips whereon the coal from Freedom's shrine hath been,
Thrilled, as but yesterday, the hearts of Berkshire's mountain men:

The echoes of that solemn voice are sadly lingering still
In all our sunny valleys, on every windswept hill.

And when the prowling man-thief came hunting for his prey
Beneath the very shadow of Bunker's shaft of gray,
How, through the free lips of the son, the father's warning spoke;
How, from its bonds of trade and sect, the Pilgrim city broke!

A hundred thousand right arms were lifted up on high,
A hundred thousand voices sent back their loud reply;
Through the thronged towns of Essex the startling summons rang.
And up from bench and loom and wheel her young mechanics sprang!

The voice of free, broad Middlesex, of thousands as of one,
The shaft of Bunker calling to that of Lexington;
From Norfolk's ancient villages, from Plymouth's rocky bound
To where Nantucket feels the arms of ocean close her round;

From rich and rural Worcester, where through the calm repose
Of cultured vales and fringing woods the gentle Nashua flows,
To where Wachuset's wintry blasts the mountain larches stir,
Swelled up to Heaven the thrilling cry of "God save Latimer!"

And sandy Barnstable rose up, wet with the salt sea spray;
And Bristol sent her answering shout down Narragansett Bay!
Along the broad Connecticut old Hampden felt the thrill,
And the cheer of Hampshire's woodmen swept down from Holyoke Hill.

The voice of Massachusetts! Of her free sons and daughters,
Deep calling unto deep aloud, the sound of many waters!
Against the burden of that voice what tyrant power shall stand?
No fetters in the Bay State! No slave upon her land!

Look to it well, Virginians! In calmness we have borne,
In answer to our faith and trust, your insult and your scorn;
You've spurned our kindest counsels; you've hunted for our lives;
And shaken round our hearths and homes your manacles and gyves!

We wage no war, we lift no arm, we fling no torch within
The fire-damps of the quaking mine beneath your soil of sin;
We leave ye with your bondmen, to wrestle, while ye can,
With the strong upward tendencies and godlike soul of man!

But for us and for our children, the vow which we have given
For freedom and humanity, is registered in heaven;
No slave-hunt in our borders — no pirate on our strand!
No fetters in the Bay State — no slave upon our land!

1844

32.

Anonymous: Criticism of the Native American Party

Local anti-immigrant or nativist parties were organized throughout the United States in the 1830s and 1840s and were especially powerful in New York City, where they had Whig support. Although workers were beginning to object to the competition of immigrants, it was the land reform or agrarian movement, spearheaded by George Henry Evans, that won the support of labor in the 1840s. Agrarians contended that if limited amounts of free land were offered to all those who would settle it, the troubles of workingmen would be ended. Agrarianism was opposed to nativism and in fact drew support from immigrant groups, especially the Germans. The Working Man's Advocate, *in which the following critique of the Nativist Party was printed in March 1844, was a land reform newspaper established by Evans.*

Source: *Working Man's Advocate*, March 23, 1844 [Commons, VII, p. 90].

The Native American Party. What has given rise to the new party now organized in this city and two or three other places under the above name? Evidently, an influx of foreign labor into a market already overstocked. The existence of this conspicuous evil is clearly the motive of those who form the body, the rank and file, of the Native American Party. The officers and leaders of the party, who are chiefly composed of the disappointed office seekers of the other parties, are incensed against the foreign population for the very disinterested reason that their occupation of office seeking has been encroached upon by adopted citizens. Another truth connected with this subject is that both of the old parties have, to curry favor with the foreign-born interest, freely dealt out to them the bribe of petty offices in order to secure their influence and votes for offices of more importance.

This state of things has very naturally led to the formation of the Native American Party. The body of the party, the suffering working classes, smarting under the effects of competition and justly incensed to see foreigners promoted to office merely because they are foreigners, are led on by men to expect a distribution of the city offices as a reward of victory. . . . Let no working-man be deluded with the idea that, even could the measures of the Native American Party, the exclusion of foreigners from the polls and from office, be accomplished, one cent would be added to their daily pittance or one hour's labor more secured to them. . . .

The plain and simple remedy for the real evils complained of by the Native Americans is to free the country from the curse of speculation in land and let the people go and cultivate the people's farm.

33.

NATHAN APPLETON: Labor and Wealth in Europe and America

The following selection originally appeared in Hunt's Merchants' Magazine, *an influential journal that, from 1839 to 1870, reflected the commercial point of view. Its author, Nathan Appleton, was a progressive Whig politician and industrialist who had helped to found the industrial enterprises at what later became Lowell, Massachusetts, and who demonstrated a concern for the welfare of labor throughout his career. The early history of the American labor movement was influenced by theories formulated in Europe, where labor constituted a social caste. Whigs endeavored to inculcate a new conception of labor in America.*

Source: *Labor, Its Relations in Europe and the United States Compared,* Boston, 1844.

WEALTH IS POWER. Its influence on society, on the character of man is the subject of frequent contemplation and examination, in all its aspects. Its possessor is the object of envy and flattery, while, in its original humble state of labor, it is passed by almost without notice, except sometimes a sigh of pity for its hardships.

Nothing is more striking than the distinction made, more especially in Europe, between labor in possession and labor in action; in other words, between capital and labor. In Europe, and especially in England, we find the inheritor of wealth, of the accumulated labor of others looking down with something like contempt, not only on labor itself in its lowest form of mere manual occupation but on all those employments whose object is the immediate accumulation of property. The possession, by the accident of birth, of wealth produced by the labor of others is held vastly more honorable than the creation of wealth by one's own labor.

In the United States it is quite otherwise. With all our inheritance of British notions and prejudices, there is nothing more striking than the change which has taken place in this country in the estimation of wealth derived by inheritance or acquired by the possessor himself. Here, all our wealth has been produced by direct labor. It has grown up in our sight, and it is impossible to attach any higher honor to him who obtains it by accident than to him who possesses it by his own acquisition.

On the contrary, the inheritor of a fortune in this country is judged wholly by the use which he makes of it. It gives him no advantage in the public estimation, any further than his own character will sustain itself independently of this circumstance.

It is not difficult to perceive the causes which have produced this different estimate of the character of labor in action, in connection with individual respectability, in the two hemispheres.

It is an interesting inquiry; still more so is an examination how far this difference of estimate is among the most active causes in giving an impress to society in America essentially different from its character in Europe. There is no circumstance in our institutions more deserving the attention of the philosophic observer. . . .

The founders of the American colonies brought with them neither wealth nor titles of nobility. They had no accumulated stores of either wealth or honors on which to subsist. Nature offered them this fertile domain on the sole condition of appropriation by labor. Their earliest political institutions, establishing perfect equality, left no avenue open to wealth or power but labor. Under these circumstances, it followed, of course, that active industry should be in the highest esteem. Industry was the only road to wealth, and wealth is power in every part of the world. There are instances of fortunes accumulated in large masses during the life of an individual, but, subject to our laws of equal distribution, they are sure to be absorbed or dissipated in the course of one or two generations.

In this state of things, it is not surprising that the acquisition of property by one's own labor and skill should be held in equal, or even higher, estimation than the inheritance by the accident of birth. It is true that the sons of the rich usually receive a better education than their fathers; and we award higher honors to the successful efforts of intellect than to those of mere industry in the accumulation of wealth. Such an estimation is, however, wholly founded on personal character.

Manual labor has a position with us which it has never possessed in any period of the world.

Agricultural labor is, in a very great measure, performed by the owners of the soil and their sons. The universal diffusion of education places our mechanics higher in the scale of intelligence than the same class has ever stood in any country. They have the elements of character which enable them to rise to any position in society.

The high reward of labor in all its branches is the great, the important distinction which diffuses comfort, intelligence and self-respect through the whole mass of the community, in a degree unknown in the previous history of civilization.

Titles of nobility we have none. We attach no respect to birth. The highest office in our little Army, and even of our Navy are of no peculiar esteem. There is a struggle for the highest political places. At the same time, political office does not, of course, carry with it a high degree of public estimation. Occupation, labor is the natural lot of all. The eloquent advocate, the learned divine, the able writer, the successful merchant, manufacturer, or agriculturist are allotted the highest places in society. These places are only obtained through an active and successful industry. We have no class, as in all the countries of Europe, born to a life of leisure, to honors and distinctions. A few sons of the rich inherit fortunes which enable them to dispense with labor or profitable occupation; but they cannot be said to constitute a class, and the wisest of them, by a sort of necessity, adopt a literary or other useful employment. Th mere possession of wealth without personal character is as little valued in this as in any other country.

It will thus be seen that the whole fabric of our society is essentially different from any which has preceded it. Society in England consists of the favored few, born to ease and independence, constituting the nobility and gentry. To them everything is subservient; from them everything takes its tone. Travelers of this class find in America a lower civilization in our highest classes than belongs to the upper class in England.

It is true, ours is a working-day world. We cannot adopt the hours nor many of the customs or opinions of a state of existence which has no counterpart among us. The attempt at imitation, which sometimes prevails, is a mistake and a blunder. We should do better to make our manners and opinions conform to our actual position, less influenced by those of Europe. There is enough in our position to be satisfied with — a diffusion of the comforts and even elegancies of life, through the whole mass of our population, in a degree never before seen. This is the result of a universal and well-paid industry.

Ours is a great novel experiment in politics and civilization. Whatever the result, it is our destiny to make it. It is our mission; our care should be to understand it and make it succeed. It is an attempt to amalgamate, equalize, and improve the whole mass of population by elevating the lower portions from their usual abject state and depressing the higher in dispensing with a privileged aristocracy. The process consists in the higher reward and higher estimation of labor, with the assurance of enjoying its own fruits.

There is another point of view in which this difference in the actual condition of our labor, compared with that of Europe, involves most important consequences; that is,

in connection with the science of political economy.

The modern school of political economy is founded on the theory of Malthus on population. That theory, as is well known, supposes a tendency in the human race to increase in population in proportion to the means of subsistence, and that that tendency is kept in check by the deficiency of those means, except during the existence of peculiar circumstances, which form an exception to the general rule. This theory, in its application to fully peopled countries with a circumscribed territory, like the British islands, is undoubtedly true; but the manner in which Malthus undertook to account for it involved the theory in some discredit which does not belong to it. He undertook to account for it by the different ratios in which population and subsistence naturally increase, applying a geometrical ratio to the former and the slower arithmetical ratio to the latter. It was a fanciful idea, but wholly false and absurd in its application.

With room for expansion, food is increased more rapidly than population, as is abundantly proved in the United States. Where there is no power of expansion the greater power of increase in food is kept in check, as well as the lesser tendency in population. By this theory of Malthus, population is constantly pressing on the means of supporting life; that is to say, a portion of the human race, in its natural condition in every country, is in an actual state or immediate danger of starvation. In this extremity there is a constant struggle on the part of laborers to obtain employment as the means of preserving life by their wages. This struggle is supposed to keep wages at the lowest point which will actually support the life of the laborer and his family. This point is thus taken to be the natural rate of wages.

The history of labor, as far as we can follow it during the whole course of European civilization, and its present actual state in

Europe, and especially in England, furnish but too sad a confirmation of the fact that this has been and now is its actual condition.

This then is taken to be the natural state of labor — a power seeking employment beyond the means of finding it, which are limited by the amount of capital devoted to this object in the payment of wages. This low and abject state of labor is the original principle from which McCulloch, Ricardo, Senior, and others of the modern school of economists have drawn most important conclusions as the foundation of their system.

Labor is thus an indefinite quantity, limited in its action by the capital devoted to its maintenance. Without capital to set it in motion it is an inert mass, useless and impotent. A result of this view is that the increase of wealth in a community goes wholly to the owner of the capital as his profits. The laborer, obliged to be content with a subsistence, is not supposed capable of any accumulation. This is the rule, subject, of course, to occasional exceptions. It is, however, on this axiom as its cornerstone that the whole modern doctrine of free trade rests. The question is the increase of national wealth.

It being admitted that profits go wholly to the owners of the capital employing labor and no part of this accumulation to the laborer himself, it follows that legislative interference can only change the application of capital from one object to another without increasing the quantity of labor which it sets in motion; and this change is sure to be from a more profitable application to one less so, since the sagacity of the capitalist, without this interference, would be sure to lead him to the most profitable employment of his capital. Hence is deduced another proposition — that no act of legislation can create wealth.

It requires little observation to perceive that views founded on such premises have no application to us. The unlimited quantity of fertile land placed within the reach of every individual is the distinguishing peculiarity of our situation in an economical point of view. This furnishes to labor the easy means of subsistence and may be considered the controlling cause, whose effects are to be traced through all the ramifications of our society. This establishes the high reward, or wages of labor, elevating the lowest laborer from the position of a mere machine, where the modern school of political economy has placed him, to one in which he becomes at his own will the possessor of capital. The labor of a single year gives to every laborer, if he choose to save his earnings, a very considerable capital. He takes at his pleasure a place in society.

It is true that the United States may be said to form an exception to the general rule, arising from the circumstance of their containing a quantity of unimproved land; but since this condition, which forms the exception, this power of expansion will necessarily continue for one or more centuries, it is sufficient for our present government and we should be cautious in adopting as rules of action theories of political economy drawn from a state of society so different from our own. They have no application to us.

When we see a house erected out of the clay of our fields and the wood of our forests, we perceive that there has been a creation of wealth; when we see that this creation has been shared by the brickmaker, the mason, and the carpenter, we cannot but laugh to scorn those theories which tell us that labor cannot accumulate capital. We see the thing done before our eyes.

With us labor is, in fact, the great accumulator. It goes to work without difficulty on its own account. It is, therefore, perfectly clear that that legislation which calls most labor into action, which gives it its fullest scope is with us most productive of wealth. The doctrine of free trade is found ed upon the assumption that labor is everywhere in excess, waiting to be employed by capital; in itself powerless, dependent, only asking to live. With us labor assumes a higher tone: it treats with capital on equal terms; it shares in the profits hand in hand with capital.

The protective system rests as its basis on the principle of an enlarged field for labor, resulting from that legislation which restricts or shuts out the competition of the cheaper and more degraded labor of Europe.

The opposition comes from capital, which alleges that this system gives to labor too great an advantage, in the power of levying a contribution in the prices of the commodities consumed by capital. The answer is that, with us labor and capital are so mixed together that, in the general prosperity resulting from an active, well-paid industry, capital is sure to get its share.

All writers on political economy recognize the high reward of labor as indicating the highest measure of general prosperity. It elevates the industrial classes in the scale of society by giving them a power and a taste in the enjoyments of civilized life and in the cultivation of their minds. With us it does more; in addition to all this it enables them to lay by a surplus as capital.

Our great advantage lies in the abundance and cheapness of our lands. This gives to the immediate tiller of the soil an easier and more abundant subsistence than can be obtained by the same labor in any other part of the world. But he requires other enjoyments than food, and the whole question is, how can these be supplied in the manner most conducive to the wealth and happiness of the whole country? It would seem to be a simple proposition that the application of a portion of our labor to the working up the raw materials which we produce into the manufactures which we consume must be the simplest and most direct mode of equalizing and diffusing the peculiar advantage which we possess in the abundance of food through all classes of society.

As a question of political economy, of the increase of national wealth, the whole consists in the inquiry whether this system does not call into action a greater amount of labor than would find employment without it? The answer would seem to be easy, and plain common sense can hardly mistake it. With the assurance of a home market, both capital and labor set freely to work to supply it.

The question is frequently complicated by the inquiry why we should make at home what we can buy cheaper from abroad? This is a question which can only be put by capital. There is nothing cheaper to labor which is purchased by idleness. A nation can buy nothing cheap which slackens the arm of its industry. The term "cheap," in such a case, has no application. The matter is only confused by reference to a money price. The real question is the best application of labor.

It is thus apparent how different is the position of labor in the United States, in relation to the science of political economy, compared with labor in England. Free trade in England is quite a different affair from free trade in the United States. Its great effort in England is directed against the Corn Laws. It is labor striving for cheaper food against a landed monopoly. It rests there on the same principle as the protective system with us — the benefit of labor. It is there resisting a monopoly against itself. It here establishes a monopoly in its own favor, if one may be allowed to apply the term to an object so universal.

It will be seen at once that both socially and politically the position of labor in this country opens a wide field for speculation and observation. We are, in this respect, a world by ourselves. The country of Europe which approximates nearest to us, theoretically, is France, since the Revolution. She has abolished the right of primogeniture and her peerage is a mere shadow; but, with a crowded population and so many old prejudices remaining, labor will find it a hard struggle to acquire much estimation there. Military glory, military command will continue to be awarded the highest honors in France, as at all the courts of the Continent, as the best security of their thrones.

It is true the present is a new era in Europe. The last half century has developed industrial power, under the direction of science, in a degree which has no parallel in previous history. This power has brought, and will continue to bring into existence a mass of wealth capable of maintaining a claim for influence with the landed interest, which has heretofore been supreme. It has already produced a considerable change in raising the industrious classes in public estimation. But there is a wide gulf in public opinion, which will continue to separate Europe and the United States in their estimates of labor and industrious occupation, and which will endure as long as their different institutions of government.

34.

Daniel Webster: For Reform of the Naturalization Laws

Lax enforcement of naturalization laws made it possible for unscrupulous politicians who needed votes to see to it that large numbers of immigrants were illegally "naturalized" almost as soon as they arrived in the country. To remedy such practices, Daniel Webster proposed in the following remarks to Boston Whigs, in November 1844, that the naturalization laws be reformed. His address was delivered shortly after the Democrat James K. Polk had defeated the Whig Henry Clay for the presidency by the narrow margin of only 38,000 votes. Webster later claimed that fraudulent votes cast for the Democrats by speedily "naturalized" citizens in Pennsylvania and New York were the factor that cost the Whigs the election.

Source: John P. Sanderson, *Republican Landmarks: The Views and Opinions of American Statesmen on Foreign Immigration,* Philadelphia, 1856, pp. 323-324.

THE RESULT of the recent elections in several states has impressed my mind with one deep and strong conviction: that is, that there is an imperative necessity for reforming the naturalization laws of the United States. The preservation of the government, and consequently the interest of all parties, in my opinion, clearly and strongly demand this.

All are willing and desirous, of course, that America should continue to be the safe asylum for the oppressed of all nations. All are willing and desirous that the blessings of a free government should be open to the enjoyment of the worthy and industrious from all countries who may come hither for the purpose of bettering their circumstances by the successful employment of their own capital, enterprise, or labor. But it is not unreasonable that the elective franchise should not be exercised by a person of a foreign birth until after such a length of residence among us as that he may be supposed to have become, in some good measure, acquainted with our Constitution and laws, our social institutions, and the general interest of the country; and to have become an American in feeling, principle, character, and sympathy, as well as by having established his domicile among us.

Those already naturalized have, of course, their rights secured; but I can conceive no reasonable objection to the different provision in regard to future cases. It is absolutely necessary, also, in my judgment, to provide new securities against the abominable frauds, the outrageous, flagrant perjuries which are notoriously perpetrated in all the great cities. There is not the slightest doubt that in numerous cases different persons vote on the strength of the same set of naturalization papers; there is as little doubt that immense numbers of such papers are obtained by direct perjury; and that these enormous offenses multiply and strengthen themselves beyond all power of punishment and restraint by existing provisions.

I believe it to be an unquestionable fact that masters of vessels, having brought over immigrants from Europe, have, within thirty days of their arrival, seen those persons carried up to the polls and give their votes for the highest offices in the national and state governments. Such voters, of course, exercise no intelligence and, indeed, no volition of their own. They can know nothing either of the questions in issue or of the candidates proposed. They are mere instruments used by unprincipled and wicked men, and made competent instruments only by the accumulation of crime upon crime.

Now it seems to me impossible that every honest man and every good citizen, every true lover of liberty and the Constitution, every real friend of the country, would not desire to see an end put to these enormous abuses. I avow it, therefore, as my opinion that it is the duty of us all to endeavor to bring about an efficient reformation of the naturalization laws of the United States.

I am well aware, gentlemen, that these sentiments may be misrepresented, and probably will be, in order to excite prejudice in the mind of foreign residents. Should such misrepresentations be made or attempted, I trust to my friends to correct it and expose it. For the sentiments themselves I am ready to take to *myself* the responsibility, and I will only add that what I have now suggested is just as important to the rights of foreigners, regularly and fairly naturalized among us, as to the rights of native-born American citizens. [*The whole assembly here united in giving twenty-six tremendous cheers.*]

The present condition of the country imperatively demands this change. The interest, the real welfare of all parties, the honor of the nation all require that subordinate and different party questions should be made to yield to this great end. And no man who esteems the prosperity and existence of his country as of more importance than a fleeting party triumph will or can hesitate to give in his adherence to these principles. [*Nine cheers.*]

Gentlemen, there is not a solitary doubt that if the elections have gone against us it has been through false and fraudulent votes. Pennsylvania, if, as they say, she has given 6,000 for our adversaries, has done so through the basest fraud. Is it not so? And look at New York. In the city there were thrown 60,000 votes, or one vote to every five inhabitants. You know that, fairly and honestly, there can be no such thing on earth. [*Cheers.*] And the great remedy is for us to go directly to the source of true popular power and to purify the elections. [*Twenty-six cheers.*]

Fellow citizens, I profess to be a lover of human liberty, especially to be devoted to the grand example of freedom set forth by the republic under which we live. But I profess my heart, my reputation, my pride of character, to be American.

35.

Nathaniel Hawthorne: Earth's Holocaust

Earth's Holocaust was originally published in Graham's Magazine in 1844, and republished in 1846 in the collection, Mosses from an Old Manse. In the parable, Hawthorne satirized the superficial efforts of the reformers of his day, who in neglecting to reform the inner man left the greater work undone. Though Hawthorne had some acquaintance with politics through his friendship with Franklin Pierce and his acceptance of minor patronage positions, he was not a political activist. Nor did he associate himself with any of the reform movements of his time.

Source: *Graham's Magazine*, May 1844.

ONCE UPON A TIME — but whether in the time past or time to come is a matter of little or no moment — this wide world had become so overburdened with an accumulation of worn-out trumpery that the inhabitants determined to rid themselves of it by a general bonfire. The site fixed upon at the representation of the insurance companies, and as being as central a spot as any other on the globe, was one of the broadest prairies of the West, where no human habitation would be endangered by the flames and where a vast assemblage of spectators might commodiously admire the show. Having a taste for sights of this kind and, imagining likewise, that the illumination of the bonfire might reveal some profundity of moral truth heretofore hidden in mist or darkness, I made it convenient to journey thither and be present.

At my arrival, although the heap of condemned rubbish was as yet comparatively small, the torch had already been applied. Amid that boundless plain, in the dusk of the evening, like a far-off star alone in the firmament, there was merely visible one tremulous gleam, whence none could have anticipated so fierce a blaze as was destined to ensue. With every moment, however, there came foot travelers, women holding up their aprons, men on horseback, wheelbarrows, lumbering baggage wagons, and other vehicles, great and small, and from far and near, laden with articles that were judged fit for nothing but to be burned.

"What materials have been used to kindle the flame?" inquired I of a bystander; for I was desirous of knowing the whole process of the affair from beginning to end.

The person whom I addressed was a grave man, fifty years old or thereabout, who had evidently come thither as a looker-on. He struck me immediately as having weighed for himself the true value of life and its circumstances and therefore as feeling little personal interest in whatever judgment the world might form of them. Before answering my question, he looked me in the face by the kindling light of the fire.

"Oh, some very dry combustibles," replied he, "and extremely suitable to the purpose — no other, in fact, than yesterday's newspapers, last month's magazines and last year's withered leaves. Here now comes some antiquated trash that will take fire like a handful of shavings."

As he spoke some rough looking men advanced to the verge of the bonfire and threw in, as it appeared, all the rubbish of the herald's office — the blazonry of coa armor, the crests and devices of illustrious families, pedigrees that extended back, like lines of light, into the mist of the Dark Ages, together with stars, garters, and embroidered collars, each of which, as paltry a bauble as it might appear to the uninstructed eye, had once possessed vast significance and was still, in truth, reckoned among the most precious of moral or material facts by the worshipers of the gorgeous past. Mingled with this confused heap, which was tossed into the flames by armfuls at once, were innumerable badges of knighthood, comprising those of all the European sovereignties, and Napoleon's decoration of the Legion of Honor, the ribbons of which were entangled with those of the ancient Order of St. Louis.

There, too, were the medals of our own Society of Cincinnati, by means of which, as history tells us, an order of hereditary knights came near being constituted out of the king quellers of the Revolution, And, besides, there were the patents of nobility of German counts and barons, Spanish grandees, and English peers, from the worm-eaten instrument signed by William the Conqueror down to the brand-new parchment of the latest lord who has received his honors from the fair hand of Victoria.

At sight of the dense volumes of smoke, mingled with vivid jets of flame, that gushed and eddied forth from this immense pile of earthly distinctions, the multitude of plebeian spectators set up a joyous shout and clapped their hands with an emphasis that made the welkin echo. That was their moment of triumph, achieved, after long ages, over creatures of the same clay and the same spiritual infirmities, who had dared to assume the privileges due only to Heaven's better workmanship.

But now there rushed toward the blazing heap a gray-haired man, of stately presence, wearing a coat from the breast of which some stars, or other badge of rank, seemed to have been forcibly wrenched away. He had not the tokens of intellectual power in his face; but still there was the demeanor, the habitual and almost native dignity, of one who had been born to the idea of his own social superiority and had never felt it questioned till that moment.

"People," cried he, gazing at the ruin of what was dearest to his eyes with grief and wonder, but nevertheless with a degree of stateliness, "people, what have you done! This fire is consuming all that marked your advance from barbarism, or that could have prevented your relapse thither. We, the men of the privileged orders, were those who kept alive, from age to age, the old chivalrous spirit; the gentle and generous thought; the higher, the purer, the more refined and delicate life. With the nobles, too, you cast off the poet, the painter, the sculptor — all the beautiful arts; for we were their patrons and created the atmosphere in which they flourish. In abolishing the majestic distinctions of rank, society loses not only its grace but its steadfastness."

More he would doubtless have spoken; but here there arose an outcry, sportive, contemptuous, and indignant, that altogether drowned the appeal of the fallen nobleman, insomuch that, casting one look of despair at his own half-burned pedigree, he shrunk back into the crowd, glad to shelter himself under his newfound insignificance.

"Let him thank his stars that we have not flung him into the same fire!" shouted a rude figure, spurning the embers with his foot. "And henceforth let no man dare to show a piece of musty parchment as his warrant for lording it over his fellows! If he have strength of arm, well and good; it is one species of superiority. If he have wit, wisdom, courage, force of character, let these attributes do for him what they may; but from this day forward no mortal must hope for place and consideration by reckoning up the moldy bones of his ancestors. That nonsense is done away."

"And in good time," remarked the grave observer by my side, in a low voice, however, "if no worse nonsense comes in its place; but, at all events, this species of nonsense has fairly lived out its life."

There was little space to muse or moralize over the embers of this time-honored rubbish; for, before it was half burned out, there came another multitude from beyond the sea bearing the purple robes of royalty, and the crowns, globes, and scepters of emperors and kings. All these had been condemned as useless baubles, playthings at best, fit only for the infancy of the world, or rods to govern and chastise it in its nonage, but with which universal manhood at its full-grown stature could no longer brook to be insulted. Into such contempt had these regal insignia now fallen that the gilded crown and tinseled robes of the player king from Drury Lane Theatre had been thrown in among the rest, doubtless as a mockery of his brother monarchs on the great stage of the world.

It was a strange sight to discern the crown jewels of England glowing and flashing in the midst of the fire. Some of them had been delivered down from the time of the Saxon princes; others were purchased with vast revenues, or perchance ravished from the dead brows of the native potentates of Hindustan; and the whole now blazed with a dazzling luster, as if a star had fallen in that spot and been shattered into fragments. The splendor of the ruined monarchy had no reflection save in those inestimable precious stones.

But enough on this subject. It were but tedious to describe how the emperor of Austria's mantle was converted to tinder, and how the posts and pillars of the French throne became a heap of coals which it was impossible to distinguish from those of any other wood. Let me add, however, that I noticed one of the exiled Poles stirring up the bonfire with the czar of Russia's scepter, which he afterward flung into the flames.

"The smell of singed garments is quite intolerable here," observed my new acquaintance, as the breeze enveloped us in the smoke of a royal wardrobe. "Let us get to windward and see what they are doing on the other side of the bonfire."

We accordingly passed around and were just in time to witness the arrival of a vast procession of Washingtonians — as the votaries of temperance call themselves nowadays — accompanied by thousands of the Irish disciples of Father Mathew, with that great apostle at their head. They brought a rich contribution to the bonfire — being nothing less than all the hogsheads and barrels of liquor in the world, which they rolled before them across the prairie.

"Now, my children," cried Father Mathew, when they reached the verge of the fire, "one shove more, and the work is done! And now let us stand off and see Satan deal with his own liquor!"

Accordingly, having placed their wooden vessels within reach of the flames, the procession stood off at a safe distance and soon beheld them burst into a blaze that reached the clouds and threatened to set the sky itself on fire. And well it might; for here was the whole world's stock of spirituous liquors which, instead of kindling a frenzied light in the eyes of individual topers as of yore, soared upward with a bewildering gleam that startled all mankind. It was the aggregate of that fierce fire which would otherwise have scorched the hearts of millions.

Meantime, numberless bottles of precious wine were flung into the blaze, which lapped up the contents as if it loved them, and grew, like other drunkards, the merrier and fiercer for what it quaffed. Never again will the insatiable thirst of the fire fiend be so pampered! Here were the treasures of famous bon vivants — liquors that had been tossed on [the] ocean, and mellowed in the sun, and hoarded long in the recesses of the earth, the pale, the gold, the ruddy juice of whatever vineyards were most delicate, the entire vintage of Tokay — all mingling in one stream with the vile fluids of the common pothouse and contributing to heighten the selfsame blaze. And while it rose in a gigantic spire that seemed to wave against the arch of the firmament and combine itself with the light of stars, the multitude gave a shout as if the broad earth were exulting in its deliverance from the curse of ages.

But the joy was not universal. Many deemed that human life would be gloomier than ever when that brief illumination should sink down. While the reformers were at work, I overheard muttered expostulations from several respectable gentlemen with red noses and wearing gouty shoes; and a ragged worthy, whose face looked like a hearth where the fire is burned out, now expressed his discontent more openly and boldly.

"What is this world good for," said the last toper, "now that we can never be jolly any more? What is to comfort the poor man in sorrow and perplexity? How is he to keep his heart warm against the cold winds of this cheerless earth? And what do you propose to give him in exchange for the solace that you take away? How are old friends to sit together by the fireside without a cheerful glass between them? A plague upon your reformation! It is a sad world, a cold world, a selfish world, a low world, not worth an honest fellow's living in, now that good fellowship is gone forever!"

This harangue excited great mirth among the bystanders; but, preposterous as was the sentiment, I could not help commiserating the forlorn condition of the last toper, whose boon companions had dwindled away from his side, leaving the poor fellow without a soul to countenance him in sipping his liquor nor, indeed, any liquor to sip. Not that this was quite the true state of

the case; for I had observed him at a critical moment filch a bottle of fourth-proof brandy that fell beside the bonfire and hide it in his pocket.

The spirituous and fermented liquors being thus disposed of, the zeal of the reformers next induced them to replenish the fire with all the boxes of tea and bags of coffee in the world. And now came the planters of Virginia, bringing their crops and tobacco. These, being cast upon the heap of inutility, aggregated it to the size of a mountain, and incensed the atmosphere with such potent fragrance that methought we should never draw pure breath again. The present sacrifice seemed to startle the lovers of the weed more than any that they had hitherto witnessed.

"Well, they've put my pipe out," said an old gentleman, flinging it into the flames in a pet. "What is this world coming to? Everything rich and racy — all the spice of life — is to be condemned as useless. Now that they have kindled the bonfire, if these nonsensical reformers would fling themselves into it, all would be well enough!"

"Be patient," responded a staunch conservative; "it will come to that in the end. They will first fling us in and, finally, themselves."

From the general and systematic measures of reform, I now turned to consider the individual contributions to this memorable bonfire. In many instances these were of a very amusing character. One poor fellow threw in his empty purse, and another a bundle of counterfeit or insolvable banknotes. Fashionable ladies threw in their last season's bonnets, together with heaps of ribbons, yellow lace, and much other half-worn milliner's ware, all of which proved even more evanescent in the fire than it had been in the fashion. A multitude of lovers of both sexes — discarded maids or bachelors and couples mutually weary of one another — tossed in bundles of perfumed letters and enamored sonnets. A hack politician, being deprived of bread by the loss of office, threw in his teeth, which happened to be false ones. The Rev. Sydney Smith, having voyaged across the Atlantic for that sole purpose, came up to the bonfire with a bitter grin and threw in certain repudiated bonds, fortified though they were with the broad seal of a sovereign state.

A little boy of five years old, in the premature manliness of the present epoch, threw in his playthings; a college graduate, his diploma; an apothecary, ruined by the spread of homeopathy, his whole stock of drugs and medicines; a physician, his library; a parson, his old sermons; and a fine gentleman of the old school, his code of manners, which he had formerly written down for the benefit of the next generation. A widow, resolving on a second marriage, slyly threw in her dead husband's miniature. A young man, jilted by his mistress, would willingly have flung his own desperate heart into the flames, but could find no means to wrench it out of his bosom. An American author, whose works were neglected by the public, threw his pen and paper into the bonfire and betook himself to some less discouraging occupation.

It somewhat startled me to overhear a number of ladies, highly respectable in appearance, proposing to fling their gowns and petticoats into the flames and assume the garb, together with the manners, duties, offices, and responsibilities, of the opposite sex. What favor was accorded to this scheme I am unable to say, my attention being suddenly drawn to a poor, deceived, and half-delirious girl, who, exclaiming that she was the most worthless thing alive or dead, attempted to cast herself into the fire amid all that wrecked and broken trumpery of the world. A good man, however, ran to her rescue.

"Patience, my poor girl!" said he, as he drew her back from the fierce embrace of the destroying angel. "Be patient and abide Heaven's will. So long as you possess a living soul, all may be restored to its first freshness. These things of matter and creations of human fantasy are fit for nothing but to be burned when once they have had their day; but your day is eternity!"

"Yes," said the wretched girl, whose frenzy seemed now to have sunk down into deep despondency; "yes, and the sunshine is blotted out of it!"

It was now rumored among the spectators that all the weapons and munitions of war were to be thrown into the bonfire, with the exception of the world's stock of gunpowder, which, as the safest mode of disposing of it, had already been drowned in the sea. This intelligence seemed to awaken great diversity of opinion. The hopeful philanthropist esteemed it a token that the millennium was already come; while persons of another stamp, in whose view mankind was a breed of bulldogs, prophesied that all the old stoutness, fervor, nobleness, generosity, and magnanimity of the race would disappear, these qualities, as they affirmed, requiring blood for their nourishment. They comforted themselves, however, in the belief that the proposed abolition of war was impracticable for any length of time together.

Be that as it might, numberless great guns, whose thunder had long been the voice of battle — the artillery of the Armada, the battering trains of Marlborough, and the adverse cannon of Napoleon and Wellington — were trundled into the midst of the fire. By the continual addition of dry combustibles, it had now waxed so intense that neither brass nor iron could withstand it. It was wonderful to behold how these terrible instruments of slaughter melted away like playthings of wax. Then the armies of the earth wheeled around the mighty furnace, with their military music playing triumphant marches, and flung in their muskets and swords. The standard bearers, likewise, cast one look upward at their banners, all tattered with shot holes and inscribed with the names of victorious fields; and, giving them a last flourish on the breeze, they lowered them into the flame, which snatched them upward in its rush toward the clouds. This ceremony being over, the world was left without a single weapon in its hands — except, possibly, a few old king's arms and rusty swords, and other trophies of the Revolution in some of our state armories.

And now the drums were beaten and the trumpets brayed all together, as a prelude to the proclamation of universal and eternal peace and the announcement that glory was no longer to be won by blood, but that it would henceforth be the contention of the human race to work out the greatest mutual good, and that beneficence, in the future annals of the earth, would claim the praise of valor. The blessed tidings were accordingly promulgated and caused infinite rejoicings among those who had stood aghast at the horror and absurdity of war.

Essex Institute, Salem

Nathaniel Hawthorne; portrait by Charles Osgood

But I saw a grim smile pass over the seared visage of a stately old commander — by his warworn figure and rich military dress, he might have been one of Napoleon's famous marshals — who, with the rest of the world's soldiery, had just flung away the sword that had been familiar to his right hand for half a century.

"Ay! ay!" grumbled he. "Let them proclaim what they please; but, in the end, we shall find that all this foolery has only made more work for the armorers and cannon founders."

"Why, sir," exclaimed I, in astonishment, "do you imagine that the human race will ever so far return on the steps of its past madness as to weld another sword or cast another cannon?"

"There will be no need," observed, with a sneer, one who neither felt benevolence nor had faith in it. "When Cain wished to slay his brother, he was at no loss for a weapon."

"We shall see," replied the veteran commander. "If I am mistaken, so much the better; but, in my opinion, without pre-

tending to philosophize about the matter, the necessity of war lies far deeper than these honest gentlemen suppose. What! Is there a field for all the petty disputes of individuals, and shall there be no great law court for the settlement of national difficulties? The battlefield is the only court where such suits can be tried!"

"You forget, general," rejoined I, "that, in this advanced stage of civilization, reason and philanthropy combined, will constitute just such a tribunal as is requisite."

"Ah, I had forgotten that, indeed!" said the old warrior, as he limped away.

The fire was now to be replenished with materials that had hitherto been considered of even greater importance to the well-being of society than the warlike munitions which we had already seen consumed. A body of reformers had traveled all over the earth in quest of the machinery by which the different nations were accustomed to inflict the punishment of death. A shudder passed through the multitude as these ghastly emblems were dragged forward. Even the flames seemed at first to shrink away, displaying the shape and murderous contrivance of each in a full blaze of light, which of itself was sufficient to convince mankind of the long and deadly error of human law. Those old implements of cruelty; those horrible monsters of mechanism; those inventions which seemed to demand something worse than man's natural heart to contrive, and which had lurked in the dusky nooks of ancient prisons, the subject of terror-stricken legend, were now brought forth to view. Headsmen's axes, with the rust of noble and royal blood upon them, and a vast collection of halters that had choked the breath of plebeian victims, were thrown in together.

A shout greeted the arrival of the guillotine, which was thrust forward on the same wheels that had borne it from one to another of the bloodstained streets of Paris. But the loudest roar of applause went up, telling the distant sky of the triumph of the earth's redemption, when the gallows made its appearance. An ill-looking fellow, however, rushed forward and, putting himself in the path of the reformers, bellowed hoarsely and fought with brute fury to stay their progress.

It was little matter of surprise, perhaps, that the executioner should thus do his best to vindicate and uphold the machinery by which he himself had his livelihood and worthier individuals their death; but it deserved special note that men of a far different sphere — even of that class in whose guardianship the world is apt to trust its benevolence — were found to take the hangman's view of the question.

"Stay, my brethren!" cried one of them. "You are misled by a false philanthropy, you know not what you do. The gallows is a heaven-ordained instrument. Bear it back, then, reverently and set it up in its old place, else the world will fall to speedy ruin and desolation!"

"Onward! onward!" shouted a leader in the reform. "Into the flames with the ac-

cursed instrument of man's blood policy! How can human law inculcate benevolence and love while it persists in setting up the gallows as its chief symbol? One heave more, good friends, and the world will be redeemed from its greatest error!"

A thousand hands, that nevertheless loathed the touch, now lent their assistance and thrust the ominous burden far, far into the center of the raging furnace. There its fatal and abhorred image was beheld, first black, then a red coal, then ashes.

"That was well done!" exclaimed I.

"Yes, it was well done," replied, but with less enthusiasm than I expected, the thoughtful observer who was still at my side; "well done, if the world be good enough for the measure. Death, however, is an idea that cannot easily be dispensed with in any condition between the primal innocence and that other purity and perfection which perchance we are destined to attain after traveling round the full circle; but, at all events, it is well that the experiment should now be tried."

"Too cold! too cold!" impatiently exclaimed the young and ardent leader in this triumph. "Let the heart have its voice here as well as the intellect. And, as for ripeness and as for progress, let mankind always do the highest, kindest, noblest thing that, at any given period, it has attained the perception of; and surely that thing cannot be wrong nor wrongly timed."

I know not whether it were the excitement of the scene or whether the good people around the bonfire were really growing more enlightened every instant, but they now proceeded to measures in the full length of which I was hardly prepared to keep them company. For instance, some threw their marriage certificates into the flames and declared themselves candidates for a higher, holier, and more comprehensive union than that which had subsisted from the birth of time under the form of the connubial tie. Others hastened to the vaults of banks and to the coffers of the rich — all of which were open to the first comer on this fated occasion — and brought entire bales of paper money to enliven the blaze and tons of coin to be melted down by its intensity.

Henceforth, they said, universal benevolence, uncoined and exhaustless, was to be the golden currency of the world. At this intelligence the bankers and speculators in the stocks grew pale, and a pickpocket, who had reaped a rich harvest among the crowd, fell down in a deadly fainting fit. A few men of business burned their daybooks and ledgers, the notes and obligations of their creditors, and all other evidences of debts due to themselves; while perhaps a somewhat larger number satisfied their zeal for reform with the sacrifice of any uncomfortable recollection of their own indebtment. There was then a cry that the period was arrived when the title deeds of landed property should be given to the flames, and the whole soil of the earth revert to the public, from whom it had been wrongfully abstracted and most unequally distributed among individuals. Another party demanded that all written constitutions, set forms of government, legislative acts, statute books, and everything else on which human invention had endeavored to stamp its arbitrary laws, should at once be destroyed, leaving the consummated world as free as the man first created.

Whether any ultimate action was taken with regard to these propositions is beyond my knowledge; for, just then, some matters were in progress that concerned my sympathies more nearly.

"See! see! What heaps of books and pamphlets!" cried a fellow, who did not seem to be a lover of literature. "Now we shall have a glorious blaze!"

"That's just the thing!" said a modern philosopher. "Now we shall get rid of the weight of dead men's thought, which has hitherto pressed so heavily on the living in-tellect that it has been incompetent to any effectual self-exertion. Well done, my lads! Into the fire with them! Now you are enlightening the world indeed!"

"But what is to become of the trade?" cried a frantic bookseller.

"Oh, by all means, let them accompany their merchandise," coolly observed an author. "It will be a noble funeral pile!"

The truth was that the human race had now reached a stage of progress so far beyond what the wisest and wittiest men of former ages had ever dreamed of that it would have been a manifest absurdity to allow the earth to be any longer encumbered with their poor achievements in the literary line. Accordingly, a thorough and searching investigation had swept the booksellers' shops, hawkers' stands, public and private libraries, and even the little bookshelf by the country fireside, and had brought the world's entire mass of printed paper, bound or in sheets, to swell the already mountain bulk of our illustrious bonfire. Thick, heavy folios containing the labors of lexicographers, commentators, and encyclopaedists were flung in, and falling among the embers with a leaden thump, smoldered away to ashes like rotten wood.

The small, richly gilt French tomes of the last age, with the hundred volumes of Voltaire among them, went off in a brilliant shower of sparkles and little jets of flame; while the current literature of the same nation burned red and blue and threw an infernal light over the visages of the spectators, converting them all to the aspect of party-colored fiends. A collection of German stories emitted a scent of brimstone. The English standard authors made excellent fuel, generally exhibiting the properties of sound oak logs. Milton's works, in particular, sent up a powerful blaze, gradually reddening into a coal, which promised to endure longer than almost any other material of the pile. From Shakespeare there gushed a flame of such marvelous splendor that men shaded their eyes as against the sun's meridian glory; nor even when the works of his own elucidators were flung upon him did he cease to flash forth a dazzling radiance from beneath the ponderous heap. It is my belief that he is blazing as fervidly as ever.

"Could a poet but light a lamp at that glorious flame," remarked I, "he might then consume the midnight oil to some good purpose."

"That is the very thing which modern poets have been too apt to do — or, at least to attempt," answered a critic. "The chief benefit to be expected from this conflagration of past literature undoubtedly is that writers will henceforth be compelled to light their lamps at the sun or stars."

"If they can reach so high," said I. "But that task requires a giant who may afterward distribute the light among inferior men. It is not everyone that can steal the fire from Heaven, like Prometheus; but when once he had done the deed, a thousand hearths were kindled by it."

It amazed me much to observe how indefinite was the proportion between the physical mass of any given author and the property of brilliant and long-continued combustion. For instance, there was not a quarto volume of the last century — nor, indeed, of the present — that would compete in that particular with a child's little gilt-covered book containing Mother Goose's melodies. The *Life and Death of Tom Thumb* outlasted the biography of Marlborough. An epic, indeed, a dozen of them — was converted to white ashes before the single sheet of an old ballad was half consumed. In more than one case, too, when volumes of applauded verse proved incapable of anything better than a stifling smoke, an unregarded ditty of some nameless bard — perchance in the corner of a newspaper — soared up among the stars with a flame as brilliant as their own. Speaking of the properties of flame, methought Shelley's poetry emitted a purer light than almost any other productions of his day, contrasting beautifully with the fitful and lurid gleams and gushes of black vapor that flashed and eddied from the volumes of Lord Byron. As for Tom Moore, some of his songs diffused an odor like a burning pastille.

I felt particular interest in watching the combustion of American authors, and scrupulously noted by my watch the precise number of moments that changed most of them from shabbily printed books to indistinguishable ashes. It would be invidious, however, if not perilous, to betray these awful secrets; so that I shall content myself with observing that it was not invariably the writer most frequent in the public mouth that made the most splendid appearance in the bonfire. I especially remember that a great deal of excellent inflammability was exhibited in a thin volume of poems by Ellery Channing; although, to speak the truth, there were certain portions that hissed and spluttered in a very disagreeable fashion. A curious phenomenon occurred in reference to several writers, native as well as foreign. Their books, though of highly respectable figure, instead of bursting into a blaze, or even smoldering out their substance in smoke, suddenly melted away in a manner that proved them to be ice.

If it be no lack of modesty to mention my own works, it must here be confessed that I looked for them with fatherly interest, but in vain. Too probably they were changed to vapor by the first action of the heat; at best, I can only hope that, in their quiet way, they contributed a glimmering spark or two to the splendor of the evening.

"Alas! and woe is me!" thus bemoaned himself a heavy looking gentleman in green spectacles. "The world is utterly ruined, and there is nothing to live for any longer. The business of my life is snatched from me. Not a volume to be had for love or money!"

"This," remarked the sedate observer beside me, "is a bookworm — one of tho men who are born to gnaw dead thoughts. His clothes, you see, are covered with the dust of libraries. He has no inward fountain of ideas; and, in good earnest, now that the old stock is abolished, I do not see what is to become of the poor fellow. Have you no word of comfort for him?"

"My dear sir," said I to the desperate bookworm, "is not nature better than a book? Is not the human heart deeper than any system of philosophy? Is not life replete with more instruction than past observers have found it possible to write down in maxims? Be of good cheer. The great book of time is still spread wide open before us; and, if we read it aright, it will be to us a volume of eternal truth."

"Oh, my books, my books, my precious printed books!" reiterated the forlorn bookworm. "My only reality was a bound volume; and now they will not leave me even a shadowy pamphlet!"

In fact, the last remnant of the literature of all the ages was now descending upon the blazing heap in the shape of a cloud of pamphlets from the press of the New World. These likewise were consumed in the twinkling of an eye, leaving the earth, for the first time since the days of Cadmus, free from the plague of letters — an enviable field for the authors of the next generation.

"Well, and does anything remain to be done?" inquired I somewhat anxiously. "Unless we set fire to the earth itself and then leap boldly off into infinite space, I know not that we can carry reform to any farther point."

"You are vastly mistaken, my good friend," said the observer. "Believe me, the fire will not be allowed to settle down without the addition of fuel that will startle many persons who have lent a willing hand thus far."

Nevertheless, there appeared to be a relaxation of effort for a little time, during which, probably, the leaders of the movement were considering what should be done

next. In the interval, a philosopher threw his theory into the flames — a sacrifice which, by those who knew how to estimate it, was pronounced the most remarkable that had yet been made. The combustion, however, was by no means brilliant. Some indefatigable people, scorning to take a moment's ease, now employed themselves in collecting all the withered leaves and fallen boughs of the forest, and thereby recruited the bonfire to a greater height than ever. But this was mere byplay,

"Here comes the fresh fuel that I spoke of," said my companion.

To my astonishment, the persons who now advanced into the vacant space around the mountain of fire bore surplices and other priestly garments, miters, crosiers, and a confusion of popish and Protestant emblems, with which it seemed their purpose to consummate this great act of faith. Crosses from the spires of old cathedrals were cast upon the heap with as little remorse as if the reverence of centuries, passing in long array beneath the lofty towers, had not looked up to them as the holiest of symbols. The font in which infants were consecrated to God, the sacramental vessels whence piety had received the hallowed draft, were given to the same destruction.

Perhaps it most nearly touched my heart to see among these devoted relics fragments of the humble communion tables and undecorated pulpits which I recognized as having been torn from the meetinghouses of New England. Those simple edifices might have been permitted to retain all of sacred embellishment that their Puritan founders had bestowed, even though the mighty structure of St. Peter's had sent its spoils to the fire of this terrible sacrifice. Yet I felt that these were but the externals of religion and might most safely be relinquished by spirits that best knew their deep significance.

"All is well," said I, cheerfully, "The wood paths shall be the aisles of our cathedral; the firmament itself shall be its ceiling.

What needs an earthly roof between the Deity and His worshiper? Our faith can well afford to lose all the drapery that even the holiest men have thrown around it and be only the more sublime in its simplicity."

"True," said my companion; "but will they pause here?"

The doubt implied in his question was well founded. In the general destruction of books already described, a holy volume, that stood apart from the catalog of human literature, and yet, in one sense, was at its head, had been spared. But the titan of innovation — angel or fiend, double in his nature and capable of deeds befitting both characters — at first shaking down only the old and rotten shapes of things, had now, as it appeared, laid his terrible hand upon the main pillars which supported the whole edifice of our moral and spiritual state. The inhabitants of the earth had grown too enlightened to define their faith within a form of words or to limit the spiritual by any analogy to our material existence. Truths which the heavens trembled at were now but a fable of the world's infancy. Therefore, as the final sacrifice of human error, what else remained to be thrown upon the embers of that awful pile except the Book which, though a celestial revelation to past ages, was but a voice from a lower sphere as regarded the present race of man?

It was done! Upon the blazing heap of falsehood and worn-out truth — things that the earth had never needed, or had ceased to need, or had grown childishly weary of — fell the ponderous church Bible, the great old volume that had lain so long on the cushions of the pulpit, and whence the pastor's solemn voice had given holy utterances on so many a Sabbath Day. There likewise fell the family Bible, which the long-buried patriarch had read to his children — in prosperity or sorrow, by the fireside and in the summer shade of trees — and had bequeathed downward as the heirloom of generations. There fell the bosom Bible, the little volume that had been the

soul's friend of some sorely tried child of dust, who thence took courage, whether his trial were for life or death, steadfastly confronting both in the strong assurance of immortality.

All these were flung into the fierce and riotous blaze; and then a mighty wind came roaring across the plain with a desolate howl, as if it were the angry lamentation of the earth for the loss of heaven's sunshine; and it shook the gigantic pyramid of flame and scattered the cinders of half consumed abominations around upon the spectators.

"This is terrible!" said I, feeling that my cheek grew pale, and seeing a like change in the visages about me.

"Be of good courage yet," answered the man with whom I had so often spoken. He continued to gaze steadily at the spectacle with a singular calmness, as if it concerned him merely as an observer. "Be of good courage, nor yet exult too much; for there is far less both of good and evil in the effect of this bonfire than the world might be willing to believe."

"How can that be?" exclaimed I impatiently. "Has it not consumed everything? Has it not swallowed up or melted down every human or divine appendage of our mortal state that had substance enough to be acted on by fire? Will there be anything left us tomorrow morning better or worse than a heap of embers and ashes?"

"Assuredly there will," said my grave friend. "Come hither tomorrow morning, or whenever the combustible portion of the pile shall be quite burned out, and you will find among the ashes everything really valuable that you have seen cast into the flames. Trust me, the world of tomorrow will again enrich itself with the gold and diamonds which have been cast off by the world of today. Not a truth is destroyed nor buried so deep among the ashes but it will be raked up at last,"

This was a strange assurance. Yet I felt inclined to credit it, the more especially as I beheld among the wallowing flames a copy of the Holy Scriptures, the pages of which, instead of being blackened into tinder, only assumed a more dazzling whiteness as the fingermarks of human imperfection were purified away. Certain marginal notes and commentaries, it is true, yielded to the intensity of the fiery test, but without detriment to the smallest syllable that had flamed from the pen of inspiration.

"Yes; there is the proof of what you say," answered I, turning to the observer; "but if only what is evil can feel the action of the fire, then, surely, the conflagration has been of inestimable utility. Yet, if I understand aright, you intimate a doubt whether the world's expectation of benefit would be realized by it."

"Listen to the talk of these worthies," said he, pointing to a group in front of the blazing pile; "possibly they may teach you something useful without intending it."

The persons whom he indicated consisted of that brutal and most earthy figure who had stood forth so furiously in defense of the gallows — the hangman, in short — together with the last thief and the last murderer, all three of whom were clustered about the last toper. The latter was liberally passing the brandy bottle which he had rescued from the general destruction of wines and spirits. This little convivial party seemed at the lowest pitch of despondency, as considering that the purified world must needs be utterly unlike the sphere that they had hitherto known, and therefore but a strange and desolate abode for gentlemen of their kidney.

"The best counsel for all of us is," remarked the hangman, "that, as soon as we have finished the last drop of liquor, I help you, my three friends, to a comfortable end upon the nearest tree, and then hang myself on the same bough. This is no world for us any longer."

"Poh, poh, my good fellows!" said a dark-complexioned personage, who now joined the group — his complexion was indeed fearfully dark, and his eyes glowed with a redder light than that of the bonfire; "be not so cast down, my dear friends; you shall see good days yet. There is one thing that these wiseacres have forgotten to throw into the fire and without which all the rest of the conflagration is just nothing at all; yes, though they had burned the earth itself to a cinder."

"And what may that be?" eagerly demanded the last murderer.

"What but the human heart itself?" said the dark-visaged stranger, with a portentous grin. "And, unless they hit upon some method of purifying that foul cavern, forth from it will reissue all the shapes of wrong and misery — the same old shapes or worse ones — which they have taken such a vast deal of trouble to consume to ashes. I have stood by this livelong night and laughed in my sleeve at the whole business. O, take my word for it, it will be the old world yet!"

This brief conversation supplied me with a theme for lengthened thought. How sad a truth, if true it were, that man's age-long endeavor for perfection had served only to render him the mockery of the evil principle, from the fatal circumstance of an error at the very root of the matter! The heart, the heart — there was the little yet boundless sphere wherein existed the original wrong of which the crime and misery of this outward world were merely types. Purify that inward sphere and the many shapes of evil that haunt the outward, and which now seem almost our only realities, will turn to shadowy phantoms and vanish of their own accord; but if we go no deeper than the intellect and strive, with merely that feeble instrument, to discern and rectify what is wrong, our whole accomplishment will be a dream, so unsubstantial that it matters little whether the bonfire, which I have so faithfully described, were what we choose to call a real event and a flame that would scorch the finger, or only a phosphoric radiance and a parable of my own brain.

36.

RALPH WALDO EMERSON: Young America

Emerson made his living as a lecturer. He often complained of the hardships of the life, which was even more difficult in his day, when transportation was relatively primitive and accommodations usually far from ideal. Yet he was a great success wherever he went; and even those who did not understand his doctrines appreciated his eloquence and his platform manner. His profoundly democratic sentiments may be deduced from a remark made by a scrubwoman who always attended his lectures in Concord. Asked if she knew what he was talking about, she said that she did not, but that she liked "to go and see him stand up there and look as though he thought everyone was as good as he." "The Young American" was a lecture delivered before the Mercantile Library Association in Boston on February 7, 1844. The theme was set by the first lines: "It is remarkable that our people have their intellectual culture from one country and their duties from another." The first country, of course, was England, the second America. Emerson, although not a fanatic literary nationalist, disapproved of this situation, which he considered to be a great waste of intellectual opportunity. A portion of the lecture is reprinted here.

Source: *Nature Addresses and Lectures*, Boston, 1903, pp. 363-395.

IT IS REMARKABLE that our people have their intellectual culture from one country and their duties from another. This false state of things is newly in a way to be corrected. America is beginning to assert herself to the senses and to the imagination of her children, and Europe is receding in the same degree. This, their reaction on education, gives a new importance to the internal improvements and to the politics of the country. Who has not been stimulated to reflection by the facilities now in progress of construction for travel and the transportation of goods in the United States?

This rage of roadbuilding is beneficent for America, where vast distance is so main a consideration in our domestic politics and trade, inasmuch as the great political promise of the invention is to hold the Union staunch, whose days seemed already numbered by the mere inconvenience of transporting representatives, judges, and officers across such tedious distances of land and water. Not only is distance annihilated but, when, as now, the locomotive and the steamboat, like enormous shuttles, shoot everyday across the thousand various threads of national descent and employment and bind them fast in one web, an hourly assimilation goes forward, and there is no danger that local peculiarities and hostilities should be preserved.

But I hasten to speak of the utility of these improvements in creating an American sentiment. An unlooked-for consequence of the railroad is the increased acquaintance it has given the American people with the boundless resources of their own soil. If this vention has reduced England to a third of its size, by bringing people so much nearer, in this country it has given a new celerity to *time* or anticipated by fifty years the planting of tracts of land, the choice of water privileges, the working of mines, and other natural advantages. Railroad iron is a magician's rod in its power to evoke the sleeping energies of land and water.

The railroad is but one arrow in our quiver, though it has great value as a sort of yardstick and surveyor's line. The bountiful continent is ours, state on state, and territory on territory, to the waves of the Pacific sea:

Our garden is the immeasurable earth,
The heaven's blue pillars are Medea's
    house.

The task of surveying, planting, and building upon this immense tract requires an education and a sentiment commensurate thereto. A consciousness of this fact is beginning to take the place of the purely trading spirit and education which sprang up while all the population lived on the fringe of seacoast. And even on the coast, prudent men have begun to see that every American should be educated with a view to the values of land. The arts of engineering and of architecture are studied; scientific agriculture an object of growing attention; the mineral riches are explored — limestone, coal, slate, and iron; and the value of timberlands enhanced.

Columbus alleged as a reason for seeking a continent in the West that the harmony of nature required a great tract of land in the Western Hemisphere to balance the known extent of land in the Eastern; and it now appears that we must estimate the native values of this broad region to redress the balance of our own judgments and appreciate the advantages opened to the human race in this country which is our fortunate home. The land is the appointed reme-

dy for whatever is false and fantastic in our culture. The continent we inhabit is to be physic and food for our mind, as well as our body. The land, with its tranquilizing, sanative influences, is to repair the errors of a scholastic and traditional education and bring us into just relations with men and things.

The habit of living in the presence of these invitations of natural wealth is not inoperative; and this habit, combined with the moral sentiment which, in the recent years, has interrogated every institution, usage, and law, has naturally given a strong direction to the wishes and aims of active young men to withdraw from cities and cultivate the soil. This inclination has appeared in the most unlooked-for quarters, in men supposed to be absorbed in business and in those connected with the liberal professions. And since the walks of trade were crowded, while that of agriculture cannot easily be, inasmuch as the farmer who is not wanted by others can yet grow his own bread, while the manufacturer or the trader, who is not wanted, cannot — this seemed a happy tendency. For beside all the moral benefit which we may expect from the farmer's profession, when a man enters it considerately, this promised the conquering of the soil, plenty, and beyond this the adorning of the country with every advantage and ornament which labor, ingenuity, and affection for a man's home could suggest. . . .

Whatever events in progress shall go to disgust men with cities and infuse into them the passion for country life and country pleasures will render a service to the whole face of this continent and will further the most poetic of all the occupations of real life, the bringing out by art the native but hidden graces of the landscape.

I look on such improvements also as directly tending to endear the land to the inhabitant. Any relation to the land, the habit of tilling it, or mining it, or even hunting

on it, generates the feeling of patriotism.
He who keeps shop on it, or he who merely uses it as a support to his desk and ledger, or to his manufactory, values it less.
The vast majority of the people of this
country live by the land and carry its quality in their manners and opinions. We in the
Atlantic states, by position, have been commercial and have, as I said, imbibed easily a
European culture. Luckily for us, now that
steam has narrowed the Atlantic to a strait,
the nervous, rocky West is intruding a new
and continental element into the national
mind, and we shall yet have an American
genius. How much better when the whole
land is a garden, and the people have
grown up in the bowers of a paradise.

Without looking then to those extraordinary social influences which are now acting
in precisely this direction, but only at what
is inevitably doing around us, I think we
must regard the *land* as a commanding and
increasing power on the citizen, the sanative
and Americanizing influence, which promises to disclose new virtues for ages to
come.

In the second place, the uprise and culmi-
nation of the new and antifeudal power of
commerce is the political fact of most significance to the American at this hour.

We cannot look on the freedom of this
country, in connection with its youth, without a presentiment that here shall laws and
institutions exist on some scale of proportion to the majesty of nature. To men legislating for the area betwixt the two oceans,
betwixt the snows and the tropics, somewhat of the gravity of nature will infuse itself into the code. A heterogeneous population crowding on all ships from all corners
of the world to the great gates of North
America, namely Boston, New York, and
New Orleans, and thence proceeding inward to the prairie and the mountains and
quickly contributing their private thought to
the public opinion, their toll to the treasury,
and their vote to the election, it cannot be
doubted that the legislation of this country
should become more catholic and cosmopolitan than that of any other.

It seems so easy for America to inspire
and express the most expansive and human
spirit; newborn, free, healthful, strong, the
land of the laborer, of the democrat, of the
philanthropist, of the believer, of the saint
she should speak for the human race. It is
the country of the future. From Washington, proverbially "the city of magnificent
distances," through all its cities, states, and
territories, it is a country of beginnings, of
projects, of designs, of expectations. . . .

It is easy to see that the existing generation are conspiring with a beneficence
which in its working for coming generations
sacrifices the passing one; which infatuates
the most selfish men to act against their private interest for the public welfare. We
build railroads, we know not for what or
for whom; but one thing is certain, that we
who build will receive the very smallest
share of benefit. Benefit will accrue, they
are essential to the country, but that will be
felt not until we are no longer countrymen.
We do the like in all matters:

Man's heart the Almighty to the
    Future set
By secret and inviolable springs.

We plant trees, we build stone houses, we
redeem the waste, we make prospective
laws, we found colleges and hospitals for
remote generations. We should be mortified
to learn that the little benefit we chanced in
our own persons to receive was the utmost
they would yield. The history of commerce
is the record of this beneficent tendency. . . .

The philosopher and lover of man have
much harm to say of trade; but the historian will see that trade was the principle of
liberty; that trade planted America and destroyed feudalism; that it makes peace and
keeps peace, and it will abolish slavery. We

omplain of its oppression of the poor and
f its building up a new aristocracy on the
uins of the aristocracy it destroyed. But the
ristocracy of trade has no permanence, is
ot entailed, was the result of toil and tal-
nt, the result of merit of some kind, and is
ontinually falling, like the waves of the sea,
efore new claims of the same sort. Trade
an instrument in the hands of that friend-
 power which works for us in our own
espite. We design it thus and thus; it turns
ut otherwise and far better. This benefi-
nt tendency, omnipotent without violence,
ists and works. . . .
I pass to speak of the signs of that which
the sequel of trade.
In consequence of the revolution in the
ate of society wrought by trade, govern-
ent in our times is beginning to wear a
umsy and cumbrous appearance. We have
ready seen our way to shorter methods.
he time is full of good signs. Some of
em shall ripen to fruit. All this beneficent
cialism is a friendly omen, and the swell-
g cry of voices for the education of the
ople indicates that government has other
ffices than those of banker and execution-
. Witness the new movements in the civi-
ed world, the Communism of France,
ermany, and Switzerland; the trades'
ions, the English League against the Corn
ws; and the whole *Industrial Statistics*, so-
lled. In Paris, the blouse, the badge of the
erative, has begun to make its appearance
 the *salons*.
Witness too the spectacle of three com-
unities which have within a very short
me sprung up within this Commonwealth,
sides several others undertaken by citizens
 Massachusetts within the territory of
her states. These proceeded from a variety
 motives, from an impatience of many uses in common life, from a wish for great-
 freedom than the manners and opinions
 society permitted, but in great part from
 feeling that the true offices of the state,
e state had let fall to the ground; that in

the scramble of parties for the public purse,
the main duties of government were omitted, — the duty to instruct the ignorant, to
supply the poor with work and with good
guidance.

These communists preferred the agricultural life as the most favorable condition for
human culture; but they thought that the
farm, as we manage it, did not satisfy the
right ambition of man. The farmer, after
sacrificing pleasure, taste, freedom, thought,
love to his work, turns out often a bankrupt, like the merchant. This result might
well seem astounding. All this drudgery,
from cockcrowing to starlight, for all these
years, to end in mortgages and the auction-
eer's flag and removing from bad to worse.
It is time to have the thing looked into, and
with a sifting criticism ascertained who is
the fool. It seemed a great deal worse because the farmer is living in the same town
with men who pretend to know exactly
what he wants.

On one side is agricultural chemistry,
coolly exposing the nonsense of our spend-
thrift agriculture and ruinous expense of
manures and offering, by means of a tea-
spoonful of artificial guano, to turn a sand-
bank into corn; and on the other, the farmer, not only eager for the information, but
with bad crops and in debt and bankruptcy,
for want of it. Here are Etzlers and mechanical projectors, who, with the Fourierists, undoubtingly affirm that the smallest
union would make every man rich; and, on
the other side, a multitude of poor men and
women seeking work and who cannot find
enough to pay their board. The science is
confident, and surely the poverty is real. If
any means could be found to bring these
two together!

This was one design of the projectors of
the associations which are now making their
first feeble experiments. They were founded
in love and in labor. They proposed, as you
know, that all men should take a part in the
manual toil and proposed to amend the

condition of men by substituting harmonious for hostile industry. It was a noble thought of Fourier, which gives a favorable idea of his system, to distinguish in his phalanx a class as the Sacred Band, by whom whatever duties were disagreeable and likely to be omitted were to be assumed.

At least an economical success seemed certain for the enterprise, and that agricultural association must, sooner or later, fix the price of bread, and drive single farmers into association in self-defense; as the great commercial and manufacturing companies had already done. The community is only the continuation of the same movement which made the joint stock companies for manufactures, mining, insurance, banking, and so forth. It has turned out cheaper to make calico by companies; and it is proposed to plant corn and to bake bread by companies. . . .

The communities aimed at a higher success in securing to all their members an equal and thorough education. And on the whole one may say that aims so generous and so forced on them by the times will not be relinquished, even if these attempts fail but will be prosecuted until they succeed.

This is the value of the communities; not what they have done but the revolution which they indicate as on the way. Yes, government must educate the poor man. Look across the country from any hillside around us and the landscape seems to crave government. The actual differences of men must be acknowledged and met with love and wisdom. These rising grounds which command the champaign below seem to ask for lords, true lords, land-lords, who understand the land and its uses and the applicabilities of men, and whose government would be what it should, namely mediation between want and supply. How gladly would each citizen pay a commission for the support and continuation of good guidance. None should be a governor who has not a talent for governing.

Now, many people have a native skill f carving out business for many hands; a g nius for the disposition of affairs; and a never happier than when difficult practic questions, which embarrass other men, a to be solved. All lies in light before the they are in their element. Could any mea be contrived to appoint only these! The really seems a progress toward such a sta of things in which this work shall be do by these natural workmen; and this, n certainly through any increased discreti shown by the citizens at elections but the gradual contempt into which offic government falls and the increasing dispo tion of private adventurers to assume fallen functions.

Thus the national post office is likely go into disuse before the private telegra and the express companies. The curren threatens to fall entirely into private han Justice is continually administered more a more by private reference and not by litig tion. We have feudal governments in commercial age. It would be but an ea extension of our commercial system to p a private emperor a fee for services, as pay an architect, an engineer, or a lawyer. any man has a talent for righting wrong, administering difficult affairs, for counseli poor farmers how to turn their estates good husbandry, for combining a hundr private enterprises to a general benefit, him in the county town or in Court Stre put up his signboard — Mr. Smith, Gove nor, Mr. Johnson, Working king.

How can our young men complain of t poverty of things in New England and n feel that poverty as a demand on their cha ity to make New England rich? Where he who seeing a thousand men useless a unhappy, and making the whole region fo lorn by their inaction, and conscious hims of possessing the faculty they want, do not hear his call to go and be their king?

We must have kings, and we must ha nobles. Nature provides such in every so ety — only let us have the real instead the titular. Let us have our leading and our inspiration from the best. In every society some men are born to rule and some to advise. Let the powers be well directed, directed by love, and they would everywhere be greeted with joy and honor. The chief is the chief all the world over, only not his cap and his plume. It is only their dislike of the pretender, which makes men sometimes unjust to the accomplished man. . . .

I call upon you, young men, to obey your heart and be the nobility of this land. In every age of the world there has been a leading nation, one of a more generous sentiment, whose eminent citizens were willing to stand for the interests of general justice and humanity at the risk of being called, by the men of the moment, chimerical and fantastic. Which should be that nation but these states? Which should lead that movement if not New England? Who should lead the leaders but the Young American?

The people and the world are now suffering from the want of religion and honor in its public mind. In America, out-of-doors all seems a market; indoors, an airtight stove of conventionalism. Everybody who comes into our houses savors of these habits; the men, of the market; the women, of the custom. I find no expression in our state papers or legislative debate, in our lyceums or churches, especially in our newspapers, of a high national feeling, no lofty counsels that rightfully stir the blood. I speak of those organs which can be presumed to speak a popular sense. They recommend conventional virtues, whatever will earn and preserve property; always the capitalist; the college, the church, the hospital, the theater, the hotel, the road, the ship of the capitalist — whatever goes to secure, adorn, enlarge these is good; what jeopardizes any of these is damnable. The "opposition" papers, so-called, are on the same side. They attack the great capitalist, but with the aim to make a capitalist of the poor man. The opposition is against those who have money, from those who wish to have money. But who announces to us, in journal or in pulpit or in the street, the secret of heroism?

Man alone
Can perform the impossible.

I shall not need to go into an enumeration of our national defects and vices which require this Order of Censors in the state. I might not set down our most proclaimed offenses as the worst. It is not often the worst trait that occasions the loudest outcry. . . . The timidity of our public opinion is our disease, or, shall I say, the publicness of opinion, the absence of private opinion. Good nature is plentiful, but we want justice, with heart of steel, to fight down the proud. The private mind has the access to the totality of goodness and truth that it may be a balance to a corrupt society; and to stand for the private verdict against popular clamor is the office of the noble.

If a humane measure is propounded in behalf of the slave or of the Irishman or the Catholic or for the succor of the poor, that sentiment, that project, will have the homage of the hero. That is his nobility, his oath of knighthood, to succor the helpless and oppressed; always to throw himself on the side of weakness, of youth, of hope; on the liberal, on the expansive side, never on the defensive, the conserving, the timorous, the lock-and-bolt system. More than our goodwill we may not be able to give. We have our own affairs, our own genius which chains each to his proper work. We cannot give our life to the cause of the debtor, of the slave, or the pauper as another is doing; but to one thing we are bound, not to blaspheme the sentiment and the work of that man, not to throw stumbling blocks in the way of the Abolitionist, the philanthropist, as the organs of influence and opinion are swift to do. It is for us to confide in the beneficent Supreme Power, and not to rely on our money and on the state, because it is the guard of money.

At this moment, the terror of old people and of vicious people is lest the Union of these states be destroyed; as if the Union had any other real basis than the good pleasure of a majority of the citizens to be united. But the wise and just man will always feel that he stands on his own feet; that he imparts strength to the state, not receives security from it; and that if all went down, he and such as he would quite easily combine in a new and better constitution. . . .

Gentlemen, the development of our American internal resources, the extension to the utmost of the commercial system, and the appearance of new moral causes which are to modify the state are giving an aspect of greatness to the future which the imagination fears to open. One thing is plain for all men of common sense and common conscience, that here, here in America, is the home of man. After all the deductions which are to be made for our pitiful politics, which stake every gravest national question on the silly die whether James or whether Robert shall sit in the chair and hold the purse; after all the deduction is made for our frivolities and insanities, there still remains an organic simplicity and liberty, which, when it loses its balance, redresses itself presently, which offers opportunity to the human mind not known in any other region.

37.

JOHN TYLER: Dorr's Rebellion

The rebellion led by Thomas Dorr in Rhode Island in 1842 had arisen over the establishment of a new constitution. The issue was whether the people of the state had the right to create a new constitution without the consent or assistance of the authorities holding office under the old constitution. The Dorr Rebellion was settled without any direct interference on the part of President Tyler. At the request of the House of Representatives, Tyler wrote the following letter of April 9, 1844, explaining his attitude toward the events in Rhode Island.

Source: Richardson, IV, pp. 283-286.

IN COMPLIANCE with a resolution of the House of Representatives of the 23rd of March last requesting the President to lay before the House

the authority and the true copies of all requests and applications upon which he deemed it his duty to interfere with the naval and military forces of the United States on the occasion of the recent attempt of the people of Rhode Island to establish a free constitution in the place of the old charter government of that state; also copies of the instructions to and statements of the charter commissioners sent to him by the then existing authorities of the state of Rhode Island; also copies of the correspondence between the executive of the United States and the charter government of the state of Rhode Island, and all the papers and documents connected with the same; also copies of the correspondence, if any, between the heads of departments and said charter government or any person or persons connected with the said government, and of any accompanying papers and documents; also copies of all orders issued by the executive of the United States, or any of the departments, to military officers for the movement or employment of troops to or in Rhode Island; also copies of all orders to naval officers to prepare steam or other vessels of the United States for service in the waters of Rhode Island; also copies of all orders to the officers of revenue cutters for the same service; also copies of any instructions borne by the secretary of war to Rhode Island on his visit in 1842 to review the troops of the charter government; also copies of any order or orders to any officer or officers of the Army or Navy to report themselves to the charter government; and that he be requested to lay before this House copies of any other papers or documents in the possession of the executive connected with this subject not above specifically enumerated,

I have to inform the House that the executive did not deem it his "duty to interfere with the naval and military forces of the United States" in the late disturbances in Rhode Island; that no orders were issued by the executive or any of the departments to military officers for the movement or employment of troops to or in Rhode Island other than those which accompany this message and which contemplated the strengthening of the garrison at Fort Adams, which, considering the extent of the agitation in Rhode Island, was esteemed necessary and judicious; that no orders were issued to naval officers to prepare steam or other vessels of the United States for service in the waters of Rhode Island; that no orders were issued "to the officers of the revenue cutters for said service"; that no instructions were borne by "the secretary of war to Rhode Island on his visit in 1842 to review the troops of the charter government"; that no orders were given to any officer or officers of the Army or Navy to report themselves to the charter govern-

ment; that "requests and applications" were made to the executive to fulfill the guarantees of the Constitution which impose on the federal government the obligation to protect and defend each state of the Union against "domestic violence and foreign invasion," but the executive was at no time convinced that the *casus foederis* had arisen which required the interposition of the military or naval power in the controversy which unhappily existed between the people of Rhode Island.

I was in no manner prevented from so interfering by the inquiry whether Rhode Island existed as an independent state of the Union under a charter granted at an early period by the Crown of Great Britain or not. It was enough for the executive to know that she was recognized as a sovereign state by Great Britain by the Treaty of 1783; that . . . she had in common with her sister states poured out her blood and freely expended her treasure in the War of the Revolution; that she was a party to the Articles of Confederation; that at an after period she adopted the Constitution of the United States as a free, independent, and republican state; and that in this character she has always possessed her full quota of representation in the Senate and House of Representatives; and that up to a recent day she has conducted all her domestic affairs and fulfilled all her obligations as a member of the Union, in peace and war, under her charter government, as it is denominated by the resolution of the House of the 23rd March.

I must be permitted to disclaim entirely and unqualifiedly the right on the part of the executive to make any real or supposed defects existing in any state constitution or form of government the pretext for a failure to enforce the laws or the guarantees of the Constitution of the United States in reference to any such state. I utterly repudiate the idea, in terms as emphatic as I can employ, that those laws are not to be enforced or those guarantees complied with because

President John Tyler

the President may believe that the right of suffrage or any other great popular right is either too restricted or too broadly enlarged.

I also, with equal strength, resist the idea that it falls within the executive competency to decide in controversies of the nature of that which existed in Rhode Island on which side is the majority of the people or as to the extent of the rights of a mere numerical majority. For the executive to assume such a power would be to assume a power of the most dangerous character. Under such assumptions the states of this Union would have no security for peace or tranquillity, but might be converted into the mere instruments of executive will.

Actuated by selfish purposes, he might become the great agitator, fomenting assaults upon the state constitutions and declaring the majority of today to be the minority of tomorrow, and the minority, in its turn, the majority, before whose decrees the established order of things in the state

should be subverted. Revolution, civil commotion, and bloodshed would be the inevitable consequences. The provision in the Constitution intended for the security of the states would thus be turned into the instrument of their destruction. The President would become, in fact, the great constitution maker for the states, and all power would be vested in his hands.

When, therefore, the governor of Rhode Island, by his letter of the 4th of April 1842, made a requisition upon the executive for aid to put down the late disturbances, I had no hesitation in recognizing the obligations of the executive to furnish such aid upon the occurrence of the contingency provided for by the Constitution and laws. My letter of the 11th of April in reply to the governor's letter of the 4th is herewith communicated, together with all correspondence which passed at a subsequent day and the letters and documents mentioned in the schedule hereunto annexed. From the correspondence between the executive of the United States and that of Rhode Island, it will not escape observation that while I regarded it as my duty to announce the principles by which I should govern myself in the contingency of an armed interposition on the part of this government being necessary to uphold the rights of the state of Rhode Island and to preserve its domestic peace, yet that the strong hope was indulged and expressed that all the difficulties would disappear before an enlightened policy of conciliation and compromise.

In that spirit I addressed to Governor King the letter of the 9th of May, 1842, marked "private and confidential," and received his reply of the 12th of May of the same year. The desire of the executive was, from the beginning, to bring the dispute to a termination without the interposition of the military power of the United States, and it will continue to be a subject of self congratulation that this leading object of policy was finally accomplished. The executive resisted all entreaties, however urgent, to depart from this line of conduct.

Information from private sources had led the executive to conclude that little else was designed by Mr. Dorr and his adherents than mere menace with a view to intimidation; nor was this opinion in any degree shaken until the 22nd of June, 1842, when it was strongly represented from reliable sources, as will be seen by reference to the documents herewith communicated, that preparations were making by Mr. Dorr, with a large force in arms, to invade the state, which force had been recruited in the neighboring states and had been already preceded by the collection of military stores in considerable quantities at one or two points. This was a state of things to which the executive could not be indifferent. Mr. Dorr speedily afterward took up his headquarters at Chepachet and assumed the command of what was reported to be a large force, drawn chiefly from voluntary enlistments made in neighboring states.

The executive could with difficulty bring itself to realize the fact that the citizens of other states should have forgotten their duty to themselves and the Constitution of the United States and have entered into the highly reprehensible and indefensible course of interfering so far in the concerns of a sister state as to have entered into plans of invasion, conquest, and revolution. But the executive felt it to be its duty to look minutely into the matter, and therefore the secretary of war was dispatched to Rhode Island with instructions (a copy of which is herewith transmitted), and was authorized, should a requisition be made upon the executive by the government of Rhode Island in pursuance of law, and the invaders should not abandon their purposes, to call upon the governors of Massachusetts and Connecticut for a sufficient number of militia at once to arrest the invasion and to interpose such of the regular toops as could be spared from Fort Adams for the defense of the city of Providence in the event of its being attacked, as was strongly represented to be in contemplation.

Happily, there was no necessity for either issuing the proclamation or the requisition or for removing the troops from Fort Adams, where they had been properly stationed. Chepachet was evacuated and Mr. Dorr's troops dispersed without the necessity of the interposition of any military force by this government, thus confirming me in my early impressions that nothing more had been designed from the first by those associated with Mr. Dorr than to excite fear and apprehension and thereby to obtain concessions from the constituted authorities which might be claimed as a triumph over the existing government.

With the dispersion of Mr. Dorr's troops ended all difficulties. A convention was shortly afterward called, by due course of law, to amend the fundamental law; and a new constitution, based on more liberal principles than that abrogated, was proposed, and adopted by the people. Thus the great American experiment of a change in government under the influence of opinion and not of force has been again crowned with success, and the state and people of Rhode Island repose in safety under institutions of their own adoption, unterrified by any future prospect of necessary change and secure against domestic violence and invasion from abroad.

I congratulate the country upon so happy a termination of a condition of things which seemed at one time seriously to threaten the public peace. It may justly be regarded as worthy of the age and of the country in which we live.

38.

Texas Without War

Mindful that 1844 was an election year, President Tyler hoped to bolster his sagging popularity by consummating the annexation of Texas before the end of his term. One of Tyler's strongest supporters in the drive for annexation was Senator Robert J. Walker of Mississippi. Early in 1844 Walker wrote a letter explaining his views on Texas in reply to a request from the people of Carroll County, Kentucky. The letter was widely circulated throughout the country as the controversy over Texas gained momentum. The following magazine editorial, quoting the major part of Walker's letter, appeared in April 1844.

Source: *United States Magazine and Democratic Review*, April 1844: "The Texas Question."

Che sarà, sarà — what must be, must be — and, in general, the sooner therefore it is, the better. Suppose a powerful magnet suspended in the air, and near it, within the full force of its attraction, suppose a piece of iron similarly suspended and free to obey the call of the mysterious metallic sympathy. While they are thus situated, so long as they are forcibly held asunder by any other sufficient counterbalancing force, their natural instinct toward cohesion may be for the time frustrated; but the moment that obstacle is removed or relaxed, they rush together — and the result is *annexation*. That Texas is to be, sooner or later, included in the Union, we have long — nay, ever since the battle of San Jacinto — regarded as an event already indelibly inscribed in the book of future fate and necessity.

The questions of time and mode we have looked upon as comparatively of minor moment. As for the latter, the question of *mode* — even if the case had presented any serious obstacle of political formality, he has read all history in vain who may yet imagine that in the larger transactions of nations there is ever much difficulty about a *way* when there is any very earnest *will* to find

one. And as for the former question, that of *time*, it has all along been manifest that time would be on the day when the South should arouse itself to a combined and determined demand for the reception of Texas into the confederation; and when that just jealousy of English power and English ambition on our continent, which is a strong pervading sentiment throughout all the sections of the Union, should become sufficiently alarmed to counterbalance the repugnance with which the first suggestion of the proposition would be received by the North.

These two conditions would probably be pretty nearly coincident, mutually connected as they indeed are with each other. Their conjunction must fix the date of the inevitably future annexation; that that conjunction is now close at hand, if not already arrived, the signs are neither few nor equivocal.

The opposition to it is doubtless to be active and vehement. As a new element in our politics, it is not, perhaps, easy to calculate its exact operation. It is believed by some that it will deeply convulse the whole North and become a subject of new party division sufficient to destroy and reconstruct our present organization of parties. This expectation we regard, however, as immensely exaggerated, if not destitute of foundation. It is not unlikely that the annexation may go into effect with a facility which will surprise us all. Resistance will be half-paralyzed in advance by the pressure of the general consciousness of its inutility — of that political certainty and that geographical fitness and propriety of the measure against which it will be ruin to contend.

Nor can the feebleness and diffusion of a mere negative opposition, on the one side, on abstract grounds of theoretical speculation unconnected with any present and palpable material interests, long withstand the attacking energy of positive determination on the other, combined, organized, and under a strong stimulus of both interest and passion. The South — and the South knows it full well — has only to call for it with that powerful influence which it derives from the close balance of the two great national parties, to secure pretty soon the emulous favor of both of the latter at the North; unless, indeed, the other great sections of the Union were excited and rallied by far stronger antagonist reasons than any existing in the present case.

Far from us the proposition that a wrong should be unresistingly acquiesced in, at the very outset of its attempt to assert itself, because it may be known in advance that resistance must be fruitless. The very magnitude of its power, on the contrary, should only stimulate a true moral bravery to those untried extremes of effort in which despair often finds successful resources which the boldest hope could not have anticipated; or at any rate, resistance in such a case is that performance of individual duty which at least satisfies conscience, discharges responsibility, and provides the best consolation for the future, when the triumphant wrong shall have established itself.

If we regarded the annexation as a measure of this character, we certainly should not allow ourselves to be found in the rear rank of those struggling against it, faint as might be the chance of success in the honorably hopeless effort. It is only because we do not so regard it — because, *if it should be carried into effect in a proper manner,* there appears to us but little sound and solid foundation for the objections with which it is denounced in advance — that we present it in this aspect and introduce into the question this element; namely, that the annexation, as a practical fact, must be and will be and therefore may as well be allowed to come peaceably into existence with as little disturbance of our temper and as little waste of our time and trouble as possible.

For ourselves we stand impartially aloof from the opposing passions which already confront each other with angry scowls on this question. We are neither Southerners, to desire the annexation for the purpose of propping up that side of the fast failing equilibrium in the federal government between the free and the slave states; nor Abolitionists, who, erroneously making the question of slavery a political and a federal question, with equal vehemence, for the same reason, deprecate that event. We occupy a position midway between the two and, as we believe, overlooking both — connected by strong sympathies with what is good and true on the side of each, yet unblinded by the peculiar and partial prejudices of either. Our range of vision, therefore, commanded by such a position, over the broad expanse of the whole question, is at least a more comprehensive, even if it should happen to be a less clear and just one, than that to be taken from either of these narrower points of view.

That Texas must sooner or later, from the very nature and necessity of things, coalesce into one political unity with the rest of the great confederacy, whose main seat is destined to be the vast valley of the Mississippi, can scarcely fail to strike the most careless eye that will cast a glance over any map of the continent of North America.

What do we there behold? Two great ranges of mountains, running parallel with the coasts of the two oceans, and converging toward each other till the one, the Alleghenies, abuts on the eastern side of the Gulf, while the other, the Rocky Mountains, continues its southward course through Mexico, and shooting off a forking branch which commences at the northeastern angle of Mexico, in latitude about 42 and longitude about 110, and in like manner abuts on the western side of the Gulf. This forking branch, composing the eastern wall of the narrow valley of the Del Norte, of which the main trunk of the Rocky Mountains or Cordilleras composes the western wall, constitutes the greater part of the western boundary of Texas, the line of which is continued to the Gulf by the river Nueces.

The broad area between these two lines of natural demarcation of territory constitutes what is usually designated as the great Valley of the West or of the Mississippi — the magnificent region allotted already, by the unequivocal finger of Providence, for the main center and home of the great republican, confederated empire of the West. On each side, between the Alleghenies and the Atlantic eastward and between the Rocky Mountains and the Pacific westward, there may be side supporters, as it were, to the vast central trunk of population and power — its outposts and outports to command the tribute of the two oceans and to connect it by the flying bridge of an illimitable commerce with the other continents, Europe and Asia.

That the whole of this valley region, thus symmetrically planned and adapted to its grand destiny, in the possession of the race sent there for the providential purpose — bounded on the north by the chain of the inland seas, which it is almost a misnomer to call lakes, and on the south resting on the northern line of the Gulf of Mexico, must, *must*, sooner or later, come together into one homogeneous unity of political system, is a simple geographical fact which

can only be questioned, as it appears to us, by one equally blind in mental and physical vision.

Of this region, Texas forms an integral and essential part. It is a huge fragment, artificially broken off from the corner, the unseemly rupture striking far inward and even approaching, in very uncomfortable nearness, to two of the most important if not vital points of the interior structure; namely, the Mississippi at the juncture of the Red River, and one of the two great arteries of communication with Oregon, through the southern pass of the mountains.

We have above admitted as the western boundary of Texas the small river Nueces, and the forking branch or offshoot from the Rocky Mountains, which forms the eastern wall of the narrow valley of the Del Norte, in accordance with the Mexican arrangement of its provincial boundaries; though, as is well known, Texas maintains the Del Norte itself as her western line, which is indeed the line of our original and foolishly ceded right; and which, as the greatest natural line of landmark and separation, affords, undoubtedly, the proper boundary between us and Mexico. As the strip of territory between these two lines is narrow and of little importance, it cannot constitute any serious difficulty in the adjustment of the main question between the two countries, which arises out of the peculiar and indeed anomalous relation of Texas to them both. In speaking of the annexation of the latter to the Union, or rather *reannexation,* to use the favorite term of its friends, we shall, of course, be understood to refer to the Del Norte as its western boundary.

On this point, of the natural fitness and propriety of the proposed reunion, as a question of political geography, as also on that of the intrinsic value of the territory in question, we cannot do better than quote Mr. Walker's clear and strong exposition of it, though we confess that we are but little influenced by the merely military bearings of the argument. After enumerating the efforts made by the last three administrations, commencing with Adams and Clay in 1825, to readjust this unhappy mutilation of our southwestern territory, Mr. Walker proceeds:

The reasons assigned in 1825, 1827, 1829, 1833 and 1835 for the reannexation of Texas apply now with full force. These reasons were: that the Sabine, as a boundary, was too near New Orleans; that the defense of that city was rendered insecure; and that the Arkansas and Red River, and all their tributaries, ought to be in our own exclusive possession. The present boundary is the worst which could be devised. It is a succession of steps and curves, carving out the great valley of the West into a shape that is absolutely hideous. It surrenders the Red River and Arkansas, and their numerous tributaries, for thousands of miles, to a foreign power. It brings that power upon the Gulf, within a day's sail of the mouth of the Mississippi, and in the interior, by the curve of the Sabine, within about 100 miles of the Mississippi.

It places that power, for many hundred miles, on the banks of the Red River, in immediate contact with 60,000 Indian warriors of our own, and with very many thousand of the fiercest savage tribes in Texas, there to be armed and equipped for the work of death and desolation. It enables a foreign power, with such aids, to descend the Red River, to the junction of the Mississippi, there to cut off all communication from above or below; to arrest at that point all boats which were descending with their troops and munitions of war for the defense of New Orleans; and fall down suddenly on that city, thus isolated from the rest of the Union, and subjected to certain ruin.

From the mouth of the Mississippi to the Sabine there is not a single harbor where an American vessel of war could find shelter; but westward of the mouth of the Sabine, in Texas, are several deep bays and harbors; and Galveston, one of these, has a depth of water equal to that at the mouth of the Mississippi. Looking into the interior, along this extraordinary boundary, we find a foreign power stretching for many hundred miles along the Sabine to the Red River, thence west

several hundred miles along that river to the western boundary of our Indian territories; thence north to the Arkansas, and up that stream to the southern boundary of the territory of Oregon, and at a point which, according to the recent most able survey of Lieutenant Fremont, is within twenty miles of the pass of the Rocky Mountains, which secures the entrance to Oregon. We thus place a foreign power there, to move eastward or westward, upon the valley of the Columbia or Mississippi. We place this power north of St. Louis, north of a portion of Iowa, and south of New Orleans, and along this line for several thousand miles in our rear.

Such is the boundary at present given to the valley of the West; such the imminent dangers to which it is subjected of Indian massacre; such the dismemberment of the great valley, and of many of the noblest streams and tributaries of the Mississippi; such the surrender of so many hundred miles of our coast, with so many bays and harbors; such the hazard to which New Orleans is subjected, and the outlet of all our commerce to the Gulf. Such is our present boundary; and it can be exchanged for one that will give us perfect security, that will place our own people and our own settlements in rear of the Indian tribes, and that will cut them off from foreign influence; that will restore to us the uninterrupted navigation of the Red River and Arkansas, and of all their tributaries; that will place us at the north, upon a point to command the pass of Oregon, and, on the south, to secure New Orleans, and render certain the command of the Gulf of Mexico.

In pursuing our ancient and rightful boundary, before we surrendered Texas, along the Del Norte, we are brought, by a western curve of that great river, to a point within 400 miles of the Pacific Ocean, and where the waters of the Del Norte almost commingle with those that flow into the Western ocean. Up to this point on the Del Norte it is navigable for steamboats; and from that point to the Pacific is a good route for caravans, and where, it is believed, the Pacific may be united with the Del Norte and the Gulf by a railroad, not longer than that which now unites Buffalo and Boston;

and where, even now, without such a road, we could command the trade of all the northern states of Mexico, and of a very large portion of the western coast of America.

The importance of Texas is thus described by Mr. Clay, in his speech of the 3rd of April, 1820:

"All the accounts concurred in representing Texas to be extremely valuable. Its superficial extent was three or four times greater than that of Florida. The climate was delicious; the soil fertile; the margins of the rivers abounding in live oak; and the country admitting of easy settlement. It possessed, moreover, if he were not misinformed, one of the finest ports in the Gulf of Mexico, the productions of which it was capable were suited to our wants. The unfortunate captive of St. Helena wished for ships, commerce, and colonies. We have them all, if we do not wantonly throw them away.

The colonies of other countries are separated from them by vast seas, requiring great expense to protect them, and are held subject to a constant risk of their being torn from their grasp. Our colonies, on the contrary, are united to, and form a part of, our continent; and the same Mississippi, from whose rich deposit the best of them (Louisiana) has been formed, will transport on her bosom the brave, the patriotic men from her tributary streams, to defend and preserve the next most valuable — the province of Texas. He was not disposed to disparage Florida; but its intrinsic value was incomparably less than that of Texas."

In the letter of instructions from Mr. Madison, as secretary of state, of the 29th of July, 1803, he says, "the acquisition of the Floridas is still to be pursued." He adds, the exchange of any part of western Louisiana, which Spain may propose for "the cession of the Floridas, is inadmissible. In intrinsic value there is no equality. We are the less disposed also to make sacrifices to obtain the Floridas, because their position and the manifest course of events *guarantee an early and reasonable acquisition of them.*"

In Mr. Madison's letter, also, as secretary of state, of the 8th of July, 1804, he announces the opposition of Mr. Jeffer-

son "to a perpetual relinquishment of *any territory* whatever eastward of the Rio Bravo." In the message of President Houston of the 5th of May, 1837, he says that Texas contains "four-fifths of all the live oak now in the world."

Cotton will be its great staple, and some sugar and molasses will be produced. The grape, the olive, and indigo and cocoa, and nearly all the fruits of the tropics will be grown there also. In Texas are valuable mines of gold and silver; the silver mine on the San Saba having been examined and found to be among the richest in the world.

In the recent debate in the British Parliament, Lord Brougham said: "The importance of Texas could not be overrated. It was a country of the greatest capabilities, and was in extent full as large as France. It possessed a soil of the finest and most fertile character, and it was capable of producing all tropical produce; and its climate was of a most healthy character. It had access to the Gulf, to the River Mississippi, with which it communicated by means of the Red River."

The possession of Texas would insure to us the trade of Santa Fe and all the northern states of Mexico. Above all, Texas is a large and indispensable portion of the valley of the West. That valley once was all our own; but it has been dismembered by a treaty formed when the West held neither of the high executive stations of the government and was wholly unrepresented in the cabinet at Washington. The Red River and Arkansas, divided and mutilated, now flow, with their numerous tributaries, for many thousand miles through the territory of a foreign power; and the West has been forced back along the Gulf, from the Del Norte to the Sabine. If, then, it be true that the sacrifice of Texas was made with painful reluctance, all those who united in the surrender will rejoice at the reacquisition.

This is no question of the purchase of new territory, but of the reannexation of that which once was all our own. It is not a question of the extension of our limits but of the restoration of former boundaries. It proposes no new addition to the valley of the Mississippi but of its reunion, and all its waters once more under our dominion. If the Creator had separated Texas from the Union by mountain barriers, the Alps or the Andes, these might be plausible objections; but he has planned down the whole valley, including Texas, and united every atom of the soil and every drop of the waters of the mighty whole. He has linked their rivers with the great Mississippi, and marked and united the whole for the dominion of one government and the residence of one people; and it is impious in man to attempt to dissolve this great and glorious Union.

Texas is a part of Kentucky, a portion of the same great valley. It is a part of New York and Pennsylvania, a part of Maryland and Virginia, and Ohio, and of all the Western states, while the Tennessee unites with it the waters of Georgia, Alabama, and Carolina. The Allegheny, commencing its course in New York, and with the Youghiogany from Maryland, and Monongahela from Virginia, merging with the beautiful Ohio at the metropolis of western Pennsylvania, embrace the streams of Texas at the mouths of the Arkansas and Red rivers, whence their waters flow in kindred union to the Gulf.

And here let me say, that New York ought to reclaim for the Allegheny its true original name, *the Ohio*, of which it is a part, and so marked and called by that name in the British maps, prior to 1776, one of which is in the possession of the distinguished representative from the Pittsburgh district of Pennsylvania. The words "Ohio" and "Allegheny," in two different Indian dialects, mean *clear*, as designating truly, in both cases, the character of the water of both streams, and hence it is that New York is upon the Ohio, and truly stands at the head of the valley of the West.

The treaty which struck Texas from the Union inflicted a blow upon this mighty valley. And who will say that the West shall remain dismembered and mutilated, and that the ancient boundaries of the republic shall never be restored? Who will desire to check the young eagle of America, now refixing her gaze upon our former limits, and repluming her pinions for her returning flight?

What American will say that the flag of the Union shall never wave again throughout that mighty territory; and that what Jefferson acquired, and Madison refused to surrender, shall never be restored? Who will oppose the reestablishment of our glorious Constitution over the whole of the mighty valley which once was shielded by its benignant sway?

Who will wish again to curtail the limits of this great republican empire, and again to dismember the glorious valley of the West? Who will refuse to replant the banner of the republic upon our former boundary, or resurrender the Arkansas and Red rivers, and retransfer the coast of the Gulf? Who will refuse to heal the bleeding wounds of the mutilated West and reunite the veins and arteries dissevered by the dismembering cession of Texas to Spain? To refuse to accept the reannexation is to *resurrender* the territory of Texas, and redismember the valley of the West. Nay, more; under existing circumstances, it is to lower the flag of the Union before the red cross of St. George, and to surrender the Florida pass, the mouth of the Mississippi, the command of the Mexican Gulf, and finally Texas itself, into the hands of England.

That Texas to the Del Norte was included in the Louisiana acquired by us from France by the treaty of 1803, is beyond dispute; we shall not consume any of our space in proving a point which Mr. Walker has already set in so clear a light. We lost it, or rather we threw it away, by the treaty with Spain of 1819; and Mr. Clay maintained in Congress, in his speech of April 3, in the following year, that that cession was unconstitutional, as being beyond the authority of the treaty-making power in our government. Mr. Walker adds a reference to the treaty of 1803 with France by which we acquired it, and by which we pledged ourselves to France and to the people of the territory, to incorporate it (Texas included) into the Union; so that "even if our subsequent treaty of cession to Spain was unconstitutional and invalid, it was a gross infraction of a previous treaty, and of one of the fundamental conditions under which Texas was acquired."

Every administration since that time, down to the year 1835, has attempted measures for the recovery of the important territory thus unfortunately lost. It was one of the earliest acts of Mr. Adams and Mr. Clay, his secretary of state, who, on the 26th of March, 1825, gave special instructions to Mr. Poinsett, our minister in that country, to endeavor to procure from Mexico the retransfer of Texas — an effort renewed on the 15th of March, 1827. General Jackson and Mr. Van Buren received similar instructions on the 25th of August, 1829, with an expression of the President's "deep conviction of the real necessity of the proposed acquisition." Through Mr. Livingston, on the 20th of March, 1833, and Mr. Forsyth, on the 2nd of July and 6th of August, 1835, General Jackson still urged, though ineffectually, the same object. And if Mr. Van Buren, within his term, did not repeat it, it was because the grounds on which the question stood had undergone material change.

Texas was no longer in the possession of Mexico to cede; the experiment was in progress whether the revolutionized province would or would not succeed in maintaining itself as an independent sovereignty — an independence which we had already recognized; and while a just and jealous respect to the relations then subsisting between Mexico and ourselves dictated at that time Mr. Forsyth's peremptory refusal of the solicitation of Texas for admission into the Union, it was at once proper then to wait the progress of events, and obvious that they must result sooner or later in the proposed annexation.

It is very certain that the reasons which caused the settled opposition of Jefferson and Madison to any relinquishment of Texas, and which, after that unlucky mistake, caused the earnest desire of all the succeeding administrations to retrace and retrieve it, by getting back the lost territory by treaty with Mexico, even though it should be at the expense of a liberal price, have not ceased to exist. This is no new thing. It is no sudden experiment of the South, as is alleged, to recruit a political strength felt to be failing before the rapid growth and extension of the free states. It is simply the revival of an old question, established by the emphatic authority of many of the elder and the most eminent sages of the republic as one of high national importance, and which has for a few past years been kept in abeyance or temporary suspension only by a peculiar state of circumstances.

Whether the proper period for its revival has arrived, may perhaps be a subject of difference of opinion. Those who regard the length of time for which Texas has maintained her independence, together with the manifest and utter hopelessness of any possible reconquest by Mexico, as now sufficient to justify disregard of the nominal rights still absurdly pretended by the latter, may certainly claim that the proper period is fully mature. And when to those considerations is added that of the danger of England's acquiring the possession of, or dominant control over, the young state, we can feel no surprise at the earnestness of their interest in the prompt settlement of the question.

Mr. Tyler has seen fit to precipitate it, in a manner much more eager than dignified, to a point which now compels an early and decisive action upon it. What may have been his personal motives in thus urging it we little care to inquire. Perhaps they were entirely disinterested and upright; perhaps in the forlorn position to which his administration had sunk, he was prompted by desire, according to the common phrase, to make "political capital" for himself; perhaps, as in the greater proportion of men's actions, his motives were a tangled web of the good and the evil. At any rate, the thing is done; the question is forced upon us; it must be fully met, and it may as well be settled promptly and quietly, on the basis to which it is perfectly palpable that it must come at last.

The two common objections against the annexation have but little real weight; namely, that of unwieldy and dangerous extension of territory, and that of its alleged bearing upon the institution of slavery. To the first, a sufficient answer might be found in the peculiar reasons above referred to, of geographical and political fitness, if not necessity. But independently of these; independently, too, of those derived from the worse evils of an English possession; independently of the commercial advantages to the rest of the Union involved in the measure; independently of the boundless facilities for smuggling by which Texas could be made the avenue for the supply of the whole West with foreign goods; independently of the evils of a hostile commercial rivalry between two contiguous countries so similar in climate, soil, productions and population, instead of that unity of nationality and policy, in all respects properly befitting them — independently of all these reasons, we say the objection has no force for us.

Our system of government is one which, rightly administered; administered on the principles of the state-rights theory — will bear indefinite extension; nor do we doubt but that in the fulness of time it is destined to embrace within its wide sweep every habitable square inch of the continent. Our rapid ratio of increase in population, together with that *diffusiveness* which appears to be a principle of our national character and which will never permit our fast multiplying millions to confine themselves within territorial limits so long as their movement remains unchecked by any great natural barriers of division, insures the arrival of a not very distant day that shall witness this consummation.

And as for what may be termed the antislavery objection, this has no greater force

than the other. The question of slavery is not a federal or national but a local question. The Abolition movement has erroneously assumed for it the former character and has chosen the federal government as the point or avenue of attack against the institution. Hence the desire of those whose conscientious views of duty make them participators in that movement, to strengthen the ascendency of the free states in the general government; and on the other hand that of the South to maintain as long as possible the equilibrium of which it has always been so jealous. The one hopes and the other fears that the federal government will fall under the control of the Abolition Party, who are urging with zeal and confidence the propagandism which they expect to extend successfully over all the free states.

For ourselves, we repeat that we do not regard the question as a *federal* but as a *local* one — not as a political but a moral and economical one, the decision of which must rest, voluntarily, with the slave states themselves. This balance of political power between the two sections we regard as of little consequence. The controlling predominance of the free states in the national government, even supposing it to be in the hands of the Abolition Party itself, though it might dissolve the Union, would not dissolve the bonds of slavery within the slave states. Nor, on the other hand, would that institution be prolonged by the reversed state of things. The eventual settlement of that unhappy question will be through the operation of much deeper and broader influences than any of these mistaken and injurious political efforts.

We have no idea that the recovery of Texas would materially affect the equilibrium referred to. Free states will be made faster than slave ones, to say nothing of the probable decay of that institution in some of the more northern of the Southern states, in proportion to its southward growth over Texas. But even if it were to have that effect — so that the annexation should preserve to the South that balancing power which should still frustrate the worse than fruitless efforts of those who aim to wield against slavery the enginery of the federal government — the wiser and truer friend of the universal cause of human liberty and of the perpetuation of the Union should witness with satisfaction rather than regret such a result; a satisfaction to be derived chiefly from his interest in the cause of the slave and his sincere desire to accelerate the day of his emancipation in the only mode either practicable or desirable.

But while we thus assent to the reception of Texas into the Union, seeing little force in the objections urged against it and viewing as a necessary political and geographical fact, let us not be supposed willing to witness its adoption in the violent and hasty manner in which Mr. Tyler, without regard either to the claims of Mexico or to political decency, appears to have urged it on. It is far too important a matter to be thus sprung upon us and hurried summarily into effect by a Vice-President and Senate, in the form of a treaty, without consultation with the representatives of the people and before time or opportunity for any popular discussion of the question and the formation of any distinct public opinion on the subject. That such process of discussion would result in general acquiescence, we have little doubt, but the precedent would be altogether too dangerous to dispense with the former in a confident reliance upon the latter.

Nor ought the annexation to be made without the consent of Mexico or her recognition of the independence of her successfully revolted province. We must avoid even the appearance of evil. It is not enough that we may be abundantly certain that Mexico can never again even hope to shake the established independence of Texas. The nominal, theoretical right is still asserted, which we cannot disregard without incurring a just liability to declaration of war by Mexico. It is not to be thought of that we should ever place ourselves in such an attitude toward any foreign power, strong or weak. Least of all, should we do so in relation to one of the feebleness of our poor neighbor on the southwest, against whom we could not but regard Mr. Tyler's blustering in his last Annual Message, as in disgustingly bad taste — contrasted too, as it was, with the honey-sweetness of his tone in the adjacent sentences in relation to England.

It would not, in all probability, be difficult to obtain the consent of Mexico, or such a recognition by her of the independence of Texas as would remove this obstacle. Her feeble and needy government, embarrassed as it already is by heavy debt to us, could, doubtless with but little difficulty be induced to surrender an imaginary title to a territory already irrecoverably lost and to exchange the neighborhood of a hostile state, now a perpetual thorn in her side, for that of a powerful and peaceful friend and ally. The proper terms of such an arrangement, this is not the place to discuss in advance. Under the guidance of the noble intellect and high and patriotic integrity, recently called to preside over our foreign relations, we feel abundantly sure that no step will be taken in this matter which any American will have to contemplate with either shame or regret.

This is no war of defense, but one of unnecessary and of offensive aggression. It is Mexico that is defending her firesides, her castles and altars, not we.

HENRY CLAY

39.

JOSHUA GIDDINGS: Texas and Slavery

A treaty providing for the annexation of Texas by the United States was presented to the Senate for ratification on April 22, 1844, and was rejected by the Senate on June 8. President Tyler had tried to make annexation a wholly national issue but, with the publication in April of a communique from the secretary of state, John C. Calhoun, to the British envoy in Washington stating that the annexation of Texas was necessary to protect the institution of slavery in the United States, the issue assumed sectional overtones. Representative Joshua Giddings of Ohio combined both Whig and Abolitionist sentiments in an address to the House on May 21, 1844, opposing annexation. A portion of his speech is reprinted below.

Source: *Globe, App.*, 28 Cong., 1 Sess., pp. 704-708.

IT IS WELL KNOWN, Mr. Chairman, that since the formation of this confederacy there has long been a supposed conflict between the interests of free labor and of slave labor, between the Southern and Northern states. I do not say that the conflict is real; I only say that in the minds of the people, both North and South, and in this hall, such conflict exists. This supposed conflict has given rise to difference of policy in our national councils. I refer to the tariff, in particular, as being a favorite measure of the North, while free trade is advocated by the South. I refer also to our harbor improvements and the improvement of our river navigation, as another measure in which the Northwest and West have felt great interest and much anxiety and to which the South [has] been constantly opposed.

But so equally balanced has been the political power between these opposing interests that for five years past our lake commerce has been entirely abandoned; and such were the deficits of the tariff that for many years our revenues were unequal to the support of government. Time eventually gave the friends of Northern interests power to amend the tariff, and, by the fixed order of nature's law, our population at the north has increased so much faster than it has in the slave states that, under the late census, the North and West now hold the balance of political power; and at the present session we have passed a bill for the protection of our lake and river commerce, which now awaits the action of the Senate and will soon become a law.

But let us admit Texas, and we shall place the balance of power in the hands of the Texans themselves. They, with the Southern states, will control the policy and the destiny of this nation; our tariff will then be held at the will of the Texan advocates of free trade. Are our friends of the North prepared to deliver over this great national policy to the people of Texas? Are the liberty-loving Democrats of Pennsylvania ready to give up our tariff? — to strike off all protection from the articles of iron and coal, and other productions of that state in order to purchase a slave market for their neighbors, who, in the words of Thomas Jefferson Randolph, "breed men for the market like oxen for the shambles?"

40.

Negro Resolutions on Segregated Schools

Laws discriminating against Negroes in Massachusetts had been largely done away with by the 1840s, through the efforts of the antislavery forces operating there, but the public school system remained segregated until 1855. In spite of opposition, the School Committee of Boston turned down several petitions to desegregate the schools. One such petition was rejected in 1844. A mass meeting of Negroes in the city on June 24 protested this denial and issued the following resolutions urging the School Committee to reconsider its action.

Source: *Liberator,* June 28, 1844.

Resolved, that, impelled by a deep sense of gratitude, we tender to Dr. D. H. Storer our unfeigned thanks for his successful efforts in instituting the late investigation of affairs connected with the Smith School, and for his unremitting attention to the same from the commencement to the close.

Resolved, that we present our most grateful acknowledgements to the Hon. John C. Park, for the late voluntary and disinterested devotion of his time and eminent talents in the cause of the wronged and neglected colored children of this city.

Whereas, we, the colored citizens of the city of Boston, have recently sent a petition to the School Committee respectfully praying for the abolition of the separate schools for colored children, and asking for the rights and privileges extended to other citizens in respect to the common-school system, viz., the right to send our children to the schools established in the respective districts in which we reside; and

Whereas, the School Committee, at their last meeting, passed a vote stating, in substance, that the prayer of our petition would not be granted, and that the separate schools for colored children would be continued; and

Whereas, we believe, and have the opinion of eminent counsel, that the institution and support of separate schools, at the public charge, for any one class of the inhabitants in exclusion of any other class is contrary to the laws of this Commonwealth; therefore,

Resolved, that we consider the late action of the School Committee, in regard to our petition asking for the entire abolition of separate schools for colored children, as erroneous and unsatisfactory.

Resolved, that while we would not turn aside from our main object, the abolition of the separate colored schools, we cannot allow this occasion to pass without an expression of our surprise and regret at the recent acquittal by the School Committee of Abner Forbes, principal of the Smith School, and of our deep conviction that he is totally unworthy of his present responsible station and that the colored parents of this city are recommended to withdraw their children from the exclusive school established in contravention of that equality of privileges which is the vital principle of the school system of Massachusetts.

Resolved, that a copy of the above preamble and resolutions be sent to the chairman of the School Committee, with a request that the petition heretofore presented may be reconsidered, and that we be allowed a hearing on said petition before them.

Resolved, that the heartfelt thanks of the colored citizens of Boston are due to Messrs. George S. Hillard and John T. Sargent for the humane and independent stand recently taken by them in the School Committee in behalf of the rights and welfare of the colored children.

Resolved, that the expression of the sense of this meeting be transmitted to the several gentlemen named in the foregoing resolutions, and be also published in the city papers.

41.

The Injustice of Tenant Farming

The Van Rensselaer estate, which comprised more than 15,000 acres of land around Albany, New York, and which dated back to the seventeenth century, was still farmed by tenants in the 1840s who held the land in perpetual lease and paid rent in wheat and personal services. In 1839 tenants formed antirent associations to repudiate the arrangement and assaulted agents who came to enforce it. In 1844 antirenters petitioned the New York state legislature to terminate Van Rensselaer's title to the land and to grant title free to those who farmed it. The petition was referred to a committee that was sympathetic to the antirenters but did not report in their favor. The following selection is taken from the committee's report.

Source: *Documents of the Assembly of the State of New-York,* 67 Session, 1844, Vol. VII, No. 189.

THE LANDS IN THE MANOR are nearly all held under perpetual leases, very similar in character, and granted, for the most part, many years since. . . .

These leases had their origin in Europe in the age of feudalism, and still preserve those restrictions which were engrafted upon them at that barbarous period, and which are so justly odious to every friend of free institutions of government.

These restrictions were devised by the sovereigns and nobles of the several nations of Europe, for the express purpose of strengthening their own power and increasing their own wealth, while at the same time they weakened and impoverished their unhappy tenants. Their sole object was to convert their tenants into abject serfs or slaves, and make them mere appendages of the soil, and to be kept forever in a condition of hopeless vassalage, without a prospect of relief.

To prevent them from leaving the estates on which they had taken up their residence, the arbitrary restrictions of exacting one quarter of the purchase money of the property of which they occupied, whenever it was transferred to a new tenant, was imposed upon them, thus virtually prohibiting them from changing their residence, without submitting to a ruinous sacrifice of their property. This restriction, known as the quarter sale, exists in many of the leases of the manor of Rensselaerwyck, and constitutes in this country, even more than in that of its origin, a most intolerable grievance.

The American people are emphatically an emigrating people. From almost every township in the older states, large colonies of farmers and mechanics have emigrated to new settlements in the West. But many of the tenants of the manor of Rensselaerwyck are unable to avail themselves, without great sacrifice, of the privilege enjoyed by their fellow citizens in other sections of the Union. If they wish to dispose of their property, one quarter of its price is liable to be forfeited to the proprietor of the manor.

A restriction of this nature, your committee feel confident, must be regarded as extremely unjust and oppressive, and as operating most effectually to check if not to arrest altogether the prosperity of that community in which it is in force. In many countries of Europe, this, as well as other barbarous features of the feudal system, have long since been abolished by express laws; shall it be suffered to remain longer as a reproach to the intelligence and civilization of a free republic? The reservation by the lessors of the manor of all water privileges, your committee regard as in the highest degree injurious to the improvement and prosperity of the two counties in which the manor is situated.

No section of the state is better adapted for a manufacturing district than this; water power is abundant, and the facilities for disposing of manufactured articles unsurpassed. But by the onerous prohibition of the leases, the tenants, unless they obtain the right by a new purchase, are forbidden to use this water power, even should it remain unoccupied for a hundred years.

Such a condition of things, the House will not fail to perceive, must be productive of serious and lasting injury to the interest of the inhabitants of the manor. While other sections of the state, untrammeled by any particle of these oppressions and antirepublican restrictions which exist in the manor of Rensselaerwyck, are advancing with giant strides in all the elements of moral and physical greatness, the inhabitants of this manor are condemned, by the hard tenure of the leases which their honest and unsuspecting ancestors bequeathed them, to toil on from year to year, in condition of comparative servitude, depressed by a constant blight upon their prosperity, and unrelieved by the prospect of a release from their burthens.

It is a source of just pride with the American farmer, that he is the proprietor of the soil which he cultivates. This honorable feeling cannot be shared by the unfortunate tenant of the manor of Rensselaerwyck. He cultivates the soil of another, and is liable at any time to have his growing crops destroyed, or his fences demolished by the proprietors of the manor, in the exercise of some one of the numerous privileges reserved to them in their leases. He is consequently depressed by these influences which tend to generate in the American farmer of more favored districts that spirit of independence which is not humbled by the payment of an annual tribute, acknowledges no superior, and which raises him a rank in the social scale never attained by the workingman of any country but our own.

42.

WILLIAM KIRKLAND: The Paradise of the Poor

According to the "safety-valve theory" of the frontier, the West would serve as a refuge for the underprivileged workers of the East. As the workers availed themselves of this refuge, the competition among those that stayed behind would cease. In the 1840s the theory was widely discussed, and on the basis of it the Democrats supported, and the Whigs opposed, a cheap land policy. However, despite the liberal land laws that were passed, workers failed to migrate West. The author of the article reprinted in part below, William Kirkland, attempted to induce the poor laborer to fulfill his theoretical role.

Source: *United States Magazine and Democratic Review*, August 1844: "The West, The Paradise of the Poor."

WE KNOW AND WE CONCLUDE that all the ends of the earth know by this time that "Westward the star of Empire takes its way." We feel it, and with all due pride; but at present we have nothing to do with the star of Empire. A humbler theme — a plain, practical theme, though a Western one — employs our pen, and we shall endeavor to treat it in a true Western (which we shall beg leave to interpret as plain and practical) manner, without "struggling to impart some impression, too mighty or too unique for words."

The impression we wish to convey respects the poor man — the really poor man. . . . For such a man the Western wilderness is a blooming field, and though there may be poetry, there is no fiction in calling the West his home.

The first aim of a poor man of that class must of course be the necessaries of life. Here he finds them at first cost. He pays for most of them in profit to nobody; not to the farmer, for if he chooses, he may dig for himself and plow for himself, since he can hire both ground and oxen if he has not money to buy them, paying the hire in a portion of the fruits raised. He pays nothing to the carrier, for articles of the first necessity are at hand; nor to the wholesale or retail dealer, for what his own hands do not procure directly he obtains by barter for their labor. In the new country the earth grants a free supply to all those who have strength and courage to take it from her bosom. . . .

The poor man in the new country has one aid not dreamed of in the older settlements — his children. These are elsewhere a subject of dread to those who depend on the day's labor for the day's food, and not always as welcome as they should be to some people who have plenty to eat. Here, "the more the merrier," and the better off, too. For six months of the year hats and shoes are out of fashion, and drapery of an almost classical simplicity is quite sufficient for the younger children. So the "outward" is easily provided for; while the inner man is solaced with bread and milk half a dozen times a day, and asks for little else.

At seven or eight years old these bread-and-milk urchins begin to be useful; to "do chores," to run on errands, and even to drive oxen and feed calves. I have seen one of these functionaries, hatless and shoeless, harrowing with a great pair of oxen, and issuing his haws and gees with all the authority of threescore, while his head reached scarcely halfway up the sides of the team he was driving. From this they become more and more useful until they reach their teens, when he must be a poor block indeed who does not pay back into the common treasury more than he takes from it. "A son and daughter are the rich man's blessing," saith the proverb, framed, no doubt, by someone who valued the riches more than son and daughter both; but our poor man is more fortunate, for he counts each one of his half dozen, or half score, a blessing. Instead of population pressing on the means of subsistence, our granaries are full to over-flowing, and stout hands and active heads are the very things we need to turn our abundance to the best account. . . .

The chief and last resource of the poor man among us which we shall mention at present is one which we have not seen laid down in any work on political, nor even on domestic, economy; nay, it is even eschewed by thrifty managers elsewhere, but here too generally practised to be omitted in our budget of ways and means. It is the system — we speak advisedly — we mean system, not practice — of borrowing. Its importance to the well-doing of him who comes into the woods with nothing is seen at a glance.

Every neighborhood is, by this plan, turned into a joint-stock association, the goods of each and every member being, in some sense, common property. It differs from other joint-stock companies in this:

that the less anyone puts in, the more he takes out. No fee is required for admission into this general loan company; mere residence confers its privileges, as it does those of citizenship. The newcomer is occasionally troubled with a little bashfulness about using his freedom, but he soon shakes it off, and becomes as perfect in the art of borrowing as those to whom it has become second nature. It requires but a short time to get the run of needful articles, so as to know pretty nearly where to find them when wanted, and then the work is done.

Elsewhere the rich give, sometimes, but they never lend. The poor cannot give much, but they are bounteous lenders of all that they possess. We find it convenient to consider all as poor, and, consequently, all as lenders. Or, if there be degrees among us, the rich man is he who has most to lend. Horace says, of the rich men of his day, *prosunt furibus,* they are a resource to pilferers, *i.e.,* can be plundered without feeling it. Our rich man is rather a resource for borrowers — one who can lend and never flinch. Now, borrowing is more respectable than begging; it is less trouble and it saves the feelings, too. As the benefit received is to be repaid only by a contra loan, and as by the principles of our company, one is required only to lend what he has, it is plain that the utterly poor man is doing a good business.

Scarcely any article is more frequently borrowed than a pair of hands, and sometimes a dozen pair at once. You pass by a stack of wheat, near which a threshing machine is planted, around which you see some twelve or twenty men and boys busily employed. The owner would seem to be a sort of rural nabob, to be able to command the services of so many active people; but so far from this being the fact, he may be the poorest of the group, since poverty is no obstacle to the early threshing of the wheat. He is to pay each of his colaborers day's work when called upon; and, so far as getting out his grain is concerned, he is no worse off than the richest man in the neighborhood. This arrangement tells plainly for the benefit of him whose hands are his all.

And these hands, well used, will soon place him above even this creditable resource of poverty, or enable him to exchange at par. Nowhere within the limits of our observation does so large a share of the returns of labor go to the pay of the laborer. The employed has nearly as much command of the necessaries and conveniences of life as the employer. Improved land, horses, cattle, farming implements have a much smaller relative value than the labor which makes them available to the owner. Aside from the cost of getting produce to market, the owner of 100 acres of improved land, with everything to correspond, is much less rich than one who owns an equally large, well-stocked, and fertile farm in western New York.

Wages, nominally higher here, are, relatively, very much higher. The services which a bushel of wheat could buy anywhere east of Lake Erie could not here be procured for less than a bushel and a half; and as to every other article of domestic production, the ratio would be still higher. This is owing, in part, to the extreme cheapness of land, and in part to the scantiness of our working population, compared with the quantity of land under cultivation. The hired laborer is, then, essentially on a par with his employer, which is the case nowhere else that we know of. . . .

The elastic feeling, incident to a new and growing country, communicates itself to all; and nowhere does the tiller of the soil so speedily recover himself from the effect of untoward circumstances. The power of self-adaptation seems inherent in the settler. He learns even to make present difficulties conduce to future prosperity by means of the habits of economy and management, which

would have been learned with far less rapidity and certainty under easier circumstances. . . .

This condition of things, which, after allowing for all the hardships and disadvantages connected with it, we may truly call blessed, in reference to the masses who are benefited by it, has its ultimate origin in the fact that the government transfers the right of property in the soil for a consideration scarce greater than the price of the title deeds. The nation virtually bestows upon each of its poor citizens as much land as he can cultivate. What other nation has the power of conferring such a boon upon the poor? We say upon the *poor*, for experience has shown that none others can profit by it. Only to the poor man, who wishes to occupy and improve the land, is it a benefit; and to him it is invaluable. It forms a practical corrective of the evils caused by the tendency of property to accumulate in large masses.

It is the aim of a good government to lessen these evils without encroaching upon the rights of individuals. Our happy position enables us to strike at the root of the difficulty, and by the virtual gift of a freehold to every poor man who is disposed to take possession of it, to prevent that excessive inequality of property which in the countries of the Old World is the worst enemy alike of individual happiness and national prosperity. It is surely no inconsiderable step toward maintaining something like an equilibrium to bestow on the poor a possession which the labor of his own hands will render ample for his support. We, in fact, secure independence to all who are able and willing to work. No man here need continue long in the service of others; and, therefore, those who desire such services are obliged to bid high for them in order to induce the strong-armed to defer for a while the satisfaction of working for themselves as masters, with that feeling of independence which is to the American as the breath of his nostrils.

In order to be impartial, we ought, perhaps, to set forth on the other side the complaints of the Western settler that what the government gives him with one hand it labors to take away with the other, by levying an enormous duty on the manufactured articles for which he may wish to barter the fruits of the soil. The agriculturist within reach of manufacturing establishments has a compensation for the extra prices he is compelled to pay in the corresponding price which he receives for his productions. To the Western farmer the burden is without an equivalent, and he feels it to be most oppressive. But to touch upon this would lead us to the vexed question of the tariff, in which wise heads labor as in a treadmill, to which we have no desire to follow them.

43.

GEORGE HENRY EVANS: A New Homestead Policy

The fundamental premise of agrarianism, as preached by George Henry Evans, was man's inherent right to the use of the soil. At a time when the East was becoming overcrowded with people in search of work, there were vast tracts of public land to the West that reformers such as Evans hoped to see made available. A new homestead policy enabling the landless citizen to take free title to a portion of the public land would ease the labor situation in the cities, push wages up, and provide occupations for those who could not find work. Evans published the following memorial to Congress in his newspaper on November 30, 1844.

Source: *Working Man's Advocate*, November 30, 1844.

THE UNDERSIGNED CITIZENS of New York respectfully represent, that in their opinion, the system of land traffic imported to this country from Europe is wrong in principle; that it is fast debasing us to the condition of a nation of dependent tenants, of which condition a rapid increase of inequality, misery, pauperism, vice, and crime are the necessary consequences; and that, therefore now, in the infancy of the republic, we should take effectual measures to eradicate the evil and establish a principle more in accordance with our republican theory, as laid down in the Declaration of Independence. To which end we propose that the general government shall no longer traffic, or permit traffic, in the public lands yet in its possession, and that they shall be laid out in farms and lots for the free use of such citizens (not possessed of other land) as will occupy them, allowing the settler the right to dispose of his possession to anyone *not possessed of other land;* and that the jurisdiction of the public lands be transferred to states only on condition that such a disposition should be made of them.

Your memorialists offer the following reasons for such a disposition of the land as they propose:

1. It would increase the number of free

holders and decrease the antirepublican dependence of those who might not become freeholders; exactly reversing the state of things now in progress.

2. As the drain of the population would gradually be to where the land was free, the price of all land held for traffic would gradually decrease, till, ultimately, the landholders would see greater advantages in an agrarian plan that would make every man a freeholder than in the system of land selling, under which their children might become dependent tenants.

3. City populations would diminish gradually, till every inhabitant could be the owner of a comfortable habitation; and the country population would be more compactly settled, making less roads and bridges necessary, and giving greater facilities of education.

4. There need be no standing army, for there would soon be a chain of townships along the frontiers, settled by independent freemen willing and able to protect the country.

5. The danger of Indian aggressions would be materially lessened if our people only took possession of land enough for their *use*.

6. The strongest motive to encroachments by whites on the rights of the Indians would be done away with by prohibiting *speculation* in land.

7. The ambition, avarice, or enterprise that would, under the present system, add acre to acre would be directed more usefully to the *improvement* of those to which each man's possession was limited.

8. There would be no repudiation of state debts, for let people settle the land compactly and they could and would make all desirable improvements without going into debt.

9. National prosperity and the prosperity of the masses would be coincident, here again reserving the present order of things, of which England is a notable example.

10. Great facilities would be afforded to test the various plans of association which now engage the attention of so large a proportion of our citizens and which have been found to work so well, so far as the accumulation of wealth and the prevention of crime and pauperism are concerned, in the case of those longest established, for instance, the Zoarites, Rappites, and Shakers.

11. The now increasing evil of office seeking would be diminished, both by doing away with the necessity of many offices now in existence and by enabling men to obtain a comfortable existence without degrading themselves to become office beggars. Cincinnatus and Washington could with difficulty be prevailed upon to take office, because they knew there was more real enjoyment in the cultivation of their own homesteads.

12. It would, in a great measure, do away the now necessary evil of laws and lawyers, as there could be no disputes about rents, mortgages, or land titles, and morality would be promoted by the encouragement and protection of industry.

13. As the people of England are now fast turning their attention to the recovery of their long-lost right to the soil, it would give them encouragement in their object and enable them the sooner to furnish happy homes for the thousands who otherwise would come among us as exiles from their native land.

14. The principle of an *equal right to the soil*, once established, would be the recognition of a truth that has been lost sight of by civilization, and which, in our opinion, would tend powerfully to realize the glorious aspirations of philanthropists — *universal peace and universal freedom.*

44.

Timothy Walker: The Right of Eminent Domain

As an Ohio judge, as a teacher in one of the pioneering law schools of the West, and as a writer on legal subjects, Timothy Walker brought distinction both to himself and to his profession. He served for a time as editor of the Western Law Journal, *and many problems of law in the West, where good lawyers were few, were referred to him for settlement. The problem of the right of eminent domain was discussed by him in his journal in May 1844.*

Source: *Western Law Journal,* May 1844: "Constitutional Power of the State Legislatures to take Private Property for Public Uses."

I HAVE RECEIVED the following letter, which, though much occupied with other matters, I have concluded to answer at once. My readers will understand that I do it in haste.

Columbus, Ind., April 9, 1844.

T. WALKER, ESQ., ED., *Law Journal,*

Sir: The members of the bar, here, are very desirous to know the rule of decision which has obtained in those states where railroads and canals have been made by corporations, in regard to the constitutional right of the legislature to invest such corporations with power to take private property for such improvements.

We have a railroad in progress here, under an act of incorporation conferring, in the broadest terms, *the power to force the right of way* by paying an assessment made exclusively by the corporation. We are generally inclined to question the constitutionality of the law, and the scarcity of reports here deprives us of adequate means to satisfy ourselves fully.

In consultation with all the gentlemen of the profession residing here, it was agreed that it might not be improper for a subscriber to your journal to request of you to notice this subject in your next number. An abbreviated notice of the current of decisions or a short editorial embracing the subject, or in such other manner as may be dictated by your better judgment, would be useful and instructive to us, here, and would be acknowledged as a courtesy.

I am, with much respect, your obedient servant,

GEO. E. TINGI

CONSTITUTIONAL PROVISIONS

THE 2ND ARTICLE of the Ordinance of 178 declares, "Should the public exigencie make it necessary, for the common preservation, to take any person's property or t demand his particular services, full compensation shall be made for the same."

The 5th Amendment of the federal Constitution declares, "Nor shall private property be taken for public use without just compensation."

The 4th Section of the 8th Article of th constitution of Ohio declares, "Privat property ought, and ever shall be forever inviolate but always subservient to the public welfare, provided a compensation b made to the owner."

The 8th Section of the 8th Article of th

onstitution of Ohio declares, "That the ght of trial by jury shall be inviolate."

The 5th Section of the 1st Article of the onstitution of Indiana declares, "That in all vil cases, where the value in controversy nall exceed the sum of $20, and in all riminal cases, except in petit misdemeanors, which shall be punishable by fine only, not xceeding $3, in such manner as the legislaure may prescribe by law, the right of trial y jury shall remain inviolate."

The 7th Section of the 1st Article of the onstitution of Indiana declares, "That no nan's particular services shall be demanded r property taken or applied to public use vithout the consent of his representatives or vithout a just compensation being made nerefor."

JUDICIAL DECISIONS

Gardner v. *Trustees of Newburgh.* . . . Gardner owned a farm through which a ream flowed, which he used for various aluable purposes. The stream issued from a oring in his neighbor's farm. The legislaure authorized the trustees to take water om the spring in pipes, for the use of the own of Newburgh, but made no provision or making up to Gardner the loss he vould sustain by diverting the water. *Held,* nat he was entitled to a fair compensation efore the water could be diverted; and as ne law made no provision therefor, an injnction was granted.

Rogers v. *Bradshaw,* in error. . . . The egislature authorized the Canal Commisioners to take lands necessary for the canal. t became necessary to use the turnpike rack for the canal and to construct a new urnpike on Bradshaw's land. He brought respass. *Held,* that trespass would not lie. Bradshaw was entitled to compensation; ut as his land was necessary for the new oad, which was rendered necessary by the anal, the Commissioners were not trespassrs. A turnpike is a public road. *Dictum,*

that even though an act taking private property for public uses makes no provision for compensation, it still shields the persons entering from liability as trespassers. . . .

Beekman v. *Saratoga Rail Road Company.* . . . The company had projected the rail road over Beekman's land, the only convenient place. He had refused his consent and would make no agreement for compensation. Pursuant to the charter, the governor had appointed commissioners, who had appraised damages, and the amount was deposited in bank for Beekman, who had notice of the fact. He applied for an injunction, which was refused. *Held,* that a rail road was a public use, if the legislature chose so to consider it, for which private property might be taken. That the government might exercise the right of eminent domain through a private corporation. That the charter must provide a fair mode of compensation, but it need not be a jury, since the constitutional guaranty of a right to a trial by jury relates only to the trial of issues of fact in civil and criminal cases in courts of justice.

Cooper v. *Williams.* . . . The law authorizing the construction of the Ohio canals empowers the Commissioners to take any land, water, or materials necessary; and if application be made within one year for compensation, they are to appoint three or five appraisers to assess damages, deducting benefits, which award the Commissioners are to pay. Cooper owned land on Mad River, commanding a large water power, part of which he was using. The Canal Commissioners constructed a dam above him and a feeder, which greatly diminished the water power Cooper might use on his land. This quantity was necessary to supply the canal. On its transit two-thirds could be sold as water power, which the Commissioners proposed to sell for the use of the state. Cooper applied for an injunction, which was refused. *Held,* that Cooper was entitled to compensation for any of his land taken or for any loss of waer flowing by or through his land. But he had no such right in the water of Mad River, that the state might not take so much as the canal required, making compensation. And having taken it, the state might use it in its transit or sell the use of it. The same affirmed in *Cooper* v. *Williams.* . . .

McArthur v. *Kelley et al.* . . . In this case the whole subject of jury trials is very fully considered. The particular point decided is that, as our constitution requires the compensation to be in money, the legislature cannot authorize the Canal Commissioners to compensate one man for the injury he will sustain in his water power by constructing a mill race on the land of another man.

Hunt's lessee v. *McMahan.* . . . In this case a construction was given to the clause relating to a trial by jury. The question was as to the constitutionality of the occupying claimant law, where three Commissioners, instead of a jury, assess the value of improvements; and the Court held the law constitutional.

Young v. *Buckingham et al.* . . . The legislature authorized the erection of a toll bridge over the Muskingum, providing that damages should be estimated by three Commissioners appointed by the Court of Common Pleas. Only two of the Commissioners concurred in the award. *Held*, that a toll bridge is a public use for which private property may be taken; and that the award of the majority of the Commissioners is sufficient.

REMARKS

THESE DECLARATIONS AND DECISIONS assert two great principles. First, the private right of an individual must yield to the *eminent domain* of government, whenever the public good requires it. And this is well, for otherwise it would be in the power of one obstinate owner to prevent the execution of any of those great public improvements which

contribute so much to the general con[venience] and happiness. Second, to equal[ize] the burden and avoid all hardship, the ow[n]er of the property so taken is to receiv[e] compensation, which shall be full and ju[st]. Any law, therefore, which should conde[mn] private property for any other than a pu[blic] use or which should not provide for suc[h] compensation would be unconstitutional.

One question which has arisen un[der] these provisions is whether the compen[sa]tion must be paid before the property [is] taken. The answer is, that if a law autho[riz]ing property to be taken provide an equi[ta]ble mode of ascertaining compensation a[nd] direct it to be paid, the law is valid; but [in] any given case, if the owner of the prope[rty] can make it appear that his compensat[ion] would be doubtful or improbable, he m[ay] obtain an injunction against taking t[he] property until compensation has been [se]cured.

Another question is whether benefits [are] to be taken into view in fixing the amou[nt] of compensation. Upon this question th[ere] has been much contrariety of opini[on.] There is an obvious distinction to be ma[de] between paying for property already tak[en] and paying for consequential injury wh[ere] property is not taken. To the latter case [the] constitutional provisions do not apply. It [is] a mere question of damages; and as th[ere] can be no actual damages where the ben[efit] exceeds the injury, there is no doubt t[hat] benefits may be properly offset against co[n]sequential injuries. But can benefits be [off]set against the value of property actua[lly] taken? In this state, where the compen[sa]tion must be "*in money*," the answer m[ust] undoubtedly be in the negative; for t[he] benefits derived from the vicinity of a pu[b]lic improvement, however great, are not l[it]erally money.

But how is it, where the compensation [is] only required to be "just" or "full," wit[h]out specifying money? Can benefits then [be] offset against property? It would seem th[ey] cannot; for while many share in the benef[it] f any great public work, besides those whose property is taken for its construction, his rule would make the burden fall wholly on the latter class, which would be *unjust*. t may be said, however, that where a man s not made absolutely poorer by taking part of his property, no injury is done to him. But the answer is, that comparatively he is made poorer by so much as the property is worth, because his neighbors, whose property is not taken, share equally in the benefits. On the whole then, the rule would seem to be that property actually taken for public benefits must be paid for, without reference to benefits, which can only be off-set against consequential damages.

Still another question is whether the amount of compensation must be determined by a jury of twelve persons. It has been decided that any fair and equitable mode will be sufficient, as by disinterested appraisers or commissioners. As to what are public uses, it has been held that canals, turnpikes, rail roads, toll bridges, supplies of water for a town, and the like are public uses; and that the legislature may exercise its right of appropriating private property for such uses through private corporations.

45.

John H. Griscom: Report on Sanitary Conditions in New York City

Between 1830 and 1840 the population of New York, since 1800 the largest city in the country, increased 50 percent (the population in 1840 was about 300,000), and a large part of the increase was made up of immigrants. Those sections of the city where the immigrant poor joined other slum dwellers were popularly known both in New York and in other cities as the "fever nest." Dr. John Griscom, a pioneer in the field of public health, was one of the first to investigate the relationship of a slum environment to health. His findings were embodied in a report, published in 1845, sections of which are reprinted here.

Source: *The Sanitary Condition of the Laboring Population of New York, A Discourse Delivered on the 30th of December, 1844, at the Repository of the American Institute,* New York, 1845, pp. 2-24.

WHEN IT WAS MY PLEASURE, as it was my duty, in 1842 and '43, to devote my small energies to the sanitary improvement of my native city, stimulated by the consciousness of being engaged in a work heretofore unried in any systematic form, and promising results of the highest and most enduring interests to my fellow citizens, I seized the occasion to recommend to the Common Council the adoption of a measure of Health Police, which I thought of serious necessity. It was the last effort I was enabled to make upon the subject, before I was again consigned to the private ranks, by removal from office.

I then hoped to see the small beginning I had made, grow into shape and usefulness under the fostering hands of whoever might be my successors. But, in common with all who had the subject so much at heart, I have been disappointed; for not only was it untouched but the seeds which I had planted were neglected, and suffered to rot in the ground.

Another political revolution brought with it the hope, strengthened by loud professions of municipal reform, that at last the day was certain and at hand, when this subject would be no longer allowed to slumber but would be regarded as one of the most urgent, and among the first, of the objects of attention by the new Common Council. The expectations of the public could not be mistaken; but an erroneous appreciation, or an entire misconception, in some quarter, of the duties and requisite qualifications of an officer of health has deferred the hopes entertained of the further prosecution of this interesting, and vitally important sanitary reform.

The desire which stimulated me in former days was, however, not suffered to sleep in my bosom; a year's reflection, and daily and more extended observation, have not only confirmed my confidence in the feasibility but increased the conviction of the necessity of the measure I had proposed, and they have enabled me to modify, enlarge, and illustrate the plan, while the determination displayed by the new chief magistrate to do *his* share of the reforms promised has inspired me afresh with the hope that the present might be a favorable time for a renewed presentation of my favorite design.

It is a measure of SANITARY REFORM. It is designed to relieve the city of a part of the heavy burden of sickness and mortality, which now oppresses its population, more especially that portion least able to relieve themselves, and most requiring the interposition and protection of law. It will be seen to be a measure of humanity, of justice to the poor, of safety to the whole people, and of economy to the public treasury.

The objects of this communication, briefly stated, are these: (1) to show that there is an immense amount of sickness, physical disability, and premature mortality, among the poorer classes; (2) that these are, to a large extent, unnecessary, being in a great degree the results of causes which are re-movable; (3) that these physical evils a[re] productive of moral evils of great magn[i]tude and number, and which, if considere[d] only in a pecuniary point of view, shou[ld] arouse the government and individuals to [a] consideration of the best means for their r[e]lief and prevention; and (4) to suggest t[he] means of alleviating these evils and preven[t]ing their recurrence to so great an e[x]tent. . . .

Our people, especially the more destitut[e] have been allowed to live out their bri[ef] lives in tainted and unwholesome atm[o]spheres, and be subject to the silent and i[n]visible encroachments of destructive age[n]cies from every direction, without o[ne] warning voice being raised to point to the[m] their danger, and without an effort to re[s]cue them from their impending fate. Fathe[rs] are taken from their children, husban[ds] from their wives, "ere they have lived o[ut] half their days"; the widows and orpha[ns] are thrown upon public or private char[ity] for support.

The money which is expended to sav[e] them from starvation, to educate them [in] the public schools, or, perchance, to mai[n]tain them in the workhouse or the prison, [if] judiciously spent in improving the sanita[ry] arrangements of the city, and instilling in[to] the population a knowledge of the mea[ns] by which their health might be protecte[d] and their lives prolonged and made happ[y] would have been not only saved but r[e]turned to the treasury in the increase[d] health of the population, a much bett[er] state of public morals, and, by consequenc[e] a more easily governed and respectab[le] community.

It is of course among the poorer labori[ng] classes that such knowledge is most wante[d] The rich, though they may be equally ign[o]rant of the laws of life and of the be[st] means of its preservation, live in larg[e] houses, with freer ventilation, and upo[n] food better adapted to support health an[d] life. Their means of obtaining greater com[-] forts and more luxuries are to them, thoug[h] perhaps unconsciously, the very reason of their prolonged lives.

Besides this, they are less harassed by the fears and uncertainty of obtaining for themselves and families a sufficiency of food and clothing. They are thus relieved of some of the most depressing influences which tend to reduce the energy of mind and body in the poor, and render the latter more susceptible to the inroads of disease.

Sanitary regulations affect the pauper class of the population more directly than any other, because they live in situations and circumstances which expose them more to attacks of disease. They are more crowded, they live more in cellars, their apartments are less ventilated, and more exposed to vapors and other emanations, etc., hence, ventilation, sewerage, and all other sanitary regulations are more necessary for them and would produce a greater comparative change in their condition. The influence of drainage upon the health and lives of the population, is too well known to require, at this day, any argument. . . .

The system of tenantage to which large numbers of the poor are subject, I think, must be regarded as one of the principal causes of the helpless and noisome manner in which they live. The basis of these evils is the subjection of the tenantry to the merciless inflictions and extortions of the sublandlord. A house, or a row, or court of houses, is hired by some person of the owner, on a lease of several years, for a sum which will yield a fair interest on the cost. The owner is thus relieved of the great trouble incident to the changes of tenants, and the collection of rents. His income is sure from one individual, and obtained without annoyance or oppression on his part. It then becomes the object of the lessee to make and save as much as possible, with his adventure, sufficient sometimes to enable him to purchase the property in a short time.

The tenements, in order to admit a great-

er number of families, are divided into small apartments, as numerous as decency will admit. Regard to comfort, convenience, and health, is the last motive; indeed, the great ignorance of this class of speculators (who are very frequently foreigners and keep a grog shop on the premises) would prevent a proper observance of these, had they the desire. These closets, for they deserve no other name, are then rented to the poor, from week to week, or month to month, the rent being almost invariably required in advance, at least for the first few terms.

The families moving in first, after the house is built, find it clean, but the lessee has no supervision over their habits, and however filthy the tenement may become, he cares not, so that he receives his rent. He and his family are often found steeped as low in depravity and discomforts as any of his tenants, being above them only in the possession of money, and doubtless often beneath them in moral worth and sensibility.

It is very frequently the case that families, after occupying rooms a few weeks, will change their location, leaving behind them all the dirt which their residence has occasioned. Upon this the next comers will sit down, being so much occupied with the hurry of moving and with the necessity of placing their furniture immediately in order, that attention to cleansing the apartment is out of the question until they are "settled," and then, if done at all, it is in the most careless and inefficient manner.

Very often, perhaps in a majority of the cases in the class of which I now speak, no cleaning other than washing the floor is ever attempted, and that but seldom. Whitewashing, cleaning of furniture, of bedding, or persons, in many cases is *never* attempted. Some have old pieces of carpet which are never shaken (they would not bear it) and are used to hide the filth on the floor. Every corner of the room, of the cupboards, of the entries and stairways, is piled up with dirt.

The walls and ceilings, with the plaster broken off in many places, exposing the lath and beams, and leaving openings for the escape from within of the effluvia of vermin, dead and alive, are smeared with the blood of unmentionable insects, and dirt of all indescribable colors. The low rooms are diminished in their areas by the necessary encroachments of the roof, or the stairs leading to the rooms above; and behind and under them is a hole into which the light of day never enters, and where a small bed is often pushed in, upon which the luckless and degraded tenants pass their nights, weary and comfortless.

In these places, the filth is allowed to accumulate to an extent [which is] almost incredible. Hiring their rooms for short periods only, it is very common to find the poor tenants moving from place to place every few weeks. By this practice they avoid the trouble of cleansing their rooms, as they can leave behind them the dirt which they have made. The same room being occupied in rapid succession by tenant after tenant, it will easily be seen how the walls and windows will become broken, the doors and floors become injured, the chimneys filled with soot, the whole premises populated thickly with vermin, the stairways, the common passage of several families, the receptacle for all things noxious, and whatever of self-respect the family might have had, be crushed under the pressure of the degrading circumstances by which they are surrounded.

Another very important particular in the arrangements of these tenements must here be noticed. By the mode in which the rooms are planned, *ventilation is entirely prevented*. It would seem as if most of these places were built expressly for this purpose. They have one or two windows, and a door at one side of the room, but no opening anywhere else. A draught of air *through* is therefore an utter impossibility. The confined position of the dwelling itself, generally, prevents the access of the external current of air, even to the outside, to any considerable extent.

The window sashes, in addition, perhaps are so arranged that the upper one (if there are two) cannot be let down, being permanently fastened up; hence the external air, poor as it is, cannot visit the upper section of the room, unless by opening the door, by which the interior of the room is exposed to view. If there is a sleeping apartment, it is placed at the extremity of the room farthest from the windows, is generally but little larger than sufficient to hold a bedstead, and its area is reduced, for air, by the bed, furniture, trunks, boxes, etc., and having no windows, fresh air and sunlight are entire strangers to its walls.

In this dark hole there is, of course, a concentrated accumulation of the effluvia of the bodies and breaths of the persons sleeping in it (frequently the whole family, several in number), and this accumulation goes on from night to night, without relief, until it can easily be believed the smell becomes intolerable, and its atmosphere productive of the most offensive and malignant diseases.

There is no exaggeration in this description. I cannot too highly color the picture if I would. What, then, will be thought of the condition of thousands of our fellow citizens in the winter season, when every crevice is closed to keep out the cold air, and when I state, that what I have described, I have repeatedly seen and felt in the summer, when the windows and doors are opened to the fullest extent, day and night, admitting all the ventilation possible, small as it is. . . .

We now naturally come, in the course of this inquiry, to two important questions preparatory to the suggestion I intend to make, of a remedy for these evils.

1. What is the effect of this degraded and filthy manner of life upon the health of the individuals, and the duration of their lives?

2. What is its influence upon their mor

als, their self-respect, and appreciation of virtue?

The answers to these queries must have an important bearing upon the moral obligations, the pecuniary expenses, and the order and character of the city government. If it can be shown that much sickness and many premature deaths are results of these residences, it will be evident that the care of the sick, and the support of the widows and orphans, must add greatly to the expenses of the city; and if it can be proved that degraded habits, bad associations, and immoral practises (though the results only of circumstances, and not of education) are their consequences, it will be equally apparent, there will thus be continued, a class in the community more difficult to govern, more disposed to robbery, mobs, and other lawless acts, and less accessible to the influences of religious and moral instruction.

With regard to the first question, an argument can hardly be necessary. Almost everyone can recall to mind some proof of the effects of nauseous odors, of the inhalation of foul air, or of sleeping in a small confined apartment, upon his own health and feelings. These effects may have been only temporary, but they will serve to show that a prolonged continuance of them, must, in reason, produce permanently bad results upon the mental and corporeal powers.

If the inhaled air (one great source of the life, health, and vigor of the animal structure) is deteriorated in quality, or diminished in quantity, below the standards necessary for a perfect decarbonization of the blood in the lungs, the blood necessarily becomes burdened with impurities, and fails to impart to the system the qualities demanded by nature for the due maintenance of health and strength. . . .

If the habitation of damp, dark cellars, and of narrow alleys and courts, and the breathing of a vitiated atmosphere, are rightly asserted to be promotive of disease, then those most subject to these causes should be sick in the greatest numbers.

Now the male part of this class breathe a totally different air through the day, at their labors in the streets, along the rivers, or upon buildings, and only at night are they subject to the worse atmosphere.

Thus more than half their hours are passed under more healthful circumstances. Even the boys who spend several hours at play, or even in a partially ventilated schoolhouse, follow an improved regimen in this particular. On the other hand, the females, both night and day, inhale the polluted atmosphere of the dwellings, and are more continually under all the other bad influences of their unfortunate situations. . . .

The influence of degraded associations, of habitual neglect of cleanliness, and prostration of health by impure living, upon the moral habits of the people, and as impediments to their social and political improvement, is a question with which I propose now to occupy the reader's attention, for a brief space, in the hope that if it can be shown that these are probable causes of misery and crime, there will be found herein an additional reason for the action of the city government upon the measures I or others may suggest, for the melioration of the condition of those classes of the community more exposed to their influences.

Let anyone ask himself the question, whether his own self-respect, his carefulness to avoid improprieties of conduct, and to maintain cleanliness of house and person, are not greatly enhanced by the examples of those around him. I believe it will not be disputed that the practices of those with whom we associate, by choice or compulsion, possess a decided influence over not only our own acts and habits but over our thoughts and even our judgments. Circumstances govern our lives, and precepts for good are feeble, unless accompanied by the strong arm of example.

"Example is better than precept," was the lesson taught us daily in our school exercises in penmanship. All society regulates the conduct of its members, and its phases of character are marked by their deportment and opinions. The "outcasts of society," constituting a very numerous tribe, form societies of their own, and stamp, in a degree, the character of the community of which they are a part. We have, as have all large cities, numbers of them with us, but they should be regarded, not as such by choice so much as by *compulsion* — as the creatures of circumstances beyond their control.

The tide of emigration which now sets so strongly toward our shores, cannot be turned back. We *must* receive the poor, the ignorant, and the oppressed from other lands, and it would be better to consider them as coming filled with the energy of hope for happier days, and more useful labors than they found at home. No one, I presume, seriously believes they come with bad intentions, and then whose fault is it that they live here in cellars more filthy than the cabins of whose wretchedness we hear so much, and for whose existence half the blame is thrown upon the government they have left.

Let us first cast the beam from our own eye. *We are parties to their degradation, inasmuch as we permit the inhabitation of places, from which it is not possible improvement in condition or habits can come.* We suffer the sub-landlord to stow them, like cattle, in pens, and to compel them to swallow poison with every breath. They are allowed, may it not be said required, to live in dirt, when the reverse, rather, should be enforced.

This depressed physical condition, and bad moral and social habits and propensities, to my mind, have an intimate relation to each other — they stand clearly in the attitudes of cause and effect. For instance, how often do we find poverty to be the instigator of theft, and immoral indulgences the results of certain circumstances in life?

Men's passions are kept in check by the restrictions of the society in which they live. Remove those checks — take from the individuals the moral atmosphere in which the move, and their evil passions will rise.

In a family composed of several person of both sexes, in circumstances admitting their living in separate apartments, the restraints of the circle of which they are part compel an observance of the separatio of the sexes, and other social proprietie They grow up habituated to correct deport ment and moral restraints which accompan them into all their relations of life. But con fine that same family to one room, comp them to perform all their personal and do mestic duties in view of each other, t sleep, dress, and undress in each other presence, and can it be doubted that th nice moral distinctions so necessary to a li of virtue will be gradually subdued, or over thrown, the heart be hardened against th teachings of the moralist, and the wave lustful passion become of increased power Yet this is the condition of hundreds families, who would gladly escape th Maelstrom of morals which threatens to e gulf them. And this is undoubtedly a princ pal source of the dreadful amount of licen tiousness infesting this city.

As breathing an impure atmosphere w produce a depressed tone of bodily feelin and positive physical disease, so will a vit ated moral atmosphere induce a relaxe state of moral feeling, and positively licen tious habits.

Whence issue, in times of riot and t mult, the disturbers of the peace, but fro the cellars and alleys, where they have neve been taught to respect themselves, muc less others.

If a family of good disposition be reduce by force of circumstances to occupy th same premises with numbers of others of different character, it will be next to impo sible to maintain their former tone of mo als, or domiciliary cleanliness and order, an they must soon lapse into the same habi and feelings as their neighbors, adding th their numbers to those who before swelle the list of the profane and evil disposed.

46.

Calvin Colton: The Relation Between Labor and Capital

In order to survive as a political entity, the Whig Party was forced to adopt many Jacksonian principles. The party's program, as thus modified, was succinctly set forth in a series of ten political pamphlets, collectively known as the Junius Tracts, *which were published during 1843 and 1844 under the pseudonym "Junius." The real name of their author was Calvin Colton, who, in the 1830s, gave up his career as a minister to become a publicist for the Whigs. The selection below is taken from Tract No. VII, "Labor and Capital."*

Source: *Junius Tracts*, No. VII, March 1844.

WHAT IS LABOR?

т is any man's or woman's efforts to live nd prosper, whether of body or of mind, or of both; whether in agriculture, or comnerce, or manufactures, or mechanics, or in ither of the numerous branches of these great and comprehensive pursuits; whether n the useful or fine arts, in digging ditches or digging out the sciences; whether in a professional career or in making books; in eaching or in study; in legislation or in government; in making pins or casting annon; in the use of hands or of feet, of ingers or of toes, of muscles or of brains; n search of knowledge or in its application; n inventions or their uses; in making canals or building ships; erecting railroads or contructing locomotives; in burning lime or brick, in quarrying or in masonry; in wielding a sledgehammer or making watches; in grinding knives or selling brick dust; in fishng for oysters or harpooning whales; in ny one of the thousand occupations of the ity or the country, on the land or on the ea; and so on and so on, to the end of that nfinite diversity of human pursuits by vhich men and women toil for a livelihood, nd to get on in the world. In a free coun-try each one chooses his own vocation, and it is not easy to say whether mind work or muscular effort is hardest.

WHAT IS CAPITAL?

Money is usually called capital. But it is not exclusively so, unless it is intended to comprehend everything that will fetch money; or everything that is *worth* money. In this sense, labor is capital. Labor, certainly, is the foundation and cause of wealth. All the world would be poor and come to nothing without it. Whatever any man has which others want, and which, being wanted, will fetch money, whether it be a capacity for labor or any species of property, it is capital. For any man, therefore, to know how rich he is or how much capital he has, he has only to inquire *what he can do and what he has* that will fetch money.

THE CAPITAL OF LABOR

He who is able to work and who can find employment with fair pay is rich to begin with, and may become rich in the usual sense of the term. A power to labor, where labor is in demand, is the best, most independent, and most productive of all capital. Money at interest, or in stocks, usually produces, in this country, an income averaging perhaps 6 percent. Some get more, some less, and some none at all. They are liable to go backward and lose principal itself. But labor, with economy, can hardly ever be worth less than 50 percent. That is, a laborer can live satisfactorily and lay up, as vested capital, half of his wages. In some kinds of employment, he can lay up three-fourths; it may be more than that.

Economy and skill in the management of his earnings may also be made productive of wealth, in addition to the profits of his labor. Some laborers, by a careful use of past earnings, soon get to realize 100 percent on their capital, including labor; and then they are growing rich, wealthy. Industrious labor of any kind, in a country like ours, with economy and being applied where labor is in demand for wages, is a sure foundation of wealth. Man does not have to labor to acquire the power. It is a capital with which he is endowed by creation, an independent faculty, and more productive than any other.

SKILL IN LABOR AND IN THE MANAGEMENT OF ITS AVAILS IS CAPITAL

MAN HAS NOT ONLY BONES, sinews, muscles, and other powers of bodily labor but he has mind to direct it, to improve in it, to make it more available, to put all its proceeds to a profitable use, and to improve even its uses. Labor turns bodily power to account, and skill multiplies the profits of labor, so that when a man gets a-going in the world, he goes fast. Riches flow in and wealth accumulates.

A man's power of labor is limited; but his skill is unlimited. Skill is often a thousand times more productive than what is commonly called labor. But it is to be remembered that skill itself is the fruit of the

labor of mind, or is the employment o mind, as muscular effort is labor of th body. But skill is capital. It is equally appl cable to agriculture as to manufactures; t the mechanic, or the useful, or fine arts. I is applicable to trade and commerce, to ev ery pursuit and occupation of life.

ENTERPRISE IS CAPITAL

IT MIGHT SEEM quite unnecessary to say, i view of what enterprise has accomplished i and for this country from the beginning our history, that enterprise is capital. Wit slender means, it has evoked unbounde wealth from the long repose of a continen and erected thereupon a vast national estat No other species of capital has contribute so largely to this stupendous result. As th collective power of national enterprise composed of individual enterprise, we fin accordingly the same character in isolate conditions, checkering the whole surface o society with great achievements effected b single persons. There was capital enough i the soul of Washington to humble th greatest nation, and to make another, wit means that would have been laughed t scorn as a subject of prophecy. In all o history, and in the various walks of life, ar to be found like miracles of enterprise, orig inating in the profound and inexhaustibl wealth and carried forward to consumma tion by the invisible power of man's mor. attributes.

MONEYED CAPITAL

MONEY IS MOST COVETED because it is mo convenient; and its convenience arises fro the fact that it will procure, in exchang everything which a man wants or desire But, in itself, it is dead capital and the lea worthy of respect or affection, as compare with labor and skill in the application of la bor and its avails. When money is put t use it is said to be active; but it has n natural, inherent productive power. Hoarded money, while in that state, is no better than rusty old iron in a farmer's garret. And when put to use, the income is not the natural product of a natural agent or natural effect of a natural cause but a mere commercial result, which is limited and small as compared with the products and avails of labor, and that little is contingent on good management and good security. The principal itself is subject to the same contingency.

Nevertheless, moneyed capital may be an important instrument in the hands of the owner, and is usually an effective power within certain limits. It will always supply wants and gratify desires so long as it lasts. But as productive capital, put to use in the hands of second and third persons, for the increase of itself, it bears no proportion to the productive power of human labor and skill. The fact that they who employ money can afford to pay interest for it, and often double, sometimes quadruple the principal sum annually, by the use of it, is proof of this point.

VESTED CAPITAL

BY VESTED CAPITAL is commonly understood money put to use for what is called interest or income. The most common forms of vested capital are bonds, mortgages, negotiable notes, silent partnerships in business firms, stocks in banks, insurances offices, turnpike and railroads, canals, fishing companies, great commercial enterprises, steamboats and steamships, navigation companies, manufactories, state and government securities, and any undertaking that is beyond the ordinary means of individuals, and which requires the combined and aggregate capital of numerous persons having money to put to use. The capital of corporate companies or bodies formed for these objects is usually divided into small shares, which, being made negotiable that anybody can buy or sell, are thence called "stocks."

CORPORATIONS

THE OBJECT OF CORPORATIONS is to combine the surplus or spare capital of numerous individuals for enterprises which are usually beyond the reach of single persons. Properly organized by the statute of incorporation, by a division of the capital into small shares, and securing to men of small means equal chances, they are well adapted to a democratic state of society by bringing down the powers of government, distributing them among the people, and vesting them in the hands of all persons who can raise $20, or $50, or $100, according to the price of shares. Few and large corporations, monopolizing power in their own specific spheres, are objects of popular jealousy, and justly so. But the multiplication of them, with moderate capital and powers, divided into small shares, spreads them out over the surface of society, and whatever powers they have, be it more or less, is so much resigned by the government, and vested immediately in the hands of the people, who are able and disposed to be owners of stock.

It is a wider and more democratic distribution of power. The responsibility of the managers is to the stockholders for the use of the capital, and to the government, and through the government, to the great body of the people for the use of their powers. That is the best, most democratic, and most beneficent system of corporations, which enables and encourages laborers and men of small means, widows and orphans, and the more dependent and helpless portions of the community to become interested in them by the investment and application of their funds, which they themselves could not employ to advantage.

For example: two men, in partnership, were joint owners of mills of great value in the state of Maine, and one of them died, leaving a widow and several children. The widow and children, of course, could not manage such a business; but by an act of incorporation from the state, the widow and the guardians of her children became corporators and managers, and the joint interest went on as before. It will be seen that cases are constantly occurring in society which require the aid of such privileges. All helpless persons who have capital enough to support them but who are unable to manage it naturally resort to such helps provided by the state, in parental care, and by considerations of humanity, as well as for the general welfare. . . .

THE LAZY CHARACTER OF MONEYED CAPITAL

WE SPEAK of the general character of its owners, and with them, it is not only lazy but often improvident. Its proposal and its terms are, *use me and give me my dividend.* When men get beyond the necessity of labor, they never like to return to it. They seek repose, enjoyment, and exemption from the rude occupations of life. It is seldom, if ever, that they realize the satisfaction they hoped for. But they have become lazy and, by their lazy position, they fall into the power of the active mind of the country. They who work are going ahead, while these fall back on their resources, can command nothing but their dividends, and are fit only to make their wills in favor of heirs, who, anticipating the future, are waiting only for the good luck that death may bring them to dissipate, it may be, the estate that falls into their possession. At best, the investments of moneyed capitalists are only valuable as they are in demand for use by the active, laborious, and industrious portion of the community, who, of the two parties, always derive the greatest benefit from them. . . .

Labor is all-powerful and destined to supplant opulent indolence by gaining possession of the means of its luxurious case. Guard their wealth however they may, "riches take to themselves wings and fly away." There is no law of inheritance i American society that can secure wealth i the same family line while it is always ope to the acquisition of industrious labor. Th gifts of fortune are always tendered to thos who toil for them and snatched from thos who riot in affluence. Already we behol no inconsiderable fraction of the large in vestments of the Lowell manufactories i the hands of those who began there b spinning and weaving, and who still spi and weave. And who that has observed th mutations of society for half a generatio or even a less time than that, does not se the same operation going on everywhere?

THE MUTUAL DEPENDENCE BETWEEN LABORERS AND MONEYED CAPITALISTS

THE RICH MAN cannot eat his money; nc clothe himself with bank notes, or gold lea or silver plate; nor shelter himself from th inclemencies of the seasons by these mater als; nor make of them any of the comfor of life. If he chooses to live at ease, for a necessaries and for all means of enjoymen he is entirely dependent on those who prc duce them. For all these he must give h money in exchange, which enables thos who minister to his convenience and con fort to better their condition and rise in th world. In these very acts of exchange, the are gradually exchanging positions in soc ety. Nor can the wealthy get a return fc their investments, or an income from the estates, if there be nobody to use the fo mer or work the latter. Both parties a served by their relative position for the tim being, though it is possible, and not unlike ly, that their children will stand in direct the opposite position of their parents in re lation to each other.

The laborer wants the reward of his to first for necessaries not in his line; next, t add to his comforts; and third, to increas his stock in trade, or augment his estat

But how could he get this reward if nobody had it to give in exchange for his services? On the other hand, the consideration paid would be of no value or use to its owners, except as it is in demand by those who carry on the active business of society and minister to its wants.

WHICH OF THESE PARTIES IS MORE BENEFITED BY THE OTHER?

IT IS TRUE that the moneyed capitalist wants his dividend; but the profits of labor, united with moneyed capital, well applied, are many times greater than the proceeds of money as an investment in the usual forms. Labor is the source of all wealth, and with money, as tools in hand, multiplies the principal in manifold quantities. The laborer, working on his own estate, gathers the rich harvest into his own barns and gives the moneyed capitalist a small fraction for the use of his sickle — for moneyed capital, in the hands of labor, is only an instrument. Or, if he works on the estate of the moneyed capitalist for wages, as at Lowell, he soon gets enough to retire in a condition to satisfy his ambition, or becomes part owner of the estate, gradually gaining on the original proprietor, with the prospect of supplanting him. Such is the advantage of labor, united with skill and enterprise, over the mere instrument which it employs.

LABOR, THE ORIGINAL AND FUNDAMENTAL POWER OF SOCIETY

THE RECOGNITION OF THE TRUE POSITION of labor in relation to moneyed capital is of no considerable political importance. We mean its position in the actual state and practical operation of American society, where labor is free and sovereign, and not as it stands under a despotism, or in the monarchical and aristocratic countries of Europe. It is our own politics and our own political powers with which *we* have to do. In this country, labor, since our independence was acquired, always has been and still is, not only an original and fundamental but a controlling power in society and in the state. We are characteristically and distinctively a nation of *workers*. There are some who do not work; but most people do. Work is the fashion and the proudest distinction in American society. Nobody looks with respect on those who live in idleness or who riot in luxurious ease. To have no business is a kind of living death. A man is lost who does not work.

Moneyed capital, with us, is a mere *tool* in the hand of labor, and is good for nothing, except as labor will bid for it. The millionaire would be scarcely better off than the owner of a single penny — not even so well off, in regard to his physical wants — if he could not call the laborer into his service; whereas the laborer is much more independent and can better do without the rich man than the rich man can do without him. This independence, this high ground of labor is perfectly well understood in this country by all parties. As the great majority are workers and all workers sympathize with each other, the ground they occupy is not only an elevated social position but a controlling political power. Just show the working power of the country what laws and what policy of government will be best for it, and the ballot box will soon demand those measures. Who will say that this demand can be successfully resisted? Who, regarding the well-being of the country, would desire it?

THE TRUE AND BEST INTEREST OF MONEYED CAPITAL

IT IS TO GIVE LABOR A FAIR REWARD and to make it profitable. But as this cannot be forced, as between the parties, trade being always a voluntary transaction, the ability to do it can not be separated from the action of government. All workers, therefore, as well as moneyed capitalists — all laborers are deeply concerned in supporting a public policy which will put labor in good demand and thus enable it to command a good price. This depends entirely upon the proceeds of moneyed investments. While these are good, labor will be in demand, and the price of it, or its wages, will be proportionately high. Moneyed investments are sure to pay well, if it can be afforded; and the more they can afford, the better for them. But, generally, this ability to give good wages depends very much, sometimes entirely, on the policy of government, in the privileges it confers on such investments, and the chances it gives to them.

If the government wars against them instead of extending to them its fostering care, if it endeavors to cripple and break them down instead of protecting and sustaining them, this hostility may and does injure the moneyed capitalist by rendering his investments insecure and unproductive; but it injures the working classes of the community much more. The rich can hide themselves in a storm of government hostility, though they may be losers; but the poor perish, or are in great distress, for want of employment. Our remark above on the comparative independence of labor applies to an ordinary state of things and not to a crisis of this description.

A FALSE NOTION

It has been a prevalent and fatal doctrine in this country, with a certain class of statesmen, that it is always a safe policy and a duty in the government to fight against moneyed capitalists, in whatever place or shape they lift up their heads, whether in banks, or in manufactories, or in any and all other forms and enterprises requiring associated capital. In this it is not considered that the employment and thriving of the people depend on the profitable investment of the

moneyed capital of the country; nor that the wages and profits of labor and the price of its products depend on the profits accruing from the use of the moneyed capital which labor employs. Moneyed capital regarded by this policy as a master, not as servant and instrument; as a hostile power not as a friendly auxiliary; as having in itself a faculty of independence, not as deriving all its value from labor; and as aiming to acquire a supremacy over society.

But a little reflection, in view of what has been said, one would think, ought to show that the condition of moneyed capital, this country, is *passive* in the hand of labor and not *active* to rule over it, and that it not possible to change this relation of dependence in the former on the latter. Moneyed capital in itself is an *inert* power a derives all its vitality from the touch of labor. For government, therefore, to open the way by its policy for the profitable use money is the same as to provide for the success and fair reward of industry at work; and that policy which destroys the profit of money destroys the profit of labor. Let government strike at the rich and blow falls on the heads of the poor. . . .

A COMPARATIVE VIEW OF THE POSITION OF LABOR IN AMERICA AND EUROPE

We have told in the outset what mean by labor. It is they who work real workers — no matter *in* what or u what or for what *end*, if it be lawful a honorable work, to supply the wants of ilized man, or the increasing wants of vancing civilization. The more wants, more work, and so much the better for where each chooses his own calling finds employment.

But the position of labor in this cou is, in a variety of important particulars new one in human society.

1. It is *free*, with the exception of Afri

slave labor. This species of freedom, which is a most important attainment in the progress of society, implies a practicable *alternative* to working on wages *at the price fixed by the employer.* In Europe, for the most part, there is no such alternative, and the laborer is *compelled* to work at a price in which he has no voice, or *he must starve;* and for the reason that he has no voice in fixing his wages, they are too scanty for comfort, much more for bettering his condition, and often too scanty for subsistence. European wages are next to a state of *starvation.* At best, it is a state of *slavery without hope.* But in this country, labor occupies *a high social and political position.* It is never *compelled* to work for wages fixed by employers, because there is always open to it the *alternative* of working *on its own hook.* American labor, therefore, does not *accept* a price imposed but *commands* its own price. At least, it is always an *independent* party in the compact. It is made *freely* and can be as freely dissolved, without incurring the doom of starvation or distressing want.

2. The *social* position of American labor is such that none but workers are held in respect, and work is held in the highest respect. No power in this country can enforce respect for the man who has nothing to do and who does nothing. Just in proportion as a rich man retires from society to wrap himself up in selfishness does he lose his influence, and the idle, lazy poor man gets little pity in his poverty. Our fathers brought with them both the necessity and spirit of work, and made it respectable. It has been transmitted as the highest recommendation and the most honorable character.

3. The *political* position of labor here is all-powerful, and so long as it is so, it cannot but be respectable. As a nation of workers, we *demand* from government a security for the interests and rights of labor, and one of those rights is that *free* American labor shall not be put on the same level with the *forced* labor of other countries, or any country. It is only necessary for the people of this country to understand correctly what the true interests and rights of labor are, and they are sure to have them secured at the ballot box. No earthly power can hinder it. What more elevated or more commanding position can labor possibly occupy? The free American laborer is the most powerful, and may well be the proudest, of men. . . .

A NEW ERA OF LABOR

IT IS IMPOSSIBLE not to observe that labor has taken up a new position on this continent, in our state of society, and that a new era in its social and political importance is opened on the world. If no interruption should take place in its progress, it will be the true millenium of labor. During the long nightmare of despotic rule over the European and Eastern world, the breast of humanity felt its heavy tread, and the toiling millions were unable to rise. But here labor has sprung to its feet, lifted up its hands on high, clapped them with joyous exultation, and learned a new song of freedom — THE REWARD OF LABOR. It has risen, at one bound, to influence and authority. There has never before been such a scene in the history of civilization. And the most remarkable and most auspicious feature of it is that it occupies a wide theater — a vast domain of political power.

Erect, in the image of God, imitating and obeying God, as a diligent worker, man here has taken possession of his primitive estate, so long alienated, and cultivates it as his own, himself the heir of his own created wealth; and not only the heir but the sovereign disposer thereof. We know not what may grow out of this new form, this apparently auspicious development of human society; but it has much contingent promise of perpetuity, enlargement, confirmation, and final consummation. . . .

THE CONTINGENCY

A *protective* TARIFF is the sole palladium of American labor. Without that defense, it is as sure to fall back prostrate on the level of European, Egyptian, and Asiatic labor, from which it has been lifted up, as the sun will rise in the East and set in the West. If American labor, having the power in its hand, will not protect itself, the fault of parting with its rights will lie at its own door. The struggle has been a great one, and it will yet be long protracted. Either the rights of American labor must give way, or the despotic rule of the Old World must yield to the claims of freedom. It is impossible that both should stand. And so long as both are in conflict, we shall not fail to realize a sturdy hostility from tottering and crumbling thrones, gathering fresh vigor from despair, assisted by their agents in our own bosom who are paid by their gold. . . .

THIS WAR UNNATURAL

IT IS CERTAINLY UNNATURAL for labor to do that which deprives it of tools to work with, cuts off its chances, and involves it in distress; for, by breaking down moneyed capital, it breaks down itself. It is moneyed capital which makes business grow and thrive, gives employment to labor, and opens to it avenues to success in life. In the state of American society, and in a prosperous condition of the country, a comfortable degree of wealth is within the reach of every honest, industrious, and enterprising man. The moneyed capitalist has no political superiority or advantage over the laborer, and no right in the republic which is not secured to both. It is, therefore, the laborer's interest that the wealth of the rich should be so invested as to impart the greatest activity to trade, and the greatest effectiveness to useful enterprise; and in nothing is this end so surely accomplished as by those moneyed and other corporations which are organized for this sole purpose.

If this capital were to lie dead, the loss to the country would be immense, and that loss would of course be divided among all classes of people and participated in by the government. It is as much the duty of the government to endow moneyed capital with the faculties of the greatest activity and effectiveness as it is the interest of its possessors to consent that it should be so used, and of labor to employ it. What supreme folly, then, for labor to go to war with moneyed capital! It thereby wars against its own life and means of success. The blow aimed at the moneyed capitalist strikes over on the head of the laborer and is sure to hurt the latter more than the former.

THE CAPACITIES OF OUR COUNTRY

WELL AND RIGHTLY GOVERNED, it is capable not only of astonishing the world but of astonishing itself. If things do not go on well it must be owing solely to the perversion of our institutions from their design. There no sufficient apology that our general prosperity should *ever* be interrupted. It is impossible that it should be, except by a violation or misapplication of the trusts reposed in our public functionaries. By a suitable protection of the interests of American labor and industry from a self-sacrificing rivalship with a foreign, oppressed, and degraded pauperism, which is in nowise mitigated but only aggravated and rendered more hopeless by the favor done to the oppressors; by a proper encouragement of the voluntary enterprises of our own citizens, the people of this country, with the rich and inexhaustible treasures of creation comprehended in our jurisdiction, are capable of producing amazing results.

That almost astonishing height of prosperity to which we had attained under the disadvantages of a defective tariff sytem, before the advent of the late destructive dynasty, is conclusive and impressive evidence of what this nation is capable of under a wise and faithful administration of our public affairs. We had been put in a train by which we were enabled to discharge with ease the entire and heavy debt incurred by the last war with Great Britain, and to overwhelm the public treasury with surplus funds; the public domain in the West was in such demand that the sales of one year amounted to $24 million. And although there were special reasons for this fact, which could not be expected to operate in perpetuity to an equal extent, nevertheless, in a prosperous state of things there would be a steady increase in those sales which, under an equitable system of distributing the proceeds among the states, whose property they are, would relieve the burdens of the indebted states and give the others a chance for such enterprises as might best promote their interests.

Providence has assigned us a rich, productive and glorious heritage, and established among us and over us a new, regenerate, and admirable system of government. It has been abused, indeed; but it is good. All we want is good and faithful men at the head of it. The wealth of the country is inexhaustible, and the enterprise of the people is unsubdued, notwithstanding all our late misfortunes. Give them a good government and they cannot help going ahead and outstripping every nation on the globe.

THE CHANCES OF LIFE IN THIS COUNTRY

OURS IS A COUNTRY where men start from a humble origin, and from small beginnings rise gradually in the world as the reward of merit and industry, and where they can attain to the most elevated positions, or acquire a large amount of wealth, according to the pursuits they elect for themselves. No exclusive privileges of birth, no entailment of estates, no civil or political disqualifications stand in their path; but one has as good a chance as another, according to his talents, prudence, and personal exertions. This is a country of *self-made men*, than which nothing better could be said of any state of society.

THE MUTUAL DEPENDENCE BETWEEN THE GOVERNMENT AND THE PEOPLE

NOTHING IS MORE INSTRUCTIVE to this point than the chapter of our own history. Except as the government, by its policy, shall enable the people to prosper in a free country like ours, where tyrannical exactions cannot be enforced, the government itself cannot prosper, but its finances will be embarrassed as soon as its own measures shall have brought embarrassment and distress on the people. A crippled and disheartened population, who have no money either to pay taxes or buy luxuries, cannot send money into the public treasury. While they are poor, the government will be poor.

A RETROSPECT

UNDERSTANDING, AS WE NOW DO, if what we have said is correct, the relation between the labor of the country and its moneyed capital, we must look back with astonishment at the policy of the federal administration from 1829 to 1841, when the cry rang through the land and never ceased — DOWN WITH THE BANKS! DOWN WITH MANUFACTORIES! DOWN WITH CORPORATIONS! DOWN WITH CAPITALISTS! It is a history that one can hardly believe in!

While memory lasts and fathers are capable of telling the story to their children; while true Americans are endowed with concern for the welfare of the country and have virtue enough to stand up for its interests; and while history may be relied upon to discharge its impartial functions, it will not fail to stand stereotyped in the minds of the American people, to be rehearsed to the listening and succeeding generation, and recorded in the annals of this nation that:

For the period above named, we had a *re*-lapse and *col*-lapse in our national welfare, never to be forgotten; that an unlucky star rose in our hemisphere, ascended to its meridian, and marched to the Western hills, leaving an *ominous tail behind*; that the people were persuaded for a time that it was the *true sun*, and were hard to be convinced of its eccentric and ill-boding character; that it brought famine, pestilence, and death; that demagoguism was the rage of its season, inoculating the poor with a mania against the rich and the laborer with jealousy against the moneyed capitalist; that the love of *one-man power* was the chief malady that afflicted the nation, and its ascendancy the most remarkable occurrence of the time; that the long-established, simple, and democratic habits of the people, social and political, were superseded by the dictation of a chief, and by the aristocratic assumptions of his menials; that new, unheard-of, and destructive doctrines were promulgated for the government of the country; that a well-ordered system of currency was broken up and destroyed; that the useful relations between capitalists and the laboring classes were violently assailed and so far dissolved as to bring great distress on the industrious and working population; that states and large corporations were first enticed to enlist in great enterprises and then forced to suspend them and to stop payment, by sudden changes in the policy and measures of the government; that our credit at home was prostrated and abroad became the byword and scorn of nations; that the shameless doctrine of the repudiation of debts was for the first time avowed and sanctioned by legislative authority; that the superstructure and very foundations of society were shaken in the general convulsion; in short, that times, modes, customs, morals, and manners underwent a complete revolution, so that the republic that *was* could hardly be recognized in the new state of things.

It was because the relation of labor to moneyed capital was entirely mistaken and misrepresented, and a war of government made upon the latter, as if it was the natural enemy of the former. . . .

REVOLUTIONS NEVER GO BACKWARD

UNDER OUR FORM OF GOVERNMENT, other revolution than that of opinion is impossible. Can anybody doubt there was a great revolution of this kind in 1840? And where is that feeling? Have the people changed their minds? They would not *act* till the time of *rescue* should come, and the silly crew at the head of affairs took the people's *disgust* as a compliment to their *treason*. The *banished* horde also took courage. But the sleeping fires have only been made hotter by that respect for order which sealed them up and for a time repressed them. The internal pressure tends upward, to open a place of utterance ere long and cast its bright light on the dark upper sky, and thence to astonish those below. A free nation once convinced of its wrongs, must be avenged; and woe to them who have done the wrong! BACKWARD? OR FORWARD? is the question for this nation to answer. And it WILL be answered. They have chosen a LEADER, the cry is — ONWARD!

47.

A Dialogue on Female Labor

The Lowell Offering *was a magazine published from 1841 to 1845 by the female operatives in the cotton mills of Lowell, Massachusetts. The articles that appeared in it — a typical example appears below — tended to confirm the impression, gained by both American and foreign visitors, that the manufacturing establishments at Lowell comprised an industrial utopia. But a rival magazine,* Factory Girl, *was also published during part of this period, having the stated intention of dispelling the myths promulgated by the* Lowell Offering.

Source: *Lowell Offering*, Lowell, 1844, pp. 199-200.

Miss S: I am very happy to see you this evening, Miss Bartlett, for I have something particular to say to you. Now, do tell me if you still persist in your resolution to return to your factory employment?

Miss B: I do. I have no objection, neither have I heard any sufficiently strong to deter me.

Miss S: The idea that it is degrading in the opinion of many would be objection enough for me without taking into the account its real tendency to promote ignorance and vice.

Miss B: By whom is factory labor considered degrading? It is by those who believe all labor degrading; by those who contemptuously speak of the farmer, the mechanic, the painter, the seamstress, and all who are obliged to toil as belonging to the lower orders; by those who seem to think the condition of labor excludes all the capacities of the mind and the virtues of humanity. They forget that circumstances over which they have little or no control place them above the necessity of labor; and that circumstances may yet compel them to engage in that at which they now scoff and spurn.

Miss S: There are objections to factory labor which serve to render it degrading — objections which cannot be urged against any other kind of female employment. For instance, to be called and to be dismissed by the ringing of a bell savors of compulsion and slavery, and cannot cease to produce mortification without having been destructive to self-respect.

Miss B: In almost all kinds of employment, it is necessary to keep regular, established hours; more particularly so where there are as many connected as in the factories. Because we are reminded of those hours by the ringing of a bell, it is no argument against our employment, any more than it would be against going to church or to school. Our engagements are *voluntarily* entered into with our employers, with the understanding that they may be dissolved at our pleasure. However derogatory to our dignity and liberty you may consider factory labor, there is not a tinge of slavery existing in it, unless there be in every kind of labor that is urged upon us by the force of circumstances.

Miss S: Objections have been brought up against the boardinghouses, and, I think, with much plausibility. The large number of females who are there thrown together are, unavoidably, intimately connected with each other. It cannot be denied that some, guilty of immoralities, find their way into the factories and boardinghouses; the example and influence of such must be pernicious and terminate in the increase of vice.

Miss B: It is true that the example and influence of immorality, wherever it exists, cannot be otherwise than evil. We know, also, that some exceptionable characters occasionally find a place among those employed in factories. We know it from the fact that dismissals do, now and then, occur as the consequence. But, my dear Miss S., did you ever know or hear of a class of people who could boast of perfection; among whom wrong of any description was never known?

Miss S: O, no! And, as I am no perfectionist, I never expect to know of one.

Miss B: Then, if in one case the guilt of a few has not corrupted the whole, why should it in the other? Living in a factory boardinghouse and working in a factory changes not "human nature": it is susceptible of good and also of evil there as it is elsewhere.

Miss S: I agree with you in thinking that among all classes and in every condition in life evil influences are at work; but in some situations in life is not the exposure to these influences much more extensive and, therefore, more dangerous, especially to the young?

Miss B: I believe there are many kinds of female employment offered in our large towns and cities far more dangerous in this respect than factory employment, although they may be considered more desirable and respectable. Now, the very fact that "factory girls" are so "intimately connected with each other" soon lays open the real character of all, and I can assure you, whenever the example of one is known to be otherwise than good, she is immediately removed, how expert soever she may be in

her business or profitable to her employer. I may add that if such ones were allowed to stay, they could not, unless they had the faculty of constantly "living in hot water." Besides, if "just as the twig is bent, the tree is inclined," the characters of most are formed before ever entering a factory.

And, yet, after all this strictness with regard to the morals and habits of female operatives, there are those who think one cannot be honest or virtuous who has ever toiled in a factory; they are sometimes spoken of, and to, as though they were destitute of sensibility and understanding, and unworthy of sympathy, kindness, or civility. Whether this is the result of erroneous opinions of factory labor or of the idea that all kinds of labor is dishonorable, it is not very gratifying to our love of approbation, though it will not deprive us of that dignity and self-respect which honesty of purpose and an industry that places us above dependence always beget.

Miss S: You will not acknowledge that factory labor is degrading or that it is productive of vice, but you must own that it fosters ignorance. When there are so many hours out of each day devoted to labor there can be no time for study and improvement.

Miss B: It is true that too large a portion of our time is confined to labor. But, first, let me remark that this is an objection which cannot be said to exist only in factory labor. It is seldom that the interest of improvement of any class of laborers is regarded by their employers in the number of hours which is called a day's work. The compensation for labor is not in proportion to the value of service rendered but is governed by the scarcity or plenty of laborers. This is an evil which has always existed, for aught I know, and I suppose is considered remediless.

We have abundant proof that unremitted toil is not always derogatory to improvement. A factory girl's work is neither hard or complicated; she can go on with perfect regularity in her duties while her mind may be actively employed on any other subject. There can be no better place for reflection, when there must be toil, than the factory. The patronage which newspapers and periodicals find in our city, our well-worn libraries, evening schools, crowded churches and Sabbath schools prove that factory operatives find leisure to use the means for improvement both in mind and heart.

But I fear I shall exhaust your patience and will bid you good evening, with an invitation to visit me after I have returned to my mill labor; and, as far as I am able, I will show you all the wonders of our "city of spindles."

48.

ROBERT OWEN: Religion and Marriage

Robert Owen, one of the founders of British socialism, introduced some of his ideas for the amelioration of the working class into America by starting the experimental community at New Harmony, Indiana. The community failed, but Owen carried on his work both in England and America. His views were generally unacceptable to Americans because he discounted the value of organized religion and the need for moral improvement. Views on religion and marriage, such as those expressed in the following "Address of Robert Owen to the People of the United States," September 1844, did much to alienate popular opinion in this country.

Source: *New-York Daily Tribune*, September 24, 1844 [Commons, VII, pp. 155-160].

AMERICANS! I HAVE COME to you a missionary from the other side of the Atlantic, to endeavor to effect in peace, for the permanent advantage of all, in every country, the greatest revolution ever yet made in human society. The general excitement and misery of the mass in nations demand it, and the signs of the times indicate its approach.

But you will naturally inquire — Who is it that is bold enough to undertake this task and what are his pretensions? He is an old man, in his seventy-fourth year, who has read and studied the various writings of the human race for five hours a day on an average for twenty years; who has been a man of extensive practice in the great department of life for more than half a century; who has traveled, seen, and heard much; who

has been for many years visited by parties in search of knowledge from all parts of the civilized world; and who has had but one object during his life, that is, to discover the cause or causes of human error and misery, and to find the remedy for both.

But this old man, because to effect this object he has been obliged in good faith to oppose all prejudices of the human race, has been more abused, vilified, and his sentiments and views more falsified by the public press than almost any other individual on either side of the Atlantic; and especially has he been misrepresented on some of the most interesting and important subjects, having reference to the permanent happiness of our race through all future ages. . . .

The impression made upon the mind of

this old man respecting religion is that upon this subject the world has been in error from the beginning, but that it is a natural and unalienable right in man to have the most unlimited religious liberty, provided he does not interfere with the liberty of others. That all that is really known on the subject of theology from the beginning of history is that, of necessity, there is an eternal, uncreated power which accomplishes whatever has been, is, or may be done throughout the universe; and that civilized nations, so-called, have agreed to call that great first uncreated power God, to which term there can be no rational objection. But what God is no man knows; it is a mystery past human penetration to find out; and the quarrels among the human race on the subject of this power, on theology, or religion are proof how far the nations of the earth are yet from being rational in their thoughts or conduct.

"Can man by searching find out God?" "Or can he do any good to God?" "Can he glorify infinite incomprehensible power?" "Can he do anything contrary to the laws of that power?" Is it not madness in men then to differ and quarrel and fight and massacre each other on account of particular, imbibed notions respecting the supposed will of a power altogether incomprehensible to man? Evidently the first step to rationality in the human race will be to abandon all angry, uncharitable, and unkind feelings for each other on account of their opinions and feelings, respecting the supposed will of a power utterly incomprehensible to the human race.

Until this effect shall be accomplished, no solid foundation can be laid for the attainment of permanent peace, progressive prosperity, and happiness among mankind; and this first and most important step can be alone gained by all agreeing to allow all in the spirit of charity the utmost religious liberty in speech, writing, and action, so long as the same liberty in others shall not be diminished or in any manner interfered with.

I, therefore, give to all others, and claim for myself, the most ample religious freedom, and the foundation stone of all true efficient, and rational liberty of mankind and without which any form of government, whatever it may be called, is a despotism.

Upon the subject of marriage, it is necessary to be equally explicit. The object of human society is to increase the happiness of each individual to the greatest extent practicable — that is, consistent with the greatest happiness of the whole. And the external laws of humanity are, in connection with the association of the sexes, that man must like that which is most agreeable to him and dislike that which is most disagreeable to him. All human laws of marriage should be based upon these divine or natural laws, and no parties, for the benefit of all, should be compelled to associate as husband and wife after the natural affection and sympathies of their nature have been so far separated that no probability remains of effecting a reunion of them.

And until an advanced state of society can be attained, and superior arrangements can be formed in a more perfect state of rational association, the following were the form, and ceremony, and mode of marriage and divorce given by the writer to the world at a most numerous public meeting in London, held for that purpose, on the 1 of May, 1838, and unanimously approved.

Many persons grossly mistake the view which I recommend of the subject of the union of the sexes. My object is to remove the causes of the immense and most melancholy and deplorable amounts of sexual crime and misery, and consequent physical and mental disease, which now exist. It is nature's laws, now disregarded, which require to be discovered and implicitly obeyed, there being none other which can produce health, virtue, and happiness.

In the present absence of real knowledge derived from experience, and with the exciting, irregular, and misdirected feelings of the population of the world created by a false education, I propose that the union and disunion of the sexes should take place under the following regulations: Persons having an affection for each other and being desirous to form a union shall first announce such intention publicly in our Sunday assemblies. If the intention remains at the end of three months, the parties, living in the meantime singly as before, make a second public declaration, in a similar manner, which declaration being registered and witnessed and entered into the book of the rational society, will constitute their rational marriage.

In the New World about to be introduced, marriages will be solely formed to promote the happiness of the sexes, and if this end be not attained, the object of the union will be defeated. Should the parties, therefore, after the termination of twelve months at the soonest, discover that their dispositions and habits are unsuited to each other, and that there is little or no prospect of happiness being derived from their union, they are to make a public declaration, as before, to that effect, after which they return home and live together six months longer, at the termination of which, if they still find their qualities discordant and both agree to make a similar second declaration, both of which being only registered and witnessed, will constitute their legal separation.

The above cases apply only when both parties unite in the last declaration. Should one alone come forward upon the last declaration and the other object to separation, they would be required to live together another six months to try if their feelings and habits could be made to accord so as to promote their happiness. But, at the end of the second six months, if the objecting party shall remain of the same mind, the separation is then to be final, and the parties may, without diminution of public opinion, form new unions more suited to their dispositions.

As all children in this new rational state of society will be trained and educated under the superintendence and care of the society, the separation of the parents will not produce any change in the condition of the rising generation.

Under these arrangements, there can be no doubt a much more virtuous and happy state of society will be enjoyed than any which has existed, at any time, in any part of the world.

These are arrangements now recommended to those who commence communities to form a rational state of society.

Unless they adopt this mode of forming their marriages, it is not probable that married persons can live long in such associations without many difficulties arising.

No parties, without actual experience, can imagine the advantages that arise from children being trained and educated from birth in these new associations, by those especially educated to educate, and who possess the most faculty for this important purpose, instead of children being brought up under the innumerable disadvantages of family arrangements and strong animal maternal affections, by which more than justice is sought for our own and less for others.

The missionary, in all his proceedings, is desirous that equal justice should be done to all of the human race; that each should be well-educated, physically, mentally, morally, and practically, which education is necessary to the well-being and happiness of all; and, also, that each should be well and efficiently employed and occupied through life, not only to produce a fair share of the wealth and knowledge which society requires from each but to keep them in the best state of health, bodily and mentally.

49.

J. W. C. DIETRICHSON: Organizing an Immigrant Church

The Norwegian clergyman J. W. C. Dietrichson came to the United States on two occasions during the 1840s to bring order and stability to the religious life of his countrymen. Cut off from the traditions of their state church, it was easy for the Norwegian immigrants either to modify their religious habits in new surroundings or to lose them altogether in the struggle to make a new life in a strange land. Dietrichson traveled to the several Norwegian settlements in the Midwest, organizing congregations and training them in the usages of their Lutheran Church background. In the following letter of September 25, 1844, from the Muskego, Wisconsin, settlement, Dietrichson described some of the problems of the frontier congregation. He evidently encountered Gustaf Unonius, a Swedish immigrant who eventually left the Lutheran Church for the Episcopalian and tried to draw his fellow Scandinavians with him.

Source: Blegen, pp. 137-138.

ON THURSDAY EVENING, July 25, I left New York on board one of the largest of the American steamboats, which have so often been described and praised for their elegance. We sailed up the beautiful, swift-flowing Hudson River; but as night came on quickly and we reached our destination, Albany, at 7 o'clock the following morning, we did not see much of the beautiful scenery which is said to be found along the banks of this river. At sunrise I was out of my berth to catch a glimpse of some of the beautiful sights. The morning was cool and misty, but gradually the weather improved so that I really discovered many fine views.

It is true that I could have taken one of the boats that make this trip in the daytime, but since the fare is then twice as high, it would have made too great inroads on my funds. And as these funds had been supplied me by the Christian sacrifices of others, I preferred here as always to go without and save, rather than cut too large a thong out of another man's leather. . . .

The first week I visited several places i the settlement [Muskego] and found tha my fear was only too well grounded tha the emigrants here have not had very goo luck. It is true that they have acquired lan 40, 80, 160, and some even 200 or 30 acres, but many of them owe money on th land and no one has succeeded in cultiva ing very much. Practically all live in smal miserable log houses consisting of one sin gle room in which everything is crowde together. So far, only a few have outhouse When they have acquired a couple of cov and a yoke of oxen they are considered be pretty well off here, since only a fe have horses. Last autumn there was muc disease and misery, but this year things ha been better.

I have made my home with Clause agreeable family and have made my excu sions from there. The first Sunday after n arrival, the tenth Sunday after Trinity, preached to a fairly large congregation one of the most spacious houses here.

small table with a white cloth was our communion table, and a beer glass and a crockery plate served as our chalice and paten at the administration of the Eucharist.

I preached my sermon, deeply moved at seeing so many of my dear countrymen in this distant foreign country, and there was general emotion among the people, who were probably even more vividly reminded of the beautiful services of their native country by hearing the Norwegian language again and seeing the complete Norwegian clerical robes. The next morning, August 12, Clausen and I set out on a journey to Chicago in Illinois to conduct a service for the Norwegians there.

During our conversation about the bishopric, we also touched on the question of ordination, and Mr. Unonius then declared that he could in no way accept Clausen as a properly ordained minister because he had not been ordained by a bishop, while he was willing to accept me. He is now trying to give others the same opinion of Clausen, and therefore it is important, also for this reason, that we get a statement from a competent authority in Norway concerning Clausen's ordination. Thus, if it had come about that our old venerable bishop in Oslo had fallen ill when I was about to be ordained and a minister had officiated at my ordination, Unonius would have had to say the same thing about me. Many of the Norwegians do not realize that this attitude is contrary to the teachings of the Lutheran Church.

50.

RUFUS CHOATE: The State and Mental Culture

In the 1840s Massachusetts enjoyed a literary renaissance spearheaded by the transcendentalists and could boast the best and most progressive educational system, from grammar school through university, in the country. Despite such cultural attainments, the state's political influence within the growing Union was dwindling, a fact that had been dramatically underlined by the Whig defeat in the election of November 1844. Rufus Choate, Whig jurist and orator, was moved to reflect upon how the Bay State should respond to its changing role. His ideas were expressed in a speech, "The Power of a State Developed by Mental Culture," delivered to the Mercantile Library Association on November 18, 1844. A part is reprinted below.

Source: *Addresses and Orations of Rufus Choate,* 5th edition, Boston, 1887, pp. 106-132.

I WONDER . . . if during the labors and excitations of the late election, and in the contemplation of possible results near and far forward, the inquiry has not occurred to you, as to me it has a thousand times, is there no way, are there no expedients by which such a state as Massachusetts, for example, may remain in the Union, performing the duties, partaking as far as may be of the good of Union, and yet be in some greater degree than now she is independent of and unaffected by the administrative and legislative policy of Union?

Is there no way to secure to ourselves a more steady, sure, progressive prosperity — such a prosperity in larger measure than we are apt to imagine — whatever national politics come uppermost? Is there no way to sink the springs of our growth and greatness so deep that the want of a little rain or a little dew, a little too much sunshine or too much shade from Washington, shall not necessarily cut off "the herd from the stalls" and cause the "fields to yield no meat"? Must it be that because the great central regions, the valley of the Mississippi, the undefined and expanding Southwest, have attracted to themselves the numerical supremacy — that our day is done? . . .

Or is there a way by which we yet may be, and forever may be, the arbiters of our own fortunes; may yet be felt in the counsels of America; may yet help to command a national policy which we approve, or at least to bear unharmed, a national policy which we condemn? Must we pale and fade and be dissolved in the superior rays of the great constellation, or yet "flame in the forehead of the morning sky" with something of the brightness of our rising?

I take it for granted in all such speculations, in all such moods as this, that we are to remain in the federal Union. With our sisters of the republic we would live — we would die —

One hope, one lot, one life, one glory.

I agree, too, that whatever we may do for Massachusetts, the influence of national politics upon our local prosperity must always be inappreciably great for evil or for good.

It is of individuals, not states, that Goldsmith exclaims,

How small, of all that human hearts
    endure,
That part which kings or laws can cause
    or cure!

The joy and sorrow, the greatness and decline, of nations, are to a vast extent the precise work of kings or laws; and although

in our system every state has its own government and its own civil polity to which important functions are assigned, yet, when you consider that it is to the great central power that war, peace, diplomacy, finance, our whole intercourse with the world, trade, as far as winds blow or waters roll, the trust of our glory, the protection of our labor, are confided, nobody can indulge the dream that a state may remain in the Union at all and yet be insensible of the good and evil, the wisdom or the folly, the honor and the shame of its successive administrations.

And yet I think that the statesmen of Massachusetts may well ask themselves whether there are no expedients of empire or imperial arts worthy her — worthy them — by which they may enable her either to retain consideration and lead in the general government, to be conspicuous and influence an American opinion, by which they may enable her either to extort what she calls good policy, or else to break the force of what she calls occasional bad policy, which she cannot hinder and to which she must submit.

Passing over all other expedients as unsuitable to the character and relations of this assembly, is it not worthwhile to consider this matter; for example, whether a higher degree of general mental culture, a more thorough exercising and accomplishing of the whole mass of our popular and higher mind, more knowledge, a wider diffusion of knowledge, loftier attainments in useful and in graceful knowledge than we have ever reached, or that any state has reached, might not help us to meet the enlarging demand of time, and the successive crises of the commonwealth? Is it certain that in our speculations on the causes of the grandeur and decay, of the wealth and the poverty, the importance and the insignificance, of states, we have given quite as high a place as it deserves to the intellect of the state?

Have we not thought too much of capacious harbors or teeming inland, navigable rivers; fleets of merchant ships and men-of-war; fields of wheat, plantations of cotton and rice and sugar; too much of tariffs and drawbacks and banks; and too little, too little of that soul by which only the nation shall be great and free? In our speculations on knowledge and the bettering of the mind, is it right or is it wise to treat them as useful or as ornamental individual accomplishments alone, and not sometimes also to think of them as mines of national riches wealthier than Ormus or Ind, as perennial and salient springs of national power, as foundations laid far below earthquake or frost, of a towering and durable public greatness?

After all, this is the thought I would present to you; is there a surer way of achieving the boast of Themistocles, that he knew how to make a small state a great one, than by making it wise, bright, knowing, apprehensive, quick-witted, ingenious, thoughtful; by communicating to the whole mass of its people the highest degree of the most improved kind of education in its largest sense, which is compatible with the system of practical things; by beginning at the cradle, by touching the infant lip with fire from heaven; by perfecting the methods of the free schools, and of all schools, so that the universal understanding shall be opened, kindled, guided at its very birth, and set forward, without the loss of a day, on the true path of intellectual life; by taking care that all the food of which the soul of the people eats shall be wholesome and nutritious; that the books and papers which they read, the sermons and speeches which they hear shall possess at least a predominance of truth, fact, honesty, of right and high thought, just and graceful feeling; by providing institutions to guide the mature mind the heights of knowledge; by collections of art and taste that shall unfold and instruct the love of beauty; by planting betimes the gardens of a divine philosophy and spreading out the pavilion of the Muses?

Let us think a little of mental culture as the true local policy of Massachusetts.

I do not propose to repeat anything quite so general and elementary as that easy commonplace which my Lord Bacon has illustrated so fondly and so gorgeously — that learned states have been usually prosperous states; that the eras of lettered glory have been eras of martial and civil glory too; that an instructed people has been for the most part a rich, laborious, energetic, and powerful people. The historical fact is undoubtedly as he records it; and it is as encouraging as it is true. . . .

In the next place, to come down to a little more detail, mental culture may contribute to our security, our independence, our local aggrandizement by informing and directing our labor.

I need not tell you that labor is the condition — I will not say of our greatness, but — of our being. What were Massachusetts without it? Lying away up under the North Star, — our winters long and cold; our springs backward and capricious; our sky ungenial; our coast ironbound; our soil not overproductive, barren almost altogether of the great staples of commerce which adorn and enrich the wheat fields of the central regions, the ocean prairies of the West, the rice grounds and sugar and cotton plantations of the South; our area small; our numbers few; our earlier occupations of navigation and fishing divided with us by a whole world at peace — what is there for us but labor — *labor improbus, labor omnia vincens* [excessive labor, labor overcoming everything]?

And what kind of labor is it which is to vanquish the antagonist powers of nature and build the palace of a commodious and conspicuous national life over against these granite mountains and this unfruitful sea? Is it one kind, or two; or is it the whole vast and various labor of intellectual civilization, not agriculture only and trade and fishing but the whole family of robust and manly arts, which furnish occupation to everybody every moment of working time — occupation to every taste and talent and faculty, that which it likes best, that which improves it most, that which it can do easiest; occupation for the strong and the weak, the bright and the dull, the young and the old, and both the sexes; occupation for winter and summer, daylight and lamplight, cold weather and warm, wet and dry; occupation that shall, with more than magnetic touch, seize on, develop, discipline, and perfect every capacity, the whole mass of ability, gathering up all fragments of mind and of time, so that nothing be lost — is not this the labor by which we are to grow great? Is not this the labor which is to be to us in the place of mines, of pearls, of vineyards, of cinnamon gardens, of enameled prairies, of wheat fields, of rice grounds and cotton fields and sugar plantations tilled by the hands of slaves?

This is that transmuting power without which we are poor, give what they will — with it rich, take what they will away! This it is, labor, ever labor, which, on the land, on the sea, in the fields, in all its applications, with all its helps, from the straw bonnet braided or plaited by the fingers, up to those vast processes in which, evoking to its aid the powers of nature and the contrivances of ages of skill, it takes the shapeless ore from its bed, the fleece from the felt, the cotton from the pod, and molds them into shapes of beauty and use and taste — the clothing, the armor, the furniture of civilization, sought for in all the markets of the world — this it is which is to enrich and decorate this unlovely nature where our lot is cast and fit it for the home of cultivated man!

Now, if the highest practicable degree of mental culture and useful knowledge is really the best instrumentality for instructing, guiding, vivifying, helping this rough power of labor; if it will supply the chemistry which teaches it how to enrich barren soils, reclaim and spare exhausted soils, irrigate parched soils, make two blades of grass grow where one grew before; if it will teach it how to build tunnels through mountains or beneath beds of rivers and under populous towns, how to fill or bridge the valley, how to stretch out and fasten in their places those long lines of iron roads which, as mighty rivers, pour the whole vast inland into a market of exchange for what trade has gathered from every quarter of the globe; if it will teach it better how to plan its voyages and make its purchases, so as most seasonably to meet the various and sudden and changing demands of men by the adequate supply; if it can teach it how to construct its tools, how to improve old ones and invent new, how to use them, by what shortest and simplest and cheapest process it can arrive at the largest results of production; if it can thus instruct and thus aid that labor, which is our only source of wealth and of all material greatness; if, above all, when rightly guided by the morality and religion which I assume everywhere to preside over our education, it communicates that moral and prudential character which is as needful and as available for thrift as for virtue, thoughtfulness, economy, self-estimation, sobriety, respect for others' rights — is it not an obvious local and industrial policy to promote, diffuse, and perfect it? . . .

It is within the knowledge of you all that Mr. Mann, in one of those reports to the Board of Education to which the community is so much indebted, I believe the fifth has developed this thought with that keenness of analysis and clearness and force of expression for which he is remarkable. You will be particularly struck with the proofs which he has there collected from several most intelligent and respectable superintendents or proprietors of manufacturing establishments, showing by precise statistical details, derived from a long course of personal observation, that throughout the whole range of mechanical industry the well educated operative does more work, does it better, wastes less, uses his allotted portion of machinery to more advantage and more profit, earns more money, commands more confidence, rises faster, rises higher, from the lower to the more advanced positions of his employments, than the uneducated operative.

And now, how interestingly and directly this fact connects itself with my subject, I need not pause to show. You speak of tariffs to protect your industry from the redundant capital; the pauper labor, the matured skill, the aggressive and fitful policy of other nations. You cannot lay a tariff under the Constitution and you cannot compel Congress to do so; but you can try to rear a class of workingmen who may help you to do something without one. You speak of specific duties, and discriminating duties, and what not! Are you sure that if everybody — *every mind,* I should say — which turns a wheel or makes a pin in this great workshop of ours, all full from basement to attic with the various hum of free labor, was educated up to the utmost degree compatible with his place in life, that this alone would not be equal to at least a uniform duty of about 28 percent ad valorem, all on the home value?

You must have more skill, you say, more skill than now, or you must have governmental protection. Very well; go to work to make it, then. You manufacture almost everything. Suppose you go into the manufacture of skill. Try your hand at the skill business. Skill in the arts is mental power exercised in arts, that is all. Begin by making mental power. You can do that as easily as you can make satinets or fustian or chain cable. You have a great deal of money. The world never saw such a provision for popular and higher education as you could make in a year in Massachusetts and not feel it. Consider how true and fine in this application would the words of the charitable

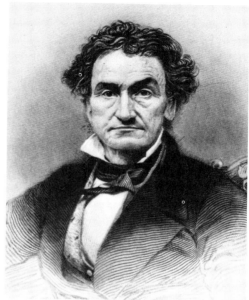

National Portrait Gallery, Smithsonian Inst.

Rufus Choate (1799-1859) was a founder of the Whig Party in Massachusetts and a senator, 1841-1845

man's epitaph be: "What I spent I had. What I kept I lost. What I gave away remains with me!"

By what precise course of instruction, elementary and advanced, by what happier methods, by what easier access to the mind and heart, by "what drugs, what charms, what conjuration, and what mighty magic," this heightened mental ability and accomplishment may be achieved, which I know is practicable and which I know is power, it is not within my plan, if I could, to suggest. I may be permitted to remember that the first time I ever ventured to open my lips in a deliberative body, I had the honor to support a bill in the House of Representatives, in Massachusetts, providing for educating teachers of common schools. I should be perfectly willing to open them for the last time, in the same place, in support of the same proposition exactly.

I can conceive of a body of teachers — I know individuals now — who would do this great work for Massachusetts, as patriotism and religion would wish it done; who would take the infant capacity of the people, as it came to life, into their arms and breathe into it the quickening breath; who, receiving it, bathed and blessed by a mother's love, would apply to it, instead of stripes, the gentle, irresistible magnet of scientific instruction, opening it as a flower to light and rain; who, when the intellectual appetite was begun to be developed, would feed it with the angels' food of the best mental and moral culture which years of reflection and experience and interchange of thought could suggest; would carry forward the heart and the reason together; would fit the whole bright tribe of childhood as completely, insofar as intellect and acquisition are concerned, for beginning to wrestle with the practical realities of life at fourteen as now at one-and-twenty.

To such teachers I leave details, with one suggestion only; that I would not take the Bible from the schools so long as a particle of Plymouth Rock was left large enough to make a gun flint of, or as long as its dust floated in the air. I would have it read, not only for its authoritative revelations and its commands and exactions, obligatory yesterday, today, and forever, but for its English, for its literature, for its pathos, for its dim imagery, its sayings of consolation and wisdom and universal truth. . . .

I have now been speaking of a way in which mental culture may help your labor to grow independent of governmental policy, and thus to disregard and endure what you cannot control. But may not the same great agent do more than this? May it not, not merely enable you to bear an administrative policy which you cannot prevent but enable you to return the more grateful power of influencing national councils and national policy, long after the numerical control has gone to dwell in the imperial valley of the West?

I will not pause to say so obvious a thing as that those you call public men, those whom you send to urge your claims and consult your interests in the national assembly, are better fitted for their task by profound and liberal studies. This were too obvious a thought; and yet I cannot help holding up to your notice a very splendid exemplification of this, in that "old man eloquent," who counts himself to have risen from the Presidency to represent the people in the House of Representatives [J. Q. Adams]. . . . If mental culture did nothing for you but send such men to consult on your welfare in the councils of the nation, it would do much to preserve your political ascendancy.

But look at this matter a little more largely. Suppose that, by succession of effort, by study, by time, you could really carry up the literary character of Massachusetts to as high a degree of superiority to the general literary character of these states, as that of Attica compared with the other states of Greece in the age after the Persian War; suppose the schoolboy boast could be achieved and you were the Athens of America; suppose the libraries, the schools, the teachers, the scholars were here, the galleries of art, the subtle thinkers, the weavers of systems, the laureled brow, "the vision and the faculty divine"; suppose the whole body of our written productions, from newspapers upward or downward, had obtained a recognized superiority over those of any other region, were purer, better expressed, more artistlike, of wider compass; suppose that the general taste of the world and the nation should authenticate and settle all this — would it or would it not profit you as an instrument of political ascendancy? It would be soothing to our pride, certainly.

Perhaps that would not be all. Knowledge is power as well as fame. You could not, perhaps, hold the lettered and moral relation to America which I have sketched — it is, alas! a sketch — without holding political relation in some degree of correspondence with it. Think of that subtle, all-embracing, plastic, mysterious, irresistible thing called public opinion, the god of this lower world, and consider what a state, or a cluster of states, of marked and acknowledged literary and intellectual lead might do to color and shape that opinion to their will. Consider how winged are words, how electrical, light-like the speed of thought, how awful human sympathy.

Consider how soon a wise, a beautiful thought uttered here — a sentiment of liberty perhaps, or word of succor to the oppressed, of exhortations to duty, to patriotism, to glory, the refutation of a sophism, the unfolding of a truth for which the nation may be better — how soon a word fitly or wisely spoken here is read on the Upper Mississippi and beneath the orange groves of Florida, all through the unequaled valley; how vast an audience it gains, into how many bosoms it has access, on how much good soil the seed may rest and spring to life, how easily and fast the fine spirit of truth and beauty goes all abroad upon the face of the world. Consider that the meditations of a single closet, the pamphlet of a single writer, have inflamed or composed nations and armies, shaken thrones, determined the policy of governments for years of war or peace. . . .

There is an influence which I would rather see Massachusetts exert on her sisters of this Union than see her furnish a President every twelve years or command a majority on any division in Congress; and that is such an influence as Athens exerted on the taste and opinion first of Greece, then of Rome, then of the universal modern world; such as she will exert while the race of man exists. This, of all the kinds of empire, was most grateful and innocent and glorious and immortal. This was won by no bargain, by no fraud, by no war of the Peloponnesus, by the shedding of no human blood.

It would rest on admiration of the beautiful, the good, the true in art, in poetry, in

thought; and it would last while the emotions, its object, were left in a human soul. It would turn the eye of America hitherward with love, gratitude, and tears, such as those with which we turn to the walk of Socrates beneath the plane tree, now sere, the summer hour of Cicero, the prison into which philosophy descended to console the spirit of Boethius, that room through whose opened window came into the ear of Scott, as he died, the murmur of the gentle Tweed — love, gratitude, and tears such as we all yield to those whose immortal wisdom, whose divine verse, whose eloquence of heaven, whose scenes of many colored life have held up the show of things to the insatiate desires of the mind, have taught us how to live and how to die! Herein were power, herein were influence, herein were security. Even in the madness of civil war it might survive for refuge and defense! . . .

And now, if anyone, any child of Massachusetts, looking round him and forward, trying to cast the horoscope of his local fortunes, feels a sentiment of despondency upon his spirit, and thinks all this exhortation to mental culture as a means of retaining endangered or receding power to be but the dream of pedantry, and begins to think that if he would belong to a great state, an historical state, an ascendant state, he must be setting out toward the tranquil sea — to him I say, turn back to her origin and be of thy unfilial fears ashamed! . . .

It took 150 years . . . one long war, one long labor, one long trial, one long sorrow, as we count sorrow, years of want and disease, of bereavements, of battle, of thought, of every heroical faculty tasked by every heroical labor, one long, varied, searching, tremendous educational process, just the process to evolve and mature these traits on which a commonwealth might repose for 1,000 years of glory — it took all this . . . to train them [the Puritan descendants] for the loftier sphere, the grander duties, the more imperial and historical renown, of independence and union.

And do you think that the energies of such a nature, so tempered and refined, are become exhausted in half a century? Who believes in such an idle expenditure of preparation? Why, that would be to hew out a throne of granite on the side of everlasting hills by the labor of generations, for one old king, the last of his line, to die on! No; be true to your origin and to yourselves, and dynasties shall fill by successive accessions the prepared and steadfast seat.

Doubtless the Pilgrim race — the Puritan race — shall go everywhere and possess largely of everything. The free Northwest, especially, will be theirs; the skies of Ontario and Erie and Michigan, the prairies of Illinois, the banks of the river of beauty, the mines of Wisconsin and Iowa shall be theirs. But the old homestead and the custody of the Rock are in the family also. Nearest of all the children to the scenes of the fathers' earthly life, be it ours the longest and the most fondly to bear their names and hold fast their virtues. Be it ours, especially, to purify, enrich, adorn this state — our own, our native land, our fathers' monument, our fathers' praise!

51.

TRUMAN MARCELLUS POST: The Need for Colleges in the West

The Society for the Promotion of Collegiate and Theological Education at the West was organized in New York City in 1843. Its purpose was to raise funds for the maintenance of Protestant colleges, many of which had foundered in the depression of 1837. A series of five articles written by Truman Marcellus Post, a minister and a teacher at Illinois College, was appended to the society's first report. The series had originally been published in the New York Observer *under the general title "Plea for Western Colleges"; the fourth article from the series is reproduced below. The anti-Catholic sentiment reflected in the article was a driving force behind Protestant support of Western education.*

Source: *Permanent Documents of the Society for the Promotion of Collegiate and Theological Education at the West,* New York, 1852, Vol. I, pp. 25-28.

COLLEGES ARE A NECESSITY of every extensive community, marked by nature as a social unity. We . . . now . . . look at some reasons why they are peculiarly needed at the West.

First, then, we find such a reason in the fact that Rome is at this time making unprecedented efforts to garrison this valle with her seminaries of education. Sh claims already to have within it between fif teen and twenty colleges and theologica schools; and this number is rapidly increas ing. To these, permanency is insured by th steadfastness of her policy; the constancy c her receipts from Catholic Europe, yearly increasing under the stimulating reports of her missionaries; and by her exacting despotism, moral if not ecclesiastic, over the earnings of her poor in this country. They are among the enduring formative forces in Western society; and the causes which sustain them will constantly add to their number.

These institutions, together with numerous grades under the conduct of their Jesuits and various religious orders, are offering (what professes to be) education almost as a gratuity in many places in the West. Whatever other qualities her education may lack, we may be sure it will not want a subtle and intense proselytism, addressing not the reason but the senses, the taste, the imagination, and the passions; applying itself diversely to the fears of the timid, and enthusiasm of the ardent, the credulity of the simple, the affections of the young, and to that trashy sentiment and mawkish charity to which all principles are the same.

Now, the policy of Rome in playing upon all these elements through her educational enginery is steadfast and profoundly sagacious. Her aim, in effect, is at the whole educational interest. The college is naturally the heart of the whole. The lower departments necessarily draw life from that. If Rome then grasps the college in the system of Western education, she virtually grasps the common school; she distills out the heart of the whole, if not a putrid superstition, at least that covert infidelity of which she is still more prolific.

Now a system so deep and so persistent must be met by a correspondent depth and persistency of policy. Protestantism can no more counteract it by temporary and spasmodic efforts than she could stop the Mississippi with a whirlwind. She can encounter it only by a system of permanent and efficient Protestant colleges. And this for two reasons. First, the Catholic seminaries in this country seem to meet a great and deeply felt social want, and can be displaced only by a supply for this want from another quarter. And second, in the nature of things, a college alone can counteract a college.

The college acts upon the public mind in a manner so peculiar, through such ages and classes, and through influences so various and subtle, so constant, noiseless, and profound that it can be successfully combated only by a similar institution. Place efficient Protestant colleges in the proximity of the Catholic and the latter will wither. For all purposes of severe intellectual discipline or masculine reason, their education is soon found to be a sham. A spiritual despotism dare not, cannot teach true history or a free and manly philosophy.

Again, other facts which constitute a peculiar necessity for colleges in the West are found in the circumstances and character of its population. First, the West is in its formative state. Never will impressions be made so easily and so enduringly for good or evil. Never will it be so important that its architect-minds — its plastic forces — should be endued with a broad and liberal intelligence. According to the elements now thrown in, it will soon permanently crystallize into dark and unshapely forms, or into order and beauty.

Another peculiar demand for colleges may be found in the immense rapidity of our growth and in the character of that growth, being a representative of almost every clime, opinion, sect, language, and social institute, not only of this country but of Christian Europe. Never was a more intense power of intellectual and moral fusion requisite to prevent the utter disorganization of society. Never was a people put to such a perilous proof of its power of assimilation, or required to incorporate with itself so rapidly such vast masses.

We have in this fact, as well as in that of the Catholic aggression, dangers and trials put upon us which our fathers never knew. Society here is new, yet vast, and with all its forces in insulation or antagonism. Never was a community in more urgent need of those institutions whose province it is profoundly to penetrate a people with a burning intelligence that shall fuse it into a unity with those great principles which are the organic life and binding forces of all society.

Again, in consequence of the incoherency of this element in a population thus heterogeneous, and broken off from the fixtures of old communities without time to form new ones, all the social forces are shifting and mutable, and yield like the particles of liquid to the last force impressed. This quality of Western society, combined with the bold, prompt, energetic, and adventurous temperament impressed generally on it by common influences in the life of the immigrant, exposes it to vehement and brief excitements, to epidemic delusion and agitation. Upon this sea of incoherent and vehement mind, every wind of opinion has been let loose and is struggling for the mastery; and the mass heaves restlessly to and fro under the thousand different forces impressed.

The West is, therefore, peculiarly perturbed with demagogism and popular agitation, not only in politics but in religion and all social interests. Amid these shifting social elements, we want principles of stability; we want a system of permanent forces; we want deep, strong, and constant influences that shall take from the changefulness and excitability of the Western mind, by giving it the tranquillity of depth, and shall protect it from delusive and fitful impulses by enduing it with a calm, profound, and pure reason.

Thus, while society with us has, on the one hand, to contend against a masked and political spiritual despotism entrenching itself in the educational interest, and, on the other, against a demagogic agitation, urged on too often by avarice, or ruffianism, or faction, or a sophistical but specious skepticism, or by fanatical or superstitious or shallow religionisms and socialisms of every hue, we find our defense against both to be the same, a thorough popular enlightenment and belief, anchored by permanent institutions gradually pervading the mass with great and tranquil and guardian truths, and adjusting the system to the fixed laws of intellectual and moral gravitation.

It may perhaps be asked, "Why not, in such a community, immediately proceed by opposing to agitation for evil, agitation for good?" This may at times be expedient but cannot be relied on permanently. First, because popular agitation, unless based on deep-wrought intellectual convictions, can only palliate; it cannot cure any evil. In the second place, in the germ of popular agitation, a freedom from the restraints of conscience and truth and honor often gives a decisive advantage, and agitating movements springing forth immediately from the people to be moved; and, possessing a quiet sympathy with its feeling and a shrewd tact in dealing with its passions and prejudices, must ever out-general any countermovement originating from a different source. Especially, movements of this kind from abroad are liable to find themselves forestalled — the popular ear and mind preoccupied, arguments closed, opposing tracts already in the hands of the people, and the Bible itself, under their elected interpreters, made to preach another gospel.

The above exigencies of Western society cannot be met without colleges. I am far from undervaluing . . . movements of Christian philanthropy toward the country. I am most grateful for them. I bless God for His word broadcast by the American Bible Society amid this people; I am thankful for the interest the American Tract Society are directing hitherward, and hail with pleasure all the living truth and hallowed thought brought by it into contact with the popular mind. The attitude and history of the American Home Missionary Society in relation to the West fill my mind with a sentiment of moral sublimity, and give it rank among the noblest and most sagacious schemes in the records of Christian benevolence. It will stand in history invested, to a great extent, with the moral grandeur of a civilizer and evangelizer of a new empire.

But these are far from excluding the scheme of colleges. The permanency of their benefits can be grounded only on a thorough and liberal popular enlightenment. The educational interest, then, must underlie them all. But the only way in which the East can lay a controlling grasp on this is by the establishment among us of permanent educational institutions. In a population, one-tenth at least of which cannot read, it is plain that education is an essential prerequisite to bringing a large class — and that most necessary to be reached — within the influence of truth through the press. And no system of foreign supply of ministers, teachers, or educated men can obviate the necessity of institutions that shall constantly send forth those that shall be the educators of this people, in the school, the pulpit, the legislature, and the various departments of social life.

Artificial irrigation cannot take the place of living waters. We are grateful for streams from abroad, but we feel there is need of opening fountains of life in the bosom of the people itself. The supplies from abroad we cannot rely on long. They are everyday becoming more inadequate in numbers, and must to some extent be deficient in adaptation to our wants; a deficiency that often for years, sometimes for life, shuts one out from the people.

The common exigencies, then, of every extensive society require colleges within itself. The peculiar evils to which that of the West is exposed obviously cannot be permanently and successfully met by other means. The question then recurs in every aspect of this subject. Will the East assist the West in establishing a Protestant system of home education, or will she leave her to grapple single-handed with Romanism and the other peculiar dangers to which she is exposed, in addition to the necessities that cluster around every infant community; or will she attempt by palliatives addressed to the symptoms to heal a disease seated in the heart?

A dangerous malady is on the patient. The peril is imminent and requires promptitude. Shall remedies be adapted to the disease or the symptoms? Or, with such fearful chances against it, shall the patient be abandoned to the conflict betwixt nature and death? Let the East remember the life thus hazarded involves her own — it is to her the brand of Meleager.

How beautiful to think of lean tough Yankee settlers, tough as guttapercha, with most occult unsubduable fire in their belly, steering over the Western Mountains to annihilate the jungle, and bring bacon and corn out of it for the Posterity of Adam. — There is no Myth of Athene or Herakles equal to this fact.
THOMAS CARLYLE, letter to Emerson

52.

ALEXANDER H. EVERETT: Greenough's Statue of Washington

In 1833 Horatio Greenough was commissioned by the U.S. government to sculpt a statue of George Washington to be placed in the Capitol rotunda. Greenough's Washington emerged as a colossal marble figure, clothed in a Roman toga and seated on an ancient throne, with right arm extended upward in majesty and left arm extended outward in conciliation. It arrived in the United States (it had been carved in Italy) in 1843. The statue prompted much comment, most of it derisive. Alexander Everett, a diplomat and a friend of Greenough's, wrote the following defense of the statue, which eventually was moved to the Smithsonian Institution.

Source: *United States Magazine and Democratic Review,* June 1844.

GREENOUGH'S GREAT WORK has surpassed my expectations, high as they were. It is truly sublime.

The statue is of colossal grandeur; about twice the size of life. The hero is represented in a sitting posture. A loose drapery covers the lower part of the figure and is carried up over the right arm, which is extended, with the elbow bent and the forefinger of the hand pointed upward. The left arm is stretched out a little above the thigh; and the hand holds a Roman sword reversed.

The design of the artist was, of course, to indicate the ascendency of the civic and humane over the military virtues, which distinguished the whole career of Washington, and which forms the great glory of his character. It was not intended to bring before the eye the precise circumstance under which he resigned his commission as commander in chief. This would have required a standing posture and a modern military costume; and, without an accompanying group of members of Congress, would have been an incomplete work. The sword re versed, and the finger pointed upward, ind cate the moral sentiment, of which the re ignation of his commission as command in chief was the strongest evidence, withou the details, which were inconsistent wit the general plan.

The face is that of Stuart's portrait, mo ified so as to exhibit the highest point manly vigor and maturity. Though not co responding exactly with any of the existin portraits, it is one of the aspects which th countenance of Washington must necessar ly have worn in the course of his progres through life and is obviously the proper on for the purpose. In expression, the counte nance is admirably adjusted to the characte of the subject and the intention of th work. It is stamped with dignity and radi ant with benevolence and moral beauty.

The execution is finished to the extrem point of perfection, as well in the accesso ries as in the statue itself. The seat is massy armchair of antique form and larg dimensions, the sides of which are covere with exquisitely wrought bas-reliefs. The subject of one is the infant Hercules strangling the serpent in his cradle; that of the other, Apollo guiding the four steeds that draw the chariot of the sun. The back of the chair is of openwork. At the left corner is placed a small statue of Columbus, holding in his hand a sphere, which he is examining with fixed attention. At the right corner is a similar small statue of an Indian chief. The effect of these comparatively diminutive images is to heighten by contrast the impression of grandeur, which is made by the principal figure.

The work stands upon a square block of granite, which bears upon its front and two sides, as an inscription, the well-known language of the resolution, adopted in Congress upon the receipt of the intelligence of Washington's death: "First in war: first in peace: first in the hearts of his countrymen."

On the back of the statue, just above the top of the chair, is placed another inscription in Latin, which is as follows:

Simulacrum istud
Ad magnum Libertatis exemplum
Nec sine ipsa duraturum
Horatius Greenough
Faciebat.

[This very image of the great example of Liberty would not endure without it. Horatius Greenough has made it.]

This inscription is not very felicitous. Independently of the objections that have been made to the grammar of the *faciebat,* which, though defended on classical authority, does not strike me as the natural form, the ideas are hardly expressed with sufficient distinctness, and, so far as they can be gathered, are not particularly appropriate. It is not easy to see in what precise or correct understanding of the terms Washington can be called an "example of liberty"; and ad-

mitting that by a rather latitudinous construction this phrase may be supposed to mean that his conduct is a proper example for the imitation of the friends of liberty, it is still more difficult to imagine why a statue of Washington may not be preserved though liberty should perish.

Two thousand years have elapsed since the fall of Grecian and Roman liberty, but Demosthenes and Cicero still survive in their "all but living busts," as well as in their "thoughts that breathe and words that burn." The precise object of this description would, perhaps, have been sufficiently provided for by a simple indication of the name of the sculptor and of the circumstances under which the work was ordered and executed.

The statue was originally placed in the Rotunda of the Capitol; but the light being found unfavorable, it was removed to a temporary building in the garden, where it now stands. The light is better than before, but the meanness of the building forms an unpleasant contrast with the grandeur of the work, and it is much to be desired that a more suitable place of deposit may soon be found for a monument so worthy of the great subject and so honorable to the artist and the country.

This magnificent product of genius does not seem to be appreciated at its full value in this metropolis of "the freest and most enlightened people on the globe." I have met with few persons here who have spoken of it in terms of strong or even moderate satisfaction. Everyone has some fault to point out that appears to withdraw his attention entirely from the grandeur and beauty of the whole, which, when they are pressed upon him, he is compelled to acknowledge. One is dissatisfied that the figure is colossal; another that the face is not an exact copy of Stuart's portrait; a third, that the posture is sitting and not standing; a fourth, that there is a want of repose in the general expression; a fifth, that one of

Statue of George Washington by Horatio Greenough

the ankles is incorrectly modeled; and so of the rest. Most of these objections proceed, as I have heard them stated, from persons who would think themselves wronged if their sensibility to the grand and beautiful in nature and art were called in question.

But how feeble must this quality be in one who can see nothing in so splendid a monument but some trifling, real or imaginary, fault! I should not blame anyone for indicating and insisting on what he might consider as blemishes if he were also to exhibit a proper feeling for the acknowledged merits of the work; but I almost lose patience when I hear a person, not without some pretensions to good taste, after a visit of an hour to the statue, making no other remark than that one of the ankles is incorrectly modeled; an error which, after a careful examination for the express purpose, I have been wholly unable to discover. This remark is nearly a repetition of the one made by an Athenian cobbler upon the first

exhibition of one of the celebrated Venuses of antiquity — that there was a wrong stitch in one of her sandals. It affords a curious though not very agreeable proof how exactly human nature repeats itself under similar circumstances, even to the slightest and apparently most accidental particulars.

The most satisfactory expression of feeling that I have met with here in regard to the statue was prompted by the finer and truer sensibility inherent in the heart of woman. It proceeded from a company of ladies whom I happened to encounter on my first visit to the building that contains this great national monument. They were strangers to me, and had not the air of persons belonging to the fashionable coteries of our large cities; but they evidently possessed — what is much more important — cultivated minds and a keen susceptibility to the influence of natural and moral beauty. They appeared to have been traveling extensively, and one of them had under her arm a large sketchbook. They expressed in various forms the highest admiration of the statue, and one of them finally remarked, as a sort of summary of the whole, that it produced upon her mind a stronger impression of sublimity and grandeur than she had received from the cataract of Niagara.

The objections above mentioned to the size, attitude, and costume of the statue, and to the character of the features, proceed upon the supposition that it was the intention of the artist to make the nearest possible approach to the person and countenance of Washington as represented in the most authentic portraits and statues; and in costume to the dress that he actually wore. This supposition is obviously an erroneous one. These are matters which have their importance as points of historical information — especially in connection with a character of so much interest. But the object of the artist in a work of this kind is much nobler than that of satisfying curiosity upon these particulars.

It was, as it should have been, his pur

pose to call forth, in the highest possible degree, the sentiment of the moral sublime, which the contemplation of the character of Washington is fitted to excite. This purpose required such a representation of his person, for instance, as, consistently with truth to nature, would tend most strongly to produce this result. A servile adherence to the existing portraits is not essential to the accomplishment of such a purpose, and might even be directly opposed to it; as, for example, if these had been executed in the early youth or extreme old age of the subject. Still less would it be necessary to preserve the costume of the period, which is already out of fashion, and for every subject, except the satisfaction of antiquarian curiosity, entirely unsuitable for effect in sculpture. The colossal size — the antique costume — the more youthful air of the face — are circumstances which, without materially impairing the truth to nature, increase very much the moral impression, and, instead of furnishing grounds for objection, are positive merits of high importance.

The question between a sitting and a standing posture is substantially the same, as whether the subject was to be presented under a civil or a military aspect. In the latter case, a standing posture would undoubtedly have been preferable. But if the ascendency given by Washington through his whole career to the virtues of the patriot citizen over the talents of the military chieftain was the noblest trait in his character, and if it was the duty of the artist to exhibit him, on this occasion, under the circumstances in which he appeared in real life to the greatest advantage, then the civil aspect of the subject, and with it the sitting posture, like the other particulars that have been mentioned, instead of being a ground of objection is a high positive merit.

It has been mentioned in private, as an objection made by a person whose judgment in some respects would be considered as entitled to respect, that there is a want of repose in the attitude. The arms are extended in a way in which they could not be placed for any length of time without producing fatigue; and we feel, it is said, the same sort of uneasiness on witnessing this attitude in a statue that we should if it were maintained permanently by a living person in our presence.

It is rather difficult to comprehend the precise meaning of this objection as applied to the statue of Washington. Where it is the intention of the artist to express repose, the indications of activity, of any kind, are, of course, out of place. Where it is intended to express activity, the indications of repose would, for the same reason, be incongruous with the subject. It is no more an objection to the statue of Washington that the arms are placed in an attitude which, after a short time, would become fatiguing to a living person, than it is an objection to the antique group of Laocoön that the muscles of a living man could not remain more than a few minutes in the state of extreme tension, indicated in that celebrated work, without convulsions; or to the Apollo Belvedere, that he stands with foot drawn back and arm extended, in the position of an archer who has just discharged an arrow from his bow. . . .

It was not the design of the artist to represent his subject in a state of repose. On the contrary, the obvious intention is to exhibit the noblest trait in his intellectual and moral character. I mean his habitual control over all the irregular propensities of his nature, at the point of time when it reached its fullest active development. In his practical career, this point was indicated by the resignation of his commission, as commander in chief, into the hands of the president of Congress. But that was a scene which comes within the province of painting rather than sculpture. A group so vast is beyond the reach of the chisel.

It was the difficult duty of the artist to embody the sentiment which governed the conduct of Washington, on that occasion, in a single figure. His success in conquering this difficulty, and producing, by a single figure, a moral emotion, superior, probably, to any that could be called forth by the finest painting of the scene before Congress, is one of the noblest triumphs of his noble art. To say that the work indicates activity and not repose is only saying, in other words, that it was executed in conformity to the leading point in a plan, which was suggested, or rather imperiously dictated, by the nature of the subject.

It is rather unpleasant to be compelled, in commenting on this splendid effort of genius, to meet such objections as these, instead of joining in the general expression of mingled admiration and delight which it ought to elicit from the whole public. I make no pretensions to connoisseurship in the art of sculpture and judge of the merit of the work merely by the impression which it makes upon my own mind; but I can say for myself that, after seeing the most celebrated specimens of ancient and modern sculpture to be found in Europe, including the Laocoön and the Apollo Belvedere, with the finest productions of Canova, Thorvaldsen, Sergell, and Chantry, I consider the Washington of Greenough as superior to any of them and as the masterpiece of the art.

The hint seems to have been taken from the Olympian Jupiter of Phidias, who said himself that he had caught the inspiration under which he conceived the plan of that great glory of ancient sculpture from a passage in the *Iliad*. In this way the noble work of Greenough connects itself by the legitimate filiation of kindred genius, transmitting its magnetic impulses through the long lines of intervening centuries with the poetry of Homer. The vast dimensions of the Jupiter of Phidias may have made it to the eye a more imposing and majestic monument; but if the voluntary submission of transcendant power to the moral law of duty be, as it certainly is, a more sublime

spectacle than any positive exercise of the same power over inferior natures, then the subject of the American sculptor is more truly divine than that of his illustrious prototype in Greece.

When Jupiter shakes Olympus with his nod, the imagination is affected by a grand display of energy, but the heart remains untouched. When Washington, with an empire in his grasp, resigns his sword to the president of Congress, admiration of his great intellectual power is mingled with the deepest emotions of delightful sympathy, and we involuntarily exclaim with one of the characters in a scene of much less importance, as depicted by an elegant female writer: "There spoke the true thing; now my own heart is satisfied."

The present location of the statue is, of course, merely provisional. It is much to be regretted that the light in the Rotunda was found to be unfavorable, as there is no other hall in any of the buildings belonging to the Union sufficiently lofty and extensive to become a suitable permanent place of deposit for this monument. How, when, and where, such a one shall be provided is a problem of rather difficult solution.

If, as has sometimes been suggested, the patrimonial estate of Washington at Mount Vernon should ever be purchased by the country, and a public building erected there to serve as a sort of National Mausoleum or Western Westminster Abbey, the statue would become, of course, its principal ornament. But the execution of this plan, should it ever be realized, is probably reserved for the good taste and liberality of some future generation. In the meanwhile, the noblest achievement of the art of sculpture, dedicated to the memory of the greatest man that ever lived in the tide of time, will be permitted by a country, which received from his hands gifts no less precious than independence and liberty, to take up its abode in a paltry barrack.

View of the courthouse at Independence, Mo., about 1850

WAGONS WEST

The Panic of 1837 ruined many small businessmen and farmers in the Midwest. As the depression dragged on, and the price of wheat fell to ten cents a bushel, a ready audience was found for rapturous descriptions of the Far West sent back by settlers in California and Oregon. Most of these reports, given wide circulation by expansionist newspapers, were exaggerated — and for a reason. Americans in northern California knew that with a few thousand fellow-countrymen they could take over control from the weak Mexican authorities. In Oregon the American settlers, supported by expansionist Congressmen, sought to displace the British by populating the area with immigrants. Propagandists advertised farms as large as kingdoms, and Oregon and California "fever" spread across the depressed Midwest. Even if only half the claims were true, why not give up the mortgaged farm and build an empire in the golden West?

The first sizable party of migrants, numbering 69 people, set out in May 1841 under the leadership of John Bidwell and John Bartleson, both farmers without experience in western travel. They were disorganized and poor; a few could not even afford wagons. They had only vague notions of how to get to the promised land; the difficulties of the overland trek were not emphasized in the advertisements. Fortunately, they were joined in Missouri by a group of mountain men, who guided them into the mountains. The party divided near Fort Hall, half heading northwest to Oregon and the rest pointing due west to California. For the latter the long stretch from the Great Salt Lake to the Sierra was a harrowing experience. They abandoned their wagons, killed their animals for food, and gave themselves up to the grueling routine. Struggling across the Sierra Nevadas through Walker Pass, they sighted the San Joaquin Valley on October 29. It was a disheartening view; the sunparched plain was hardly the paradise of their dreams. But they had arrived and soon scattered to find work. They were the first major immigrant party to reach California.

Camp at St. Joseph (Black Snake Hill), Mo.; drawn by J. Gainsborough Bruff during a trip west

Ferry at Council Bluffs, Iowa

The Start

Each summer brought larger numbers of migrants in the footsteps of the Bidwell-Bartleston party. The wagons gathered near Independence or St. Joseph, Missouri, from all over the Midwest. At the appointed time in early spring the plains teemed with activity. Around thousands of campfires last minute repairs were being made, meat was being smoked for the journey, animals bought and sold, and wagons packed. Meanwhile, the men met to elect a captain and draw up a body of rules to govern the train and maintain order. Mountain men appeared to offer themselves as guides. Finally, the parties crossed the Missouri River and set out across the plains.

Landing at Weston on the Missouri River; drawing by an unknown artist going west in 1849

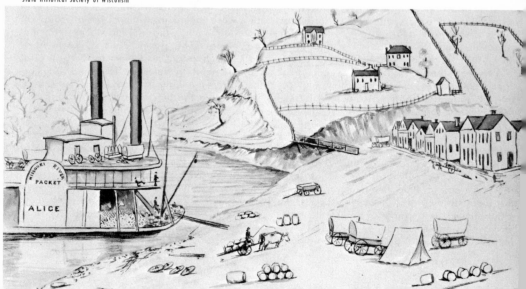

(Above) Perilous ferriage of the Missouri, seven miles below Ft. Kearny, by Bruff; (center right) Chimney Rock, one of the natural landmarks that guided the course of wagon trains

(Above) Pawnee Indian village; (below) ferrying wagons on the Platte River

(Top) Fort Laramie, painted by A. J. Miller; (center) wagon train fording Laramie Creek; (right) view to the southeast from the top of Independence Rock showing a wagon train camped on the Sweetwater River

Once underway, the wagon trains traveled on a northwesterly course along the Platte River to Ft. Laramie in eastern Wyoming. From there the trail led up the North Platte to the Sweetwater River and through a rugged canyon passage to South Pass, the first important milestone. In the pass, the migrants crossed the Continental Divide and began, at least symbolically, the descent to the Pacific. But it was an anti-climactic turning point. The arid plateau of the pass offered no sudden view of rivers flowing dramatically westward, and the most difficult part of the trip was still to come. There was little game, and the trail to Fort Hall on the Snake River passed through rocky, desolate country. At Fort Hall the trail divided, with the Californians heading southwest to the Humboldt River and those bound for Oregon following the Snake north and west. This final portion of the journey was a disheartening test of endurance. At times the Oregon Trail was so steep the wagons had to be held upright with ropes. Further on the wagons had to be dragged through narrow canyon passages. The final barrier, the Cascade Mountains, was often bypassed by converting the wagons into boats and floating downstream.

(Above) Fort Bridger and (below) Fort Hall, two old fur-trading forts which offered protection to wagon trains moving west on the Oregon Trail

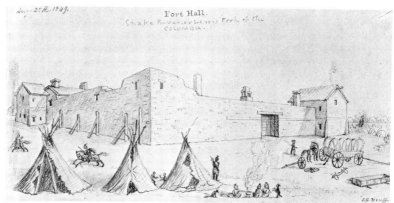

Oregon City on the Willamette River, 1846

Humboldt Pass viewed from a high peak east of the pass in the Sierra Nevada range

In spite of its hardships the Oregon Trail wc shorter and less demanding than the route to Ca ifornia, and the majority of migrants before th Gold Rush went to Oregon. The major difficulti on the California Trail were getting from Sout Pass to the Humboldt River and then gettin across the Sierra Nevada. The least torturo route to the Humboldt, by way of Fort Hall, wc also the longest. Since the Sierra had to b crossed before the snows of early November, va ious "cut-offs" were devised to shorten the rout each one named after its discoverer.

In 1844 a group led by Elisha Stevens, an o mountain man, pioneered the usual migrant rou across the Sierra. With the aid of an Indic named "Truckee," the Stevens party struck we from Humboldt Sink and hauled their wago over a pass that led directly to Sutter's Fort the other side. Theirs was the first party to arri with their wagons intact.

(Above) Jim Baker, who went west with Jim Bridger in 1838 and first served as a trapper. He became a guide for wagon trains after the fur trade died out; (right) hunting the grizzly bear; sketch by William H. Myers, 1845

(Above) Jim Bridger, trapper who remained in the mountains after the fur trading ceased and served as a guide to the parties migrating to California and Oregon; (right) descent from the Blue Mountains; (below) dead animals at Rabbit Hole Spring on the California Trail in the Nevada desert; (bottom) Lassen's Rancho Bosquejo in northern California

THE RABBIT-HOLE SPRINGS.

View of Pike's Peak from forty miles distant; from Fremont's report of his expedition

The government responded to interest in the Far West by sending John C. Fremont, a young Army engineer, on a series of expeditions to survey and map the trails to Oregon and California. Fremont spent 1842 in the Wind River Mountains and in 1843-44 led an expedition that marched from St. Louis to Oregon, then south into Nevada and across the Sierra into California, returning East by way of Nevada and Utah. A third expedition in the following year arrived in California in time for Fremont and his men to play a leading role in the Bear Flag Revolt of American settlers and the establishment of the Republic of California. Fremont's exploring contributed scientific information and accurate maps, and his popularity as the "Pathfinder" stimulated public interest in the West, but he covered no territory not already explored by the fur traders and produced little information directly useful to the migrants.

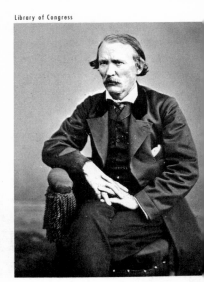

(Above right) John C. Fremont, photograph dated c. 1850; (right) Kit Carson, Fremont's guide on most of the expeditions; (below) Pass of the Standing Rock

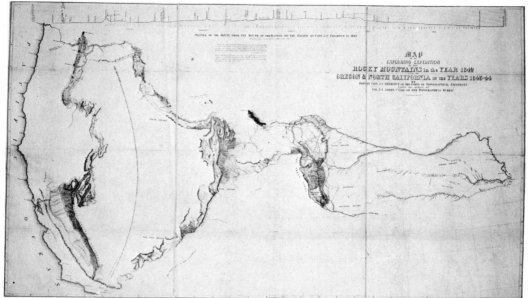

(Above) Map of Fremont's expedition in the Rocky Mountains of
Oregon and north California during 1843 and 1844. Fremont was
the first to name the area between the Sierra and Colorado
Rockies "The Great Basin";
(right) Pyramid Lake in the Sierra
Nevada range; (below) pass in
the Sierra Nevadas of California

View of Sutter's Fort in Sacramento, Calif., 1847

Gold

James Marshall, who discovered gold at Sutter's Mill

On January 24, 1848, James Marshall, an employee of John Sutter, discovered gold in the American River. News of the find spread across the country, and California fever became gold fever. Farms were abandoned, San Francisco was virtually deserted, and the migrations across the plains and around the Horn became a flood. In less than two years the population of California multiplied six times, to over 100,000.

Portrait of Captain John A. Sutter by Samuel Osgood

San Francisco in 1847; drawing by William Rich Hutton

1845

53.

WENDELL PHILLIPS: Concerning the Impossibility of Union with Slaveholders

As early as 1841, the Abolitionist leader William Lloyd Garrison maintained that since slavery could not be abolished under the existing Constitution, the North must in justice secede from the Union. In January 1843 the Massachusetts Anti-Slavery Society adopted his idea, and later in the same year the national society endorsed disunion by a vote of 59 to 21. In 1845 the society published a pamphlet, Can Abolitionists Vote or Take Office Under the United States Constitution?, *supporting its decision. The Introduction to the pamphlet was written by Wendell Phillips and is reproduced below.*

Source: *Anti-Slavery Examiner,* No. 13, New York, 1845.

THE AMERICAN ANTI-SLAVERY SOCIETY, at its annual meeting in May 1844, adopted the following resolution:

> *Resolved,* that secession from the present United States government is the duty of every Abolitionist; since no one can take office or throw a vote for another to hold office, under the United States Constitution, without violating his anti-slavery principles and rendering himself an abettor of the slaveholder in his sin.

The passage of this resolution has caused two charges to be brought against the Society: First, that it is a *no-government* body, and that the whole doctrine of nonresistance is endorsed by this vote; and second,

that the Society transcended its proper sphere and constitutional powers by taking such a step.

The logic which infers that because a man thinks the federal government bad he must necessarily think *all* government so, has, at least, the merit and the charm of novelty. There is a spice of arrogance just perceptible in the conclusion that the Constitution of these United States is so perfect that one who dislikes it could never be satisfied with any form of government whatever!

Were O'Connell and his fellow Catholics nonresistants because, for 200 years, they submitted to exclusion from the House of Lords and the House of Commons rather

Wendell Phillips; etching by J. Andrews, 1845

is its duty to find out all the sources of pro-slavery influence in the land. It is its right, it is its duty to try every institution in the land, no matter how venerable or sacred, by the touchstone of anti-slavery principle; and if it finds anyone false, to proclaim that fact to the world, with more or less of energy according to its importance in society. It has tried the Constitution and pronounced it unsound.

No member's conscience need be injured; the qualification for membership remains the same — "the belief that slaveholding is a heinous crime." No new test has been set up; but the majority of the Society, for the time being, faithful to its duty of trying every institution by the light of the present day, of uttering its opinion on every passing event that touches the slave's welfare, has seen it to be duty to sound forth its warning —

No Union with Slaveholders!

No one who did not vote for the resolution is responsible for it. No one is asked to quit our platform. We, the majority, only ask him to extend to our opinions the same toleration that we extend to him, and, agreeing to differ on this point, work together where we can. We proscribe no man for difference of opinion.

It is said that, having refused in 1840 to say that a man *ought to vote* on the ground that such a resolution would be tyrannical and intolerant, the Society is manifestly inconsistent now in taking upon itself to say that no Abolitionist *can* consistently vote. But the inconsistency is only apparent and not real.

There may be a thousand reasons why a particular individual ought not to do an act, though the act be innocent in itself. It would be tyranny, therefore, in a society which can properly take notice of but one subject, slavery, to promulgate the doctrine that all its members ought to do any partic-

than qualify themselves for a seat by an oath abjuring the pope? Were the *nonjuring* bishops of England nonresistants when they went down to the grave without taking their seats in the House of Lords rather than take an oath denying the Stuarts and to support the House of Hanover? Both might have purchased power at the price of one annual falsehood.

There are some in this country who do not seem to think that price at all unreasonable. It were a rare compliment indeed to the nonresistants if every exhibition of rigid principle on the part of an individual is to make the world suspect him of leaning toward their faith.

The Society is not opposed to government but only to *this* government, based upon and acting for slavery.

With regard to the second charge, of exceeding its proper limits and trespassing on the rights of the minority, it is enough to say that the object of the American Anti-Slavery Society is the "entire abolition of slavery in the United States." Of course it

ular act, as, for instance, to vote, to give money, to lecture, to petition, or the like. The particular circumstances and opinions of each one must regulate his actions. All we have a right to ask is that he do for the slave's cause as much as he does for any other of equal importance.

But when an act is wrong, it is no intolerance to say to the whole world that it ought *not to be done*. After the Abolitionist has granted that slavery is wrong, we have the right to judge him by his own principles and arraign him for inconsistency that, so believing, he helps the slaveholder by his oath. . . .

I am aware that we nonvoters are rather singular. But history, from the earliest Christians downward, is full of instances of men who refused all connection with government and all the influence which office could bestow rather than deny their principles or aid in doing wrong. Yet I never heard them called either idiots or overscrupulous. Sir Thomas More need never have mounted the scaffold had he only consented to take the oath of supremacy. He had only to tell a lie with solemnity, as we are asked to do, and he might not only have saved his life but, as the trimmers of his day would have told him, doubled his influence. Pitt resigned his place as prime minister of England rather than break faith with the Catholics of Ireland. Should I not resign a petty ballot rather than break faith with the slave?

But I was specially glad to find a distinct recognition of the principle upon which we have acted applied to a different point, in the life of that patriarch of the anti-slavery enterprise, Granville Sharpe. It is in a late number of the *Edinburgh Review*. While an underclerk in the War Office, he sympathized with our fathers in their struggle for independence. "Orders reached his office to ship munitions of war to the revolted colonies. If his hand had entered the account of such a cargo, it would have contracted in

his eyes the stain of innocent blood. To avoid this pollution, he resigned his place and his means of subsistence at a period of life when he could no longer hope to find any other lucrative employment." As the thoughtful clerk of the War Office takes his hat down from the peg where it has used to hang for twenty years, methinks I hear one of our opponents cry out, "Friend Sharpe, you are absurdly scrupulous." "You may innocently aid government in doing wrong," adds another. While Liberty Party yelps at his heels, "My dear sir, you are quite losing your influence!" And indeed it is melancholy to reflect how, from that moment, the mighty underclerk of the War Office (!) dwindled into the mere Granville Sharpe of history! The man of whom Mansfield and Hargrave were content to learn law, and Wilberforce, philanthropy.

One friend proposes to vote for men who shall be pledged not to take office unless the oath of the Constitution is dispensed with, and who shall then go on to perform in their offices only such duties as we, their constituents, approve. He cites, in support of his view, the election of O'Connell to the House of Commons, in 1828, I believe, just one year before the "oath of supremacy," which was the objectionable one to the Catholics, was dispensed with. Now, if we stood in the same circumstances as the Catholics did in 1828, the example would be in point. When the public mind is thoroughly revolutionized and ready for the change, when the billow has reached its height and begins to crest into foam, then such a measure may bring matters to a crisis. But let us first go through, in patience, as O'Connell did, our twenty years of agitation.

Waiving all other objections, this plan seems to me mere playing at politics and an entire waste of effort. It loses our high position as moral reformers; it subjects us to all that malignant opposition and suspicion of motives which attend the array of parties;

and while thus closing up our access to the national conscience, it wastes in fruitless caucusing and party tactics the time and the effort which should have been directed to efficient agitation.

The history of our Union is lesson enough, for every candid mind, of the fatal effects of every, the least, compromise with evil. The experience of the fifty years passed under it shows us the slaves trebling in numbers, slaveholders monopolizing the offices and dictating the policy of the government, prostituting the strength and influence of the nation to the support of slavery here and elsewhere, trampling on the rights of the free states and making the courts of the country their tools. To continue this disastrous alliance longer is madness. The trial of fifty years only proves that it is impossible for free and slave states to unite on any terms without all becoming partners in the guilt and responsible for the sin of slavery. Why prolong the experiment? Let every honest man join in the outcry of the American Anti-Slavery Society.

NO UNION WITH SLAVEHOLDERS!

54.

Resolutions of a New York Antirent Convention

The great estates in New York that had been granted to wealthy settlers in colonial times still existed in the 1830s. The land was parceled out among hundreds of tenants who worked it and paid the owners rent and services. This vestige of European feudalism was unpopular in a democratic country where family ownership of farms was the rule. From 1839 to 1846 New York was the scene of antirent agitation and occasional rioting by tenants. By 1844 the antirenters had organized an association that convened at Bern, New York, in January 1845. The resolutions below were adopted by the convention. The antirent faction was strong enough in 1846 to influence the state's constitutional convention to abolish feudal land tenure.

Source: *Albany Argus*, February 11, 1845.

Whereas, the time has arrived when it becomes necessary for us, as citizens and tenants, residing on manors claimed and leased by landlords under grants from foreign governments, thus in a formal and public manner to correct false representations and misapplied constructions of the designs and purposes of the antirent associations in the various counties in this state. Public functionaries, and also the press, both powerful organs, have widely spread charges of combination of tenants for the secret purpose of hiring persons disguised as Indians to set law at defiance and obtaining right by might. When the public mind is abused, it is calculated to defeat the objects sought for, and tends to bring associations into disrepute; therefore, we publicly declare, before God and man, that no such combinations have been made within our knowledge or belief, and can exist in imagination.

The associations of tenants are for honorable and legal redress of grievances to be obtained from the proper tribunals. The only services employed are legal counsels; the only expenses those for publications, the attendance on courts and sessions of the legislature. Over the acts of individuals the associations have no control, and therefore disclaim any accountability.

Resolved, that we, as a pure and patriotic party, will, in future, discountenance and discontinue all public and mercenary prints of every kind and nature that are publishing falsehoods against us and alleging things against us, as a body, which they know at the time of giving publicity to are utterly destitute of every shadow of truth, and all for their own supposed pecuniary benefit.

Resolved, that, in the opinion of this convention, the late and lamentable scenes in the county of Rensselaer, in which sacrifice of human life occurred, present a case which calls loudly for the censure of a civilized and enlightened community against all and every act infringing in the least upon law and order, and that we entirely disavow all and any connection with lawless and reckless desperadoes.

Resolved, that, while we deeply regret the illegal acts and recent loss of human life in Columbia County, we are rejoiced to learn through the report of the coroner's inquest that the death of Rifenburgh was caused by accident and was not a foul murder, as charged by a corrupt and partisan press.

Resolved, that we will discard and discountenance any man or men pretending to be our friend who grasp at any adverse report, and who countenance, exaggerate, and circulate such as truths, to the detriment of our individual and party rights.

Resolved, that we will adhere to our heretofore expressed opinion through the ballot boxes, and sustain nominations made as *antirent*, laying aside all old party lines, either Whig or Democratic, and in nominating our candidates, we will endeavor to select men who have been with us in our days of adversity as well as prosperity, who are and have been antirent men at all times.

Resolved, that we deeply regret that the governor of this state should "feel himself precluded from inviting the careful attention of the legislature to the consideration" of the acknowledged grievances of the tenants, by reason of the lawless and indefensible acts of a misguided few, with whose acts and doings he truly expresses his conviction that the great body of the "tenant farmers" are in nowise connected, and which they totally discountenance; but we cannot but deprecate this act of injustice, in making the sins of others the ground of withholding all relief from the acknowledged burden of oppression resting upon us.

Resolved, that we cannot conceive of any sufficient cause for the countinuance of "contracts" which are acknowledged to be "onerous in their exactions, and tenures which in their nature and character are uncongenial with the habits and opinions of a free people," and the principles of a free government.

Resolved, that we fully and heartily concur in the sentiment of our state executive that the "theory upon which our government is instituted is equal protection to all." Yet, while we make this concession, we most deeply deplore that the practical effect of our laws relating to landlord and tenant is diametrically opposed to such theory.

Resolved, that we view with surprise that an executive of the state of New York should shrink from the responsibility of his own acts, and call for legislative action to shield him from such responsibility and the just award of public sentiment.

The Committee on Petitions was then announced, and through Mr. Thompson, chairman of the Committee, reported the following, which was unanimously adopted:

> To the Hon. the Legislature of the State of New York. The undersigned, legal voters and citizens of the county of ———— , conceiving the existing laws of this state relating to landlord and tenant to be unjust, oppressive, and diametrical-

ly opposed to the spirit of free and republican institutions, do hereby petition your honorable body for the passage of an act repealing all laws granting special privileges to landlords in the collection of their rents, so that they shall be permitted to use and enjoy the common right of other creditors in the collection of their dues and none other.

And the undersigned do further petition your honorable body for the passage of an act authorizing tenants, when prosecuted for rents, to set up as a defense against such prosecution the want of a good and sufficient title to the premises in the landlord or prosecutor; and that such defense be a bar to any recovery against such tenant until the title of the landlord be fully established; to apply in those cases where lands have been leased for a long series of years or in perpetuity.

And your petitioners do further ask for the passage of a law authorizing and directing the assessors of the several towns of this state to estimate and consider the amount of rents charged on leasehold premises, leased for a term of fifteen years and upward, situated in their respective towns, as the interest of a principal, which principal shall be assessed to the owners of such premises and the taxes thereon to be paid in the towns within which such lands are situated; for their benefit, and in case of default of payment of such taxes, that such leasehold premises be returned in like manner as nonresident lands, and the interest of the landlord sold therefore.

55.

The Restless Pursuit of Wealth

The American Review: A Whig Journal of Politics, Literature, Art
and Science *was a monthly magazine published from 1845 to 1852. The editorial
printed below is taken from its first issue. The* American Review *(the title was
changed to* American Whig Review *in 1850) was intended to counter the popularity
of the Democratic journal launched in 1837, the* United States Magazine and
Democratic Review. *Generally the* American Review *promoted Whig principles
and defended the interests of commerce and industry. Although the criticisms of the
American character in the following article were made by Democrats as well as Whigs,
the view of society put forth in the editorial was held typically by Whigs.*

Source: *American Review,* January 1845: "Influence of the Trading Spirit
         upon the Social and Moral Life of America."

THOSE INFLUENCES which affect the characters of a whole people are less observed, although more important, than such as are peculiar to classes or individuals. The exertions which one may make to protect himself from error or demeaning influences are sometimes rendered ineffectual from his ignorance of the tremendous biases which he receives from a corrupt public opinion; as the most careful observations of the mariner are sometimes vitiated by an unknown current which insensibly drifts him from his supposed position. What everybody does in our own community we are apt to suppose to be universal with men; and universal custom is, by general consent, not to be disputed. We are not disposed to suspect public opinion or to question common custom. Nay, we do not even, for the most part, distinguish between a prevailing sentiment and an innate idea, between a universal or national habit and a law of nature. The customs of the city in which we are brought up seem to most persons of Divine appointment. We are apt to account a foreigner who prefers (in accordance with his own national manners and prejudices) a different division of the day, different hours at the table, a different style of dress, as almost immoral. This proves how little aware we may be of the nature of the social habits and sentiments which greatly influence our characters. We propose to offer a few observations upon some of our national habits and tendencies.

There is but one thing to discourage such an inquiry, and that is, that after understanding the direction and force of the current on which we are borne, there is little hope of withstanding it, or guiding ourselves upon it. But to this it must be replied that public opinion is made up of private opinions, and that the only way of ever changing it is by commencing to correct, be it ever so little, the judgments of one's own mind and of the few others under our influence. We must not despise humble means of influence, nor hesitate to do a little good, because an almost hopeless amount of evil surrounds us.

All strangers who come among us remark the excessive anxiety written in the American countenance. The widespread comfort, the facilities for livelihood, the spontaneous and cheap lands, the high price of labor are equally observed, and render it difficult to account for these lines of painful thoughtfulness. It is not poverty, nor tyranny, nor overcompetition which produces this anxi-

ety; that is clear. It is the concentration of the faculties upon an object which in its very nature is unattainable — the perpetual improvement of the outward condition.

There are no bounds among us to the restless desire to be better off; and this is the ambition of all classes of society. We are not prepared to allow that wealth is more valued in America than elsewhere; but in other countries the successful pursuit of it is necessarily confined to a few, while here it is open to all. No man in America is contented to be poor, or expects to continue so. There are here no established limits within which the hopes of any class of society must be confined, as in other countries. There is consequently no condition of hopes realized; in other words, of contentment. In other lands, if children can maintain the station and enjoy the means, however moderate, of their father, they are happy. Not so with us. This is not the spirit of our institutions. Nor will it long be otherwise in other countries.

That equality, that breaking down of artificial barriers which has produced this universal ambition and restless activity in America is destined to prevail throughout the earth. But because we are in advance of the world in the great political principle and are now experiencing some of its first effects, let us not mistake these for the desirable fruits of freedom. Commerce is to become the universal pursuit of men. It is to be the first result of freedom, of popular institutions everywhere. Indeed, every land not steeped in tyranny is now feeling this impulse.

But while trade is destined to free and employ the masses, it is also destined to destroy for the time much of the beauty and happiness of every land. This has been the result in our own country. We are free. It is a glorious thing that we have no serfs, with the large and unfortunate exception of our slaves; no artificial distinctions; no acknowledged superiority of blood; no station which merit may not fill; no rounds in the social ladder to which the humblest may not aspire.

But the excitement, the commercial activity, the restlessness to which this state of things has given birth is far from being a desirable or a natural condition. It is natural to the circumstances, but not natural to the human soul. It is good and hopeful to the interests of the race, but destructive to the happiness and dangerous to the virtue of the generation exposed to it.

Those unaccustomed, by reading or travel, to other states of society are probably not aware how very peculiar our manner of life here is. The laboriousness of Americans is beyond all comparison, should we except the starving operatives of English factories. And when we consider that here, to the labor of the body is added the great additional labor of mental responsibility and ambition, it is not to be wondered at that as a race, the commercial population is dwindling in size and emaciated in health, so that pallor is the national complexion.

If this devotion to business were indispensable to living, it would demand our pity. It is unavoidable, we know, in one sense. That is, it is customary — it is universal. There is no necessity for the custom; but there is a necessity, weakly constituted as men are, that every individual should conform greatly to the prevailing habits of his fellows and the expectations of the community in and with which he deals. It is thus that those who deeply feel the essentially demoralizing and wretched influences of this system are yet doomed to be victims of it. Nay, we are all, no matter what our occupations, more or less, and all greatly, sufferers from the excessive stimulus under which everything is done.

We are all worn out with thought that does not develop our thinking faculties in a right direction, and with feeling expended upon poor and low objects. There is no profession that does not feel it. The lawyer must confine himself to his office, without vacation, to adjust a business which never sleeps or relaxes. The physician must labor day and night to repair bodies, never well from overexertion, overexcitement, and overindulgence. The minister must stimulate himself to supply the cravings of diseased moral appetites and to arouse the attention of men deafened by the noise and dizzy with the whirl in which they constantly live.

We call our country a *happy* country; happy, indeed, in being the home of noble political institutions, the abode of freedom; but very far from being happy in possessing a cheerful, lighthearted, and joyous people. Our agricultural regions even are infected with the same anxious spirit of gain. If ever the curse of labor was upon the race, it is upon us; nor is it simply now "by the sweat of thy brow thou shalt earn thy bread." Labor for a livelihood is dignified. But we labor for bread, and labor for pride, and *labor* for pleasure.

A man's life with us *does* consist of the abundance of the things which he possesses. To get, and to have the reputation of possessing, is the ruling passion. To it are bent all the energies of nine-tenths of our population. Is it that our people are so much more miserly and earthborn than any other? No, not by any constitutional baseness; but circumstances have necessarily given this direction to the American mind. In the hard soil of our common mother — New England — the poverty of our ancestors, their early thrift and industry, the want of other distinctions than those of property, the frown of the Puritans upon all pleasures; these circumstances combined, directed our energies from the first into the single channel of trade. And in that they have run till they have gained a tremendous head, and threaten to convert our whole people into mere money changers and producers. Honor belongs to our fathers, who in times of great necessity met the demand for a most painful industry with such manly and un-flinching hearts. But what was their hard necessity we are perpetuating as our willing servitude! What they bore as evil we seek as good.

We cannot say that the destiny of this country did not demand that the spirit of trade should rule it for centuries. It may be that we are now carrying out only the decree of Providence. But if so, let us consider ourselves as in the wilderness and not in the promised land. Let us bear the dispensation of God, but not glory in our bondage. If we are doomed to be tradesmen, and nothing but tradesmen; if money and its influences and authority are to reign for a season over our whole land, let us not mistake it for the Kingdom of Heaven, and build triumphal arches over our avenues of trade, as though the Prince of Peace and Son of God were now and thus to enter in.

It is said that we are not a happy people. And it is true; for we most unwisely neglect all those free fountains of happiness which Providence has opened for all its children. Blessed beyond any people with the means of living, supplied to an unparalleled extent with the comforts and luxuries of life, our American homes are somber and cheerless abodes. There is even in the air of comfort which their well-furnished apartments wear something uncomfortable. They are the habitations of those who do not live at home. They are wanting in a social and cheerful aspect. They seem fitted more to be admired than to be enjoyed. The best part of the house is for the occasional use of strangers and not to be occupied by those who might, day by day, enjoy it, which is but one proof among many that we love to appear comfortable rather than to be so.

Thus miserable pride hangs like a millstone about our hospitality. "We sacrifice the hospitality of a year to the prodigality of a night." We are ashamed of anything but affluence, and when we cannot make an appearance, or furnish entertainments as showy as the richest, we will do nothing. Thus does pride close our doors. Hospitality becomes an event of importance. It is not our daily life, one of our chiefest enjoyments, but a debt, a ceremony, a penance. And not only pride but anxiety of mind interferes with sociality.

Bent upon one aim, the merchant grudges his thoughts. He cannot expend his energies in social enjoyment. Nay, it is not enjoyment to him; society has nothing of the excitement of business. The excessive pursuit of gain begets a secrecy of thought, a contradiction of ideas, a barrenness of interest, which renders its votary anything but social or companionable. Conversation incessantly takes an anxious and uninteresting turn; and the fireside becomes only a narrower exchange, and the parlor a more private newsroom.

It is rare to see a foreigner without some taste for amusement, some power of relaxing his mind, some interest in the arts or in literature. This is true even of the less privileged classes. It is rare, on the contrary, to find a *virtuous* American past middle life who does not regard amusements of all sorts either as childish or immoral; who possesses any acquaintance with or taste for the arts, except it be a natural and rude taste for music; or who reads anything except newspapers, and only the political or commercial columns of those. It is the want of tastes for other things than business which gives an anxious and unhappy turn to our minds. It cannot be many years before the madness of devoting the whole day to the toils of the countinghouse will be acknowledged; before the claim of body and mind to relaxation and cheerful, exhilarating amusement will be seen.

We consider the common suspicion which is felt of amusements among thoughtful people to be one of the most serious evils to which our community is exposed. It outlaws a natural taste and violates and ruins the consciences of the young by stamping as sinful what they have not the force to refrain from. It makes our places of amusement low, divides the thoughtful and the careless, the grave and the gay, the old and the young in their pleasures. Children are without the protection of their parents in their enjoyments. And thus, too, is originated one of the greatest curses of our social state — the great want of intimacy and confidence between children and their parents, especially between fathers and sons.

The impulses that incline to pleasure, if opposed, tend to vice. Nature finds a vent for her pent-up forces. Alas! for what are called *strict morals* in this view; when, by an unnatural restriction, innocent and open pleasures make way for secret vices or sins of the heart.

While the commercial spirit in this extravagant form gives a certain sobriety and moral aspect to society, it occasions an excessive barrenness of real moral excellencies. This is a very difficult and delicate distinction to render popularly apparent, although of the most vital and substantial reality. There is a very great difference between what are called strict morals, and morals that are really profound in their sources and pervading in their influence. We are more strict in our morals in these Northern states than anywhere in the world, but it is questionable whether our morality is not of a somewhat inferior quality and in a too narrow view. It is artificial, conventional. There is no quarter of the earth where the Sabbath is more scrupulously observed, where religious institutions are so well supported, or where more abstinence from pleasure is practised. The great virtue of industry prevails. Overt sins are more rare here than elsewhere.

As far as morality is restrictive in its nature, it has accomplished a great work in America. The vices or sins which are reducible to statute, or known by name, are generally restrained. We have a large class of

persons of extraordinary propriety and faultlessness of life. Our view of morals has a tendency to increase this class. Our pursuits are favorable to it. The love of gain is one of the most sober of all desires. The seriousness of a miser surpasses the gravity of a devotee. Did not every commercial city draw a large body of strangers to it, and attract many reckless and vicious persons, it would wear a very solemn aspect. The pleasure-seeking, the gay, the disorderly, are never the trading population. Large commercial cities tend to great orderliness and decency of manners and morals. But they also tend to very low and barren views of moral excellence.

And the American spirit of our own day illustrates this. Our moral sense operates only in one direction. Our virtues are the virtues of merchants and not of men. We run all to honesty and mercantile honesty. We do not cultivate the graces of humanity. We have more conscience than heart, and more propriety than either. The fear of evil consequences is more influential than the love of goodness. There is nothing hearty, gushing, eloquent in the national virtue. You do not see goodness leaking out from the full vessel at every motion it feels. Our goodness is formal, deliberate, premeditated. The upright man is not benevolent, and the just man is not generous. The good man is not cheerful. The religious man is not agreeable.

In other words, our morals are partial, and therefore barren. It is not generally understood how great scrupulousness of character may be united with great selfishness, and how, along with a substantial virtue, there may exist the most melancholy deficiencies. This seems to be very common with us, and to be the natural result of our engrossing pursuits. Everyone minds his own business to the extreme peril of his own soul. The apostolic precept, "Mind not thine own things, but also the things of another," is in danger of great neglect. Our social condition makes us wary, suspicious, slow to commit ourselves too far in interest for others.

The shyness of the tradesman communicates itself to the manners of the visitor; we learn to live within ourselves; we grow unsocial, unfraternal in feeling; and the sensibility, the affection, the cordiality, the forthputting graces of a warm and virtuous heart die of disuse. For our part, we are ready to say, let us have more faults and more virtues; more weaknesses and more graces; less punctilio and more affluence of heart. Let us be less dignified and more cordial; less sanctimonious and more unselfish; less thriving and more cheerful; less toilsome and more social.

We want, as a people, a rounder character. Our humanity is pinched; our tastes are not generous. The domestic and social virtues languish. The dearest relations of life are stripped of beauty; a wretched utility usurps that proper theater of beautiful sentiment, our very homes. Children grow up unknown to their parents. The mature despise their own youth, and have no sympathy with the romance, the buoyancy, the gayety of their children. Enterprise is our only enthusiasm. We grow to be ashamed of our best affections. We are afraid to acknowledge that we derive enjoyment from trifles, and make apologies for being amused with anything. Thus is the beautiful field of life burnt over, and all its spontaneous flowers and fruitage destroyed; a few towering trunks alone redeeming the landscape.

Happiness is made up of little things, and he who would be happy at all, must enjoy the little things day by day. So fraternal love, benevolence, virtue, consist in small acts prompted by love, and binding the day with a chain of delicate moral links. Character, too, is the result of right purposes, and pure feelings, and generous emotions, exercised upon trivial occasions day after day;

and heroic and high virtue is the necessary result of this mode of life.

We fear that the ruling passion of our community, the habits of business which it has established, the anxious and self-concentrated mind which ensues, the morals which it engenders are very hostile to anything like perfected humanity. It is very probable that we may have erred in supposing a greatly better state of things to exist in other communities. But we know that we are right as to the positive state of our own, whatever it may be relatively to others. We know, too, very well the almost insuperable difficulties in the way of any individual who shall attempt to withstand the prevailing current of sentiment or of business habits.

But if *none* are to escape, it is well to be aware of the danger; nor must it be assumed that a firm will cannot do much to emancipate a man from the general bondage of trade. Sooner than slave from morning to night at business, we would counsel any man conscious of inward resources, of the desire to cultivate his better nature, his social feelings, his tastes, his generous and cheerful sentiments, to give it up altogether as soon as the most moderate competency is secured; to seek the country — to occupy some of our rich Western lands — to do anything which will give him time to enjoy domestic pleasures, to rear his children, to acquaint himself with nature, to read, to meditate.

The excitement, the bustle, the toil of our life render us dead to the voice of the highest truth. We cannot stop to consider the matter. How few are aware that Christianity is a call to freedom, a call to happiness. Would we but listen, it would break these very chains whose galling wounds we have been opening; it would allay these feverish anxieties; it would restore to us contentment; it would legitimate our pleasures; it would reestablish or for the first time build our homes; it would give our children parents, and us parents children; it would teach us that happiness resides ever in the simple and impartial bounties of God: in a domestic love, in social intercourse, in generous sympathy, in a mind pleased with little things, in the gratification of our various innocent tastes, in the love of nature, in thought, in doing good.

We meanwhile barter the substance for the shadow — delve for the means instead of quietly enjoying the end — keep up appearances, deceive others with the show of happiness, and fall at length from the top of life's laborious gains into our graves, worn out with anxieties that have benefited no one, and carrying neither the recollection nor the capacity of happiness with us into a spiritual existence.

56.

Asa Whitney: A Railroad to the Pacific

On January 28, 1845, Asa Whitney, a New York merchant who had made a fortune in the Orient, proposed in the following memorial to both houses of Congress that he be granted a tract of land sixty miles wide from Lake Michigan to the Pacific Ocean in return for constructing a railroad. The Senate Committee on Public Lands reported in favor of the scheme in July 1846, but a House committee found it impractical. For the next decade, Whitney conducted a propaganda campaign, lecturing, writing, and memorializing Congress. By 1853 there was agreement in Congress that a railroad should be built, but by that time the increasing sectional sentiment precluded an agreement on the route. Not until 1862, with only Republicans in Congress, was legislation passed to forward the project.

Source: 28 Congress, 2 Session, Senate Document No. 69.

Your memorialist begs respectfully to represent to your honorable body that, by rivers, railroads, and canals, all the states east and north of the Potomac connect directly with the waters of the Great Lakes.

That there is a chain of railroads in projection and being built from New York to the southern shore of Lake Michigan, which, crossing all the veins of communication to the ocean through all the states south and east of the Ohio River, will produce commercial, political, and national results and benefits which must be seen and felt through all our vast Confederacy. Your memorialist would further represent to your honorable body that he has devoted much time and attention to the subject of a railroad from Lake Michigan, through the Rocky Mountains, to the Pacific Ocean; and that he finds such a route practicable, the results from which would be incalculable, far beyond the imagination of man to estimate. To the interior of our vast and widely spread country it would be as the heart is to the human body.

It would, when completed, cross all the mighty rivers and streams which wend their way to the ocean through our vast and rich valleys, from Oregon to Maine, a distance of more than 3,000 miles. The incalculable importance of such a chain of roads will readily be seen and appreciated by your honorable body. It would enable us in the short space of eight days (and perhaps less) to concentrate all the forces of our vast country at any point, from Maine to Oregon, in the interior or on the coast.

Such easy and rapid communication, with such facilities for exchanging the different products of the different parts, would bring all our immensely widespread population together as one vast city, the moral and social effects of which must harmonize all together as one family with but one interest — the general good of all.

Your memorialist respectfully represents to your honorable body that the roads from New York to Lake Michigan, a distance of 840 miles, will no doubt be completed by the states through which they pass or by individuals; that from Lake Michigan to the mouth of the Columbia River is 2,160 miles, making from New York to the Pacific Ocean 3,000 miles; from the Columbia River to the Sandwich Islands is 2,100 miles, making from New York to the Sandwich Islands 5,100 miles; from Columbia River to Japan is 5,600 miles, making from New York to Japan 8,600 miles; from the Columbia River to Amoy, in China (the port nearest the tea and silk provinces) is 6,200 miles, making from New York to Amoy only 9,200 miles, which, with a railroad to the Pacific, thence to China by steam, can be performed in 30 days, now being a sailing distance of nearly 17,000 miles, requiring from 100 to 150 days for its performance.

Then the drills and sheetings of Connecticut, Rhode Island, and Massachusetts can be transported to China in thirty days, and the teas and rich silks of China in exchange come back to New Orleans, to Charleston, to Washington, to Baltimore, to Philadelphia, to New York, and to Boston in thirty

days more. Comment is unnecessary. Your honorable body will readily see the revolution by this to be wrought in the entire commerce of the world, and that this must inevitably be its channel, when the rich freights from the waters of the Mississippi and the Hudson will fill to overflowing with the products of all the earth, the storehouses of New York and New Orleans, the great marts dividing the commerce of the world, while each state and every town in our vast Confederacy would receive its just proportion of influence and benefits, compared with its vicinity to or facility to communicate with any of the rivers, canals, or railroads crossed by this great road.

Your memorialist would respectfully represent to your honorable body its political importance that, affording a communication from Washington to the Columbia River in less than eight days, a naval depot with a comparatively small navy would command the Pacific, the South Atlantic, and the Indian oceans, and the Chinese seas.

Your memorialist begs respectfully to represent, further, to your honorable body, that he can see no way or means by which this great and important work can be accomplished, for ages to come, except by a grant of a sufficient quantity of the public domain; and your memorialist believes that from the proceeds of such a grant he will be enabled to complete said road within a reasonable period of time and at the same time settle the country through which it passes, so far as the lands may be found suited to cultivation, with an industrious, frugal people — thus, in a comparatively short space of time, accomplishing what will otherwise require ages and thus at once giving us the power of dictation to those who will not long remain satisfied without an attempt to dictate to us.

Our system of free government works so well, diffusing so much intelligence, dispensing equal justice, and insuring safety to all, and producing so much general comfort and prosperity that its influence must, like a mighty flood, sweep away all other systems. Then let us not flatter ourselves that this overwhelming current is not to meet resistance, for to us directly will that resistance be applied; and your memorialist believes that we must yet meet that desperate and final struggle which shall perpetuate our system and religious and civil liberty.

Your honorable body are aware of the overpopulation of Europe; and your memorialist would respectfully represent that, by the application of machinery and its substitution for manual labor, the latter no longer receives its just or sufficient reward; and thousands, in the fear of starvation at home, are driven to our shores, hoping, from our widespread and fertile soil, to find a rich reward for their labor — most of them ignorant and all inexperienced.

Having been herded together in large numbers at home, they dread separation even from misery; they fear the wilderness or prairie; they refuse to leave the city; their small means are soon exhausted; they see abundance around them, almost without price, but that small price they can no longer pay; necessity plunges them into vice, and often crime, and they become burdensome to our citizens — and which evil is increasing to an alarming extent. And your memorialist believes it must increase, unless there can be some great and important point in our interior to which they can be attracted immediately on their landing, where their little means, with their labor, can purchase lands, where they will escape the tempting vices of our cities, where they will have a home with their associates, and where their labor from their own soil will not only produce their daily bread but in time an affluence of which they could never have dreamed in their native land.

Your memorialist believes that this road will be the great and desirable point of attraction; that it will relieve our cities from a vast amount of misery, crime, and taxation; that it will take the poor unfortunates to a land where they will be compelled to labor for a subsistence; and as they will soon find that their labor and efforts receive a just reward — finding themselves and their little ones surrounded with comfort and plenty, the recompense for their own toil — their energies will kindle into a flame of ambition and desire; and we shall be enabled to educate them to our system — to industry, prosperity, and virtue. Your memorialist confidently expects all this, and more.

Your memorialist would respectfully represent, further, to your honorable body that, from an estimate as nearly accurate as can be made short of an actual survey, the cost of said road, to be built in a safe, good, and substantial manner, will be about $50 million; and as the road cannot (from the situation of the uninhabited country through which it will pass) earn anything or but little before its completion, therefore a further sum of $15 million will be required to keep in operation, expenses, etc. — making the total estimated cost of said road, when completed, $65 million.

It may require some years before the earnings of said road (at the low rates of tolls necessary for its complete success) can be much if anything beyond its current expenses for repairs, etc.; but that after a period of —— years, and at the very lowest possible rates of tolls, it must earn more than ample for its repairs and expenses. It would be the only channel for the commerce of all the western coast of Mexico and South America, of the Sandwich Islands, of Japan, of all China, Manila, Australia, Java, Singapore, Calcutta, and Bombay — not only all ours but the commerce of all Europe.

To the most of these places must pass this road — your memorialist says *must* because the saving of time (so all-important to the merchant) from the long and hazardous voyage around either of the capes would force it; and in a few years would be built up cities, towns, and villages, from the lake to the ocean, which would alone support the road.

Being built from the public lands, the road should be free, except so far as sufficient for the necessary expenses of operation, repairs, etc. And your memorialist believes that, at a very low rate of tolls, a sum would be gained, after all current expenses, sufficient to make a handsome distribution for public education; and, as a part of the earnings will be from foreign commerce, your memorialist begs respectfully to submit the subject to your wise consideration.

Your memorialist respectfully represents, further, to your honorable body, that, from the knowledge he can procure, he finds that the lands, for a long distance east of the mountains, are bad, of little or no value for culture; that through and for some distance beyond the mountains would also be of but little if any value; therefore, your memorialist is satisfied that it will require an entire tract of sixty miles in width, from as near to Lake Michigan as the unappropriated lands commence to the Pacific Ocean.

Therefore, in view of all the important considerations here set forth, your memorialist is induced to pray that your honorable body will grant to himself, his heirs, and assigns such tract of land, the proceeds of which to be strictly and faithfully applied to the building and completing the said road, always with such checks and guarantees to your honorable body as shall secure a faithful performance of all the obligations and duties of your memorialist; and that, after the faithful completion of this great work, should any lands remain unsold or any moneys due for lands or any balance of moneys received for lands sold, which have not been required for the building of said road, then all and every of them shall belong to your memorialist, his heirs, and assigns, forever.

Your memorialist further prays that your honorable body will order a survey of said route, to commence at some point to be fixed upon as most desirable on the shore of Lake Michigan, between the 42° and 45° north latitude, thence west to the gap or pass in the mountains, and thence the most practicable route to the Pacific Ocean.

Your memorialist would respectfully represent one further consideration to your honorable body: that, in his opinion, Oregon must fast fill up with an industrious, enterprising people from our states; that they will soon attract and draw to them large numbers from the states of Europe — all expecting to share in the benefits from our free government — claiming its care and protection; but the difficulty of access to them either by land or water will forbid such a hope.

And your memorialist believes that the time is not far distant when Oregon will become a state of such magnitude and importance as to compel the establishment of a separate government — a separate nation, which will have cities, ports, and harbors, all free, inviting all the nations of the earth to a free trade with them; when they will control and monopolize the valuable fisheries of the Pacific; control the coast trade of Mexico and South America, of the Sandwich Islands, Japan, and all China, and be our most dangerous and successful rivals in the commerce of the world.

But your memorialist believes that this road will unite them to us, enabling them to receive the protecting care of our government, sharing in its blessings, benefits, and prosperity, and imparting to us our share of the great benefits from their local position, enterprise, and industry. But your honorable body will see all this, and more. And, as in duty bound, your memorialist will ever pray.

57.

WILLIAM GREGG: Southern Manufacturing

For a generation, Southern manufacturers like William Gregg tried to induce their wealthy landowning neighbors to take an active role in promoting industry, especially cotton manufacturing. Gregg's goal was Southern economic independence, in order to lessen the emigration from the South of its enterprising population, and to employ the poor. He felt that the raw materials for manufacturing abounded and that their exploitation was blocked only by state of mind. The essays in which his appeal was put forward appeared originally in the Charleston Courier *in 1845 signed "South Carolina," and in pamphlet form under the author's true name in the same year. Of the twelve essays, the third and fourth are reprinted below.*

Source: D. A. Tompkins, *Cotton Mill, Commercial Features,* Charlotte, N.C., 1899, Appendix.

HOWEVER UNPOPULAR the doctrine of encouraging domestic industry in South Carolina may be, I feel satisfied that there are few individuals so ultra in their notions, with regard to our being exclusively agricultural, that will not feel charmed with the idea of *domestic industry;* it carries with it the idea of an improved condition of our country — of compensated industry and comforts around us. It is to be lamented that our great men are not to be found in the ranks of those who are willing to lend their aid in promoting this good cause.

Are we to commence another ten-years' crusade to prepare the minds of the people of this state for revolution,[1] thus unhinging every department of industry and paralyzing

the best efforts to promote the welfare of our country? Already do we hear of persons, high in the estimation of our state, largely engaged in cotton planting and, on the side of state resistance, expressing doubts as to the permanency and safety of any investments that can be made in South Carolina. Lamentable, indeed, is it to see so wise and so pure a man as Langdon Cheves putting forth the doctrine, to South Carolina, that manufactures should be the last resort of a country. With the greatest possible respect for the opinions of this truly great man and the humblest pretensions on my part, I will venture the assertion that a greater error was never committed by a statesman.

No good is without its evil, and I am free to confess that when a people become so infatuated with the spirit of manufactures as to undertake to force large establishments into unnatural existence, at the expense of other pursuits, they are committing an error by making an evil of that which would otherwise be a great blessing. I admit, also

1. Those who are disposed to agitate the state and prepare the minds of the people for resisting the laws of Congress, and particularly those who look for so direful a calamity as the dissolution of our Union, should, above all others, be most anxious to diversify the industrial pursuits of South Carolina, as to render her independent of all other countries; for as sure as this greatest of calamities befalls us, we shall find the same causes that produced it, making enemies of the nations which are at present the best customers for our agricultural productions.

that agriculture is the natural and "blessed employment of man"; but that a country should become eminently prosperous in agriculture, without a high state of perfection in the mechanic arts, is a thing next to impossible — to be dreamed of, not realized — a picture of the imagination, not to be found in reality on the face of the globe.

What does this gentleman mean by agriculture? Does he intend that we shall follow the footsteps of our forefathers and still further exhaust our soil by the exclusive culture of cotton? Does he not know that this system has already literally destroyed our state, and driven from it wealth and population; that many of its wealthiest and most enterprising citizens have left it in search of new and more productive lands? Does he not know that money is not wealth to a nation unless it is spent within its borders in the improvement, mental and physical, of the condition of its inhabitants, in the renovation of its soil, in the construction of roads and bridges, in the erection of fine houses, and in planting orchards and making barns for the protection of produce and livestock?

This is indeed a kind of wealth that will never be realized in South Carolina without domestic manufactures. And, lest I be misunderstood as to what I mean by domestic manufactures, I will here state that I mean the erection of steam mills in Charleston for every purpose that our mechanics may desire, to enable them to compete with foreigners in the manufacture of thousands of articles now imported into the state; the erection of steam cotton manufactories to employ the poor and needy of this city and the hundreds who seem to have little else to do than follow our military parades through the streets; the erection of cotton manufactories throughout the state to employ our poor and half-starved population, whose condition could not but be improved in working up a part of our cotton into cloth to cover their nakedness and to clothe

our Negroes and ourselves at a cost, for the manufacture of the coarse fabrics (osnaburgs), of 2¼ cents per pound and for the finer, such as brown and bleached shirtings, drillings, and cotton flannels, of from 3 to 8 cents per pound, instead of sending the same abroad to be returned to us, charged with 12 cents per pound for osnaburgs and from 20 to 65 cents for the other articles named.

I mean that, at every village and crossroad in the state, we should have a tannery, a shoemaker, a clothier, a hatter, a blacksmith (that can make and mend our ploughshares and trace chains), a wagon maker and a carriage maker, with their shops stored with seasoned lumber, the best of which may be obtained in our forests. This is the kind of manufactures I speak of as being necessary to bring forth the energies of a country and give healthful and vigorous action to agriculture, commerce, and every department of industry, and, without which, I ventured the assertion that this state can never prosper. This is the state of things that every true friend of South Carolina ought to endeavor to bring about.

If he wishes to see her worn-out and desolate old fields turned into green pastures, her villages brightened up with the hand of industry, her dilapidated farmhouses taken down to be replaced by opulent mansions, her muddy and almost impassable roads graded and macadamized, let him use his endeavors to make the people of South Carolina think less of their grievances and more of the peaceable means of redress; let our politicians, instead of teaching us to hate our Northern brethren, endeavor to get up a good feeling for domestic industry; let them teach our people that the true mode of resistance will be found in making more and purchasing less; let them endeavor to satisfy our capitalists that we are not on the verge of revolution but that there is safety in investments in South Carolina and no necessity of seeking, for such purposes, the stocks of others or readily convertible ones of our own.

There is no lack of capital in South Carolina. Charleston herself possesses all the requisites, and it is only necessary that public attention should be properly directed to this vast field for profitable investments in this state, and to give assurances of political stability and safety; to bring it out and to stop the millions which are being all the time transferred from the South to the North, and with it would be retained among us the enterprising merchant, who, on his retirement from the toils of business, would forget the green fields and pleasant ways of his native land to mingle with us in domestic industry.

Let the manufacture of cotton be commenced among us, and we shall soon see the capital that has been sent out of our state to be invested in Georgia state and other foreign stocks returned to us. We shall see the hidden treasures that have been locked up, unproductive and rusting, coming forth to put machinery in motion and to give profitable employment to the present unproductive labor of our country.

To give an idea of the various sources from which capital is drawn for such purposes, I will state how the Merrimack Company at Lowell is made up. It is composed of 390 stockholders, of whom there are 46 merchants and traders; 68 females; 52 individuals retired from business; 80 administrators, executors, guardians, and trustees; 23 lawyers; 18 physicians; 3 literary institutions; 15 farmers; 40 secretaries, clerks, and students; 45 mechanics and persons employed in the service of the company, who hold stock to the amount of $60,000.

Cotton manufactures have been the pioneers which have introduced and given an impetus to all other branches of mechanism in Great Britain, the continent of Europe, and this country. Taking this for granted, one would suppose that the persons who established the extensive iron establishment now in operation in the mountainous parts of our state, although actuated by an enterprising spirit, counted without their host; it was really putting the cart before the horse. I trust, however, that a change in our industrial pursuits is soon to take place which will give a new aspect to things in that quarter; that those establishments are yet to thrive, proving to be inexhaustible sources of wealth to our state and monuments to the enterprise of their projectors. If South Carolina commence the manufacture of cotton in earnest, these works will be brought into requisition, and the iron produced by them will no longer be sent to the Eastern states to be turned into ploughshares for us. The endless sources of demand which will spring up for it will cause a home consumption for it all.

The cheapness of waterpower, if not the chief, will at least constitute one important element of success with us. There is probably no state in the Union in which water power is more abundant. Leaving out of the question as being too tedious to enumerate the great number of waterfalls on the tributary streams of the Peedee, Wateree, Broad, and Saluda rivers, we will notice those only, in the immediate vicinity of our two lines of railroad to Columbia and Hamburg, that is, within five miles of them. In the most healthy regions of the state, abounding with granite and building timber, waterpower may be found, sufficient to work up half the crop of South Carolina, all of which is nearly valueless at the present time.

For the information of such as are not acquainted with the manner of computing the force of falling water, I will state that the quantity of water used by the generality of sawmills, running but one saw, with a head of 10 feet, will be sufficient to produce, if raised to a head of 15 feet, 50 horsepower. From this statement, persons may easily calculate what such waterfalls would be worth if located at Lowell or near

Philadelphia. In Lowell, waterpower is sold at $4 per spindle, which is equal to $262 for each horsepower. At Manayunk, five miles from Philadelphia, it is sold for $100 for every square inch of under a 3-feet head, and over a 20-feet fall; this is equal to $1,016 for each horsepower. It is not so valuable at places unfavorably located; but the price at which it sells in those above mentioned accounts at once for the eagerness with which such property is sought after in situations remote from navigation, and even in mountainous countries.

Godspeed on the glorious result that may be anticipated from so great a change in our industrial pursuits. Were all our hopes in this particular consummated, South Carolina would present a delightful picture. Every son and daughter would find healthful and lucrative employment; our roads, which are now a disgrace to us, would be improved; we would no longer be under the necessity of sending to the North for half-made wagons and carriages to break our necks; we would have, if not as handsome, at least as honestly and faithfully made ones, and mechanics always at hand to repair them. Workshops would take the place of the throngs of clothing, hat, and shoe stores, and the watchword would be — from the seaboard to the mountains, success to domestic industry.

WE WANT NO LAWS for the protection of those that embark in the manufacture of such cotton fabrics as we propose to make in South Carolina; nor does it follow, as a matter of course, that because we advocate a system which will diversify the pursuits of our people and enable them to export a portion of one of our valuable staples in a manufactured state, that we wish manufactures to predominate over other employments. All must admit that, to a certain extent, the system we advocate could not operate otherwise than to produce beneficial results, by regulating prices, by insuring a certain reward to labor, a profitable income to capital, and by infusing health, vigor, and durability into every department of industry.

It is a well-established fact that capital employed in this state in the culture of cotton does not, with ordinary management, yield more than 3 or 4, and in some instances, 2 percent. This being the only mode of employing our capital, except in the culture of rice, how can we expect to retain men of *capital* and *enterprise* among us? Those having the first must be wholly wanting in the last; or they must possess an extraordinary attachment to the land of their nativity to remain with us under such a state of affairs.

With this fact before us, is it surprising that South Carolina should remain stationary in population? And let it be remembered that the same cause which has produced this result will continue to operate hurtfully in the same ratio as the price of our great staple declines. In all probability an additional outlet will soon be opened to drain us of our people and our capital. How much this is to take from us remains to be seen. Unless we betake ourselves to some more profitable employment than the planting of cotton, what is to prevent our most enterprising planters from moving, with their Negro capital, to the Southwest? What is to keep our businessmen and moneyed capital in South Carolina? Capital will find its way to places that afford the greatest remuneration, and, in leaving our state, it will carry with it its enterprising owner.

These are truly unpleasant reflections, but they force themselves upon us. Who can look forward to the future destiny of our state, persisting as she does with such pertinacity in the exclusive and exhausting system of agriculture, without dark forebodings? If we listen much longer to the *ultras* in agriculture and *croakers* against mechani-

William Gregg (1800-1867), president of the first cotton mill in the South, organized the S.C. Institute to encourage mechanical arts

cal enterprise, it is feared that they will be the only class left to stir up the indolent sleepers that are indisposed to action and that are willing to let each day provide for itself.

Since the discovery that cotton would mature in South Carolina, she has reaped a golden harvest; but it is feared it has proved a curse rather than a blessing; and I believe that she would at this day be in a far better condition had the discovery never been made. Cotton has been to South Carolina what the mines of Mexico were to Spain: it has produced us such an abundant supply of all the luxuries and elegancies of life, with so little exertion on our part, that we have become enervated, unfitted for other and more laborious pursuits, and unprepared to meet the state of things which sooner or later must come about.

Is it out of place here to predict that the day is not far distant, yea, is close at hand, when we shall find that we can no longer *live* by that which has heretofore yielded us, not only a bountiful and sumptuous living at home but has furnished the means for carrying thousands and tens of thousands of our citizens abroad to squander their gold in other countries; that we have wasted the fruits of a rich, virgin soil in ease and luxury; that those who have practised sufficient industry and economy to accumulate capital have left, or are leaving us, to populate other states?

We shall indeed soon be awakened to look about us for other pursuits, and we shall find that our soil has to be renovated, our houses and workshops have to be built, our roads and bridges have to be made, all of which ought to have been done with the rich treasures that have been transferred to other states. Let us begin at once, before it is too late, to bring about a change in our industrial pursuits; let us set about it before the capital and enterprise of our state has entirely left us; let croakers against enterprise be silenced; let the workingmen of our state who have, by their industry, accumulated capital turn out and give a practical lesson to our political leaders that are opposed to this scheme.

Even Mr. Calhoun, our great oracle — a statesman whose purity of character we all revere, whose elevation to the highest office in the gift of the people of the United States would enlist the undivided vote of South Carolina — even he is against us in this matter. He will tell you that no mechanical enterprise will succeed in South Carolina; that good mechanics will go where their talents are better rewarded; that to thrive in cotton spinning one should go to Rhode Island; that to undertake it here will not only lead to loss of capital but disappointment and ruin to those who engage in it.

If we look at this subject in the abstract only, we shall very naturally come to the above conclusions; it is, however, often the case that practical results contradict the plainest abstract propositions, and it is hoped that in the course of these remarks it will be proved to the satisfaction of at least some of our men of capital and enterprise that the spinning of cotton may be undertaken with a certainty of success in the two Carolinas and Georgia; and that the failures which have taken place ought not to deter others from embarking in the business, they being the result of unpardonable ignorance and just such management on the part of those interested as would prove ruinous in any other undertaking.

There are those who understand some things as well as, if not better, than other people, who have taken the pains to give this subject a thorough investigation and who could probably give even Mr. Calhoun a practical lesson concerning it. The known zeal with which this distinguished gentleman has always engaged in everything relating to the interest of South Carolina forbids the idea that he is not a friend to domestic manufactures, fairly brought about; and, knowing, as he must know, the influence which he exerts, he should be more guarded in expressing opinions adverse to so good a cause.

Those who project new enterprises have in all ages and countries had much to contend with; and, if it were not that we have such immense advantages in the cheapness of labor and of the raw material, we might despair of success in the manufacture of cotton in South Carolina. But we must recollect that those who first embarked in this business in Rhode Island had the prejudice of the whole country against them. There were croakers then as well as now, and, in addition to all the disadvantages we have to contend with, the wide ocean lay between them and the nations skilled in mechanic arts; the laws of England forbade the export of machinery and affixed heavy penalties to prevent the emigration of artisans, and it was next to impossible to gain access to her manufacturing establishments, so that these men were completely shut out from knowledge.

How is it with us? We find no difficulty in obtaining the information which money could not purchase for them and which cost them years of toil. The New England people are anxious for us to go to spinning cotton, and they are ready and willing to give us all the requisite information. The workshops of England and America are thrown open to us, and he who has the capital at command may, by a visit to England or to our Northern machine shops, supply himself with the best machinery that the world affords and also the best machinists and most skillful manufacturers to work and keep it in order. With all these advantages, what is to prevent the success of a cotton factory in South Carolina? It may safely be asserted that failure will be the result of nothing but the grossest mismanagement.

It will be remembered that the wise men of the day predicted the failure of steam navigation and also of our own railroad; it was said we were deficient in mechanical skill and that we could not manage the complicated machinery of a steam engine, yet these works have succeeded. We have found men competent to manage them; they grow up among us and we are not only able to keep such machines in order but to build and fit them to steamboats, mills, locomotives, carriages, etc. And the shops engaged in this sort of manufactures do away with much of the reproach that attaches to our city; they remove many of the obstacles in erecting cotton factories, for they can furnish steam engines, water-wheels, shafting, and all the running gear to put machinery in operation.

58.

Songs of the Underground Railroad

*Estimates of the effectiveness of the Underground Railroad in helping slaves escape
to freedom in the North vary widely, ranging between forty and one hundred thousand
persons, between 1830 and 1860. But there is no disputing the emotions created by the
Railroad in the South — among slaves, for whom it was the only hope for freedom, and
among slaveholders, for whom it was at best organized thievery. The two famous
spirituals reprinted here, both of which have been traced to the mid-1840s, are
expressive of both points of view. Each reveals the intensity of the Negro's desire to
be free — which combined in his mind with the Christian idea of salvation — and each
also reveals the necessity for secrecy in any and all discussions of the Railroad's
activities. One of the most celebrated of the "conductors" of the Railroad was an
escaped slave named Harriet Tubman (c. 1821-1913), who was known as "Moses."
"Go Down, Moses" is supposed to have been about her. "Steal Away" is supposed
to have been sung at many a Negro meeting as a signal for one or more slaves to begin
the long dangerous journey northward. And "Follow the Drinking Gourd" was a kind of
musical map for the slaves who were already on their way. The "Drinking Gourd" is
another name for the Big Dipper, which pointed north and to freedom.*

Source: *The Story of the Jubilee Singers with Their Songs,* J. B. T. Marsh, ed., Boston, 1880.

GO DOWN, MOSES

When Israel was in Egypt's land,
  Let my people go;
Oppressed so hard they could not stand,
  Let my people go.

  Chorus:
  Go down, Moses, way down
      in Egypt's land;
  Tell old Pharoah, to let my people go.

Thus saith the Lord, bold Moses said,
  Let my people go;
If not I'll smite your first born dead,
  Let my people go.

No more shall they in bondage toil,
  Let my people go;
Let them come out with Egypt's spoil,
  Let my people go.

O 'twas a dark and dismal night,
  Let my people go;
When Moses led the Israelites,
  Let my people go.

The Lord told Moses what to do,
  Let my people go;
To lead the children of Israel through,
  Let my people go.

O come along, Moses, you won't get lost,
  Let my people go;
Stretch out your rod and come across,
  Let my people go.

As Israel stood by the water side,
  Let my people go;
At the command of God it did divide,
  Let my people go.

And when they reached the other side,
  Let my people go;
They sang a song of triumph o'er,
  Let my people go.

You won't get lost in the wilderness,
  Let my people go;
With a lighted candle in your breast,
  Let my people go.

O let us all from bondage flee,
  Let my people go;
And let us all in Christ be free,
  Let my people go.

We need not always weep and moan,
  Let my people go;
And wear these slavery chains forlorn,
  Let my people go.

What a beautiful morning that will be,
  Let my people go;
When time breaks up in eternity,
  Let my people go.

❧ STEAL AWAY

Steal away, steal away,
Steal away to Jesus.
Steal away, steal away home,
I ain't got long to stay here.

  My Lord calls me
  He calls me by the thunder;
  The trumpet sounds it in my soul:
  I ain't got long to stay here.

  My Lord calls me,
  He calls me by the lightning;
  The trumpet sounds it in my soul:
  I ain't got long to stay here.

❧ FOLLOW THE DRINKING GOURD

Follow the drinking gourd,
Follow the drinking gourd,
For the old man is a-waiting
For to carry you to freedom,
Follow the drinking gourd.

59.

The Natural Right to Property

In 1844 George Henry Evans revived the agrarian movement by organizing a political party, first called the Agrarian League and later the National Reform Association, and by bringing out again the Working Man's Advocate, *which had been discontinued in 1837. Newspapers generally ignored the new movement until the beginning of 1845, when an article in the January issue of the* United States Magazine and Democratic Review *provoked a hostile response. The following selection, which appeared in the* Advocate, *includes an attack on agrarianism by the* New York Sun *and numbered comments by the editor of the* Advocate.

Source: *Working Man's Advocate,* February 15, 1845.

THE FRENCH REVOLUTION gave rise to singular doctrines. Animated by a love of liberty and a hatred to tyranny, anxious to get rid of an effeminate monarchy and develop the true resources and energies of the country, the poorer and middling classes seized the reins of power and France became a republic, and the monarchy was overthrown. During the existence of that republic, France achieved great victories over its enemies and brought forward the most illustrious men the world ever saw; but, instead of profiting by the example of this country, in the calm exercise of its newborn liberties, the Convention of France was filled with men of violent passions, licentiousness, and furious democracy, who not only desecrated by their cruelties a pure love of liberty (1) but who were constantly bringing forward new and strange theories of government.

One was an agrarian law for an equal division of property, or what was then and has since been called the natural rights of man to property. (2) We have in this country a class of philosophers of this character who have, from time to time, for many years, pressed their peculiar doctrines upon the people. While confined to mere essays, debates, and lectures, this new philosophy was harmless; but when mingled with the political discussions of the day, and made to assume the form of a principle, and urged as a sound one, it becomes dangerous to the institutions of the country, and men of all parties should unite to PUT DOWN doctrines which strike at the root of the social system because they involve reforms which cannot, without revolution and bloodshed, be carried into effect. (3)

A partisan magazine belonging to this peculiar school, has, in a recent number, broached the doctrine of the natural rights of property in a very elaborate article, and attempts to show that the "conventional laws of property, counteracting the natural laws and the natural rights of man, are among the foremost of the causes of the ignorance, poverty, suffering, and sin which, in all ages, have degraded the masses of mankind." To enable the writer to carry out this principle, he says, "There is a natural right of property (land), as a natural right of life and liberty — equally conferred by the Creator — belonging to man as man — equally necessary to enable him to accomplish the destiny assigned him. Whatever deprives men of a natural right is a robbery — whoever does it is a robber. "The

earth," it says, "was created for the subsistence of man; by the law of nature it is the common patrimony of the race. If, by virtue of his creation as a son of God, every man has a natural essential right to life and liberty, by virtue of the same relation, every man must have a right to equal portion of the earth, or an equivalent, for his subsistence and use."

This doctrine is based upon the principle of *liberty and equality*, but this school of philosophers, and they are as old as they are unsuccessful, forget that *equality* relates to political rights. (4) There shall be no ranks (such as landlords and tenants), no titles, no hereditary principles, no exclusive privileges (some protected to a superfluity of land and others with none at all); laws are made for the benefit of all and bind all equally.

This is the equality which is the twin sister of liberty. It is the equality of law, not of property. It is not because *A* owns a three-story house that *B*, having none of his own, claims to be proprietor of the adjoining building. By "equality" it is not intended because I own a farm which I have acquired by hard labor that I must divide my farm with a person who probably has neither industry, temperance, nor enterprise to acquire one for himself. (5) This "equality" does not imply, as the philosophers imagine, that one man having a dollar must divide that dollar with his neighbor who has none. (Who said it did, Alderman?)

Political liberty is not the parent of equality in the social system, and for this simple reason: the moment man is free to pursue any occupation he pleases, his energy and his intellect are free, and such a man must acquire property, whereas the man without intellect or energy remains poor. (Invariably so!) Here both are politically equal, but not socially. Would you take from the intelligent and active to give to the indolent? (6) If all men were intellectually endowed alike by nature then there would be something in this equality. (7)

Suppose that we should [enact] laws in

carrying out such doctrines, to prevent men bequeathing their property to whoever they please, and compel them to leave that property to the public to be equally divided, who would ever exert himself to acquire any property? Who would care for it, beyond the wants of the day? This doctrine of the "rights of property" is unnatural and unreasonable. (8) It teaches man not to depend upon his own industry and energy but upon the energy and industry of others. Connected with our political discussions, it is wicked and mischievous.

The man without means is at war with himself and with all mankind; he is willing to take what he knows belongs to another, and to accomplish this he becomes radical and revolutionary. The democracy of large cities partake already of a portion of this spirit. Men become politicians who are unwilling to labor, and, after shouting at the polls and at ward meetings, they demand to be paid in the offices of the people, which probably they have not character to claim nor capacity to fill. We must avoid the errors of the French Revolution. Democracy does not mean vandalism. (9)

(1) A very natural result of a long series of atrocities to which they had been subject, and one which ought to be a lesson to those who are the props of oppression everywhere.

(2) An agrarian law relates to a division of *land* and not a division of the products of labor, or *property,* as the *Sun* artfully pretends. If France had adopted an agrarian law, all Europe would have been republics long ago.

(3) Those who have read Dickens' "Chimes" will call to mind the worthy of the "put down" school portrayed in that little work. We poor, landless fellows may talk and debate and lecture on agrarianism as much as we please, it seems (we are very thankful for the smallest favors); but when we come to "mingle our notions with the political discussions of the day," and "make them assume the form of a principle," O dear! it is *there* the shoe pinches, and the Alderman Cute of the *Sun* decrees that we must be "put down." Alas! that we should have been born without "saddles on our backs" ready for Alderman Cute to mount, and with such thoughts running through our brains as to make us imagine that we have a right to a bit of the earth! We *must* be desperately "bad."

(4) It is a *political* right that our natural rights shall be protected, or what is your political organization good for, Alderman?

(5) Certainly not, Alderman; but if there is land that *nobody* has acquired by hard labor, nor even by gift or purchase from somebody who *stole* it, might not the possession of this land make some industrious and temperate and enterprising who would otherwise be the reverse?

(6) Not unless they had got what did not belong to them. Would *you?*

(7) And since they are *not,* it is the more necessary that they should have an equality of *rights.*

(8) You are battling here a windmill of your own imagining; but, if we may be allowed to cross-examine you, what objection have you to the right to *land?* May the poor not have a bit of it?

(9) Neither does democracy mean that there should be 80,000 persons receiving pauper relief or charity in a population of 400,000, or that those who produce the least should enjoy the most of the products of labor. The grand "error of the French Revolution" was in not making every citizen a freeholder, and *that* is the error that "we should avoid" if we would not split on the same rock. However, if these doctrines are to be "put down," it is hoped that Alderman Cute will let us know how he is going to work at it. That is what we are curious about.

60.

JAMES K. POLK: The Annexation of Texas and Oregon

In the presidential election of 1844, the Democrats nominated thoroughgoing expansionist James K. Polk to oppose the Whig candidate, Henry Clay, who had spoken out against the immediate annexation of Texas. One of Polk's campaign slogans was "the reannexation of Texas and the reoccupation of Oregon," the prefix intended to give historic sanction to an expansionist program. Oregon was coupled with Texas in order to gain Northern support for westward expansion. After Polk's victory, but before he took office, a joint resolution inviting Texas to join the Union as a state was passed by Congress. Tyler signed it on March 1, 1845, three days before Polk delivered the inaugural address from which the following selection is taken.

Source: Richardson, IV, pp. 373-382.

THE REPUBLIC OF TEXAS has made known her desire to come into our Union, to form a part of our Confederacy and enjoy with us the blessings of liberty secured and guaranteed by our Constitution. Texas was once a part of our country, was unwisely ceded away to a foreign power, is now independent, and possesses an undoubted right to dispose of a part or the whole of her territory and to merge her sovereignty as a separate and independent state in ours. I congratulate my country that by an act of the late Congress of the United States the assent of this government has been given to the reunion, and it only remains for the two countries to agree upon the terms to consummate an object so important to both.

I regard the question of annexation as belonging exclusively to the United States and Texas. They are independent powers, competent to contract; and foreign nations have no right to interfere with them or to take exceptions to their reunion. Foreign powers do not seem to appreciate the true character of our government. Our Union is a confederation of independent states, whose policy is peace with each other and all the world. To enlarge its limits is to extend the dominions of peace over additional territories and increasing millions.

The world has nothing to fear from military ambition in our government. While the Chief Magistrate and the popular branch of Congress are elected for short terms by the suffrages of those millions who must in their own persons bear all the burdens and miseries of war, our government cannot be otherwise than pacific. Foreign powers should therefore look on the annexation of Texas to the United States, not as the conquest of a nation seeking to extend her dominions by arms and violence but as the peaceful acquisition of a territory once her own, by adding another member to our confederation with the consent of that member, thereby diminishing the chances of war and opening to them new and ever increasing markets for their products.

To Texas the reunion is important because the strong protecting arm of our government would be extended over her, and the vast resources of her fertile soil and genial climate would be speedily developed, while the safety of New Orleans and of our whole Southwestern frontier against hostile aggression, as well as the interests of the whole Union, would be promoted by it.

In the earlier stages of our national existence the opinion prevailed with some that our system of confederated states could not operate successfully over an extended territory, and serious objections have at different times been made to the enlargement of our boundaries. These objections were earnestly urged when we acquired Louisiana. Experience has shown that they were not well founded. The title of numerous Indian tribes to vast tracts of country has been extinguished; new states have been admitted into the Union; new territories have been created and our jurisdiction and laws extended over them. As our population has expanded, the Union has been cemented and strengthened. As our boundaries have been enlarged and our agricultural population has been spread over a large surface, our federative system has acquired additional strength and security.

It may well be doubted whether it would not be in greater danger of overthrow if our present population were confined to the comparatively narrow limits of the original thirteen states than it is now that they are sparsely settled over a more expanded territory. It is confidently believed that our system may be safely extended to the utmost bounds of our territorial limits, and that as it shall be extended the bonds of our Union, so far from being weakened, will become stronger.

None can fail to see the danger to our safety and future peace if Texas remains an independent state or becomes an ally or dependency of some foreign nation more powerful than herself. Is there one among our citizens who would not prefer perpetual peace with Texas to occasional wars which so often occur between bordering independent nations? Is there one who would not prefer free intercourse with her to high duties on all our products and manufactures which enter her ports or cross her frontiers? Is there one who would not prefer an unrestricted communication with her citizens to the frontier obstructions which must occur if she remains out of the Union?

Whatever is good or evil in the local institutions of Texas will remain her own, whether annexed to the United States or not. None of the present states will be responsible for them any more than they are for the local institutions of each other. They have confederated together for certain specified objects. Upon the same principle that they would refuse to form a perpetual union with Texas because of her local institutions, our forefathers would have been prevented from forming our present Union.

Perceiving no valid objection to the measure and many reasons for its adoption vitally affecting the peace, the safety, and the prosperity of both countries, I shall, on the broad principle which formed the basis and produced the adoption of our Constitution, and not in any narrow spirit of sectional policy, endeavor by all constitutional, honorable, and appropriate means to consummate the expressed will of the people and government of the United States by the reannexation of Texas to our Union at the earliest practicable period.

Nor will it become in a less degree my duty to assert and maintain by all constitutional means the right of the United States to that portion of our territory which lies beyond the Rocky Mountains. Our title to the country of the Oregon is "clear and unquestionable," and already are our people preparing to perfect that title by occupying it with their wives and children. But eighty years ago our population was confined on the west by the ridge of the Alleghenies.

Within that period — within the lifetime, I might say, of some of my hearers — our people, increasing to many millions, have filled the eastern valley of the Mississippi, adventurously ascended the Missouri to its headsprings, and are already engaged in establishing the blessings of self-government in valleys of which the rivers flow to the Pacific.

The world beholds the peaceful triumphs of the industry of our emigrants. To us belongs the duty of protecting them adequately wherever they may be upon our soil. The jurisdiction of our laws and the benefits of our republican institutions should be extended over them in the distant region which they have selected for their homes. The increasing facilities of intercourse will easily bring the states, of which the formation in that part of our territory cannot be long delayed, within the sphere of our federative Union. In the meantime, every obligation imposed by treaty or conventional stipulations should be sacredly respected.

61.

John L. O'Sullivan: Our Manifest Destiny

The phrase "manifest destiny" both defined and encouraged the spirit of expansionism, and was used to promote and to justify the spread of democracy across the North American continent. The phrase was probably coined by the editor of the United States Magazine and Democratic Review, *John O'Sullivan, and was first used by him in an editorial in July 1845 calling for the annexation of Texas. Sections of the article appear below. It was used again by O'Sullivan in the December 27, 1845, issue of another paper that he edited, the* New York Morning News, *this time to prove that the United States had "true title" to the Oregon Territory. It was in the context of the Oregon question that the phrase gained wide currency, first in Congress and then in the general press.*

Source: *United States Magazine and Democratic Review*, July 1845: "Annexation."

IT IS TIME NOW for opposition to the annexation of Texas to cease, all further agitation of the waters of bitterness and strife, at least in connection with this question, even though it may perhaps be required of us as a necessary condition of the freedom of our institutions, that we must live on forever in a state of unpausing struggle and excitement upon some subject of party division or other. But, in regard to Texas, enough has now been given to party. It is time for the common duty of patriotism to the country to succeed; or if this claim will not be recognized, it is at least time for common sense to acquiesce with decent grace in the inevitable and the irrevocable.

Texas is now ours. Already, before these words are written, her convention has undoubtedly ratified the acceptance, by her congress, of our proffered invitation into the Union; and made the requisite changes in her already republican form of constitution to adapt it to its future federal relations. Her star and her stripe may already be said to have taken their place in the glorious blazon of our common nationality; and the sweep of our eagle's wing already includes within its circuit the wide extent of her fair and fertile land.

She is no longer to us a mere geographical space — a certain combination of coast, plain, mountain, valley, forest, and stream. She is no longer to us a mere country on the map. She comes within the dear and sacred designation of our country; no longer a *pays* [country], she is a part of *la patrie;* and that which is at once a sentiment and a virtue, patriotism, already begins to thrill for her too within the national heart.

It is time then that all should cease to treat her as alien, and even adverse — cease to denounce and vilify all and everything connected with her accession — cease to thwart and oppose the remaining steps for its consummation; or where such efforts are felt to be unavailing, at least to embitter the hour of reception by all the most ungracious frowns of aversion and words of unwelcome. There has been enough of all this. It has had its fitting day during the period when, in common with every other possible question of practical policy that can arise, it unfortunately became one of the leading topics of party division, of presidential electioneering.

But that period has passed, and with it let its prejudices and its passions, its discords and its denunciations, pass away too. The next session of Congress will see the representatives of the new young state in their places in both our halls of national legislation, side by side with those of the old Thirteen. Let their reception into "the family" be frank, kindly, and cheerful, as befits such an occasion, as comports not less with our own self-respect than patriotic duty towards them. Ill betide those foul birds that delight to file their own nest, and disgust the ear with perpetual discord of ill-omened croak.

Why, were other reasoning wanting, in favor of now elevating this question of the reception of Texas into the Union, out of the lower region of our past party dissensions, up to its proper level of a high and broad nationality, it surely is to be found, found abundantly, in the manner in which other nations have undertaken to intrude themselves into it, between us and the proper parties to the case, in a spirit of hostile interference against us, for the avowed object of thwarting our policy and hampering our power, limiting our greatness and checking the fulfillment of our manifest destiny to overspread the continent allotted by Providence for the free development of our yearly multiplying millions. This we have seen done by England, our old rival and enemy; and by France, strangely coupled with her against us, under the influence of the Anglicism strongly tinging the policy of her present prime minister, Guizot.

The zealous activity with which this effort to defeat us was pushed by the representatives of those governments, together with the character of intrigue accompanying it, fully constituted that case of foreign interference, which Mr. Clay himself declared should, and would unite us all in maintaining the common cause of our country against the foreigner and the foe. We are only astonished that this effect has not been more fully and strongly produced, and that the burst of indignation against this unauthorized, insolent, and hostile interference against us, has not been more general even among the party before opposed to annexation, and has not rallied the national spirit and national pride unanimously upon that policy. We are very sure that if Mr. Clay himself were now to add another letter to his former Texas correspondence, he would express this sentiment, and carry out the idea already strongly stated in one of them, in a manner which would tax all the powers of blushing belonging to some of his party adherents.

It is wholly untrue, and unjust to ourselves, the pretense that the annexation has been a measure of spoliation, unrightful and unrighteous — of military conquest under forms of peace and law — of territorial aggrandizement at the expense of justice, and justice due by a double sanctity to the weak. This view of the question is wholly unfounded, and has been before so amply refuted in these pages, as well as in a thousand other modes, that we shall not again dwell upon it.

The independence of Texas was complete and absolute. It was an independence, not only in fact, but of right. No obligation of duty toward Mexico tended in the least degree to restrain our right to effect the desired recovery of the fair province once our own — whatever motives of policy might have prompted a more deferential consideration of her feelings and her pride, as involved in the question. If Texas became peopled with an American population, it was by no contrivance of our government, but on the express invitation of that of Mexico herself; accompanied with such guaranties of state independence, and the maintenance of a federal system analogous to our own, as constituted a compact fully justifying the strongest measures of redress on the part of those afterward deceived in this guaranty, and sought to be enslaved under the yoke imposed by its violation.

She was released, rightfully and absolutely released, from all Mexican allegiance, or duty of cohesion to the Mexican political body, by the acts and fault of Mexico herself, and Mexico alone. There never was a clearer case. It was not revolution; it was resistance to revolution: and resistance under such circumstances as left independence the necessary resulting state, caused by the abandonment of those with whom her former federal association had existed. What then can be more preposterous than all this clamor by Mexico and the Mexican interest, against annexation, as a violation of any rights of hers, any duties of ours? . . .

Nor is there any just foundation for the charge that annexation is a great pro-slavery measure — calculated to increase and perpetuate that institution. Slavery had nothing to do with it. Opinions were and are greatly divided, both at the North and South, as to the influence to be exerted by it on slavery and the slave states. That it will tend to facilitate and hasten the disappearance of slavery from all the northern tier of the present slave states, cannot surely admit of serious question. The greater value in Texas of the slave labor now employed in those states, must soon produce the effect of draining off that labor southwardly, by the same unvarying law that bids water descend the slope that invites it.

Every new slave state in Texas will make at least one free state from among those in which that institution now exists — to say nothing of those portions of Texas on which slavery cannot spring and grow — to say nothing of the far more rapid growth of new states in the free West and Northwest, as these fine regions are overspread by the emigration fast flowing over them from Europe, as well as from the Northern and Eastern states of the Union as it exists. On the other hand, it is undeniably much gained for the cause of the eventual voluntary abolition of slavery, that it should have been thus drained off toward the only outlet which appeared to furnish much probability of the ultimate disappearance of the Negro race from our borders.

The Spanish-Indian-American populations of Mexico, Central America, and South America, afford the only receptacle capable of absorbing that race whenever we shall be prepared to slough it off — to emancipate it from slavery, and (simultaneously necessary) to remove it from the midst of our own. Themselves already of mixed and confused blood, and free from the "prejudices" which among us so insuperably forbid the social amalgamation which can alone elevate the Negro race out of a virtually servile degradation; even though legally free the regions occupied by those populations must strongly attract the black race in that direction; and as soon as the destined hour of emancipation shall arrive, will relieve the question of one of its worst difficulties, if not absolutely the greatest. . . .

California will, probably, next fall away from the loose adhesion which, in such a country as Mexico, holds a remote province in a slight equivocal kind of dependence on the metropolis. Imbecile and distracted, Mexico never can exert any real government authority over such a country. The impotence of the one and the distance of the other, must make the relation one of virtual independence; unless, by stunting the province of all natural growth, and forbidding that immigration which can alone develope its capabilities and fulfill the purposes of its creation, tyranny may retain a military dominion, which is no government in the legitimate sense of the term.

In the case of California this is now impossible. The Anglo-Saxon foot is already on its borders. Already the advance guard of the irresistible army of Anglo-Saxon emigration has begun to pour down upon it, armed with the plough and the rifle, and marking its trail with schools and colleges, courts and representative halls, mills and meetinghouses. A population will soon be in actual occupation of California, over which it will be idle for Mexico to dream of dominion. They will necessarily become independent. All this without agency of our government, without responsibility of our people — in the natural flow of events, the spontaneous working of principles, and the adaptation of the tendencies and wants of the human race to the elemental circumstances in the midst of which they find themselves placed.

And they will have a right to independence — to self-government — to the possession of the homes conquered from the wilderness by their own labors and dangers, sufferings and sacrifices — a better and a truer right than the artificial title of sovereignty in Mexico, a thousand miles distant, inheriting from Spain a title good only against those who have none better. Their right to independence will be the natural right of self-government belonging to any community strong enough to maintain it — distinct in position, origin and character, and free from any mutual obligations of membership of a common political body, binding it to others by the duty of loyalty and compact of public faith. This will be their title to independence; and by this title, there can be no doubt that the population now fast streaming down upon California will both assert and maintain that independence.

Whether they will then attach themselves to our Union or not, is not to be predicted with any certainty. Unless the projected railroad across the continent to the Pacific be carried into effect, perhaps they may not; though even in that case, the day is not distant when the empires of the Atlantic and Pacific would again flow together into one, as soon as their inland border should approach each other. But that great work, colossal as appears the plan on its first suggestion, cannot remain long unbuilt.

Its necessity for this very purpose of binding and holding together in its iron clasp our fast-settling Pacific region with that of the Mississippi Valley — the natural facility of the route — the ease with which any amount of labor for the construction can be drawn in from the overcrowded populations of Europe, to be paid in the lands made valuable by the progress of the work itself — and its immense utility to the commerce of the world with the whole eastern coast of Asia, alone almost sufficient for the support of such a road — these considerations give assurance that the day cannot be distant which shall witness the conveyance of the representatives from Oregon and California to Washington within less time than a few years ago was devoted to a similar journey by those from Ohio; while the magnetic telegraph will enable the editors of the *San Francisco Union*, the *Astoria Evening Post*, or the *Nootka Morning News*, to set up in type the first half of the President's inaugural before the echoes of the latter half shall have died away beneath the lofty porch of the Capitol, as spoken from his lips.

Away, then, with all idle French talk of balances of power on the American Continent. There is no growth in Spanish America! Whatever progress of population there may be in the British Canadas, is only for their own early severance of their present colonial relation to the little island 3,000 miles across the Atlantic; soon to be followed by annexation, and destined to swell the still accumulating momentum of our progress.

And whosoever may hold the balance, though they should cast into the opposite scale all the bayonets and cannon, not only of France and England, but of Europe entire, how would it kick the beam against the simple, solid weight of the 250, or 300 million — and American millions — destined to gather beneath the flutter of the stripes and stars, in the fast hastening year of the Lord 1945!

62.

Robert Owen: An Open Letter to Capitalists

The socialist Robert Owen was originally critical of the Associationist communities and of their joint stock method of organization, but by 1845 he had come to regard Associationism as a possible stepping-stone to the ideal society. He wished to establish a model of his perfect society in America, and by organizing it on the joint stock principle, hoped to induce American capitalists to finance it. Hence his call of March 31, 1845, "To the Capitalists and Men of Extensive Practical Experience in New York," reprinted below.

Source: *New-York Daily Tribune*, April 2, 1845 [Commons, VII, pp. 164-166].

Your position is, at this period, owing to a singular combination of fortunate circumstances, one the most to be desired for the attainment of great individual and national objects.

The funds of the one, directed to be practically applied by the experience of the other, could insure, without risk, larger returns for capital than can be obtained by any other investment of it, without great risk, in any other direction in these states or in Europe.

The expenditure of the capital in the way to be proposed would, by the mode of its application, double its value in four or five years and give most advantageous occupation to operatives of every description, create a demand for all kinds of materials, and insure beneficial employment for the unemployed females; in fact, place the continually increasing prosperity of these states on a solid foundation and prevent the recurrence of what is technically called "bad times" ever being again known.

Had the capitalists and men of business in extensive operations been trained to understand their own interests and the interests of their country and of society generally, the late disasters which produced such overwhelming distress throughout the commercial world, arising solely from artificial causes, could never have occurred.

You desire to be independent of pecuniary circumstances, and to enjoy the advantages of wealth to the greatest extent when wisely expended. The time has arrived when you may accomplish these objects without risk, first, for yourselves and children through succeeding generations, and second, for the population of these states, as they shall be trained through the means to be proposed, to make a judicious and proper use of these advantages.

The mode to accomplish these most desirable objects will be to form joint stock companies with unlimited amount of capital — for any amount may be immediately advantageously employed — to form new superior establishments for producing and distributing wealth, for educating the children of the persons to be employed so that they shall acquire from their infancy a sound, practical, and active character, both physical and mental, under a new combination of greatly improved external circumstances, by which these establishments will, after paying a liberal interest for the capital during the intermediate time, always repay the capital by a sinking fund annually appropriated for that purpose, and will be easily governed on such principles as will be highly beneficial to the capitalists and operatives.

These establishments will enable the capitalists and men of extensive practical experi-

Museum of Fine Arts, Boston; Karolik Collection

Robert Owen, pencil sketch by Rembrandt Peale

ence to solve without difficulty the great problem of the age, that is, how to apply the enormous and ever growing new scientific powers for producing wealth beneficially for the entire population, instead of allowing them to continue, as heretofore, most injuriously to create enormous riches for the few and to impoverish the many, driving them toward a desperation that will ultimately, if not untimely prevented by this measure, involve the overwealthy in utter destruction?

It is my intention to make this — now the most important subject that can engage the attention of all parties, rich and poor, capitalists and operatives — so plain in the lectures which I have agreed to deliver . . . as will make the subject far better understood than the gross misrepresentations of the ill informed have permitted it to be up to this period. My great desire is, without regard to class, party, sect, or present condition, permanently to benefit all.

63.

Immigrant Labor and the War Against Capitalism

In the mid-1840s, immigration for the first time began to create a surplus of unskilled laborers in the Eastern states. One of the first protests against the influx of immigrants to be published in an important labor paper is reprinted here. The article reflects the dilemma of the American workingman, who depended on immigrant votes to elect candidates sympathetic to labor, but who had also to compete with the newly arrived workers in the labor market.

Source: *Voice of Industry* (Fitchburg, Mass.), October 9, 1845.

WE COPY THE FOLLOWING item from the *Lowell Journal*. "Two hundred workmen from England arrived at the Iron Works at Danville, Penn., where they are to be employed."

The above few lines contain an important lesson for every workingman and woman in America; they clearly exhibit to the unbiased, investigating, and reflecting mind the onward, rapid strides of the great, deep-rooted, inhuman monster system of capital against labor which is fast devouring every tangible and valuable right that belongs to the working classes of this country, as moral, physical, and intellectual beings, capable of filling the land with an abundance and generating peaceful industry, virtue, and happiness.

Just as sure as there is a sun at noonday, capital, under its present hostile and unnatural state, is fast reducing labor to utter dependence and slavish beggary. The above quotation is but one of the countless demonstrations of this sad reality, which daily manifest themselves among us, and though political demagogues, for the sake of the emoluments of society, laud and eulogize the "freedom of equality of our people," though false philosophers theorize and glowingly set forth the "virtuous tendencies of our institutions," and blinded bigots or sectarian devotees sanctimoniously reason of the "pious relations" existing between the employer and the employed, the master and the slave, capital and labor, and the justice and morality of our organization; yet the true state and condition of the laboring people are fast being developed — truth cannot always be stifled or light hid from those who sit in darkness.

This talk about the continued prosperity, happy condition, and future independence of the producing class of this country, as a class, is all fiction, moonshine. There is at this very moment a great strife between capital and labor, and capital is fast gaining the mastery — the gradual abasement of the workingmen and women of this country abundantly sustain this position — the various "strikes" among the operatives and workingmen in New England and other sections of the country, which have almost invariably proved abortive and ineffectual, evidently show that combined, incorporated, and protected capital can "starve out" and dismay the disorganized, competing, and dependent laborers, whose daily toil provides the scanty portion to satisfy the pinching necessities of those dependent upon them.

The *democratic republican* capital of this country, which has been so amply fortified against foreign *despotic* capital by the suffrages of American workingmen ("all for their especial benefit"), says there are not enough "free, independent, and well-paid" workingmen and women in this country; consequently; foreign operatives and workmen must be imported. No tariff on these! No, no, it won't do to protect the capital of American workingmen and women (their labor) against foreign competition! for this would be antirepublican. But "protect the rich capitalist and he will take care of the laborer."

Now the capitalists of the Danville Iron Works wish to protect themselves against these "disorderly strikes" by importing a surplus of help; the Lowell capitalists entertain the same republican idea of self-protection, the Pittsburgh and Allegheny city capitalists, whose sympathies (if they have any) have been recently appealed to, wish to secure themselves against "turn-outs" by creating a numerous poor and dependent populace. Isolated capital everywhere and in all ages protects itself by the poverty, ignorance, and servility of a surplus population who will submit to its base requirements.

Hence the Democratic or Whig capital of the United States is striving to fill the country with foreign workmen — English workmen, whose abject condition in their own country has made them tame, submissive, and "peaceable, orderly citizens"; that is, work *fourteen* and *sixteen* hours per day for what capital sees fit to give them; and if it is not enough to provide them a comfortable house to shelter their wives and children and furnish them with decent food and clothes, why, they must live in cellars, go hungry and ragged! And for this state of things, capitalists are not answerable. O! no — "they (the laborers) ain't obliged to take it — they are free to go when they please!"

How long will the working people of this country remain indifferent to these important considerations? How long will they continue blinded to the monopolizing tendencies of our system of capital against labor? They are at war with each other, and Art has taken sides as an ally with capital against humanity and the defenseless laborer; they are all antagonistical whereas they should be united and harmonious; even labor is at war with itself, wasting and consuming what strength and union capital has been unable to destroy.

Let the American laborers recollect that the same grasping system which has driven thousands from the Old World in utter destitution to this country, for refuge, is here being nourished; and should they suffer it to go on, their children will look in vain for an asylum for their ills and oppressions; and, perchance, in their wild breathing after that rational freedom which God gave to *all* and which brings peace, plenty, and happiness, curse the day that gave them existence and the beautiful heavens and earth that mock and aggravate their misery.

———◆———

I accept the universe.
      MARGARET FULLER. Carlyle commented, "Gad! she'd better!"

64.

MARGARET FULLER: On the Emancipation of Women

Margaret Fuller, Marchioness Ossoli, ardent feminist, literary critic, and journalist, was the only woman who was sufficiently intellectual to be acceptable to the high standards of the Transcendentalists, and she helped edit their literary journal, the Dial, *from 1840 to 1842. At the same time she was conducting informal classes, called "conversations," in a private home in Boston, which were attended by many of the leading citizens. The substance of her teaching appeared in a book,* Woman in the Nineteenth Century, *which was published in 1845; an earlier version had been called* The Great Law Suit or Man vs. Woman. *A selection from the work appears below.*

Source: *Woman in the Nineteenth Century,* Arthur B. Fuller, ed., Boston, 1855 pp. 30-38.

MANY WOMEN ARE CONSIDERING within themselves what they need that they have not, and what they can have if they find they need it. Many men are considering whether women are capable of being and having more than they are and have, *and* whether, if so, it will be best to consent to improvement in their condition.

This morning, I open the *Boston Daily Mail* and find in its "poet's corner" a translation of Schiller's *Dignity of Woman.* In the advertisement of a book on America, I see in the table of contents this sequence, "Republican Institutions. American Slavery. American Ladies." . . .

The past year has seen action in the Rhode Island legislature, to secure married women rights over their own property, where men showed that a very little examination of the subject could teach them much; an article in the *Democratic Review* on the same subject more largely considered, written by a woman, impelled, it is said, by glaring wrong to a distinguished

friend, having shown the defects in the existing laws, and the state of opinion from which they spring; and an answer from the revered old man, J. Q. Adams, in some respects the Phocion of his time, to an address made him by some ladies. . . .

These symptoms of the times have come under my view quite accidentally: one who seeks, may, each month or week, collect more.

The numerous party, whose opinions are already labeled and adjusted too much to their mind to admit of any new light, strive, by lectures on some model woman of bride-like beauty and gentleness, by writing and lending little treatises, intended to mark out with precision the limits of Woman's sphere, and Woman's mission, to prevent other than the rightful shepherd from climbing the wall, or the flock from using any chance to go astray.

Without enrolling ourselves at once on either side, let us look upon the subject from the best point of view which today offers; no better, it is to be feared, than a high housetop. A high hilltop, or at least a cathedralspire, would be desirable.

It may well be an antislavery party that pleads for Woman, if we consider merely that she does not hold property on equal terms with men; so that, if a husband dies without making a will, the wife, instead of taking at once his place as head of the family, inherits only a part of his fortune, often brought him by herself, as if she were a child, or ward only, not an equal partner.

We will not speak of the innumerable instances in which profligate and idle men live upon the earnings of industrious wives; or if the wives leave them, and take with them the children, to perform the double duty of mother and father, follow from place to place, and threaten to rob them of the children, if deprived of the rights of a husband, as they call them, planting themselves in their poor lodgings, frightening them into paying tribute by taking from them the children, running into debt at the expense of these otherwise so overtasked helots. Such instances count up by scores within my own memory.

I have seen the husband who had stained himself by a long course of low vice, till his wife was wearied from her heroic forgiveness, by finding that his treachery made it useless, and that if she would provide bread for herself and her children, she must be separate from his ill fame — I have known this man come to install himself in the chamber of a woman who loathed him, and say she should never take food without his company. I have known these men steal their children, whom they knew they had no means to maintain, take them into dissolute company, expose them to bodily danger, to frighten the poor woman, to whom, it seems, the fact that she alone had borne the pangs of their birth, and nourished their infancy, does not give an equal right to them.

I do believe that this mode of kidnapping

— and it is frequent enough in all classes of society — will be by the next age viewed as it is by Heaven now, and that the man who avails himself of the shelter of men's laws to steal from a mother her own children, or arrogate any superior right in them, save that of superior virtue, will bear the stigma he deserves, in common with him who steals grown men from their motherland, their hopes, and their homes.

I said, we will not speak of this now; yet I *have* spoken, for the subject makes me feel too much. I could give instances that would startle the most vulgar and callous; but I will not, for the public opinion of their own sex is already against such men, and where cases of extreme tyranny are made known, there is private action in the wife's favor. But she ought not to need this, nor, I think, can she long. Men must soon see that as, on their own ground, Woman is the weaker party, she ought to have legal protection, which would make such oppression impossible. But I would not deal with "atrocious instances," except in the way of illustration, neither demand from men a partial redress in some one matter, but go to the root of the whole. If principles could be established, particulars would adjust themselves aright. Ascertain the true destiny of woman; give her legitimate hopes, and a standard within herself; marriage and all other relations would by degrees be harmonized with these.

But to return to the historical progress of this matter. Knowing that there exists in the minds of men a tone of feeling toward women as toward slaves, such as is expressed in the common phrase, "Tell that to women and children"; that the infinite soul can only work through them in already ascertained limits; that the gift of reason, Man's highest prerogative, is allotted to them in much lower degree; that they must be kept from mischief and melancholy by being constantly engaged in active labor, which is to be furnished and directed by those better able to think, etc., — we need not multiply instances, for who can review the experience of last week without recalling words which imply, whether in jest or earnest, these views, or views like these, — knowing this, can we wonder that many reformers think that measures are not likely to be taken in behalf of women, unless their wishes could be publicly represented by women?

"That can never be necessary," cry the other side. "All men are privately influenced by women; each has his wife, sister, or female friends, and is too much biased by these relations to fail of representing their interests; and, if this is not enough, let them propose and enforce their wishes with the pen. The beauty of home would be destroyed, the delicacy of the sex be violated, the dignity of halls of legislation degraded, by an attempt to introduce them there. Such duties are inconsistent with those of a mother"; and then we have ludicrous pictures of ladies in hysterics at the polls, and senate chambers filled with cradles.

But if, in reply, we admit as truth that Woman seems destined by nature rather for the inner circle, we must add that the arrangements of civilized life have not been, as yet, such as to secure it to her. Her circle, if the duller, is not the quieter. If kept from "excitement," she is not from drudgery. Not only the Indian squaw carries the burdens of the camp, but the favorites of Louis XIV accompany him in his journeys, and the washerwoman stands at her tub, and carries home her work at all seasons, and in all states of health. Those who think the physical circumstances of Woman would make a part in the affairs of national government unsuitable, are by no means those who think it impossible for Negresses to endure fieldwork, even during pregnancy, or for sempstresses [seamstresses] to go through their killing labors.

As to the use of the pen, there was quite as much opposition to Woman's possessing herself of that help to free agency as there is now to her seizing on the rostrum or the desk; and she is likely to draw, from a permission to plead her cause that way, opposite inferences to what might be wished by those who now grant it.

As to the possibility of her filling with grace and dignity any such position, we should think those who had seen the great actresses, and heard the Quaker preachers of modern times, would not doubt that Woman can express publicly the fullness of thought and creation, without losing any of the peculiar beauty of her sex. What can pollute and tarnish is to act thus from any motive except that something needs to be said or done. Woman could take part in the processions, the songs, the dances of old religion; no one fancied her delicacy was impaired by appearing in public for such a cause.

As to her home, she is not likely to leave it more than she now does for balls, theatres, meetings for promoting missions, revival meetings, and others to which she flies, in hope of an animation for her existence commensurate with what she sees enjoyed by men. Governors of ladies'-fairs are no less engrossed by such a charge, than the governor of a state by his; presidents of Washingtonian societies no less away from home than presidents of conventions. If men look straitly to it, they will find that, unless their lives are domestic, those of the women will not be. A house is no home unless it contain food and fire for the mind as well as for the body. . . . For human beings are not so constituted that they can live without expansion. If they do not get it in one way, they must in another, or perish.

As to men's representing women fairly at present, while we hear from men who owe to their wives not only all that is comfortable or graceful, but all that is wise, in the arrangement of their lives, the frequent remark, "You cannot reason with a woman," — when from those of delicacy, nobleness, and poetic culture, falls the contemptuous phrase "women and children," and that in no light sally of the hour, but in works intended to give a permanent statement of the best experiences, — when not one man, in the million, shall I say? No, not in the hundred million, can rise above the belief that Woman was made *for Man*, — when such traits as these are daily forced upon the attention, can we feel that Man will always do justice to the interests of Woman?

Can we think that he takes a sufficiently discerning and religious view of her office and destiny *ever* to do her justice, except when prompted by sentiment, — accidentally or transiently, that is, for the sentiment will vary according to the relations in which he is placed? The lover, the poet, the artist, are likely to view her nobly. The father and the philosopher have some chance of liberality; the man of the world, the legislator for expediency, none.

Metropolitan Museum of Art; Stokes-Hawes gift

Margaret Fuller (Marchioness Ossoli); daguerreotype by Southworth and Hawes, about 1845

Under these circumstances, without attaching importance, in themselves, to the changes demanded by the champions of Woman, we hail them as signs of the times. We would have every arbitrary barrier thrown down. We would have every path laid open to Woman as freely as to Man. Were this done, and a slight temporary fermentation allowed to subside, we should see crystallizations more pure and of more various beauty. We believe the divine energy would pervade nature to a degree unknown in the history of former ages, and that no discordant collision, but a ravishing harmony of the spheres, would ensue.

Yet, then and only then will mankind be ripe for this, when inward and outward freedom for Woman as much as for Man shall be acknowledged as a *right*, not yielded as a concession. As the friend of the Negro assumes that one man cannot by right hold another in bondage, so should the friend of Woman assume that Man cannot by right lay even well meant restrictions on Woman. If the Negro be a soul, if the woman be a soul, apparelled in flesh, to one Master only are they accountable. There is but one law for souls, and, if there is to be an interpreter of it, he must come not as man, or son of man, but as son of God.

Were thought and feeling once so far elevated that Man should esteem himself the brother and friend, but nowise the lord and tutor, of Woman, — were he really bound with her in equal worship, — arrangements as to function and employment would be of no consequence. What woman needs is not as a woman to act or rule, but as a nature to grow, as an intellect to discern, as a soul to live freely and unimpeded, to unfold such powers as were given her when we left our common home. If fewer talents were given her, yet if allowed the free and full employment of these, so that she may render back to the giver his own with usury, she will not complain; nay, I dare to say she will bless and rejoice in her earthly birthplace, her earthly lot.

65.

Strike of Pittsburgh Women

In the 1840s the main goal of labor was the ten-hour work day. Women workers, although organized separately, were among the most enthusiastic unionists of the decade. The following notice appeared concerning a strike of the female operatives of Pittsburgh, Pennsylvania, in 1845. The Pennsylvania legislature reviewed petitions for a ten-hour law in 1844 and 1846, but it was not until March 1848 that any law limiting the hours of labor was passed.

Source: *United States Journal,* (Washington City), October 18, 1845.

THE PATRIOTIC FEMALES employed in the Pittsburgh factories recently struck for the ten-hour system. A portion of them were compelled by dire necessity to return to the slavery of their iron-hearted employers; the others raised a fund, and, what is more, raised the d————l! They marched in a body to the various mills, and in spite of all opposition from the mayor, police, etc., released the operatives from their employment, stopped the works, distributed the money collected for the use of those who had been compelled to go to work, and then all was quiet.

This is a refreshing spot in life's wilderness. It is the most glorious mob since that on Bunker Hill, in old revolutionary times — if we except the one in Cincinnati which riddled the shaving shops in that city a few years ago. Patriotism is not yet wholly extinct in our tariff-ridden country.

The editor of the *Louisville Democrat* moralizes upon the subject as follows:

The strike at Pittsburgh among the factory hands has not only failed but the magnanimous employers have increased the number of working hours. This is always the end of a struggle of poverty against wealth. It is almost uniformly within the power of the employer to take exemplary vengeance; and he rarely fails to do it. We hope that the next Congress will bear all these matters in mind. These manufacturers are public beneficiaries. They come begging to Congress for protection, for the shillings to be extracted out of the pocket of the consumers, among whom are these poor operatives. We have now a Democratic Congress, and we insist that when these gentlemen beggars come importuning for favors, that that body shall recollect that American industry does indeed need protection from these beggars who live upon the spoils which partial legislation takes from the industry of the country.

It should be remembered that legislative favors are always mischievous, especially when they concentrate wealth or increase the power of capital over labor. These have power enough without any artificial aid. One thing is clear, these strikes and failures will satisfy all workingmen as to how much protection of capital benefits them. The enormous per cents of manufactures are not for them. Submission, submission — that's the word for laborers, especially little boys and girls in the factories.

66.

James K. Polk: Reaffirmation of the Monroe Doctrine

In his message to Congress of December 2, 1845, President Polk reinterpreted the Monroe Doctrine in terms of the prevailing spirit of Manifest Destiny. Whereas Monroe had said only that the Western Hemisphere was no longer open to European colonialism, Polk now stated that European nations had better not interfere with projected territorial expansion by the United States. The occasion of this message was recent publicity concerning attempts of Great Britain and France to thwart annexation of Texas. Polk also asserted the United States' title to Oregon and California.

Source: Richardson, IV, pp. 385-416.

IT IS SUBMITTED to the wisdom of Congress to determine whether, at their present session, and until after the expiration of the year's notice, any other measures may be adopted consistently with the convention of 1827 for the security of our rights and the government and protection of our citizens in Oregon. That it will ultimately be wise and proper to make liberal grants of land to the patriotic pioneers, who amidst privations and dangers lead the way through savage tribes inhabiting the vast wilderness intervening between our frontier settlements and Oregon, and who cultivate and are ever ready to defend the soil, I am fully satisfied. To doubt whether they will obtain such grants as soon as the convention between the United States and Great Britain shall have ceased to exist would be to doubt the justice of Congress; but, pending the year's notice, it is worthy of consideration whether a stipulation to this effect may be made consistently with the spirit of that convention.

The recommendations which I have made as to the best manner of securing our rights in Oregon are submitted to Congress with great deference. Should they in their wisdom devise any other mode better calculated to accomplish the same object, it shall meet with my hearty concurrence.

At the end of the year's notice, should Congress think it proper to make provision for giving that notice, we shall have reached a period when the national rights in Oregon must either be abandoned or firmly maintained. That they cannot be abandoned without a sacrifice of both national honor and interest is too clear to admit of doubt.

Oregon is a part of the North American continent, to which, it is confidently affirmed, the title of the United States is the best now in existence. For the grounds on which that title rests I refer you to the correspondence of the late and present secretary of state with the British plenipotentiary during the negotiation. The British proposition of compromise, which would make the Columbia the line south of 49°, with a trifling addition of detached territory to the United States north of that river, and would leave on the British side two-thirds of the whole Oregon territory, including the free navigation of the Columbia and all the valuable harbors on the Pacific, can never for a moment be entertained by the United States without an abandonment of their just and clear territorial rights, their own self-respect, and the national honor. For the information of Congress, I communicate herewith the correspondence which took place between the two governments during the late negotiation.

The rapid extension of our settlements over our territories heretofore unoccupied, the addition of new states to our confederacy, the expansion of free principles, and our rising greatness as a nation are attracting the attention of the powers of Europe, and lately the doctrine has been broached in some of them of a "balance of power" on this continent to check our advancement. The United States, sincerely desirous of preserving relations of good understanding with all nations, cannot in silence permit any European interference on the North American continent, and should any such interference be attempted will be ready to resist it at any and all hazards.

It is well known to the American people and to all nations that this government has never interfered with the relations subsisting between other governments. We have never made ourselves parties to their wars or their alliances; we have not sought their territories by conquest; we have not mingled with parties in their domestic struggles; and believing our own form of government to be the best, we have never attempted to propagate it by intrigues, by diplomacy, or by force. We may claim on this continent a like exemption from European interference. The nations of America are equally sovereign and independent with those of Europe. They possess the same rights, independent of all foreign interposition, to make war, to conclude peace, and to regulate their internal affairs. The people of the United States cannot, therefore, view with indifference attempts of European powers to interfere with the independent action of the nations on this continent.

The American system of government is entirely different from that of Europe. Jealousy among the different sovereigns of Europe, lest any one of them might become too powerful for the rest, has caused them anxiously to desire the establishment of what they term the "balance of power." It cannot be permitted to have any application on the North American continent, and especially to the United States. We must ever maintain the principle that the people of this continent alone have the right to decide their own destiny. Should any portion of them, constituting an independent state propose to unite themselves with our confederacy, this will be a question for them and us to determine without any foreign interposition. We can never consent that European powers shall interfere to prevent such a union because it might disturb the "balance of power" which they may desire to maintain upon this continent.

Near a quarter of a century ago the principle was distinctly announced to the world, in the annual message of one of my predecessors, that:

> The American continents, by the free and independent condition which they have assumed and maintain, are henceforth not to be considered as subjects for future colonization by any European powers.

This principle will apply with greatly increased force should any European power attempt to establish any new colony in North America. In the existing circumstances of the world the present is deemed a proper occasion to reiterate and reaffirm the principle avowed by Mr. Monroe and to state my cordial concurrence in its wisdom and sound policy. The reassertion of this principle, especially in reference to North America, is at this day but the promulgation of a policy which no European power should cherish the disposition to resist. Existing rights of every European nation should be respected, but it is due alike to our safety and our interests that the efficient protection of our laws should be extended over our whole territorial limits, and that it should be distinctly announced to the world as our settled policy that no future European colony or dominion shall with our consent be planted or established on any part of the North American continent.

67.

Robert J. Walker: Tariffs and Revenue Laws

President Polk wished to reestablish the independent treasury that had originated with President Van Buren, and he wanted a tariff that would not produce a surplus in the treasury, that would not raise the price of imported necessities, and that would not favor the interests of any one section. These objectives underlay the first report submitted to Congress by Polk's secretary of the treasury, Robert J. Walker of Mississippi. The sub-treasury system proposed in Walker's report was incorporated into the Independent Treasury Act of August 6, 1846, and Walker's tariff program formed the basis of the Revenue Bill (sometimes called "Walker's Tariff") signed on July 30, 1846. The report, which was presented on December 3, 1845, and is reprinted in part below, is among the classics of free-trade literature.

Source: 29 Congress, 1 Session, House Document No. 6.

In suggesting improvements in the revenue laws, the following principles have been adopted:

1. That no more money should be collected than is necessary for the wants of the government, economically administered.

2. That no duty be imposed on any article above the lowest rate which will yield the largest amount of revenue.

3. That below such rate discrimination may be made, descending in the scale of duties; or, for imperative reasons, the articles may be placed in the list of those free from all duty.

4. That the maximum revenue duty should be imposed on luxuries.

5. That all minimums and all specific duties should be abolished, and ad valorem duties substituted in their place — care being taken to guard against fraudulent invoices and undervaluation, and to assess the duty upon the actual market value.

6. That the duty should be so imposed as to operate as equally as possible throughout the Union, discriminating neither for nor against any class or section.

No horizontal scale of duties is recommended; because such a scale would be a refusal to discriminate for revenue and might sink that revenue below the wants of the government. Some articles will yield the largest revenue at duties that would be wholly or partially prohibitory in other cases. Luxuries, as a general rule, will bear the highest revenue duties: but even some very costly luxuries, easily smuggled, will bear but a light duty for revenue, while other articles of great bulk and weight will bear a higher duty for revenue. There is no instance within the knowledge of this department of any horizontal tariff ever having been enacted by any one of the nations of the world.

There must be discrimination for revenue, or the burden of taxation must be augmented, in order to bring the same amount of money into the treasury. It is difficult, also, to adopt any arbitrary maximum to which an inflexible adherence must be demanded in all cases. Thus, upon brandy and spirits, a specific duty, varying as an equivalent ad valorem from 180 to 261 percent, yields a large revenue; yet no one would propose either of these rates as a maximum. These duties are too high for revenue from the encouragement they present for smuggling these baneful luxuries; yet a duty of 20 percent upon brandy and spirits would be far below the revenue standard, would greatly diminish the income on these imports, require increased burdens upon the necessaries of life, and would revolt the moral sense of the whole community.

There are many other luxuries which will bear a much higher duty for revenue than 20 percent; and the only true maximum is that which experience demonstrates will bring, in each case, the largest revenue at the lowest rate of duty. Nor should maximum revenue duties be imposed upon all articles; for this would yield too large an income, and would prevent all discrimination within the revenue standard, and require necessaries to be taxed as high as luxuries. But, while it is impossible to adopt any horizontal scale of duties, or even any arbitrary maximum, experience proves that, as a general rule, a duty of 20 percent ad valorem will yield the largest revenue. . . .

It is believed that sufficient means can be obtained at the lowest revenue duties on the articles now subjected to duty; but if Congress desire a larger revenue, it should be procured by taxing the free articles rather than transcend, in any case, the lowest revenue duties. It is thought, however, that,

without exceeding that limit in any case, an adequate revenue will still be produced and permit the addition to the free list of salt and guano. In one of his annual messages, Mr. Jefferson recommended to Congress "the suppression of the duties on salt." A large portion of this duty is exhausted in heavy expenses of measuring salt, and in large sums paid for fishing bounties and allowances in lieu of the drawback of the duty, both which expenditures would fall with a repeal of the duty; which repeal, therefore, can cause no considerable reduction of the revenue.

Salt is a necessary of life, and should be as free from tax as air or water. It is used in large quantities by the farmer and planter; and to the poor this tax operates most oppressively, not only in the use of the article itself but as combined with salted provisions. The salt made abroad by solar evaporation is also most pure and wholesome, and, as conservative of health, should be exempt from taxation.

The duty on cotton bagging is equivalent to 55.2 percent ad valorem on the Scotch bagging, and to 123.11 percent on the gunny bag; and yet the whole revenue from these duties has fallen to $66,064.50. Nearly the entire amount, therefore, of this enormous tax makes no addition to the revenue, but inures to the benefit of about thirty manufacturers. As five-sixths of the cotton crop is exported abroad, the same proportion of the bagging around the bale is exported and sold abroad at a heavy loss, growing out of a deduction for tare. Now, as duties are designed to operate only on the domestic consumption, there ought to be a drawback of the whole duty on cotton bagging re-exported around the bale, on the same principles on which drawbacks are allowed in other cases. The cotton planting is the great exporting interest, and suffers from the tariff in the double capacity of consumer and exporter.

Cotton is the great basis of our foreign exchange, furnishing most of the means to purchase imports and supply the revenue. It is thus the source of two-thirds of the revenue, and of our foreign freight and commerce, upholding our commercial marine and maritime power. It is also a bond of peace with foreign nations, constituting a stronger preventive of war than armies or navies, forts or armaments. At present prices, our cotton crop will yield an annual product of $72 million and the manufactured fabric $504 million, furnishing profits abroad to thousands of capitalists and wages to hundreds of thousands of the working classes; all of whom would be deeply injured by any disturbance, growing out of a state of war, to the direct and adequate supply of the raw material. . . .

The condition of our foreign relations, it is said, should suspend the reduction of the tariff. No American patriot can desire to arrest our onward career in peace and prosperity; but if, unhappily, such should be the result, it would create an increased necessity for reducing our present high duties in order to obtain sufficient revenue to meet increased expenditures. The duties for the quarter ending September 30, 1844, yielded $2,011,885.90 more of revenue than the quarter ending September 30, 1845; showing a very considerable decline of the revenue growing out of a diminished importation of the highly protected articles and the progressive substitution of the domestic rivals. Indeed, many of the duties are becoming dead letters, except for the purpose of prohibition, and, if not reduced, will ultimately compel their advocates to resort to direct taxation to support the government.

In the event of war, nearly all the high duties would become prohibitory from the increased risk and cost of importations; and if there be, indeed, in the opinion of any, a serious danger of such an occurrence, it appeals most strongly to their patriotism to impose the lowest revenue duties on all articles as the only means of securing, at such a period, any considerable income from the tariff.

The whole power to collect taxes, whether direct or indirect, is conferred by the same clause of the Constitution. The words are, "The Congress shall have the power to lay and collect taxes, duties, imposts, and excises." A direct tax or excise, not for revenue but for protection, clearly would not be within the legitimate object of taxation; and yet it would be as much so as a duty imposed for a similar purpose. The power is "to lay and *collect* taxes, duties, imposts, and excises." A duty must be laid only that it may be *collected*; and if it is so imposed that it cannot be collected, in whole or in part, it violates the declared object of the granted power. To lay all duties so high that none of them could be collected would be a prohibitory tariff. To lay a duty on any one article so high that it could not be collected would be a prohibitory tariff upon that article.

If a duty of 100 percent were imposed upon all or upon a number of articles, so as to diminish the revenue upon all or any of them, it would operate as a partial prohibition. A partial and a total prohibition are alike in violation of the true object of the taxing power. They only differ in degree and not in principle. If the revenue limit may be exceeded 1 percent, it may be exceeded 100. If it may be exceeded upon any one article, it may be exceeded on all; and there is no escape from this conclusion but in contending that Congress may lay duties on all articles so high as to collect no revenue, and operate as a total prohibition.

The Constitution declares that "all bills for raising revenue shall originate in the House of Representatives." A tariff bill, it is conceded, can only originate in the House because it is a bill for *raising revenue*. That is the only proper object of such a bill. A tariff is a bill to "lay and collect taxes." It is a bill for "raising revenue"; and whenever it departs from that object, in whole or in part, either by total or partial prohibition, it violates the purpose of the granted power.

In arranging the details of the tariff, it is

believed that the maximum revenue duties should be imposed upon luxuries. It is deemed just that taxation, whether direct or indirect, should be as nearly as practicable in proportion to property. If the whole revenue were raised by a tax upon property, the poor, and especially those who live by the wages of labor, would pay but a very small portion of such tax; whereas, by the tariff, the poor, by the consumption of various imports or domestic articles enhanced in price by the duties, pay a much larger share of the taxes than if they were collected by an assessment in proportion to property.

To counteract, as far as possible, this effect of the tariff — to equalize its operation and make it approximate as nearly as may be to a system of taxes in proportion to property — the duties upon luxuries, used almost exclusively by the rich, should be fixed at the highest revenue standard. This would not be discriminating in favor of the poor, however just that might be within the revenue limit, but it would mitigate, as far as practicable, that discrimination against the poor which results from every tariff by compelling them to pay a larger amount of taxes than if assessed and collected on all property in proportion to its value. In accordance with these principles, it is believed that the largest practicable portion of the aggregate revenue should be raised by maximum revenue duties upon luxuries, whether grown, produced, or manufactured at home or abroad.

An appeal has been made to the poor by the friends of protection on the ground that it augments the wages of labor. In reply, it is contended that the wages of labor have not augmented since the tariff of 1842, and that in some cases they have diminished.

When the number of manufactories is not great, the power of the system to regulate the wages of labor is inconsiderable; but as the profit of capital invested in manufactures is augmented by the protective tariff, there is a corresponding increase of power, until the control of such capital over the wages of labor becomes irresistible. As this power is exercised from time to time, we find it resisted by combinations among the working classes, by turning out for higher wages or for shorter time; by trades unions; and in some countries, unfortunately, by violence and bloodshed.

But the government, by protective duties, arrays itself on the side of the manufacturing system, and, by thus augmenting its wealth and power, soon terminates in its favor the struggle between man and money — between capital and labor. When the tariff of 1842 was enacted, the maximum duty was 20 percent. By that act, the average of duties on the protected articles was more than double. But the wages of labor did not increase in a corresponding ratio, or in any ratio whatever. On the contrary, while wages in some cases have diminished, the prices of many articles used by the working classes have greatly appreciated.

A protective tariff is a question regarding the enhancement of the profits of capital. That is its object, and not to augment the wages of labor, which would reduce those profits. It is a question of percentage, and is to decide whether money vested in our manufactures shall, by special legislation, yield a profit of 10, 20, or 30 percent, or whether it shall remain satisfied with a dividend equal to that accruing from the same capital invested in agriculture, commerce, or navigation.

The present tariff is unjust and unequal as well in its details as in the principle upon which it is founded. On some articles the duties are entirely prohibitory and on others there is a partial prohibition. It discriminates in favor of manufactures and against agriculture by imposing many higher duties upon the manufactured fabric than upon the agricultural product out of which it is made. It discriminates in favor of the manufacturer and against the mechanic by many higher duties upon the manufacture than upon the article made out of it by the mechanic.

It discriminates in favor of the manufacturer and against the merchant by injurious restrictions upon trade and commerce; and against the shipbuilding and navigating interest by heavy duties on almost every article used in building or navigating vessels. It discriminates in favor of manufactures and against exports, which are as truly the product of American industry as manufactures. It discriminates in favor of the rich and against the poor by high duties upon nearly all the necessaries of life, and by minimums and specific duties, rendering the tax upon the real value much higher on the cheaper than upon the finer article.

Minimums are a fictitious value, assumed by law, instead of the real value; and the operation of all minimums may be illustrated by a single example. Thus, by the tariff of 1842, a duty of 30 percent ad valorem is levied on all manufactures of cotton; but the law further provides that cotton goods "not dyed, colored, printed, or stained, not exceeding in value 20 cents per square yard, shall be valued at 20 cents per square yard." If, then, the real value of the cheapest cotton goods is but 4 cents a square yard, it is placed by the law at the false value of 20 cents per square yard, and the duty levied on the fictitious value — raising it five times higher on the cheap article consumed by the poor than upon the fine article purchased by the more wealthy. . . .

The operation of the specific duty presents a similar discrimination against the poor and in favor of the rich. Thus, upon salt: the duty is not upon the value, but it is 8 cents a bushel, whether the article be coarse or fine — showing, by the same document, from actual importation, a discrimination of 64 percent against the cheap and in favor of the finer article; and this, to a greater or less extent, is the effect of all specific duties. . . .

If direct taxes were made specific, they would be intolerable. Thus, if an annual tax of $30 was assessed on all houses without respect to their actual value, making the owner of the humble tenement or cabin pay a tax of $30 and the owner of the costly mansion a tax of but $30 on their respective houses, it would differ only in degree, but not in principle, from the same unvarying specific duty on cheap as on fine articles. If any discrimination should be made, it should be the reverse of the specific duty and of the minimum principle by establishing a maximum standard above which value the duties on the finer article should be higher, and below which they should be lower on the cheaper article. The tax upon the actual value is the most equal. . . .

At least two-thirds of the taxes imposed by the present tariff are paid, not into the treasury but to the protected classes. . . . This estimate is based upon the position that the duty is added to the price of the import, and also of its domestic rival. If the import is enhanced in price by the duty, so must be the domestic rival; for, being like articles, their price must be the same in the same market. The merchant advances in cash the duty on the import and adds the duty, with a profit upon it, and other charges, to the price — which must therefore be enhanced to that extent. . . . The duty, therefore, must be added to the price and paid by the consumer — the duty constituting as much a part of the price as the cost of production. . . .

The truest comparison is between the present price of the same article at home and abroad; and to the extent that the price is lower in the foreign market than in our own, the duty, if equal to that difference, must to that extent enhance the price, and in the same ratio with the lower duty. The difference in price at home or abroad is generally about equal to the difference in the cost of production and presents, in a series of years, the surest measure of the effect of the duty — the enhancement in price being equal to that difference. . . .

The great argument for the tariff is that foreign labor being cheaper than our own, the cost of foreign productions, it is said, is lessened to that extent, and that we must make up this difference by an equivalent duty and a corresponding enhancement of price in our own market, both of the foreign article and of its rival domestic product — thus rendering the duty a tax on all consumers for the benefit of the protected classes. If the marshal were sent by the federal government to collect a direct tax from the whole people to be paid over to manufacturing capitalists to enable them to sustain their business, or realize a larger profit, it would be the same in effect as the protective duty. . . .

Legislation for classes is against the doctrine of equal rights, repugnant to the spirit of our free institutions, and, it is apprehended by many, may become but another form for privileged orders, under the name of protection instead of privilege; indicated here not by rank or title, but by profits and dividends extracted from the many, by taxes upon them, for the benefit of the few.

No prejudice is felt by the secretary of the treasury against manufacturers. His opposition is to the protective system and not to classes or individuals. He doubts not that the manufacturers are sincerely persuaded that the system which is a source of so much profit to them is beneficial also to the country. He entertains a contrary opinion, and claims for the opponents of the system a settled conviction of its injurious effects. While a due regard to the just and equal rights of all classes forbids a discrimination in favor of the manufacturers by duties above the lowest revenue limit, no disposition is felt to discriminate against them by reducing such duties as operate in their favor below that standard.

Under revenue duties it is believed they would still receive a reasonable profit, equal to that realized by those engaged in other pursuits; and it is thought they should desire no more, at least through the agency of governmental power. Equal rights and profits, so far as laws are made, best conform to the principles upon which the Constitution was founded, and with an undeviating regard to which all its functions should be exercised, looking to the whole country and not to classes or sections.

Soil, climate, and other causes vary very much in different countries the pursuits which are most profitable in each; and the prosperity of all of them will be best promoted by leaving them, unrestricted by legislation, to exchange with each other those fabrics and products which they severally raise most cheaply. This is clearly illustrated by the perfect free trade which exists among all the states of the Union, and by the acknowledged fact that any one of these states would be injured by imposing duties upon the products of the others. It is generally conceded that reciprocal free trade among nations would best advance the interest of all. But it is contended that we must meet the tariffs of other nations by countervailing restrictions.

That duties upon our exports by foreign nations are prejudicial to us is conceded, but while this injury is slightly felt by the manufacturers, its weight falls almost exclusively upon agriculture, commerce, and navigation. If those interests which sustain the loss do not ask countervailing restrictions, should not be demanded by the manufacturers, who do not feel the injury, and whose fabrics, in fact, are not excluded by the foreign legislation of which they complain. That agriculture, commerce, and navigation are injured by foreign restrictions constitutes no reason why they should be subject to still severer treatment by additional restrictions and countervailing tariffs enacted at home. Commerce, agriculture, and navigation, harassed as they may be by foreign restrictions, diminishing the amount of exchangeable products which they could otherwise purchase abroad, are burdened with heavier impositions at home.

Nor will augmented duties here lead to a reduction of foreign tariffs, but the reverse, by furnishing the protected classes there with the identical argument used by the protected classes here against reduction. By countervailing restrictions we injure our own fellow citizens much more than the foreign nations at whom we propose to aim their force; and in the conflict of opposing tariffs we sacrifice our own commerce, agriculture, and navigation. As well might we impose monarchical or aristocratic restrictions on our own government or people, because that is the course of foreign legislation. Let our commerce be as free as our political institutions. Let us, with revenue duties only, open our ports to all the world, and nation after nation will soon follow our example. . . .

If [the manufacturing] interest desired reciprocal free trade with other nations, it would have desired a very different tariff from that of 1842. It would have sought to confine the high duties to those cases where the foreign importer would sell his imports for cash only, and admitted a drawback of one-half of the duty where American exports would be taken abroad in exchange — not an actual barter of foreign imports for an equal amount in value of our products, but without any barter where a sum equal to the value of their exports was used in purchasing here an equal amount in value of any of our products; and the shipment made abroad of these products upon the same principle under which a drawback of duties is now allowed on the re-exportation of foreign imports. This would be less simple and is not recommended in lieu of that absolute reduction of the duties which will accomplish the same object of unrestricted exchange. But such a provision would be a self-executing reciprocity law, and should be desired by those believing in countervailing tariffs against foreign nations,

Library of Congress

Robert J. Walker (1801-1869)

but in reciprocal free trade with all — thus enabling our farmers and planters to sell their products for cheaper foreign manufactures, getting more for what they sell and paying less for what they purchase in exchange.

It seems strange that while the profit of agriculture varies from 1 to 8 percent, that of manufactures is more than double. The reason is that, while the high duties secure nearly a monopoly of the home market to the manufacturer, the farmer and planter are deprived to a great extent of the foreign market by these duties. The farmer and planter are, to a great extent, forbidden to buy in the foreign market, and confined to the domestic articles enhanced in price by the duties. The tariff is thus a double benefit to the manufacturer and a double loss to the farmer and planter; a benefit to the former in nearly a monopoly of the home market and in enhanced prices of their fabrics; and a loss to the latter in the payment of those high prices and a total or partial exclusion from the foreign market.

The true question is whether the farmer and planter shall, to a great extent, supply our people with cheap manufactures purchased abroad with their agricultural products, or whether this exchange shall be forbidden by high duties on such manufactures, and their supply thrown, as a monopoly, at large prices, by high tariffs, into the hands of our own manufacturers. . . . The farmer and planter are asked to sacrifice the markets of the world, containing a population of 800 million, disabled from purchasing our products by our high duties on all they would sell in exchange. The farmer and planter have the home market without a tariff, and they would have the foreign market also to a much greater extent but for the total or partial prohibition of the last tariff.

We have more fertile lands than any other nation, can raise a greater variety of products, and, it may be said, could feed and clothe the people of nearly all the world. The home market, of itself, is wholly inadequate for such products. They must have the foreign market, or a large surplus, accompanied by great depression in price, must be the result. . . . The growing West in a series of years must be the greatest sufferers by the tariff, in depriving them of the foreign market and that of the cotton-growing states. . . .

Agriculture is our chief employment; it is best adapted to our situation; and, if not depressed by the tariff, would be the most profitable. We can raise a larger surplus of agricultural products, and a greater variety, than almost any other nation, and at cheaper rates. Remove, then, from agriculture all our restrictions, and by its own unfettered power it will break down all foreign restrictions, and, ours being removed, would feed the hungry and clothe the poor of our fellowmen throughout all the densely peopled nations of the world. But now we will take nothing in exchange for these products but specie, except at very high duties; and nothing but a famine breaks down all foreign restrictions and opens for a time the ports of Europe to our breadstuffs. . . .

Connected with this department and t[he] finances is the question of the sales of t[he] public lands. The proceeds of these sales, is believed, should continue to constitute portion of the revenue, diminishing to th[e] extent the amount required to be raised [by] the tariff. . . . The average annual sal[es] have been much less than 2 million acre[s] yet the aggregate net proceeds of the sal[es] in 1834, 1835, 1836, and 1837 w[as] $51,268,617.82. Those large sales were a[l]most exclusively for speculation; and th[is] can only be obviated at all times by confi[n]ing the sales to settlers and cultivators limited quantities, sufficient for farms [or] plantations.

The price at which the public land[s] should be sold is an important question the whole country, but especially to t[he] people of the new states, living mostly r[e]mote from the seaboard, and who ha[ve] scarcely felt the presence of the governme[nt] in local expenditures but chiefly in the e[x]haustion of their means for purchases public lands and for customs. The publ[ic] lands are not of the same value, yet th[ey] are all fixed at one, unvarying price, whi[ch] is far above the value of a large portion these lands. The quantity now subject [to] entry at the minimum price of $1.25 p[er] acre is 133,307,457 acres, and 109,035,34[?] in addition, to which the Indian title h[as] been extinguished — being an aggregate 242,342,802 acres, and requiring a centu[ry] and a quarter to complete the sales at t[he] rate they have progressed heretofore, with[out including any of the unsold lands [of] Texas or Oregon, or of the vast region b[e]sides to which the Indian title is not y[et] extinguished. It is clear, then, that there is vast and annually increasing surplus of pub[lic] lands, very little of which will be sol[d] within any reasonable period at the prese[nt] price, and in regard to which the public i[n]terest would be promoted and the reven[ue] augmented by reducing the price.

The reduction of the price of the publ[ic] lands in favor of settlers and cultivato[rs] would enhance the wages of labor. It is an argument urged in favor of the tariff that we ought to protect our labor against what is called the pauper labor of Europe. But while the tariff does not enhance the wages of labor, the sales of the public lands at low prices and in limited quantities to settlers and cultivators would accomplish this object. If those who live by the wages of labor could purchase 320 acres of land for $80, 160 acres for $40, or 80 acres for $20, or a 40-acre lot for $10, the power of the manufacturing capitalist in reducing the wages of labor would be greatly diminished; because, when these lands were thus reduced in price, those who live by the wages of labor could purchase farms at these low rates and cultivate the soil for themselves and families, instead of working for others twelve hours a day in the manufactories.

Reduce the price which the laborer must pay for the public domain; bring thus the means of purchase within his power; prevent all speculation and monopoly in the public lands; confine the sales to settlers and cultivators in limited quantities; preserve these hundreds of millions of acres, for ages to come, as homes for the poor and oppressed; reduce the taxes by reducing the tariff and bringing down the prices which the poor are thus compelled to pay for all the necessaries and comforts of life, and more will be done for the benefit of American labor than if millions were added to the profits of manufacturing capital by the enactment of a protective tariff.

The secretary of the treasury, on coming into office, found the revenues deposited with banks. . . . One of the great evils of banks is the constant expansion and contraction of the currency; and this evil is augmented by the deposits of the revenue with banks, whether state or national. The only proper course for the government is to keep its own money separate from all banks and bankers, in its own treasury — whether in the Mint, branch mints, or other government agencies — and to use only gold and silver coin in all receipts and disbursements. The business of the country will be more safe when an adequate supply of specie is kept within our limits and its circulation encouraged by all the means within the power of the government.

If this government and the states and the people unite in suppressing the use of specie, an adequate supply, for want of a demand, cannot be kept within our limits, and the condition of the business and currency of the country will be perilous and uncertain. It will be completely within the power of the banks, whose paper will constitute the exclusive circulation of the whole community. Nor will it be useful to establish a constitutional treasury if it is to receive or disburse the paper of banks. Separation from banks in that case would only be nominal, and no addition would be made to the circulation of gold and silver.

Various forms of paper credit have been suggested, as connected with the operations of the constitutional treasury; but they are all considered as impairing one of the great objects of such a treasury — namely, an augmented circulation of specie. If paper, in whatever form, or from whatever source it may issue, should be introduced as a circulation by the constitutional treasury, it would, precisely to that extent, diminish its use as a means of circulating gold and silver. . . .

There is nothing which will advance so surely the prosperity of the country as an adequate supply of specie, diffused throughout every portion of the Union, and constituting, to a great extent, the ordinary circulation everywhere among the people. It is a currency that will never break nor fail; it will neither expand nor contract beyond the legitimate business of the country; it will lead to no extravagant speculations at one time, to be followed by certain depression at another; nor will labor ever be robbed of its reward by the depreciation of such currency. There is no danger that we shall have too much gold and silver in actual circulation, or too small an amount of bank paper, or that any injury ever will be inflicted upon the business of the country, by a diminution of the circulation of the paper of banks, and the substitution in its place, to that extent, of gold and silver. Even their most ardent advocates must admit that banks are subject to periodical expansions and contractions, and that this evil would be increased by giving them the funds of the government to loan, and by receiving and disbursing nothing but their paper.

It is believed that the permanent interest of every class of the people will be advanced by the establishment of the constitutional treasury, and that the manufacturers especially will derive great benefit from its adoption. It will give stability to all their operations, and insure them, to a great extent, against those fluctuations, expansions, and contractions of the currency so prejudicial to their interests. By guarding against inflations of the currency, it will have a tendency to check periodical excesses of foreign importations purchased in fact upon credit; while loans from banks, or dangerous enlargements of their business, and excessive issues of their paper will be greatly diminished. While a sound and stable currency guards the manufacturer against excessive importations from abroad, it protects him from disasters at home, and from those ruinous revulsions in which so many thousands are reduced to bankruptcy.

The tariff, if followed, as in the absence of adequate checks it certainly soon will be, by an inflated currency, while it thus enhances the expenses of manufacturing at home, will speedily and certainly raise prices up to the whole amount of the duty, so as to repeal the operation of that duty in favor of the manufacturer and enable the foreign importer again to flood the market at the enhanced prices arising from an inflated currency. But soon the revulsion comes, and all are overwhelmed in a common ruin. The currency is reduced below the wants of the country by a sudden and ruinous contraction; and the labor and industry of years are required to repair the mischief. Stability, both in the tariff and the currency, is what the manufacturer should most desire.

Let the tariff be permanently adjusted by a return to reasonable and moderate revenue duties, which, even when imposed truly and in good faith for that purpose, will yield sufficient advantage to afford reasonable profits; and let this permanent system (and none other can be permanent) be established and accompanied by a stable currency, and the manufacturer, in a series of years, will derive the greatest benefits from the system.

The present system cannot be permanent. It is too unequal and unjust, too exorbitant and oppressive, and too clearly in conflict with the fundamental principles of the Constitution. If the manufacturer thinks that this system can be permanent, let him look to the constant changes which have attended all attempts to establish and continue a protective tariff. The first tariff was based in part upon the principle of very moderate protection to domestic manufactures; and the result has been . . . that the tariff has been changed and modified thirty times since that period — being more than once, on an average, for every Congress since the government was founded; and one of these tariffs was in itself a system of successive biennial changes, operating through a period of ten years.

Of these changes, fourteen have been general and sixteen special. From 1816 onward, these changes have been most frequent; and it is vain to expect permanency from anything but a revenue tariff. Stability is what the manufacturer should desire, and especially that the question should be taken out of the arena of politics by a just and permanent settlement.

68.

Lewis C. Levin: Native Americans and the Foreign-Born

Robert C. Winthrop, a Whig representative from Massachusetts, transmitted resolutions from the Massachusetts legislature to the House of Representatives, on December 15, 1845, calling for an investigation of alleged election frauds associated with immigrants and for changes in the country's naturalization laws if warranted. It was moved that the resolutions be referred to the Judiciary Committee, but the Nativist Lewis C. Levin of Pennsylvania, fearing that the Judiciary Committee would not be sympathetic, proposed that a select committee be created to review the issue. On December 17 and 18, ostensibly in defense of his motion, Levin delivered the following speech in the House. Levin's motion was overruled; the resolutions were referred to the Judiciary Committee; and the Committee reported against changing the naturalization laws.

Source: *Globe, App.,* 29 Cong., 1 Sess., pp. 46-50.

THE GENTLEMAN who last occupied the floor has been anxious to proclaim the death of native Americanism. Sir, it is a principle that can never die. It is part and parcel of the country itself, and as natural to our soil as the mountains that rise in the clouds, or the rivers that water our plains. The principle which binds us together is one so irresistibly attractive, as to promise us a large majority of the people of these United States as friends and supporters — arrayed in the armor of truth, and inspired by the enthusiasm of patriotism. That principle, sir, is a living principle. It is no abstraction. It is an embodied vitality of all that is pure in life, lofty in patriotism, and sublime in achievement. It is identified with the birth of the republic — the day-flash of our liberty — the maturity of our independence, and the establishment of our glorious Constitution. It is recognized as fame. It is consecrated as glory.

The farmer at his plow feels its warmth in his heart. The boy at school, as his peach-bloom cheek flushes with pride, shoots a brighter glance from his eye at the thought of the name, that is itself that principle, and which equally defies slander, repels calumny, conquers argument, and soars above scorn, contempt, and hatred. Is it necessary that I should mention the name, when there is but one that corresponds with the definition? And yet, so heavy have become the foreign mists that obscure men's minds, who lose all pride of the past in the selfishness of the present, that I find myself constrained to give breath to a charm that shall usher our adversaries into the very flood of noonday light.

The name, sir, that embodies our principles is that of George Washington! If, then, any discredit can attach to being a native American, I for one plead guilty, and fling myself upon the mercy of an age recreant to the principles of the Revolution, and dead to the claims of country. Will those who prefer to worship the pagan idols of foreign altars (I speak politically) show mercy to one who claims the feelings and sympathies incident to a fellowship of birthright with George Washington — one who dare, without quailing before ridicule, or blushing at the ribald jest of the infidel scorner, lay his hand upon the Bible as the rock of his faith, and hold the Constitution to his heart as the monitor of his political duty — one who, whatever may be his fate on this stage of action, is content to abide by the verdict of a tribunal in which human frailty has no share. As native Americans, we desire to erect additional bulwarks for the protection of American institutions from foreign influence. . . .

But we have been told that we belong to a party of "one idea." Is that a reason why we should not be privileged to bring this great subject in proper form to the full consideration of the House? The term conveys no disparagement; and, if designed as a sarcasm, it has lost its point in the literal truth of the praise that lies enveloped in its meaning. All great achievements originate from "one idea." . . .

Democracy is "one idea" — the popular element in the ascendant, though it be the foreign element. Whigism is "one idea" — an aristocracy of talent, or the conservatism of the moneyed interest. The two old parties are most emphatically based on "one idea." Not so, however, the native American. Our great object is to attain to unity of national character; and as necessary to that end, we embrace every measure and policy decidedly American, or that can, in the most remote degree, contribute to establish the national character. We go for everything American in contradistinction to everything foreign. That, too, may be called "one idea"; but it is a glorious idea. . . .

Is our Constitution placed above the danger of subversion by the influx of that horde of aliens who combine to break down its barriers that they may command in the citadel, or overrun the land? And do you propose to stifle inquiry on questions like these, and then, in justification of your anti-American course, tell us that we belong to a party of "one idea"? Yes, sir; we have one great leading idea on all great questions involving free institutions, as well as national policy, which, when traced to its roots, or followed out in all its ramifications, is found to embrace the perfection of every science and principle, every art and scheme of life that stamps man as an immortal and responsible being. Other parties, sir, may boast their 10,000 ideas of imbecility and corruption. We boast of but one; and that one, thank God, is honest, wise, benevolent, comprehensive; and last, not least, American. But, even on the supposition that we aimed at but one idea — the extension of the naturalization law to twenty-one years — still that would not subject us to the imputation of one idea; for such a law involves more ideas than some of our opponents appear able to comprehend. . . .

The gentleman from Alabama has likened our cause to that of Abolition. Is this charge just? Is it true? Abolition seeks to overthrow an institution which exists under the Constitution, and which Abolition is willing to overleap. Native Americanism seeks to defend every institution that exists under that glorious Constitution, which we venerate as the ark of our political covenant. Surely the gentleman from Alabama has not been made acquainted with the origin of the native American movement in that state which I have the honor to represent in part.

A foreign demagogue addresses a political missive to a certain body of so-called American citizens, banded together as a distinct political organization, and tells them *"Where you have the elective franchise, giv your votes to none but those who will assist you in carrying out the intentions"* — of what? The American Constitution? Oh, no! Of what? American freedom? Oh, no! But poll your votes to carry out the intentions of a foreign despot who aims at the overthrow of American institutions. Was it a crime, sir, for native Americans to repel this aggression, and proclaim to the world that no foreign potentate, or agent, or demagogue, should invade the constitutional rights of any portion of our American population?

And now, sir, when we propose to erect bulwarks in defense of American rights, American institutions, and the American Constitution, a spurious appeal is made in behalf of the banded foreign legion, and we are asked to substitute the liberal spirit of the Declaration of American Independence for the venerated charter of our republican rights. This suggestion has long since been made by the demagogue of Europe to whom I have alluded, and I blush to find it reechoed on our republican shores. By which document are we bound as citizens of these United States? The Declaration of American Independence is an exposition of the rights of man, which applies to the whole human family. The Constitution is a settled system of government for the American people only. The cry raised here of natural rights, under an organized government, is little better than the ravings of insanity. Natural rights are the offspring of revolution, that struggle through anarchy to settled system of law. Nations have a natural right to independence, but individuals under an organized government can claim no rights not embraced in their legal institutions. Life, liberty, and the pursuit of happiness, are recognized, defined, and limited by the law.

All such fallacies produce mischief, Mr. Speaker, and none more than that which supposes naturalization to be a right, a boon, or a favor granted to the alien. No alien has a right to naturalization; neither is it granted as a boon. We grant it in self-defense as a protection to American institutions; it is one of the political fortifications of our free system of government; it is a Bunker Hill entrenchment to repel foreign assault. Exclusion is the original object of naturalization — not admission to citizenship; for, if that were the object, we should have no naturalization laws; in which case, all foreigners would become American citizens the moment they landed on our shores. To prevent this universal admission to citizenship, we frame naturalization laws, and prescribe forms that operate as a check upon the interference of foreigners in our institutions. . . .

Mr. Speaker, all that I have said has been drawn from me by the latitude that has been given to this debate, which ought to have been confined to the naked question of *reference*. I have avoided touching upon the merits of the main question, which we ask to bring in proper form to the consideration of the House, and which, I repeat, a select committee will alone enable us to accomplish. Will the House permit us to place before the nation such records, drawn from the proper departments, as will show that, unless some remedy be applied to this great and growing evil, THE DAY IS NOT FAR DISTANT WHEN THE AMERICAN-BORN VOTER WILL FIND HIMSELF IN A MINORITY IN HIS OWN LAND! Or will you continue to tell us that because we are not as liberal as we might be to foreign ignorance and foreign crime, you will shut out this appeal, which comes up to you in all its freshness from the hearts of the American people? . . .

Sir, I disclaim all pretensions to "liberality" on this question, in which lies coiled up the future happiness or misery of millions of unborn American citizens. We are now struggling for national character and national identity, and not for the meed of courtesy, or the extent of a generous disposition.

We stand now on the very verge of overthrow by the impetuous force of invading foreigners. Europe can no longer contain the growing population that is swelling her to bursting. She must disgorge it at any price, no matter what. Each hour will behold this tide of foreign immigration, rising higher and higher, growing stronger and stronger, and rushing bolder and bolder. . . .

If the heart of the alien is in his native land — if all his dearest thoughts and fondest affections cluster around the altar of his native gods — let us not disturb his enjoyments by placing this burden of new affections on his bosom, through the moral force of an oath of allegiance, and the onerous obligation of political duties that jar against his sympathies, and call on him to renounce feelings that he can never expel from his bosom. Let us secure him the privilege at least of mourning for his native land, by withholding obligations that he cannot discharge either with fidelity, ability, or pleasure. Give him time, sir, to wean himself from his early love. Why should he not, like our own sons, enjoy twenty-one years of infant freedom from political cares, to look around him, grow familiar with the new scene in which he finds himself placed — become acquainted with all the new and intricate relations by which man is made a

sovereign by the voice of his fellowman, and yet still retains all the responsibilities of the citizen, even while he exercises all the power of a monarch.

A long list of innumerable duties will engage all his attention during his political novitiate, in addition to those comprised in reforming the errors and prejudices of the nursery, and in creating and forming new opinions, congenial to the vast field which lies spread before him in morals, politics, and life. A due reflection will convince every alien, when his passions are not inflamed by the insidious appeals of selfish demagogues, that his highest position is that of a moral agent in the full enjoyment of all the attributes of civil freedom, preparing the minds and hearts of his children to become faithful, intelligent, and virtuous republicans, born to a right that vindicates itself by the holy ties of omnipotent nature, and which, while God sanctions and consecrates, no man can dispute.

We, as native Americans, and the people of these United States, as patriots and republicans, have now attained that climax of foreign influence, when to pause in our onward career of reforming the abuse that subjects us to the degradation is to surrender forever the high dignity of moral independence, and the peculiar exalted, distinctive character of a homogeneous nation.

———————◆———————

The best business you can go into you will find on your father's farm or in his workshop. If you have no family or friends to aid you, and no prospect open to you there, turn your face to the great West and there build up your home and fortune.

HORACE GREELEY, *To Aspiring Young Men*, 1846; often quoted as "Go West, young man, and grow up with the country"

1846

69.

Robert C. Winthrop: The Oregon Question

In 1846 a resolution directing the President to give Great Britain a year's notice (as required by conventions of 1818 and 1827) before terminating joint occupancy of the Oregon Territory was debated in Congress. In a speech delivered on January 3 and reprinted here in part, Robert C. Winthrop, a Whig representative from Massachusetts, argued against the resolution. The Whigs were willing to accept a British settlement of the disputed Oregon boundary along the 49th parallel. But Western Democrats, who had helped elect President Polk in 1844, now proclaimed "Fifty-four forty or fight" and clamored for acquisition of the whole territory. Although the Democrats succeeded in passing the resolution in a modified form, the boundary was amicably settled along the 49th parallel by a treaty proclaimed on June 15.

Source: *Globe, App.*, 29 Cong., 1 Sess., pp. 98-101.

I AM PERFECTLY AWARE, Mr. Speaker, that, express the views which I entertain when I may, I shall not escape reproach and imputation from some quarters of the House. I know that there are those by whom the slightest syllable of dissent from the extreme views which the administration would seem recently to have adopted will be eagerly seized upon as evidence of a want of what *they* call patriotism and American spirit. I spurn all such imputations in advance. I spurn the notion that patriotism can only be manifested by plunging the nation into war, or that the love of one's own country can only be measured by one's hatred to any other country. Sir, the American spirit that is wanted at the present moment, wanted for our highest honor, wanted for our dearest interests, is that which dares to confront the mad impulses of a superficial popular sentiment, and to appeal to the sober second thoughts of moral and intelligent men. Every schoolboy can declaim about honor and war, the British lion and the American eagle; and it is a vice of our nature that the calmest of us have heartstrings which may vibrate for a moment even to such vulgar touches.

But (thanks to the institutions of education and religion which our fathers founded), the great mass of the American people have, also, an intelligence and a moral sense which will sooner or later respond to appeals of a higher and nobler sort, if we will only have the firmness to make them. It was a remark of an old English courtier, a century and a half ago, to one who threatened to take the sense of the people on some important question, that he would take the *nonsense* of the people and beat him twenty to one. And it might have been something better than a good joke in relation to the people of England at the time it was uttered. But I am not ready to regard it as applicable to our own intelligent and educated American people at the present day. An appeal to the nonsense of the American people may succeed for an hour; but the stern sense of the country will soon reassert itself, and will carry the day in the end.

But, Mr. Speaker, there are other reproaches, beside those of my opponents, to which I may be thought to subject myself, by the formal promulgation of the views which I entertain on this subject. It has been said, in some quarters, that it was not good party policy to avow such doctrines; that the friends of the administration desire nothing so much as an excuse for branding the Whigs of the Union as the peace party; and that the only course for us in the minority to pursue is to brag about our readiness for war with those that brag loudest. Now, I am entirely sensible that if an opponent of the present administration were willing to make a mere party instrument of this Oregon negotiation, he might find in its most recent history the amplest materials for throwing back upon the majority in this House the imputations in which they have been heretofore so ready to indulge.

How easy and obvious it would be for us to ask: Where, where, was the heroic determination of the executive to vindicate our title to *the whole of Oregon* — yes, sir, "THE WHOLE OR NONE"— when a deliberate offer of more than 5° of latitude was recently made to Great Britain? Made, too, at a moment when the President and his secretary of state tell you that they firmly believed that our right to the whole was clear and unquestionable! How easy it would be to taunt the secretary of state with the policy he has pursued in his correspondence, of keeping back those convincing arguments upon which he now relies to justify him in claiming the whole of this disputed territory, until his last letter — until he had tried in vain to induce Great Britain to accept a large part of this territory — as if he were afraid to let even his own country understand how good our title really was in case he could succeed in effecting a compromise!

For myself, however, I utterly repudiate all idea of party obligations or party views in connection with this question. I scorn the suggestion that the peace of my country is to be regarded as a mere pawn on the political chessboard, to be periled for any mere party triumph. We have seen enough of the mischief of mingling such questions with party politics. We see it at this moment. It has been openly avowed elsewhere, and was repeated by the honorable member from Illinois (Mr. Douglas) in this House yesterday, that Oregon and Texas were born and cradled together in the Baltimore Convention; that they were the twin offspring of that political conclave; and in that avowal may be found the whole explanation of the difficulties and dangers with which the question is now attended.

I honor the administration, Mr. Speaker, for whatever spirit of conciliation, compromise, and peace it has hitherto manifested on this subject, and have no hesitation in saying so. If I have anything to reproach them with, or taunt them for, it is for what appears to me as an unreasonable and precipitate abandonment of that spirit. And if anybody desires on this account, or any other account, to brand me as a member of the peace party, I bare my bosom, I hold out both my hands to receive that brand. I am willing to take its first and deepest impression, while the iron is sharpest and hottest. If there be anything of shame in such a brand, I certainly glory in my shame. . . .

But who, who is willing to bear the brand of being a member of the war party? Who will submit to have that Cain mark stamped upon his brow? I thank heaven that all men, on all sides, have thus far refused to wear it. No man, of ever so extreme opinions, has ventured yet to speak upon this question without protesting, in the roundest terms, that he was for peace. Even the honorable member from Illinois, who was for giving the notice to quit at the earliest day, and for proceeding at once to build forts and stockades, and for asserting an exclusive jurisdiction over the whole Oregon territory at the very instant at which the twelve months should expire, was as stout as any of us for preserving peace. My venerable colleague [Mr. Adams], too, from whom I always differ with great regret, but in differing from whom on the present occasion I conform not more to my own conscientious judgment than to the opinions of my constituents, and of a great majority of the people of Massachusetts, as I understand them — he, too, I am sure, even in that very torrent of eloquent indignation which cost us for a moment the order and dignity of the House, could have had nothing but the peace of the country at heart. So far as peace, then, is concerned, it seems that we are all agreed. "Only it must be an honorable peace"; that, I think, is the stereotyped phrase of the day; and all our differences are thus reduced to the question: What constitutes an honorable peace?

Undoubtedly, Mr. Speaker, the answer to this question must depend upon the peculiar circumstances of the case to which it is applied. . . . I maintain —

1. That this question, from its very nature, is peculiarly and eminently one for negotiation, compromise, and amicable adjustment.

2. That satisfactory evidence has not yet been afforded that no compromise which

the United States ought to accept can be effected.

3. That, if no other mode of amicable settlement remains, arbitration ought to be resorted to; and that this government cannot relieve itself from its responsibility to maintain the peace of the country while arbitration is still untried.

I perceive, sir, that the brief time allowed us in debate will compel me to deal in the most summary way with these propositions, and that I must look to other opportunities for doing full justice either to them or to myself. Let me hasten, however, to do them what justice I may.

There are three distinct views in which this question may be presented, as one peculiarly for negotiation and compromise. In the first place, there is the character of the subject matter of the controversy. Unquestionably there may be rights and claims not of a nature to admit of compromise, and as to which there must be absolute and unconditional relinquishment on one side or the other, or a conflict is inevitable. I may allude to the impressment of our seamen as an example — a practice which could not be renewed by Great Britain at any moment, or under any circumstances, without producing immediate hostilities.

But here we have, as the bone of our contention, a vast and vacant territory, thousands of miles distant from both countries, entirely capable of division, and the loss of any part, I had almost said of the whole, of which, would not be of the smallest practical moment to either of them — a territory the sovereignty of which might remain in abeyance for a half century longer without serious inconvenience or detriment to anybody, and in reference to which there is certainly not the slightest pretense of a necessity for summary or precipitate action. We need ports on the Pacific. As to land, we have millions of acres of better land still unoccupied on this side of the mountains. What a spectacle it would be, in the sight of men and angels, for the two countries which claim to have made the greatest advances in civilization and Christianity, and which are bound together by so many ties of nature and art, of kindred and of commerce, each of them with possessions so vast and various, to be seen engaging in a conflict of brute force for the immediate and exclusive occupation of the whole of Oregon! The annals of barbarism would afford no parallel to such a scene!

In the second place, sir, there is the character of the *title* to this territory on both sides. I shall attempt no analysis or history of this title. I am certainly not disposed to vindicate the British title; and as to the American, there is nothing to be added to the successive expositions of the eminent statesmen and diplomatists by whom it has been illustrated. But, after all, what a title it is to fight about! Who can pretend that it is free from all difficulty or doubt? Who would take an acre of land upon such a title as an investment without the warranty of something more than the two regiments of riflemen for which your bill provides? Of what is the title made up? Vague traditions of settlement, musty records of old voyages, conflicting claims of discovery, disputed principles of public law, acknowledged violations of the rights of aboriginal occupants — these are the elements — I had almost said the beggarly elements — out of which our clear and indisputable title is compounded. I declare to you, sir, that as often as I thread the mazes of this controversy, it seems to me to be a dispute as to the relative rights of two parties to a territory, to which neither of them has any real right whatever; and I should hardly blame the other nations of the world for insisting on coming in for scot and lot in the partition of it. Certainly, if we should be so false to our character as civilized nations as to fight about it, the rest of Christendom would be justified, if they had the power, in treating us as we have always treated the savage tribes of our own continent, and turning us both out altogether. . . .

Mr. Speaker, there is a third, and, in my judgment, a still more conclusive reason for regarding this question as one for negotiation and compromise. I refer to its history, and to the admissions on both sides which that history contains. For thirty years this question has been considered and treated as one not of *title* but of *boundary*. To run a boundary line between Great Britain and the United States from the Rocky Mountains to the Pacific Ocean — this has been the avowed object of each successive negotiation. It has been so treated by Mr. Monroe, and Mr. Adams, and Mr. Gallatin, and Mr. Rush, and by all the other American statesmen who have treated of it at all. Offers of compromise and arrangement have been repeatedly made on both sides on this basis. Three times we have offered to Great Britain to divide with her on the 49th parallel of latitude, and to give her the navigation of the Columbia into the bargain. Mr. Polk and Mr. Buchanan themselves have acted upon the same principle up to the moment of the final abrupt termination of the negotiations. They have offered again to make the 49th parallel the boundary line between the possessions of Great Britain and the United States in the Northwestern Territory. With what face, then, can we now turn round and declare that there is no boundary line to be run, nothing to negotiate about, and that any such course would involve a cession and surrender of American soil! Such a course would be an impeachment of the conduct of the distinguished statesmen whose names I have mentioned. It implies an imputation upon the present President of the United States and his secretary of state. And, explain it as we may, it would be regarded as an unwarrantable and offensive assumption by the whole civilized world. . . .

I am under no particular obligation to

vindicate the course of the present administration. But, as an American citizen, without regard to party and with a single eye to the honor of my country, I would indignantly repel the idea that our government, in whosoever hands it might be, could be guilty of so scandalous and abominable an act as that which has now been imputed to it by one of its peculiar defenders. But the honorable member admits that any man of common sense must have understood that the minister of Great Britain would refuse the offer which was thus made (hypocritically made, as he believes,) and would refuse it precisely as it has been refused, without even transmitting it across the water. What, then, becomes of all the indignation which has been expressed and implied by the administration and its friends, from the secretary of state downward, at the rejection, and more particularly at the manner of the rejection, of that offer?

Robert C. Winthrop (1809-1894); Brady photo

Why, it seems, after all, that the honorable member and myself are not so very far apart. This admission of his is entirely in accordance with the view which I have already expressed, that if any compromise whatever was to be made (and I rejoice to find that even the chairman of the Committee on Foreign Affairs has this morning emphatically denominated himself a *compromiser*) the rejection of this precise offer does not authorize us to leap at once to the conclusion that "no compromise which the United States ought to accept can be effected." If our government has thus far made no offer, except one which "any man of common sense might have known would be rejected precisely as it has been," I trust it will bethink itself of making another hereafter, which will afford to Great Britain a less reasonable pretext for so summary a proceeding.

But, Mr. Speaker, it is certainly possible that, with the best intentions on both sides of the water, all efforts at negotiating a compromise may fail. It may turn out hereafter, though I deny that it is yet proved, that no compromise which the United States ought to accept can be effected. What then? Is there no resort but war? Yes, yes; there is still another easy and obvious mode of averting that fearful alternative. I mean *arbitration*; a resort so reasonable, so just, so conformable to the principles which govern us in our daily domestic affairs, so conformable to the spirit of civilization and Christianity that no man will venture to say one word against it in the abstract. But then we can find no impartial arbiter, say gentlemen; and, therefore, we will have no arbitration. Our title is so clear and so indisputable that we can find nobody in the wide world impartial enough to give it a fair consideration! . . .

If there be a jealousy of crowned heads, why not propose a commission of civilians? If you will put no trust in princes, there are profound jurists, accomplished historians, men of learning, philosophy, and science, on both sides of the water, from whom a tribunal might be constituted, whose decision upon any question would command universal confidence and respect. The venerable Gallatin (to name no other American name), to whose original exposition of this question we owe almost all that is valuable in the papers by which our title has since been enforced, would add the crowning grace to his long life of patriotic service by representing his country once more in a tribunal to which her honor, her interests, and her peace might safely be entrusted. At any rate, let us not reject the idea of arbitration in the abstract; and, if the terms cannot be agreed upon afterward, we shall have some sort of apology for not submitting to it. General Jackson, sir, did not regard arbitration as a measure unfit either for him or his country to adopt. Indeed, it is well understood that he was so indignant at the king of Holland's line not being accepted by us that he declined to take any further steps on the subject of the Northeastern boundary.

I cannot but regret, Mr. Speaker, that the President, in making up an issue before the civilized world, upon which he claims to be relieved from all responsibility which may follow the failure to settle this question, has omitted all allusion to the fact that arbitration on this subject of Oregon has been once solemnly tendered to us by Great Britain. I am willing, however, to put the very best construction on this omission of which it is susceptible, and to believe that the President desired to leave himself still uncommitted upon this point. Without some such explanation, it certainly has a most unfortunate and disingenuous look. This omitted fact is, indeed, enough to turn the scale of the public judgment upon the whole issue. Arbitration offered by Great Britain, and perseveringly rejected by us, leaves the responsibility for the preservation of peace upon our own shoulders. The administration cannot escape from the burden

of that responsibility; and a fearful responsibility it is, both to man and to God! . . .

I am ready to go as far as Great Britain has gone in establishing our jurisdiction there; and no interest, either of those who are going there, or of those who are staying here, calls on us to go further at present. The best interests of both parties, on the contrary, forbid any such proceeding. Gentlemen talk about following up this notice by taking immediate possession of the territory. This is sooner said than done. What if Great Britain should happen to get the start of us in that proceeding? Such a thing would not be matter of very great astonishment to those who remember her celerity in such movements, and her power to sustain them when once made. Where should we be then? Would there be no war?

And what would be the consequences of a war under such circumstances — the consequences, not upon cotton or upon commerce, not upon Boston or Charleston or New York, but what would be the consequences so far merely as Oregon itself is concerned? The cry is now, "the whole of Oregon or none," and echo would answer, under such circumstances, *"none!"* I see not how any man in his senses can resist the conviction that, whatever compensation we might console ourselves with, by a cut out of Canada, or by the whole of Canada — that under whatever circumstances of success we might carry on the war in other quarters of the world or of our own continent, the adoption of such a course would result in the immediate loss of the whole of the territory in dispute. This, at least, is my own honest opinion.

As a friend, then, to Oregon, with every disposition to maintain our just rights to that territory, with the most sincere desire to see that territory in the possession of such of our own people as desire to occupy it — whether hereafter as an independent nation, as was originally suggested by a distinguished senator from Missouri [Mr. Benton] and more recently by a no less distinguished senator from Massachusetts [Mr. Webster] or as a portion of our own widespread and glorious republic — I am opposed to the steps which are now about to be so hotly pursued. . . .

But while I am thus opposed to war for Oregon, or to any measures which, in my judgment, are likely to lead to war, I shall withhold no vote from any measure which the friends of the administration may bring forward for the defense of the country. Whether the bill be for two regiments or for twenty regiments, it shall pass for all me. To the last file, to the uttermost far-thing which they may require of us, they shall have men and money for the public protection. But the responsibility for bringing about such a state of things shall be theirs, and theirs only. They can prevent it if they please. The peace of the country and the honor of the country are still entirely compatible with each other. The Oregon question is still perfectly susceptible of an amicable adjustment, and I rejoice to believe that it may still be so adjusted. We have had omens of peace in the other end of the Capitol, if none in this. But if war comes, the administration must take the responsibility for all its guilt and all its disgrace.

70.

Anonymous: California and the National Interest

President Polk's California policy was partly based on his fear that if the United States did not quickly acquire California, Great Britain would. In the fall of 1845 Polk directed his confidential agent in California, Thomas Larkin, to encourage sentiment there for a voluntary union with the United States, and dispatched John Slidell to Mexico with an offer to purchase the area. President Herrera of Mexico, who was disposed to reestablish relations with the United States, had agreed, in October 1845, to receive a "commissioner," but in December, bowing to public opposition, refused to grant Slidell an audience on the pretext his appointment had not been confirmed. Within the United States the desire to acquire California was widespread, and the following article, reprinted in part from a Whig journal, the American Review, *was one of many evaluations of the California question.*

Source: *American Review,* January 1846: "California."

LETTERS FROM WASHINGTON, on which we rely, render it probable that Mr. Slidell, our newly appointed minister to Mexico, goes clothed with power to treat with that government for the cession of California to the United States. The intelligence is vague, but we trust it is true, and that the negotiation may prove successful. The natural progress of events will undoubtedly give us that province just as it gave us Texas. Already American emigrants thither are to be numbered by thousands, and we may, at almost any moment, look for a declaration, which shall dissolve the slight bonds that now link the province to Mexico, and prepare the way for its ultimate annexation to the United States.

Regarding, therefore, the accession of California as an event which present tendencies, if not checked or counteracted, must render inevitable, we should prefer to see it accomplished by an agency, at once more direct and less questionable in point of national morality. It cannot be disguised that we stand open to the charge of having colonized Texas, and recognized her independence, for the express purpose of seizing her soil — that we wrested her territory from Mexico, peacefully and by a gradual process, to be sure, but as really and as wrongfully as if we had conquered her by arms in the field of battle. It cannot but be, at least, suspected that the grounds of the revolution which made Texas independent of the central state lacked those essential elements which alone redeem rebellion from crime, and justify the disruption of those political bonds which constitute a state — that no overwhelming necessity for such a step existed — and that the reasons assigned, where not palpably false, were unsound and frivolous. We were not slow to recognize this independence, nor to avail ourselves of it, to transfer to ourselves that sovereignty which had thus been annulled.

It will be impossible, under all the circumstances of this transaction, to persuade the world that these events had no connection with each other, either in fact or in the intentions of our government which, directly or indirectly, gave vigor and success to them all. Until the memory of this achievement shall have somewhat faded, we do not desire to see the experiment renewed. If we are to have a further accession of territory, we hope to see it effected by an open purchase and a voluntary cession. Thus did we come in possession of Florida, including the Oregon dispute, and on terms which the

country, we believe, thus far at least, does not deem extravagant. Texas, it seems not at all unlikely, may yet cost us more than would in the beginning have bought it outright; and California, it may fairly be presumed, may now be purchased, at least *nemine contradicente,* for a sum which the country will deem small for so valuable an acquisition.

For, certainly, we do regard it as extremely desirable that California — a part, at least, of the province known by that name — should become the property, and remain forever under the exclusive jurisdiction, of the United States. Lower California, as it is called, embracing the long, narrow peninsula between the Gulf and the Pacific, stretching from the 21° to 33° latitude, a distance of above 800 miles, with an average breadth of about 60, is universally represented by travelers as sterile and hopelessly desolate. It consists, indeed, of a chain of volcanic, treeless, barren mountains of rock, broken only by still more dreary plains of sand, destitute of streams, swept by fierce tornadoes, and of necessity abandoned almost entirely to sterility and desolation.

Scattered spots now and then occur where the torrents of rain have not washed away the soil, or where, being surrounded by rocks on every side, it has been protected from those influences which have made the peninsula, on the whole, the most uninhabitable region of the northern temperate zone. These, however, are neither frequent enough nor large enough to redeem, or relieve, the general character of the country; and Lower California must always remain an undesirable possession for any country, except one that sways a barren scepter and to which extent, not fertility, of territory seems attractive. It may well, therefore, be left to Mexico.

With Upper California the case is different. The southern and eastern portions — indeed nearly the whole province except that part bordering on the Pacific — is scarcely more valuable than the lower province. Through the eastern section extends the chain of the Rocky Mountains, broken into fragments, and converting a wide space of the country, through its entire length, into a waste perfectly uninhabitable, producing very little vegetation, and through which the traveler, with danger and difficulty, finds a casual and precarious path. West of this chain lies a vast, sandy plain, nearly 700 miles in length, with a width of 100 miles at its southern, and 200 at its northern, extremity. The whole valley of the Colorado is utterly barren, and is described by an American traveler as a great burial place of former fertility, which can never return.

Like its branches the river is not navigable. The Gila, which forms the southeastern boundary of the province, is a rapid stream, and its upper portion flows through rich and beautiful valleys, capable of supporting a numerous population. In the center of the northern section of Upper California lies the Timpanigos Desert, between 400 and 500 miles square, and probably the most utterly desolate region of so great an extent upon the western continent. On its northwest border Mary's River takes its rise, and flows southwestwardly about 160 miles, into its own lake, which is about 60 miles in length, and half as wide. The valley of the stream has a rich soil, which, were not the atmosphere too dry, would be well adapted to agricultural purposes, and contains many fine groves of aspen and pine, that shelter deer, elk, and other game.

The remaining part of Upper California — that which lies nearest the Pacific coast — is not only by far the best portion of the province but one of the most beautiful regions on the face of the earth. It embraces the whole country drained by the waters which empty into the Bay of San Francisco. These are, first, beginning at the south, the San Joaquin, which rises in a lake called Bonavista, in latitude 36°, and about 300

miles northwest of the mouth of the Colorado; it runs thence, northwest some 600 miles, with a deep and tranquil current, navigable for 250 miles above its mouth, and through a valley 600 miles in length, and from 40 to 100 in width; bounded on every side by mountains, which thus enclose a prairie surface, covered with trees which skirt the streams, of above 40,000 square miles in superficial extent.

Among the highlands which enclose this valley are vast forests filled with the loftiest and finest cedars and pines in the world, with every variety of soil, freshwater lakes, and every element of unbounded agricultural wealth, except a propitious climate. From November to March the whole valley is flooded by heavy and incessant rains; and from April until autumn an intolerable heat converts this vast fen of stagnant waters into a valley of the Shadow of Death. This evil, however, it is confidently asserted, is susceptible of an easy remedy by draining these accumulated waters into the river. . . .

Here, then, lies upon the Pacific coast, adjoining our western border, included between the parallels which embrace the southern sections of the United States and stretching northward to the southern boundary of Oregon, a region of country capable of sustaining a greater population than now inhabits the entire American Union. Traversed, through its entire length and from its most remote corners, by noble rivers all concentrating their waters, and forming at their common mouth, the finest harbor perhaps in the world; abounding in timber of the best quality for shipbuilding and all naval purposes, easily floated to a common point, and that the beautiful and capacious harbor of San Francisco, containing measureless waterpower, immense agricultural resources, and all the elements which nature can furnish of national wealth and national consequence — it is yet shut out from the influences of Christian civilization and abandoned to a people who neither know its capacities, nor feel the pressure of any obligation to develop and expand them.

The aggregate population is probably below 20,000. The harvested crops in 1839 amounted to 69,000 bushels of wheat, 22,000 of maize, and 15,000 of barley; and the whole annual merchantable production of the country, including cattle and furs, its staple commodities, is estimated by Captain Wilkes at less than $1 million. Nor is there anything in the history of the country to induce the hope that under its present control it will ever attain that position, and serve those ends in the great scheme of the world's civilization, for which Providence has so clearly designed it. . . .

No one who cherishes a faith in the wisdom of an overruling Providence, and who sees, in the national movements which convulse the world, the silent operation of an invisible but omnipotent hand, can believe it to be for the interest of humanity, for the well-being of the world, that this vast and magnificent region should continue forever in its present state. Capable of sustaining millions of people, of conferring upon them all the physical comforts of life, and of raising them to the highest point of mental and moral cultivation, if only they have the energy and the ability to use its resources — so long as desolation broods upon it, so long as the shadows of ignorance, indolence and moral degradation hang around it — the manifest designs of Providence are unfulfilled, and the paramount interests of the world lack due advancement. While California remains in possession of its present inhabitants and under control of its present government, there is no hope of its regeneration. This will demand a life, an impulse of energy, a fiery ambition of which no spark can ever be struck from the soft sluggishness of the American Spaniard. . . .

California, to become the seat of wealth and power for which nature has marked it, must pass into the hands of another race.

And who can conjecture what would now have been its condition, had its first colonists been of the stock which peopled the Atlantic coast? . . .

It seems to us improbable that a government marked and swayed by Mexican temper, which persisted against the advice and example of the leading nations of the earth in refusing to recognize the independence of Texas for a long series of years of enforced inaction; which has, from first to last, charged upon the United States the robbery and despoilment of the fairest of her possessions, should now, so soon after the obnoxious deed is finally and fully accomplished, manifest even an intemperate eagerness to resume with us friendly relations, and to negotiate for a boundary upon so liberal a basis as she is said to have proposed. We fear these measures are but the fair-seeming dictates of a "necessity of present life."

They have already relieved her seaboard from the presence of our squadron, and her Texan frontier from the pressure of our troops. They have averted, or at least deferred, a blow against which she had found it impossible to interpose the shield of British power, and have released her from the fatal necessity of engaging, single-handed, the power of the United States. Of such a struggle the result has repeatedly been predicted in Europe. The French *Journal des Débats* has declared that "the conquest of Mexico would be a wide step toward the enslavement of the world by the United States, and a levy of bucklers by the Mexicans *at this moment* would lead the way to this subjection." The London *Times* remarks that Mexico has had the sagacity to perceive that a declaration of war would enable the United States to seize upon and retain the Mexican territory. These views were doubtless enforced upon the Mexican administration by the representatives of both France and Great Britain; and the result has been that all thought of immediate war has passed away.

Meantime, a negotiation has been set on

foot with Great Britain for the cession of California, and is "now in progress." Suppose it to be successful, and the British power to be planted in the Bay and around the tributary waters of San Francisco. Will not the European powers be then in a condition to attempt to reduce to practice the theory of M. Guizot, that "the integrity of existing powers in America must be maintained"? "Between the autocracy of Russia on the East, and the democracy of America, aggrandized by the conquest of Mexico on the West," says the *Journal des Débats,* the official paper of the French government, "*Europe may find herself more compressed than she may one day think consistent with her independence and dignity.*"

It cannot be disguised that apprehensions of the future power of the American people are arousing the fears and influencing the policy of the principal nations of Europe. The leading journal of Great Britain but a few days since, declared that "no European politician can look forward to the power of the United States, within the present century, but with the most *appalling* prospects." And so the Paris *Débats* remarks that "for the political balance of the world, the conquest of Mexico by the United States may create eventual dangers, which, although distant, it may not be superfluous to *guard against.*"

And so again, upon another occasion, the same official journal employed this still more emphatic language:

A cry of war between America and Mexico has been raised; although it is not believed that the threats will be followed by acts, yet it would be well for us to be prepared for anything. North America presents her ambitious plans for conquering all the American continent. She began by the annexation of Texas, by which she divides Mexico, and a war will give her a welcome pretense for possessing herself of all Mexico. Soon the smaller states will follow, and the Isthmus of Panama fall into the hands of North America. *Europe should not tolerate this,* NOR SUFFER NORTH AMERICA TO IN-

CREASE, or the independence of Europe might sooner or later be wedged in by the two colossuses of Russia and North America, and suffer from their oppression.

It seems well-nigh incredible that any or all the European powers should seriously resolve upon measures to prevent and check the growth, in power and influence, of the United States. To the casual observer we seem to be so far removed from them, the ocean that rolls between us seems so broad, as to stifle and destroy that envy and jealousy which, under other circumstances, might ripen into displeasure and end in open and effective hostility. But further reflection, we apprehend, will weaken the force of these considerations. The affairs of the whole world are, in many very important respects, linked and even fused together. Commerce, which has come to be the ruling power upon this globe, makes its home upon the broad sea that knows no bounds — its familiar paths are upon the world's great highways; and it knows comparatively little, in its highest and most far-reaching relations, of those national limits which divide, and therefore weaken, the aggregate of human power.

That nation of the earth which has most power, upon land and sea, must have over every other, and over all others, advantages, the weight of which no distance from them can ever seriously impair. Supremacy of this kind long enjoyed will never be readily yielded; nor can any prospect, however remote, that it will be snatched away by some vigorous and growing competitor fail to be met with discontent which may ripen into scowling defiance and open hostility. These considerations, and others which must readily occur to everyone upon slight reflection, must remove or at least modify the incredulity with which the chance of European intervention for the purpose, whether avowed or not, of checking and fixing limits to the growth of American power, is very naturally received. . . .

The existence of this feeling among the sovereigns of Europe toward this country cannot be cloaked by honied diplomatic assurances of distinguished consideration, nor disproved by angry or contemptuous denial. We look upon it as a fact — a *fixed fact* — which must have weight in any speculations that claim to be intelligent, concerning our present and future foreign relations. We have introduced it here for the purpose of saying that Mexico cannot be ignorant of its existence, and that, in our judgment, she intends, with more of wisdom than we have given her credit for, to make it serviceable in "feeding fat the grudge" she bears us.

She cannot lack the sagacity to perceive that, with Great Britain firmly fixed in California, she could not engage in war with the United States without a certainty, or, at the least, a very strong probability of having Great Britain for an active ally. This is an object worthy her endeavor. It is one likely, we fear, to be attained through the "negotiation now in progress for the adoption of a frontier parallel," on her northern border, deemed, by Great Britain, *"necessary to British interests."* Should it prove successful, our government, we fear, will find reason to regret its forbearance in not having regarded the declarations and acts of Mexico, consequent upon the annexation of Texas, as, in fact declarations of war against a portion of the American Union, and thus forcing her to a speedy and final adjustment of all points of disagreement.

We deem it impossible that Great Britain should expect to occupy California, either as a colony or "somewhat in the manner of the East India Company," with the acquiescence or indifference of the United States. In no spot upon the continent could she establish her power where it could be so effectually wielded to our lasting injury. It can scarcely be doubted that the Pacific Ocean is hereafter to bear upon its bosom a far greater commerce than now floats upon the Atlantic. Whatever may be its relation to Europe, to the United States, it is destined to be the highway to Asia, the avenue to the unbounded wealth of the "gorgeous East." . . .

With this port for her naval depot, Great Britain would indeed be *mistress of the seas,*

——— not for a day, but for all time!

An armed squadron, sailing thence, by a single blow could sink millions of American property, seize upon tens of thousands of our citizens, sweep our commerce, and drive our flag from the Pacific seas. With California in that part of our dominions, Canada upon our northern frontier, Halifax overhanging our northeastern coast, a portion of the West India Islands whence to hurl her brands of open war, and her infernal enginery for exciting civil contention, in our southern section, with Mexico for an ally, and her ports as *points d'appui* for assailing our southern and southwestern cities, she would certainly have enfolded us as completely in her net as the bloodiest intentions of extermination could possibly desire!

Such a consummation, we venture to say, and England must know, can never be effected with the acquiescence, or without the utmost possible resistance, on the part of the United States.

Uncle Joshua always says, in nine cases out of ten it costs more to rob an orchard than it would to buy the apples.
SEBA SMITH ("MAJOR JACK DOWNING"), to General Pierce, of the Mexican War

71.

ABBOTT LAWRENCE: A New England View of Tariffs

*New England businessmen generally favored high tariffs as a protection for home
industries. The free trade policies of the Polk administration were not at all to their
liking. The special target of New England animosity was Secretary of the Treasury
Robert J. Walker, who had set forth the administration's policies in his report for 1845.
To counter the free-trade program, Massachusetts manufacturer Abbott Lawrence
wrote a series of letters to former Senator William C. Rives of Virginia. These
letters reached the public through publication in the* Richmond Whig. *But neither the
South nor the West could be persuaded to support New England protectionist goals, and
the Walker Tariff was passed, establishing a trend toward free trade that lasted until
the Civil War. One letter from Lawrence to Rives, dated January 16, 1846, is reprinted here.*

Source: *Letters from the Hon. Abbott Lawrence to the Hon. William C. Rives,
of Virginia,* Boston, 1846, pp. 8-23.

I STATED IN MY LETTER of the 7th that I should write to you again upon the subject of the entire change proposed by the President of the United States, and the secretary of the treasury, in our revenue laws. It is no other than the adoption of ad valorem for specific duties, and a reduction of the whole to 20 percent; this being the maximum at which the secretary supposes the largest revenue can be obtained. I shall not now discuss the rates of duty that will produce the greatest amount of revenue. I will leave the secretary to settle that question; but shall endeavor to show what the effect will be upon the country if his recommendation should be adopted by Congress.

I deem the scheme proposed to Congress, in the main, a *currency* question, and one which, if carried out, will reach, in its operation, the occupation and business of every man in the United States. I believe the most economical member of Congress will agree that $30 million will be required, annually, to carry on this government, for the next five years, and that this estimate does not include large sums that may be wanted to settle our affairs with Mexico, Texas, etc.; and that this sum is to be raised from foreign importations and the public lands.

The goods, subject to duty, imported the last year, amounted, in round numbers, to $90 million, and the goods free of duty to about $25 million. I have not the returns at hand, and may not be exactly correct as to amounts, but they are near enough to illustrate my arguments. The former paid an average duty of about 32 percent, creating a revenue, say of $28 million. If the revenue derived from an importation of $90 million gave $28 million, what amount must be imported, to produce the same sum at 20 percent ad valorem?

The answer is, $140 million. Add to this the free goods, about $25 million, and we have an importation of $165 million. Our exports have not exceeded, nor are they likely at present to exceed $120 million; we then have a deficit of $45 million to provide for; and how is this balance to be paid? State stocks are no longer current in Europe. Even the stocks of the United States cannot be negotiated on favorable terms.

We who are merchants can answer this question, having often been obliged to make our remittances in coin when our imports have exceeded our exports.

If we are obliged to import $140 million of goods subject to duty to meet the wants of the government, it is quite certain that the coin must be exported to meet the deficiency. If the importations fall short of $140 million, we then have an empty Treasury. In one case, the country will be made bankrupt to fill the Treasury; and, in the other, the Treasury will be bankrupt and resort to Congress for Treasury notes and loans. It may be said that our exports will increase with our imports; this supposition I think fallacious.

The policy of Great Britain, and that of all Europe, has been, and is likely to continue, to protect everything produced either at home or in their colonies. In Great Britain, the article of cotton is now admitted free, the duty having been repealed the very last year. This was owing to repeated representations of the Manchester spinners to Parliament as to the necessity of such a measure, in consequence of the competition from foreign countries in the coarse fabrics manufactured from cotton produced in, and shipped from, the United States. The argument presented in the House of Commons was that the Americans had taken possession of every market where they were admitted on the same terms with their coarse goods. This is a true representation, and I apprehend the repeal of the duty on cotton

will not enable the British manufacturer to again obtain possession of those markets for the heavy descriptions of cotton fabrics.

What other article of importance does the government of Great Britain admit free of duty? I know of none. Cotton is admitted free of duty from necessity. How is it with tobacco? A duty is paid of 1,200 percent. Wheat is prohibited by the "sliding scale," and, in case of a total repeal of the Corn Laws, very little wheat would be shipped from this country, inasmuch as it can be laid down, in ordinary years of harvest, much cheaper from the Baltic. Beef and pork are burdened with a heavy duty. The duty and charges on a barrel of American pork laid down in Liverpool, with the commissions for sales, amount to $5.75; so that the quantity of this article shipped to England must be inconsiderable, unless the prices here should be so low as to be ruinous to the farmer.

I cannot find in the catalog of our strictly agricultural products a single article that is not burdened with a high duty in England, or other parts of Europe, if it comes in competition with their own products; nor can I discover that there is a disposition on the part of a single European nation to relax the stringent system of duties on imports from this country. It is possible that Great Britain may abate her Corn Laws so far as to admit Indian corn at a nominal duty. If it should be done, I have little faith in our being able to ship it to advantage.

I state the fact, then, that exports will not increase in consequence of a reduction, or even a total repeal, of the present tariff. The duty in Great Britain, on all the products of the United States received in that Kingdom, including cotton, is not less than 48 percent, and, exclusive of cotton, 300 percent; and this, too, on raw produce, generally, where the charge of freight constitutes from one-tenth to one-quarter of the cost here — and this is *free trade!*

I hope you of Virginia will examine this

matter and ask yourselves where the best customers are to be found for your agricultural products. I will just state to you here that Massachusetts takes annually more flour, Indian corn, pork, and many other articles, the productions of the West, as well as of Virginia, than all Europe.

The question then arises, what will be our condition after the proposed plan of low duties goes into operation? In twenty days after the bill becomes a law, it will have reached every country in Europe with which we have trade. The manufactories are all set in motion for the supply of the American market; the merchandise is shipped on account of foreigners, in many cases with double invoices; one set for the customhouse and another for the *sales,* so that instead of the duty amounting to 20 percent, it will not, probably, exceed 15 percent. This has been the experience of the American importers in New York, who, previously to the passage of the tariff of 1842, had (most of them) abandoned the business, not being able to compete successfully with fraudulent foreigners. I will not say that all foreigners commit frauds on the revenue — far from it; but I do say that enormous frauds have been perpetrated by foreigners on the revenue, under ad valorem duties, and will be again, prostrating the business of honest foreign and American importers.

In less than twelve months after the new plan shall have been in operation, this whole country will be literally surfeited with foreign merchandise (if it be not so, the revenue will fall short of the wants of the government); we shall then owe a debt abroad of millions of dollars, which must be paid in coin. The exchanges go up to a point that makes it profitable to ship specie; money becomes scarce in the Atlantic cities; yet bills on England and France do not fall; the loans made to the South and West are called in; demands for debts due from those sections of country are made; exchange

cannot be obtained; produce is purchased and shipped; and when it arrives at the North, it will not command the cost in the West.

A paralysis will have struck the business of the country; produce will no longer answer to pay debts due at the North, and the next resort is to coin, which is to be collected and sent down the Mississippi, or over the mountains, to Baltimore, Philadelphia, New York, and Boston. Western and Southern credits are cut off, as the people of those sections can no longer promptly meet their engagements. The new states and the outer circle of the republic are the weak points; and the first giving way of the banks is heard from those places where there is the least amount of capital.

We see the storm approaching like a thundershower in a summer's day; we watch its progress but cannot escape its fall. It at last reaches the great marts of trade and the exchanges, having swept everything in its course; and the banks of the Atlantic cities, after a violent effort to maintain their credit and honor, are forced to yield to this utopian experiment on the currency. I have no hesitation in stating that all this will take place within the space of eighteen months from the time this experimental bill goes into operation; and not a specie-paying bank, doing business, will be found in the United States.

Where will be the revenue which was to produce such a mighty sum under low duties? Where is the Treasury and the secretary and the President and his cabinet? The Treasury is empty; the secretary is making his estimates of income for 1849, and preparing to ask Congress for a large *batch* of Treasury notes; or perhaps the deficit is so large that a loan may be required.

We have now come to a point of depression in the great business of the country which has attracted the attention and anxiety of all classes of people, *all* having felt its blight, excepting the great capitalists and money holders, who are reaping golden harvests by the purchase of property, which the wants of the unfortunate throw into the market at ruinous rates. It is now seen and felt from the low wages of labor and the great number of persons unemployed, with the cries of distress from all quarters that it is the labor and not the capital of the country that suffers by violent revulsions caused by unwise legislation. Have the people of the South and West forgotten their troubles of 1837 to 1842, to the hour of the passage of that law, which has redeemed the credit of the government and restored prosperity to the country.

I have intimated that there is less capital in the new states than in many of the old ones; it will not be denied that the moneyed capital of this country is held in the Northern and Eastern states, and that the South and West are usually largely indebted to them. Now, I should be glad to be informed what benefit is to be derived by a planter in Alabama or Mississippi, or a farmer in Ohio or Illinois, by a change like that I have described, particularly, if by chance, he should be in debt? Do the people of the South believe they can raise the price of cotton, or be able to negotiate loans, to prosecute the construction of their contemplated railroad? Do Ohio, Louisiana, Illinois, Michigan believe they are to create a better market for their produce, or sooner complete the harbors, so much desired on the shores of those "Inland Seas," and be able to negotiate loans and obtain subscribers to the stock of their intended railroads, by the adoption of this new system of political economy?

And now what say the *great states* of New York and Pennsylvania to this proposed experiment? Can they afford to try it, and are they ready? If they are, it will be adopted; if they are not, the present law will stand and the country will repose for awhile in happiness and prosperity. Anyone would suppose that those states that are now just emerging from embarrassment, which at one time seemed almost sufficient to overwhelm them in ruin, would be unwilling to try an experiment which is certain, in my judgment, to place them in a position that will be the means of destroying the fair prospects of thousands who are resting in quiet security upon the faith of what they deem a paternal and wise government.

The question of an important alteration in our revenue laws should not be kept in suspense. The Treasury will feel its effects before the end of the present year. The expectation of a great reduction of duties prevents the merchants from going on with their usual business. Voyages are delayed and orders for goods are held back until this important question shall be settled. I say, therefore, if we are to go through this fiery ordeal, let it come at once. We cannot probably place ourselves in a better condition than we are now to meet the troubles that await us.

Mr. Walker proposes to substitute ad valorem for specific duties, in opposition to our own experience and that of almost every other country. I have never yet found an American merchant who has not been in favor of specific duties, wherever it can be done with convenience to the importer and the government. I confess it is a bold measure to propose a total and entire change of a revenue system which was established with the government, and has stood the test of experience through all the trials of political parties and administrations, from General Washington to Mr. Polk. It appears more extraordinary at this time, as the country is in a high state of prosperity. The revenue is enough for all the reasonable wants of the government, and the people appear to be satisfied with their condition.

The resources of the country were never developing more rapidly; the increase of our population, the present year, will probably equal that of the last, which I estimate at

600,000 souls; our wealth too has been wonderfully augmented by the construction of railroads; there has been a great increase of our shipping engaged in the domestic commerce of the country, not only by sea but upon our rivers and Great Lakes. The manufacturing interest has been largely extended; and the soil, too, has been made to produce vastly more than at any former period. The whole productive power of the country has been greater in three years (that is, since the passage of the tariff of 1842) than during any equal space of time in our national history.

There have been three periods of universal distress throughout our land since the peace of 1783, and in each case under low duties. I appeal to those who remember those periods; and to others, I refer to the annals of our country. Those periods were from 1783 (the conclusion of the Revolutionary War) to 1789, 1815 to 1824, 1837 to 1842.

I would respectfully recommend to the secretary of the treasury, who appears to have received new light upon the subject of our national economy, to examine the history of the legislation of Congress at the above periods. He will find in his own department of the government abundant evidence of the distress that existed under low duties and a deranged currency.

There is a prevalent idea abroad that the capital of the country will suffer exceedingly by a revulsion in its business, and that the tariff of 1842 has operated in favor of the capital and not the labor of the country. There can be no doubt that capital is generally profitably and safely employed, and well paid. The profits of capital are low when wages are low; but capital has usually had the power to take care of itself, and does not require the aid of Congress to place it in any other position than to put the labor in motion. Congress should legislate for the labor, and the capital will take care of itself. I will give you an example of

the rate of wages under low duties and under the tariff of 1842. In 1841 and 1842, the depression in all kinds of business became so oppressive that many of the manufacturing establishments in New England were closed, the operatives dismissed, the mechanical trades were still, and every resource for the laboring man seemed dried up.

In the city of Lowell, where there are more than thirty large cotton mills, with from 6 to 16,000 spindles each, it was gravely considered by the proprietors whether the mills should be stopped. It was concluded to reduce the wages; this was done several times, until the reduction brought down the wages from about $2.00 to $1.50 per week, exclusive of board; this operation took place upon between 7,000 and 8,000 females. The mills run on; no sales were made of the goods; the South and West had neither money nor credit; and, finally, it was determined to hold out till Congress should act upon the tariff. The bill passed, and of course the mills were kept running, which would not have been the case if the act had been rejected; and now the average wages paid at Lowell, taking the same number of females for the same service, is $2.00 per week, exclusive of board. Yet Mr. Walker says labor has fallen. Where are the wages for labor, I ask, lower than they were in 1842? Who is to be benefited by the adoption of a system that gives up everything and gives no reasonable promise of anything?

I have succeeded, I trust, in showing that there is no probability of our exports increasing in consequence of a reduction of the tariff, and that the products of the Western states find the best market among the manufacturers at home. In regard to the Southern and cotton-growing states, they are to be greatly benefited by the increase of consumption of their staples at home. No appreciable quantity can be shipped to England if the tariff should be repealed, it being already free of duty. The establishment and successful prosecution of the spinning of cotton in this country has enabled the planters to obtain, for several years past, at least an additional cent per pound on the whole crop, and perhaps even more.

The Americans are the greatest spinners of cotton in the world, the British excepted. The competition has kept the price from falling to a ruinous point on several occasions, and it has been acknowledged by many of the most intelligent planters in the South. Our consumption reached, the last year, 176 million pounds, which is equal to the whole crop of the Union in 1825, and equal to the whole consumption of Great Britain in 1826. This is a striking fact, and one that should be remembered by the planters.

The history of the production and manufacture of cotton is so extraordinary, that I propose to send to you some statistics on the subject, furnished me by a friend. I hope you will not deem me oversanguine when I tell you that it is my belief that the consumption of cotton in this country will double in eight or nine years, and that it will reach 400 million pounds in 1856; and, further, that we are not only destined to be the greatest cotton growers but the most extensive cotton spinners in the world. We have all the elements among ourselves to make us so.

The manufacture of cotton is probably in its infancy; but a moderate portion of mankind have yet been clothed with this healthful and cheap article. Nothing can stop the progress of this manufacture but some suicidal legislation that will prostrate the currency of the country and deprive the people of the means of consuming. There can be no legislation that will break down the manufacture of cotton and wool excepting through the operations of the currency. We may be disturbed by low duties; the finer descriptions of cotton and woolens, printed goods, and worsted fabrics would be seri-

ously affected by low ad valorem duties; but the coarser fabrics, such as are generally consumed by the great body of the people, will be made here under any and all circumstances. If we have competition from abroad, the labor must and will come down; this has been often tested and our experience establishes the fact.

In Virginia and other Southern states, and even at the West, many persons have believed that the protective system was made by and for New England, and that New England, and particularly Massachusetts, could not thrive without it. Now, this is an error; the South and West began the system of high protective duties for the purpose of creating a market for their produce (although the principle of discrimination was recognized and established when the first tariff was enacted). It is not true that we are more dependent on a protective tariff than the Middle, Western, or Southern states. Those states that possess the smallest amount of capital are the most benefited by a protective tariff.

We have in New England a great productive power; in Massachusetts, far greater than any other state in proportion to population. We have a hardy, industrious, and highly intelligent population, with a perseverance that seldom tires; and we have also acquired a considerable amount of skill, which is increasing everyday. Besides this, we have already accomplished a magnificent system of intercommunication between all parts of this section of the country by railroads; this is the best kind of protective power, having reduced the rate of carriage to a wonderful extent. This being done, we have money enough remaining to keep all our labor employed and prosecute our foreign and domestic commerce without being in debt beyond the limits of our own state.

Now, I ask how *we* shall stand, compared with Pennsylvania, Ohio, Alabama, Georgia, or Louisiana, when the day of financial trial shall come. I do not deny we shall suffer, but as it has been in times past, we shall go into and come out of the troubles far stronger than any other state out of New England. It is not my purpose to present to you the balance sheet of Massachusetts, but it is due to her character and her dignity that she should stand before you in her true position. I have never advocated a protective tariff for my own or the New England states exclusively, nor have those gentlemen with whom I have been associated in this cause at any time entertained a narrow or sectional view of the question. We have believed it to be for the interest of the whole country that its labor should be protected, and so far as I have had to do with the adjustment of those difficult combinations embraced in a tariff bill, I have endeavored to take care that the interests of all the states were protected, whether they were large or small. I say now to you, and it should be said in Congress and to the country, that Massachusetts asks no exclusive legislation.

If Pennsylvania, New York, and Ohio, the three great states, with Kentucky, Georgia, Missouri, Alabama, and Louisiana, wish to try an experiment on iron, coal, hemp, cotton bagging, sugar, etc. I am ready, as one citizen of Massachusetts, to meet it and await in patient submission the result, which I doubt not will be found, within eighteen months, in the realization of all I have predicted. I say again, I would not, if I could, have a tariff made for Massachusetts alone. If, however, there should be a new one, let *our* interests, with those of every other in the Union, share that protection to which we are all entitled, and of which *we* claim our *full* share. I can with confidence assure you that we shall go upward and onward. *We will work.* If twelve hours' labor in the twenty-four will not sustain us, we can, and will work fourteen; and at the same time feel that Congress cannot take the sinews from our arms, or rob us of the intelligence acquired from our

public schools, established by the foresight and wisdom of our fathers.

At the risk of writing a long letter, I cannot forbear alluding to the fact that the habitual agitation of this question of the tariff has worked, in the main, to the advantage of New England.

We were, previous to the War of 1812, an agricultural and navigating people. The American system was forced upon us and was adopted for the purpose of creating a home market for the products of the soil of the South and West. We resisted the adoption of a system which we honestly believed would greatly injure our navigation and drive us from our accustomed employments into a business we did not understand. We came into it, however, reluctantly, and soon learned that, with the transfer of our capital, we acquired skill and knowledge in the use of it; and that, so far from our foreign commerce being diminished, it was increased, and that our domestic tonnage and commerce were very soon more than quadrupled.

The illustrations were so striking in every department of labor that those who, fifteen years ago, were the strongest opponents of the protective tariff among us, have given up their theories and acknowledged that the revelations are such as to satisfy the most skeptical. We have gone forward steadily, till many descriptions of manufactures are as well settled in New England as the raising of potatoes. Our experience has given us skill; and, of course, we have confidence in our own resources that does not exist elsewhere.

When I converse with gentlemen from the South and West respecting the establishment of manufactures, they reply that they should long ago have engaged in them, but the repeal of the tariff, the action of the government, prevented them. Now you cannot blame us if this constant agitation of the tariff question has tended to give New England not a monopoly but advantages which she has not been instrumental in bringing about. I have no doubt we have been gainers, on the whole, by these agitations, yet we have at times been great sufferers. I wish those states that have withheld their energies from entering upon these industrial pursuits to examine this matter, and, if I am right, to *take an observation and a new departure.*

We have no jealousy, whatever, concerning the establishment of manufactories in all parts of the country; on the contrary, I believe those gentlemen from the South and West who have been here will bear witness to the desire on the part of the people who are engaged in manufactures to impart all the information in their power; there is room for us all. When the Southern and Western states shall manufacture their own clothing, we shall have become extensive exporters of the variety of manufactures

produced here. We have the ships and the men to navigate them. We shall pursue an extensive foreign commerce with manufactures and bring home the produce of other countries, such as coffee, tea, etc., and pay for the produce of the South and West with foreign luxuries and necessaries of life. . . .

To place the people in a condition of permanent and solid prosperity, we must encourage home industry by obtaining the greatest amount of production; this can only be obtained by diversifying labor, which will bring with it high wages; and, unless the labor is well paid, our country cannot prosper. Agriculture, the foundation of all wealth, depends on production and a market for those products. The encouragement of agriculture is found in the establishment of manufactures, which if maintained, will be certain to secure a market.

72.

JOHN C. CALHOUN: Against General Resolutions on Foreign Affairs

On December 2, 1845, President Polk had restated the Monroe Doctrine in terms appropriate to the prevailing sense of Manifest Destiny that had helped elect him to office. On January 14, 1846, Senator William Allen of Ohio, chairman of the Senate Foreign Relations Committee, introduced a resolution designed to commit Congress to the principles laid down by Monroe and Polk. Twelve days later in a debate with Senator Lewis Cass of Michigan, John C. Calhoun, who had been a member of Monroe's Cabinet in 1823, inveighed against the resolution. The substance of his argument is given in the selection below.

Source: *Globe*, 29 Cong., 1 Sess., pp. 245-246.

Mr. Calhoun. We all remember the Holy Alliance to overthrow Bonaparte. England refused to join it, although she acted with it. In the process of time, the Holy Alliance contemplated an interference with the affairs of South America in order to restore

the dominion of Spain over her revolted provinces. Our government received an intimation from Mr. Canning, who was then at the head of the British Ministry — a man of extraordinary sagacity and talent — stating at the same time that if the American

overnment would back the British government, she would discountenance such inter-
erence. And this general declaration had
eference to a specific case, and stopped
here.

Mr. Monroe was a wise man, and had no
lesign of burdening the country with a task
vhich it could not perform. He knew there
vas a broader declaration made by the gen-
leman then secretary of state. As far as my
nowledge extends, it was never brought
orward for cabinet deliberation. It has been
long time since, and I will not be positive.
have no doubt that the gentleman to
vhom reference has been made is entitled
o the paternity. I say so, because out of
his grew the Panama Convention, although
t was not legitimately an offspring. But if
his declaration was right, the Panama Con-
ention was no bad conception, and the
ropriety of our sending a minister could
ardly be resisted. It was a more sensible
orm of carrying out a broad proposition.

But Mr. President, you and all the older
enators know what would have been the
esult. If, when we were called on, we had
aid we would join Great Britain against
he rest of the world, we would have been
peedily called on to act. I did, when the
roposition first came up, give my assent to
:; but, after reflection, thought that it had a
ernicious effect elsewhere, and would have
t now. I made no opposition to this in
onsequence of a deference to Great Britain
r the other European powers, but a defer-
nce to ourselves. Our own good sense
hould teach us that we ought not to un-
ertake what we cannot perform. It should
e so with individuals and with nations. By
he adoption of the principle of the resolu-
ion, we would be called on to interfere
vhenever a European nation, right or
vrong, should bring on a conflict of arms
etween one or another nation on this con-
inent. I would ask the senator from Michi-
an, where is the limitation?

Mr. Cass. Will the gentleman allow me

to explain? The principle for which I contend is this: By such a declaration as that
contemplated in the resolution, we would
merely place our protest on record, not being thereby bound to any definite course of
action but being left free to maintain neutrality or actively engage in enforcing the
principle, as we might see fit.

Mr. Calhoun. Well, would it not be better to wait for the emergency in which we
would have sufficient interest to interfere,
and sufficient power to make that interference influential? Why make any such declaration now? What good purpose can it
serve? Only to show to the men that are to
come after us that we were wiser and more
patriotic than we feared they might be! I
cannot, for my life, see a single good likely
to result from this measure. . . .

Will mere vaporing bravado have any
practical effect? No. You must adopt a very
different course of policy. You must arm,
equip, fit out your navies, raise a powerful
revenue, and resist them by practical measures, if you think proper to resist them.
Will not the effect of such a declaration be
the very reverse of all this practical course
of policy? Will it not create jealousy on the
part of England? Will it not militate against
the formation of alliances on the part of nations favorably disposed toward us? No
good effects can come from it. From first to
last, in my opinion, it will be followed by
unqualified evil consequences. In this spirit
I resisted it on a former occasion; in this
spirit I resist it now. . . .

As to Texas, Mr. President, as far as I
had any share in the management of that
particular question, I can only say that the
declaration of Mr. Monroe had not the
weight of that piece of paper; and if a thousand such declarations, in even stronger
terms, had been made and passed the Senate, they would not have had that weight.
Declarations, sir, are easily made. The affairs of nations are not controlled by mere
declarations. If a declaration of opinion
were sufficient to change the whole course

of events, no nation would be more prompt than we.

But we must meet interference in our affairs in another way. We must meet it as it was met in the case of Texas — decidedly, boldly, and practically. We must meet each particular case by itself, and according to its own merits, always taking care not to assert our rights until we feel ourselves able to sustain our assertions. As to general abstract declarations of that kind, I would not give a farthing for a thousand of them. They do more harm than good, or rather no good at all, but a great deal of harm.

73.

ANONYMOUS: Vote Yourself a Farm

"Vote yourself a farm" was the motto of the National Reform Association, an organization of agrarians founded by George Henry Evans in 1844. A small but vociferous group, the association backed politicians who agreed to support its policies and wielded a strong influence in various trade unions. Although the association broke up in the 1850s after Evans died, its motto was used until 1862 when a homestead bill was finally passed. The appeal reprinted below was originally circulated as a handbill, and subsequently reprinted in Evans' newspaper.

Source: *True Workingman*, January 24, 1846 [Commons, VII, pp. 305-307].

ARE YOU AN AMERICAN CITIZEN? Then you are a joint owner of the public lands. Why not take enough of your property to provide yourself a home? Why not vote yourself a farm?

Remember Poor Richard's saying: "Now I have a sheep and a cow, everyone bids me 'good morrow.' " If a man have a house and a home of his own, though it be a thousand miles off, he is well received in other people's houses; while the homeless wretch is turned away. The bare right to a farm, though you should never go near it, would save you from many an insult. Therefore, vote yourself a farm.

Are you a party follower? Then you have long enough employed your vote to benefit scheming office seekers; use it for once to benefit yourself. Vote yourself a farm.

Are you tired of slavery, of drudging for others, of poverty and its attendant miseries? Then, vote yourself a farm.

Are you endowed with reason? Then you must know that your right to life hereby includes the right to a place to live in, the right to a home. Assert this right so long denied mankind by feudal robbers and their attorneys. Vote yourself a farm.

Are you a believer in the Scriptures? Then assert that the land is the Lord's because He made it. Resist then the blasphemers who exact money for His work even as you would resist them should they claim to be worshiped for His holiness. Emancipate the poor from the necessity of encouraging such blasphemy. Vote the freedom of the public lands.

Are you a man? Then assert the sacred rights of man, especially your right to stand upon God's earth and to till it for your own profit. Vote yourself a farm.

Would you free your country and the sons of toil everywhere from the heartless, irresponsible mastery of the aristocracy of avarice? Would you disarm this aristocracy of its chief weapon, the fearful power of banishment from God's earth? Then join with your neighbors to form a true American party, having for its guidance the principles of the American Revolution, and whose chief measures shall be: (1) to limit the quantity of land that any one man may henceforth monopolize or inherit; and (2) to make the public lands free to actual settlers only, each having the right to sell his improvements to any man not possessed of other land. These great measures, once carried, wealth would become a changed social element; it would then consist of the accumulated products of human labor instead of a hoggish monopoly of the products of God's labor; and the antagonism of capital and labor would forever cease.

Capital could no longer grasp the largest share of the laborer's earnings as a reward for not doing him all the injury the laws of the feudal aristocracy authorize, viz., the denial of all stock to work upon and all place to live in. To derive any profit from the laborer, it must first give him work; for it could no longer wax fat by levying a dead tax upon his existence. The hoary iniquities of Norman land pirates would cease to pass current as American law. Capital, with its power for good undiminished, would lose the power to oppress; and a new era would dawn upon the earth and rejoice the souls of a thousand generations. Therefore, forget not to vote yourself a farm.

74.

ANONYMOUS: Work, Wealth, and Free Land

Among the German immigrants who came to America in the 1840s were German communists seeking political asylum in the New World. One communist immigrant, Hermann Kriege, organized the Social Reform Association, a group of workingmen who collaborated with the National Reform Association, led by George Henry Evans, in promoting agrarian reform. Unlike Evans, Kriege regarded land reform as an initial step toward the eventual overthrow of capitalism. In January 1846, Kriege established the German language Volks Tribun *in New York as the organ of the Social Reform Association. An article from the May 9, 1846, issue is reprinted below in translation.*

Source: *Volks Tribun* (New York), May 9, 1846 [Commons, VII, pp. 92-93].

WHILE HARDHEARTED ARISTOCRATS of this country may, with suppressed rage, look forward to the new arrivals, who in ever greater numbers land on these shores from Germany, and while even German editors may try to represent to the overtimid workingmen this increasing immigration as a misfortune, all staunch republicans in America will receive the distressed fugitives with open arms; for they know that whoever has been compelled by the oppression of despotism to leave his native hearth must become a valuable support to democracy.

But if, indeed, all these poor workingmen were destined to be in each other's way in the cities, if they could not be given the means to support themselves and families by the work of their hands and to assist in producing general prosperity, then we might well shed hot tears at each incoming immigrant ship; for each would bring so much new misery and new sorrow, each would decrease the wages and raise the price of provisions. And what would become of us in the end? Would we not miserably starve in spite of democracy and republicanism?

Self-willed people, as you are, will you then never learn to comprehend that you have the means in your hands to help yourselves and all the unfortunate immigrants at the same time? Will you never learn to realize that you need not starve so long as you still have something to eat, and that you can get plenty to eat so long as you have uncultivated land and hands to cultivate it? Grow wise at last and use your sound sense to make yourselves happy. Hold fast what you have, and do not let the last remnant be stolen away before your eyes, for truly you have been robbed enough. Say to the speculators, "Hands off of our land; what is still ours shall be ours, and from now on we shall reserve it for honest labor and free use. We know now that we cannot satisfy our hunger with your bank notes; we need other means of sustenance and these must be produced; therefore we shall keep the soil so that we may be assured that we will not become your bondmen!"

If once the soil is free, then every honest workingman who leaves his old home in order to lead a happier life in the free air on this side of the ocean becomes a blessing to our republic, and we shall be able to welcome every immigrant ship with a thousand guns; for work gives abundance, and the more producing hands, the more wealth.

75.

"Elanoy"

Transportation companies, speculators in Western land, and underpopulated Western communities all advertised in the East for settlers. Not infrequently, the areas they promoted were likened to paradise. The author of the following song contrasted the promise with the reality in the state of Illinois.

ELANOY

Way down upon the Wabash, such land was never known;
If Adam had passed over it, the soil he'd surely own.
He'd think it was the garden he played in as a boy,
And straight pronounce it Eden in the state of Elanoy.

'Twas here the Queen of Sheba came, with Solomon of old,
With a donkey load of spices, pomegranates and fine gold.
And when she saw this lovely land, her heart was filled with joy,
Straightway she said, "I'd like to be a queen in Elanoy."

She's bounded by the Wabash, the Ohio and the Lakes,
There's crawfish in the swampy lands, the milk-sick and the shakes.
But these are slight diversions and take not from the joy
Of living in this garden land, the state of Elanoy.

Away up in the northward, right on the borderline,
A great commercial city, Chicago, you will find.
Her men are all like Abelard, her women like Heloise,
All honest virtuous people, for they live in Elanoy.

Chorus:
Then move your family westward, good health you will enjoy,
And rise to wealth and honor in the state of Elanoy.

76.

Walt Whitman: The Duty of a Government

*Walt Whitman, an ardent believer in democracy, delighted in the rough and tumble of
politics and actively supported radical reform Democrats and Free Soil advocates.
During the 1840s he lived in Manhattan and Brooklyn and worked for several local
magazines and newspapers. For two years, 1846 to 1848, he was editor of the*
Brooklyn Eagle. *This position enabled him to make public his views on a wide
variety of issues. It was open criticism of the Democratic Party's position on slavery
that eventually cost him his job, for the* Eagle *was a spokesman for Democratic
Party policy. Following is an editorial by Whitman published on April 4, 1846.*

Source: *Brooklyn Eagle*, April 4, 1846.

THE END OF ALL GOVERNMENT is the happiness of the whole community; and whenever it does not secure that, it is a bad government, and it is time it *was altered.* — *N.Y. Globe, March 28.*

We snip out this little paragraph from our New York contemporary because it affords us a chance of nailing a very wide though very foolish error. It is only the novice in political economy who thinks it the duty of government to *make* its citizens happy. Government has no such office. To protect the weak and the minority from the impositions of the strong and the majority, to prevent anyone from positively working to render the people unhappy (if we may so express it), to do the labor not of an officious intermeddler in the affairs of men but of a prudent watchman who prevents outrage — these are rather the proper duties of a government.

Under the specious pretext of effecting "the happiness of the whole community," nearly all the wrongs and intrusions of government have been carried through. The legislature may, and should, when such things fall in its way, lend its potential weight to the cause of virtue and happiness, but to legislate in direct behalf of those objects is never available and rarely effects any even temporary benefit. Indeed, sensible men have long seen that "the best government is that which governs least." And we are surprised that the spirit of this maxim is not oftener and closer to the hearts of our domestic leaders.

77.

Samuel J. May: The Enfranchisement of Women

When the Reverend Samuel J. May delivered his sermon, "The Rights and Condition of Women," to his New York congregation on November 8, 1846, the movement for women's rights had not yet been organized. When it was organized, a few years later, the notion that the suffrage should be extended to women was disputed so hotly even among females that the movement almost failed at its inception. The suggestion in May's sermon that the suffrage must be the ultimate goal of women was therefore a bold one. Male support for women's rights came mostly from Transcendentalists and Abolitionists, and May was prominent in the latter group.

Source: *The Rights and Condition of Women*, Syracuse, 1846.

ALLOW ME AGAIN TO SPEAK plainly to you of the rights and condition of women. My thoughts were urgently drawn to this subject last spring by the fact that, at that time, the people of this state were called, in their primary capacity, to decide whether the sale of intoxicating drinks should be licensed, a question of the highest personal, domestic, and social consequence; and yet more than half of the people, the women, were not only not expected but not allowed to influence directly a decision in which they were so much interested.

About the same time, the *men* of our nation presumed to plunge us into the multiform calamities, crimes, and expenditures of a war, without so much as consulting the women who will have to share equally, if not to endure the larger part of the losses and sufferings that are inevitable upon such a measure of folly and wickedness.

Again, during the past summer, a large convention of delegates, elected by the people of this state, have been in session at the capitol, framing a new constitution which is to affect as vitally the lives, liberties, properties, happiness of women as of men; and yet not a female was there to represent the interests of her sex; nor would one hardly suspect, from the document they have spread before their fellow citizens, that there were any women in the body politic. Nor is this all; but last Tuesday, when the constituents of that convention were called upon to signify whether they would ratify the new constitution, the women of New York were not expected, nor would they have been permitted, to say by their votes

hether or not they were willing to live
nder such a frame of government.

Now this is all unequal, all unrighteous,
his utter annihilation, politically considered,
f more than one-half of the whole community. It is a piece of assumption just as
gregious as it would be for the females to
all a convention, frame a state government,
nd go on to administer it by officers of
heir own choosing, without any recogni-
ion of the rights and hardly any of the ex-
stence even of our sex.

This entire disfranchisement of females is
s unjust as the disfranchisement of the
nales would be; for there is nothing in
heir moral, mental, or physical nature that
isqualifies them to understand correctly the
rue interests of the community or to act
isely in reference to them. . . .

To prove, however, that woman was not
ntended to be the equal of man, the argu-
ent most frequently alleged is that she is
he weaker vessel, inferior in stature, and
as much less physical strength. This physiological fact, of course, cannot be denied;
though the disparity in these respects is
ery much increased by neglect or misman-
gement. But allowing women generally to
ave less bodily power, why should this
onsign them to mental, moral, or social de-
endence? Physical force is of special value
nly in a savage or barbarous community.

is the avowed intention and tendency of
hristianity to give the ascendancy to man's
oral nature; and the promises of God,
ith whom is all strength and wisdom, are
 the upright, the pure, the good, not to
e strong, the valiant, or the crafty.

The more men receive of the lessons of
hristianity, the more they learn to trust in
od, in the might of the right and true, the
ss reliance will they put upon brute force.
nd as brute force declines in public esti-
ation, the more will the feminine qualities
 the human race rise in general regard and

confidence, until the meek shall be seen to
be better than the mighty, and the humble
only be considered worthy of exaltation.
Civilization implies the subordination of the
physical in man to the mental and moral;
and the progress of the melioration of the
condition of our race has been everywhere
marked by the elevation of the female sex.

But some would eagerly ask, should
women be allowed to take part in the constructing and administering of our civil institutions? Allowed, do you say? The very
form of the question is an assumption of
the right to do them the wrong that has
been done them. Allowed! Why, pray tell
me, is it from us their rights have been received? Have we the authority to accord to
them just such prerogatives as we see fit
and withhold the rest? No! woman is not
the creature, the dependent of man but of
God. We may with no more propriety assume to govern women than they might assume to govern us. And never will the nations of the earth be well-governed until
both sexes, as well as all parties, are fairly
represented and have an influence, a voice,
and, if they wish, a hand in the enactment
and administration of the laws.

One would think the sad mismanagement
of the affairs of our own country should, in
all modesty, lead us men to doubt our own
capacity for the task of governing a nation,
or even a state, alone; and to apprehend
that we need other qualities in our public
councils, qualities that may be found in the
female portion of our race. If woman be the
complement of man, we may surely venture
the intimation that all our social transactions will be incomplete, or otherwise imperfect, unless they have been guided alike
by the wisdom of each sex. The wise, virtuous, gentle mothers of a state or nation
(should their joint influence be allowed)
might contribute as much to the good order, the peace, the thrift of the body politic
as they severally do to the well-being of

Samuel J. May

their families, which for the most part, all know is more than the fathers do.

Even for the restraint of the unruly and the reformation of the vicious, women would be found to possess a power and a skill which far transcend the force and coarse appliances on which men are wont to rely. In support of this last supposition, I need only point you to Mrs. Fry in England, and to Mrs. Farnham and Miss Dix in our own country. These women have evinced a fortitude and courage, as well as a degree of sound sense, which very few men possess.

Undoubtedly some of you are ready to say to me, "Pray, would you have women public instructors, lecturing upon moral and political science, and haranguing the people upon their special duties as citizens?" Hear my reply. It is not for me, nor for us men, to prescribe the mode in which the women shall operate. Let us leave this to their own good sense and taste. There is a great deal of lecturing and haranguing that does not profit. Would that neither men nor women

should ever speak in public unless they have somewhat to say worth hearing. But if a valuable thought is suggested to anyone, I see not why that thought should be suppressed because it was started in the mind of a female. And if she to whom it has come has power to utter it and is moved so to do, I see not why she should be forbidden.

To me, it is as grateful to hear words of wisdom and eloquence from a woman as a man; and quite as uninstructive and wearisome to listen to a vapid, inane discourse from the one as from the other. I know not why silly men should be encouraged to speak more than silly women; nor why the wise of one sex should be forbidden, any more than the wise of the other, to communicate what they possess to those who may need it and in the manner they prefer. To whomsoever God has given the power to instruct and control others by their learning, their eloquence, or their wit, to them He has given the authority to do so. I have heard some women speak in a manner far more convincing and impressive than most men that I have known were able to; and so as amply to vindicate their right to stand up in the pulpit or the forum as teachers of men.

"Ah," say some, "would you then have women engage in the acrimonious contests of the political parties, attend the angry meetings, witness the passion, hear the ribaldry and abuse that are poured upon each other by the excited opponents; and be tempted perhaps to commit the same offenses themselves?" No. Surely not. Neither would I have *men* guilty of such indecorum, folly, and wickedness. If political meetings must needs be disgraced by such scenes, they ought not to be held; and those men who would attend them show that they are careless of their own moral health. It were no more unseemly, no worse anyway, for women to be thus defiled than for us men

We are called to be upright, pure, and holy beings as well as they. Propriety of conduct, courtesy of manners, purity of speech, delicacy, refinement, gentleness are just as becoming in one sex as the other.

For one, I do not allow it to be a matter of course that we men should be rough, violent, passionate, abusive, profane, obscene. It is unworthy of any man to be so. He is as much bound as a woman can be "to keep himself unspotted from the world," and to keep himself away from places where, and from persons by whom, he may be tempted to become thus vile. Is it not indeed a mortifying confession, one that we men ought to be ashamed to make, that political meetings are occasions from which the delicate and pure would shrink, and yet that we attend them?

Nay, more, friends, if it be true that they are such, if our primary political gatherings, at which the people are called to consider their true interests and duties, and to exercise their high prerogatives as a self-governing community, if these primary meetings are indeed such scenes that our mothers, wives, sisters, and daughters would be disgusted if not corrupted at them, may we not seriously apprehend that our civil institutions are unsound, rotten at the very core; and anxiously look about us for healing and purifying influences, from any quarter, to save us from the impending ruin?

The terms in which the two sexes are generally spoken of seem to imply that men must, of course, go forth, take part in the collisions of political party, pecuniary interest, or local concernment; get themselves careworn, perplexed, irritated, soured, angry; while women are to stay at home and prepare themselves, with all the blandishments of maternal, sisterly, conjugal, or filial affection, to soothe our irritated tempers, mollify the bruises we have received in our conflicts with other men, and so prepare us to strive with renewed resolution, and

bruise or get bruised again. Now this seems to me like a perfect caricature of the true business of life; and still more of the relation in which God has placed man and woman. . . .

If, therefore, there be any untoward influences in political, professional, or mercantile transactions *that cannot be withstood*, but necessarily harden the heart, blunt the moral sensibilities, and sour the temper, men ought to keep aloof from such intercourses no less than women; for goodness of heart is as indispensable to the well-being of the one as of the other. The preservation and growth of godliness in us should be with all the great object of life. For the sake of this, the sacrifice of everything else, if necessary, ought to be made.

It may sometimes, ay, often, be right that men and women should yield up their time, property, lives even, in the service of their country, much more in the cause of humanity. But it can never be required of either, under the moral government of God, to sacrifice their integrity, their purity, the health, the life of their souls. If, without this sacrifice, either men or women can render special service to the state or the nation, by private or public speech or action, they may, they ought so to do.

Here the question comes: "Would you have women leave their homes, neglecting their children and the duties of their households, that they may take part in the management of public affairs?" No; certainly not. No more would I encourage men to do this great wrong, as they too often do. The *family* is the most important institution upon earth. If the duties of father and mother were generally well discharged, there would be little of importance left for civil governments to take care of. The family, therefore, ought never to be neglected for the service of the state by the father any more than the mother.

Indeed, there is one reason why the father should be even more especially careful to make himself an object of reverence and deep affection to his children. In the Sacred Scriptures, in the preaching and conversations which children hear, and the religious instructions they receive, God is represented as the Father of the human family. Now they must, of course, get their ideas of a father from the character and conduct of the earthly parent who wears that name. If, therefore, he be not what the name imports, he will only obscure the Divine Being to the minds of his children. Whenever, therefore, public offices are incompatible with the faithful, kind, and wise discharge of domestic duties, they ought to be declined by the father no less than by the mother.

But where either men or women are without families; or where their children have come to years of discretion; or where they have such talent or tact that they can fulfill well all their parental obligations, and have time, wisdom, and strength to spare to the public use, they ought so to bestow them. It is as much the duty of women as of men to do this; and the institution or the custom of that community must be unwise, unnatural, unchristian that would forbid them thus to contribute to the commonweal. . . .

Women are coaxed, flattered, courted, but they are not respected by many men as they ought to be; neither do they respect themselves as they should. They are not regarded and treated as equals; nor do they claim to be. So long has this been the case, so long have they and we all been used to that organization of society in which they are assigned to an inferior place that most of us, and most too of themselves, acquiesce in the wrong as if it were right. But this does not make it so; nor avert the evil consequences which are flowing through society from the entire exclusion of the wisdom and virtue of half of mankind from the councils of state and the administrations of justice and mercy.

The intellectual and moral powers of the female sex generally are not half developed, because no adequate demands are made upon them. Excluded as they are from all direct influence in the decision of many of the greatest questions of social and national interest, they seldom take the trouble even to consider them; and so we lose the benefit we might derive from their perceptions of right, which are often clearer than our own. When we see what has been done for the redemption of mankind by the few women who have broken through the enclosure, in which custom would keep them, and have thought and spoken and written freely in behalf of humanity, we cannot repress the apprehension that states and nations are suffering immeasurably from that waste of intellect and moral sense which are expending themselves upon the inanities of fashion and the follies of personal or household display. . . .

Women are too dependent upon men. We have too much power over them; and they are often cruelly oppressed. See how pitifully their labors are requited. The disclosures that have been made of the incessant, wasting toils to which they are subjected, especially in or near large cities, for a compensation utterly insufficient to provide them amply with the bare necessaries of life; the degradation of their persons to which they are often driven by the pressure of absolute want; the ease with which the base, heartless seducer escapes the condemnation which his villainy deserves; and the unforgiving censure with which his victim is pursued — these disclosures alone are enough to show how unequal, how unfair is the dealing of our race with that portion which, if either, should be treated with the greater leniency, enough to show how false, hypocritical is much of the adulation that is bestowed on women. Can those men feel any proper respect for females who make them their drudges from morning to night, or who are willing to pay them the miserable pittances which they do, for labors that consume the livelong day and oft the sleepless night? Yes, about as much as the slaveholders feel for their slaves.

Again, as it respects education, that grand leveler as well as elevator of mankind, how much more liberal are the provisions which are made to give our sons than our daughters a generous culture in all the arts and sciences that open to the human soul perennial sources of high, pure satisfaction; and give to their possessor not only abilities for greater usefulness to others but multiplied means of self-subsistence. I know the majority of female children are so much more disposed to study and are so much quicker to learn than those of the other sex that there may be found in the community a greater number of pretty well-instructed women than of men. But let their thirst for knowledge be ever so ardent, let their powers of acquisition be ever so good, females are nowhere admitted into the highest seminaries of learning.

And even as it respects property, a due portion of which is in this life convenient for all, which the majority seem to regard as "the one thing needful," our being's end and aim, which therefore ought in all fairness to be made alike accessible to all — even as it respects property, women are nowhere allowed the same opportunities to acquire it, nor have they the same securities for its preservation.

Furthermore, the current literature of the day, the fashionable novels, the poetry, and the newspapers, are inimical to the independence and true welfare of women. These are continually intimating that *marriage* is indispensable to the respectability and usefulness of females. Not only the silliest jokes but often also the most cruel taunts are flung at "single" women. So that, in addition to the urgencies of pecuniary necessity, they are impelled by the dread of ridicule (of which strong and wise men often stand in awe) to rush into wedlock on the first opportunity, consenting it may be to the most ill-assorted alliances from which only sorrow and sin can flow.

These circumstances operate powerfully to depress and oppress women, to make them too dependent, to leave them at the mercy of men. And I do not believe their condition will be essentially improved until their rights are recognized as equal every way, nor until these are secured in the very framework of society.

I hope and pray that what has now been said may not fall to the ground. I have alluded to our new constitution as furnishing one evidence of the great social wrong against which I have now entered my earnest protest. That constitution, however, I consider a great improvement upon the present one. It contains several important provisions for the melioration of our social state. I voted for its adoption. I hope it will be ratified. But its defects should be noted, and all good men and true should do what they may to obtain a still more perfect basis of our civil fabric so soon as the people can be brought to feel the need of another revision. I fain would hope that, when next the people frame a constitution for this state, the stupendous fact will not be overlooked *that more than one-half of our population are females, to whom equal rights and equal privileges ought to be accorded.*

We hold these truths to be self-evident: that all men and women are created equal.

Seneca Falls Declaration of Sentiments, 1848

78.

JAMES RUSSELL LOWELL: War and Slavery

Below is reprinted the first in the series of poems that came to be called The Biglow
Papers. *The poem with its introduction was published in the* Boston Courier *on
June 17, 1846, about five weeks after war with Mexico was declared. The series was
continued for the duration of the war and was published as a single volume in 1848.
(A second series of* Biglow Papers *was written during the Civil War and published in
1867.) The Yankee dialect and pungent satire in conjunction with the topical theme
brought Lowell fame, and helped popularize the theory that the Mexican War was
instigated by a conspiracy of slaveholders headed by President Polk.*

Source: *The Biglow Papers*, Cambridge, Mass., 1848, pp. 1-12.

Mister Eddyter:

Our Hosea wuz down to Boston last week, and he see a cruetin Sarjunt a struttin round as popler as a hen with 1 chicking, with 2 fellers a drummin and fifin arter him like all nater. the sarjunt he thout Hosea hedn't gut his i teeth cut cos he looked a kindo's though he'd jest com down, so he cal'lated to hook him in, but Hosy woodn't take none o' his sarse for all he hed much as 20 Rooster's tales stuck onto his hat and eenamost enuf brass a bobbin up and down on his shoulders and figureed onto his coat and trousis, let alone wut nater hed sot in his featers, to make a 6 pounder out on.

wal, Hosea he com home considerabal riled, and arter I 'd gone to bed I heern Him a thrashin round like a short-tailed Bull in fli-time. The old Woman ses she to me ses she, Zekle, ses she, our Hosee's gut the chollery or suthin anuther ses she, don't you Bee skeered, ses I, he's oney amakin pottery [poetry] ses i, he's ollers on hand at that ere busynes like Da & martin, and shure enuf, cum mornin, Hósy he cum down stares full chizzle, hare on eend and cote tales flyin, and sot rite of to go reed his varses to Parson Wilbur bein he haint aney grate shows o' book larnin himself, bimeby he cum back and sed the parson wuz dreffle tickled with 'em as i hoop you will Be, and said they wuz True grit.

Hosea ses taint hardly fair to call 'em hisn now, cos the parson kind o' slicked off sum o' the last varses, but he told Hosee he didn't want to put his ore in to tetch to the Rest on 'em, bein they wuz verry well As thay wuz, and then Hosy ses he sed suthin a nuther about Simplex Mundishes or sum sech feller, but I guess Hosea kind o' didn't hear him, for I never hearn o' nobody o' that name in this villadge, and I've lived here man and boy 76 year cum next tater diggin, and thair aint no wheres a kitting spryer 'n I be.

If you print 'em I wish you'd jest let folks know who hosy's father is, cos my ant Keziah used to say it's nater to be curus ses she, she aint livin though and he's a likely kind o' lad.   EZEKIEL BIGLOW

Thrash away, you'll *hev* to rattle
　On them kittle drums o' yourn —
'Taint a knowin' kind o' cattle
　Thet is ketched with moldy corn;
Put in stiff, you fifer feller,
　Let folks see how spry you be —
Guess you'll toot till you are yeller
　'Fore you git ahold o' me!

Thet air flag's a leetle rotten,
　Hope it aint your Sunday's best; —
Fact! it takes a sight o' cotton
　To stuff out a soger's chest:
Sence we farmers hev to pay fer 't,
　Ef you must wear humps like these,
Sposin' you should try salt hay fer 't,
　It would du ez slick ez grease.

'T would n't suit them Southun fellers,
　They 're a dreffle graspin' set,
We must ollers blow the bellers
　Wen they want their irons het;
May be it's all right ez preachin',
　But *my* narves it kind o' grates,
Wen I see the overreachin'
　O' them nigger-drivin' States.

Them thet rule us, them slave-traders,
　Haint they cut a thunderin' swarth
(Helped by Yankee renegaders,)
　Thru the vartu o' the North!
We begin to think it's nater
　To take sarse an' not be riled;
Who 'd expect to see a tater
　All on eend at bein' biled?

Ez fer war, I call it murder —
　There you hev it plain an' flat;
I don't want to go no furder
　Than my Testyment fer that;
God hez sed so plump an' fairly,
　It's ez long ez it is broad,
An' you've gut to git up airly
　Ef you want to take in God.

'Taint your eppyletts an' feathers
　Make the thing a grain more right;
'Taint afollerin' your bell-wethers
　Will excuse ye in His sight;
Ef you take a sword an' dror it,
　An' go stick a feller thru,
Guv'ment aint to answer for it,
　God 'll send the bill to you.

Wut's the use o' meetin -goin'
　Every Sabbath, wet or dry,
Ef it's right to go amowin'
　Feller-men like oats an' rye?
I dunno but wut it's pooty
　Trainin' round in bobtail coats —
But it 's curus Christian dooty
　This ere cuttin' folks's throats.

They may talk o' Freedom's airy
　Tell they're pupple in the face —
It 's a grand gret cemetary
　Fer the barthrights of our race;
They jest want this Californy
　So 's to lug new slave-states in
To abuse ye, an' to scorn ye,
　An' to plunder ye like sin.

Aint it cute to see a Yankee
　Take sech everlastin' pains,
All to git the Devil's thankee
　Helpin' on 'em weld their chains?
Wy, it 's jest ez clear ez figgers,
　Clear ez one an' one makes two,
Chaps thet make black slaves o' niggers
　Want to make wite slaves o' you.

Tell ye jest the eend I've come to
　Arter cipherin' plaguy smart,
An' it makes a handy sum, tu,
　Any gump could larn by heart;
Laborin' man an' laborin' woman
　Hev one glory an' one shame.
Ev'y thin' thet 's done inhuman
　Injers all on 'em the same.

'Taint by turnin' out to hack folks
  You 're agoin' to git your right,
Nor by lookin' down on black folks
  Coz you 're put upon by wite;
Slavery aint o' nary color,
  'Taint the hide thet makes it wus,
All it keers fer in a feller
  'S jest to make him fill its pus.

Want to tackle *me* in, du ye?
  I expect you'll hev to wait;
Wen cold lead puts daylight thru ye
  You'll begin to kal'late;
S'pose the crows wun't fall to pickin'
  All the carkiss from your bones,
Coz you helped to give a lickin'
  To them poor half-Spanish drones?

Jest go home an' ask our Nancy
  Wether I'd be sech a goose
Ez to jine ye — guess you 'd fancy
  The etarnal bung wuz loose!
She wants me fer home consumption,
  Let alone the hay's to mow —
Ef you're arter folks o' gumption,
  You've a darned long row to hoe.

Take them editors thet's crowin'
  Like a cockerel three months old —
Don't ketch any on 'em goin',
  Though they *be* so blasted bold;
Aint they a prime set o' fellers?
  'Fore they think on 't they will sprout
(Like a peach thet's got the yellers,)
  With the meanness bustin' out.

Wal, go 'long to help 'em stealin'
  Bigger pens to cram with slaves,
Help the men thet 's ollers dealin'
  Insults on your fathers' graves;
Help the strong to grind the feeble,
  Help the many agin the few,
Help the men thet call your people
  Witewashed slaves an' peddlin' crew!

Massachusetts, God forgive her,
  She 's akneelin' with the rest,
She, thet ough' to ha' clung fer ever
  In her grand old eagle-nest;
She thet ough' to stand so fearless
  Wile the wracks are round her hurled,
Holdin' up a beacon peerless
  To the oppressed of all the world!

Haint they sold your colored seamen?
  Haint they made your env'ys wiz?
Wut 'll make ye act like freemen?
  Wut 'll get your dander riz?
Come, I 'll tell ye wut I 'm thinkin'
  Is our dooty in this fix,
They 'd ha' done 't ez quick ez winkin'
  In the days o' seventy-six.

Clang the bells in every steeple,
  Call all true men to disown
The tradoocers of our people,
  The enslavers o' their own;
Let our dear old Bay State proudly
  Put the trumpet to her mouth,
Let her ring this messidge loudly
  In the ears of all the South:

"I 'll return ye good fer evil
  Much ez we frail mortils can,
But I wun't go help the Devil
  Makin' man the cus o' man;
Call me coward, call me traiter,
  Jest ez suits your mean idees —
Here I stand a tyrant-hater,
  An' the friend o' God an' Peace!"

Ef I 'd *my* way I hed ruther
  We should go to work an' part —
They take one way, we take t'other,
  Guess it would n't break my heart;
Man hed ough' to put asunder
  Them thet God has noways jined;
An' I should n't gretly wonder
  Ef there 's thousands o' my mind.

'The Painter's Triumph'' painted in 1838 by William Sidney Mount

A NATIVE VISION

Shortly after the Hudson River painters had challenged the old guard with their call to nature, a school of "genre" painters emerged with a new interpretation of the American experience. Theirs was an explicitly democratic response that celebrated the common man. It gloried happily in detailed accounts of daily activities of rural Americans, during that brief period of illusory optimism and well-being before industrialization and the Civil War brought an end to innocence.

The genre painters never comprised a coherent school, as did the Hudson River artists. They were largely self-taught and stayed close to the locales that they knew. They did, however, share a common outlook, expressed by William Sidney Mount: "Never paint for the few, but for the many." In the opinion of these painters, the excited recognition of their work by a neighbor was a "painter's triumph."

A related, if more profound, spirit permeated American letters during the same period. The romantic poetry of Longfellow, the moral philosophy of Channing and Emerson, and the dark introspection of Hawthorne and Poe had moved beyond the need for self-conscious assaults on alien traditions. For the most part these men responded with stylistic and intellectual integrity to the substance of their particular experience, turning only occasional glances in the direction of Europe.

"Exhibition Gallery of the Louvre" (1832) by Morse shows aspiring painters copying the master

Outside a small circle of artists and patrons in New York and a few other cities, a painter could gain little recognition. When a wider popularity was found at all it usually came through the reproduction of a particularly sentimental painting such as Cole's "Kindred Spirits." There were simply too few people with the taste or the money to buy paintings. A few embittered artists turned to Europe for solace. For most genre painters the desire to paint "for the many" precluded this alternative. Both Bingham and Mount found even New York unpalatable.

"Art Versus Law" by Blythe laments the artist's lot in America while "Studio Reception, Paris" by Rossiter presents a contrasting view

"The Sailor's Wedding," painted by Woodville in 1852, is filled with humorous characterizations

Woodville

Of the qualities common to the genre painters, humor was the most general. It was not a condescending humor depicting its subjects as rustic bumpkins, but the wry comment of one man about the foibles of his neighbors. This view is particularly explicit in the work of Richard Caton Woodville. He was one of the earliest to develop something of the flavor of everyday life in his paintings. His characters are types and his paintings describe only one dimension of their lives, but their jovial optimism captures an important strain in the American consciousness.

"Politics in an Oysterhouse," 1848 (above) and "Waiting for the Stage" (below) are comic interpretations of the man's world at mid-century, down to the cigars and cigarettes littering the floor

(Above) "Poor Author and Rich Bookseller" by Allston; (right) Longfellow

The first flowering of American literature had centered on New York and the Knickerbocker School, with which Washington Irving and William Cullen Bryant were identified. Shortly thereafter the focus of American literary and intellectual life shifted to Boston, in what is commonly described as the New England Renaissance. Springing from liberal Unitarianism, the new air of intellectual freedom fostered the classic period of American literature. At the forefront of this movement were the Transcendentalists, who brought a new and mystical view of life into American thought.

Nathaniel Hawthorne, photographed by Brady

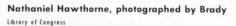

Edgar Allen Poe (1809-1849)

William Ellery Channing (1780-1842)

Under the stimulus of Emerson's moral philosophy, several American writers turned for the first time to introspective examination of the human condition. Hawthorne saw life as a confrontation with evil and could not share Emerson's optimistic views. The spirit of this renaissance also brought forth literary crusaders like Whittier, who fixed the antislavery cause in its passionately moral context. Outside Boston literary circles, Longfellow achieved immense popularity with his romantic epics, and Poe brought a melancholy genius to his short stories and poems that had considerable influence outside America. Greenough's persistent study of classical sculpture and designs seemed out of touch with the spirit of his times.

Ralph Waldo Emerson (1803-1882)

Horatio Greenough in his studio in Italy

John Greenleaf Whittier (1807-1892)

"Bargaining for a Horse" (1853) by Mount

Mount

William Sidney Mount seldom left his home in Long Island. He was devoted to the locale and its citizens, representing them in his paintings as the expression of the best in rural life. His literal style was perfectly suited to its subject. There is nothing powerful about the scenes, but taken together they constitute a statement of belief in the virtues of rural America. In retrospect it seems an exercise in nostalgia, but at the time about 80 percent of the population lived off the land.

Mount, photographed by Brady in 1856; (right) "Eel Spearing at Setauket," 1845

"Long Island Farmhouses"

"Raffling for the Goose" and "Ringing the Pig" are both typical of Mount's interpretation of farm life on Long Island

"Fur Traders Descending the Missouri"

Bingham

Like other genre painters, George Caleb Bingham spent most of his life far from cosmopolitan centers. His best-known works are studies of life in his native Missouri and on the western rivers. Bingham, too, was largely self-taught and was dedicated to depicting the common man. His paintings, however, are much more formally structured and for this reason occasionally achieve greater visual impact. Bingham tried to live in Washington and become a portrait painter but soon gave it up.

Sketch by Bingham of a musician entertaining other passengers on a flatboat trip (above); Self-portrait by Bingham, 1835 (left)

1847

79.

Ralph Waldo Emerson: "Ode Inscribed to W. H. Channing"

Believing as they did in the spark of divinity in man and in the perfectibility of society, many of the Transcendentalists felt compelled to practise what they preached in the reform movements of the 1830s and 1840s. Until fairly late in life, Emerson remained aloof from direct involvement in reform, although many of his disciples, including William Henry Channing, encouraged him to take an active role. In the "Ode" reprinted here Emerson explained his reluctance to act, on both philosophic and personal grounds.

Source: *Complete Works*, Centenary Edition, Boston, 1903.

ODE *Inscribed to W. H. Channing*

Though loathe to grieve
The evil time's sole patriot,
I cannot leave
My honied thought
For the priest's cant,
Or statesman's rant.

If I refuse
My study for their politique,
Which at the best is trick,
The angry Muse
Puts confusion in my brain.

But who is he that prates
Of the culture of mankind,
Of better arts and life?
Go, blindworm, go,
Behold the famous States
Harrying Mexico
With rifle and with knife!

Or who, with accent bolder,
Dare praise the freedom-loving
    mountaineer?
I found by thee, O rushing Contoocook!
And in thy valleys, Agiochook!
The jackals of the negro holder.

The God who made New Hampshire
Taunted the lofty land
With little men;
Small bat and wren
House in the oak:
If earth fire cleave
The upheaved land, and bury the folk,
The southern crocodile would grieve.
Virtue palters; Right is hence;
Freedom praised, but hid;
Funeral eloquence
Rattles the coffin lid.

What boots thy zeal,
O glowing friend,
That would indignant rend
The northland from the south?
Wherefore? to what good end?
Boston Bay and Bunker Hill
Would serve things still;
Things are of the snake.

The horseman serves the horse,
The neatherd serves the neat,
The merchant serves the purse,
The eater serves his meat;
'T is the day of the chattel,
Web to weave, and corn to grind;
Things are in the saddle,
And ride mankind.

There are two laws discrete,
Not reconciled —
Law for man, and law for thing;
The last builds town and fleet,
But it runs wild,
And doth the man unking.

'T is fit the forest fall,
The steep be graded,
The mountain tunneled,
The sand shaded,
The orchard planted,
The glebe tilled,
The prairie granted,
The steamer built.

Let man serve law for man;
Live for friendship, live for love,
For truth's and harmony's behoof;
The state may follow how it can,
As Olympus follows Jove.

 Yet do not I implore
The wrinkled shopman to my sounding
  woods, ·
Nor bid the unwilling senator
Ask votes of thrushes in the solitudes.
Every one to his chosen work;
Foolish hands may mix and mar;
Wise and sure the issues are.
Round they roll till dark is light,
Sex to sex, and even to odd;
The over-god
Who marries Right to Might,
Who peoples, unpeoples,
He who exterminates
Races by stronger races,
Black by white faces,
Knows to bring honey
Out of the lion;
Grafts gentlest scion
On pirate and Turk.

The Cossack eats Poland,
Like stolen fruit;
Her last noble is ruined,
Her last poet mute:
Straight, into double band
The victors divide;
Half for freedom strike and stand;
The astonished Muse finds thousands at
  her side.

80.

Charles Sumner: A War to Strengthen the Slavery Interests

The condemnation of the Mexican War that is reprinted here in part was written by the Abolitionist and crusader for peace Charles Sumner and adopted by the Massachusetts legislature in 1847. That the war was provoked by the United States, as Sumner maintained, is no longer disputed; but that it was a "war designed to confirm and fortify the 'Slave Power'" is doubtful. Most of the pro-war sentiment came from the Western states. Practically all the Southern Whigs and some Southern Democrats, including John C. Calhoun, opposed the war. Calhoun wanted Texas, but without war. He feared the acquiring of too much new land would reopen the unsolved problem of slavery in the territories.

Source: OSL 132: "Report on the War with Mexico."

IT IS A WAR FOR THE EXTENSION OF SLAVERY

A WAR OF CONQUEST IS BAD; but the present war has darker shadows. It is a war for the extension of slavery over a territory which has already been purged by Mexican authority from this stain and curse. Fresh markets of human beings are to be established; further opportunities for this hateful traffic are to be opened; the lash of the overseer is to be quickened in new regions; and the wretched slave is to be hurried to unaccustomed fields of toil. It can hardly be believed that now, more than eighteen hundred years since the dawn of the Christian era, a government, professing the law of charity and justice, should be employed in war to extend an institution which exists in defiance of these sacred principles.

It has already been shown that the annexation of Texas was consummated for this purpose. The Mexican War is a continuance, a prolongation, of the same efforts; and the success which crowned the first emboldens the partisans of the latter, who now, as before, profess to extend the area of freedom, while they are establishing a new sphere for slavery.

The authorities already adduced in regard to the objects of annexation illustrate the real objects of the Mexican War. Declarations have also been made, upon the floor of Congress, which throw light upon it. Mr. Sims, of South Carolina, has said that "he had no doubt that every foot of territory we shall permanently occupy, south of thirty-six degrees thirty minutes, will be slave territory"; and, in reply to his colleague, Mr. Burt, who inquired whether this opinion was "in consequence of the known determination of the Southern people that their institutions shall be carried into that country, if acquired," said, in words that furnish a key to the whole project, "It is founded on the known determination of the Southern people that their institutions shall be carried there; it is founded in the laws of God, written on the climate and soil of the country: nothing but slave labor can cultivate, profitably, that region of country."

The recent rejection, in both houses at Washington, of the Wilmot proviso, by which slavery was to be excluded from all new territorial acquisitions, reveals to the world the fixed determination of a majority of Congress to make the war an instrument for the extension of slavery, and the establishment in new regions of what Mr. Upshur called "the grand domestic institution."

IT IS A WAR TO STRENGTHEN THE "SLAVE POWER"

BUT IT IS NOT MERELY proposed to open new markets for slavery: it is also designed to confirm and fortify the "Slave Power." Here is a distinction which should not fail to be borne in mind. Slavery is odious as an institution, if viewed in the light of morals and Christianity. On this account alone we should refrain from rendering it any voluntary support. But it has been made the basis of a political combination, to which has not inaptly been applied the designation of the "Slave Power."

The slaveholders of the country — who are not supposed to exceed 200,000 or at most 300,000 in numbers — by the spirit of union which animates them, by the strong sense of a common interest, and by the audacity of their leaders, have erected themselves into a new "estate," as it were, under the Constitution. Disregarding the sentiments of many of the great framers of that instrument, who notoriously considered slavery as *temporary*, they proclaim it a *permanent* institution; and, with a strange inconsistency, at once press its title to a paramount influence in the general government, while they deny the right of that government to interfere, in any way, with its existence. According to them, it may never be restrained or abolished by the general government, though it may be indefinitely extended.

And it is urged that, as new free states are admitted into the Union, other slave states should be admitted, in order to preserve, in the Senate, what is called the "balance of power"; in other words, the equipoise between slavery and freedom, though

it might, with more propriety, be termed the preponderance of slavery. The bare enunciation of this claim discloses its absurdity. Is it not a mockery of the principles of freedom, which moved the hearts and strengthened the hands of our fathers, to suppose that they contemplated any such perverse arrangement of political power?

It cannot be doubted that His Excellency is entirely right when he says, in his message, that "at the time of the adoption of the Constitution of the United States the final extinction of the institution of slavery was looked for at no very distant day," and that "so carefully was the Constitution formed that, when the event took place, not one word or phrase of it would require to be altered, and no expression in it would give notice to posterity that such an institution ever existed"; and, further, that "the Constitution leaves slavery where it found it, a state institution; and though, as a compromise, it did confer political power upon states which had slaves, by reason of their slaves, *it was not intended* that that power should be extended *beyond the states who were parties to the compromise.*"

But the slave power has triumphed over the evident intentions of the framers of the Constitution. It appears that only one new free state has been formed out of territory acquired by treaty, while four new slave states have been established, and the foreign slave state of Texas has been incorporated into the Union by joint resolutions of Congress.

The object of the bold measure of annexation was not only to extend slavery, but to strengthen the "Slave Power." The same object is now proposed by the Mexican War. This is another link in the gigantic chain by which our country and the Constitution are to be bound to the "Slave Power." This has been proclaimed in public journals. The following passage from the *Charleston* (S.C.) *Courier* avows it: "Every battle fought in Mexico, and every dollar spent there, but insures the acquisition of territory which must widen the field of *Southern enterprise and power in future.* And the final result will be to readjust the balance of power in the confederacy, *so as to give us control over the operations of government in all time to come."*

IT IS A WAR AGAINST THE FREE STATES

REGARDING IT as a war to strengthen the "Slave Power," we are conducted to a natural conclusion, that it is virtually, and in its consequences, a war against the free states of the Union. Conquest and robbery are attempted in order to obtain a political control at home; and distant battles are fought, less with a special view of subjugating Mexico than with the design of overcoming the power of the free states, under the Constitution. The lives of Mexicans are sacrificed in this cause; and a domestic question, which should be reserved for bloodless debate in our own country, is transferred to fields of battle in a foreign land. . . .

UNCONSTITUTIONALITY OF THE WAR

THE WAR SHOULD NOT FAIL, also, to be regarded in the light of the Constitution. And here we must be brief. The stages by which the country has reached it have been as unconstitutional as its objects. First, Texas was annexed, by joint resolutions of Congress, in violation of the Constitution. Second, the President, in undertaking to order General Taylor, without the consent of Congress, to march upon territory in possession of Mexico, assumed a power which belongs to Congress alone. To Congress has been committed the dread thunderbolt of war. "Congress shall have power to declare war," are the words of the Constitution. But the President has usurped its most terrible authority. His order to General Taylor was an unauthorized act of war.

Third, as a war of conquest, and for the

Metropolitan Museum of Art; Stokes-Hawes gift

Charles Sumner, taken by Southworth and Hawes about 1847

extension of slavery, it is contrary to the principles of our Constitution, which, according to the words of the preamble, was formed "to provide for the *common defense,* promote the general welfare, and secure *the blessings of liberty to ourselves and our posterity."* Such a war as that in which we are now engaged can find no sanction in these words: it is *not* for the *common defense,* nor to *secure the blessings of liberty.* Fourth, as a war to strengthen the "Slave Power," it is also unconstitutional. Thus it may be branded as a fourfold infraction of the fundamental law of the land.

CRIMINALITY OF THE WAR

AND IT IS ALSO a violation of the fundamental law of Heaven, of that great law of Right which is written by God's own finger on the heart of man. His Excellency said nothing beyond the truth when, in his message, he declared that "an offensive and unnecessary war was the highest crime which man can commit against society." It is so; for all the demons of hate are then let loose in mad and causeless career. Misrule usurps the place of order, and outrage of all kinds stalks "unwhipt of justice." An unjust and unnecessary war is the dismal offspring of national insensibility, steeping the conscience in forgetfulness, and unkenneling the foul brood of murder, rapine, and rape.

How, then, must we regard the acts in the present war? Have they any extenuation beyond the sanction of mortals, like ourselves, who have rashly undertaken to direct them? The war is a crime, and all who have partaken in the blood of its well-fought fields have aided in its perpetration. It is a principle of military law that the soldier shall not question the orders of his superior. If this shall exonerate the Army from blame, it will be only to press with accumulated weight upon the government, which has set in motion this terrible and irresponsible machine. . . .

RESTRAINT AND OVERTHROW OF THE "SLAVE POWER"

A CAREFUL EXAMINATION of the history of our country, exposing the tyranny and usurpation of the "Slave Power," has not yet been attempted. Our object will be to call attention to a few undeniable facts. The "Slave Power" has predominated over the federal government from its first establishment. It has always absorbed to itself a large portion of all offices of honor and profit under the Constitution. It has held the presidency for fifty-six years, while the free states have held it for twelve years only. It has for several years rejected the petitions of the free states, thus virtually denying the right of petition.

It has denied, to free colored citizens of the free states, the privileges secured to them by the Constitution of the United States, by imprisoning them, and sometimes selling them into slavery. It has insulted and exiled, from Charleston and New Orleans, the honored representatives of Massachu-

setts, who have been sent to those places in order to throw the shield of the Constitution and law over her colored citizens. It first imposed upon the country the policy of protecting domestic manufactures, contrary to the interests of the free states, and now, when those interests have changed, at a later day has defeated the same policy, contrary to the interests of the same states.

It required the action of the national government to endeavor to secure compensation for certain slaves who, in the exercise of the natural rights of men, had asserted and achieved their freedom on the Atlantic Ocean, and sought shelter in Bermuda. It instigated and carried on a most expensive war in Florida, mainly to recover certain fugitive slaves. It wrested from Mexico the province of Texas, and finally secured its annexation to the United States. And now it has involved the whole country in a causeless, cruel, and unjust war with Mexico. All these things have been done by the "Slave Power."

Their bare enumeration, without further argument, furnishes a sufficient reason for calling for the restraint and overthrow of this influence. And here we do not encounter any difficulties arising from constitutional doubts. It is true that slavery is recognized by the Constitution, and a certain political importance is attached to it by the manner in which it is represented in the House of Representatives and the electoral colleges. But the "Slave Power," *as such*, is an element and influence unknown to the original framers of that instrument.

It is not to be supposed that they who anxiously looked for the abolition of slavery could ever have regarded it as the legitimate foundation of an association which was to control the counsels and conduct of the country, and dictate its most important measures. There are but two elements in its existence: first, slavery; and, second, combination among all interested in the preservation of slavery.

The principles of opposition to the "Slave Power" are the natural correlative or complement of these. They are, first, freedom; and, second, a combination among all interested in the preservation of freedom. If it be right, under the Constitution, for men to combine for slavery, they may surely combine for freedom. The country has suffered much under the "Slave Power." It remains to be seen if it may not be restored by a combination not yet attempted, — the "Freedom Power."

And here, as in other movements for the good of the country, Massachusetts must take the lead. She must be true to the spirit of her fathers in the colonial struggles. She must be true to the sentiments of her Bill of Rights. She must be true to the resolutions which she has put forth against the outrages of the "Slave Power" in imprisoning her colored citizens, and in annexing Texas. She must be true to the moral and religious sentiments of her citizens. In one word, she must be true to her CONSCIENCE, and not allow it to be longer "unquiet" by submission to the "Slave Power."

All of which, with the accompanying Resolutions, is respectfully submitted.

RESOLVES

CONCERNING THE MEXICAN WAR
AND THE INSTITUTION OF SLAVERY

Resolved, that the present war with Mexico has its primary origin in the unconstitutional annexation to the United States of the foreign state of Texas, while the same was still at war with Mexico; that it was unconstitutionally commenced by the order of the President, to General Taylor, to take military possession of territory in dispute between the United States and Mexico, *and in the occupation of Mexico;* and that it is now waged ingloriously, — by a powerful nation against a weak neighbor, — unnecessarily and without just cause, at immense cost of treasure and life, for the dismemberment of Mexico, and for the conquest of a portion of her territory, from which slavery has already been excluded, with the triple object of extending slavery, of strengthening the "Slave Power," and of obtaining the control of the Free States, under the Constitution of the United States.

Resolved, that such a war of conquest, so hateful in its objects, so wanton, unjust, and unconstitutional in its origin and character, must be regarded as a war against freedom, against humanity, against justice, against the Union, against the Constitution, and *against the Free States;* and that a regard for the true interests and the highest honor of the country, not less than the impulses of Christian duty, should arouse all good citizens to join in efforts to arrest this gigantic crime, by withholding supplies, or other voluntary contributions, for its further prosecution, by calling for the withdrawal of our army within the established limits of the United States, and in every just way aiding the country to retreat from the disgraceful position of aggression which it now occupies towards a weak, distracted neighbor and sister republic.

Resolved, that our attention is directed anew to the wrong and "enormity" of slavery, and to the tyranny and usurpation of the "Slave Power," as displayed in the history of our country, particularly in the annexation of Texas, and the present war with Mexico; and that we are impressed with the unalterable conviction that a regard for the fair fame of our country, for the principles of morals, and for that righteousness which exalteth a nation, sanctions and requires all constitutional efforts for the abolition of slavery within the limits of the United States, while loyalty to the Constitution, and a just self-defense, make it specially incumbent on the people of the free states to cooperate in strenuous exertions to restrain and overthrow the "Slave Power."

81.

Territorial Expansion and the Extension of Slavery

In August 1846 David Wilmot moved that a proviso barring slavery from the territories acquired as a result of the Mexican War be attached to an appropriations bill being discussed in the House of Representatives. Although never passed, the Wilmot Proviso was reintroduced on several occasions, and ignited a political war that helped bring about the deterioration of both major parties. Northern Whigs and radical Democrats united to support the Proviso, while Democrats and Southern Whigs denounced it. John C. Calhoun denied the right of Congress to exclude slavery from the territories, and in the editorial that follows, his arguments were endorsed. The editorial also endorsed the vigorously expansionist "all Mexico movement."

Source: *United States Magazine and Democratic Review,* October 1847:
"New Territory versus No Territory."

THE WAR, which the insane folly of the Spaniards has forced upon us after fifty years of threatening and surrendering of territory reluctantly as we have pressed upon their front, has the disadvantage of acquiring territory too fast, "before our population is sufficiently advanced to gain it from them piece by piece." That was a wise policy ascribed in the early stages of the war to Almonte and his party, who, learning more from the experience of the past than our own politicians have done, saw in the last fifty years of peace the steady and resistless approach of the American people. They saw territory after territory, no matter by whom owned or by what people inhabited, swallowed up in the great Union, the march of which was not perceptibly stayed, even when Louisiana and its French citizens became an American republic. They saw Texas suddenly grow into a state through Anglo-Saxon energy, and as promptly fall into the line of the Union, while its pioneers were already taking root in California and New Mexico.

The "coquetry" of the Texan rulers with

Great Britain and Mexico was not more successful than that of former similar attempts; and Captain Elliot won no more fame than Arbuthnot in Florida, Powers in Kentucky, or Germaine in Vermont. If ten years sufficed to swallow up Texas, as many more would involve a province in Mexico, and to this progress an obstinate war might be a barrier. But alas! their power to resist an American Army was less even than their ability to resist the approach of settlers. The occupation of their soil by volunteer troops, who are precisely the most enterprising class of a race unequaled for energy, only clears the way for the no less adventurous settlers. The 30,000 intelligent men who visit the admirable climate, fertile fields, and boundless mineral resources of Mexico will at least familiarize the minds of the people at home with the advantages there offered and possibly stimulate the emigration.

It matters not whether a treaty stipulates for more or less territory, it will all come into the country "piece by piece" as "our population are sufficiently advanced to gain it." The surrender of Texas by the Treaty of 1819 was fondly hoped by the "No Territory" Party to have put that matter at rest, and no doubt many a purblind Federalist looked upon the Sabine as the utmost southern limit of the Union. That dishonorable dismemberment, however, has brought its own punishment in the pretext it offered the Spaniards for an attack which must end in a removal of the boundary still farther south and a completion of its western progress.

This occupation of territory by the people is the great movement of the age, and until every acre of the North American continent is occupied by citizens of the United States, the foundation of the future empire will not have been laid. The chief evil of Europe, that which oppresses England and destroys Ireland, is the exclusion of the people from the soil. England, with a population larger than our Union, has but 32,000 proprietors of the soil. That which constitutes the strength of the Union, the wealth and independence of its people, is the boundless expanse of territory laid open to their possession; and the more rapidly it is overrun by needy settlers, the greater is the security that it will be equally and extensively distributed, and the more impossible it becomes for any section or clique to exercise "control over them," or to encroach upon the rights they enjoy under our Constitution.

All the territory of the Union is the common property of all the states — every member, new or old, of the Union, admitted to partnership under the Constitution, has a perfect right to enjoy the territory, which is the common property of all. Some of the territory was acquired by treaty from England; much of it by cession from the older states; yet more by treaties with Indians, and still greater quantities by purchase from Spain and France; large tracts again by the annexation of Texas; and the present war will add still more to the quantity yet to be entered by citizens of the United States, or of those of any of the countries of Europe that choose to migrate thither.

All this land, no matter whence it was derived, belongs to all the states jointly. That acquired from England by treaty was in their joint capacity as a federal government; that purchased from Indians and foreign governments was paid for with the money drawn through customs duties from the citizens of all the states; and funds derived from those sources, backed by blood drawn mostly from the South, is the price paid for conquered territory; and no citizen of the United States can be debarred from moving thither with his property and enjoying the liberties guaranteed by the Constitution.

The lands ceded to the United States collectively, by individual states that claimed them, were accepted by acts of Congress that specified "that no regulations made or to be made by Congress shall tend to emancipate slaves." The right of all the citizens of the older states to emigrate with all their property whatsoever, and enjoy therewith the vacant lands, is perfect. The instrument by which the thirteen original slave states entered into a union which admitted Vermont as a slave state recognizes and guarantees slaves as the property of their owners. That instrument expressly allowed the importation of slaves into the Union until 1808, at a duty not to exceed $10 per head; and Section 2, Article IV, providing for the recovery of fugitive slaves from labor, manifestly admits and asserts the exercise of a positive, unqualified right on the part of the owner of the slave, which no state law or regulation can in any way qualify, regulate, control, or restrain.

Any law or regulation which interrupts, limits, delays or postpones the rights of the owner to the immediate command of his service or labor, operates a discharge of the slave from service, and is a violation of the Constitution. This right of property in slaves is guaranteed as a municipal regulation; it in no shape bears a national character under the Constitution, and the original states enjoyed that property as long as it was profitable to them. When it ceased to be so, some of them abolished the institution without reference to the federal government. It was a species of property that they had a right to sell elsewhere or relinquish at their pleasure. Other states, however, are yet in possession of that property as well as their rights in the new territory. To set up, therefore, a pretense that if they adhere to the property they possess they shall be deprived of their rights in the states to be formed in any acquired territory is an unprincipled violation of a solemn treaty, an attack upon the Constitution, and a gross injustice to the rights of neighboring states.

If the Constitution is respected, then the rights of no member in the common property can be impaired, because it is possessed of other property distasteful to other members. If the Constitution is not respected, then the right of one state to interfere with the internal affairs of another is no greater than to meddle with serfdom in Russia or slavery in India. Unfortunately, this institution in the South, once common to all the states, has on several occasions received somewhat of a national character, particularly in the Missouri Compromise, where a line of latitude was fixed to the north of which no slave state should be erected; and, on several other occasions, in a less marked manner. It is, therefore, the more necessary that its purely municipal character should be distinctly borne in mind, and that it should not be permitted to be used as a means of checking the expansion of the Union by preventing any description of emigrants from occupying any territory best suited to their means and interests. . . .

The whole tendency of these attempts to enforce, through conditions of admission into the Union, a control over the states by Congress, not authorized by the Constitution, is dangerously and illegally to enlarge the powers of the federal government and produce inequality among the states. The Constitution does not prohibit slavery in any of the states, and, yet, through the Missouri Compromise, it is sought to usurp for Congress the power to prohibit it in a number of states that will hereafter grow up. When these new states come into the Union, they are controlled by the Constitution only; and as that instrument permits slavery in all the states that are parties to it, how can Congress prevent it? To attempt it is clearly such a departure from the spirit of the Constitution as is at war with the whole course of the Democratic Party, and as such cannot have a prosperous issue.

That the question of slavery — a purely municipal matter and, as such, entirely without the range of congressional control — has, unfortunately, on more than one occasion, approached a national form by being made the subject of official documents, not in defense of any foreign aggression upon our domestic rights is matter of regret; but does not, therefore, confer the right to confirm that national appearance by national action. On the other hand, it calls for a more rigid acknowledgment of the immunities due to each member of the Union, present and to come.

A great deal of controversy seems to arise from misunderstanding, as thus: One party states that "if territory is to be conquered or purchased *for the purpose* of extending slavery," it is a violation of the Constitution. Nothing can be more clear. But when, through the results of war, territory comes into the possession of the Union, it is equally a violation of the Constitution for Congress to undertake to say that there shall be no slavery then. The people of the United States were nearly unanimous for the admission of Texas into the Union; but probably not an insignificant fraction required its annexation *"for the purpose"* of extending slavery.

The acquirement of territory by Congress is in accordance with the policy of the Union, but no more "for the purpose of extending slavery" than for the extension of Mormonism, or any sect of religion or school of philosophy. There is a vast distinction between "annexation for the purpose of extending slavery" and making the exclusion of slavery the condition of annexation; both are equally at war with the Constitution, which permits the acquirement of territory but forbids meddling with slavery, pro or con.

82.

ALBERT GALLATIN: The Unjust War with Mexico

By 1847 Albert Gallatin's long and distinguished career of public service was behind him. Most of the men with whom he had worked and sometimes fought were dead, and at the age of eighty-six he was now mainly involved in scholarly activities. President of the New York Historical Society and founder, in 1842, of the American Ethnological Society, he devoted his time to study and writing, especially on the subject of the American Indian. But the Mexican War revived his old interest in politics, and he wrote a pamphlet, Peace with Mexico, *in which he expressed his conviction that the war had been unjustly begun by the United States and his anxiety over whether such a war could be brought to an honorable conclusion. The portion of the pamphlet titled "The Mission of the United States" is reprinted here.*

Source: *Peace with Mexico*, New York, 1847, pp. 25-30.

THE PEOPLE OF THE UNITED STATES have been placed by Providence in a position never before enjoyed by any other nation. They are possessed of a most extensive territory with a very fertile soil, a variety of climates and productions, and a capacity of sustaining a population greater in proportion to its extent than any other territory of the same size on the face of the globe.

By a concourse of various circumstances, they found themselves, at the epoch of their independence, in the full enjoyment of religious, civil, and political liberty, entirely free from any hereditary monopoly of wealth or power. The people at large were in full and quiet possession of all those natural rights for which the people of other countries have for a long time contended and still do contend. They were, and you still are, the supreme sovereigns, acknowledged as such by all. For the proper exercise of these uncontrolled powers and privileges, you are responsible to posterity, to the world at large, and to the Almighty Being who has poured on you such unparalleled blessings.

Your mission is to improve the state of the world, to be the "model republic," to show that men are capable of governing themselves, and that this simple and natural form of government is that also which confers most happiness on all, is productive of the greatest development of the intellectual faculties, above all, that which is attended with the highest standard of private and political virtue and morality.

Your forefathers, the founders of the republic, imbued with a deep feeling of their rights and duties, did not deviate from those principles. The sound sense, the wisdom, the probity, the respect for public faith with which the internal concerns of the nation were managed made our institutions an object of general admiration. Here, for the first time, was the experiment attempted with any prospect of success and, on a large scale, of a representative democratic republic. If it failed, the last hope of the friends of mankind was lost or indefinitely postponed, and the eyes of the world were turned toward you. Whenever real or pretended apprehensions of the imminent danger of trusting the people at large with power were expressed, the answer ever was, "Look at America!"

In their external relations, the United States, before this unfortunate war, had, while sustaining their just rights, ever acted in strict conformity with the dictates of justice and displayed the utmost moderation. They never had voluntarily injured any other nation. Every acquisition of territory from foreign powers was honestly made, the result of treaties not imposed but freely assented to by the other party. The preservation of peace was ever a primary object. The recourse to arms was always in self-defense. On its expediency there may have been a difference of opinion; that in the only two instances of conflict with civilized nations which occurred during a period of sixty-three years (1783 to 1846) the just rights of the United States had been invaded by a long-continued series of aggressions is undeniable.

In the first instance, war was not declared, and there were only partial hostilities between France and England. The Congress of the United States, the only legitimate organ of the nation for that purpose, did, in 1812, declare war against Great Britain. Independent of depredations of our commerce, she had for twenty years carried on an actual war against the United States. I say actual war since there is now but one opinion on that subject; a renewal of the impressment of men sailing under the protection of our flag would be tantamount to a declaration of war. The partial opposition to the War of 1812 did not rest on a denial of the aggressions of England and of the justice of our cause but on the fact that, with the exception of impressments, similar infractions of our just rights had been committed by France, and on the most erroneous belief that the administration was partial to that country and insincere in their apparent efforts to restore peace.

At present all these principles would seem to have been abandoned. The most just, a purely defensive war, and no other is justifiable, is necessarily attended with a train of great and unavoidable evils. What shall we say of one, iniquitous in its origin and provoked by ourselves, of a war of aggression, which is now publicly avowed to be one of intended conquest?

If persisted in, its necessary consequences will be a permanent increase of our military establishment and of executive patronage; its general tendency to make man hate man, to awaken his worst passions, to accustom him to the taste of blood. It has already demoralized no inconsiderable portion of the nation.

The general peace which has been preserved between the great European powers during the last thirty years may not be ascribed to the purest motives. Be these what they may, this long and unusual repose has been most beneficial to the cause of humanity. Nothing can be more injurious to it, more lamentable, more scandalous than the war between two adjacent republics of North America.

Your mission was to be a model for all other governments and for all other less-favored nations; to adhere to the most elevated principles of political morality; to apply all your faculties to the gradual improvement of your own institutions and social state; and by your example to exert a moral influence most beneficial to mankind at large. Instead of this, an appeal has been made to your worst passions; to cupidity; to the thirst of unjust aggrandizement by brutal force; to the love of military fame and of false glory; and it has even been tried to pervert the noblest feelings of your nature. The attempt is made to make you abandon the lofty position which your fathers occupied, to substitute for it the political morality and heathen patriotism of the heroes and statesmen of antiquity.

I have said that it was attempted to pervert even your virtues. Devotedness to country, or patriotism, is a most essential virtue, since the national existence of any society depends upon it. Unfortunately, our most virtuous dispositions are perverted, not only by our vices and selfishness but also by their own excess. Even the most holy of our attributes, the religious feeling, may be perverted from that cause, as was but too lamentably exhibited in the persecutions, even unto death, of those who were deemed heretics. It is not, therefore, astonishing that patriotism carried to excess should also be perverted.

In the entire devotedness to their country, the people everywhere and at all times have been too apt to forget the duties imposed upon them by justice toward other nations. It is against this natural propensity that you should be specially on your guard. The blame does not attach to those who, led by their patriotic feelings, though erroneous, flock around the national standard. On the contrary, no men are more worthy of admiration, better entitled to the thanks of their country than those who, after war has once taken place, actuated only by the purest motives, daily and with the utmost self-devotedness brave death and stake their own lives in the conflict against the actual enemy. I must confess that I do not extend the same charity to those civilians who coolly and deliberately plunge the country into any unjust or unnecessary war.

We should have but one conscience; and most happy would it be for mankind were

Library of Congress

Albert Gallatin (1761-1849), daguerreotype made shortly before his death

statesmen and politicians only as honest in their management of the internal or external national concerns as they are in private life. The irreproachable private character of the President and of all the members of his administration is known and respected. There is not one of them who would not spurn with indignation the most remote hint that, on similar pretenses to those alleged for dismembering Mexico, he might be capable of an attempt to appropriate to himself his neighbor's farm.

In the total absence of any argument that can justify the war in which we are now involved, resort has been had to a most extraordinary assertion. It is said that the people of the United States have a hereditary superiority of race over the Mexicans, which gives them the right to subjugate and keep in bondage the inferior nation. This, it is also alleged, will be the means of enlightening the degraded Mexicans, of improving their social state, and of ultimately increasing the happiness of the masses.

It is compatible with the principle of democracy, which rejects every hereditary claim of individuals, to admit a hereditary superiority of races? You very properly deny that the son can, independent of his own merit, derive any right or privilege whatever from the merit or any other social superiority of his father. Can you for a moment suppose that a very doubtful descent from men who lived 1,000 years ago has transmitted to you a superiority over your fellowmen? But the Anglo-Saxons were inferior to the Goths, from whom the Spaniards claim to be descended; and they were in no respect superior to the Franks and to the Burgundians. It is not to their Anglo-Saxon descent but to a variety of causes, among which the subsequent mixture of Frenchified Normans, Angevins, and Gascons must not be forgotten, that the English are indebted for their superior institutions.

In the progressive improvement of mankind, much more has been due to religious and political institutions than to races. Whenever the European nations, which from their language are presumed to belong to the Latin or to the Sclavonian race, shall have conquered institutions similar to those of England, there will be no trace left of the pretended superiority of one of those races above the other. At this time the claim is but a pretext for covering and justifying unjust usurpation and unbounded ambition.

But admitting, with respect to Mexico, the superiority of race, this confers no superiority of rights. Among ourselves the most ignorant, the most inferior, either in physical or mental faculties, is recognized as having equal rights, and he has an equal vote with anyone, however superior to him in all those respects. This is founded on the immutable principle that no one man is born with the right of governing another man. He may, indeed, acquire a moral influence over others, and no other is legitimate.

The same principle will apply to nations. However superior the Anglo-American race may be to that of Mexico, this gives the Americans no right to infringe upon the

rights of the inferior race. The people of the United States may rightfully, and will, if they use the proper means, exercise a most beneficial moral influence over the Mexicans and other less enlightened nations of America. Beyond this they have no right to go.

The allegation that the subjugation of Mexico would be the means of enlightening the Mexicans, of improving their social state, and of increasing their happiness is but the shallow attempt to disguise unbounded cupidity and ambition. Truth never was or can be propagated by fire and sword, or by any other than purely moral means. By these, and by these alone, the Christian religion was propagated, and enabled, in less than 300 years, to conquer idolatry. During the whole of that period Christianity was tainted by no other blood than that of its martyrs.

The duties of the people of the United States toward other nations are obvious. Never losing sight of the divine precept, "Do to others as you would be done by," they have only to consult their own conscience. For our benevolent Creator has implanted in the hearts of men the moral sense of right and wrong, and that sympathy for other men the evidences of which are of daily occurrence.

It seems unnecessary to add anything respecting that false glory which, from habit and the general tenor of our early education, we are taught to admire. The task has already been repeatedly performed in a far more able and impressive manner than anything I could say on the subject. It is sufficient to say that at this time neither the dignity nor honor of the nation demand a further sacrifice of invaluable lives, or even of money. The very reverse is the case. The true honor and dignity of the nation are inseparable from justice. Pride and vanity alone demand the sacrifice. Though so dearly purchased, the astonishing successes of the American arms have at least put it in the power of the United States to grant any terms of peace without incurring the imputation of being actuated by any but the most elevated motives. It would seem that the most proud and vain must be satiated with glory, and that the most reckless and bellicose should be sufficiently glutted with human gore.

A more truly glorious termination of the war, a more splendid spectacle, an example more highly useful to mankind at large cannot well be conceived than that of the victorious forces of the United States voluntarily abandoning all their conquests, without requiring anything else than that which was strictly due to our citizens.

83.

"Green Grow the Lilacs"

The Mexican War was thought for many years to have given the language two expressive words: "doughboy" and "gringo." The former, the common term for an American soldier, did originate during the war, and lasted until World War II, when it was replaced by "GI." "Gringo," an uncomplimentary Spanish term for Yankee or American, was supposed to be a contraction (complete with Spanish accent) of the first two words of the following song. The etymology does not stand up, but it remains true that the song was a sentimental favorite all over the United States, and especially among soldiers, in the decade and a half before 1860.

GREEN GROW THE LILACS

Green grow the lilacs, all sparkling with dew;
I'm lonely, my darling, since parting from you.
But by our next meeting I hope to prove true,
And change the green lilacs to the red, white, and blue.

I passed my love's window, both early and late,
The look that she gave me, it made my heart ache.
Oh the look that she gave me was painful to see,
For she loves another one better than me.

I wrote her a letter all wet with my tears,
She sent me an answer confirming my fears,
Saying, "Keep your love letters and I will keep mine,
Just you write to your love and I'll write to mine."

I once had a sweetheart, but now I have none,
Since she's gone and left me, I care not for one.
Since she's gone and left me, contented I'll be,
For she loves another one better than me.

84.

James K. Polk: California and Mexico

In his third annual message to Congress on December 7, 1847, which is reprinted here in part, President Polk reiterated the minimal territorial objectives for which the United States had originally gone to war with Mexico. New Mexico and the Californias (divided into upper and lower at that time), as Polk had instructed special envoy Nicholas Trist in June to insist upon, were the only basis for an honorable peace. Trist, however, had failed to negotiate a treaty and was recalled to the States in October. By the time Polk was addressing Congress, sentiment in favor of annexing all of Mexico had increased, partly because the Mexicans had refused Trist's terms but also because of the ease with which the army had overrun Mexico. Had another envoy been sent at this time it is likely that he would have gone demanding additional territory, but Trist refused to resign, stayed on in Mexico as an unauthorized agent, and in February 1848 negotiated a treaty that conformed to his original instructions. Polk was reluctant to change the treaty once he had it in hand and on May 30 the Treaty of Guadalupe Hidalgo was ratified. Trist, however, was repudiated and Polk refused to pay his salary and expenses.

Source: Richardson, IV, pp. 532-564.

A STATE OF WAR abrogates treaties previously existing between the belligerents, and a treaty of peace puts an end to all claims for indemnity for tortious acts committed under the authority of one government against the citizens or subjects of another, unless they are provided for in its stipulations. A treaty of peace which would terminate the existing war without providing for indemnity would enable Mexico, the acknowledged debtor and herself the aggressor in the war, to relieve herself from her just liabilities. By such a treaty our citizens who hold just demands against her would have no remedy either against Mexico or their own government. Our duty to these citizens must forever prevent such a peace, and no treaty which does not provide ample means of discharging these demands can receive my sanction.

A treaty of peace should settle all existing differences between the two countries. If an adequate cession of territory should be made by such a treaty, the United States should release Mexico from all her liabilities and assume their payment to our own citizens. If instead of this the United States were to consent to a treaty by which Mexico should again engage to pay the heavy amount of indebtedness which a just indemnity to our government and our citizens would impose on her, it is notorious that she does not possess the means to meet such an undertaking. From such a treaty no result could be anticipated but the same irritating disappointments which have heretofore attended the violations of similar treaty stipulations on the part of Mexico. Such a treaty would be but a temporary cessation of hostilities, without the restoration of the friendship and good understanding which should characterize the future intercourse between the two countries.

That Congress contemplated the acquisition of territorial indemnity when that body made provision for the prosecution of the war is obvious. Congress could not have meant, when in May 1846, they appropriated $10 million and authorized the President to employ the militia and naval and military forces of the United States and to accept the services of 50,000 volunteers to enable him to prosecute the war, and when, at their last session, and after our Army had invaded Mexico, they made additional appropriations and authorized the raising of additional troops for the same purpose, that no indemnity was to be obtained from Mexico at the conclusion of the war; and yet it was certain that if no Mexican territory was acquired, no indemnity could be obtained.

It is further manifest that Congress contemplated territorial indemnity from the fact that at their last session an act was passed, upon the executive recommendation, appropriating $3 million with that express object. This appropriation was made "to enable the President to conclude a treaty of peace, limits, and boundaries with the Republic of Mexico, to be used by him in the event that said treaty, when signed by the authorized agents of the two governments and duly ratified by Mexico, shall call for the expenditure of the same or any part thereof." The object of asking this appropriation was distinctly stated in the several messages on the subject which I communicated to Congress. Similar appropriations made in 1803 and 1806, which were referred to, were intended to be applied in part consideration for the cession of Louisiana and the Floridas.

In like manner it was anticipated that in settling the terms of a treaty of "limits and boundaries" with Mexico a cession of territory estimated to be of greater value than the amount of our demands against her might be obtained, and that the prompt payment of this sum in part consideration for the territory ceded, on the conclusion of a treaty and its ratification on her part, might be an inducement with her to make such a cession of territory as would be satisfactory to the United States; and although the failure to conclude such a treaty has rendered it unnecessary to use any part of the $3 million appropriated by that act, and the entire sum remains in the treasury, it is still applicable to that object should the contingency occur making such application proper.

The doctrine of no territory is the doctrine of no indemnity, and if sanctioned would be a public acknowledgment that our country was wrong and that the war declared by Congress with extraordinary unanimity was unjust and should be abandoned — an admission unfounded in fact and degrading to the national character.

The terms of the treaty proposed by the United States were not only just to Mexico but, considering the character and amount of our claims, the unjustifiable and unprovoked commencement of hostilities by her, the expenses of the war to which we have been subjected, and the success which had attended our arms, were deemed to be of a most liberal character.

The commissioner of the United States was authorized to agree to the establishment of the Rio Grande as the boundary from its entrance into the Gulf, to its intersection with the southern boundary of New Mexico, in north latitude about 32°, and to obtain a cession to the United States of the provinces of New Mexico and the Californias and the privilege of the right of way across the Isthmus of Tehuantepec. The boundary of the Rio Grande and the cession to the United States of New Mexico and Upper California constituted an ultimatum which our commissioner was under no circumstances to yield.

That it might be manifest, not only to Mexico but to all other nations, that the United States were not disposed to take advantage of a feeble power by insisting upon wresting from her all the other provinces, including many of her principal towns and cities which we had conquered and held in our military occupation, but were willing to conclude a treaty in a spirit of liberality, our commissioner was authorized to stipulate for the restoration to Mexico of all our other conquests.

As the territory to be acquired by the boundary proposed might be estimated to be of greater value than a fair equivalent for our just demands, our commissioner was authorized to stipulate for the payment of such additional pecuniary consideration as was deemed reasonable.

The terms of a treaty proposed by the Mexican commissioners were wholly inadmissible. They negotiated as if Mexico were the victorious, and not the vanquished party. They must have known that their ultimatum could never be accepted. It required the United States to dismember Texas by surrendering to Mexico that part of the territory of that state lying between the Nueces and the Rio Grande, included within her limits by her laws when she was an independent republic, and when she was annexed to the United States and admitted by Congress as one of the states of our Union.

It contained no provision for the payment by Mexico of the just claims of our citizens. It required indemnity to Mexican citizens for injuries they may have sustained by our troops in the prosecution of the war. It demanded the right for Mexico to levy and collect the Mexican tariff of duties on goods imported into her ports while in our military occupation during the war, and the owners of which had paid to officers of the United States the military contributions which had been levied upon them; and it offered to cede to the United States, for a pecuniary consideration, that part of Upper California lying north of latitude 37°. Such were the unreasonable terms proposed by the Mexican commissioners.

The cession to the United States by Mexico of the provinces of New Mexico and the Californias, as proposed by the commissioner of the United States, it was believed would be more in accordance with the convenience and interests of both nations than any other cession of territory which it was probable Mexico could be induced to make.

It is manifest to all who have observed the actual condition of the Mexican government, for some years past and at present, that if these provinces should be retained by her she could not long continue to hold and govern them. Mexico is too feeble a power to govern these provinces, lying as they do at a distance of more than 1,000 miles from her capital; and if attempted to be retained by her they would constitute but for a short time even nominally a part of her dominions. This would be especially the case with Upper California.

The sagacity of powerful European nations has long since directed their attention to the commercial importance of that province, and there can be little doubt that the moment the United States shall relinquish their present occupation of it and their claim to it as indemnity, an effort would be made by some foreign power to possess it, either by conquest or by purchase. If no foreign government should acquire it in either of these modes, an independent revolutionary government would probably be established by the inhabitants and such foreigners as may remain in or remove to the country as soon as it shall be known that the United States have abandoned it. Such a government would be too feeble long to maintain its separate independent existence, and would finally become annexed to or be a dependent colony of some more powerful state.

Should any foreign government attempt to possess it as a colony, or otherwise to incorporate it with itself — the principle avowed by President Monroe in 1824 and reaffirmed in my first annual message — that no foreign power shall with our consent be permitted to plant or establish any new colony or dominion on any part of the North American continent must be maintained. In maintaining this principle and in resisting its invasion by any foreign power, we might be involved in other wars more expensive and more difficult than that in which we are now engaged.

The provinces of New Mexico and the Californias are contiguous to the territories of the United States, and if brought under the government of our laws their resources — mineral, agricultural, manufacturing, and commercial — would soon be developed.

Upper California is bounded on the north by our Oregon possessions, and if held by the United States would soon be settled by a hardy, enterprising, and intelligent portion of our population. The bay of San Francisco and other harbors along the Californian coast would afford shelter for our Navy, for our numerous whale ships, and other merchant vessels employed in the Pacific Ocean, and would in a short period become the marts of an extensive and profitable commerce with China and other countries of the East.

These advantages, in which the whole commercial world would participate, would at once be secured to the United States by the cession of this territory; while it is certain that as long as it remains a part of the Mexican dominions they can be enjoyed neither by Mexico herself nor by any other nation. . . .

In proposing to acquire New Mexico and the Californias, it was known that but an inconsiderable portion of the Mexican people would be transferred with them, the country embraced within these provinces being chiefly an uninhabited region.

These were the leading considerations which induced me to authorize the terms of peace which were proposed to Mexico. They were rejected, and negotiations being at an end, hostilities were renewed. An assault was made by our gallant Army upon the strongly fortified places near the gates of the city of Mexico and upon the city itself, and after several days of severe conflict the Mexican forces, vastly superior in number to our own, were driven from the city, and it was occupied by our troops.

Immediately after information was received of the unfavorable result of the negotiations, believing that his continued presence with the Army could be productive of no good, I determined to recall our commissioner. A dispatch to this effect was transmitted to him on the 6th of October last. The Mexican government will be informed of his recall, and that in the existing state of things I shall not deem it proper to make any further overtures of peace, but shall be at all times ready to receive and consider any proposals which may be made by Mexico.

Since the liberal proposition of the United States was authorized to be made, in April last, large expenditures have been incurred and the precious blood of many of our patriotic fellow citizens has been shed in the prosecution of the war. This consideration and the obstinate perseverance of Mexico in protracting the war must influence the terms of peace which it may be deemed proper hereafter to accept.

Our arms having been everywhere victorious, having subjected to our military occupation a large portion of the enemy's country, including his capital; and negotiations for peace having failed, the important questions arise, in what manner the war ought to be prosecuted and what should be our future policy. I cannot doubt that we should secure and render available the conquests which we have already made, and that with this view we should hold and occupy by our naval and military forces all the ports, towns, cities, and provinces now in our occupation or which may hereafter fall into our possession; that we should press forward our military operations and levy such military contributions on the enemy as may, as far as practicable, defray the future expenses of the war.

Had the government of Mexico acceded to the equitable and liberal terms proposed, that mode of adjustment would have been preferred. Mexico having declined to do this and failed to offer any other terms which could be accepted by the United States, the national honor, no less than the public interests, requires that the war should be prosecuted with increased energy and power until a just and satisfactory peace can be obtained. In the meantime, as Mexico refuses all indemnity, we should adopt measures to indemnify ourselves by appropriating permanently a portion of her territory.

Early after the commencement of the war, New Mexico and the Californias were taken possession of by our forces. Our military and naval commanders were ordered to conquer and hold them, subject to be disposed of by a treaty of peace. These provinces are now in our undisputed occupation, and have been so for many months, all resistance on the part of Mexico having ceased within their limits. I am satisfied that they should never be surrendered to Mexico. Should Congress concur with me in this opinion, and that they should be retained by the United States as indemnity, I can perceive no good reason why the civil jurisdiction and laws of the United States should not at once be extended over them.

To wait for a treaty of peace such as we are willing to make, by which our relations toward them would not be changed, cannot be good policy; while our own interest and that of the people inhabiting them require that a stable, responsible, and free government under our authority should as soon as possible be established over them. Should Congress, therefore, determine to hold these provinces permanently, and that they shall hereafter be considered as constituent parts of our country, the early establishment of territorial governments over them will be important for the more perfect protection of persons and property; and I recommend that such territorial governments be established. It will promote peace and tranquillity among the inhabitants, by allaying all apprehension that they may still entertain of being again subjected to the jurisdiction of Mexico. I invite the early and favorable consideration of Congress to this important subject.

———————◆———————

General Taylor never surrenders.

THOMAS L. CRITTENDEN, reply, on behalf of General Zachary Taylor, at the Battle of Buena Vista, Feb. 22, 1847, when summoned to surrender by General Santa Anna. The phrase became the slogan of the presidential campaign of 1848, when Taylor was elected.

85.

George C. Beckwith: War and Its Remedies

George Beckwith became the leader of the American Peace Society after William Ladd died in 1841. However, his leadership was challenged by the "non-resistors," those members who condemned all war, even including defensive war. In 1846 the non-resistors left the parent body (just as a similar group had done in the 1830s), and Beckwith stayed on to lead the remaining moderate faction. In 1847 he published The Peace Manual: or, War and Its Remedies, *intended to be the definitive work on peace, a portion of which is reprinted here.*

Source: *The Peace Manual: or, War and its Remedies,* Boston, 1847, pp. 187-195, 229-244.

INFLUENCE OF WAR UPON THE ENTERPRISES OF CHRISTIAN BENEVOLENCE

THE CHURCH OF CHRIST, after centuries of comparative slumber, has at length girded herself in earnest for the work of reclaiming the whole world to God, and has organized her Sabbath schools, and her Peace and Temperance, Tract and Bible, Missionary and kindred societies, as the special machinery wherewith to work out this grand and glorious result.

But war either stops or cripples all this machinery. It impedes every enterprise of Christian benevolence. Would you roll back the waves of intemperance? War would open its floodgates wider than ever, and pour over the whole land its waves of liquid fire and death. It has ever been a hotbed of this evil; nor could a war rage throughout our country, without putting back the cause of temperance a whole generation. Its fleets, its camps, and recruiting rendezvous, are all so many nurseries of drunkenness and kindred vices. So all experience, all observation, testify. The war-system, even in peace is a most prolific source of intemperance; for its musters, its parades, and its military visits, and dinners, and balls, and other displays, are so many incentives to habits of intoxication.

Would you fain convert our seamen to God? Alas! War would soon carry them beyond your reach, on board those warships which warriors themselves have sometimes called "floating hells." This department of benevolence a vigorous naval war would almost entirely suspend, and leave at its close nearly our whole marine in a state of moral degeneracy, from which it would perhaps require a score of years fully to reclaim them.

Would you check the tide of impurity? War would multiply its reeking Sodoms all over the land. Would you follow hard upon the farthest wave of Western population, or thread the dark alleys and lanes of our cities, to gather the young into Sabbath schools, and there bring them under the power of God's truth? War would thwart you at every step, and either drive the children from you, or paralyze no small part of your efforts.

Would you plant on the very confines of the wilderness, churches that shall one day make the moral desert there bud and blossom like the rose, and send back thence men, and money, and prayers for the world's evangelization? War would drive your home missionaries from their field, or well-nigh neutralize their power. The mere anticipation of a war in Canada once disbanded a whole presbytery of missionaries, and drove them out of the country; and, amid the whirlwind of war excitement that swept for a time down the great valley of the West, when our troops rushed to the Rio Grande, what could the best preachers in the world have done for the conversion of sinners, or the sanctification of Christians? . . .

Peace fosters the spirit of missions. It was the spirit of peace that brought our Savior from the bosom of His Father; that breathed through His whole life, and drew from His cross the prayer, "Father, forgive them, for they know not what they do." The same spirit animated the martyr at the stake, and carried the apostles from continent to continent, through fire and blood, with their message of salvation to perishing men. Look at Brainerd in the Indian's wigwam; track the Moravian through the snows of Greenland; follow the footsteps of Schwartz across the burning plains of India, or of Martyn over the mountains of Persia; and you find in each case the same spirit that loves its enemies, turns the other cheek to the smiter, and seeks to overcome evil only with good. Such is the spirit of peace; nor can it exist without nourishing the disposition to bless the world with our religion of peace.

How unlike such a spirit is that of war! They are antagonistic, utterly incompatible. Could two neighbors, while fiercely panting each for the other's blood, seek one another's salvation? No more can two nations, while putting forth their utmost energies in vindictive, murderous strife, labor one for the spiritual good of the other. So of the world; and, if all its myriads were simultaneously engaged in war, the work of its Christianization must cease for the time, nor could ever begin again until the fires of war were quenched. . . .

Peace is also indispensable to secure the men and the money requisite for the world's conversion. It has been estimated that 30,000 heralds of the cross would suffice for this purpose; but the wars of Europe alone sacrificed, in twenty-two years, three hundred times that number, and the war-system of Christendom employs for its support, even in peace, about one hundred times as many! . . .

But war, moreover, dries up or poisons the very fountains of those moral influences which sustain the missionary enterprise. These are all found in the general prosperity of the church at home — in the growth of her members and her graces; in her frequent and glorious revivals of religion; in the multitude and ceaseless activity of her Sabbath schools; in her system of educating a body of able, devoted men for her ministry; in the success of her efforts to stay the ravages of intemperance, and fill the land with tracts, and Bibles, and churches, and the benign influences of a Sabbath devoted to the worship of God, and the salvation of souls. Here are the mainsprings of the missionary cause; and every one of them a vigorous, long-protracted war would either destroy, suspend, or seriously paralyze. . . .

The heathen are not ignorant of our war character. Have they read none of our history written for ages in blood? Know they not that Christendom is now covered with barracks, and bristling with millions of bayonets? Nay, have we not ourselves carried the proof of our guilt to the very doors of the heathen? Show us in the wide world any considerable country which nominal Christians have not drenched in blood. Traverse all Asia, all Africa, all America; and where will you not find their war tracks in fire, and blood, and tears?

Thus has war made the very name of Christianity a hissing, a scorn, and a loathing through the pagan world; and the missionary, go where he will, must meet these deep, bitter, almost incurable prejudices against our religion of peace, so strangely belied for fifteen centuries by her warring votaries. Not a sea can he cross, not a country reach, scarce an island touch, but the war dogs from Christendom have been there before him, to throw in his way obstacles which ages can hardly suffice to remove. Abolish war among nominal Christians; and you pave the way for the speedy, thorough conversion of the whole world to God, and peace will be found to be quite indispensable to the full success of the missionary enterprise. . . .

SUBSTITUTES FOR WAR

ALL OUR METHODS OF PEACE, or substitutes for war, resolve themselves into the simple principle of having nations adjust their difficulties as individuals do theirs. The latter, when any dispute arises, either agree between themselves, or refer the case to umpires mutually chosen, or carry it into a court of law for a fair and equitable decision; and, in pursuance of the same policy, nations should first employ negotiation, next resort, by arbitration or mediation, to some form of amicable reference, or, better than all, should establish a system of justice between nations, like our codes and courts of law for individuals. Some of these expedients are occasional, others would be permanent; and we will just glance at each of these classes.

Temporary Substitutes for War

The first of these temporary expedients, then, would be *negotiation*. So long as na-

tions keep cool and kind enough to adjust their own difficulties, this method is decidedly the best of all. If they made the sword really their last resort, instead of their first; or if popular sentiment should always hold them back from conflict till mutual forbearance, explanation, and concession, had exhausted their utmost power, this expedient alone would, in nine cases out of ten, prevent an appeal to arms.

Our next resort would be to *arbitration;* a substitute adopted when the parties are unable to adjust their own difficulties, or prefer the decision of an impartial umpire. Better for the parties to agree among themselves, if they can; but, if they cannot, nations should in every case settle their disputes by some mode of reference. Nor is there any objection in their case, that would not apply to individuals; for it is just as feasible and safe, as equitable and honorable, for the former as for the latter.

But there is another form of reference in the principle of *mediation.* When rulers become so exasperated against each other, as to withdraw from official intercourse, and the strange, semi-barbarous code of national honor requires them to keep aloof, or to meet only on the field of battle, a third power, friendly to both, occasionally interposes with the offer of its services as mediator. Such services the parties are now bound in courtesy to accept; and this simple expedient, a new development of the pacific tendencies of the age, promises to obviate the most delicate and difficult cases of misunderstanding.

It is well known, that duellists cannot fight so long as a mutual friend stands between them as mediator; and, if so effectual for the prevention of duels, the principle, equally applicable to war, would be likely to prove still more successful here, from the longer delay necessary, from the greater publicity of the transaction, and from the overwhelming majority on both sides interested in a peaceful issue of the dispute.

Thus might a single cabinet, by the well-timed tender of its services, hold in check the war-spirit of the whole civilized world, and do much to keep its nations in permanent peace.

Another occasional substitute for war is *nonintercourse*. If a neighbor habitually maltreats us, and will neither make reparation, nor come to any reasonable terms, we sometimes find it best simply to let him alone, and have nothing whatever to do with him, until he proves himself worthy of our renewed confidence and intercourse. So the church, and all voluntary associations, when a member can no longer be tolerated within their pale, merely exclude him, and leave him to the recoil of his own misdeeds.

The principle is equally applicable to nations. If a government neglects its treaty engagements, or violates in other respects the law of nations, and persists in its refusal to make due reparation, it would be far better to withdraw from all intercourse with a nation so unreasonable, and wait for the frowns of the world, and a returning sense of justice and self-respect to set them right, than to embroil scores of innocent millions in war. Such a contest would soon hide or change the real, original issue, while nonintercourse would keep that issue steadily before all men, and thus concentrate the rays of truth, and right, and public opinion, in a burning focus upon the offender's conscience.

It could do very little injury in comparison with war, while it would be likely to accomplish far more good. Had France, in 1835, persisted in her refusal to pay the $5 million confessedly due to us, such a course as this would in time have secured the payment; but, had we gone to war for it, she would have fought till doomsday before she would have paid a farthing. To this principle of nonintercourse as a pacific measure, or substitute for war in extreme cases, Jefferson gave the seal of his approbation and example.

Permanent Substitutes for War

I. Stipulated Arbitration

Not content with palliatives, we seek effectual remedies for war; and, for this purpose, we urge the adoption of permanent substitutes. The first of these is stipulated arbitration; by which we mean, that nations incorporate in every treaty a clause, binding themselves to adjust whatever difficulties may arise between them, in no case by the sword, but always by reference to umpires mutually chosen, and agree either to abide by their decision, or to claim, if dissatisfied, only a new hearing, or a different reference.

To such a substitute, what objection can be urged? It relinquishes no right; it sacrifices no interest; it would startle few, if any prejudices; it can offend neither the strong nor the moderate peace-man, neither the Quaker nor the warrior; it is adapted to the present state of the world, and consistent alike with the precepts of Christianity, and the dictates of sound policy; a measure level to the comprehension of all, and commending itself to their common sense as simple, feasible, and likely to prove successful.

The plan speaks for itself. Common sense decides, that no man should be allowed to judge in his own case; and this principle is quite as applicable to communities as to individuals. The former, equally liable to all the influences that bias the judgment, and lead to wrong conclusions, should never be permitted, any more than individuals, to act as witness, jury, and judge in their own case. Nor is this principle new or untried. It is as old as human society; it has been acted upon more or less from the earliest dawn of civilization; we often find the wisest and best men preferring it even to a regular course of law, for the adjustment of their own differences; and we simply ask, that nations should exercise an equal degree of sense, candor, and justice, by referring their disputes, in like manner, to competent and impartial arbiters.

The same principle lies at the bottom of all our courts. Every trial in them is a reference. No litigant is allowed to decide, or even to testify in his own case; but he must, whether willing or unwilling, submit to the judgment of his peers on the testimony of credible witnesses. Nor has he any direct voice in the selection of his arbiters; society chooses them for him; and before a judge and jury thus appointed, he is compelled to go, and abide their decision. Such is the ordinary course of justice . . . and ought not governments, in the adjustment of their difficulties, to act on principles as equitable and elevated, as those which they prescribe to their own subjects? Shall common sense, common honesty, the established rules of right and wrong, never be extended to the intercourse of nations?

In behalf of this plan, we might quote the highest authorities, the voice of public opinion fast growing in favor of the principle, and the example of nearly all Christendom, now beginning to adopt it in some form as their last resort, instead of the sword. Do you deem it disreputable? It certainly cannot be more so than occasional reference, which all the world approve. Do you say that nations cannot, or should not, thus pledge themselves *in advance*? They do and must in every treaty. Such a pledge is quite as proper in the former as in the latter case, and is just the thing we need to prevent a sudden, passionate rush to arms.

Do you plead that arbitration is at best uncertain? Not half so much so as war confessedly is. Do you say you can judge for yourself? So can the other party; but, since you differ, and consequently cannot both be right, nor each have his own way, how shall the dispute be settled? Can you find a cheaper, juster, surer way, than reference to umpires in whom you both have confidence, and before whom you are allowed a full and fair hearing?

II. A Congress of Nations

We shall not enter into the details of a plan for a congress of nations. We are not sticklers for any particular plan or name, but propose merely to incorporate the grand principle of reference in some standing tribunal for the peaceful adjustment of all international difficulties.

This plan includes two measures — one temporary, the other settled and permanent. We would first have a diplomatic congress of nations, a grand convention of delegates plenipotentiary, from all parts of the civilized world, that could be brought into the measure, to deliberate and agree upon a code of international law. We would have them invested, like ambassadors, with power, not to establish such a code themselves, but merely to recommend its principles in detail to their respective governments for their adoption or rejection. The next measure would be the establishment of an international tribunal to interpret that code, and adjudicate whatever cases any nations in dispute might refer to their decision. Its jurisdiction should extend only to matters connected with the intercourse of nations; and no case should come before it except by consent and choice of parties. Its decisions should be final, and preclude, by mutual agreement, all right of appealing to any further means of adjustment, except a new hearing, an amicable consultation, or reference to special umpires mutually chosen.

Its decrees, however, should be merely advisory. Whether legislative or judicial, they should bind no party without their consent, and depend for success entirely on the high repute of the tribunal, on the obvious equity of its decisions, and the strong tide of public opinion in their favor. It should act as a diet of ambassadors, to mature terms for the ratification of their respective constituents, or as a board of referees, whose arbitrament the parties would still be at liberty to accept or reject. Nor should its sanctions ever include or involve a resort to the sword. Its decrees should be enforced only by moral or peaceful means. Penalties there might be; but they should all be pacific, and consist in the recoil of public opinion, in the withdrawal of friendly intercourse, or the curtailment of commercial and other privileges.

These outlines should be constantly borne in mind; for they obviate most of the objections hitherto brought against the project of a congress of nations, and would at least render such a tribunal perfectly harmless. . . .

Such a congress would remove the grand incentives to war. It would crush, or chain, or neutralize the war-spirit. It would make the warrior's business odious, and render it the chief glory of rulers, not to wage war, but to preserve unbroken, universal peace. It would give a new direction to the energies of all Christendom, and turn the ambition of princes and statesmen into peaceful channels. It would sweep away the grand nurseries of war, by superseding all war establishments. It would eventually convert standing armies into handfuls of policemen, and leave warships to rot, arsenals to molder, and fortifications to crumble into ruins. Here are the chief combustibles of war; and, when these are all removed, it will be well-nigh impossible to kindle its fires on any emergency.

Such a congress, moreover, would obviate nearly all the occasions of war. These are now found in points of national honor — in sudden bursts of passion among rulers — in occasional outrages of officers or citizens — in clashing views, customs, or interests — in temporary misconceptions and animo-sities — in claims for redress denied, or unduly delayed — in mutual jealousies, suspicions and fears. Most of these difficulties, such a tribunal would either prevent, or easily settle; and for the rest, it would provide an antidote sufficient to supersede ninety-nine wars in a hundred.

Nay; would not this grand expedient suffice for the worst emergency? It would make nations, just like the members of a Christian church, cease to think of settling their disputes by arms. They could never draw the sword at the outset; and the long delay occasioned by an appeal to the congress, and by subsequent preparations for conflict, would give ample time for passion to cool, and reason to gain such an ascendency as she seldom, if ever, had in any declaration of war by men. If the parties disliked the first decision, they might claim repeated hearings; and every new trial would create new obstructions in the way of appealing to the sword.

But why suppose such a tribunal powerless for the preservation of peace? Because it would wear no crown, wield no sword, hold no purse? Such logic mistakes the age. Opinion is now the mistress of the world. Her voice could light or quench the fires of a thousand battlefields. It changed the government of France in a day, and reformed the Parliament of England without bloodshed. It made us free. It once marshaled all Europe in the Crusades. It called up the demonspirits of the French Revolution, and sent hurricane after hurricane of war howling in wrath over the fairest portions of Christendom. All this it has done; and when embodied in the grand Areopagus of the world, would it then be powerless?

86.

Anonymous: Hired Help on the Farm

In the late 1830s and 1840s immigration to America rapidly increased and its character changed; immigrant mechanics and laborers significantly outnumbering immigrant farmers for the first time. The representatives of American labor seriously protested against the incursion of laborers from abroad. Some social effects of the new immigration are described in the following letter, which was published originally in the official organ of Brook Farm, the Harbinger, *on July 3, 1847. The letter, signed only "Wendell," is reprinted in part below.*

Source: *Harbinger,* July 3, 1847: "Trip to Vermont."

No one of the social tendencies of this state is more striking than that relating to labor. There has been, within fifteen years, almost a complete revolution in this regard. Time was, when the sons and daughters of farmers deemed it no disgrace to labor for wages on a neighbor's farm or in his domestic employment. The employer considered himself in no way superior to the employed; they stood on a basis of equality and regarded each other with mutual respect. Now it is among the rarest things to find the son of a farmer, or even a native of the state, working by the month or by the day upon a farm, and it is equally rare to find a farmer's daughter performing domestic service in a neighbor's family, and if any are found doing it, it is because they can command unusual wages, and at the same time feel that they do not compromise their social standing.

It was little thought when it commenced that the employment of Irish and Canadian helps would so soon accomplish such a revolution. But would employers give $12 per month, and $1 per week, for the help of their neighbors' sons and daughters, when they could get far more compliant and servile ones for half the money, and with a little instruction, equally skillful? And would those who had formerly performed this labor, continue to do it, when attended with such a reduction of wages, and when their social standing was affected by it?

The Irish girl and Canadian were not treated as equals. They were not allowed to eat with their employers, were never allowed to entertain company in the parlor, and go to parties with the sons and daughters of the farmer; and here was a distinction odious, and till then unheard of, broadly and clearly drawn between the farmer and his helps — between the employer and the employed. This was a language, whose significance could not fail to be understood, by those who had formerly officiated in the capacity of hired men and girls. To be a "hired man" or a "hired girl" was no disgrace, but to be a mere "help" was odious and abominable.

Moderate farmers instead of seeing, as formerly, their daughters securely and honorably employed in a neighbor's service, watched over, and cared for, as children and friends, now see them quitting home, friends, and paternal guardianship, to throng the factories of Manchester, Lowell, and Andover, where they are shut up for thirteen hours a day, where they are allowed but ten minutes to eat their dinners and forced to sleep in brick pens rather than comfortable rooms, exposed to the tyranny of corporation's odious Black List; to the thousand temptations of a crowded city; a promiscuous population and ill-chosen associates, and without home, friends or counsellors, wearing life to decay, and weaving themselves shrouds whilst earning a gown.

This is only a single paragraph in the record of calamity, which results from a system of repugnant hired labor, but it clearly indicates the great work of this age to be, the association of men, in *attractive, united industry*.

87.

The Ten-Hour Day

After the Panic of 1837 the labor movement faltered, and, unlike its precursor of the 1830s, the movement for reorganization in the 1840s was dominated by reformers. The only cause of immediate benefit to the workers for which it pressed was the ten-hour day, which had been largely established among artisans in the 1830s but not among factory hands. By 1853 the ten-hour day was upheld by legislation in most of the Northern states. The first ten-hour law was passed in 1847 in New Hampshire and its provisions are included in the editorial printed below. The special contract provision, making it possible for individual workers to agree to longer hours, made the law ineffective.

Source: *New-York Weekly Tribune*, August 14, 1847.

HAVING BEEN FAR AWAY at the West when this act was passed, and not having been able to lay hands on a copy for some days after our return, we have been constrained to listen to the discussion of its merits without being qualified to participate therein. If we mistake not, most of those out of the state who have most volubly debated this measure have refrained from publishing it, leaving at least one of their readers imperfectly enlightened by their dissertations. Having at length, however, obtained a copy of the act itself, we give place to it, as follows:

An Act regulating the Hours of Labor in Manufactories.

Section 1. *Be it enacted by the Senate and House of Representatives in General Court convened*, that in all contracts for or relating to labor, ten hours of actual labor shall be taken to be a day's work, unless otherwise agreed by the parties; and no person shall be required or held to perform more than ten hours labor in one day, except in pursuance of an express contract requiring greater time.

Section 2. No minor under the age of fifteen shall be employed in any manufacturing establishment more than ten hours the day, in any labor, without the written consent of the parent or guardian of such minor first obtained. If any manufacturer, or any corporation, or the agent of any manufacturer or corporation shall employ any such minor in violation of the provisions of this section, he or they shall be punished by a fine not exceeding $100.

Approved July 3, 1847.

This certainly seems to us a very poor affair, but not at all for the reasons assigned by the mass of its adversaries. They condemn it for attempting to limit the hours per day of hired labor; we, for doing so little toward the accomplishment of that important end. With regard to minors, especially, we did hope to find this act far better than the mockery it is. The policy of legislative interference with the contracts of adults for their own services may be questioned; but who can seriously doubt that it is the duty of the Commonwealth to see that the tender frames of its youth are not shattered by excessively protracted toil?

Will anyone pretend that ten hours per day, especially at confining and monotonous avocations, which tax at once the brain and the sinews, are not quite enough for any child to labor statedly and steadily? Is it not a chief and powerful argument for any legislation on the subject that the constitutions of the future fathers and mothers of the nation may be and are undermined and broken down by persistent labor through twelve to fourteen hours per day? If this be so (and we have the most irrefragable testimony that it is), why should "the consent of the parent or guardian of such minor" be allowed to overrule the demands of justice, humanity, and the public weal? On what ground is this manifest recreancy to the vital principle of the act defended?

So of the provision "under the age of fifteen." Girls of fifteen to eighteen or twenty should be most carefully shielded from the life-long evils which result from excessively severe or protracted toil, not only for their own sakes but in view of their duty and destiny as the future wives and mothers of the nation. There is no reason for legislative interference in favor of a younger class which does not equally plead for them. And if ten hours per day be enough for anyone to labor steadily — as the spirit of this law clearly implies — it should not be within the power of a father or mother (who may be living in drunken idleness on the earnings of a child's overtaxed energies) to make void the immunity of the law.

We apprehend, too, that with regard to farming and other outdoor labor the act might well have provided for an hour longer per day in summer, to be balanced by working an hour less than ten in winter, which would very nearly conform to the general usage. But we shall hear further on this point.

We apprehend this act will prove worthless as a practical measure and leave everything very nearly as it was. We believe nothing less than a peremptory prohibition of the employment of minors for more than ten hours per day, without regard to the consent of parents or guardians, will effect much, if anything. Still, we are willing to see a trial made even of this milk-and-water enactment. Should it be found to answer no purpose but that of appeasing popular demand, it will not be likely to effect even that for any considerable time.

As to those consistent Free Traders like the *Journal of Commerce,* or inconsistent Protectionists like the *Express,* who talk of the folly of legislating in the premises, and the wisdom of letting such matters regulate themselves, our response to them is the same as to the same kind of logic regarding tariffs, excise, etc. — Gentlemen, we do know that these things have not regulated themselves in accordance with the demands of justice and beneficence in the absence of legislative interference: we will see if law, which cannot well make them worse, will not make them better.

If you have so much faith in "moral sua-sion" and its adjuncts, just try them on in some state where legal interference is condemned and let us see how you succeed. If your plan shall work better than ours, so be it: we are perfectly willing that both should be tried and the most effective commended and relied on.

88.

Daniel Webster: A Railroad in New Hampshire

On August 28, 1847, ceremonies celebrating the completion of the Northern Railroad from Franklin to Grafton in New Hampshire were held at Grafton. When it became known to the gathering that Daniel Webster was at his farm in nearby Salisbury, he was summoned to make a few remarks. His extemporaneous response comprises the selection below.

Source: *The Works of Daniel Webster*, 16th edition, Boston, 1872, Vol. II, pp. 409-419.

I AM VERY HAPPY, fellow citizens, to be here on this occasion, to meet here the directors of the Northern Railroad, the directors of various other railroads connected with it below, and such a number of my fellow citizens, inhabitants of this part of the state. Perhaps my pleasure and my surprise at the success of this great enterprise so far are the greater in consequence of my early acquaintance with this region and all its localities.

But, gentlemen, I see the rain is beginning to descend fast, and I pray you to take shelter under some of these roofs. [*Cries of "Go on! go on! Never mind us!"*]

In my youth and early manhood, I have traversed these mountains along all the roads or passes which lead through or over them. We are on Smith's River, which, while in college, I had occasion to swim. Even that could not always be done; and I have occasionally made a circuit of many rough and tedious miles to get over it. At that day, steam as a motive power, acting on water and land, was thought of by nobody; nor were there good, practicable roads in this part of the state. At that day, one must have traversed this wilderness on horseback or on foot. So late as when I left college, there was no road from river to river for a carriage fit for the conveyance of persons.

I well recollect the commencement of the system of turnpike roads. The granting of the charter of the fourth turnpike, which led from Lebanon to Boscawen, was regarded as a wonderful era. The champion in the legislature of this great enterprise was Benjamin J. Gilbert, then a lawyer at Hanover, always a most amiable and excellent man, and now enjoying a healthful old age in the city of Boston. I think he is eighty-four

years old. He is well known to the elder
inhabitants of this county, and I am glad of
this opportunity to allude to him as a highly valued friend of long standing.

I remember to have attended the first
meeting of the proprietors of this turnpike
at Andover. It was difficult to persuade men
that it was possible to have a passable carriage road over these mountains. I was too
young and too poor to be a subscriber, but
I held the proxies of several absent subscribers, and what I lacked in knowledge and
experience I made up in zeal. As far as I
now remember, my first speech after I left
college was in favor of what was then regarded as a great and almost impracticable
internal improvement, to wit, the making of
a smooth, though hilly, road from Connecticut River, opposite the mouth of the White
River, to the Merrimack River at the mouth
of the Contoocook. Perhaps the most valuable result of making these and other turnpike roads was the diffusion of knowledge
upon roadmaking among the people; for, in
a few years afterward, great numbers of the
people went to church, to electoral and other meetings, in chaises and wagons, over
very tolerable roads.

The next step after turnpikes was canals.
Governor Sullivan, Dr. Dexter, Colonel
Baldwin, and other eminent citizens of
Massachusetts had planned the Middlesex
Canal, connecting the Merrimack River at
Pawtucket Falls, near where Lowell now is,
with Boston. And a canal was built around
those falls, also, to complete a water conveyance to Newburyport. Great expense
was incurred afterward in locking the various falls higher up the river, until at length
the river was made navigable for boats as
high up as Concord. This was thought to
be a great and most useful achievement, and
so indeed it was.

But a vastly greater was now approaching, the era of steam. That is the invention
which distinguishes this age. The application of steam to the moving of heavy bod-

ies, on the water and on the land, towers
above all other inventions of this or the
preceding age, as the Cardigan Mountain
now before us lifts itself above the little
hillocks at its base.

Fellow citizens, can we without wonder
consider where we are and what has
brought us here? Several of this company
left Boston and Salem this morning. They
passed the Kearsarge on the left, the Ragged Mountain on the right, have threaded
all the valleys and gorges, and here they
now are, at 2 o'clock, at the foot of the
Cardigan Hills. They probably went to the
market this morning, ordered their dinners,
went home to a leisurely breakfast, and set
out on their journey hither. Here they now
are, enjoying the collation of our hospitable
friend Mr. Cass, at the hour when their
families are dining at home. By the way, if
they had thought fit (and it would have
been a happy thought), they might have
brought us a few fish taken out of the sea
at sunrise this morning, and we might here
enjoy as good a fish dinner as our friends
are now enjoying at Phillips' Beach or Na-
hant. This would have been rather striking
— a chowder at the foot of the Cardigan
Hills would have been a thing to be talked
about.

Fellow citizens, this railroad may be said
to bring the sea to your doors. You cannot,
indeed, snuff its salt water, but you will
taste its best products, as fresh as those who
live on its shores. I cannot conceive of any
policy more useful to the great mass of the
community than the policy which established these public improvements. Let me
say, fellow citizens, that in the history of
human inventions there is hardly one so
well calculated as that of railroads to equalize the condition of men. The richest must
travel in the cars, for there they travel fast-
est; the poorest can travel in the cars, while
they could not travel otherwise, because this
mode of conveyance costs but little time or
money. Probably there are in the multitude

before me those who have friends at such distances that they could hardly have visited them had not railroads come to their assistance to save them time and to save them expense. Men are thus brought together as neighbors and acquaintances who live 200 miles apart.

We sometimes hear idle prejudices expressed against railroads because they are close corporations; but so, from the necessity of the case, they necessarily must be, because the track of a railway cannot be a road upon which every man may drive his own carriage. Sometimes, it is true, these railroads interrupt or annoy individuals in the enjoyment of their property; for these cases the most ample compensation ought to be made. I have myself had a little taste of this inconvenience. When the directors of the road resolved to lay it out upon the river (as I must say they were very wise in doing), they showed themselves a little too loving to me, coming so near my farmhouse that the thunder of their engines and the screams of their steam whistles, to say nothing of other inconveniences, not a little disturbed the peace and the repose of its occupants. There is, besides, an awkward and ugly embankment thrown up across my meadows. It injures the looks of the fields.

But I have observed, fellow citizens, that railroad directors and railroad projectors are no enthusiastic lovers of landscape beauty; a handsome field or lawn, beautiful copses, and all the gorgeousness of forest scenery pass for little in their eyes. Their business is to cut and to slash, to level or deface a finely rounded field and fill up beautifully winding valleys. They are quite utilitarian in their creed and in their practice. Their business is to make a good road. They look upon a well-constructed embankment as an agreeable work of art; they behold with delight a long, deep cut through hardpan and rock such as we have just passed; and if they can find a fair reason to run a tunnel under a deep mountain, they are half in raptures.

To be serious, gentlemen, I must say I admire the skill, the enterprise, and that rather bold defiance of expense which have enabled the directors of this road to bring it with an easy ascent more than 500 feet above the level of the Merrimack River. We shall soon see it cross yonder mountainous ridge, commonly called "the Height of Land," and thence pitch down into the fair valley of the Connecticut.

Fellow citizens, you who live along the line of the road must already begin to feel its beneficial effects. Your country is rather a rough one. There are, indeed, good lands about the base of the Kearsarge, on Beach Hill, Babcock's Hill, and other places adjacent to the road. There are other portions not so fertile. We may infer this from the names they bear. We have come through "Little Gains," "Hard Scrabble," and "Dungeswamp," which latter, I understand, is an Indian word to signify the poorest land in creation. But, fellow citizens, health and industry, good morals, and good government have made your homes among these mountains prosperous and happy.

This great improvement comes to your further assistance. It will give you new facilities, connect you more readily with other portions of the state, and most assuredly, according to all experience, create new objects for the application of your enterprise and your labor. You do not yet begin to feel the benefits which it will confer on you. I rejoice most heartily that my native state has adopted a policy which has led to these results. I trust that policy may be steadily pursued till internal improvement in some really and intrinsically useful form shall reach every glen and every mountainside of the state.

And now, my friends, having thus shortly complied with the wish expressed by you that I should address you in a few words, I take a respectful leave of you, tendering to you all at parting my best wishes for your health and prosperity.

89.

"Pat Works on the Railway"

From 1830 to 1850 more than 2 million immigrants came to the United States, and of these, more than 40 percent were Irish. During this period many shortline railroads and canals were built and the Irish in particular made up the labor force that built them. "Pat Works on the Railway" tells of their trials. Versions of this song were sung by entertainers, seamen, and Irish railroad workers as far away as England.

PAT WORKS ON THE RAILWAY

In eighteen hundred and forty-one
I put my corduroy breeches on.
I put my corduroy breeches on
To work upon the railway.

   Chorus:
   Fill-i-me-oo-ree-i-ree-ay (three times)
   To work upon the railway.

In eighteen hundred and forty-two
I left the Old World for the New.
Bad cess to the luck that brought me
   through
To work upon the railway.

In eighteen hundred and forty-three
'Twas then that I met sweet Molly McGee.
An elegant wife she's been to me
While working on the railway.

In eighteen hundred and forty-four
I traveled the land from shore to shore,
I traveled the land from shore to shore
To work upon the railway.

In eighteen hundred and forty-five
I found myself more dead than alive.
I found myself more dead than alive
From working on the railway.

It's "Pat do this" and "Pat do that,"
Without a stocking or cravat,
Nothing but an old straw hat
While I worked on the railway.

In eighteen hundred and forty-seven
Sweet Biddy McGee she went to heaven;
If she left one kid she left eleven,
To work upon the railway.

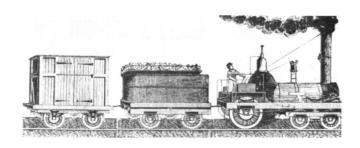

90.

Joseph Henry: First Annual Report on the Smithsonian Institution

When the Englishman James Smithson died in 1829, he left a bequest to be used to found an institution under his name in Washington, D.C. Not until 1846 did Congress set up the Smithsonian Institution, under a board of regents, with Joseph Henry, scholar and physicist, as its first secretary and director. For the next thirty-two years Henry developed and guided the Institution under the terms of Smithson's will, which called for "an establishment for the increase and diffusion of knowledge among men." The following portion from Henry's first annual report of December 8, 1847, outlines his intentions for the Institution.

Source: *The Eight Annual Reports of the Board of Regents of the Smithsonian Institution*, Washington, 1854, pp. 119-133.

THAT THE INSTITUTION is not a national establishment, in the sense in which institutions dependent on the government for support are so, must be evident when it is recollected that the money was not absolutely given to the United States, but entrusted to it for a special object; namely, the establishment of an institution for the benefit of men, to bear the name of the donor, and consequently to reflect upon his memory the honor of all the good which may be accomplished by means of the bequest. The operations of the Smithsonian Institution ought, therefore, to be mingled as little as possible with those of the government, and its funds should be applied exclusively and faithfully to the increase and diffusion of knowledge among men.

That the bequest is intended for the benefit of men in general, and that its influence ought not to be restricted to a single district, or even nation, may be inferred not only from the words of the will but also from the character of Smithson himself; and I beg leave to quote from a scrap of paper in his own hand the following sentiment bearing on this point: "The man of science has no country; the world is his country — all men his countrymen." The origin of the funds, the bequest of a foreigner, should also preclude the adoption of a plan which does not, in the words of Mr. Adams, "spread the benefits to be derived from the Institution not only over the whole surface of this Union but throughout the civilized world."

"Mr. Smithson's reason for fixing the seat of his Institution at Washington obviously was that *there* is the seat of government of the United States, and *there* the Congress, by whose legislation, and the executive, through whose agency, the trust committed to the honor, intelligence, and good faith of the nation is to be fulfilled." The center of operations being permanently fixed at Washington, the character of this city for literature and science will be the more highly exalted in proportion as the influence of the Institution is more widely diffused.

That the terms "increase" and "diffusion" of knowledge are logically distinct, and should be literally interpreted with reference to the will, must be evident when we reflect that they are used in a definite sense and not as mere synonyms by all who are engaged in the pursuits to which Smithson devoted his life. In England there are two classes of institutions founded on the two ideas conveyed by these terms. The Royal Society, the Astronomical, the Geological, the Statistical, the Antiquarian societies, all have for their object the increase of knowledge; while the London Institution, the Mechanics' Institution, the Surry Institution, the Society for the Diffusion of Religious Knowledge, the Society for the Diffusion of Useful Knowledge, are all intended to diffuse or disseminate knowledge among men. In our own country, also, the same distinction is observed in the use of the terms by men of science. Our colleges, academies, and common schools are recognized as institutions partially intended for the diffusion of knowledge; while the express object of some of our scientific societies is the promotion of the discovery of new truths.

The will makes no restriction in favor of any particular kind of knowledge; though propositions have been frequently made for devoting the funds exclusively to the promotion of certain branches of science having more immediate application to the practical arts of life, and the adoption of these propositions has been urged on the ground of the conformity of such objects to the pursuits of Smithson. But an examination of his writings will show that he excluded from his own studies no branch of general knowledge, and that he was fully impressed with the important philosophical fact that all subjects of human thought relate to one great system of truth. To restrict, therefore, the operations of the Institution to a single science or art would do injustice to the character of the donor, as well as to the cause of general knowledge.

If preference is to be given to any branches of research, it should be to the higher and apparently more abstract; to the discovery of new principles rather than of isolated facts. And this is true even in a

practical point of view. Agriculture would have forever remained an empirical art had it not been for the light shed upon it by the atomic theory of chemistry; and incomparably more is to be expected as to its future advancement from the perfection of the microscope than from improvements in the ordinary instruments of husbandry.

The plan of increasing and diffusing knowledge . . . will be found in strict accordance with the several propositions deduced from the will of Smithson. . . . It embraces, as a leading feature, the design of interesting the greatest number of individuals in the operations of the Institution and of spreading its influence as widely as possible. It forms an active organization, exciting all to make original researches who are gifted with the necessary power, and diffusing a kind of knowledge, now only accessible to the few, among all those who are willing to receive it. In this country, though many excel in the application of science to the practical arts of life, few devote themselves to the continued labor and patient thought necessary to the discovery and development of new truths. The principal cause of this want of attention to original research is the want, not of proper means but of proper encouragement. The publication of original memoirs and periodical reports . . . will act as a powerful stimulus on the latent talent of our country by placing in bold relief the real laborers in the field of original research, while it will afford the best materials for the use of those engaged in the diffusion of knowledge.

The advantages which will accrue from the plan of publishing the volumes of the *Smithsonian Contributions to Knowledge* are various. In the first place, it will serve to render the name of the founder favorably known wherever literature and science are cultivated, and to keep it in continual remembrance with each succeeding volume, as long as knowledge is valued. A single new truth, first given to the world through these volumes, will forever stamp their character as a work of reference. The *Contributions* will thus form the most befitting monument to perpetuate the name of one whose life was devoted to the increase of knowledge, and whose ruling passion, strong in death, prompted the noble bequest intended to facilitate the labors of others in the same pursuit.

Again, the publication of a series of volumes of original memoirs will afford to the Institution the most ready means of entering into friendly relations and correspondence with all the learned societies in the world, and of enriching its library with their current transactions and proceedings. But perhaps the most important effect of the plan will be that of giving to the world many valuable memoirs, which, on account of the expense of the illustrations, could not be otherwise published. Everyone who adds new and important truths to the existing stock of knowledge must be, of necessity, to a certain degree, in advance of his age. Hence the number of readers and purchasers of a work is often in the inverse ratio of its intrinsic value; and, consequently, authors of the highest rank of merit are frequently deterred from giving their productions to the world on account of the pecuniary loss to which the publication would subject them.

When our lamented countryman Bowditch contemplated publishing his commentary on La Place, he assembled his family and informed them that the execution of this design would sacrifice one-third of his fortune, and that it was proper his heirs should be consulted on a subject which so nearly concerned them. The answer was worthy of the children of such a father: "We value," said they, "your reputation more than your money." Fortunately, in this instance, the means of making such a sacrifice existed; otherwise, one of the proudest monuments of American science could not have been given to the world. In the majority of cases, however, those who are most capable of extending human knowledge are least able to incur the expense of the publication.

Wilson, the American ornithologist, states, in a letter to Michaux, that he has sacrificed everything to publish his work. "I have issued," he says, "six volumes, and am engaged on the seventh; but as yet I have not received a single cent of the proceeds." In an address on the subject of natural history, by one of our most active cultivators of this branch of knowledge, we find the following remarks, which are directly in point:

Few are acquainted with the fact that from the small number of scientific works sold, and the great expense of plates, our naturalists not only are not paid for their labors but suffer pecuniary loss from their publications. Several works on different branches of zoology, now in the course of publication, will leave their authors losers by an aggregate of $15,000. I do not include in this estimate works already finished — one, for instance, the best contribution to the natural history of man extant, the publication of which will occasion its accomplished author a loss of several thousand dollars. A naturalist is extremely fortunate if he can dispose of 200 copies of an illustrated work, and the number of copies printed rarely exceeds 250.

It may be said that these authors have their reward in the reputation which they thus purchase; but reputation should be the result of the talents and labor expended in the production of a work, and should not in the least depend upon the fact that the author is able to make a pecuniary sacrifice in giving the account of his discoveries to the public.

Besides the advantage to the author of having his memoir published in the Smithsonian *Contributions,* free of expense, his labors will be given to the world with the stamp of approval of a commission of learned men; and his merits will be generally made known through the reports of the Institution. Though the premiums offered may be small, yet they will have considerable effect in producing original articles. Fifty or a hundred dollars awarded the author of an original paper will, in many instances, suffice to supply the books, or to pay for the materials, or the manual labor required in prosecuting the research.

There is one proposition . . . which has given rise to much discussion, and which, therefore, requires particular explanation. I allude to that which excludes from the *Contributions* all papers consisting merely of unverified speculations on subjects of physical science. The object of this proposition is to obviate the endless difficulties which would occur in rejecting papers of an unphilosophical character; and though it may in some cases exclude an interesting communication, yet the strict observance of it will be found of so much practical importance that it cannot be dispensed with.

It has been supposed, from the adoption of this proposition, that we are disposed to undervalue abstract speculations; on the contrary, we know that all the advances in true science — namely, a knowledge of the laws of phenomena — are made by provisionally adopting well-conditioned hypotheses, the product of the imagination, and subsequently verifying them by an appeal to experiment and observation. Every new hypothesis of scientific value must not only furnish an exact explanation of known facts but must also enable us to predict, in kind and quantity, the phenomena which will be exhibited under any given combination of circumstances.

Thus, in the case of the undulatory hypothesis of light, it was inferred, as a logical consequence, that if the supposition were true that light consisted of waves of an ethereal medium, then two rays of light, like two waves of water under certain conditions, should annihilate each other, and darkness be produced. The experiment was tried, and the anticipated result was obtained. It is this exact agreement of the deduction with the actual result of experience

that constitutes the verification of a hypothesis, and which alone entitles it to the name of a theory, and to a place in the transactions of a scientific institution. It must be recollected that it is much easier to speculate than to investigate, and that very few of all the hypotheses imagined are capable of standing the test of scientific verification.

For the practical working of the plan for obtaining the character of a memoir, and the precaution taken before it is accepted for publication, I would refer to the correspondence . . . relative to the memoir now in process of publication by the Institution. As it is not our intention to interfere with the proceedings of other institutions but to cooperate with them, so far as our respective operations are compatible, communications may be referred to learned societies for inspection . . . and abstracts of them given to the world through the bulletins of these societies; while the details of the memoirs and their expensive illustrations are published in the volumes of the *Smithsonian Contributions*. The officers of several learned societies in this country have expressed a willingness to cooperate in this way.

Since original research is the most direct way of increasing knowledge, it can scarcely be doubted that a part of the income of the bequest should be appropriated to this purpose, provided suitable persons can be found and their labors be directed to proper objects. The number, however, of those who are capable of discovering scientific principles is comparatively small; like the poet, they are "born, not made"; and, like him, must be left to choose their own subject and wait the fitting time of inspiration. In case a person of this class has fallen on a vein of discovery and is pursuing it with success, the better plan will be to grant him a small sum of money to carry on his investigations, provided they are considered worthy of assistance by competent judges. This will have the double effect of encouraging him in the pursuit and of facilitating his progress.

The Institution, however, need not depend upon cases of this kind, even if they were more numerous than they are, for the application of its funds in the line of original research. There are large fields of observation and experiment, the cultivation of which, though it may afford no prospect of the discovery of a principle, can hardly fail to produce results of importance both in a practical and theoretic point of view. As an illustration of this remark, I may mention the case of the investigations made a few years ago by a committee of the Franklin Institute of Philadelphia. The secretary of the treasury of the United States placed at the disposal of this society a sum of money for the purpose of making experiments with reference to the cause of the explosion of steam boilers. A committee of the society was chosen for this purpose, which adopted the ingenious plan of writing to all persons in the United States engaged in the application of steam, and particularly to those who had observed the explosion of a steam boiler. In this way, opinions and suggestions in great variety as to the cause of explosions were obtained. The most plausible of these were submitted to the test of experiment; the results obtained were highly important, and are to be found favorably mentioned in every systematic work on the subject of steam which has appeared in any language, within the last few years. New and important facts were established; and, what was almost of as much consequence, errors which had usurped the place of truth were dethroned. . . .

In carrying out the spirit of the plan adopted — namely, that of affecting men in general by the operations of the Institution — it is evident that the principal means of diffusing knowledge must be the *press*. Though lectures should be given in the city in which Smithson has seen fit to direct the establishment of his Institution, yet, as a plan of general diffusion of knowledge, the system of lectures would be entirely inadequate; every village in our extended country

would have a right to demand a share of the benefit, and the income of the Institution would be insufficient to supply a thousandth part of the demand. It is also evident that the knowledge diffused should, if possible, not only embrace all branches of general interest, so that each reader might find a subject suited to his taste, but also that it should differ in kind and quality from that which can be readily obtained through the cheap publications of the day.

These requisites will be fully complied with in the publications of the series of reports proposed. . . . A series of periodicals of this kind, posting up all the discoveries in science from time to time, and giving a well-digested account of all the important changes in the different branches of knowledge, is a desideratum in the English language. The idea is borrowed from a partial plan of this kind in operation in Sweden and Germany; and for an example of what the work should be, I would refer to the annual report to the Swedish Academy of its perpetual secretary, Berzelius, on physical science.

The reports can be so prepared as to be highly interesting to the general reader, and at the same time of great importance to the exclusive cultivator of a particular branch of knowledge. Full references should be given in footnotes to the page, number, or volume of the work from which the information was obtained and where a more detailed account can be found. It is scarcely necessary to remark that the preparation of these reports should be entrusted only to persons profoundly acquainted with the subjects to which they relate; namely, to those who are devoted to particular branches while they possess a knowledge of general principles. Sufficient explanations should be introduced to render the report intelligible to the general reader without destroying its scientific character. Occasionally, reports may be obtained from abroad — as, for example, accounts of the progress of certain branches of knowledge in foreign countries

— and these may be translated, if necessary, and incorporated into other reports by some competent person in this country.

Besides the reports on the progress of knowledge, the program proposes to publish, occasionally, brief treatises on particular subjects. There are always subjects of general interest of which brief expositions would be of much value. The preparation of these, however, should be entrusted to none but persons of character and reputation, and should be subjected to a revision by competent and responsible judges before they are given to the public. They may be presented in the form of reports on the existing state of knowledge relative to a given subject, and may sometimes consist of memoirs and expositions of particular branches of literature and science translated from foreign languages. The reports and treatises of the Institution, sold at a price barely sufficient to pay the expense of printing, will find their way into every school in our country, and will be used, not as first lessons for the pupil but as sources of reliable information for the teacher. . . .

The two plans, namely, that of publication and original research and that of collections of objects of nature and art are not incompatible, and may be carried on harmoniously with each other. The only effect which they will have on one another is that of limiting the operation of each on account of the funds given to the other. Still, with a judicious application and an economical expenditure of the income, and particularly by rigidly observing the plan of finance suggested by Dr. Bache in the construction of the building, much good may be effected in each of the two branches of the Institution.

To carry on the operations of the first, a working library will be required, consisting of the past volumes of the transactions and proceedings of all the learned societies in every language. These are the original sources from which the most important principles of the positive knowledge of our day have been drawn. We shall also require

a collection of the most important current literature and science for the use of the collaborators of the reports; most of these, however, will be procured in exchange for the publications of the Institution, and, therefore, will draw but little from the library fund. . . .

The collections of the Institution, as far as possible, should consist of such articles as are not elsewhere to be found in this country, so that the visitors at Washington may see new objects, and the spirit of the plan be kept up of interesting the greatest possible number of individuals. A perfect collection of all objects of nature and of art, if such could be obtained and deposited in one place, would form a museum of the highest interest; but the portion of the income of the bequest which can be devoted to the increase and maintenance of the museum will be too small to warrant any attempt toward an indiscriminate collection. It is hoped that, in due time, other means may be found of establishing and supporting a general collection of objects of nature and art at the seat of the general government with funds not derived from the Smithsonian bequest.

For the present, it should be the object of the Institution to confine the application of the funds; first, to such collections as will tend to facilitate the study of the memoirs which may be published in the *Contributions,* and to establish their correctness; second, to the purchase of such objects as are not generally known in this country, in the way of art and the illustration of antiquities, such as models of buildings, etc.; and, third, to the formation of a collection of instruments of physical research which will be required both in the illustration of new physical truths and in the scientific investigations undertaken by the Institution.

Much popular interest may be awakened in favor of the Institution at Washington by throwing the rooms of the building open on stated evenings, during the session of Congress, for literary and scientific assemblies, after the manner of the weekly meetings of the Royal Institution in London. At these meetings, without the formality of a regular lecture, new truths in science may be illustrated and new objects of art exhibited. Besides these, courses of lectures may be given on particular subjects by the officers of the Institution or by distinguished individuals invited for the purpose.

I was authorized, in connection with the Committee on Organization, to commence the publication of the *Smithsonian Contributions to Knowledge* and to receive any memoir which might be presented on any subject, provided it was found, on examination, to furnish an interesting addition to the sum of human knowledge, resting on original research. The first memoir presented and found to be of the character prescribed by the resolution of the Board was one on the remains of the ancient inhabitants of the North American continent. It contains the result of several years' labor in the survey and exploration of the mounds and earthworks of the Mississippi Valley, and will furnish a highly interesting addition to the antiquities of our country which could not have been given to the world but for the timely aid extended to it by this Institution. The memoir was referred to the American Ethnological Society with a request that a committee of its members might be appointed to examine and report on its character, as to fitness for publication in the *Smithsonian Contributions to Knowledge.* On the favorable report of this committee, and on the responsibility of the society, the memoir has been accepted for publication.

91.

Ole M. Raeder: Norwegian Immigrants in America

In 1847 Ole Raeder, a distinguished Norwegian jurist, was sent to the United States by the Norwegian government to study the American jury system. Raeder recorded his impressions of America in general and the Norwegian settlements in particular in discerning letters addressed "to my countrymen." These he sent home regularly for publication in Norwegian newspapers. Examples are given below.

Source: *America in the Forties: The Letters of Ole Munch Raeder,* Gunnar J. Malmin, translator and editor, Minneapolis, 1929, pp. 18-28.

I CANNOT CONVINCE MYSELF that all these countrymen of ours, as they leave our own country, are to be regarded as completely lost and as strangers to us. On the contrary, I believe that they are carrying on a great national mission — in accordance with the wishes of Providence, working through their instinctive desire to wander. Their mission consists in proclaiming to the world that the people of the Scandinavian countries, who in former days steered their course over every sea and even found their way to the distant shores of Vinland and Hvidmannaland, have not been blotted out from among the peoples of the earth, nor have they degenerated.

After having regained their independence, so that they again can show themselves in the world, they come to demand their place in that country upon which their fathers cast the first ray of light, no matter how flickering and uncertain, and to take part in the great future which is in store for this youthful, but already mighty, republic. Let them become Americans, as is the duty of holders of American soil, but this need not prevent them from remaining Norwegian for a long time to come. The American character is not yet so fixed and established that it excludes all others.

The Americans are satisfied with demanding a few general traits of political rather than of really national significance. Under such lenient influences, the aliens are elevated and improved, rather than changed; they lose their sharp edges and adopt some of the good qualities of others. Even if America, fulfilling also in this respect a great and providential purpose, shall in the end absorb and mold together into a compact whole all the various nationalities which now are making their contributions in such rich measure, and shall not only blot out the many prejudices which now separate people in their home countries but also absorb some of the individual characteristics which now constitute the peculiar qualities of each nation; even if such be the case, then surely it will be for us, as well as for every other European nation, not merely a source of satisfaction as an historical fact, but perhaps also, in the course of events, a factor of real benefit that our Scandinavian North has become one of the parent nations for this nation to whose lot will undoubtedly some day fall the place of leadership in the affairs of the world.

There are, even now, so many of our people out here in the West that they already appear as a group and thereby are protected against influences foreign to themselves, because their relationship to one another is stronger than their relationship to other races. But if this condition is to be at all lasting, there must be more intelligence among them; they must realize that this instinct of theirs is quite consistent with good sense and honor; they must learn to appreciate their own nationality more than they do and to cause others to respect it, too.

For these reasons the establishment of a press among them is undoubtedly of the greatest importance. The reading material they have had so far in their own language, with the exception of the few books they brought with them and what has been sent to them for their religious instruction by upright men in Norway, has consisted, for the most part, of a few religious and moral pamphlets, printed by the Episcopalian religious tract society in New York.

The question now will be if there are men who are able and willing to use this means of instructing and influencing their countrymen. Unfortunately it cannot be denied that such men are few and far between — if, indeed, there are any. The natural result of the fact that so far almost exclusively men of the least educated classes have emigrated from our country will probably make itself felt in the use they make of their press. This tendency will be all the stronger because of the fact that the great majority of people, influenced by the examples round about them, realize the need of progress and of getting away from the sense of inferiority, which they now undoubtedly feel, and rightly enough, toward the Americans in so many respects. . . .

I have been greatly interested in finding out how far the Norwegians have progressed in their understanding of American affairs, for example, as to the differences between the political parties. I must say I believe they have not reached beyond the first rudiments of a republican education. To be sure, I shall not lay too much stress on the fact that a couple of them called the government price on land "the king's price," because it would be stretching the point a bit to charge a mere thoughtless expression to their political ignorance; even in Norway there are still many who, following a custom dating from the time of Christian VII, speak of "the king," when they should say "the state."

On the other hand, there are undoubtedly not a few to whom can be applied what an American told me of one whom he had asked if he were a Whig or a Democrat. The American had soon discovered after questioning the Norwegian about the meaning of the terms, and particularly about what he had against the Whig doctrine concerning banks and the protection of industry, that the man did not have the least idea that these matters were the main issues involved in the political struggle. If he had been asked not if he were a Democrat, with which expression he is well acquainted from his home country, but if he were a Locofoco, he would presumably at once have admitted his inability to answer.

It is the common accusation of the Whigs against the Locofocos that they decoy the immigrants to their side at the elections and on other public occasions where voting is done through the use they make of the name Democrat, which the Whigs claim rightfully belongs to themselves. Especially the Irishmen and the Germans are deceived in this manner, while, on the other hand, it has been observed that the Englishmen, who have a constitutional education and have learned to think for themselves or, as the Locofocos would say, have been corrupted by the aristocracy which infests Great Britain, willingly take sides with the Whigs.

The Norwegians . . . often understand the true state of affairs just as little as do the Irishmen and the Germans, and most of them if asked will affirm that they are Democrats, but most of them, on the other hand, seem to be sensible enough not to be enticed into voting either for the one party or the other until they have learned a little more about what they stand for. Furthermore, most of them have as yet had no opportunity to vote, because it is necessary to have lived five years in the country and to have renounced all allegiance to their mother country in order to obtain American citizenship.

Thus almost the only opportunity to vote that the great mass of the Norwegians have had was on the question of the proposed constitution [of Wisconsin], on which the legislature declared that every man over twenty-one years who had been six months in the territory and had declared his intention of becoming a citizen should be entitled to vote. On the occasion of the election of members to the assembly summoned last winter to prepare the constitution, I understand that the votes of the Norwegians were much divided, and I have not been able to find out whether the Whigs or the Locofocos won the majority among them.

At Koshkonong Prairie the Whigs are said to have voted for the candidates of the opposite party. To be sure, I have heard that the Locofocos in the neighboring town of Janesville had done not a little to gain the favor of the Norwegians by collecting about $100 toward the erection of their church, but the Norwegians of course deny that this had any influence on them, and I really do not know what the truth of the matter is. Be that as it may, the support of the Norwegians for the Locofocos did not extend further than strictly to the support of their candidates in the election.

When the constitution was framed and came up for a referendum of all the voting citizens, most of the Norwegians at Rock Prairie and, as far as I have discovered, the great majority of the Norwegians in the whole territory voted against it. Their votes were not without influence, because the Norwegian population, according to what I have heard from dependable men in the various settlements, must be at the very least 6,000 and, presumably, 7 - or 8,000.

The outcome of the whole affair was that the constitution was rejected and as a result Wisconsin must still be content to be classed as a territory without the privileges of a state. The truth of the matter is that the Locofocos, who made up the majority of the assembly, were a little too ambitious and passed regulations which offended both the common sense and the prejudices of the people, so that many allowed themselves to thrust aside party considerations and vote quite independently. There was, indeed, such a turmoil in the camp of the Locofocos themselves that it was generally declared that the votes on the adoption or rejection of the constitution could not be taken as a true test of party strength. Every Loco was permitted to vote against the constitution without being struck off the list of party members. Thus it happened, in spite of the fact that the Locofocos have the majority in this territory, that their constitution was rejected because of its rather far-fetched provisions, much to the joy of the Whigs.

This was, as already stated, almost the first political affair in which the Norwegians took any real part; and, as far as I know, it was the first time that any official notice was taken of them, through the publication and circulation at public expense of a Norwegian translation of the draft of the constitution. I have obtained a copy of this remarkable document and shall bring it home with me. The translation is said to be the work of a Dane at Milwaukee, and it is, by the way, a rather poor job.

Several circulars by private citizens were also spread among them, stressing the good or the bad features of the constitution. One of these is said to have been written by a Danish painter, Søborg (or some such name), at Milwaukee; it takes a stand against the constitution and its composition bears evidence of a man of considerable ability and familiarity with conditions. Mr. Reymert is also said to have written a circu-

lar against the constitution. A third, in support of the draft, is said to be a translation of a German or English original and to be the work of the same man who translated the draft itself. I have not read these last two.

The objections which seem to have borne the most weight with the Norwegians were concerned with what a couple of them, when I inquired as to their motives, spoke of as the "women's law" and the "money-law"; married women were to be given the right to separate property, and paper money was outlawed. Furthermore, twenty-four acres or property to the value of $1,000 was made exempt from distraint for debts. I think, however, that these regulations were by no means the worst provisions in the constitution.

I am sure I should not have hesitated to vote for the provision in regard to the property of married women, since it is by no means an absolute and unqualified rule. The provision as to distraint goes a little too far, perhaps, and would probably have reduced credit in a territory which as yet is almost entirely dependent on eastern capital; but it cannot be denied that the humane experiments made by New York in this direction are well worth copying. On the other hand, I should most certainly not have voted for the absolute prohibition of banks, although it is easy to understand that people in the West have become alarmed as the result of the bitter experiences they have had with the disastrous effects of giving the banks a free hand.

In Illinois, where a new constitution is just being formulated, the constitutional assembly is said to have discovered a quite novel method of dealing with this situation; it does not absolutely forbid the establishment of banks, but every new venture in this respect is to be brought to a referendum in the primary assemblies. The people are now about to vote on the adoption of the new constitution, and plans are being made to have it printed in English, German, and Norwegian.

The chief objection raised by the Locofocos against banks is the same in Illinois as here and everywhere in America, namely, that they will encourage the growth of an aristocracy; and it is, for that matter, the same question which at an earlier period split the people in the whole Union when the national bank was being discussed. It is an affair which extends back to the time when the national constitution was formulated, and the attitude of the parties on this as well as on almost every other problem of importance has changed so often that it is easy enough to get it all confused; one really cannot blame a Norwegian much if he is not at once able to decide whether he ought to be a Whig or a Loco.

Nevertheless it is interesting to follow the course of the more recent events in this country, and especially for a Norwegian, because the development in so many respects resembles that which has taken place in our own country — much more than in any other European country. The tendencies of their political parties much resemble those of our own, although differing on so many points. After the Federalists had become unpopular, the name "Democrats," which at first very few cared to use, became more and more popular as the principles of the constitution developed and the sovereignty of the majority became more and more recognized. Both parties, naturally, claim to be the true Democrats and call the opposing party Federalists. "We," the Whigs declare, "are the descendants of Jefferson, who wished to protect industry, of Madison and Monroe, who established the National Bank; these very men you praise to the skies as Democrats! We are the ones who are complaining of the authority your Locofoco President is assuming in carrying on his unfortunate and destructive war with Mexico."

No matter what name the respective parties assume, it is certain that the Locos, who now are in power at Washington, have reduced the tariff and destroyed the National Bank, and their President has vetoed a bill providing for the construction of harbors and the like on the Great Lakes at government expense. It is also certain that if anyone tries to remain neutral, he merely exposes himself to the hatred of both parties. It is much the same as in ancient Athens and, to some extent, in Norway at the present time — very difficult to remain outside of a party. To be sure, there is no legal punishment for it, but the press at once picks up such an individual and places him in a party which is called the "no-party" party and gives him thus an exemplary punishment.

Foreigners are, thank goodness, an exception to the rule, unless they intend to become American citizens. To be on the safe side, though, I have declared myself to be a Whig, which I can do quite honestly, as I really must give this party my preference in the two main issues involved. *Nordlyset* declares that it wishes to remain nonpartisan and has rejected attempts to make it a prohibition paper. It is strange, by the way, that there are so few who have ventured to belong to the one party on one issue and to the other party on the other.

I have been assured that such a thing simply does not occur; and yet there is no other connection between the two questions of banks and protective tariff than the rather far-fetched one, that factories and banks could center fortunes in the hands of a few individuals and thus create a sort of aristocracy. While the question dealt with a *national* bank, to be sure, the case was somewhat different, because the rights of the central government were involved. The fact of the matter is that the party organizations are so well established that very few venture beyond the traditional regulations and arguments.

1848

92.

JOHN HUMPHREY NOYES: The Oneida Community

The Oneida Community, founded by John Humphrey Noyes in central New York in 1847, was the most successful socialist utopian community of the nineteenth century. Noyes had arrived some years before at a doctrine of Christian perfectionism that lost him his churchly affiliation, but it was his rejection of monogamous marriage that led his home community at Putney, Vermont, to reject him and his followers, and caused his removal to New York. Of the roots of his community Noyes said: "As Unitarianism ripened into Transcendentalism at Boston, and Transcendentalism produced Brook Farm; so Orthodoxy ripened into Perfectionism at New Haven, and Perfectionism produced the Oneida Community." The community prospered financially after establishing several successful industries, and it remained intact until 1879, when outside pressures, largely religious, caused it to disband. These pressures arose mostly because of the system of "complex marriage" practised by the community. Noyes's beliefs on the proper relations between the sexes are explained in the following selection from his book Bible Communism, *published in 1848.*

Source: *History of American Socialisms,* Philadelphia, 1870, pp. 623-637.

SOCIAL THEORY

[Leading propositions of *Bible Communism* slightly condensed.]

Chapter I. Showing what is properly to be anticipated concerning the coming of the Kingdom of Heaven and its institutions on earth.

Proposition 1. The Bible predicts the coming of the Kingdom of Heaven on earth. Dan. 2:44; Isa. 25:6-9.

2. The administration of the will of God in His kingdom on earth will be the same as the administration of His will in heaven. Matt. 6:10; Eph. 1:10.

3. In heaven, God reigns over body, soul, and estate, without interference from human governments. Dan. 2:44; 1 Cor. 15:24, 25; Isa. 26:13, 14, and 33:22.

4. The institutions of the Kingdom of Heaven are of such a nature that the general disclosure of them in the apostolic age would have been inconsistent with the continuance of the institutions of the world through the times of the Gentiles. They

were not, therefore, brought out in detail on the surface of the Bible but were disclosed verbally by Paul and others to the interior part of the church. 1 Cor. 2:6; 2 Cor. 12:4; John 16:12, 13; Heb. 9:5.

Chapter II. Showing that marriage is not an institution of the Kingdom of Heaven, and must give place to communism.

Proposition 5. In the Kingdom of Heaven, the institution of marriage, which assigns the exclusive possession of one woman to one man, does not exist. Matt. 22:23-30.

6. In the Kingdom of Heaven, the intimate union of life and interest, which in the world is limited to pairs, extends through the whole body of believers; *i.e.,* complex marriage takes the place of simple. John 17:21. Christ prayed that all believers might be one, even as He and the Father are one. His unity with the Father is defined in the words, "All mine are thine, and all thine are mine." John 17:10. This perfect community of interests, then, will be the condition of all when his prayer is answered. The universal unity of the members of Christ is described in the same terms that are used to describe marriage unity. Compare 1 Cor. 12:12-27 with Gen. 2:24. See also 1 Cor. 6:15-17 and Eph. 5:30-32.

7. The effects of the effusion of the Holy Spirit on the day of Pentecost present a practical commentary on Christ's prayer for the unity of believers, and a sample of the tendency of heavenly influences, which fully confirm the foregoing proposition. "All that believed were together and had all things common; and sold their possessions and goods, and parted them to all, as every man had need." "The multitude of them that believed were of one heart and of one soul; neither said any of them that aught of the things which he possessed was his own; but they had all things common." Acts 2:44, 45, and 4:32. Here is unity like that of the Father and the Son: "All mine thine, and all thine mine."

8. Admitting that the community principle of the day of Pentecost, in its actual operation at that time, extended only to material goods, yet we affirm that there is no intrinsic difference between property in persons and property in things; and that the same spirit which abolished exclusiveness in regard to money, would abolish, if circumstances allowed full scope to it, exclusiveness in regard to women and children. Paul expressly places property in women and property in goods in the same category, and speaks of them together, as ready to be abolished by the advent of the Kingdom of Heaven. "The time," says he, "is short; it remaineth that they that have wives be as though they had none; and they that buy as though they possessed not; for the fashion of this world passeth away." 1 Cor. 7:29-31.

9. The abolishment of appropriation is involved in the very nature of a true relation to Christ in the Gospel. This we prove thus: The possessive feeling which expresses itself by the possessive pronoun *mine* is the same in essence when it relates to persons as when it relates to money or any other property. Amativeness and acquisitiveness are only different channels of one stream. They converge as we trace them to their source. Grammar will help us to ascertain their common center; for the possessive pronoun *mine* is derived from the personal pronoun *I;* and so the possessive feeling, whether amative or acquisitive, flows from the personal feeling, that is, it is a branch of egotism.

Now, egotism is abolished by the Gospel relation to Christ. The grand mystery of the Gospel is vital union with Christ; the merging of self in His life; the extinguishment of the pronoun *I* at the spiritual center. Thus Paul says, "I live, yet not I, but Christ liveth in me." The grand distinction between the Christian and the unbeliever, between heaven and the world, is that in one reigns the We-spirit and in the other the I-spirit.

From *I* comes *mine,* and from the I-spirit comes exclusive appropriation of money, women, etc. From *we* comes *ours,* and from the We-spirit comes universal community of interests.

10. The abolishment of exclusiveness is involved in the love-relation required between all believers by the express injunction of Christ and the apostles, and by the whole tenor of the New Testament. "The new commandment is that we love one another," and that, not by pairs, as in the world, but *en masse.* We are required to love one another fervently. The fashion of the world forbids a man and woman who are otherwise appropriated to love one another fervently. But if they obey Christ they must do this; and whoever would allow them to do this, and yet would forbid them (on any other ground than that of present expediency) to express their unity, would "strain at a gnat and swallow a camel"; for unity of hearts is as much more important than any external expression of it, as a camel is larger than a gnat.

11. The abolishment of social restrictions is involved in the antilegality of the Gospel. It is incompatible with the state of perfected freedom toward which Paul's Gospel of "grace without law" leads, that man should be allowed and required to love in all directions, and yet be forbidden to express love except in one direction. In fact, Paul says, with direct reference to sexual intercourse, "All things are lawful for me, but all things are not expedient; all things are lawful for me, but I will not be brought under the power of any" (1 Cor. 6:12), thus placing the restrictions which were necessary in the transition period on the basis, not of law but of expediency and the demands of spiritual freedom, and leaving it fairly to be inferred that in the final state, when hostile surroundings and powers of bondage cease, all restrictions also will cease.

12. The abolishment of the marriage system is involved in Paul's doctrine of the end of ordinances. Marriage is one of the "ordinances of the worldly sanctuary." This is proved by the fact that it has no place in the resurrection. Paul expressly limits it to life in the flesh. Rom. 7:2-3. The assumption, therefore, that believers are dead to the world by the death of Christ (which authorized the abolishment of Jewish ordinances) legitimately makes an end of marriage. Col. 2:20.

13. The law of marriage is the same in kind with the Jewish law concerning meats and drinks and holy days, of which Paul said that they were "contrary to us, and were taken out of the way, being nailed to the cross." Col. 2:14. The plea in favor of the worldly social system, that it is not arbitrary but founded in nature, will not bear investigation. All experience testifies (the theory of the novels to the contrary notwithstanding) that sexual love is not naturally restricted to pairs. Second marriages are contrary to the one-love theory, and yet are often the happiest marriages. Men and women find universally (however the fact may be concealed) that their susceptibility to love is not burned out by one honeymoon or satisfied by one lover. On the contrary, the secret history of the human heart will bear out the assertion that it is capable of loving any number of times and any number of persons, and that the more it loves, the more it can love. This is the law of nature, thrust out of sight and condemned by common consent, and yet secretly known to all.

14. The law of marriage "worketh wrath": (1) it provokes to secret adultery, actual or of the heart; (2) it ties together unmatched natures; (3) it sunders matched natures; (4) it gives to sexual appetite only a scanty and monotonous allowance, and so produces the natural vices of poverty, contraction of taste, and stinginess or jealousy. (5) it makes no provision for the sexual appetite at the very time when that appetite is the strongest.

By the custom of the world, marriage in the average of cases takes place at about the age of twenty-four, whereas puberty commences at the age of fourteen. For ten years, therefore, and that in the very flush of life, the sexual appetite is starved. This law of society bears hardest on females, because they have less opportunity of choosing their time of marriage than men. This discrepancy between the marriage system and nature is one of the principal sources of the peculiar diseases of women, of prostitution, masturbation, and licentiousness in general.

Chapter III. Showing that death is to be abolished, and that, to this end, there must be a restoration of true relations between the sexes.

Proposition 15. The Kingdom of Heaven is destined to abolish death in this world. Rom. 8:19-25; 1 Cor. 15:24-26; Isa. 25:8.

16. The abolition of death is to be the last triumph of the Kingdom of Heaven; and the subjection of all other powers to Christ must go before it. 1 Cor. 15:24-26; Isa. 33:22-24.

17. The restoration of true relations between the sexes is a matter second in importance only to the reconciliation of man to God. The distinction of male and female is that which makes man the image of God, *i.e.*, the image of the Father and the Son. Gen. 1:27. The relation of male and female was the first social relation. Gen. 2:22. It is therefore the root of all other social relations. The derangement of this relation was the first result of the original breach with God. Gen. 3:7; compare 2:25.

Adam and Eve were, at the beginning, in open, fearless, spiritual fellowship — first with God, and second with each other. Their transgression produced two corresponding alienations, viz.: first, an alienation from God, indicated by their fear of meeting Him and their hiding themselves among the trees of the Garden; and second, an alienation from each other, indicated by their shame at their nakedness and their hiding themselves from each other by clothing. These were the two great manifestations of original sin — the only manifestations presented to notice in the record of the apostasy. The first thing then to be done, in an attempt to redeem man and reorganize society, is to bring about reconciliation with God; and the second thing is to bring about a true union of the sexes. In other words, religion is the first subject of interest and sexual morality the second in the great enterprise of establishing the Kingdom of Heaven on earth.

18. We may criticize the system of the Fourierists, thus: The chain of evils which holds humanity in ruin has four links, viz.: (1) a breach with God (Gen. 3:8), (2) a disruption of the sexes, involving a special curse on woman (Gen. 3:16), (3) the curse of oppressive labor, bearing specially on man (Gen. 3:17-19), (4) the reign of disease and death (Gen. 3:22-24). These are all inextricably complicated with each other.

The true scheme of redemption begins with reconciliation with God, proceeds, first, to a restoration of true relations between the sexes, then to a reform of the industrial system, and ends with victory over death. Fourierism has no eye to the final victory over death, defers attention to the religious question and the sexual question till some centuries hence, and confines itself to the rectifying of the industrial system. In other words, Fourierism neither begins at the beginning nor looks to the end of the chain but fastens its whole interest on the third link, neglecting two that precede it and ignoring that which follows it.

The sin-system, the marriage-system, the work-system, and the death-system are all one and must be abolished together. Holiness, free love, association in labor, and immortality constitute the chain of redemption and must come together in their true order.

19. From what precedes, it is evident

that any attempt to revolutionize sexual morality before settlement with God is out of order. Holiness must go before free love. Bible communists are not responsible for the proceedings of those who meddle with the sexual question before they have laid the foundation of true faith and union with God.

20. Dividing the sexual relation into two branches, the amative and propagative, the amative or love-relation is first in importance, as it is in the order of nature. God made woman because "he saw it was not good for man to be alone" (Gen. 2:18); i.e., for social, not primarily for propagative purposes. Eve was called Adam's "helpmeet." In the whole of the specific account of the creation of woman, she is regarded as his companion, and her maternal office is not brought into view. Gen. 2:18-25.

Amativeness was necessarily the first social affection developed in the Garden of Eden. The Second Commandment of the eternal law of love, "Thou shalt love thy neighbor as thyself," had amativeness for its first channel; for Eve was at first Adam's only neighbor. Propagation and the affections connected with it did not commence their operation during the period of innocence. After the fall, God said to the woman, "I will greatly multiply thy sorrow and thy conception"; from which it is to be inferred that, in the original state, conception would have been comparatively infrequent.

21. The amative part of the sexual relation, separate from the propagative, is eminently favorable to life. It is not a source of life (as some would make it) but it is the first and best distributive of life. Adam and Eve, in their original state, derived their life from God. Gen. 2:7. As God is a dual being, the Father and the Son, and man was made in His image, a dual life passed from God to man. Adam was the channel specially of the life of the Father, and Eve of the life of the Son. Amativeness was the natural agency of the distribution and mu-

tual action of these two forms of life. In this primitive position of the sexes (which is their normal position in Christ), each reflects upon the other the love of God; each excites and develops the divine action in the other.

22. The propagative part of the sexual relation is in its nature the expensive department: (1) while amativeness keeps the capital stock of life circulating between two, propagation introduces a third partner; (2) the propagative act is a drain on the life of man and, when habitual, produces disease; (3) the infirmities and vital expenses of woman during the long period of pregnancy waste her constitution; (4) the awful agonies of childbirth heavily tax the life of woman; (5) the cares of the nursing period bear heavily on woman; (6) the cares of both parents through the period of the childhood of their offspring are many and burdensome; (7) the labor of man is greatly increased by the necessity of providing for children.

A portion of these expenses would undoubtedly have been curtailed if human nature had remained in its original integrity, and will be when it is restored. But it is still self-evident that the birth of children, viewed either as a vital or a mechanical operation, is in its nature expensive; and the fact that multiplied conception was imposed as a curse indicates that it was so regarded by the Creator.

Chapter IV. Showing how the sexual function is to be redeemed and true relations between the sexes restored.

Proposition 23. The amative and propagative functions are distinct from each other and may be separated practically. They are confounded in the world, both in the theories of physiologists and in universal practice. The amative function is regarded merely as a bait to the propagative and is merged in it. But if amativeness is, as we have seen, the first and noblest of the social affections, and if the propagative part of the sexual relation was originally secondary and became paramount by the subversion of order in the fall, we are bound to raise the amative office of the sexual organs into a distinct and paramount function. [Here follows a full exposition of the doctrine of self-control or male continence; which is an essential part of the Oneida theory, but may properly be omitted in this history.]

Chapter V. Showing that shame, instead of being one of the prime virtues, is a part of original sin and belongs to the apostasy.

Proposition 24. Sexual shame was the consequence of the fall, and is factitious and irrational. Gen. 2:25; compare 3:7. Adam and Eve, while innocent, had no shame; little children have none; other animals have none.

Chapter VI. Showing the bearings of the preceding views on socialism, political economy, manners and customs, etc.

Proposition 25. The foregoing principles concerning the sexual relation open the way for association: (1) they furnish motives. They apply to larger partnerships the same attractions that draw and bind together pairs in the worldly partnership of marriage. A community home in which each is married to all and where love is honored and cultivated will be as much more attractive than an ordinary home, as the community outnumbers a pair; (2) these principles remove the principal obstructions in the way of association. There is plenty of tendency to crossing love and adultery, even in the system of isolated households. Association increases this tendency. Amalgamation of interests, frequency of interview, and companionship in labor inevitably give activity and intensity to the social attractions in which amativeness is the strongest element.

The tendency to extramatrimonial love will be proportioned to the condensation of interests produced by any given form of as-

sociation; that is, if the ordinary principles of exclusiveness are preserved, association will be a worse school of temptation to unlawful love than the world is, in proportion to its social advantages. Love in the exclusive form has jealousy for its complement; and jealousy brings on strife and division. Association, therefore, if it retains one-love exclusiveness, contains the seeds of dissolution; and those seeds will be hastened to their harvest by the warmth of associate life.

An association of states with customhouse lines around each is sure to be quarrelsome. The further states in that situation are apart, and the more their interests are isolated, the better. The only way to prevent smuggling and strife in a confederation of contiguous states is to abolish customhouse lines from the interior, and declare free trade and free transit, collecting revenues, and fostering home products by one customhouse line around the whole. This is the policy of the heavenly system — "that they *all* (not two and two) may be one."

26. In vital society, strength will be increased and the necessity of labor diminished, till work will become sport, as it would have been in the original Eden state. Gen. 2:15; compare 3:17-19. Here we come to the field of the Fourierists — the third link of the chain of evil. And here we shall doubtless ultimately avail ourselves of many of the economical and industrial discoveries of Fourier. But as the fundamental principle of our system differs entirely from that of Fourier (our foundation being his superstructure, and vice-versa), and as every system necessarily has its own complement of external arrangements, conformed to its own genius, we will pursue our investigations for the present independently, and with special reference to our peculiar principles.

Labor is sport or drudgery according to the proportion between strength and the work to be done. Work that overtasks a child is easy to a man. The amount of work remaining the same, if man's strength were doubled, the result would be the same as if the amount of work were diminished one-half. To make labor sport, therefore, we must seek, first, increase of strength, and second, diminution of work; or (as in the former problem relating to the curse on woman), first, enlargement of income, and second, diminution of expenses. Vital society secures both of these objects. It increases strength by placing the individual in a vital organization, which is in communication with the source of life and which distributes and circulates life with the highest activity; and, at the same time, by its compound economies, it reduces the work to be done to a minimum.

27. In vital society, labor will become attractive. Loving companionship in labor, and especially the mingling of the sexes, makes labor attractive. The present division of labor between the sexes separates them entirely. The woman keeps house and the man labors abroad. Instead of this, in vital society, men and women will mingle in both of their peculiar departments of work. It will be economically as well as spiritually profitable to marry them indoors and out, by day as well as by night. When the partition between the sexes is taken away and man ceases to make woman a propagative drudge, when love takes the place of shame and fashion follows nature in dress and business, men and women will be able to mingle in all their employments, as boys and girls mingle in their sports; and then labor will be attractive.

28. We can now see our way to victory over death. Reconciliation with God opens the way for the reconciliation of the sexes. Reconciliation of the sexes emancipates woman and opens the way for vital society. Vital society increases strength, diminishes work, and makes labor attractive, thus removing the antecedents of death. First we abolish sin; then shame; then the curse on woman of exhausting childbearing; then the

curse on man of exhausting labor; and so we arrive regularly at the tree of life.

Chapter VII. A concluding caveat that ought to be noted by every reader of the foregoing argument.

Proposition 29. The will of God is done in heaven and of course will be done in His kingdom on earth, not merely by general obedience to constitutional principles but by specific obedience to the administration of His spirit. The constitution of a nation is one thing and the living administration of government is another. Ordinary theology directs attention chiefly, and almost exclusively, to the constitutional principles of God's government; and the same may be said of Fourierism, and all schemes of reform based on the development of "natural laws." But as loyal subjects of God, we must give and call attention to His actual administration; *i.e.,* to His will directly manifested by His spirit and the agents of His spirit, viz., His officers and representatives.

We must look to God, not only for a constitution but for presidential outlook and counsel; for a cabinet and corps of officers; for national aims and plans; for direction, not only in regard to principles to be carried out but in regard to time and circumstance in carrying them out. In other words, the men who are called to usher in the Kingdom of God will be guided, not merely by theoretical truth but by the spirit of God and specific manifestations of His will and policy, as were Abraham, Moses, David, Jesus Christ, Paul, etc.

This will be called a fanatical principle because it requires bona fide communication with the Heavens and displaces the sanctified maxim that the "age of miracles and inspiration is past." But it is clearly a Bible principle; and we must place it on high, above all others, as the palladium of conservatism in the introduction of the new social order.

93.

BENJAMIN HALLETT: The Sovereignty of the People

The events leading up to the case of Luther v. Borden occurred during Dorr's Rebellion in Rhode Island. The appeal, as brought before the U.S. Supreme Court, sought more than a personal redress of grievances. It was a case to test the legality of the Dorr constitution and, by implication, to ascertain whether a majority of citizens in a state could create a new government to supersede an unpopular, constituted authority. Benjamin Hallett represented Luther, and Daniel Webster represented Borden. In spite of the intent of the case, the Supreme Court failed to consider the fundamental issues raised and sustained a lower court decision against Luther. Following is a portion of Hallett's argument before the Supreme Court in January 1848.

Source: *Mr. Hallett's Argument in the Rhode Island Causes*, Boston, 1848, pp. 3-55.

THE FIRST OF THESE CAUSES comes before this Court by writ of error to the Circuit Court of the United States for the District of Rhode Island, upon a judgment pro forma against the plaintiff in error. The second is sent up from the same Court upon a certificate of division of opinion between the two judges.

Both causes involve similar questions and principles, and therefore may with great propriety be argued together, the distinction between them being, that in the first the distinct issue raised is the validity of the people's constitution, which the plaintiff claims was in force in Rhode Island; and in the second the question is definitely raised as to the force and validity of martial law, under which the defendants justify their acts of trespass.

If the new constitution, and laws under it, were in force in Rhode Island, and the old charter government rightfully superseded thereby, then the justification of the defendants fails in both cases. If, on the other hand, that constitution was not in force, but the charter legislature was in fact the law-making power, yet, if they had not the

power to declare martial law in the manner they did, or if the act itself and the proceedings under it were illegal or defective, or if the defendants have failed to show their authority as subordinates, then also the defense in both cases, but especially in the latter, fails.

The first is an action for trespass to the property of the plaintiff, Martin Luther; the second is an action for trespass to the person of the plaintiff, Rachael Luther.

The facts which appear upon the record and are to be taken as fully proved are these:

In June 1842, Martin Luther was living in the town of Warren, in the state of Rhode Island, in his own house (which was also occupied by his mother, Rachael Luther), and had lived there for nearly forty years. On the 29th of June, in the nighttime, the defendants, Luther M. Borden, Stephen Johnson, William L. Brown, John H. Munroe, William B. Snell, James Gardner, and John Kelly, are charged with breaking into the plaintiff's dwelling house, they being armed with muskets and other dangerous weapons, and in a menacing manner breaking and tearing down the doors, glasses, windows, and furniture, and otherwise defacing and injuring the house.

They are also charged, in the second suit, with a personal trespass upon the plaintiff, Mrs. Luther, an elderly lady of some eighty years of age, by forcibly, in the nighttime, breaking into her chamber in which she was sleeping with her maidservant, driving them from their beds in their nightclothes, and with bayonets pointed to the breast and body of the plaintiff and her servant, menacing and threatening to stab and kill them if they did not disclose where Martin Luther was, and detaining them in their nightdress and not permitting them to dress for more than an hour, to their great terror and alarm.

These trespasses are obviously of a highly aggravated character; a midnight invasion of the rights of domicile, and an outrage upon personal security, under circumstances that would call for the highest exemplary damages. The parties in both suits, by these violent proceedings of armed men against them, were compelled to leave the state in which they could find no protection from law, and became citizens of the state of Massachusetts. It was vain for them to have sought redress in the state courts of Rhode Island. Hence this was precisely the case for a resort to the courts of the United States, contemplated by the framers of the Constitution, in order to lift the questions that might arise between citizens of different states above the partial influences of the local tribunals. . . .

I then submit the preliminary proposition, that upon the pleadings and the record of this case the Court cannot determine the issue, whether a trespass was or was not committed, without first deciding what were the constitution and frame of government in force in Rhode Island at the time. And with this view, and under the permission of the Court, I shall proceed to open this cause upon the broad basis of this argument, in its full force and extent, covering the whole ground of *rightful changes of government by the people of the states of this Union.*

These preliminary suggestions embrace within the issue three general propositions:

1. That the assumed authority, legislative and military, and the acts and orders under which defendants justify, are invalid and insufficient.

2. That the issue was properly before the Court below, and it is necessary for this Court to pass upon it in order to determine the rights of the parties on the record in this cause.

3. That it is a judicial power and not a political power which the Court is called upon to exercise in applying the rule of decision that is to govern this case.

The burden of proof is on the defendants to show their justification, but the plaintiff, doubtless, must show, at least, so far as to set aside the authority of the defendant's plea, that the new government had superseded the old form.

I propose, therefore, to maintain in the argument the following points which were ruled against the plaintiff, merely formally, in the Court below.

1. That the people's constitution was in force in Rhode Island in June 1842.

2. That the legislature chosen under it was the law-making power.

3. That consequently, the preexisting charter government was superseded; and

4. That the plaintiff need show such change of government only so far as the justification the defendants set up, under the first, is concerned.

In order to sustain these propositions we must first establish the great basis upon which alone they can rest in the American system of government, viz.:

1. That the majority of the people, or of the legal voters of a state, have a right to establish a written constitution.

2. That this is preeminently their right in

the absence of any provision in the existing frame of government for its amendment.

3. That this right is independent of the will or sanction of the legislature, and can be exercised by the right of eminent sovereignty in the people without the form of a precedent statute law.

In maintaining these positions I shall not assume to rely upon my own opinions, for it would manifestly be presumptuous to attempt to establish before this tribunal any fundamental theory of government sustained only by the opinions of counsel. This is, of all causes, not one to be carried on either side by eloquence or assertion. It is, preeminently, a case for argument, authority, and constitutional construction. . . .

The American doctrine of a paramount written constitution, binding the legislature, and subject only to the people, was lost in Rhode Island if it did not exist in the whole people. Admitting the right of the people to make a constitution and overthrow the British colonial government to have been acquired or confirmed by the Revolution, how did they lose it? When regrant it? If never, how can this right be denied to the people of Rhode Island, in setting aside their charter government and adopting a written constitution to control their legislature and officers? Then if the right existed, how was it to be exercised? The subsisting government had no power or right to make a constitution. All their declarations of rights in the digests of laws were only repealable legislative acts, without guarantee.

Our opponents, doubtless, will concede a *right* of revolution, but say we must take it by *physical force!* The value of that sort of right to a state of this Union I will consider presently, but the right of revolution being admitted, does it follow that it must be by force? If the people have a right, they must also have a right to exercise it peaceably. If they do so without attacking the existing government, and peaceably set up a government of organic law defined in a written

constitution, and if after this is done, the old government, which is virtually superseded, attacks the new, then to defend the latter is not revolution but law and order, and the old disbanded government is the aggressor. . . .

The Revolution, being successful, established this new fundamental principle of government, and in Rhode Island it was distinctly recognized "that the powers of government may be reassumed by the people whensoever it shall become necessary to their happiness."

This the people did, and no more. They made no attack on existing institutions. They changed no organic relations of the people to the government. They violated no allegiance, they dissolved no community, they changed no relation of the state to the Union. The identity and integrity of the state remained the same. It was no more a change of identity, of relations of people and rulers, of the government and the governed, or of the federal relations to the Union, than a change in the codes of legislation.

The fundamental law was changed by peaceful, popular process. If the right to do so was with the people, the form was legal and even legitimate, for it was sanctioned by the fundamental rule of government, lying at the foundation of all government. If they had this right, they exercised it as peacefully and legally as the legislature could exercise their right in revising the code of state laws.

The theory of the opposite side assumes that the people of the states of this Union have acquired no rights in regard to government, by the Revolution, that the people under old governments did not possess. That is physical right, natural right. The *right of might* which is no right but mere physical power to do wrong or right. But there was no such thing as a peaceful change of government under old systems, and consequently no change of government without the consent of government. On the other hand, American institutions recognize three great principles:

1. The elective power to change rulers.

2. The representative power substituting agency from the people for irresponsibility to the people.

3. And behind all this, the power and right of the majority of the community to change at pleasure the organic law of the state and prescribe forms of constitutions as the supreme law.

This makes the distinction in principle and fact: the distinction between attacking an existing government with lawless violence and the peaceful organization of a new frame of the same government, and then, after it is so established, sustaining it under the forms of law. This is the Rhode Island case, and this is shown by the history of the proceedings up to the first attempts of the chartists to resist the operations of the people's constitution.

At the first step the charter assembly fell into a self-convicted absurdity. They had looked on and said nothing except resort to the old deceptive mode of diverting the people from a constitution by calling a Landholders' Convention. But, in January 1842, they were officially informed by their governor that the people had made a constitution and demanded of them to surrender up their agency to the new frame of government. Then they spoke for the first time, but it was only declaratory. They resolved that —

> *Whereas a portion of the people* of this state, *without the forms of law,* have undertaken to form and establish a constitution of government, and have declared such constitution to be the supreme law, and have communicated such constitution to the General Assembly; *and whereas* many of the good people of this state are in danger of being misled by these *informal* proceedings; therefore *resolved* by this General Assembly, that all acts done by the persons aforesaid, for the purpose of imposing upon this state a constitution, are *an assumption of the powers of government,* in violation of the rights of the existing government, and of the people at large!

Here we have, in a very little space, the concession of the whole argument. The old Assembly, in this resolution, wrote their own epitaph. They admitted that "a portion of the people" had undertaken to form and establish a constitution, that they had declared it to be the supreme law, and had communicated it to the Assembly.

This yielded the point that those who had made this constitution were a "portion of the people" of Rhode Island. This shuts up their argument that none but legal voters are people. It was not aliens, non-voters, strangers, or disqualified persons but whoever made that constitution were a *part* of the political society and community of Rhode Island! Now add to this admission the great fact in this case, on which both parties stand here, that those who made that constitution were a majority of the *whole* people of Rhode Island, and here we have it legislatively declared, before the old Assembly expired, that a majority of people of Rhode Island have formed and established a constitution, and have declared it to be the supreme law, and communicated it to the legislature as such!

The only trouble was this had been done, as the Assembly say, "without the form of law." That was, at best, a mere matter of form which should never override substance in a great right. But the Assembly relieved the difficulty at once, by declaring that what they meant by making a constitution without the form of law was, "*an assumption of the powers* of government, in violation of the *rights* of the existing government."

And there stood their own Bill of Rights, solemnly adopted by the Convention of 1790, "that the powers of government may be reassumed by the people"! How, then,

Benjamin Hallett

could it be "a violation of the rights of the existing government" for the people to do just what they had declared in 1790, by a Convention paramount to the Assembly, that they might do "whenever it shall become necessary to their happiness"?

This they had done, and no more. In doing this there was no *rebellion* because a new fundamental law was established, and new duties created between the people and their *agent,* the government. There was no *treason,* for a new oath and a new allegiance grew out of this fundamental change of law. Under the old system it was treason. Under the American system it was the exercise of an inherent, inalienable, fundamental right. And the quality of this right could not depend upon the mere fact whether it was resisted or tolerated by the old form of government. If the latter resisted they made war, and not the people who exercised the right and sustained it against the war made upon them by the old government. . . .

Whether it was a constitution of *right* depends solely upon the *first step* in making it, viz.: whether the action of the legislature, and that merely a *request,* was indispensable.

It all comes back to this: Is a constitution void and inoperative unless the legislature request the people to make it?

Must the legislature alone permit, and cannot the people go behind such permission? Can the legislature refuse to act for half a century, and then punish the people for acting?

If of right, without such beginning, it takes effect proprio vigore. The obstinacy of the General Assembly caused the whole difficulty. If they had done in 1841 what they did in June 1842, all dissension would have ceased. The result shows that they were only contending for dogmatism, for they have done in the last constitution just what they charge us with rebellion and treason for doing. The surrender of land suffrage, as the only means of saving the collision that would have shattered the old dynasty, shows the necessity of the change demanded by the people; and the whole point of law and order is that the Assembly would not do, in answer to the wishes of the people, what they afterward did do, and thereby admit they ought to have done at first. . . .

We are now prepared, in the argument to apply the foregoing facts in the Rhode Island case to the broad and general proposition which embraces all free American states, of *the right of the people to change government, and to judge of the occasion.* Did this right vest in the people of the colonies by the operation of the Declaration of Independence? This has already been demonstrated, and will hardly be denied from any quarter.

Then have American institutions in the states or in the Union changed, modified, limited, or restricted this right, as it originally was declared to exist, "inherent and unalienable" in the people? In short, is the sovereignty in the people, and how may they exercise it?

It may safely be assumed that no man, or set of men, in a government where suffrage is in the hands of the masses, will venture to deny, in so many words, that the people are sovereign. Doubtless this will be conceded, gracefully if not graciously, by the distinguished counsel on the other side. But how conceded, is the question. I apprehend, from the tenor of the defendants' abstract of points, that while this same sovereignty may *seem* to be yielded to the people in terms, it will be qualified away, and in effect denied and abrogated, in detail and in all efficient operation.

By their limitations and constructions the people will turn out to be very great sovereigns with very great powers but without any possible *right* to exercise that sovereign power short of *rebellion* against the governments of their own creation! That is the question we are to try: whether this virtue of sovereignty has gone out of the people by some sort of prescription, grant, acquiescence or submission, and become vested in the government, so that the people can never have the free use of it again, without some process of license or regrant from the legislature?

We are not discussing revolutions by mere physical force but a fundamental principle of right; and to test this, we must first see what the right is, and then whether it is a mere abstraction or active and operative. When they talk of sovereignty, what is the sovereignty they mean? That which we rest our argument upon is the sovereignty defined by the enlightened advocates of liberty in the Old World, and its founders and expounders in the new. Here I leave all speculation and abide by the highest sanction of precedents. If dry in detail, it is vital in principle. Then *what is the sovereignty of the people as defined by the American principles of government?*

The theory of the other side, and the only theory they can stand on to invalidate a constitution framed by a clear majority, through the peaceful forms of conventions, is, that the people are sovereign not in themselves but through the forms of law emanating from the legislature. In short, that the sovereignty has no power to make fundamental law, except through the permissive agency of statute law. . . .

Then, if the people have the right, how may they exercise it? Who shall begin, the people or the government, conventions or legislatures? We say the former. The proposition on the other side is: You must have a statute law to call your convention and count your votes, and say who shall vote and how, or you cannot take a step to make or alter the frame of government.

It is not so, unless this boasted sovereignty is but a mockery, a delusion, and a snare. Will this Court say to the people of each state in this Union that true it is they are the source of all political power, but if they presume to exercise their sovereignty in establishing or changing constitutions of government, without consent of the legislature, they shall be followed with pains and penalties, enforced by the lawless despotism of martial law, and backed by the whole military power of the United States, called out by the President to suppress insurrection and domestic violence!

Whenever this tribunal shall proclaim this to be the law, it will have decreed that, in contemplation of law, the people here, as in Great Britain, do not exist. Such is not the law of this land here nor elsewhere. On the contrary, all American precedents and practice of government demonstrate that the assumption — that the first step in reforms and changes of government — must emanate from the established government, and not from the people, is the dogma of *despotism!* . . .

Now let us go back to the first step in free government, and having the source of power in the people, trace its practical operation in making constitutions.

The position may seem plausible and eminently conservative that it will not do to trust the mass of community with the power to assemble together, and ascertain the will of the majority in any other form except by a statute, prescribing who shall vote, and when, and where, and how! But this is not an American principle.

The serious objection to this position is, that it resolves sovereignty into the government, and takes it from the people. This is plain because he who *alone* can take the first step is the sovereign. At his will all progress stands still. . . .

The fundamental distinction between the American principle of *popular* government and the European principle of *legitimate* government is this.

1. In the former the people are the ultimate source of power and can change government without a law permitting them to do so.

2. In the latter the reigning dynasty, or at best the Parliament, is the sovereign power in the state, and the people can make no change in government whatever; they can only take what is granted and submit to what is decreed. . . .

Let the people of this country, whatever else they may yield, NEVER YIELD BY REMOTEST IMPLICATION THE GREAT RIGHT TO ORIGINATE, FRAME, REMODEL AND AMEND GOVERNMENT!

The moment they descend to become mere acceptors or rejectors of amendments emanating from any other source, they are *slaves of government* and no longer sovereign. For this is the vital distinction between the American principle of free institutions and the European principle of legitimate government. . . .

Now we find the majority of the people of Rhode Island adopting a constitution. Must it not be treated as an act of the sovereign power? They answer no, because the Assembly refused to request the Convention to meet. Then, the basis of the defendants' proposition is this:

1. That when any commonwealth or state exists under an organic law and has created a legislature, no convention with a view to a change of the organic law by the whole people can be rightfully held, without the previous consent of the legislature, however constituted, and whether chosen by a minority or majority of the whole people.

2. That if held without such previous consent, it is revolutionary, and its acts, though ratified by the whole people, invalid, unauthorized and insurrectionary.

In short, that the fundamental law depends upon the legislature and not upon the people. The inference from this theory is unavoidable, viz.:

1. That the legislature is sovereign, and that however oppressed the majority may be under a system of minority suffrage, no change can take place unless the people conquer it in battle by force, or unless the legislature grants them leave to assemble in convention to make a constitution!

2. That if the majority of the people (or if all except a quorum of the legislature and the executive) should attempt by force to put down the government, or to change it at all without legislative consent, this constitutes a case of "domestic violence," which the whole naval and military forces of the Union may be called out to suppress!

3. That there are no inherent liberties in the people, and the entire substance must yield to the mere shadow of form.

Such is not the American theory of government. On the contrary, the preliminary forms in making a constitution are nothing to the substance. "They are but the scaffolding of the building, which is of no further use after the edifice is completed and occupied."

It may be suggested that the people's constitution is not proved. It is proved by the facts in the record. But how prove a constitution? How does the present constitution of Rhode Island or of any state exist, and how could it be proved? Would it depend upon no one objecting to the present constitution in Rhode Island? It received not 7,000 votes; much less than a majority of the whole legal voters under it. The people's party might have objected or may now object. The seal of the state might be abstracted. This is no test of authenticity. The people's officers had their seal. The record shows no seal on either side. In fact the only distinction between the present constitution and the people's, as to authenticity, for the time they were in force or to be in force, is the act of the Assembly calling the Convention, and that was a mere request.

Then we must fall back on the system of paramount right. Where is it? Where is the *power behind* all, *beyond* all constitutions? What is outside of the frame of government? Can a constitution be altered only by its own terms, and in its own forms? Even if this were conceded, it cannot apply to Rhode Island. But if only this were true, then we have made at least one step beyond the doctrines of the Laybach Circular. We have made one step in getting constitutions that authorize change.

The doctrine then would be, "All changes in government must emanate from those whom *the constitution* has entrusted with the power to recommend such change." But if it also applies to the case of Rhode Island, then we have not advanced a step beyond the divine right of kings — only to the divine right of the king's charter.

They will contend that the American practice has been to make all changes through the organized government. Such is not the fact. It may be convenient, desirable, but it is not the ultimatum, neither is it a rule. It is, at most, a question of concurrence between the people and the government. Where the voters are the great majority, this might be in practical operation sufficient. But suppose they do not concur? Suppose the government gets into the hands of a minority and won't yield?

This provision for concurrence does not take away the reserved right of the people to act. *They* give all the validity, and not the act calling the Convention. The form prescribed is mere direction to the agents, not a bar to the people. If the necessity arises, the people may act.

It did arise in Rhode Island, and the people acted. The preliminary call, had it emanated from the Assembly, could give no validity or precedent authority until the people voted on it and confirmed it. The confirmation made it the act of the people. But it would have been just as much their act had they originated the call without the unauthorized *request* of the Assembly. . . .

Now, shall this be affirmed of a mere legal right against natural right, and at the same time shall the people be denied the exercise of a great natural and civil right, above law and above constitutions, because it cannot execute itself, in calling conventions and counting votes, without the aid of a special statute!

If the foregoing positions are well founded, they prove that the people in their aggregate capacity as a political community are sovereign as to government, and have a right to exercise that sovereignty and to judge of the occasion.

But who constitute the people who hold this sovereignty? Is it the legal voters, the whole body of adult males, or all the human beings in a state? Standing by itself, each community, being independent, may establish its own rules as to qualifications of voters. The question, so circumscribed, would be one of convenience and acquiescence. It could conclude no right of the majority. With this qualification, the states being independent by the Revolution, each might establish the limitations and exceptions it chose to, as to the rule which they all laid down that the sovereignty resided in the people. When they formed the Union and conceded some of the attributes of sovereignty, they yielded nothing on this point, except that the United States were to guarantee to each state a republican form of government.

The power to frame their own government, subject only to this limitation, was unrestricted. Each state might adopt its own construction as to the organic law and the rights of voting. It left each state as an independent community, and the question who were the people in that community was to be determined by the community, but subject always to the right of the majority to change the organic law. And however this maxim was restricted in practice, its force was not destroyed whenever the rightful majority chose to act.

Now from what source does the rightful majority spring? Who are the people? To answer this, what was the doctrine promulgated by the American Revolution? There can be but one reply, "That the sovereignty in all the free states was placed in the whole body of the adult male population, with exceptions, and in the other states in the whole body of the free white adult males." There is no case of exclusion of citizens who demanded a voice. The exceptions to the rule in all these states were those persons not competent to form a contract. In one class of states, this excluded children under twenty-one years, idiots and insane, strangers and women. In another class of states, slaves are to be added.

The reasons of these exclusions it is unnecessary to discuss because all our governments were formed without any innovation on this common consent of mankind in all governments. *But if a doubt were raised here, it is no argument in favor of limiting the sovereignty to a less number* than all the adult males. If that argument is good, it is the strongest against their theory. So slaves are excluded for the same reason that minors and incompetent persons are, because by the laws of the community in which they are found, they are incapable of making contracts. They are not citizens, and by no qualifications placed within their reach, can become such.

The case, as applied to Rhode Island, or any state where the minority held the right of suffrage, and the political power, would be parallel, only in case the non-voters were not only excluded for want of qualification *but could never become qualified!*

The attempt to alarm the South on this point is absurd. It is not necessary, in order to sustain the relation of slavery in the states where it exists, to limit the rights of a majority of a free people and make them the subjects of a minority. If it were, it would be the strongest possible argument against slavery! Admit it and it gives no security to the voters. The physical force of the slave to rise upon his master remains the same in either case, and the recognition of the right of the majority of the whole citizens to form government recognizes no more right in the slave to act as a citizen in that organization than does the opposite doctrine. . . .

What is the right of revolution as applied to a state of this Union? Even if the right of revolution is conceded, in what practical form does it exist under our institutions?

If by revolution is meant overthrowing the existing government and setting up another by military force, this is no political right. In this form, the same right exists to revolutionize for monarchy as for republicanism. It can only be a natural and physical right, the right of minorities as well as majorities. It exists in every despotic or monarchical government.

It was proclaimed in the Declaration — looking, however, to a new source of sovereignty in the people. A revolution in government, not like that of 1688, which was only a revolution in men and dynasties. But in the American system, in opposition to the European, the moral was first combined with the physical and natural right to resist oppression. It became a voting as well as a fighting right. "It is the right of the people to alter or to abolish government, and to institute new government."

The Confederation of 1777 left the right of revolution in each state, except so far as limited by the pledge of perpetual union, and prohibiting each state from engaging in war without the consent of Congress. The Constitution of the United States went farther. It explained and reduced to practice the right of change of government recognized in the Declaration. It secured the right of the people peaceably to assemble and to keep and bear arms. It left to them all rights not conceded. It gave to Congress the power of calling forth the militia to execute the laws of the Union, suppress insurrection and repel invasion, and to declare war; but no state to engage in war unless invaded. It required the United States to guarantee to every state in this Union a republican form of government, and protect each of them against invasion, and (on application of the legislature, etc.) against "domestic violence."

And here we are met with the objection that the revolution in Rhode Island, though perfected by voting and legislating, yet not having been sustained by military force against the old government and the threats of the President, it became rebellion, insurrection and domestic violence. So that, the moment they give us the right of revolution, they send the President, at the head of all the troops of the United States, to suppress it.

This phrase "domestic violence" becomes most important in the construction of this highest of all state rights, the right to model and remodel its own local institutions. We contend it can only mean resistance to the statute or common law of a state, and hence there was no case of domestic violence in Rhode Island, except on the part of the men of the old government against the new. It was no case of domestic violence, because

First, the whole people there had a right

to participate in government. It was not a question between slaves and masters, subjects and sovereigns, but between the majority of the citizens who possessed every civil right except that of voting — unless they could buy land of the landholders — and the minority who held the land and restricted suffrage.

Second, in point of fact there was no violence and no act done against existing laws of the old government until the new constitution was adopted.

Third, in point of fact the new constitution was adopted by a majority of the legal voters in Rhode Island.

This fact renders it unnecessary to consider the question of domestic violence as applied to the body of non-voters in a state forming a new government, aside from the action of the voters. We do not admit that the people could have been restrained by laws forbidding their meeting, but this is another question and we need not consider its effect. It is enough that all their acts were within existing laws until the new government went into effect. Then it was too late to interfere.

Now if "revolution" in a state of this Union necessarily involves a case of "domestic violence," this right of revolution is held by the whole people of a state, subject to the arbitrary will of the governor, or the quorum of a legislature of a state, and the President of the United States. This would make all state institutions subservient, in effect, to the military power of the President. If the legislature are to determine, in the first instance, whether a movement of the people is revolution or "domestic violence," then the right of revolution is made to depend upon the legislature. This brings back the sovereign power in subserviency to the legislature, for "the legislature will always make the power it wishes to exercise." . . .

This presents the question as to what is the practical value to the people of the states, of the right of revolution, which is conceded by those who deny the right of the people to change government, without the previous consent of the legislature. If in conceding that right they reserve the power in the legislature to call it insurrection or domestic violence, and the power of the President to call out the militia by his mere will, the right of the majority is shrunk into the will of a minority legislature, and the caprice, mistake, impulse, or ambition of the President. It is a right that can, upon such construction, be maintained successfully only against the whole military force of the Union. Such a construction would be to legalize civil war and disunion.

If the President should send his troops to invade a state when changing its form of government, public opinion would enlist the people of other states to join in resisting such invasion; and civil war would blaze through the Union. Suppose a reelection of the President depending on the vote of a state or two where the legislature desired his reelection and the people were against it, and a call to disperse the voters at the polls?

The order of the President to call out the militia might protect the militia; but the order must issue from the President, in conformity to law, and must be executed by officers duly commissioned through all the forms of law, or it would be no justification. And if an unreasonable interference with state rights, it would never be submitted to by the rest of the Union to crush a single state.

This discretionary power of the President can be rightly or safely construed only as applying to resistance to state or United States laws; plain insurrection and rebellion. At best, it is a dangerous power, and the most alarming executive prerogative in our institutions, and public opinion would go far to restrain it.

But it need not be considered in reference to the Rhode Island question. However dangerous the power, the President did not

exercise it in any form to give effect to his constitutional right of decision as to the existing cause; and in any event, his acting with either of the two legislatures would decide nothing as to their constitutional or legal right, and conclude nothing. The threat of interference and of military demonstration may have compelled the people to abandon the further support of their government, but the President did nothing under the provisions or sanction of the constitution. All his acts were private and never consummated. In his message to the House of Representatives, April 10, 1844, the President says:

I have to inform the House that the executive did not deem it his duty to interfere with the naval and military forces of the United States in the late disturbance in Rhode Island; the executive was at no time convinced that the *casus foederis* had arisen which required the interposition of the military power.

This view has been followed out to test the practical value of what is called the right of revolution in the people of a state of this Union. It fails, and we fall back upon the great conservative right of the people: the American doctrine of popular government, viz: that peaceful changes of government are provided as the substitute of violence and bloodshed, "for the people possess over our constitutions control in *act* as well as in right."

The right is left to the people in each state peacefully to reassume the powers of government whenever it shall become necessary to their happiness, "and to institute new government, laying its foundation in such principles and organizing its power in such form as shall to them seem most likely to effect their safety and happiness." This right the people have never surrendered, but if they have only the right of the strongest, nothing is gained over old forms of government.

94.

"No Irish Need Apply"

Substantial Irish immigration began in 1809 and resumed after the close of the War of 1812; Irish represented 44 percent of the total immigration between 1830 and 1840. But Irish immigration reached its peak after the great famine of 1846, constituting 49 percent of the total in the decade 1841-1850. Because of their numbers, their poverty, and, especially, their religion, the Irish were widely disliked; and numerous social and political organizations were formed to foment anti-Irish sentiment. This song, which dates from the period, dramatizes both such feelings and the brash temper often attributed to the Irish immigrants.

NO IRISH NEED APPLY

I'm a decent boy just landed from the town of Ballyfad;
I want a situation and I want it very bad.
I've seen employment advertised, "It's just the thing," says I,
But the dirty spalpeen ended with "No Irish Need Apply."
"Whoo," says I, "that is an insult, but to get the place I'll try,"
So I went there to see the blackguard with his "No Irish Need Apply."

Chorus:
Some do think it is a misfortune to be christened Pat or Dan,
But to me it is an honor to be born an Irishman.

I started out to find the house, I got there mighty soon;
I found the old chap seated — he was reading the *Tribune*.
I told him what I came for, when he in a rage did fly;
"No!" he says, "You are a Paddy, and no Irish need apply."
Then I gets my dander rising, and I'd like to black his eye
For to tell an Irish gentleman "No Irish Need Apply."

I couldn't stand it longer so a-hold of him I took,
And I gave him such a welting as he'd get at Donnybrook.
He hollered "Milia Murther," and to get away did try,
And swore he'd never write again "No Irish Need Apply."
Well, he made a big apology; I told him then goodbye,
Saying, "When next you want a beating, write 'No Irish Need Apply.' "

95.

FREDERICK DOUGLASS: A Negro View of the Mexican War

The treaty that terminated the Mexican War was signed at Guadalupe Hidalgo on February 2, 1848. With minor modifications it was approved by the U.S. Senate on March 10 and by the Mexican congress on May 25, and it was ratified by both parties on May 30. The treaty was opposed in America both by those who wanted more territory from Mexico than the treaty secured and by those who wanted no territory at all. Frederick Douglass, a Negro Abolitionist and editor of the North Star, *belonged to the latter group. An editorial that originally appeared in his newspaper on March 17, 1848, is reprinted below.*

Source: *North Star* (Rochester, N.Y.), March 17, 1848.

PEACE! PEACE! PEACE!

THE SHOUT IS ON EVERY LIP, and emblazoned on every paper. The joyful news is told in every quarter with enthusiastic delight. We are such an exception to the great mass of our fellow countrymen in respect to everything else, and have been so accustomed to hear them rejoice over the most barbarous outrages committed upon an unoffending people, that we find it difficult to unite with them in their general exultation at this time; and, for this reason, we believe that by *peace* they mean *plunder.*

In our judgment, those who have all along been loudly in favor of a vigorous prosecution of the war, and heralding its bloody triumphs with apparent rapture, and glorifying the atrocious deeds of barbarous heroism on the part of wicked men engaged in it, have no sincere love of peace, and are not now rejoicing over *peace* but *plunder.* They have succeeded in robbing Mexico of her territory, and are rejoicing over their success under the hypocritical pretense of a regard for peace. Had they not succeeded in robbing Mexico of the most important and most valuable part of her territory, many of those now loudest in their professions of favor for peace would be loudest and wildest for war — war to the knife.

Our soul is sick of such hypocrisy. We presume the churches of Rochester will return thanks to God for peace they did nothing to bring about, and boast it as a triumph of Christianity! That an end is put to the wholesale murder in Mexico is truly just cause for rejoicing; but we are not the people to rejoice; we ought rather blush and hang our heads for shame, and, in the spirit of profound humility, crave pardon for our crimes at the hands of a God whose mercy endureth forever.

96.

Roger S. Baldwin: The Executive Prerogative in Foreign Policy

In February 1848 the French monarchy was overthrown and a provisional government, espousing democratic principles, was established. On April 6, Senator Edward Hannegan of Indiana submitted a joint resolution, framed by the Committee on Foreign Relations, tendering the congratulations of the American people to the people of France for effecting this change in their government. Although sympathy for the French was widespread, the resolution aroused the opposition both of those who thought that congratulations were premature and of those who questioned the propriety of congressional involvement in foreign affairs. Both reservations were expressed in a speech by Senator Roger Baldwin of Connecticut on March 31. Portions of his remarks are printed below.

Source: *Globe, App.,* 30 Cong., 1 Sess., pp. 453-454.

When these resolutions came before the Senate yesterday, I moved to refer them to the Committee on Foreign Relations. Subsequently, after the remarks which were made by the honorable senator from South Carolina [Mr. Calhoun] I acquiesced in the motion made by that senator to lay them on the table. The Senate, however, did not adopt the motion, and it is now proposed by the honorable senator who moved the resolutions that a day be specially assigned for their consideration by the Senate. I am opposed, sir, to the assignment at this time of any day for that purpose, because I am still of opinion that a reference of the resolutions to the Committee on Foreign Relations, as originally moved, is the proper course to be pursued in regard to them.

The first resolution declares, "that in the name and behalf of the American people, the congratulations of Congress are tendered to the people of France, upon their success in their efforts to consolidate liberty, by embodying its principles in a republican form of government." The second requests the President to transmit the preceding resolution to the American minister at Paris, with instructions to present it to the French government. Personally, sir, as one of the American people, I yield to no senator in the expression of my sympathy with the great movement which is now going on for the amelioration of the political and social condition of the people of France and of the other European states. But as a member of this Senate, I am not prepared to act on these resolutions, or to assign a day for that purpose, until I am better satisfied of our right to act in the manner proposed.

I want first to be assured, that we are entitled, as senators — as members of the Congress of the United States — to speak at all in the name and behalf of the American people, in a matter relating to the intercourse of this government with a foreign nation. I had supposed, sir, that everything relating to the foreign intercourse of the people of the United States pertained, in the first instance, to the executive. I had supposed that in the distribution of powers and duties among the several departments of our government, the people had confided to the President alone the trust of speaking in their name and behalf to foreign nations; and to Congress, the trust of legislating for their benefit.

I am aware, sir, that questions may arise in relation to our foreign intercourse, on which it may be proper and expedient that the sentiments of Congress should be declared. But these are cases where legislation is required, to enable the executive to carry out his views in regard to the foreign intercourse of the nation.

If the President, deeming it his duty to recognize the independence of a foreign government, or to send a minister to a nation with which the United States have before had no diplomatic intercourse, calls on Congress to make provision for the exigency, then, sir, the matter comes up legitimately for discussion before Congress, acting in its legislative capacity, in deciding upon the expediency of granting or withholding the appropriation required. . . .

Congress is not called on to legislate for any purpose connected with the recognition of the French Republic. We are not asked to aid the executive by an appropriation to carry into effect any suggestion or purpose of his in relation to our foreign intercourse. We are called upon by this resolution to undertake, ourselves, the direction of the foreign intercourse of this government; to declare that we, as the representatives of the American people, are authorized to speak in their name — announce their sentiments — and request the President to direct them to be communicated, as such, to the French government, by the American minister at Paris.

Now, sir, I say the American people are able to speak for themselves. They are able to manifest their own sympathies. They are doing it, sir, from one end of the Union to the other; and that is the proper way for the sympathies of the American people to be manifested on this occasion, unless it be done through that organ of the government whom they have specially entrusted with the duty of conducting their foreign intercourse. When and how have they ever delegated to us the power to speak in their name in relation to the concerns of a foreign people?

Sir, if we can tender congratulations in the name of the American people to the republicans of France on the achievement of their liberties, can we not also tender the expression of their regrets to the downtrodden subjects of other empires, who yet groan beneath the scepter of a despot? There are many governments with whom we hold diplomatic intercourse whose institutions are as little accordant with the views and wishes of the American people as those which have just been so signally overthrown; but have they ever authorized Congress to express their disapprobation for those institutions? To what inconsistencies in the action of the government would not such a course inevitably lead? To what derangement of the system established by the executive of conducting its foreign intercourse? By what imperfect lights would Congress necessarily be guided in its action in comparison with the sources of intelligence, which constant and confidential correspondence with our ministers abroad, places at all times at the command of the President?

It appears to me, therefore, to be obviously proper that the executive should take the initiative in all such proceedings; and unless he is under the necessity of applying to Congress for an appropriation to enable him to accomplish his purpose, that Congress should confine itself to the legislative duties assigned to it by the Constitution. By the second resolution, the President is "requested to transmit this resolution to the American minister at Paris, with *instructions* to present it to the French government."

Is not this, I ask, the first time in the history of this government that Congress has undertaken to give instructions to the President in regard to our foreign intercourse? If there be any other instance of record, I am not aware of it. I know of no precedent for such a resolution; but I do know that this matter — of the interference of Congress with the appropriate duties of the executive — has been discussed on more than one occasion, and the sentiments of both Houses of Congress expressed against it. . . .

Sir, I am for maintaining the responsibility of the separate departments of the government. I would neither interfere with the duties of the executive, nor suffer the executive to interfere with the duties of Congress. If each department of the government confines itself to the proper discharge of the functions committed to it by the American people, we shall go on harmoniously and regularly, and the voice of the people will be authoritatively declared whenever, and in whatever form, the occasion may require it to be uttered. But, if Congress is to be made the arena for the discussion, with a view to their promulgation, of any sentiments, no matter what, which any member may think proper to propose in regard to the concerns of a foreign government or people, can we fail to perceive the dangerous consequences to which it will inevitably lead? . . .

Regarding, as I do, the resolutions on your table as liable, in an eminent degree, to the same objections, I am neither prepared at this time to give them my support, nor even to assign a day for their consideration. I do not believe it to be our province to speak for the American people in this matter. I believe they are competent to speak much more effectively themselves than we can speak for them; and that the voice of the people, in the warm language of their own hearts, embodied in their own resolutions, will be much more acceptable to the people of France than any cold declarations in their name by the Congress of the United States, whom they never authorized to speak in their behalf.

But, Mr. President, if I was satisfied that it was proper for Congress to speak in the name of the American people on this subject, I entirely concur with the senator from South Carolina in the opinion that the time has not arrived in which we can, with propriety, adopt the sentiment embodied in these resolutions. The resolutions declare, if I understand their true meaning, that the people of France have succeeded in their efforts to consolidate liberty, by embodying its principles in a republican constitution.

Sir, they are only making, now, the first effort to accomplish this purpose. The government of France is not in the hands of those who have been elected by the people. It is either self-constituted or it derives its power from the spontaneous movement of the people of Paris, with whom the Revolution commenced. The Provisional Government is taking its first measures for obtaining a full representation of the French people in a convention, to lay the foundation for the establishment and maintenance of constitutional liberty.

Have they accomplished it? Is liberty consolidated in the language of the resolution? I do not like the word, sir. It is rather too much in the style of the Holy Alliance to suit my taste. I remember, in the famous declaration of their policy, sent out to the world by the allied monarchs, they spoke of it as the only means of "consolidating human institutions and remedying their imperfections." I should prefer some other word, of less equivocal import. I had much rather see liberty diffused through France, to the utmost limits of the realm, than consolidated in the hands of a Parisian regency. It sounds too much like the consolidation of power that centralizes here. And I think, sir, that the Congress of the United States would be much better employed in taking measures to prevent that consolidation of power which is so rapidly going on within the precincts of this Capitol, by means of the enormous increase of executive patronage, than in undertaking to conduct, unasked, the foreign intercourse of the American people.

97.

Debate on the Yucatan Bill

*In April 1848 an envoy of Yucatán transmitted a message from the Yucatán governor
offering the United States "dominion and sovereignty" over the peninsula if the
American Army would put down an Indian uprising that threatened to exterminate
the white population there. Similar offers, the message added, had been made to
Great Britain and Spain. President Polk transmitted the document to Congress on
April 29, along with an appeal for U.S. involvement on military and moral grounds.
The Senate Committee on Foreign Relations framed a bill providing for the American
occupation of Yucatán. In the subsequent debate over the bill, Senators John Niles
and John C. Calhoun opposed intervention in speeches delivered during the month of
May, portions of which appear below. The issue was dropped when the white and
Indian inhabitants of Yucatán reached an independent settlement.*

Source: *Globe, App.,* 30 Cong., 1 Sess., pp. 609-613, 630-633.

I.

JOHN NILES: Against Intervention in the Internal Affairs of Other Nations

MR. PRESIDENT, to judge of the propriety of passing this bill and to appreciate the force of the objections which stand in the way of its passage, we must first consider what the bill is, what it proposes to do. The first section authorizes and directs the president to take temporary military occupation of Yucatán and to employ the Army and Navy of the United States to assist the white population of the country in the war in which they are now engaged with the Indians. This is certainly a very important and a very extraordinary measure. It is not exactly a declaration of war, yet it involves a war and all its responsibilities — a war which may be protracted and troublesome. But it is something more than a declaration of war, as the bill on its face looks to acquisition and conquest. War may lead to con-

quest; but this bill, on its face, directs the President to take possession of a foreign country, and establish a military government over it.

A military occupation will of course supersede the existing government, as has been the case in other parts of Mexico where we have had a military occupation. This, then, is a bill to take possession of Yucatán and establish our authority over it. I know it is said that the occupation is to be temporary; but when will a temporary occupation cease? Not certainly until the causes which induced the occupation have ceased to exist, and, as they will not be likely soon to disappear, the occupation will become permanent.

And on what grounds is it claimed that so extraordinary a measure as this can be justified? Two have been assigned: first, on the ground of policy; and second, on the ground of humanity, our interference having been solicited by the government of Yucatán. These two grounds do not stand well together. If we interfere and take possession of the country from considerations of policy, the world will give us very little credit for our humanity. They are inconsistent with each other: one looks to our own interest, the other to the interest of the people of Yucatán. That we might interfere and assist the people of that country in a way to rest on grounds of humanity will not be denied; but the manner provided in this bill really excludes all idea of humanity and makes all the measure strictly one of policy; and the honorable chairman who reported the bill had the candor to admit that this was mainly a measure of policy. His remarks were almost entirely confined to that view of the question.

To justify the measure on either ground, it becomes important to see what is the political condition of Yucatán. Like every other people, Yucatán must be regarded in one of three political aspects: either as an independent state, possessing and exercising the right of sovereignty; as a dependency of Mexico; or in a state of revolution, having thrown off the yoke of Mexico, yet not having established its independence, so as to be recognized as one of the family of nations.

No one claims that Yucatán is an independent state; she does not claim it herself. The most that she claims is that she has thrown off the authority of Mexico and that she has been neutral in the war between the United States and Mexico. Our government has in some respects recognized her neutrality but in others has regarded her as a part of Mexico. We have taken and still hold Laguna, one of her ports, where we have collected duties as in other ports of Mexico in our possession. But in what light does Mexico regard Yucatán? She certainly regards her as one of the states of that Republic.

How, then, can we take possession of that country without giving offense to Mexico? If we establish our authority there, it will exclude the authority of Mexico; we

must hold the country against Mexico. If we were not now in a war with Mexico, this would be regarded by her as an invasion of her territory and would certainly involve us in a war with Mexico. That our occupation was in pursuance of a request of Yucatán would be no justification to Mexico as long as she regards Yucatán as a part of her territory. It would be another Texas affair with this important difference — that Yucatán has not yet asserted her independence and has not been recognized as an independent state by any nation, not even by the United States. Her consent, therefore, would amount to nothing. It would be no answer to the complaints of Mexico to say that we had taken possession of this department of hers for purposes of humanity, to assist the people in defending themselves against the Indian population. . . .

Mr. President, in whatever light we regard the people of Yucatán, whether as an independent people or as a dependency upon Mexico or as in a state of revolution, you cannot pass this bill consistently with what I believe we admit to be the settled principles of policy which have ever governed the conduct of this government in its intercourse with foreign powers. In accordance with these principles, it makes no difference whether Yucatán is regarded in any one of these three lights. We have no more right to interfere in the domestic concerns of a state or province under the jurisdiction of some other country.— no more right to interfere in domestic affairs, local in their character — than we have to interfere in the domestic affairs of a great independent state. Upon what principle, sir, can this military occupation of this province be justified in reference to the established principles which have governed the action of the United States? View it in whatever aspect you please, I ask upon what ground can it be justified?

Sir, there are two great principles which have been held sacred by this country from its earliest history; and I am not prepared to admit that the declaration of Mr. Monroe, so often referred to, if properly understood, gives any sanction or recognizes any policy of this government which involves a departure from these principles. What are these principles?

First, there is the principle of neutrality with regard to belligerents. This principle our government has ever maintained, and a majority of our most distinguished statesmen have endeavored to impress its importance upon the minds of our people and upon every other nation in the world, in every possible mode and form. They have held it as one of the most sacred of principles in regard to our intercourse with the other powers of the world and the surest guaranty of peace. Can we, consistently with what is due to this great principle, interfere in this civil war, whether we regard Yucatán as an independent state or as a dependent province? She is no part of the United States; she is a country foreign to us. There is a war there, sir; and can we forcibly interfere in it without invalidating the great principle of neutrality toward belligerents? I see no answer to this query, and I believe there can be no answer.

The second principle we have hitherto held equally sacred, the principle of nonintervention. It is the principle which this government, above all others, ought to hold sacred because it strikes at the very foundations of free government. It is the principle which belongs to a free people; which is, that they should take care of their own affairs. Is it consistent with this principle to take possession of a foreign state and take part in a civil war in which it is engaged? Why, sir, a proposition of this kind needs but to be fully understood in order to show its fallacy. It does not admit of argument, because stating it carries with it the argument. Are we to undertake to control by force the destinies of this people? And because they are in a terrible state of tumult and civil anarchy, are we to settle their difficulties by taking possession of the country, putting down one party and setting up another? What sort of government will you give them? Will you attempt to force your own principles of government upon them, or will you consult their wishes, and attempt to set up such a government as they may ask at your hands? Sir, this matter is beset with difficulties at every step.

I wish to say something, Mr. President, in regard to this doctrine which has been said to have been held by President Monroe and which is very gravely spoken of as the settled and established policy of this country. We must look to the circumstances of the nations in this hemisphere and in Europe at the time the declarations of Mr. Monroe were made, and to which they were applied, to form a correct opinion of them. These were not abstract declarations of principles to govern the action of this government but declarations applied to the then existing state of the countries in Europe and America.

I have examined the two messages of 1823 and 1824 which contain his doctrines. Some years previous to that, the Spanish colonies in this hemisphere had asserted and declared their independence; but Spain refused to acknowledge them and still asserted her dominion over them. Mr. Monroe did not deny the right of Spain to reestablish her dominion over them; much less did he assert the right of the United States to interfere between Spain and her colonies or to set itself up as the arbitrator and guardian of all the nations in this hemisphere. What he declared was that the political system of Europe must not be extended to America to control the destinies of these Spanish-American countries. He did not mean the monarchical system of Europe, as some seem to suppose, but that combination among the great powers, sometimes called the Holy Alliance, which divided and disposed of the small states of Europe according to their pleasure. This is the system to which he alludes when he says, "we should consider any attempt on their part to extend their system to any portion of this hemisphere as dangerous to our peace and safety." It was that arbitrary system of the balance of power, maintained by the allied powers of Europe and which virtually annihilated all the small states, which Mr. Monroe declared could not be extended to this hemisphere. This was to prevent the allied powers from assisting Spain in the resubjugation of her revolted colonies, which he said had assumed and were capable of maintaining their independence.

When the time had arrived for acknowledging the independence of those countries, Mr. Monroe acted cautiously and prudently. A resolution was introduced in the other chamber urging and stimulating the executive on to action. He acted in a manner which it would be well, perhaps, to imitate in this case. He sent out commissioners to ascertain the condition of these countries, and whether they had effectually secured and were able to maintain their independence as states. Being satisfied of this fact, he acknowledged their independence. In the meantime, a peculiar state of things had transpired in Europe. The several powers on that great continent had combined against one great power, one great man. The result of that combination, called the Holy Alliance, was the overthrow of this one great power. This Holy Alliance, or combination among the great powers of Europe, was intended to control the power and direct the destinies of all the governments of Europe. Spain was a member of this alliance and, at this time, was attempting to reclaim her possessions in this country. She refused to acknowledge the independence of these states years and years after we acknowledged it.

Mr. Monroe, then looking at the state of affairs in this country and then at the situa-tion of things in Europe, considered that it belonged to the United States, as the great power on this continent, so far to interfere in behalf of the Spanish-American states as to declare to the civilized world that we would not permit this European alliance to extend its system to any portion of the American continents. It was this combined system, this assumption of power on the part of the great powers of Europe to dispose of the nations of the earth according to their sovereign will that Mr. Monroe said should not be extended to this hemisphere, taking in the Southern as well as the Northern continent. Gentlemen may well say with propriety that this sentiment was heartily responded to by his countrymen, though there has been no occasion to put it into practice. After a while, the combination was broken up, and, soon after, Spain acknowledged the independence of these states on this continent.

This is one of the positions of Mr. Monroe and has no connection whatever with the right of intervention, as now asserted, in the concerns of foreign powers — no connection with the idea which seems to be assumed that Mr. Monroe claimed for the United States as the principal and only great nation in this hemisphere, the right to dictate to or to control the destinies of all others or assumed the obligation to protect them. His was not the doctrine of interference but of resistance to the interference of others. He was a man of too much good sense to have contended for the right of intervention in the manner which is asserted. He had no such idea.

What further does Mr. Monroe say? In connection with this view, he says, in direct reference to the condition of the Spanish-American states in this hemisphere that —

The American continents, by the free and independent condition assumed and maintained, are henceforth not to be considered as subjects of future colonization for any European power.

John Niles (1787-1856), senator from Connecticut

What did he mean by this? I think nothing more than what is contained in his first position, as it has direct reference to the ability of the countries on these continents to maintain their independence. He meant no more than that those countries ought not to be forcibly reduced to colonies by any European power. Did he mean that no European power could establish colonies in any unoccupied territory they might have in this country? Certainly he could not mean that; because he admits that the existing rights of European powers could not be disturbed. It was, then, only an elaboration of the first doctrine, that the countries here are capable of maintaining their own independence and could not be disturbed or subjugated by any European power. What is there in all this that supports the idea that it was the purpose of Mr. Monroe to watch over all the countries of this hemisphere and to repel interference in any one of them without regard to the idea whether it was an encroachment upon our rights or such an invasion of the rights of other independent nations as might endanger our own safety, but merely as being the great power on this continent, we had the right and were under obligation to regulate the affairs of all other

countries, at least so far as regards European interference? Has Mr. Monroe ever laid down any such principles of power on our part? . . .

This is no trivial concern. This is not a question as to the right of intervention but whether we know enough about the merits of the controversy to justify our adopting and carrying out the extraordinary measures proposed. We are to take sides on this question. We are to become a party to this war and are to assume that it is, on the one hand, a war of extermination carried on by barbarians and on the other, a war of self-defense, a resistance to the murderous incursions of savages. It may be so. But I ask whether there is anything before us to justify our assuming such a position, attached to which are consequences so very solemn, not only to that country, but to our own citizens. Why, I have just read from this report that these so-called savages are citizens of the state of Yucatán. They have been admitted as equals into society. The white citizens of that country, says Mr. Sierra, have made great efforts to elevate, educate, instruct, and even to Christianize them. They are, then, according to this authority, a portion of the people of that country. To a great extent they are a civilized and a Christian people. They are Catholics, I believe; and we are called upon to aid in what? Why, in their utter extermination. This is, as is said, truly a war of extermination.

For one, sir, I would hesitate long before I would give a vote to take the responsibility of exterminating this race, to say nothing about exposing and hazarding the lives of my own countrymen. I should like, for one, to know more upon this subject. I find that the correspondence laid before us sheds no light on the question how this controversy began. The statement also of Mr. Sierra, affirming that there were no factions existing in the state, does not seem to be entirely true. He doubtless supposed it so at the time, and there may be a total absence of the exhibition of factions today, and yet tomorrow they may come forth in all their evils. We know that during the short period of our war with Mexico, the condition of Yucatán has assumed three or four different phases. But there are factions. There are two parties, and dissensions among the whites as well as this controversy with the natives.

No longer than the 5th of last month, I find that the then governor, believing it might tend to harmonize and unite the people and thus strengthen their hands in the struggle in which they were engaged, resigned his office, doubtless in favor of the rival leader of the other hostile party. Mendez, the then governor, resigned in favor of Barbachina. This measure seems to have been designed to unite the two parties and to enable them more effectually to defend themselves against the assaults of their savage foe and to strengthen their hands against their common enemy, the Indians. But such was the bitterness of feeling between the two parties that it had a directly contrary effect, for, of the 8,000 men who composed their army at the time, about one-half, comprising the partisans of Mendez, immediately returned to their homes, reducing the army to some 4,000 men.

Sir, we know nothing of the occasion of this difficulty. I believe that the report received today, containing the correspondence with the Navy Department, throws some light on the origin and causes of this war; but I have not had an opportunity to examine it. The correspondence in the two messages afforded very little light; in fact, Mr. Sierra seems to avoid going into the origin of the controversies. Traced to its source, I think it will be found that this war at present existing in that country is one of the deplorable evils resulting from their divisions. Sir, is it not improbable that the degraded native population of that country, who for three long centuries have been in a state of complete subjugation and whose natural characteristic, according to Mr. Sierra, is stupidity, should, of their own accord, after having endured oppression so long, from some strange feeling newly sprung up in their breasts, unite their strength and form an offensive league against their ancient oppressors? Sir, there are, there must have been, other causes of this difficulty, of which we at present know nothing. . . .

Mr. President, the policy on which this bill rests — fear of a supposed extension of the dominion of a foreign power on the one hand, and a design of extending our own dominion on the other, if such an idea can be allowed — I regard as unsound and dangerous. This spirit of jealousy in regard to the strength of any power on this continent is, in my judgment, not only a very unwise but a very dangerous policy. What is to be the result if we resist every attempt — which seems to be the idea of the honorable chairman and others — on the part of any foreign government to establish or extend their dominion here? Will we not be kept in a constant state of war or preparation for war? Will not the adoption of such a policy change our character, perhaps imperceptibly, to that of a military people and lead to a steady enlargement of our military and naval establishments? Will it not entail upon us a national debt and change in some degree the spirit of the people and, in process of time, the spirit if not the form of our institutions?

While seeking to avoid imaginary evils, we may fall upon real evils. These evils we may run into under a republican form of government as well as under a monarchical. The evils resulting from overgrown military establishments are a public debt and the withdrawal of so large a portion of the industrial power of the country to be maintained at the expense of the remaining portion. Look at France, with a military establishment of 500,000 men. If she expects to get relief from the burdens arising from this military establishment and a national debt, its legitimate offspring, by a mere change in the form of government, she will find herself entirely mistaken. My honorable friend, the chairman of the Committee on Foreign Relations, in alluding to the remarks of the gentleman from South Carolina, who adverted to the impolicy of hazarding an additional war at the time when we were involved in a heavy public debt, said that when any great measure for extending our dominion — I suppose he meant our resisting foreign colonization in this country or the carrying out the great principle of lust of dominion — whenever there was any occasion for adopting any such great measure, the senator from South Carolina was constantly bringing forward the "phantom of a national debt."

Sir, the people of England and France and all the states of Europe seem at last to have found that a national debt was no phantom but rather a sad reality. And shall we enter upon a policy which has brought such calamities upon Europe? And I hope the senator will pardon me for saying that I think we are progressing in this matter very respectably and that a national debt, of $100 million is not to be called a phantom. I think, if not sensible now of the reality of a national debt, with this convenient mode of getting along by making loans, that when we get peace and shall find it hardly admissible to go on by a system of loans, and we come to be thrown back upon our own real resources, the actual revenues, that then the honorable gentleman will be convinced that a national debt is something more than a phantom. And with my views of our present revenue and looking to the present disturbed condition of Europe and the effect it must have upon our trade, I am inclined to fear that the senator may find that the public debt is a reality, and our revenue a phantom. I hope it may not be so, Mr. President.

I have got through what I have to say in opposition to this bill. In regard to the request contained in the message and the appeal made to us, I would go for assisting this suffering people as far as may be consistent with the established principles of this government — with maintaining our neutrality in this war as in all other wars and of abstaining from improper interference with the domestic concerns of this as of all other nations. I am of the opinion that something might be done without violating these principles. Whatever measure may be proposed in accordance with those principles for their relief, I assure the honorable chairman I will go as far, if not farther, than himself, in carrying it out. Possibly we might go so far as to supply that people with arms and ammunition; I am not prepared to say but that I would go to that length, but that would be the extent to which I would go.

We have hitherto maintained a prudent, just, and safe course of policy upon this subject, and I earnestly hope that no untoward circumstances, no emergency in neighboring states, no affecting appeal to our feelings, will induce us to depart from it. Any departure might be fatal to our best interests, and we might find it difficult to get back into the path in which we have so far walked with safety and which has given to this country a degree of prosperity, an exemption from the evils of war, and a freedom from disturbances and entanglements which has fallen to the lot of no other nation. If, then, we have thus far steadily pursued this policy with a success and prosperity almost unequaled, I hope and trust the Senate will consider long and seriously upon the subject before they pass a bill, which, in my judgment, involves a departure from established principles and which will expose us to new sources of difficulty and become an example for the future, fraught with danger and evils which no one can foresee and no human sagacity control.

II.

John C. Calhoun: The Inapplicability of the Monroe Doctrine

THE PRESIDENT in his message recommends to Congress to adopt such measures as they may deem expedient to prevent, in the first place, Yucatán from becoming a colony of any European power; and, in the next, to prevent the white inhabitants of that territory from being exterminated or expelled. In support of the latter, he informed the Senate that there is now raging a cruel and devastating war on the part of the Indians against the whites; and that, unless some foreign power should aid, they will be destroyed or driven from the country. In support of the other recommendation, he states that the government of Yucatán has offered to the governments of Great Britain, Spain, and the United States the dominion over the country in order to obtain aid. The President also informs the Senate that unless we grant aid, some other power will; and that ultimately it may assert its dominion and sovereignty over the territory — a result which, he informs us, would be in contravention of the declaration of Mr. Monroe and which must on no account be permitted. The Committee on Foreign Relations, in order to carry out these recommendations, have reported a bill which is now before us, the first section of which provides for taking military occupation of Yucatán, as recommended by the President.

Such are the recommendations of the President, and such the measure recommended by the committee. The subject is one of great magnitude. It is pregnant with consequences, both near and remote, which may deeply affect the peace and interests of this country. It demands the most serious deliberation. I have bestowed upon it full attention and have arrived at a conclusion adverse to the recommendations of the President and the report of the committee. I propose to show, in the first place, that the case of Yucatán, even as stated by the President himself, does not come within the declarations of Mr. Monroe and that they do not furnish the slightest support to the measure reported by the committee. . . .

When the chairman of the Committee on Foreign Relations addressed the Senate a few days since, he related a conversation which he had with Mr. Adams in reference to this declaration, and, according to his statement, if I heard him aright and he be correctly reported, Mr. Adams, in applying his observations to the whole of these declarations, stated that they all originated with himself and were unknown to the other members of the cabinet until they appeared in Mr. Monroe's message. There certainly must be a mistake either on the part of Mr. Adams or that of the chairman of the Committee on Foreign Relations as to the two first of these declarations. The history of the transaction, the senator will perceive if he examines the documents, shows distinctly that they came through Mr. Rush, originating not with Mr. Adams but Mr. Canning, and were first presented in the form of a proposition from England. I recollect, as distinctly as I do any event of my life, that all the papers in connection with this subject were submitted to the members before the cabinet met and were duly considered. Mr. Adams, then, in speaking of the whole as one, must have reference to the declaration relative to colonization.

As respects that, his memory does not differ much from mine. My impression is that it never became a subject of deliberation in the cabinet. I so stated when the Oregon question was before the Senate. I stated it in order that Mr. Adams might have an opportunity of denying it or asserting the real state of the fact. He remained silent, and I presume that my statement is correct; that this declaration was inserted after the cabinet deliberation. It originated entirely with Mr. Adams, without being submitted to the cabinet, and it is, in my opinion, owing to this fact that it is not made with the precision and clearness with which the two former are. It declares without qualification that these continents have asserted and maintained their freedom and independence and are no longer subject to colonization by any European power. This is not strictly accurate. Taken as a whole, these continents had not asserted and maintained their freedom and independence. At that period Great Britain had a larger portion of the continent in her possession than the United States. Russia had a considerable portion of it, and other powers possessed some portions of the Southern part of this continent. The declaration was broader than the fact and exhibits precipitancy and want of due reflection.

Besides, there was an impropriety in it when viewed in conjunction with the foregoing declarations. I speak not in the language of censure. We were as to them acting in concert with England, on a proposition coming from herself — a proposition of the utmost magnitude and which we felt at the time to be essentially connected with our peace and safety; and of course it was due to propriety as well as policy that this declaration should be strictly in accordance with British feeling. Our power then was not what it is now, and we had to rely upon her cooperation to sustain the ground we had taken. We had then only about 6 or 7 million people, scattered, and without such means of communication as we now possess to bring us together in a short period of time. The declaration accordingly, with respect to colonization, striking at England as well as Russia, gave offense to her, and that to such an extent that she refused to cooperate with us in settling the Russian question. Now, I will venture to say that if that declaration had come before that cau-

National Archives

John C. Calhoun; photo by Mathew Brady, about 1850

tious cabinet — for Mr. Monroe was among the wisest and most cautious men I have ever known — it would have been modified and been expressed with a far greater degree of precision and with much more delicacy in reference to the feelings of the British government.

In stating the precise character of these declarations and the manner in which they originated, I have discharged a double duty; a duty to my country, to whom it is important that these declarations should be correctly understood, and a duty to the cabinet of which I was a member and am now the only survivor. I remove a false interpretation, which makes safe and proper declarations improper and dangerous.

But it is not only in these respects that these famous declarations are misunderstood by the chief magistrate of the country, as well as by others. They were but declarations, nothing more; declarations announcing in a friendly manner to the powers of the world that we should regard certain acts of interposition of the allied powers as dangerous to our peace and our safety; interposition of European powers, to oppress the republics which had just arisen upon this continent, as manifesting an unfriendly disposition; and that this continent, having become free and independent, was no longer the subject of colonization by European powers. Not one word in any one of them in reference to resistance. There is nothing said of it; and with great propriety was it omitted. Resistance belonged to us — to Congress; it is for us to say whether we shall resist or not and to what extent.

But such is not the view taken by the present chief magistrate. He seems to hold these declarations as imposing a solemn duty on him as chief magistrate to resist on all occasions; and not only to resist but to judge of the measure of that resistance. He tells us in this very message that it is not to be permitted in any event that any foreign power should occupy Yucatán. That is language for us to hold, not for the chief magistrate. And in conformity with that, he sends in a message without giving us one particle of evidence as to those great political considerations which influenced the cabinet decisions, as stated on this floor, in declaring whether we shall occupy the country or not. I speak it not in the way of censure. I state it only as a matter of fact, deducible from the message itself, and as evincing undoubtedly a great and dangerous misconception of these celebrated declarations.

But that is not all. He tells you in the same message that these declarations have become the settled policy of this country. What! the declarations? Declarations are not policy and cannot become settled policy. He must mean that it has become the settled policy of this country to resist what these declarations refer to; and to resist, if need be, by an appeal to arms. Is this the fact? Has there been one instance in which these declarations have been carried into effect by resistance? If there be, let it be

pointed out. Have there not been innumerable instances in which they have not been applied? Certainly. Still stronger declarations, under this broad interpretation, were disavowed entirely three years afterward by the vote of the Republican Party, when the administration of Mr. Adams endeavored to apply them by sending ministers to the congress at Panama, as will be seen by reading the debates and the proceedings on the subject.

And let me say — for it is proper that I should make the declaration on this occasion — that there has been an entire revolution between the two parties in this country in reference to our foreign relations. At the commencement of our government and down to a late period — I will mark it the commencement of Jackson's administration — the policy of the Republican Party was to avoid war as long as war could be avoided and to resort to every means to avert its calamities. The opposite party, without being a war party, had not so decided an aversion to war. The thing is now reversed; and hence I, who endeavored to maintain the old ground of the party, have for years on all questions connected with our foreign relations, been compelled to cooperate with gentlemen on the opposite side, and to resist those in the midst of whom I stand. No; it is not, and never has been, the established policy of the country. And if it should ever become so, to the wide extent to which these declarations have been interpreted to go, our peace would ever be disturbed; the gates of our Janus would ever stand open; wars would never cease.

What the President has asserted in this case is not a principle belonging to these declarations; it is a principle which, in his misconception, he attempts to ingraft upon them, but which has an entirely different meaning and tendency. The principle which lies at the bottom of his recommendation is, that when any power on this continent becomes involved in internal warfare, and the weaker side chooses to make application to us for support, we are bound to give them support for fear the offer of the sovereignty of the country may be made to some other power and accepted. It goes infinitely and dangerously beyond Mr. Monroe's declaration. It puts it in the power of other countries on this continent to make us a party to all their wars; and hence I say, if this broad interpretation be given to these declarations, we shall forever be involved in wars.

But, in disavowing a principle which will compel us to resist every case of interposition of European powers on this continent, I would not wish to be understood as defending the opposite, that we should never resist their interposition. . . . There are cases of interposition where I would resort to the hazard of war with all its calamities.

Am I asked for one? I will answer. I designate the case of Cuba. So long as Cuba remains in the hands of Spain — a friendly power, a power of which we have no dread — it should continue to be, as it has been, the policy of all administrations ever since I have been connected with the government, to let Cuba remain there; but with the fixed determination, which I hope never will be relinquished, that if Cuba pass from her, it shall not be into any other hands but ours — this, not from a feeling of ambition, not from a desire for the extension of dominion but because that island is indispensable to the safety of the United States; or rather, because it is indispensable to the safety of the United States that this island should not be in certain hands. . . .

I have now stated my reasons against the measure reported by the committee to carry into effect the message of the President recommending that we should adopt the measure to prevent Yucatán from becoming a colony of a foreign power. I now proceed to consider the next — to adopt measures to prevent the white population from being exterminated or expelled from Yucatán. And

here let me express my regret that the President should, in the same message, unite two measures of such different characters — one an appeal to our humanity, which I would, as far as we could with propriety, act upon promptly, and at once; the other, involving the highest considerations of policy and which requires much time and much deliberation. It is among the most complicated questions ever presented to this body, and by no means the least important. Why these different questions have been mingled I am not prepared to say. The emergency for the one seems to have existed long before the other. Danger to the white population has been known to exist since the middle of February, but the message has only been recently communicated to us. During this long interval, if the case appealing to our humanity had been brought forward, we might long ere this have rendered efficient aid. But, whatever may be the effects of the delay in reference to the Yucatánese, they are not chargeable to us. Higher considerations in reference to ourselves — considerations of policy — demand of us deliberation, and that deliberation, I trust, will be given, in despite of the charge of unnecessary delay. But I pass on to the question of humanity.

If this be a war of races in reality; if the white race be not responsible for this war; if they have used all manly exertions and exhibited due courage in repelling the danger, strong indeed would be the appeal to my sympathies. I have no aversion to any race, red or black, but my sympathies are for the white race. I am not so much sophisticated by misguided philosophy or false philanthropy as to lose the natural feelings which belong to me. I go further. If this is a case of war between races; if the Indians have, without just cause, risen and threatened the massacre and extermination of the white race, who have acted so generously toward them as to raise them from the condition of slaves or serfs to that of citizens and freemen, this would present a strong case, on the score of policy, for interposition, connected with considerations belonging to progress, civilization, and liberty.

It was the Spanish or white race, and in that we include the mixed races, who overthrew the Spanish power and have throughout evinced the greatest attachment, under all circumstances, to republican government. They have all the wealth and comprise nearly all the intelligence of the country; and on their ascendency, in my opinion, depends the future progress of civilization and liberty of Yucatán. It is true, they are not very elevated in their sentiments nor very well informed on political subjects but they are far better informed and far more elevated in sentiment than the Indian race can possibly be. If they can maintain themselves, there is some hope that Yucatán may go forward, that intelligence may increase, and that, at some future day, they may be prepared to take a higher position in civilization than at present. If the white race overthrown and Indian ascendency established, there will be a directly opposite tendency to end in a despotic government, like that of Haiti. Perhaps a capable man may at first be elevated to power and may govern tolerably well, but it will undoubtedly follow the course of Haiti. The tendency of power will be downward, until it come down to the very bottom and end in a savage state. . . .

How far ought we go, then, on the score of humanity? I am of the opinion that all the naval force which we can spare should be sent to relieve these helpless people and that we should supply food and raiment for their present necessities and convey them wheresoever they desire — to Cuba or elsewhere. In a word, we should do all that humanity requires. But I cannot agree to carry out the provisions of a bill which authorizes the President to use the Army and Navy to take military occupation of the country. No considerations of humanity, or of the ascendency of the white race in Yucatán, justify, in my opinion, the adoption of such a course of policy.

It is now clear that the white population including the mixed race, is so prostrated and feeble, and the Indians so powerful, that not a hope remains of reestablishing the permanent ascendency of the former. We can, doubtless, by force, subject the Indians and reinstate the whites in power; but the moment that we withdraw, the former state of things will recur. We will thus be perpetually engaged in this work. Now, I am not willing to incur the danger and the cost of maintaining the ascendency of the whites. I am not willing to have this task, which does not belong to us, assumed by our government.

This is the last of earth! I am content.
JOHN QUINCY ADAMS, "The Old Man Eloquent," last words, Feb. 21, 1848

98.

The Seneca Falls Declaration on Women's Rights

The movement for equal rights for women got formally under way with the Seneca Falls (New York) Convention, called by two female Abolitionists, Lucretia Mott and Elizabeth Cady Stanton, and held on July 19 and 20, 1848. A Declaration of Sentiments and twelve resolutions, both reproduced below, were adopted at the meeting. The eleventh resolution may not have been adopted by the full convention. At a second convention in August, the movement took organizational shape and thereafter spread quickly throughout the North and Northwest.

Source: *History of Woman Suffrage*, Elizabeth C. Stanton *et al.*, eds., Vol. I, New York, 1881, pp. 70-73.

DECLARATION OF SENTIMENTS

WHEN, IN THE COURSE OF HUMAN EVENTS, it becomes necessary for one portion of the family of man to assume among the people of the earth a position different from that which they have hitherto occupied, but one to which the laws of nature and of nature's God entitle them, a decent respect to the opinions of mankind requires that they should declare the causes that impel them to such a course.

We hold these truths to be self-evident: that all men and women are created equal; that they are endowed by their Creator with certain inalienable rights; that among these are life, liberty, and the pursuit of happiness; that to secure these rights governments are instituted, deriving their just powers from the consent of the governed. Whenever any form of government becomes destructive of these ends, it is the right of those who suffer from it to refuse allegiance to it, and to insist upon the institution of a new government, laying its foundation on such principles, and organizing its powers in such form, as to them shall seem most likely to effect their safety and happiness.

Prudence, indeed, will dictate that governments long established should not be changed for light and transient causes; and, accordingly, all experience has shown that mankind are more disposed to suffer, while evils are sufferable, than to right themselves by abolishing the forms to which they were accustomed. But when a long train of abuses and usurpations, pursuing invariably the same object, evinces a design to reduce them under absolute despotism, it is their duty to throw off such government and to provide new guards for their future security. Such has been the patient sufferance of the women under this government, and such is now the necessity which constrains them to demand the equal station to which they are entitled.

The history of mankind is a history of repeated injuries and usurpations on the part of man toward woman, having in direct object the establishment of an absolute tyranny over her. To prove this, let facts be submitted to a candid world.

He has never permitted her to exercise her inalienable right to the elective franchise.

He has compelled her to submit to laws in the formation of which she had no voice.

He has withheld from her rights which are given to the most ignorant and degraded men, both natives and foreigners.

Having deprived her of this first right of a citizen, the elective franchise, thereby leaving her without representation in the halls of legislation, he has oppressed her on all sides.

He has made her, if married, in the eye of the law, civilly dead.

He has taken from her all right in property, even to the wages she earns.

He has made her, morally, an irresponsible being, as she can commit many crimes with impunity, provided they be done in the presence of her husband. In the covenant of marriage, she is compelled to promise obedience to her husband, he becoming, to all intents and purposes, her master — the law giving him power to deprive her of her liberty and to administer chastisement.

He has so framed the laws of divorce, as to what shall be the proper causes and, in case of separation, to whom the guardianship of the children shall be given, as to be wholly regardless of the happiness of women — the law, in all cases, going upon a false supposition of the supremacy of man and giving all power into his hands.

After depriving her of all rights as a married woman, if single and the owner of property, he has taxed her to support a government which recognizes her only when her property can be made profitable to it.

He has monopolized nearly all the profitable employments, and from those she is permitted to follow, she receives but a scanty remuneration. He closes against her all the avenues to wealth and distinction which he considers most honorable to himself. As a teacher of theology, medicine, or law, she is not known.

He has denied her the facilities for obtaining a thorough education, all colleges being closed against her.

He allows her in church, as well as state, but a subordinate position, claiming apostolic authority for her exclusion from the

Metropolitan Museum of Art, Stokes-Hawes gift

Southworth and Hawes daguerreotype thought to be of Susan B. Anthony as a young woman

ministry, and, with some exceptions, from any public participation in the affairs of the church.

He has created a false public sentiment by giving to the world a different code of morals for men and women, by which moral delinquencies which exclude women from society are not only tolerated but deemed of little account in man.

He has usurped the prerogative of Jehovah himself, claiming it as his right to assign for her a sphere of action, when that belongs to her conscience and to her God.

He has endeavored, in every way that he could, to destroy her confidence in her own powers, to lessen her self-respect, and to make her willing to lead a dependent and abject life.

Now, in view of this entire disfranchisement of one-half the people of this country, their social and religious degradation, in view of the unjust laws above mentioned, and because women do feel themselves aggrieved, oppressed, and fraudulently deprived of their most sacred rights, we insist that they have immediate admission to all the rights and privileges which belong to them as citizens of the United States.

In entering upon the great work before us, we anticipate no small amount of misconception, misrepresentation, and ridicule; but we shall use every instrumentality within our power to effect our object. We shall employ agents, circulate tracts, petition the state and national legislatures, and endeavor to enlist the pulpit and the press in our behalf. We hope this Convention will be followed by a series of conventions embracing every part of the country.

RESOLUTIONS

Whereas, the great precept of nature is conceded to be that "man shall pursue his own true and substantial happiness." Blackstone in his *Commentaries* remarks that this law of nature, being coeval with mankind and dictated by God himself, is, of course, superior in obligation to any other. It is binding over all the globe, in all countries and at all times; no human laws are of any validity if contrary to this, and such of them as are valid derive all their force, and all their validity, and all their authority, mediately and immediately, from this original; therefore,

Resolved, That such laws as conflict, in any way, with the true and substantial happiness of woman, are contrary to the great precept of nature and of no validity, for this is "superior in obligation to any other."

Resolved, that all laws which prevent woman from occupying such a station in society as her conscience shall dictate, or which place her in a position inferior to that of man, are contrary to the great precept of nature and therefore of no force or authority.

Resolved, that woman is man's equal, was intended to be so by the Creator, and the highest good of the race demands that she should be recognized as such.

Resolved, that the women of this country

ought to be enlightened in regard to the laws under which they live, that they may no longer publish their degradation by declaring themselves satisfied with their present position, nor their ignorance, by asserting that they have all the rights they want.

Resolved, that inasmuch as man, while claiming for himself intellectual superiority, does accord to woman moral superiority, it is preeminently his duty to encourage her to speak and teach, as she has an opportunity, in all religious assemblies.

Resolved, that the same amount of virtue, delicacy, and refinement of behavior that is required of woman in the social state should also be required of man, and the same transgressions should be visited with equal severity on both man and woman.

Resolved, that the objection of indelicacy and impropriety, which is so often brought against woman when she addresses a public audience, comes with a very ill grace from those who encourage, by their attendance, her appearance on the stage, in the concert, or in feats of the circus.

Resolved, that woman has too long rested satisfied in the circumscribed limits which corrupt customs and a perverted application of the Scriptures have marked out for her, and that it is time she should move in the enlarged sphere which her great Creator has assigned her.

Resolved, that it is the duty of the women on this country to secure to themselves their sacred right to the elective franchise.

Resolved, that the equality of human rights results necessarily from the fact of the identity of the race in capabilities and responsibilities.

Resolved, that the speedy success of our cause depends upon the zealous and untiring efforts of both men and women for the overthrow of the monopoly of the pulpit, and for the securing to woman an equal participation with men in the various trades, professions, and commerce.

Resolved, therefore, that, being invested by the Creator with the same capabilities and the same consciousness of responsibility for their exercise, it is demonstrably the right and duty of woman, equally with man, to promote every righteous cause by every righteous means; and especially in regard to the great subjects of morals and religion, it is self-evidently her right to participate with her brother in teaching them, both in private and in public, by writing and by speaking, by any instrumentalities proper to be used, and in any assemblies proper to be held; and this being a self-evident truth growing out of the divinely implanted principles of human nature, any custom or authority adverse to it, whether modern or wearing the hoary sanction of antiquity, is to be regarded as a self-evident falsehood, and at war with mankind.

99.

"Buffalo Gals"

The original of this song was composed in 1844 by a blackface minstrel, "Cool" White, whose group, the Virginia Serenaders, popularized it throughout the country under the title "Lubly Fan." Other minstrel groups took up the song and changed the title to fit the town where it was performed; thus it was variously "Charleston Gals," "Pittsburgh Gals," "Louisiana Gals," and so forth. One particularly famous group, the Ethiopian Serenaders, introduced a Buffalo version about 1848, and Buffalo it has remained ever since.

Source: *Minstrel Songs, Old and New,* Boston, 1882.

✦ BUFFALO GALS

As I was lumbering down the street
Down the street, down the street,
A handsome gal I chanced to meet —
Oh! she was fair to view.

I asked her would she have some talk,
Have some talk, have some talk,
Her feet covered up the whole sidewalk
As she stood close by me.

I asked her would she have a dance,
Have a dance, have a dance,
I thought that I might get a chance
To shake a foot with her.

I'd like to make that gal my wife,
Gal my wife, gal my wife,
I'd be happy all my life
If I had her by me.

Chorus:
Buffalo gals, won't you come out tonight,
Won't you come out tonight, won't you come out tonight?
Buffalo gals, won't you come out tonight
And dance by the light of the moon?

100.

A. J. Downing: In Praise of Farming

A. J. Downing was the leading American landscape architect and horticulturist of the first half of the nineteenth century. In 1846 he accepted the editorship of a new periodical, Horticulturist, *a position retained until his death in 1852. His editorials were published in 1853 in a collection called* Rural Essays; *a typical example, which originally appeared in June 1848, is reprinted here.*

Source: *Rural Essays,* New York, 1853: "Cultivators: The Great Industrial Class of America."

AT THIS MOMENT, when the Old World's monarchical institutions are fast falling to pieces, it is interesting to look at home, at the prosperous and happy condition of our New World republic.

Abroad, the sovereign springs from a privileged class and holds his position by the force of the army. His state and government are supported by heavy taxes wrung from the laboring classes, often entirely without their consent. At home the people are the sovereign power. The safety of their government lies in their own intelligence; and the taxes paid for the maintenance of public order or to create public works fall with no heavy or unequal pressure, but are wisely and justly distributed throughout all classes of society.

In the United States, the *industrial classes* are the true sovereigns. *Idleness* is a condition so unrecognized and unrespected with us that the few professing it find themselves immediately thrown out of the great machine of active life which constitutes American society. Hence, an idle man is a cipher. Work he must, either with his head, his hands, or his capital; work in some mode or other, or he is a *dethroned sovereign.* The practical and busy spirit of our people repu-

diates him, and he is of no more absolute consequence than the poor fugitive king — denied and driven out by his subjects.

The CULTIVATORS OF THE SOIL constitute the great industrial class in this country. They may well be called its "bone and sinew"; for, at this moment, they do not only feed all other classes but also no insignificant portion of needy Europe, furnish the raw material for manufactures, and raise the great staples which figure so largely in the accounts of the merchant, the shipowner and manufacturer, in every village, town, and seaport in the Union.

The sovereign people has a better right to look over its "rent roll" to examine the annual sum total of the products of its industry than any other sovereign whatever; and it has accordingly employed Mr. Burke, the excellent commissioner of patents, to collect statistical facts and publish them in the annual report of his office. An examination of the condition of this country as exhibited in Mr. Burke's report of its industrial resources will, we think, afford the best proof ever exhibited of the value of the American Union and the extraordinary wealth of our territory.

The total value of the *products of the soil,*

alone, for the past year, he estimates at more than $1,500,000,000. The value of the grain crops and great agricultural staples of the country, for 1847, amounts to $815,863,688. The value of all horticultural products (gardens, orchards, and nurseries) is estimated at $459,577,533. The value of the livestock, wool, and dairy products amounts to $246,054,579. The value of the products of the woods and forests amounts to $59,099,628.

It is also estimated that there were produced last year 224,384,502 bushels of *surplus* grains of various kinds, over and above what was amply sufficient for home consumption. This is much more than enough to meet the ordinary demand of all the corn-buying countries of Europe.

Over $1,500,000,000 in the products of the soil for a single year! Does not this fully justify us in holding up the cultivators of the American soil as the great industrial class? But let us compare them a little, by Mr. Burke's aid, with the other industrial classes.

The annual product of all the manufactures in the Union, for 1847, is estimated at $500 million. The profits of trade and commerce at $23,458,345. The profits of fisheries, $17,069,262; and of banks, money institutions, rents, and professions, $145 million. Total, $809,697,407.

Here we have the facts, or something, at least, like an approximation to the facts, of the results of the yearly industrial labor of the republic. The average amount is the enormous sum of over $2,389,000,000. Of this, the agricultural class produces *nearly double that of all other classes*, or over $1,579,000,000; while all other classes, merchants, manufacturers, professional men, etc., produce but little more than $809 million.

There are a few among the great traders and "merchant princes" who do not sufficiently estimate the dignity or importance of any class but their own. To them we commend a study of Mr. Burke's statistical tables. There are some few farmers who think their occupation one of narrow compass and resources; we beg them to look over the aggregate annual products of their country and take shame to themselves.

It is no less our duty to call the attention of our own readers to the great importance of the horticultural interest of the country. Why, its products ($459 million) are more than half as great in value as those strictly agricultural; they are almost as large as the whole manufacturing products of the country; and half as large as the manufacturing and all other interests, excepting the agricultural, combined.

In truth, the profits of the gardens and orchards of the country are destined to be enormous. Mr. Burke's estimate appears to us very moderate; and from the unparalleled increase in this interest very recently, and the peculiar adaptation of our soil and climate to the finest fruits and vegetables, the next ten years must exhibit an amount of horticultural products which will almost challenge belief. The markets of this country will not only be supplied with fruit in great abundance and excellence but thousands of orchards will be cultivated solely for foreign consumption.

The system of railroads and cheap transportation already begins to supply the seaboard cities with some of the fair and beautiful fruits of the fertile West. When the orchards of Massachusetts fail, the orchards of western New York will supply the Boston market with apples; and, thus, wherever the finest transportable products of the soil are in demand, there they will find their way.

There are, however, many of the finer and more perishable products of the garden and orchard which will not bear a long journey. These it should be the peculiar business of the cultivator of the older and less fertile soil in the seaboard states to grow. He may not, as an agriculturalist, be able to compete with the fertile soils of the

West; but he may still do so as a horticulturist by devoting his attention and his land to orchards and gardens. If it is too difficult and expensive to renovate an old soil that is worn out, or bring up a new one naturally poor, for farm crops, in the teeth of Western grain prices, he may well afford to do so for the larger profit derived from orchard and garden culture, where those products are raised for which a market must be found without long transportation.

He who will do this most successfully must not waste his time, labor, and capital by working in the dark. He must learn gardening and orcharding as a practical art and a science. He must collect the lost elements of the soil from the animal and mineral kingdoms, and bring them back again to their starting point. He must seek out the food of plants in towns and villages where it is wasted and thrown away. He must plant and prune so as to aid and direct nature, that neither time nor space are idly squandered.

Certainly we have just pride and pleasure in looking upon the great agricultural class of America. Landholders and proprietors of the soil, as they are, governing themselves and developing the resources of a great nation; how different is their position from that of the farmers of England: hundreds of thousands of men, working, generation after generation, upon lands leased by a small privileged body, which alone owns and entails the soil; or even from that of France, where there are millions of proprietors, but proprietors of a soil so subdivided that the majority have half a dozen acres, or, perhaps, even a half or fourth of an acre in extent, often scarcely sufficient to raise a supply of a single crop for a small family.

If we have said anything calculated to inspire self-respect in the agricultural class of this country, it is not with a view to lessen that for any other of its industrial classes. Far from it. Indeed, with the versatility of power and pursuits which characterize our people, no class can be said to be fixed. The farming class is the great nursery of all the professions and the industrial arts of the country. From its bosom go out the shrewdest lawyers and the most successful merchants of the towns; and back to the country return these classes again, however successful, to be regenerated in the primitive life and occupation of the race.

But the agricultural class perhaps is still wanting in a just appreciation of its importance, its rights, and its duties. It has so long listened to sermons, lectures, and orations from those who live in cities and look upon country life as "something for dull wits," that it still needs apostles who draw their daily breath in green fields and are untrammeled by the schools of politics and trade.

The agricultural journals over the whole country have done much to raise the dignity of the calling. They have much still to do. The importance of agricultural schools of a high grade should be continually insisted upon, until every state legislature in the Union comes forward with liberal endowments. And if pledges ought ever to be demanded of politicians, then farmers should not be slow to require them of their representatives for legislation favorable to every sound means of increasing the intelligence of this great bulwark of the country's safety and prosperity — the *cultivators of the soil.*

———◆———

We inscribe on our banner Free Soil, Free Speech, Free Labor, and Free Men.
Motto of the Free-Soil Party, insurgent Democrats who nominated Van Buren in 1848

Daguerreotype from late 1840s showing President James Polk and his wife with a group of friends

PROBLEMS OF DIVERSITY

By 1840, the population of the United States had risen to 17,000,000, and the flood of immigration that was to double this figure in 25 years had begun. The delicate balance between freedom and order was repeatedly tested, as political and social institutions strained to assimilate and accomodate their new members, with their diverse problems and needs. The issues of the maintenance and expansion of slavery continued to arouse bitter sectional antagonism. Widening democracy, encouraged by the removal of religious and property restrictions from the right to vote, brought a new class of men to the polls. In cities with a large immigrant population, powerful and flagrantly corrupt political machines flourished.

The upheaval and insecurity of rapid change caused a nativist reaction that was often violent. Many of the communal societies that appeared during the period were treated with derision; the Mormons were unable to find a community where they could be accepted. Exclusive religious and fraternal societies with strictly limited memberships multiplied. The debates over education revealed that the democratic notion of public responsibility for the education of all was by no means taken for granted. Requests by Roman Catholics for public funds were rejected, not entirely on constitutional grounds. In addition, the Mexican War aroused a nationalistic excitement more jingoist in character than the self-assurance seen earlier in the War of 1812.

EMIGRATION.

Detailing the Progress and Vicissitudes of an Emigrant!!

Dedicated to all those, who would leave their native Country to seek a better condition in a distant Foreig...

Embarking with your Family for America — taking leave of Albion's white Cliffs — No more Taxes —

On the wide and boundless Sea — Rolling mountains high, a month on the Atlantic Provisions nearly exhausted or spoild, but no lack of hard Junk and Putrid Water —

Landing at an American Port more ? alive — the Cholera raging — Coffins as packing cases — half a mind to go b...

Sailing up the St Laurence in an American Boiler — stowd in a hold very like the Black hole of Calcutta — all got a Fit of the American Ague — Thermometer at 100 —

Arrived at your allotment on the borders of a huge Canadian Forest under the guidance of a imposing agent — and which must be cut, cleard, spaded & till'd, before you can Settle (no work no eat) —

Strolling in the Woods — and ? an interview with the Natives —

A view of your Log Hut — digging under a burning Sun — Thermometer at 90 in the shade — infested day Musquitoes with stings like Stocking Needles —

In exploring the neighbouring land, you tumble over an Alligator — makes him run — the devil catch the hindmost!

Visited by a Set not the Tax gatherer —

A Twelve months' residence — having an addition to your family already too many — sitting after a day's toil at your door — drop a tear for deserted England yet England with all thy faults I love thee still — a Spider at day at a creak spins a web in your hat, & a Scorpion creeps into your Hut unobserved takes a lodging under the bed & gives birth to a numerous brood —

Sleeping under Buffalo skins lined with fleas as big as blue bottles — alarmed in the night by a colony of Rats in your room — where Ferocity almost bids fair to take final possession —

A melancholy prospect — after 4 years industril can turn it to no account — Visited by a neighbour nearest by 8 miles, who came on purpose, why Farmer with a large family should not do like about 12 or 14 years by dint of perseverance — openly condoles with you, is laughing in his sleeve quitting the land of Prayers Taxes & Petitions —

Your Hut on Fire for the 3d time — goods & chattels included — no engines no water nor neighbourly assistance had incured — & no prospect of Subscription or Parish relief — sits down unable to do any thing & witness the destruction of your little all — untill the dry grass catches fire & compels you to run off your own estate —

Fall into the hands of the Cannibals — you & your family victims of State — being roasted for a Feast yourself escapes by a miracle —

The Finale or wind up — Poor Friendless down — like Robinson Crusoe on an uninhabited looking out for a Ship to convey you back to work your passage back & land once M— cares Friends & cares every thing !!!

C J Grant Invent Del & Lith

Pub. by J. Pattie, Bookseller, 15 High St Bloomsbury opposite St Giles Church, London 18??

Emigrant ship arriving at the New York Battery in 1847; painting by Samuel B. Waugh

Immigration

Immigrants to the New World poured in at an unheard of rate. In the decade from 1831 to 1840, about 600,000 foreigners arrived in America; in the next decade, well over 1,700,000 arrived. Immigration was largely from the British Isles, Germany, and Scandinavia. The demand for cheap labor to build railroads and canals assured jobs for most. The Irish famines of 1845-49 resulted in a great wave of newcomers and in increasing hostility toward immigrants and Catholicism among the "Native Americans."

(Right) Irish emigrants leaving their home for America; (below) Swedish emigrants going west

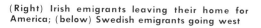

Lithograph of the riot in Philadelphia in 1844 between the Catholics and non-Catholics

SHALL IT COME TO THIS?

ROMISH INTOLERANCE MUST NOT TRIUMPH!

"DANGER IN THE DARK"

IS DESTINED TO BE READ BY EVERY AMERICAN.

THE AIM OF POPE PIUS IX.

"BEWARE! THERE IS DANGER IN THE DARK!"

(Left) Cartoon of the Know-Nothing Party; (right) ad for agents to sell the anti-Catholic book, "Danger in the Dark"; (below) riot in Hoboken involving Germans and a New York street gang

Nativism was anti-Irish, anti-German, and anti-Catholic in expression. In the Philadelphia riots in 1844, 9 people were killed, scores injured, and two Catholic churches burned to the ground. Since many immigrant groups formed social, economic, and political blocs, they seemed to threaten the democracy of the common man. Boston, New York, and Baltimore all suffered from xenophobia. In this climate arose the political grouping called "Know-Nothings," which later entered national politics as the Native American Party. Secret societies flourished and were attacked. In defense against the nativists, the Irish organized fraternal groups such as the Ancient Order of Hibernians.

George Eastman House

Chicago Historical Society

(Above) "The True Origin of Freemasonry"; (below) "The Great Secret of Odd-Fellowship Exposed"

Library of Congress

Extermination of the Latter-day Saints from Missouri in 1838 by orders of Gov. Boggs

The alien was not alone in suffering from intolerance. The Latter-day Saints, or Mormons, first appearing as an organized group in 1830, were driven from New York State to Ohio, then to Missouri, then to Illinois, and finally to Salt Lake City. They represented a fairly solid bloc in the midst of diversity; their religious views appeared utterly alien to their neighbors. Inevitably hostility arose. The killing of seventeen Mormons in Missouri in 1838 led to their settlement of Nauvoo, Illinois. But by 1845 Illinois was as hostile as Missouri. At last the long trek was undertaken to the forbidding land of Utah, in hopes that nothing about the country would attract outsiders. But even in Utah the Saints had to battle with their persecutors.

Brigham Young

View of Salt Lake City, Utah, in 1858

National Academy of Design

Public enthusiasm for the Mexican war is seen in these illustrations: (left) "War News from Mexico" by R. C. Woodville; (below) "Soldier's Adieu," an 1847 lithograph

On May 11, 1846, Congress declared that "By an act of the Republic of Mexico, a state of war exists between that Government and the United States." After a long series of territorial disputes, charges and countercharges of aggression, both sides were ready for battle and confident of victory. The war captured popular imagination; Winfield Scott and Zachary Taylor became national heroes. Mexico was forced to cede Texas, New Mexico, and upper California. Some Northerners charged that the war was in reality a campaign to extend slavery.

Library of Congress

"A Little More Grape, Capt. Bragg" depicts the triumph of Zachary Taylor at Buena Vista

Library of Congress

George Eastman House

Daguerreotype of a soldier, c. 1850

Mrs. Ralph S. Mackay

Bridal couple; man in national guard uniform

Militia drill in the 1830s; drawing by D. C. Johnston, 1862
Library of Congress

Pennsylvania Historical and Museum Commission

Library of Congress

(Above) Philadelphia private school; (left)
George Wolf, governor favoring free schools

Education

A concerted drive toward expanded public education had begun in the 1830s. Massachusetts, largely under Horace Mann's influence, was first with a statewide tax system for the benefit of public schools. In
Pennsylvania Gov. George Wolf put
through a public education act that led to
much antagonism — taxes were inevitably
raised to support the system, and Wolf was
defeated for re-election. In spite of these
and similar efforts, the idea of public education was still open to question, and in
many states schooling was haphazard.

Library of Congress

The unrewarding role of the schoolmaster as depicted in two lithographs of the 1840s

American Antiquarian Society

Mississippi Female College, Hernando, Miss.

(Above) Rev. Daniel Sharp, founder of Boston University; 1848 daguerreotype; (center right) view of Girard College by Langenheim; (bottom right) pencil drawing of the summer dress of students at Harvard, about 1840

(Above) **Professor performing chemistry experiment**; (right) **Louis Agassiz, zoologist**

Higher education continued to reflect the diverse aims of the portions of the population that supported it. Most colleges retained church affiliation. Most women, when educated at all, attended tiny female seminaries that concentrated on social refinements, music, and literature. At Harvard and a few other schools, more attention was given to the natural sciences. A number of medical schools were established, and efforts were made to insure at least minimum standards in medical education.

(Above) **Rush Medical College, Chicago, 1843;** (below) **Harvard Society for Medical Improvement**

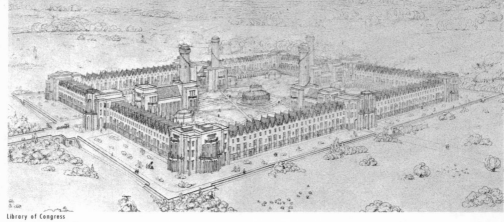

Robert Owen's sketch for the proposed communities at New Harmony, Indiana

(Above) George Rapp; (right) Robert Owen, 1834 portrait by W. H. Brooke

New Harmony as it looked in 1832; watercolor by Karl Bodmer

(Left) Adin Ballou, Hopedale; (center) John H. Noyes, Oneida; (right) Charles Fourier, advocate of Utopian society

Utopia

The generally free atmosphere in the United States attracted a number of social reformers convinced of the virtues of communal organization of society. Two such communities were founded at Harmony, Indiana. In 1814 George Rapp established a communistic theocracy that prospered for a decade before moving to Pennsylvania. Robert Owen, a Scots industrialist, bought the site in 1825 and started a community, called New Harmony, based on equal distribution of wealth. Several cooperative societies, among them Brook Farm, were organized on the principles of Charles Fourier, a French social philosopher.

Recruit arriving at Oneida Community

Brook Farm, painting by Josiah Wolcott

Engraving of the religious exercises of the Shakers at Niskayuna

The Oneida Community, founded by John H. Noyes, was the most radical in concept. It was also the most successful financially, as a result of its prospering crafts industry. However, the community aroused public outrage with an elaborate marriage ceremony that made all the women the wives of all the men. Other communal societies had a more religious orientation. Ballou's Hopedale Community sought to create the "Kingdom of God on earth," and the Shakers awaited the second coming of Christ. The Shakers first came to America in 1774 and thrived for several decades. But, like the Rappists, their vow of celibacy made recruiting of converts a condition of survival.

(Above) "Obediah Puzzled"; satire on Quakers; (below) Bishop's Hill, communistic colony in Illinois

101.

Factory Rules at Lowell, Massachusetts

By setting up carefully supervised boarding houses, providing religious instructions, and establishing strict rules of conduct, the founders of the textile mills at Lowell, Massachusetts, had tried to create safe and congenial working conditions for their female operatives. In the late 1840s, however, life at Lowell began to change. Wages were lowered, the work load was increased, and the living quarters deteriorated. The change was owing in part to the availability of cheap immigrant labor, especially from Ireland, after 1846. The relationship between owners and operatives also became more businesslike, and less paternalistic. Indicative of the altered conditions is the following set of regulations laid down by one of the factories for its employees in 1848.

Source: *Handbook to Lowell,* 1848, pp. 42-44 [Commons, VII, pp. 135-136].

REGULATIONS TO BE OBSERVED by all persons employed . . .

The overseers are to be always in their rooms at the starting of the mill, and not absent unnecessarily during working hours. They are to see that all those employed in their rooms are in their places in due season and keep a correct account of their time and work. They may grant leave of absence to those employed under them when they have spare hands to supply their places, and not otherwise, except in cases of absolute necessity.

All persons in the employ of the Hamilton Manufacturing Company are to observe the regulations of the room where they are employed. They are not to be absent from their work without the consent of the overseer, except in cases of sickness, and then they are to send him word of the cause of their absence. They are to board in one of the houses of the company and give information at the counting room: where they board, when they begin, or whenever they change their boarding place; and are to observe the regulations of their boardinghouse.

Those intending to leave the employment of the company are to give at least two weeks' notice thereof to their overseer.

All persons entering into the employment of the company are considered as engaged for twelve months, and those who leave sooner or do not comply with all these regulations will not be entitled to a regular discharge.

The company will not employ anyone who is habitually absent from public worship on the Sabbath or known to be guilty of immorality.

A physician will attend once in every month at the counting room to vaccinate all who may need it, free of expense.

Anyone who shall take from the mills or the yard any yarn, cloth, or other article belonging to the company will be considered guilty of stealing and be liable to prosecution.

Payment will be made monthly, including board and wages. The accounts will be made up to the last Saturday but one in every month and paid in the course of the following week.

These regulations are considered part of the contract with which all persons entering into the employment of the Hamilton Manufacturing Company engage to comply.

102.

Horace Mann: Twelfth Annual Report

The selection below comprises a part of the twelfth and last of the famous annual reports that Horace Mann, as secretary of the Massachusetts Board of Education, submitted to the state legislature. In 1848, the year it was submitted, Mann resigned his post to take the late John Quincy Adams' seat in Congress. During the twelve years he served as secretary, Mann increased the length of the school year, established fifty new common schools, and founded three normal schools (the first in America). He also founded the Common School Journal, a biweekly publication dealing with school administration, and in general set the standards for educational reform everywhere in America.

Source: *Annual Reports of the Secretary of the Board of Education of Massachusetts for the Years 1845-1848*, Boston, 1891, pp. 222-340.

PHYSICAL EDUCATION

MODERN SCIENCE HAS MADE nothing more certain than that both good and ill health are the direct result of causes mainly within our own control. In other words, the health of the race is dependent upon the conduct of the race. The health of the individual is determined primarily by his parents, secondarily by himself. The vigorous growth of the body, its strength and its activity, its powers of endurance, and its length of life, on the one hand; and dwarfishness, sluggishness, infirmity, and premature death on the other, are all the subjects of unchangeable laws. These laws are ordained of God; but the knowledge of them is left to our diligence, and the observance of them to our free agency.

These laws are very few; they are so simple that all can understand them, and so beautiful that the pleasure of contemplating them, even independent of their utility, is a tenfold reward for all the labor of their acquisition. . . . And hence the uncompromising necessity that all children should be instructed in these laws; and not only instructed, but that they should receive such a *training* during the whole course of pupilage as to enlist the mighty forces of habit on the side of obedience; and that their judgment also should be so developed and matured, that they will be able to discriminate between different combinations of circumstances, and to adapt, in each case, the regimen to the exigency. . . .

Not only will a general knowledge of human physiology, or the laws of health, do much to supersede the necessity of a knowledge of pathology, or the laws of disease, but the former is as much better than the latter as prevention is better than remedy, as much better as all the comforts and securities of an unburnt dwelling are than two-thirds of its value in money from the insurance office. A general diffusion of physiological knowledge will save millions annually to the state. It will gradually revolutionize many of the absurd customs and usages of society, conforming them more and more to the rules of reason and true enjoyment, and withdrawing them more and more from the equally vicious extremes of barbarism and of artificial life. It will restrain the caprices and follies of fashion in regard to dress and amusement, and subordinate its ridiculous excesses to the laws of health and decency. It will reproduce the obliterated lines that once divided day and night. It will secure cleanliness and purity, more intimate and personal than any the laundress can supply. It will teach men "to eat that they may live, instead of living that they may eat." . . .

My general conclusion, then, under this head, is that it is the duty of all the governing minds in society — whether in office or out of it — to diffuse a knowledge of these beautiful and beneficent laws of health and life throughout the length and breadth of the state; to popularize them; to make them, in the first place, the common acquisition of all and, through education and custom, the common inheritance of all, so that the healthful habits naturally growing out of their observance shall be inbred in the people, exemplified in the personal regimen of each individual, incorporated into the economy of every household, observable in all private dwellings and in all public edifices, especially in those buildings which are erected by capitalists for the residence of their work people or for renting to the poorer classes; obeyed, by supplying cities with pure water; by providing public baths, public walks, and public squares; by rural cemeteries; by the drainage and sewerage of populous towns; and by whatever else may promote the general salubrity of the atmosphere — in fine, by a religious observance of all those sanitary regulations with which modern science has blessed the world.

For this thorough diffusion of sanitary intelligence, the common school is the only agency. It is, however, an adequate agency. Let human physiology be introduced as an indispensable branch of study into our public schools; let no teacher be approved who is not master of its leading principles and of their applications to the varying circumstances of life; let all the older classes in the schools be regularly and rigidly examined upon this study by the school committees, and a speedy change would come over our personal habits, over our domestic usages, and over the public arrangements of society.

Temperance and moderation would not be such strangers at the table. Fashion, like European sovereigns, if not compelled to abdicate and fly, would be forced to compromise for the continued possession of her throne by the surrender to her subjects of many of their natural rights. A sixth order of architecture would be invented, the hygienic, which, without subtracting at all from the beauty of any other order, would add a new element of utility to them all. The "health regulations" of cities would be issued in a revised code — a code that would bear the scrutiny of science.

And, as the result and reward of all, a race of men and women, loftier in stature, firmer in structure, fairer in form, and better able to perform the duties and bear the burdens of life, would revisit the earth. The minikin specimens of the race, who now go on dwindling and tapering from parent to child, would reascend to manhood and womanhood. Just in porportion as the laws of health and life were discovered and obeyed would pain, disease, insanity, and untimely death cease from among men. Consumption would remain; but it would be consumption in the active sense.

INTELLECTUAL EDUCATION

ANOTHER CARDINAL OBJECT which the government of Massachusetts, and all the influential men in the state, should propose to themselves is the physical well-being of all the people — the sufficiency, comfort, competence, of every individual in regard to food, raiment, and shelter. And these necessaries and conveniences of life should be obtained by each individual for himself, or by each family for themselves, rather than accepted from the hand of charity or extorted by poor laws. It is not averred that this most desirable result can, in all instances, be obtained; but it is, nevertheless, the end to be aimed at. True statesmanship and true political economy, not less than true philanthropy, present this perfect theory as the goal, to be more and more closely approximated by our imperfect practice. The desire to achieve such a result cannot be regarded as an unreasonable ambition; for, though all mankind were well fed, well clothed, and well housed, they might still be but half civilized. . . .

According to the European theory, men are divided into classes, some to toil and earn, others to seize and enjoy. . . . Our ambition as a state should trace itself to a different origin and propose to itself a different object. Its flame should be lighted at the skies. Its radiance and its warmth should reach the darkest and the coldest abodes of men.

It should seek the solution of such problems as these: To what extent can competence displace pauperism? How nearly can we free ourselves from the low-minded and the vicious, not by their expatriation but by their elevation? To what extent can the resources and powers of nature be converted into human welfare, the peaceful arts of life be advanced, and the vast treasures of human talent and genius be developed? How much of suffering, in all its forms, can be relieved; or, what is better than relief, how much can be prevented? Cannot the classes of crimes be lessened, and the number of criminals in each class be diminished?

Our exemplars, both for public and for private imitation, should be the parables of the lost sheep and of the lost piece of silver. When we have spread competence through all the abodes of poverty; when we have substituted knowledge for ignorance in the minds of the whole people; when we have reformed the vicious and reclaimed the criminal, then may we invite all neighboring nations to behold the spectacle and say to them, in the conscious elation of virtue, "Rejoice with me," for I have found that which was lost. Until that day shall arrive, our duties will not be wholly fulfilled, and our ambition will have new honors to win.

But is it not true that Massachusetts, in some respects, instead of adhering more and more closely to her own theory, is becoming emulous of the baneful examples of Europe? The distance between the two extremes of society is lengthening, instead of being abridged. With every generation, fortunes increase on the one hand, and some new privation is added to poverty on the other. We are verging toward those extremes of opulence and of penury, each of which unhumanizes the human mind. A perpetual struggle for the bare necessaries of life, without the ability to obtain them, makes men wolfish. Avarice, on the other hand, sees, in all the victims of misery around it, not objects for pity and succor but only crude materials to be worked up into more money.

I suppose it to be the universal sentiment of all those who mingle any ingredient of benevolence with their notions on political economy, that vast and overshadowing private fortunes are among the greatest dangers to which the happiness of the people in a republic can be subjected. Such fortunes would create a feudalism of a new kind, but one more oppressive and unrelenting than that of the Middle Ages. . . .

Now, surely nothing but universal education can counterwork this tendency to the domination of capital and the servility of labor. If one class possesses all the wealth and the education, while the residue of society is ignorant and poor, it matters not by what name the relation between them may be called: the latter, in fact and in truth, will be the servile dependants and subjects of the former. But, if education be equably diffused, it will draw property after it by the strongest of all attractions; for such a thing never did happen, and never can happen, as that an intelligent and practical body of men should be permanently poor. Property and labor in different classes are essentially antagonistic; but property and labor in the same class are essentially fraternal.

The people of Massachusetts have, in some degree, appreciated the truth, that the unexampled prosperity of the state — its comfort, its competence, its general intelligence and virtue — is attributable to the education, more or less perfect, which all its people have received. But are they sensible of a fact equally important; namely, that it is to this same education that two-thirds of the people are indebted for not being today the vassals of as severe a tyranny, in the form of capital, as the lower classes of Europe are bound to in the form of brute force?

Education, then, beyond all other devices of human origin, is the great equalizer of the conditions of men, the balance wheel of the social machinery. I do not here mean that it so elevates the moral nature as to make men disdain and abhor the oppression of their fellowmen. This idea pertains to another of its attributes. But I mean that it gives each man the independence and the means by which he can resist the selfishness of other men. It does better than to disarm the poor of their hostility towards the rich: it prevents being poor.

Agrarianism is the revenge of poverty against wealth. The wanton destruction of the property of others — the burning of hayricks and cornricks, the demolition of machinery because it supersedes hand labor, the sprinkling of vitriol on rich dresses — is only agrarianism run mad. Education prevents both the revenge and the madness. On the other hand, a fellow feeling for one's class or caste is the common instinct of hearts not wholly sunk in selfish regards for person or for family. The spread of education, by enlarging the cultivated class or caste, will open a wider area over which the social feelings will expand; and, if this education should be universal and complete, it would do more than all things else to obliterate factitious distinctions in society. . . .

POLITICAL EDUCATION

THE NECESSITY of general intelligence — that is, of education (for I use the terms as substantially synonymous, because general intelligence can never exist without general education, and general education will be sure to produce general intelligence) — the necessity of general intelligence under a republican form of government, like most other very important truths, has become a very trite one. It is so trite, indeed, as to have lost much of its force by its familiarity. . . .

That the affairs of a great nation or state are exceedingly complicated and momentous, no one will dispute. Nor will it be questioned that the degree of intelligence that superintends should be proportioned to the magnitude of the interests superintended. He who scoops out a wooden dish needs less skill than the maker of a steam engine or a telescope. The dealer in small wares requires less knowledge than the merchant who exports and imports to and from all quarters of the globe. An ambassador cannot execute his functions with the stock of attainments or of talents sufficient for a parish clerk. Indeed, it is clear that the want of *adequate* intelligence — of intelligence *commensurate* with the nature of the duties to be performed — will bring ruin or disaster upon any department.

A merchant loses his intelligence, and he becomes a bankrupt. A lawyer loses his intelligence, and he forfeits all the interests of his clients. Intelligence abandons a physician, and his patients die with more than the pains of natural dissolution. Should judges upon the bench be bereft of this guide, what havoc would be made of the property and the innocence of men! Let this counselor be taken from executive officers, and the penalties due to the wicked would be visited upon the righteous, while the rewards and immunities of the righteous would be bestowed upon the guilty. And so, should intelligence desert the halls of legislation, weakness, rashness, contradiction, and error would glare out from every page of the statute book.

Now, as a republican government represents almost all interests, whether social, civil, or military, the necessity of a degree of intelligence adequate to the due administration of them all is so self-evident, that a bare statement is the best argument. But, in the possession of this attribute of intelligence, elective legislators will never far surpass their electors. By a natural law, like that which regulates the equilibrium of fluids, elector and elected, appointer and appointee, tend to the same level. It is not more certain that a wise and enlightened constituency will refuse to invest a reckless and profligate man with office, or discard him if accidentally chosen, than it is that a foolish or immoral constituency will discard or eject a wise man. . . .

It may be an easy thing to make a republic; but it is a very laborious thing to make republicans; and woe to the republic that rests upon no better foundations than ignorance, selfishness, and passion! Such a republic may grow in numbers and in wealth. As an avaricious man adds acres to his lands, so its rapacious government may increase its own darkness by annexing provinces and states to its ignorant domain. Its armies may be invincible, and its fleets may strike terror into nations on the opposite sides of the globe at the same hour. Vast in its extent, and enriched with all the prodigality of nature, it may possess every capacity and opportunity of being great and of doing good.

But, if such a republic be devoid of intelligence, it will only the more closely resemble an obscene giant who has waxed strong in his youth and grown wanton in his strength; whose brain has been developed only in the region of the appetites and passions, and not in the organs of reason and conscience; and who, therefore, is boastful of his bulk alone, and glories in the weight of his heel, and in the destruction of his arm. Such a republic, with all its noble capacities for beneficence, will rush with the speed of a whirlwind to an ignominious end; and all good men of aftertimes would be fain to weep over its downfall, did not their scorn and contempt at its folly and its wickedness repress all sorrow for its fate. . . .

However elevated the moral character of a constituency may be; however well informed in matters of general science or history, yet they must, if citizens of a republic, understand something of the true nature and functions of the government under which they live. That anyone who is to participate in the government of a country when he becomes a man should receive no instruction respecting the nature and functions of the government he is afterward to administer is a political solecism. . . .

Had the obligations of the future citizen been sedulously inculcated upon all the children of this republic, would the patriot have had to mourn over so many instances where the voter, not being able to accomplish his purpose by voting, has proceeded to accomplish it by violence; where, agreeing with his fellow citizens to use the machinery of the ballot, he makes a tacit reservation that, if that machinery does not move according to his pleasure, he will wrest or break it? If the responsibleness and value of the elective franchise were duly appreciated, the day of our state and national elections would be among the most solemn and religious days in the calendar.

Men would approach them, not only with preparation and solicitude, but with the sobriety and solemnity with which discreet and religious minded men meet the great crises of life. No man would throw away his vote through caprice or wantonness, any more than he would throw away his estate or sell his family into bondage. No man would cast his vote through malice or revenge, any more than a good surgeon would amputate a limb or a good navigator sail through perilous straits, under the same criminal passions.

But perhaps it will be objected, that the Constitution is subject to different readings, or that the policy of different administrations has become the subject of party strife; and, therefore, if anything of constitutional or political law is introduced into our schools, there is danger that teachers will be chosen on account of their affinities to this or that political party, or that teachers will feign affinities which they do not feel in order that they may be chosen; and so each schoolroom will at length become a miniature political clubroom, exploding with political resolves, or flaming out with political addresses, prepared by beardless boys in scarcely legible handwriting and in worse grammar.

With the most limited exercise of discretion, all apprehensions of this kind are wholly groundless. There are different readings of the Constitution, it is true; and there are partisan topics which agitate the country from side to side; but the controverted points, compared with those about which there is no dispute, do not bear the proportion of one to a hundred. And, what is more, no man is qualified, or can be qualified, to discuss the disputable questions, unless previously and thoroughly versed in those questions about which there is no dispute. In the terms and principles common to all, and recognized by all, is to be found the only common medium of language and of idea by which the parties can become intelligible to each other; and there, too, is the only common ground whence the arguments of the disputants can be drawn.

It is obvious, on the other hand that, if the tempest of political strife were to be let loose upon our common schools, they would be overwhelmed with sudden ruin. Let it be once understood that the schoolroom is a legitimate theater for party politics, and with what violence will hostile partisans struggle to gain possession of the stage and to play their parts upon it! Nor will the stage be the only scene of gladiatorial contests; these will rage in all the avenues that lead to it.

A preliminary advantage, indispensable to ultimate success, will be the appointment of a teacher of the true faith. As the great majority of the schools in the state are now organized, this can be done only by electing a prudential committee, who will make what he calls political soundness paramount to all other considerations of fitness. Thus, after petty skirmishings among neighbors, the fierce encounter will begin in the district's primary assembly, in the schoolroom itself.

This contest being over, the election of the superintending or town's committee must be determined in the same way; and this will bring together the combustibles of each district to burn with an intenser and a more devouring flame in the town meeting. It is very possible, nay, not at all improbable, that the town may be of one political complexion, while a majority of the districts are of the opposite.

Who shall moderate the fury of these conflicting elements when they rage against each other? And who shall save the dearest interests of the children from being consumed in the fierce combustion? If parents

Horace Mann, Southworth and Hawes daguerreotype

find that their children are indoctrinated into what they call political heresies, will they not withdraw them from the school? And, if they withdraw them from the school, will they not resist all appropriations to support a school from which they derive no benefit?

But, could the schools themselves survive these dangers for a single year, it would be only to encounter others still more perilous. Why should not the same infection that poisons all the relations of the schoolroom spread itself abroad and mingle with all questions of external organization and arrangement? Why should not political hostility cause the dismemberment of districts already too small; or, what would work equal injury, prevent the union of districts whose power of usefulness would be doubled by a combination of their resources? What better could be expected than that one set of schoolbooks should be expelled, and another introduced, as they might be supposed, however remotely, to favor one party or the other, or as the authors of the books might

belong to one party or the other? And who could rely upon the reports, or even the statistics, of a committee chosen by partisan votes, goaded on by partisan impulses, and responsible to partisan domination, and this, too, without any opportunity of control or check from the minority?

Nay, if the schools could survive long enough to meet the crisis, why should not any and every measure be taken, either to maintain an existing political ascendency, or to recover a lost one, in a school district, or in a town, which has even been taken by unscrupulous politicians to maintain or to recover an ascendency at the polls? Into a district, or into a town, voters may be introduced from abroad to turn the scale. An employer may dismiss the employed for their refusal to submit to his dictation, or make the bread that is given to the poor man's children perform the double office of payment for labor to be performed and of a bribe for principle to be surrendered. And beyond all this, if the imagination can conceive anything more deplorable than this, what kind of political doctrines would be administered to the children amid the vicissitudes of party domination — their alternations of triumph and defeat?

This year, under the ascendency of one side, the Constitution declares one thing; and commentaries, glosses, and the authority of distinguished names, all ratify and confirm its decisions. But victory is a fickle goddess. Next year, the vanquished triumph; and Constitution, gloss, and authority make that sound doctrine which was pestilent error before, and that false which was true. Right and wrong have changed sides. The children must now join in chorus to denounce what they had been taught to reverence before, and to reverence what they had been taught to denounce. In the meantime, those great principles, which, according to Cicero, are the same at Rome and at Athens, the same now and forever, and which, according to Hooker, have their seat in the bosom of God, become the fittest emblems of chance and change.

Long, however, before this series of calamities would exhaust itself upon our schools, these schools themselves would cease to be. The plowshare would have turned up their foundations. Their history would have been brought to a close — a glorious and ascending history, until struck down by the hand of political parricide; then suddenly falling with a double ruin, with death and with ignominy.

But, to avoid such a catastrophe, shall all teaching relative to the nature of our government be banished from our schools; and shall our children be permitted to grow up in entire ignorance of the political history of their country? In the schools of a republic, shall the children be left without any distinct knowledge of the nature of a republican government, or only with such knowledge as they may pick up from angry political discussions or from party newspapers, from caucus speeches, or 4th of July orations — the Apocrypha of Apocrypha?

Surely, between these extremes, there must be a medium not difficult to be found. And is not this the middle course, which all sensible and judicious men, all patriots, and all genuine republicans must approve? Namely, that those articles in the creed of republicanism which are accepted by all, believed in by all, and which form the common basis of our political faith, shall be taught to all. But when the teacher, in the course of his lessons or lectures on the fundamental law, arrives at a controverted text, he is either to read it without comment or remark; or, at most, he is only to say that the passage is the subject of disputation, and that the schoolroom is neither the tribunal to adjudicate, nor the forum to discuss it.

Such being the rule established by common consent, and such the practice observed with fidelity under it, it will come to be universally understood that political proselytism is no function of the school, but

that indoctrination into matters of controversy between hostile political parties is to be elsewhere sought for and elsewhere imparted. Thus may all the children of the Commonwealth receive instruction in all the great essentials of political knowledge — in those elementary ideas without which they will never be able to investigate more recondite and debatable questions; thus will the only practicable method be adopted for discovering new truths, and for discarding, instead of perpetuating, old errors; and thus, too, will that pernicious race of intolerant zealots, whose whole faith may be summed up in two articles, that they themselves are always infallibly right and that all dissenters are certainly wrong, be extinguished; extinguished, not by violence, nor by proscription, but by the more copious inflowing of the light of truth.

MORAL EDUCATION

MORAL EDUCATION is a primal necessity of social existence. . . . Every law in the statute book might be obeyed, so as to leave no penalty to be awarded by the courts, or inflicted by executive officers, and yet myriads of private vices, too subtle and intangible for legislative enactments, and too undefinable to be dealt with by the tribunals of justice, might still imbitter all domestic and social relations, and leave nothing in life worth living for.

Were the greater plagues of public crime and open violence to be stayed still the lesser ones might remain; like the plagues of Egypt, they might invade every house, penetrate to every chamber, corrupt the water in the fountains and the bread in the kneading troughs, and turn the dust into loathsome life, so that the plague of hail and the plague of darkness might seem to be blessings in the comparison. In offenses against what are usually called the "minor morals," — against propriety, against decency, against the domestic relations, and against good neighborhood, as they are illustrated and enjoined by the example of Christ, the precepts of the gospel, and the perfect law of love, — here is a vast region where offenses may grow, and where they do grow, thick-standing and rankly luxuriant.

Against these social vices in all ages of the world, the admonitions of good men have been directed. The moralist has exposed their deformity in his didactic page; the satirist has chastised them in his pungent verse; the dramatist has held them up to ridicule on the mimic stage; and, to some extent, the Christian minister has exhibited their gross repugnancy to the character of a disciple of Jesus. Still they continue to exist. . . . The race has existed long enough to try many experiments for the solution of this greatest problem ever submitted to its hands; and the race has experimented, without stint of time or circumscription of space to mar or modify legitimate results. . . .

But to all doubters, disbelievers, or despairers in human progress, it may still be said, there is one experiment which has never yet been tried. It is an experiment, which, even before its inception, offers the highest authority for its ultimate success. Its formula is intelligible to all; and it is as legible as though written in starry letters on an azure sky. It is expressed in these few and simple words: "Train up a child in the way he should go; and, when he is old, he will not depart from it." This declaration is positive. If the conditions are complied with, it makes no provision for a failure. Though pertaining to morals, yet, if the terms of the direction are observed, there is no more reason to doubt the result than there would be in an optical or a chemical experiment.

But this experiment has never yet been tried. Education has never yet been brought to bear with one-hundredth part of its potential force upon the natures of children, and, through them, upon the character of men and of the race. In all the attempts to reform mankind which have hitherto been made, whether by changing the frame of government, by aggravating or softening the severity of the penal code, or by substituting a government-created for a God-created religion, — in all these attempts, the infantile and youthful mind, its amenability to influences, and the enduring and self-operating character of the influences it receives, have been almost wholly unrecognized. Here, then, is a new agency, whose powers are but just beginning to be understood, and whose mighty energies hitherto have been but feebly invoked; and yet, from our experience, limited and imperfect as it is, we do know, that, far beyond any other earthly instrumentality, it is comprehensive and decisive. . . .

RELIGIOUS EDUCATION

BUT IT WILL BE SAID that this grand result in practical morals is a consummation of blessedness that can never be attained without religion, and that no community will ever be religious without a religious education. Both these propositions I regard as eternal and immutable truths. Devoid of religious principles and religious affections, the race can never fall so low but that it may sink still lower; animated and sanctified by them, it can never rise so high but that it may ascend still higher. . . .

I here place the argument in favor of a religious education for the young upon the most broad and general grounds, purposely leaving it to every individual to add for himself those auxiliary arguments which may result from his own peculiar views of religious truth. But such is the force of the conviction to which my own mind is brought by these general considerations, that I could not avoid regarding the man who should oppose the religious education of the young as an insane man; and, were it proposed to debate the question between us, I should desire to restore him to his reason before entering upon the discussion. If, suddenly summoned to eternity, I were able to give but one parting word of advice to my own children, or to the children of others; if I were sinking beneath the wave, and had time to utter but one articulate breath; or were wasting away upon the deathbed, and had strength to make but one exhortation more, — that dying legacy should be, "Remember thy Creator in the days of thy youth." . . .

On this subject I propose to speak with freedom and plainness, and more at length than I should feel required to do but for the peculiar circumstances in which I have been placed. It is matter of notoriety, that the views of the Board of Education, and my own, perhaps, still more than those of the Board, on the subject of religious instruction in our public schools, have been subjected to animadversion. Grave charges have been made against us, that our purpose was to exclude religion, and to exclude that, too, which is the common exponent of religion — the Bible — from the common schools of the state; or, at least, to derogate from its authority, and destroy its influence in them.

Whatever prevalence a suspicion of the truth of these imputations may have heretofore had, I have reason to believe that further inquiry and examination have done much to disabuse the too credulous recipients of so groundless a charge. Still, among a people so commendably sensitive on the subject of religion as are the people of Massachusetts, any suspicion of irreligious tendencies will greatly prejudice any cause, and, so far as any cause may otherwise have the power of doing good, will greatly impair that power.

It is known, too, that our noble system of free schools for the whole people is strenuously opposed by a few persons in our own state, and by no inconsiderable numbers in some of the other states of this Union; and

that a rival system of "parochial" or "sectarian schools" is now urged upon the public by a numerous, a powerful, and a well-organized body of men. It has pleased the advocates of this rival system, in various public addresses, in reports, and through periodicals devoted to their cause, to denounce our system as irreligious and antichristian. They do not trouble themselves to describe what our system is, but adopt a more summary way to forestall public opinion against it by using general epithets of reproach, and signals of alarm.

In this age of the world, it seems to me that no student of history, or observer of mankind, can be hostile to the precepts and the doctrines of the Christian religion, or opposed to any institutions which expound and exemplify them; and no man who thinks, as I cannot but think, respecting the enduring elements of character, whether public or private, can be willing to have his name mentioned while he is living, or remembered when he is dead, as opposed to religious instruction and Bible instruction for the young. In making this final report, therefore, I desire to vindicate my conduct from the charges that have been made against it; and, so far as the Board has been implicated in these charges, to leave my testimony on record for their exculpation. . . .

After years of endurance, after suffering under misconstructions of conduct, and the imputation of motives whose edge is sharper than a knife, it was at my suggestion, and by making use of materials which I had laboriously collected, that the Board made its Eighth Annual Report, — a document said to be the ablest argument in favor of the use of the Bible in schools anywhere to be found. This report had my full concurrence. Since its appearance, I have always referred to it as explanatory of the views of the Board, and as setting forth the law of a wise commonwealth and the policy of a Christian people. Officially and unofficially, publicly and privately, in theory and in practice, my course has always been in conformity with its doctrines. And I avail myself of this, the last opportunity which I may ever have, to say, in regard to all affirmations or intimations that I have ever attempted to exclude religious instruction from school, or to exclude the Bible from school, or to impair the force of that volume, that they are now, and always have been, without substance or semblance of truth. . . .

The very terms "public school" and "common school" bear upon their face that they are schools which the children of the entire community may attend. Every man not on the pauper list is taxed for their support; but he is not taxed to support them as special religious institutions: if he were, it would satisfy at once the largest definition of a religious establishment. But he is taxed to support them as a *preventive* means against dishonesty, against fraud, and against violence, on the same principle that he is taxed to support criminal courts as a *punitive* means against the same offenses.

He is taxed to support schools, on the same principle that he is taxed to support paupers, because a child without education is poorer and more wretched than a man without bread. He is taxed to support schools, on the same principle that he would be taxed to defend the nation against foreign invasion, or against rapine committed by a foreign foe, because the general prevalence of ignorance, superstition, and vice, will breed Goth and Vandal at home more fatal to the public well-being than any Goth or Vandal from abroad. And, finally, he is taxed to support schools, because they are the most effective means of developing and training those powers and faculties in a child, by which, when he becomes a man, he may understand what his highest interests and his highest duties are, and may be in fact, and not in name only, a free agent.

The elements of a political education are not bestowed upon any school child for the purpose of making him vote with this or that political party when he becomes of age, but for the purpose of enabling him to choose for himself with which party he will vote. So the religious education which a child receives at school is not imparted to him for the purpose of making him join this or that denomination when he arrives at years of discretion, but for the purpose of enabling him to judge for himself, according to the dictates of his own reason and conscience, what his religious obligations are, and whither they lead.

But if a man is taxed to support a school where religious doctrines are inculcated which he believes to be false, and which he believes that God condemns, then he is excluded from the school by the divine law, at the same time that he is compelled to support it by the human law. This is a double wrong. It is politically wrong, because, if such a man educates his children at all, he must educate them elsewhere, and thus pay two taxes, while some of his neighbors pay less than their due proportion of one; and it is religiously wrong, because he is constrained by human power to promote what he believes the Divine Power forbids. The principle involved in such a course is pregnant with all tyrannical consequences. . . .

It is still easier to prove that the Massachusetts school system is not antichristian nor unchristian. The Bible is the acknowledged expositor of Christianity. In strictness, Christianity has no other authoritative expounder. This Bible is in our common schools by common consent. Twelve years ago, it was not in all the schools. Contrary to the genius of our government, if not contrary to the express letter of the law, it had been used for sectarian purposes, — to prove one sect to be right, and others to be wrong. Hence it had been excluded from the schools of some towns by an express vote. But since the law, and the reasons on which it is founded, have been more fully explained and better understood, and since sectarian instruction has, to a great extent, ceased to be given, the Bible has been restored.

I am not aware of the existence of a single town in the state in whose schools it is not now introduced, either by a direct vote of the school committee, or by such general desire and acquiescence as supersede the necessity of a vote. In all my intercourse for twelve years, whether personal or by letter, with all the school officers in the state, and with tens of thousands of individuals in it, I have never heard an objection made to the use of the Bible in school, except in one or two instances; and, in those cases, the objection was put upon the ground that daily familiarity with the book in school would tend to impair a reverence for it. . . .

And further: our law explicitly and solemnly enjoins it upon all teachers, without any exception, "to exert their best endeavors to impress on the minds of children and youth committed to their care and instruction the principles of piety, justice, and a sacred regard to truth, love to their country, humanity, and universal benevolence, sobriety, industry, and frugality, chastity, moderation, and temperance, and those other virtues which are the ornament of human society, and the basis upon which a republican constitution is founded." Are not these virtues and graces part and parcel of Christianity? In other words, can there be Christianity without them? While these virtues and these duties towards God and man are inculcated in our schools, anyone who says that the schools are antichristian or unchristian expressly affirms that his own system of Christianity does not embrace any one of this radiant catalog; that it rejects them all; that it embraces their opposites.

And further still: our system makes it the express duty of all the "resident ministers of the gospel" to bring all the children within the moral and Christian inculcations above enumerated; so that he who avers that our system is an antichristian or an unchristian one avers that it is both antichristian and unchristian for a "minister of the gospel" to promote, or labor to diffuse, the moral attributes and excellences which the statute so earnestly enjoins.

So far, the argument has been of an affirmative character. Its scope and purpose show, or at least tend to show, *by direct proof*, that the school system of Massachusetts is not an antichristian nor an unchristian system. But there is still another mode of proof. The truth of a proposition may be established by showing the falsity or absurdity of all conflicting propositions. So far as this method can be applied to moral questions, its aid may safely be invoked here.

What are the other courses which the state of Massachusetts might adopt or sanction in relation to the education of its youth? They are these four:

1. It might establish schools, but expressly exclude all religious instruction from them, making them merely schools for secular instruction.

2. It might adopt a course directly the reverse of this. It might define and prescribe a system of religion for the schools, and appoint the teachers and officers, whose duty it should be to carry out that system.

3. It might establish schools by law, and empower each religious sect, whenever and wherever it could get a majority to determine what religious faith should be taught in them. And,

4. It might expressly disclaim and refuse all interference with the education of the young, and abandon the whole work to the hazards of private enterprise, or to parental will, ability, or caprice.

1. A system of schools from which all religious instruction should be excluded might properly be called unchristian, or rather non-Christian, in the same sense in which it could be called non-Jewish or non-Mahometan; that is, as having no connection

with either. I do not suppose a man can be found in Massachusetts who would declare such a system to be his first choice.

2. Were the state to establish schools, and prescribe a system of religion to be taught in them, and appoint the teachers and officers to superintend it, could there be any better definition or exemplification of an ecclesiastical establishment? Such a system would create at once the most formidable and terrible hierarchy ever established upon earth. It would plunge society back into the Dark Ages at one precipitation. . . .

3. As a third method, the government might establish schools by law, and empower each religious sect, whenever and wherever it could get a majority, to determine what religious faith should be taught in them.

Under such a system, each sect would demand that its own faith should be inculcated in all the schools, and this on the clear and simple ground that such faith is the only true one. . . .

Now, it is almost too obvious to be mentioned, that such a claim as the above reduces society at once to this dilemma: if one religious sect is authorized to advance it for itself, then all other sects are equally authorized to do the same thing for themselves. The right being equal among all the sects, and each sect being equally certain and equally determined, what shall be done? Will not each sect, acting under religious impulses — which are the strongest impulses that ever animate the breast of man — will not each sect do its utmost to establish its supremacy in all the schools? Will not the heats and animosities engendered in families and among neighbors burst forth with a devouring fire in the primary or district school meetings? And, when the inflammable materials of all the district meetings are gathered together in the town meeting, what can quell or

quench the flames till the zealots themselves are consumed in the conflagration they have kindled? . . .

Is there not, on the contrary, an unspeakable value in the fact, that, under the Massachusetts system, the Bible is allowed to speak for itself? Under a system opposite to ours, this right of speaking for itself would never be vouchsafed to it. And how narrow is the distance between those who would never allow the Bible to be read by the people at all, and those who will allow it to be read only in the presence of a government interpreter! If government and teachers really believe the Bible to be the word of God, — as strictly and literally given by His inspiration as the tables of the law which Moses brought down from the mount were written by His finger, — then they cannot deny, that, when the Bible is read, God speaks, just as literally and truly as an orator or a poet speaks when his oration or his poem is rehearsed. With this belief, it is no figure of speech to say, when the lids of the Bible are opened in school that its oracles may be uttered, that the lips of Jehovah are opened that He may commune with all His children, of whatever faith, who may be there assembled. . . .

I hold it, then, to be one of the excellences, one of the moral beauties, of the Massachusetts system, that there is one place in the land where the children of all the different denominations are brought together for instruction, where the Bible is allowed to speak for itself; one place where the children can kneel at a common altar, and feel that they have a common Father, and where the services of religion tend to create brothers, and not Ishmaelites. If this be so, then it does violence to truth to call our system antichristian or unchristian.

4. One other system, if it may be so called, is supposable; and this exhausts the number of those which stand in direct conflict with ours. It is this: Government might

expressly disclaim and refuse all interference with the education of the young, abandoning the whole work to the hazards of private enterprise, or to parental will, ability, or caprice.

The first effect of this course would be the abandonment of a large portion of the children of every community to hopeless and inevitable ignorance. Even with all the aids, incitements, and bounties now bestowed upon education by the most enlightened states in this Union, there exists a perilous and a growing body of ignorance, animated by the soul of vice. Were government systems to be abolished, and all government aids to be withdrawn, the number of American children, who, in the next generation, would be doomed to all the wants and woes that can come in the train of ignorance and error, would be counted by millions. This abandoned portion of the community would be left, without any of the restraints of education, to work out the infinite possibilities of human depravity.

In the more favored parts of the country, the rich might educate their own children; although it is well known, even now, that, throughout extensive regions of the South and West, the best education which wealth can procure is meager and stinted, and alloyed with much error. The "parochial" or "sectarian" system might effect something in populous places; but what could it do in rural districts, where so vast a proportion of all the inhabitants of this country reside? . . .

I know of but one argument, having the semblance of plausibility, that can be urged against this feature of our system. It may be said, that if questions of doctrinal religion are left to be decided by men for themselves, or by parents for their children, numerous and grievous errors will be mingled with the instruction. Doubtless the fact is so. If truth be one, and if many contradictory dogmas are taught as truth, then it is mathematically certain that all the alleged truths but one is a falsity.

But, though the statement is correct, the inference which is drawn from it in favor of a government standard of faith is not legitimate; for all the religious errors which are believed in by the free mind of man, or which are taught by free parents to their children, are tolerable and covetable, compared with those which the patronage and the seductions of government can suborn men to adopt, and which the terrors of government can compel them to perpetuate. The errors of free minds are so numerous and so various, that they prevent any monster-error from acquiring the ascendency, and therefore truth has a chance to struggle forward amid the strifes of the combatants; but if the monster-error can usurp the throne of the civil power, fortify itself by prescription, defend its infallibility with all the forces of the state, sanctify its enormities under sacred names, and plead the express command of God for all its atrocities, — against such an antagonist, truth must struggle for centuries, bleed at every pore, be wounded in every vital part, and can triumph at last, only after thousands and tens of thousands of her holiest disciples shall have fallen in the conflict.

If, then, a government would recognize and protect the rights of religious freedom, it must abstain from subjugating the capacities of its children to any legal standard of religious faith with as great fidelity as it abstains from controlling the opinions of men. It must meet the unquestionable fact, that the old spirit of religious domination is adopting new measures to accomplish its work, — measures which, if successful, will be as fatal to the liberties of mankind as those which were practised in bygone days of violence and terror.

These new measures are aimed at children instead of men. They propose to supersede the necessity of subduing free thought *in the mind of the adult*, by forestalling the development of any capacity of free thought *in the mind of the child*. They expect to find it easier to subdue the free agency of children by binding them in fetters of bigotry than to subdue the free agency of men by binding them in fetters of iron.

For this purpose, some are attempting to deprive children of their right to labor, and, of course, of their daily bread, unless they will attend a government school, and receive its sectarian instruction. Some are attempting to withhold all means even of secular education from the poor, and thus punish them with ignorance, unless, with the secular knowledge which they desire, they will accept theological knowledge which they condemn. Others still are striving to break down all free public school systems where they exist, and to prevent their establishment where they do not exist, in the hope, that, on the downfall of these, their system will succeed. The sovereign antidote against these machinations is free schools for all, and the right of every parent to determine the religious education of his children.

103.

Pennsylvania Child Labor Law

In December 1847 the Pennsylvania senate conducted hearings on child labor in factories. The senators heard testimony that children often worked from sunrise to sunset, that their wages were not based on hours worked, and that in at least one factory employing eighty to ninety persons, fifteen or sixteen were under twelve years old, and twenty were between twelve and twenty-one years old. In March 1848 the Pennsylvania legislature passed "An Act to Limit the Hours of Labor, and to Prevent the Employment, in Factories, of Children under Twelve Years of Age," which is reprinted below. By 1860 fewer than ten states had child labor regulations of any sort and in only four states was a minimum age of employment set for specified types of factory work. In most states that had such laws evasion was usually easy for employers.

Source: *Laws of the General Assembly of the Commonwealth of Pennsylvania, Passed at the Session of 1848*, Harrisburg, 1848, No. 227, pp. 278-279.

Section 1. *Be it enacted* by the Senate and House of Representatives of the commonwealth of Pennsylvania in General Assembly met, and *it is hereby enacted* by the authority of the same, that labor performed during a period of ten hours, on any secular day, in all cotton, woolen, silk, paper, bagging, and flax factories shall be considered a legal day's labor; and that, hereafter, no minor or adult engaged in any such factories shall be held or required to work more than ten hours on any secular day or sixty hours in any secular week; and that after the 4th day of July, of the present year, no minor shall be admitted as a worker, under the age of twelve years, in any cotton, woolen, silk, or flax factory within this commonwealth; that if any owner of or employer in any such factories aforesaid shall employ any such minor, he shall be adjudged to pay a penalty of $50, one-half thereof to the party so employed and the other half to the commonwealth, to be received in like manner as fines of like amount are now recoverable by law:

Provided, that nothing contained in this act shall be construed to prevent minors above the age of fourteen years from being employed more than ten hours in any day, if the same be done by special contract with their parents or guardians.

104.

JAMES RUSSELL LOWELL: English Thought and American Writers

Lowell worked sporadically at his Fable for Critics *for about a year, beginning in the summer of 1847 and ending the following summer; the work was published on October 31, 1848. It appeared anonymously, which it well might have, considering that it made more or less fun of all of Lowell's contemporaries; "the secret was kept," the author wrote a friend, "till after several persons had laid claim to its authorship." In another letter he declared that he had "a sort of presentiment . . . that this little bit of pleasantry will* take," *which indeed it did, becoming almost the best-known work of this poet who was otherwise a serious, not to say a solemn, writer. The portion of the* Fable *printed here is serious enough; in it Lowell expounds the proper attitude for Americans to assume toward John Bull — that is, the English. But the "rocking horse rhythm" that Lowell maintains throughout is a sign, of course, of the essential lightheartedness of the piece.*

Source: *A Fable for Critics*, New York, 1848, pp. 48-51.

> There are truths you Americans need to be told,
> And it never'll refute them to swagger and scold;
> John Bull, looking o'er the Atlantic, in choler
> At your aptness for trade, says you worship the dollar;
> But to scorn such i-dollar-try's what very few do,
> And John goes to that church as often as you do.
> No matter what John says, don't try to outcrow him,
> 'Tis enough to go quietly on and outgrow him;
> Like most fathers, Bull hates to see Number One
> Displacing himself in the mind of his son,
> And detests the same faults in himself he'd neglected
> When he sees them again in his child's glass reflected;
> To love one another you're too like by half,
> And tear your own pasture for naught but to show
> What a nice pair of horns you're beginning to grow.
>
> There are one or two things I should just like to hint,
> For you don't often get the truth told you in print;

The most of you (this is what strikes all beholders)
Have a mental and physical stoop in the shoulders;
Though you ought to be free as the winds and the waves,
You've the gait and the manners of runaway slaves;
Tho' you brag of your New World, you don't half believe in it,
And as much of the Old as is possible weave in it;
Your goddess of freedom, a tight, buxom girl,
With lips like a cherry and teeth like a pearl,
With eyes bold as Herè's, and hair floating free,
And full of the sun as the spray of the sea,
Who can sing at a husking or romp at a shearing,
Who can trip through the forests alone without fearing,
Who can drive home the cows with a song through the grass,
Keeps glancing aside into Europe's cracked glass,
Hides her red hands in gloves, pinches up her lithe waist,
And makes herself wretched with transmarine taste;
She loses her fresh country charm when she takes
Any mirror except her own rivers and lakes.

You steal Englishmen's books and think Englishmen's thought,
With their salt on her tail your wild eagle is caught;
Your literature suits its each whisper and motion
To what will be thought of it over the ocean;
The cast clothes of Europe your statesmanship tries
And mumbles again the old blarneys and lies;
Forget Europe wholly, your veins throb with blood
To which the dull current in hers is but mud;
Let her sneer, let her say your experiment fails,
In her voice there's a tremble e'en now while she rails,
And your shore will soon be in the nature of things
Covered thick with gilt driftwood of runaway kings,
Where alone, as it were in a Longfellow's Waif,
Her fugitive pieces will find themselves safe.
O, my friends, thank your God, if you have one, that He
'Twixt the Old World and you set the gulf of a sea;
Be strong-backed, brown-handed, upright as your pines,
By the scale of a hemisphere shape your designs,
Be true to yourselves and this new nineteenth age,
As a statue by Powers, or a picture by Page,
Plough, dig, sail, forge, build, carve, paint, make all things new,
To your own New-World instincts contrive to be true,
Keep your ears open wide to the Future's first call,
Be whatever you will, but yourselves first of all,
Stand fronting the dawn on Toil's heaven-scaling peaks,
And become my new race of more practical Greeks.
Hem! your likeness at present, I shudder to tell o't,
Is that you have your slaves, and the Greek had his helot.

1849

105.

ALEXANDER MACKAY: Apostles of the Democratic Creed

In The Western World; or, Travels in the United States in 1846-47, *the Scottish journalist, Alexander Mackay, set out to portray "the social life of America, the working of its political institutions, and the bearing of its policy upon its moral development." Mackay felt that too many authors had attempted to portray the United States after spending only a few months there. Mackay, on the contrary, spent several years in the States studying the national character before embarking on the 1846-1847 tour that directly inspired his book. Mackay's was one of the most sympathetic and knowledgeable accounts written in the pre-Civil War period. The following selection is from a chapter entitled "American Character — Physical Condition of Society in America."*

Source: *The Western World; or, Travels in the United States in 1846-47,*
  4th edition, London, 1850, Vol. III, pp. 317-342.

MANY EUROPEANS QUIT the shores of the republic with unfavorable impressions of American character, in the broadest acceptation of the term. But in the majority of instances, those who do so, enter the country with preconceived notions of it and leave it ere they have learned to discern objects through the right medium. The Americans as a people, for instance, are characterized by some as gloomy and reserved; whereas, if properly approached, they are frank, communicative, and not infrequently even mercurial in their dispositions. Anyone who has mingled much in American society must have seen that gloom was far from being its predominant characteristic, at least in the case of American women. If they have any fault in this respect as a class, it is not that of coldness and reserve but of overvivaciousness and a tendency to the frivolous and amusing. In parts of the country where fanaticism in religion has for some time prevailed, a settled gloom may be discerned on the majority of countenances; but it does not so much indicate a morose spirit as a real or affected habit of looking serious.

From a pretty long and intimate acquaintance with American society in most of its phases, I can confidently say that the traveler who finds the people of America habitually keeping him at a distance, and otherwise treating him coldly, must be himself chiefly to blame for the reception which he experiences. During my peregrinations through the Union — and they were many and long — I had frequent opportunity of seeing how English travelers demeaned themselves on passing through the country. I invariably found that those who met the Americans frankly and ingenuously were treated with the utmost kindness and warmheartedness and were consequently favorably impressed with the character of the people; whereas, such as traveled through the country as if it were a compliment to the republic that they touched its democratic soil and as if the mere fact of their being Englishmen entitled them to treat all who came in their way with ill-dissembled hauteur and contumely were left to find their way as they best could, the cold shoulder being turned to them wherever they went.

This is not done from any feeling of vindictiveness toward them, for they are generally laughed at on assuming insolent airs and demanding extra attentions. Those who will not treat them frankly, the Americans will not put themselves out of their way to receive kindly nor will they give their confidence to such as expect to gain it without an equivalent. But be frank, fair, and honest with them, treating them not with marked deference but with ordinary courtesy, and a more kindhearted, accessible, hospitable, and manageable people are not to be found.

The Americans are almost universally known to be a sensitive people. They are more than this; they are oversensitive. This is a weakness which some travelers delight to play upon. But if they understood its source aright, they would deal more tenderly with it. As a nation, they feel themselves to be in the position of an individual whose permanent place in society has not yet been ascertained. They have struggled in little more than half a century into the first rank among the powers of the earth; but, like all

new members of a confined and very particular circle, they are not yet quite sure of the firmness of their footing. When they look to the future, they have no reason to doubt the prominency of the position — social, political, and economical — which they will assume. But they are in haste to be all that they are yet destined to be; and although they do not exact from the stranger a positive recognition of all their pretensions, they are sensitive to a degree to any word or action on his part which purports a denial of them.

It must be confessed that this weakness has of late very much increased. A sore that is being constantly irritated will soon exhibit all the symptoms of violent inflammation. The feelings of the American people have been wantonly and unnecessarily wounded by successive travelers who have undertaken to depict them, nationally and individually, and who, to pander to a prevailing taste in this country, have generally viewed them on the ludicrous side. It is a mistake to fancy that the Americans are impatient of criticism. They will submit to any amount of that is fair when they discover that it is tendered in an honest spirit. What they most wince at is the application to them and their affairs of epithets tending to turn them into ridicule. You may be as severe as you please with them, even in their own country as well as out of it, without irritating them, provided it appears that your intention is not simply to raise a laugh at their expense.

When I first went to Washington I was cautioned by one who knew the Americans well not to suppress my real sentiments concerning them, but to be guarded as to the terms and the manner in which I gave utterance to them. They have been so frequently unjustly dealt with by English writers that they now suspect every Englishman of a predetermination to treat them in a similar manner. I acted upon the advice which I received, and for the six months during which I resided in the capital, I freely indulged in criticism of men and things, without, so far as I could ascertain, giving the slightest offense to anyone. But there are cases in which a look, a shrug of the shoulder, or a verbal expression may cause the greatest irritation.

In this country it is difficult to understand this sensitiveness on the part of the American people. England has her fixed position in the great family of nations and at the head of civilization — a position which she has long occupied and from which it will be some time ere she is driven. We care not, therefore, what the foreigner says or thinks of us. He may look or express contempt as he walks our streets or frequents our public places. His praise cannot exalt nor can his contempt debase us, as a people. The desire of America is to be at least abreast of England in the career of nations; and every expression which falls from the Englishman showing that in his opinion she is yet far behind his own country grates harshly upon what is after all but a pardonable vanity, springing from a laudable ambition.

The Americans are much more sensitive at home than they are abroad. Their country is but yet young; and when they hear parties abroad who have never seen it, expressing opinions in any degree derogatory to it, they console themselves with the reflection that the disparaging remark has its origin in an ignorance of the country, which is judged of, not from what it really is but simply as a state of but 70 years' growth.

Now in Europe it is but seldom that 70 years of national existence accomplishes much for a people. It is true that more has been done for mankind during the last 70 than perhaps during the previous 700; but the development of a nation in Europe is a slow process at the best, as compared with the course of things in this respect in America. The American, therefore, feels that if the European would suspend his judgment until he saw and heard for himself, it would be very different from what it is when begotten in prejudice and pronounced in ignorance. This takes the sting from such disparaging criticism abroad as he may chance to hear. But if it is offered at home, unless it is accompanied with all the candor and honesty in which such criticism should alone be indulged in, he has no such reflection to take refuge in, and it wounds him to the quick.

If, notwithstanding all the evidences which the country affords of unexampled prosperity, universal contentment, social improvement, and material progress, the foreigner still speaks of it, not in terms of severity but in those of contempt — in terms, in short, which the American feels and knows are not justifiable — he can only refer the criticism to a predetermination to turn everything into ridicule and is consequently not unjustly offended. Such, unfortunately, is the predetermination with which a large proportion of English travelers in America enter the country, demeaning themselves during their peregrinations through it with an ill-disguised air of self-importance, unpalatable to a people who have become jealous from unmerited bad treatment. The consequence is that every Englishman in America is now on his good behavior. He is not regarded as candid until he proves himself the reverse, but as prejudiced and unfriendly until he gives testimony of his fairness and honesty.

If the Americans are more sensitive at home than they are abroad, they are more boastful abroad than they are at home. The one is a mere weakness, the other frequently an offense. Many in Europe judge of the American people from the specimens of them who travel. There are, of course, many Americans that travel, who, if they partake largely of the national vanity attributed to them all, have the tact and the courtesy to conceal it. Indeed, some of the best specimens of Americans are, for obvious reasons, those who have traveled much from home. But the great mass of American travelers enter foreign countries with as thick a coat of prejudice about them as Englishmen generally wear in visiting America. The consequence is that they commit the fault abroad at which they are so irritated when committed in regard to themselves by the foreigner in America.

With the American abroad, however, this fault assumes the reverse phase of that taken by it when committed by the foreigner in America. The Englishman, for instance, who is disposed to view everything in America through a jaundiced eye and to draw invidious comparisons between the two countries, exalts his own by running down the other. The American, on the other hand, having the same object in view, approaches it from the opposite side, drawing comparisons favorable to his country, not by disparaging others but by boasting of his own. This may be the weaker, but it is certainly the less offensive manifestation of a common fault.

It would be erroneous to suppose that the national vanity which so many Americans exhibit abroad is prominently manifested at home. At all events it is not obtruded upon the stranger. The evidences of the country's greatness, both present and prospective, are before him when in the country; and to recapitulate them to him under these circumstances would be but to tell a tale twice over. If he does not draw favorable conclusions from what he sees, it is hopeless to expect him to do so from anything that he could hear. The American may be amazed at his real or annoyed at his willful blindness, but he generally leaves him to his own inferences. It is only abroad, and when in contact with those who have not had ocular demonstration of it, that he is prone to dwell in a vaunting spirit upon his country's greatness.

Some allowance, however, should be made for the American, even in his most boastful humor. If he has nothing in a national point of view to be vain of, he has certainly much of which he can and should feel proud. There is no other country on earth which in so short a time has accomplished so much. It has but just passed the usual term allotted as the period of life to man, and yet it takes rank as a first-rate power. But let it not be supposed that all this has been achieved in seventy years. The American republic has never had a national infancy, like that through which most European nations have passed. The Colonies were, in a measure, old while they were yet new. They were as old as England herself in point of moral, and new only in point of material, civilization. They were not savages who laid the foundations of our colonial dominion in America but emigrants from a highly civilized society, carrying with them all the moral results of centuries of social culture. . . .

Intimately connected with the pride of country which generally distinguishes the Americans is the feeling which they cherish toward their institutions. Indeed, when the national feeling of an American is alluded to, something very different is implied from that which is generally understood by the term. . . . But the American exhibits little or none of the local attachments which distinguish the European. His feelings are more centered upon his institutions than his mere country. He looks upon himself more in the light of a republican than in that of a native of a particular territory. His affections have more to do with the social and political system with which he is connected than with the soil which he inhabits. The national feelings, which he and a European [cherish], being thus different in their origin and their object, are also different in their results.

The man whose attachments converge upon a particular spot of earth is miserable if removed from it, no matter how greatly his circumstances otherwise may have been improved by his removal; but give the American his institutions, and he cares but little where you place him. In some parts of the Union the local feeling may be comparatively strong, such as in New England; but it is astonishing how readily even there an American makes up his mind to try his fortunes elsewhere, particularly if he contemplates removal merely to another part of the Union, no matter how remote or how different in climate and other circumstances from what he has been accustomed to, provided the flag of his country waves over it and republican institutions accompany him in his wanderings.

Strange as it may seem, this peculiarity, which makes an American think less of his country than of the institutions which characterize it, contributes greatly to the pride which he takes in his country. He is proud of it, not so much for itself as because it is the scene in which an experiment is being tried which engages the anxious attention of the world. The American feels himself much more interested in the success of his scheme of government, if not more identified with it, than the European does in regard to his. . . .

He feels himself, therefore, to be directly interested in the success of the political system under which he lives, and all the more so because he is conscious that in looking to its working mankind are divided into two great classes — those who are interested in its failure and those who yearn for its success. Every American is thus, in his own estimation, the apostle of a particular political creed, in the final triumph and extension of which he finds both himself and his country deeply involved. This gives him a peculiar interest in the political scheme which he represents and invests his country with an additional degree of importance in his sight, as in that of many others, from being the scene of an experiment in the success of which not only Americans but mankind are interested.

Much, therefore, of the self-importance which the American assumes, particularly abroad, is less traceable to his mere citizenship than to his conscious identification with the success of democracy. Its manifestation may not always be agreeable to others, but the source of his pride is a legitimate and a noble one. It involves not only his own position but also the hopes and expectations of humanity.

It is this feeling which renders the establishment of monarchy an impossibility in the United States. The American not only believes that his material interests are best subserved by a democratic form of government but his pride is also mixed up with its maintenance and its permanency. It is a common thing for Europeans to speculate upon the disintegration of the Union and the consequent establishment in some part or parts of it, of the monarchical principle. These speculations are generally based upon precedents but upon precedents which have, in reality, no application to America. The republics of old are pointed to as affording illustrations of the tendencies of republicanism. But the republics of old afford no criterion by which to judge of republicanism in America. The experiment which is being tried there is one *sui generis*. Not only are the political principles established different from those which have heretofore been practically recognized but the people are also in a better state of preparation for the successful development of the experiment.

The social condition of the ancient republics was as different from that of America as night is from day. The political superstructures which arose in them conformed themselves more or less to the nature of their bases. The result was not republicanism but oligarchy. All that can be said of these so-called republics is that they were not monarchies. But it does not follow that they were republican. The elementary principle of republicanism is that government, to be stable, must be deeply rooted in the public will. The governments of the older republics were not so, and they perished — as all usurpations will and must do. The more modern republics, again, are divisible into two classes — such as were assimilated in the principles and in the form of their government to the more ancient, and such as too hastily and inconsiderately assumed the true democratic type. If the former shared the fate of the older republics, it was because they resembled them in the faultiness of their construction. If the latter were evanescent and speedily relapsed into monarchy, it was but the natural result of hasty and violent transition.

But the mistake lies in arguing from these cases, particularly the latter, in our speculations as to the future of America. It is but natural that a people who have been for ages inured to monarchy, whose sentiments are more or less intertwined and whose sympathies are bound up with it, should, after having been for a season, either through their own madness or through the folly of others, divorced from it, revert to it again on the first favorable opportunity. But in doing so they are only following the true bent of their inclinations, to which their inconsiderate republican experiment in reality did violence. Generations must elapse ere a people trained and educated to monarchy can be really converted into republicans; in other words, a people cannot be suddenly or violently diverted from that to which they have been trained and accustomed.

This is a very simple rule; but simple though it be, it is precisely that which Europeans overlook in judging of the stability of democracy in America. The American republic, in the first place, differs essentially from all that have preceded it in the principles on which it is founded: it is not a republic in simply not being a monarchy; it is a democratic republic in the broadest sense of the term. If it is not a monarchy, neither is it an oligarchy. It is the people in reality that rule; it is not a mere fraction of them

that usurps authority. The success of the American experiment depended, as it still depends, upon the character of the people. . . . Their associations are all republican — their principles and practice have ever been so — their interests have been subserved by republican institutions, and their pride is now involved in their maintenance and extension. The circumstances of the country and the character and genius of the people are as much now, as in 1776, inimical to monarchy. On what, therefore, rests the supposition so often hazarded by parties in this country that violence will be done, and that ere long, to the republic in America? Unless the people can be persuaded to do violence to their feelings, tastes, habits, and associations and to adopt institutions incompatible with their position and circumstances, there is no fear of democracy in America.

Many point to the accumulation of wealth as that which will work the change. It is quite true that some of the millionaires of America would have no objection to the establishment of a different order of things. But both in numbers and influence they are insignificant, as compared with the great mass even of the commercial and manufacturing communities, who are staunch democrats at heart. Much more are they so when we take the great agricultural body of America into account. Here, after all, is the stronghold of democracy on the continent. However it may be undermined in the town, its foundations are deeply and securely laid in the township. No one who has mingled much with the American farmers can entertain any serious doubts of the stability of democracy in America. . . .

Many of what some regard as the more inflated peculiarities of the American character may be attributed to the faith which Americans cherish in the destiny of their country. Whatever may be its future social and political influence, they have no doubt that, as regards territorial extension, it will yet embrace the continent. The issues which such a consummation involves are enough to make a people feel proud of their country. The realization of their hopes in this respect they regard as a mere question of time. They feel that there is, in reality, no power on the continent that can ultimately resist them.

I was forcibly impressed with the extent to which this feeling prevails, on listening one day to a speech delivered by Mr. Crittenden of Kentucky, in the Senate, shortly after the breaking out of the Mexican War. It was in reply to Mr. Sevier from Arkansas, who was complaining that a portion of one of the counties of that state had been reserved to the Indians. Mr. Crittenden, in showing him how unworthy such a complaint was, reminded him that the whole state had been taken from the Indians and, not only it but every state in the Confederacy. He then recapitulated the accessions made to the territory of the Union since the period of its independence. He alluded to the boundary, particularly the south and southwest, as ever changing so as to embrace new acquisitions. It had first swept from the St. Mary's round the peninsula of Florida and crept up the Gulf to the Mississippi and Sabine. It afterward fled westward to the Nueces and was then, he reminded the House, alluding to the cause of the war, supposed to be on the Rio Grande. It fled, he continued, before the Anglo-American race as it advanced. "Where is it now?" he asked in conclusion. "Just," he added, "where we please to put it."

Many fall into the mistake of supposing that an indulgence in hatred of England is a chronic state of the American mind. In the Irish population of the United States is the true source of the enmity toward this country which is sometimes exhibited. Originating among these, unscrupulous politicians fan the flame to serve their own purposes; but it has to be constantly supplied with fuel or it speedily dies out. The feeling is not a general one nor is it permanent with any section of the native population not directly of Irish extraction. In all disputes with this country there is more of bluster than bad feeling.

The American desires to see his country in advance of all nations, in power, wealth, and moral influence. Great Britain is the only power which he now regards as standing in the way. The Americans treat us as the only enemies, when enemies, worthy of a thought as such. It is this that makes them so touchy in all their quarrels with us. They are far more likely to be reasonable and conciliatory in a dispute with Spain than with Great Britain. They may give way in the one case, but they fear that if they did so in the other, it would seem as if they had been bullied into so doing. We, again, have been the only enemy with which they have ever been in serious collision. But after all, a friendly and kindly feeling with regard to us pervades the American mind; they would not willingly see us injured by a third party if they could prevent it.

"We have had many quarrels with you," said a lady to me once in Washington, "but we are proud of our descent from the English! We court the French when it suits our purpose, but," she added, with great emphasis, "we would not be descended from them on any account."

The Americans are charged by some as being guilty of inconsistency in the fondness which they manifest for titles. But those who make this charge do so without reflection. The Americans are fond of titles, but that does not argue that they are inconsistent republicans. The fondness for titles which they display is but a manifestation of the fondness for distinction natural to the human mind. And what sane man ever inculcated the idea that republicanism was inconsistent with the love of distinction? Constitute society as you may, there must be posts of honor, power, influence, dignity, and emolument to strive for. These exist in republics as well as under any other form of government.

Are they not to be striven for without compromising one's political creed? And if the office is obtained, why not be called by its name? The presidency of the republic is an office — he who obtains it is called the "President." Does a man cease to be a republican because he aspires to both? Is it not rather a laudable ambition that prompts the aspiration? Or should he who obtains the office drop the title? As it is with the title of President, so it is with all other titles in America. A judgeship is a distinction. On him who obtains it, it confers the appellation of "judge." A governorship of a state is a distinction. He who is appointed to it is called the "governor." And so on through all the offices in the state, civil and military.

There is this broad and essential difference, however, between titles as coveted in America and titles as existing in Europe. There the title pertains to a distinction acquired by the individual himself, for himself, and has always connected with it some office of trust or responsibility. Here we have similar titles, but we have others also which spring from the mere accident of birth, which are connected with no duties and which do not necessarily indicate any merit on the part of those possessing them. The time was in England when marquis, earl, and viscount indicated something more than mere arbitrary social rank. There are in America no titles analogous to these. There duties are inseparable from titles. So long as there are offices in the republic to be filled and so long as republicans may legitimately aspire to fill them, so long may they, without sacrificing their consistency, assume the titles of the offices to which they are appointed.

The love of money is regarded by many as a striking trait in the American character. I fear that this is a weakness to which humanity must universally plead guilty. But it is quite true that it is an absorbing passion with the Americans. This cannot be denied, but it may be explained. America is a country in which fortunes have yet to be made. Wealth gives great distinction, and wealth is, more or less, within the grasp of all. Hence the universal scramble. All cannot be made wealthy, but all have a chance of securing a prize. This stimulates to the race, and hence the eagerness of the competition. In this country, however, the lottery is long since over, and with few exceptions the great prizes are already drawn. To the great bulk of the people wealth is utterly unattainable. All they can hope for is competency, and numbers fall short even of that. Men soon flag in a hopeless pursuit. Hence it is that, in this country, the scramble is neither so fierce nor universal.

The American people discover an extraordinary talent for invention. The Patent Office in Washington is a most creditable monument to their inventive powers. They are also quick in the adoption of an improvement, no matter from what source it proceeds.

They are excessively fond of being well dressed. The artisans among them are particularly so, not so much from personal vanity as from the fact that they make dress a test of respectability. Almost every man who is not an immigrant wears superfine broadcloth in America, if we except the hardworking farmer, who generally attires himself in homespun. You seldom meet with a fustian jacket, except on an immigrant's back, in an American town.

This leads me . . . briefly to glance at the physical condition of society in America. If the social structure in the republic has no florid Corinthian capital rising into the clear air above, neither has it a pedestal in the mire beneath. If it is devoid of much of the ornamental, so is it also wanting in much of the painful and degrading. It may not be so picturesque as many of the social fabrics which have sprung from chivalry and feudalism, but it is nevertheless compact, elegant, symmetrical, and commodious. It is to English society what a modern house is to an Elizabethan mansion — it is not built so much to attract the eye as to accommodate the inmates.

The most important feature of American society, in connection with its physical condition, is that competence is the lot of all. No matter to what this is attributable, whether to the extent and resources of the country or to the nature of its institutions or to both, such is the case, and one has not to be long in America to discover it. It is extremely seldom that the willing hand in America is in want of employment, while the hardworking man has not only a competency on which to live but, if frugal, may soon save up sufficient to procure for himself in the West a position of still greater comfort and independence.

There are paupers in America, but, fortunately, they are very few. They are generally confined to the large towns; nor need they subsist upon charity, if they had the energy to go into the rural districts and seek employment. This, however, is not applicable to the majority of them who are aged and infirm. It may be laid down as a general rule, without qualification, that none are deprived of competency in America except such as are negligent, idle, or grossly improvident. The general effect of this upon society has been already considered. Both in their social and political relations, all classes are thus able to act an independent part — an important consideration in connection with the peculiar polity of America.

This being the broad and wholesome basis on which society, so far as regards its physical condition, rests, the character of the superstructure may easily be inferred.

Where all classes have a competency, no class demurs to the luxuries enjoyed by another. There is but little jealousy of wealth in America for reasons already explained. It is but in extremely rare instances that gigantic accumulations have as yet been made. Nor are they likely to be speedily multiplied, the whole spirit of legislation being against them.

There is no legislation against accumulations of personal property, for the very good reason that it would be difficult to prevent its distribution. It is sure to circulate through the community, so that all, by turns, can have the advantage of it. But the whole spirit of American legislation is decidedly averse to accumulations of landed property. Such the people conceive would be incompatible with the safety of their institutions. They have accordingly removed all restrictions upon its alienation, and land is now as marketable a commodity as the wheat that is raised upon it.

It is seldom indeed that you find a native American or the descendant of an immigrant occupying a lower position than that of an artisan. Those who are mere laborers are almost exclusively immigrants and, in nineteen cases out of twenty, Irish immigrants. Such as emigrate from England, Scotland, or Germany are soon absorbed into the rural population, and become, by-and-by, proprietors of land themselves. But the Irish congregate in masses in the large towns, as they do here, to do the drudgery of the community. It is thus that, if a canal is being dug or a railway constructed, you meet with gangs of laborers almost entirely composed of Irishmen. Their descendants, however, become ambitious and thrifty and form the best of citizens.

Enough has here been said to show that America is the country for the industrious and hardworking man.

106.

Theodore Parker: A Critique of American Churches

Such phrases as "the Great American Preacher" and "the Great Reformer" have been used to describe the Transcendentalist minister, Theodore Parker. Emerson called him "an excellent scholar, in frank and affectionate communication with the best minds of the day, yet the tribune of the people. . . ." On October 4, 1849, Parker gave an address before the Onondaga Teachers' Institute at Syracuse, New York, in which he argued the value of education for all citizens. He asserted that in America public education is strongly influenced by four "educational forces": the state, business, the church, and the press. His critique of the churches follows.

Source: *The Public Education of the People*, Boston, 1850, pp. 30-34.

THE CHURCHES have the same faults as the state. There is the same postponement of justice and preference of force, the same neglect of the Law of God in their zeal for the statutes of men; the same crouching to dollars or to numbers. However, in the churches these faults appear negatively, rather than as an affirmation. The worldliness of the church is not open, self-conscious and avowed; it is not that injustice is openly defended but rather justice goes by default. But if the churches do not positively support and teach injustice, as the state certainly does, they do not teach the opposite and, so far as that goes, are allies of the state in its evil influence.

The fact that the churches, as such, did not oppose the war and do not oppose slavery, its continuance, or its extension; nay, that they are often found its apologists and defenders, seldom its opponents; that they not only pervert the sacred books of the Christians to its defense but wrest the doctrines of Christianity to justify it; the fact that they cannot, certainly do not, correc the particularism of the political parties, th love of wealth in one, of mere majorities i the other; that they know no patriotism no bounded by their country, none coextensiv with mankind; that they cannot resist th vice of party spirit — these are real proof that the church is but the ally of the stat in this evil influence.

But the church has also certain specifi faults of its own. It teaches injustice by con tinually referring to the might of God, nc His justice; to His ability and will to dam mankind, not asking if He has the right? I teaches that in virtue of His infinite powe He is not amenable to infinite justice and t infinite love. Thus, while the state teache in the name of expediency and by practice that the strong may properly be the tyran of the weak, the mighty nation over th feeble, the strong race over the inferior, th: the government may dispense with right : home and abroad — the church, as theor and in Christ's name, teaches that God ma repudiate His own justice and His own love.

The churches have little love of truth, as such, only of its uses. It must be such a truth as they can use for their purposes; canonized truth; truth long known; that alone is acceptable and called "religious truth"; only that is "of God"; all else is "profane and carnal," as the reason which discovers it. They represent the average intelligence of society; hence, while keeping the old, they welcome not the new. They promote only popular forms of truth, popular in all Christendom, or in their special sect. They lead in no intellectual reforms; they hinder the leaders. Negatively and positively, they teach, that to believe what is clerically told you in the name of religion, is better than free, impartial search after the truth. They dishonor free thinking and venerate constrained believing.

When the clergy doubt, they seldom give men audience of their doubt. Few scientific men not clerical believe the Bible account of creation — the universe made in six days and but a few thousand years ago — or that of the formation of woman, and of the deluge. Some clerical men still believe these venerable traditions, [in] spite of the science of the times; but the clerical men who have no faith in these stories not only leave the people to think them true and miraculously taught but encourage men in the belief, and calumniate the men of science who look the universe fairly in the face and report the facts as they find them.

The church represents only the popular morality, not any high and aboriginal virtue. It represents not the conscience of human nature, reflecting the universal and unchangeable moral laws of God, touched and beautified by His love, but only the conscience of human history, reflecting the circumstances man has passed by, and the institutions he has built along the stream of time. So, while it denounces unpopular sins, vices below the average vice of society, it denounces also unpopular excellence, which is above the average virtue of society. It blocks the wheels rearward, and the car[t] of humanity does not roll down hill; but it blocks them forward also.

No great moral movement of the age is at all dependent directly on the church for its birth; very little for its development. It is in spite of the church that reforms go forward; it holds the curb to check more than the rein to guide. In morals, as in science, the church is on the anti-liberal side, afraid of progress, against movement, loving "yet a little sleep, a little slumber"; conservative and chilling, like ice; not creative, nor even quickening, as water. It doffs to use and wont; has small confidence in human nature, much in a few facts of human history. It aims to separate piety from goodness, her natural and heaven-appointed spouse, and marry her to bigotry, in joyless and unprofitable wedlock.

The church does not lead men to the deep springs of human nature, fed ever from the far heights of the divine nature, whence flows that river of God, full of living water, where weary souls may drink perennial supply. While it keeps us from falling back, it does little directly to advance mankind. In common with the state, this priest and Levite pass by on the other side of the least developed classes of society, leaving the slave, the pauper, and the criminal to their fate, hastening to strike hands with the thriving or the rich.

These faults are shared in the main by all sects; some have them in the common, and some in a more eminent degree, but none is so distinguished from the rest as to need emphatic rebuke, or to deserve a special exemption from the charge. Such are the faults of the church of every land, and must be from the nature of the institution; like the state, it can only represent the average of mankind.

I am not speaking to clergymen, professional representatives of the church, not of the church as an ecclesiastical machine for keeping and extending certain opinions and symbols, not for an ecclesiastical purpose; I speak to teachers, for an educational purpose, of the church as an educational machine, one of the great forces for the spiritual development of the people.

107.

Anonymous: Letter from the Sierra Nevadas

In January 1848 gold was discovered in the Sacramento Valley. By the end of the year, people from every walk of life and all parts of the world were rushing to California to make their fortunes. Ships chartered in Europe made their way nonstop to the American West Coast. These European expeditions were stimulated, in part, by letters such as the one reprinted below. It was dated July 15, 1849, and was published in a Norwegian newspaper in November.

Source: Blegen, pp. 225-228.

ONCE MORE I HAVE THE PLEASURE of writing you, though I am 1,000 miles away from you and more than 250 miles from the coast. At present I am staying in the Sierra Nevada Mountains in California.

You will recall that I told you that I had decided to go on to California. As a result of this decision, I left New York on February 1, and, after a very pleasant voyage of eight days on board the steamship *Falcon,* I arrived with 300 other passengers at Havana, where we stayed one day. From there we sailed to Chagres, a four days' voyage. Here we left the *Falcon* and took another steamboat up the lovely River Chagres, which is from 60 to 100 feet wide but very shallow.

As the steamboat could not go up more than about twenty-five miles, we had to continue our journey in canoes. These are from 20 to 80 feet long and in proportion to their length are paddled by from one to eight naked Negroes. I was in one of the smallest canoes with only one Negro. These Negroes are extremely good-natured, honest people. They excel in particular in the exceptional endurance and strength with which they paddle the canoes up against the strong current all day long without resting, except when they eat their simple meals.

After spending forty hours in the canoe, I arrived at Gorgona, a small town of about 1,500 inhabitants, where four of my friends and I pitched our tent to wait for the arrival of the rest of the company. From here, is about twenty-three miles through very mountainous country to Panama. Transportation of baggage is very cheap here. We bought six horses at from $14 to $25 apiece, and a friend of mine and I thus transported all our baggage to Panama. . . .

On March 10 we left Panama on board a steamship bound for San Francisco, where we duly arrived on April 1, exactly two months after we had left New York. Since this city, to judge by all indications, is some day to become the greatest emporium on the Pacific, I shall try to give you a description of it. The city is located on the southern side of the entrance from the Pacific at the first large bay, part of which is called Santa Clara Bay. For the main part, the city has been laid out in a small valley between two rows of hills. Its appearance from the anchorage is completely American, except for the lack of church steeples, of which American cities always have a very large number. The surroundings of the city are quite barren. There are two hotels in town, where you pay $5 a day, and a great many gambling houses, where thousands of dollars are lost every day. The population is about 5,000.

After four days' stay in San Francisco, I once more boarded a small vessel and went about 120 miles up the Sacramento River. Here we took three wagons drawn by oxen to carry our baggage to the mountains, where we hoped to make our fortune by washing and digging for gold. After four days' troublesome journey on foot, we arrived at our destination; but for two reasons we discovered that we could not make our fortune right away. In the first place, the water in the river where we hoped to find gold was too high and, besides, the hostility of the Indians presented a serious obstacle.

On one occasion the Indians had killed five people and burned the bodies. The angry gold diggers, about forty in number, got together and set out to find the Indians. They did find them, killed about fifty and took sixty prisoners, who were all released, however, except seven. The next day these were taken out of their prison, one to be

shot and the others to watch. But as soon as the unfortunate creatures were out in the open, they tried to run away. Shouts of "Shoot them! Shoot them!" were heard. Guns were fired, and three of them fell on the spot, three others threw themselves in the river, but all were shot. One fell only a few steps from me, riddled by six bullets, another by three. This shocked me very much, and I also think that it is wrong to shoot them wherever you catch sight of them. As a rule the Indians are both cowardly and cunning. If one of them can find an opportunity to shoot an arrow — they are extremely skillful with bow and arrow — into the heart of a white man, he does so. Besides, they steal a lot of horses, which they kill and eat.

Every man here is armed with a gun, pistols, and knives. My six-barreled pistols which I bought in New York for $12 I have sold here for $100. To give you an idea of the prices of various things here and of the cost of living in this place, I shall give you a list of the current prices of the most necessary and common articles. A horse costs from $200 to $500; an ox, $100; and a sheep, $16. Hard bread (for there is no soft bread here), $1.25; flour, 75 cents, dried apples, $1.25; ham, $1.25 — all a pound — molasses, $4 a bottle; sugar, 80 cents a pound; tea, $5 a pound, etc. Boards cost $700 for 1,000 cubic feet, and three small boxes of matches are $1. Potatoes are $1.25 a pound. A pair of boots that cost $2.50 in New York are $20 here. A pair of shoes that were 75 cents in New York are $8 here, and so on. These are high prices, to be sure, but if you work hard you can still make money. In May, I saved $223; in June, $295. Yesterday alone I made $35. All my earnings from May 1 to July 14 amount to $750, which is $120 more than the cost of the journey here.

The work is extremely hard. I start at 4 o'clock in the morning and keep on till 12 noon. After that I rest for three or four hours, for at that time of day the heat is unbearable, and then I work again till 8 o'clock in the evening. The nights here are exceedingly cold. We live in tents; I have not been inside a house since April 1. The ground is our bed and a saddle or something like that our pillow.

This kind of life agrees with me, and my health is excellent. We live a free life, and the best thing of all, that which I have always considered one of the supreme blessings of existence, is that no human being here sets himself up as your lord and master. It is true that we do not have many of the luxuries of life, but I do not miss them, with the exception of cigars, which are too expensive here, as you only get three for $1.

Fine order and peace prevail here. It seems to me as if one person were afraid of the other, since he knows very well that an insult will usually be paid back with a piece of lead. Thefts and robberies have been very rare, up to the last two weeks when a lot of horses were stolen. Everyone may safely leave his tent without having to fear in the least that something has been stolen when he returns.

But if this does happen and the thief is caught, all the neighbors assemble and elect a judge. If the thief is found guilty by the judge, he is punished with a certain number of lashes and is given a respite of twelve or eighteen hours to enable him to clear out of

the mountains. If he is still there after the respite has expired, he is shot. This is the usual procedure; but three Frenchmen who had gone a little too far were hanged to a tree without further ceremony.

It would be too detailed a matter to describe to you how the gold is found. I hope that Almighty God, who so far has guided my way through life with the greatest love and goodness, will grant me the happiness to see you and all my dear ones again; then I will tell you everything that I now have to leave out of my writing.

Here it must be enough to say that the gold we find is almost completely pure. The size of the nuggets varies. In some places pieces have been found that weighed up to seven pounds. Here, at the river where I am staying, it is found almost like fish scales, very thin and in all kinds of forms. You obtain it by washing out the dirt in a machine which looks like a roller, and that is what it is called. You throw the dirt in one end of the machine, which is somewhat higher than the other, and start the machine, all the time adding a certain quantity of water. By this process, lighter particles, like dirt and pebbles, are washed away, and the gold is left behind, together with a sort of fine black sand which consists mainly of iron particles. This is taken out of the machine and carefully washed out in a pan.

The frontiers are not east or west, north or south but wherever a man fronts a fact.

HENRY DAVID THOREAU, *A Week on The Concord and Merrimac Rivers, 1849*

108.

"Days of Forty-Nine"

*The Forty-niners loved to sing. They sang as they worked, they sang as they sat
around their campfires in the soft California night, they sang when they came into
San Francisco to spend, often in one wild night or week of nights, the gold they had
so laboriously dug out of the ground. "Days of Forty-Nine" is a good example of their
songs; it probably does not exaggerate the hardships and the roughness of life in
California during the Gold Rush, and it reflects the insouciant attitude of the gold
diggers toward the "refinements" of civilization. It was probably written, if formally
written at all, some years after 1849, but it belongs here as a memorial of those
exciting days when San Francisco was new.*

Source: Allen, pp. 152-154.

DAYS OF FORTY-NINE

You are gazing now on old Tom Moore,
A relic of bygone days;
'Tis a bummer too they call me now,
But what care I for praise?
It's oft, says I, for the days gone by,
It's oft do I repine,
For the days of old when we dug out gold
In the days of Forty-Nine.

My comrades they all loved me well,
That jolly, saucy crew;
A few hard cases, I will admit,
But they were brave and true.
Whatever the pinch, they never would flinch;
They never would fret nor whine,
Like good old bricks they stood the kicks
In the days of Forty-Nine.

There's old "Aunt Jess," that hard old cuss,
Who never would repent;
He never missed a single meal,
Nor never paid a cent.
But old "Aunt Jess," like all the rest,
At death did he resign,
And in his bloom he went up the flume
In the days of Forty-Nine.

There is Ragshag Jim, the roaring man,
Who could out-roar a buffalo, you bet;
He roared all day and he roared all night,
And I guess he's roaring yet.
One night Jim fell in a prospect hole,
It was a roaring bad design,
For in that hole Jim roared out his soul
In the days of Forty-Nine.

There was Monte Pete, I'll never forget
The luck he always had;
He would deal for you, both day and night,
Or as long as he had a scad.
It was a pistol shot that laid Pete out;
It was his last resign;
And it caught Pete shore, right in the door,
In the days of Forty-Nine.

Of all the comrades that I've had,
There's none that's left to boast;
And I'm left alone in my misery,
Like some poor wandering ghost.
And as I pass from town to town,
They call me the rambling sign,
Since the days of old when we dug out gold
In the days of Forty-Nine.

109.

Frank Soulé *et al.:* San Francisco During and After the Gold Rush

Within a very few years after 1849 San Francisco grew from a village into a city of more than 20,000 inhabitants. It served as a debarkation point, a supply depot, and an amusement center for the thousands of gold seekers who rushed to California from all over the world. The city's growth and characteristics were depicted in a volume called The Annals of San Francisco, *from which the following selections are taken.*

Source: *The Annals of San Francisco,* New York, 1855, pp. 224-226, 243-249, 350-353, 364-366, 411-412, 423-426.

A SHORT EXPERIENCE of the mines had satisfied most of the citizens of San Francisco that, in vulgar parlance, all was not gold that glittered, and that hard work was not easy — sorry truisms for weak or lazy men. They returned very soon to their old quarters and found that much greater profits with far less labor were to be found in supplying the necessities of the miners and speculating in real estate.

For a time, everybody made money, in spite of himself. The continued advance in the price of goods, and especially in the value of real estate, gave riches at once to the fortunate owner of a stock of the former or of a single, advantageously situated lot of the latter. When trade was brisk and profits so large, nobody grudged to pay any price or any rent for a proper place of business. Coin was scarce, but bags of gold dust furnished a circulating medium, which answered all purposes. The gamblers at the public saloons staked such bags, or were supplied with money upon them by the "banks" till the whole was exhausted.

There were few regular houses erected, for neither building materials nor sufficient labor were to be had; but canvas tents or houses of frame served the immediate needs of the place. Great quantities of goods continued to pour in from the nearer ports, till there were no longer stores to receive and cover them. In addition to Broadway Wharf, Central Wharf was projected, subscribed for, and commenced. Several other small wharves at landing places were constructed at the cost of private parties. All these, indeed, extended but a little way across the mud flat in the bay and were of no use at low tide; yet they gave considerable facilities for landing passengers and goods in open boats.

The different religious denominations were beginning to make movements as to creating churches and appointing clergymen; while the Freemasons and Odd Fellows were likewise beginning to take their characteristic first steps. Seamen deserted their vessels, as a matter of course, so soon as they dropped anchor in the bay, and hastened to the mines. Society, not merely there, but in San Francisco, was in a state of utter disorganization, which became worse and more terrible as the autumn and winter months brought new thousands of immigrants upon the place. . . .

There was neither a proper government for the state nor recognized municipal authorities, who could have protected the citizens and established order and made provision for the systematic extension of the town and reception of the coming crowds. There was a military governor, indeed, and martial law could have been adopted, but the governor had not sufficient force at his command to curb the wild elements of the population; nor, at best, would his forcible interference have satisfied American ideas of civil independence and the national privilege of self-government. Thefts, robberies, murders, and other outrages of the most desperate and criminal nature were taking place, and there were no proper officials to take cognizance of them and bring the offenders to justice. Every man was intent on merely making money; and, provided an outrage did not, in a direct manner, personally or pecuniarily affect himself, he was content to shut his eyes to the ultimate consequences.

By the beginning of 1849, the population of San Francisco had increased to 2,000. Two months later it was probably about 3,000; while in July, when the riots and outrages of the "hounds" came to a height, it might be nearly 5,000. This was what might be called the usual and permanent population of the time, if anything could be supposed permanent in so frail and fluctuating a place; although everyday new arrivals of immigrants added temporarily to the number, till they flocked off to Sacramento, Stockton, and the mines.

THE POPULATION OF THE STATE, and of San Francisco in particular, had been largely increasing during the last six months. Between the 1st of January, 1849, and the 30th of June following, it was estimated that 15,000 had been added to the population of the country; of which number nearly 10,000 came by sea and landed at San Francisco. Only about 200 of these were females. The next half year gave an average of 4,000 immigrants per month, by sea alone, about 500 of whom, in all, were females; and the whole of which numbers landed at San Francisco. In the early part of 1849, the arrivals were principally from Chile, Mexico, and other countries on the Pacific coasts of America; but, later in the year, an immense number of Americans came direct from the Atlantic states, around Cape Horn or by way of Panama, while many foreigners also arrived from China and from various parts of Europe.

Hitherto, the departures were comparatively few. Altogether, nearly 40,000 immigrants landed at San Francisco during 1849. Besides that great number, some 3,000 or 4,000 seamen deserted from the many hundred ships lying in the bay. Probably two-thirds of all these proceeded to the mines or to various parts of the interior; but, on the other hand, numerous fortunate diggers, or those who had tried gold digging and been disappointed, visited town to spend their gains, recruit their health, or follow out some new pursuit there.

It will be remembered also that somewhere about 30,000 American immigrants had reached California across the Plains, many of whom ultimately settled in San Francisco. Therefore, it may be reasonably estimated that, at the close of 1849, the population of the town numbered at least 20,000 and probably nearer 25,000 souls. A very small proportion of these were females; a still smaller one, children of either sex; while the vast majority of inhabitants were adult males in the early prime of manhood. This circumstance naturally tended to give a peculiar character to the aspect of the place and habits of the people.

There was no such thing as a *home* to be found. Scarcely even a proper *house* could be seen. Both dwellings and places of business were either common canvas tents or small, rough-board shanties or frame buildings of one story. Only the great gambling saloons, the hotels, restaurants, and a few public buildings and stores had any pretensions to size, comfort, or elegance.

The site on which the town is built was then still covered with numberless sandhills. The streets were therefore uneven and irregular. By the continued passage of men, and of horses and drays with building materials and goods, while the rainy season (which commenced earlier than usual and was remarkably severe) was shedding torrents from the clouds, the different thoroughfares were soon so cut up as to become almost, if not quite, impassable. Indeed, both horse or mule and dray were sometimes literally swallowed up in the mud, while their owner narrowly escaped a similar fate. The town authorities caused numberless cartloads of brushwood and limbs of trees to be cut from the surrounding hills and thrown into the streets; but these only answered a limited and temporary purpose. The difficulty could not thus be remedied.

Nobody troubled himself to remove any rubbish from the way; but inmates of tents and houses satisfied themselves with placing a few planks, tobacco boxes, bags of coffee, barrels of spoiled provisions, or any other available object across and along the worst parts of the roads to enable them safely to reach their own dwellings. It was not for everybody, however, to attempt to navigate these perilous places or hope to keep on the narrow, slippery, unsteady, and often interrupted path which spanned the unfathomed abysses of mud and water which lay on all sides. Lanterns were indispensable to pedestrians at night, and even in daylight not a few would lose their footing and find it difficult to extricate themselves from their unpleasant predicaments.

In those miserable apologies for houses, surrounded by heaps and patches of filth, mud, and stagnant water, the strange, mixed population carried on business, after a fashion. It is not to be supposed that people could or did manage matters in the strict orderly manner of older communities. Very few were following that particular business to which they had been bred or for which they were best fitted by nature. Every immigrant on landing at San Francisco became a new man in his own estimation and was prepared to undertake anything or any piece of business whatsoever. And truly he did it; but it was with a deal of noise, bustle, and unnecessary confusion.

The great recognized orders of society were tumbled topsy-turvy. Doctors and dentists became draymen, or barbers, or shoeblacks; lawyers, brokers, and clerks turned waiters or auctioneers or, perhaps, butchers; merchants tried laboring and lumping, while laborers and lumpers changed to merchants. The idlest might be tempted, and the weakest were able, to do something — to drive a nail in frame buildings, lead a burdened mule, keep a stall, ring a bell, or run a message.

Adventurers, merchants, lawyers, clerks, tradesmen, mechanics, and every class, in turn, kept lodging houses, eating and drinking houses, billiard rooms and gambling saloons, or single tables at these. They dabbled in "beach and water lots," 50-vara [about 46 feet] blocks, and new town allotments over the whole country; speculated in flour, beef, pork, and potatoes; in lumber and other building materials; in dry goods and soft, hard goods and wet; bought and sold, wholesale and retail, and were ready to change their occupation and embark in some new nondescript undertaking after two minutes' consideration.

All things seemed in the utmost disorder. The streets and passages, such as they were, and the inside of tents and houses were heaped with all sorts of goods and lumber. There seemed no method in anything. People bustled and jostled against each other, bawled, railed, and fought, cursed and swore, sweated and labored lustily, and somehow the work was done. A spectator would have imagined the confusion inextricable but soon had reason to change his opinion. Everybody was busy and knew very well what he himself had to do.

Heaps of goods disappeared, as if by magic, and new heaps appeared in their place. Where there was a vacant piece of ground one day, the next saw it covered with half a dozen tents or shanties. Horses, mules, and oxen forced a way through, across, and over every obstruction in the streets; and men waded and toiled after them. Hundreds of rude houses and tents were daily in the course of erection; they nestled between the sandhills, covered their tops, and climbed the heights to the north and west of the town.

As we have said, there were no *homes* at this period in San Francisco, and time was too precious for anyone to stay within doors to cook victuals. Consequently, an immense majority of the people took their meals at restaurants, boarding houses and hotels, the number of which was naturally, therefore, very great; while many lodged as well as boarded at such places. Many of these were indeed miserable hovels, which showed only bad fare and worse attendance, dirt, discomfort, and high prices. A few others again were of a superior class; but, of course, still higher charges had to be made for the better accommodation. At best, all were inconveniently crowded, heated, and disagreeable.

The whole population was constantly moving and always visible, which added greatly to its apparent numbers. If only people did not sleep in public, they at least worked, ate, and amused themselves in crowds. But even at night, they lay from half a dozen to twoscore in a room — on the floor, in rows of cots or contracted and filthy bunks fastened to the weatherboards from floor to ceiling, in which were immense swarms of fleas and other troublesome vermin. At some lodging houses and hotels, every superficial inch — on floor, tables, benches, shelves, and beds — was covered with a portion of weary humanity.

While wages and profits were so high, and there was no comfort at their sleeping quarters, men spent money freely at different places of riotous excess and were indeed forced to pass their hours of leisure or recreation at drinking bars, billiard rooms, and gambling saloons. Such places were accordingly crowded with a motley crew, who drank, swore, and gamed to their hearts' content. *Everybody did so;* and that circumstance was a sufficient excuse, if one were needed, to the neophyte in debauchery.

To vary amusements, occasionally a fancy-dress ball or masquerade would be announced at high prices. There the most extraordinary scenes were exhibited, as might have been expected where the actors and dancers were chiefly hotheaded young men, flush of money and half frantic with excitement, and lewd girls freed from the necessity of all moral restraint. A concert or a lecture would at other times help to entertain the weary spirits of the town. But of all their haunts, the gambling saloons were the most notorious and best patronized.

Gambling was a peculiar feature of San Francisco at this time. It was *the* amusement, *the* grand occupation of many classes, apparently the life and soul of the place. There were hundreds of gambling saloons in the town. The barroom of every hotel and public house presented its tables to attract the idle, the eager, and covetous. Monte, faro, roulette, rondo, rouge et noir, and vingt-[et-]un were the games chiefly played. In the larger saloons, beautiful and well-dressed women dealt out the cards or turned the roulette wheel, while lascivious pictures hung on the walls. A band of music and numberless blazing lamps gave animation and a feeling of joyous rapture to the scene. No wonder the unwary visitor was tempted and fell before he had time to awake from the pleasing delusion.

To make a fortune in the turning of a card was delightful; the very mingled hope and fear of eventual success was a charming excitement. For the moment, men felt as great conquerors may be supposed sometimes to feel; they maneuvered on the green cloth, the field of their operations, thinking their own skill was playing the game, when chance alone gave the result. At the end of a long evening's campaign of mingled victories and defeats, petty skirmishes, they would either draw off their forces to renew the game next day or hazard their all, thousands of dollars perhaps, on the issue of one great battle, and a moment afterward leave the table richer or poorer by a moderate fortune. Again and again were such campaigns fought, till the excitement and intense desire of playing became chronic. When great sums could no longer be had, small ones served the same purpose; and were, in the end, lost like the others. Gambling became a regular business; and those who followed it professionally were really among the richest, most talented, and influential citizens of the town. . . .

The Vigilance Committee agreed to suspend indefinitely further operations regarding crime and criminals in the city. The old extensive chambers in Battery Street were relinquished, and new rooms, "open at all times, day and night, to the members," were taken in Middleton and Smiley's buildings, corner of Sansome and Sacramento Streets. During the three preceding months, this association had been indefatigable in collecting evidence and bringing the guilty to justice. It had been formed, not to supersede the legal authorities but to strengthen them when weak; not to oppose the law but to sanction and confirm it.

The members were mostly respectable citizens who had, and could have, only one object in view — the general good of the community. They exercised an unceasing *vigilance* over the hidden movements of the suspected and criminal population of the place and unweariedly traced crime to its source, where they sought to stop it. They had hanged four men without observing ordinary legal forms, but the persons were

fairly tried and found guilty, while three, at least, of the number confessed to the most monstrous crimes and admitted death to be only a due punishment. At this small cost of bloodshed, the Vigilance Committee freed the city and country of many reckless villains who had been long a terror to society.

When these had disappeared, outrages against person and property almost disappeared, too, or were confined to petty cases. The legal and municipal authorities now acquired what previously they lacked, sufficient power to master the remaining criminals; and the Committee, having no longer a reason for continued action, gladly relinquished the powers they had formerly exercised. Grand juries, instead of offering presentments against them, only praised in the usual reports their useful exertions, while, like all good citizens, they lamented their necessity.

Judges occasionally took offense at the terms of such reports and sought to have them modified; but the grand juries were firm. Judge Levi Parsons applied to the Supreme Court to have certain obnoxious sentences in one of these reports struck out; but his petition was refused. People felt that there was much truth in the repeated declarations of the grand juries, and they hailed with delight their expressions of implied confidence in the Vigilance Committee. The weak, inefficient, and sometimes corrupt courts of law were denounced as strongly by the juries as by that association itself. In one report the grand jury said:

The facilities with which the most notorious culprits are enabled to obtain bail, which, if not entirely worthless, is rarely enforced when forfeited, and the numerous cases in which, by the potent influence of money and the ingenious and unscrupulous appliance of legal technicalities, the most abandoned criminals have been enabled to escape a deserved punishment meets with their unqualified disapprobation.

But the worst days were over, and comparative peace was restored to society. Therefore, the Vigilance Committee ceased to act. The members, however, did not dissolve the association, but only appointed a special or executive committee of forty-five to exercise a general watchfulness and to summon together the whole body when occasion should require. This was shortly afterward done in one or two instances, when instead of being opposed to the authorities the members now firmly supported them by active personal aid against commotions and threatened outrages among the populace. They had originally organized themselves to protect the city from arson, murder, and rapine, when perpetrated as part of a general system of violence and plunder by hardened criminals.

In ordinary crimes, and when these stood alone and did not necessarily lead to general destruction, the Vigilance Committee did not interfere further than as good citizens and to merely aid the ordinary officials whose duty it was to attend to all cases of crime. When, therefore, some six months later, a body of 2,000 excited people sought to "lynch" the captain and mate of the ship *Challenge* for cruelty to the crew during the passage from New York to San Francisco, the Vigilance Committee, instead of taking the side of the enraged multitude, firmly supported the legal authorities.

On many occasions, both before and after this time, the Committee were of great service to the authorities. At their own cost, they collected evidence, apprehended criminals and delivered them into the hands of legal justice. When the city offered a reward of $2,500 to any person who would give information which might lead to the apprehension and conviction of an incendiary, the Committee offered a reward of $5,000 for the same services. The members gave large contributions to hasten the completion of the public jail; and, in many ways, by money, counsel and moral aid, and active personal assistance, sought earnestly to raise the character of the judicial tribunals and strengthen their action.

There could not be a greater calumny uttered against high-minded men than to represent, as was frequently done in other countries and in the Atlantic states, the members of the Vigilance Committee as a lawless mob who made passion their sole guide and their own absolute will the law of the land. Necessity formed the Committee and gave it both irresistible moral and physical force. One might as well blame a drowning wretch for clinging to a sinking brother, or to a straw, as say that the inhabitants of San Francisco did wrong — some in joining the association and others in not resisting but applauding its proceedings.

People out of California could know little at best of the peculiar state of society existing there; and such as condemned the action of the Vigilance Committee positively either knew nothing on the subject or they outraged the plainest principles of self-preservation. We all defend the man who, with his own hand, violently and unscrupulously slays the midnight robber and assassin because he would otherwise lose his own life and property, and where the time and place make it ridiculous to call for legal protection. So also should we defend the community that acts in a similar manner under analogous circumstances. Their will and power form new *ex tempore* laws, and if the motives be good and the result good, it is not very material what the means are. . . .

Formerly, that is only two years before, the San Franciscans were careless in personal appearance and rude in manners. Now, they dressed richly and extravagantly and assumed the polished airs of gentlemen. A striking change was observable everywhere and in everything. The houses were growing magnificent and their tenants fashionable. Perhaps this fashion was not quite *à la mode de Paris,* but rather *sui generis.* Balls and convivial parties of the most brilliant character were constantly taking place. The great number of flaunting women of pleasure, particularly the French, mightily encouraged this universal holiday and gave ease, taste, and sprightly elegance to the manners of the town.

There is perhaps no place in the world where money is so little regarded as in San Francisco. A man spends there like a prince, as he gains like one. The "almighty dollar" to him appears of less worth than a shilling does to people in England or in our Eastern states. At these balls, and at all public and private entertainments, immense sums were squandered. Trade might be dull, bad, ruinous; rents might rise or fall and people be really insolvent; still they spent money on all sides. Business losses generally fell on distant correspondents, and the half-burned and supposed bankrupt and ruined city showed still the same brilliant bustle; and its inhabitants still pursued the same expensive round of amusements.

Gold must come from the placers, and San Francisco never could in a certain sense be poor. The riches of the Californian mines on the one side, and the luxuries and conveniences of all countries in the world on the other, met in San Francisco. It would be hard, indeed, for its hot-blooded and venturous population if they did not make the treasures within their grasp minister to every enjoyment that youth and sanguine constitutions could crave.

Ever since the first great immigration, many of the inhabitants carried some weapon of defense secretly about them. During the disturbed times in the early part of 1851, when nobody was safe from the assaults of desperadoes even in the public street or in his own dwelling, the practice of wearing deadly weapons became still more common. These were often used, though not so much against the robber and assassin as upon the old friend and acquaintance, or the stranger, when drink and scandal, time and circumstance had converted them into supposed enemies. The number of duels, and especially of sudden personal affrays, was fearfully great. The general population of San Francisco — with shame it must be confessed, in those days, as is still the case to a considerable extent — drank largely of intoxicating liquors. A great many tippled at times, and quite as many swore lustily.

They are an adventurous people, and their enjoyments are all of an exciting kind. They are bold and reckless from the style of the place and the nature both of business and amusement. Newcomers fall naturally into the same character. It may therefore be imagined that personal rencontres frequently occur among such a population. In 1851 these were constantly happening. One man perhaps called another a "liar," and straightway revolvers were produced on both sides. Repeated shots were hastily fired, with sometimes as much damage to the bystanders as to the half-drunken quarrelers themselves. Some scenes of a most savage and atrocious description, ending occasionally in death, took place between parties who were reputed to be of the first class of citizens.

Among the lower American orders, and in all classes of foreigners, down to the vilest "greasers," the same violent spirit of personal revenge and deadly outrage was common. On the slightest occasion, at a look or touch, an oath, a single word of offense, the bowie knife leaped from its sheath, and the loaded revolver from the breast pocket or the secret case, and death or severe wounds quickly closed the scene. The spectators often shared in the same wild feelings and did not always seek to interfere. The law was powerless to prevent such personal conflicts. Men thought as little of their blood and lives as of their money and, to gratify high, swelling passion, would madly waste them all alike.

One considerable cause of personal disputes and bloodshed was the uncertainty of legal titles to property, which encouraged squatterism. Owing to recent conflicting decisions by the courts of law, it almost appeared that the only, or the best, title to real estate was actual possession. A great many people made a practice of settling down upon any vacant lot they fancied and, perhaps, in the course of a night, would fence it in and erect some small house on the ground. When daylight and the proprietor came, the intruder defied ejection. To seek redress from the tribunals whose judgments had led to these encroachments was only ridiculous; so the parties generally fought it out among themselves, with the aid of friends and long purses to hire help, until both suffered considerably in the battle.

The effect of these conflicting legal decisions on the titles to real estate had otherwise a very prejudicial effect. They hindered the immediate and permanent improvement of property, since no man would expend large sums in that way when his title to the ground was in jeopardy. Lenders, already alarmed at the foolish proposals of usury bills in the legislature, became shy in advancing money on the security of many properties; the value of real estate fell considerably; in some instances, no price whatever could be obtained where the title was disputed; and all was painful doubt on the subject.

In 1850, real estate in the city was assessed at the value of $16,849,024; while, in 1851, it was only $10,518,273; and this was notwithstanding the vast improvements that had taken place in the interval. In the end, certain acts passed by the state, which confirmed sales of the beach and water lots by the city and sanctioned its title to those lots still unsold, and also later and more satisfactory decisions of the Supreme Court in the matter of titles, helped to reestablish confidence on the subject and secure the old owner in his property against the mere squatter. . . .

THE POPULATION of both the state and city was largely increased in 1852. The departures by sea from San Francisco were only 23,196, while there were 66,988 arrivals. This immigration was about double the amount that had taken place in 1851. The immigrants from the Atlantic states generally crossed the Isthmus, while the greater number of European foreigners came round Cape Horn. The Germans, a most valuable and industrious class of men, and the French, perhaps by nature not quite so steady and hardworking a race though still a useful body of citizens, were year by year arriving in large numbers, and were readily remarked among the motley population.

The most untutored eye could distinguish and contrast the natural phlegm and common-sense philosophy of the fat Teuton and the "lean and hungry look" and restless gestures of the Celt. Both races were generally "bearded like the pard," though in this respect they were only like the commonalty of San Francisco who pride themselves much upon hair. The people named cherished many of their old nationalities and generally frequented their own particular boarding and eating houses and places of recreation. The English, Scotch, and Irish immigrants were also numerous but their characteristics, although something different, were less distinguishable from those of native Americans than were the manners and customs of other foreigners.

Besides these, there were always arriving numerous specimens of most other European nations — Spaniards, Portuguese, Italians, Swiss, Greeks, Hungarians, Poles, Russians, Prussians, Dutch, Swedes, Danes, Turks, too — all visited California. Many of them went to the mines, although a considerable proportion never left San Francisco. The country and city were wide enough to hold them all and rich enough to give them all a moderate independence in the course of a few years. A considerable number of German and French women were constantly arriving, as also many more of the sex from the Atlantic states. The female part of the population, though still numerically very far below the male portion, was increasing, perhaps faster in proportion to their previous numbers.

Upward of 20,000 Chinese are included in the general number of arrivals above given. Such people were becoming very numerous in San Francisco, from whence the recent immigrants from their country scattered themselves over the various mining regions of California. At one period of 1852 there were supposed to be about 27,000 Chinese in the state. A considerable number of people of "color" (*par excellence*) also arrived. These were probably afraid to proceed to the mines to labor beside the domineering white races, and therefore they remained to drudge and to make much money and spend it in San Francisco like almost everybody else.

Mexicans from Sonora and other provinces of Mexico and many Chileans and a few Peruvians from South America were likewise continually coming and going between San Francisco and the ports of their own countries. The Chinese immigrants had their mandarins, their merchants, rich, educated and respectable men, in San Francisco; but all the Mexicans and Chileans, like the people of Negro descent, were only of the commonest description. The women of all these various races were nearly all of the vilest character and openly practised the most shameful commerce. The lewdness of fallen white females is shocking enough to witness, but it is far exceeded by the disgusting practices of these tawny visaged creatures. . . .

No important change had occurred in the social or moral condition of San Francisco during 1852. . . . The old dizzy round of business and pleasure continued. There were now only more people, greater wealth, finer houses, more shops and stores, more work, trade, and profits, more places of dissipation and amusement, more tippling and swearing, more drunkenness and personal outrages, nearly as much public gambling, and more private play. There were also a few more modest women, and many more of another class; more benevolent institutions and orphans' asylums; more fire companies, military companies, and Masonic lodges.

Likewise, there were more newspapers that discoursed eloquently, ever railing "in good set terms" against corruption in high places, but which, not being supported by the sincere feeling of a pure and honest people, made no such irresistible body of public opinion as they sometimes do in other countries. Then there were more churches, more moral teachers and religious publications, more Sabbath and day schools; and, too, more of everything that was beautiful and bad, more vice, debauchery, and folly, and, perhaps, also a little more real religion, and sometimes a deal of outward decency. The moral sepulcher was occasionally receiving a fresh coat of paint.

It should not be forgotten, at the same time, that, with the increase of population, there was also an increase of occasional charities and high-minded liberal deeds. These things are done in secret or they lose their noble character. The public generally know not of them. However much the sordid pursuit of wealth may cloud the true friendships and generous actions of many of the San Franciscans, the native worth of heroic and pure souls will at times shine through all. As kings reigned before Agamemnon, so there are here great and worthy, honest and true men, as well as there have been elsewhere. Their exact number cannot be counted, but the student of human nature, according to his temperament and means of information, may hazard an estimate on the subject.

Residents of a few years' standing, the landmarks, by turns, of the ancient village, town, and city, began now to disappear. These perhaps had made a fortune and sown their "wild oats" in the place. They now retired to the Atlantic states or Europe, — to *home*, in short — to enjoy their gains at ease, astonish quiet neighbors with their wondrous tales, speculate on the future of San Francisco, and become disgusted and ennuied with the slowness, tameness, decorum, and insipidity of the conventional mode of existence they were leading.

New faces and new names were rising into importance in place of the earliest pioneers and the "forty-niners." The majority, however, of the first settlers had faith in the place; they relished its excitements as well of business as of pleasure; they had no family or fond ties elsewhere, or these had been long rudely broken; and so they adhered to San Francisco. Many of these persons had waxed very rich, in spite of themselves, by the sudden rise in the value of real estate or by some unexpected circumstance, while others, after expending a world of ingenuity, wickedness, and hard work, remained almost as poor as when, hopeful and daring, they landed in the ship's boat at Clark's Point or, when the tide was high, at the first rude wharf that ran a short distance out from the beach at Montgomery Street.

There is a fascination in even the loose, unsettled kind of life at San Francisco. Of many who have left the city after a residence of years, and when they have accumulated a handsome fortune, a considerable number have gladly returned. For many months, perhaps for even a year or two, the immigrant thinks he can never worthily or rationally enjoy existence in such a place; so he determines to make a fortune as soon as possible and decamp forever. But fortunes are now made more slowly, and the old citizen — a few years here make one old in sensation, thought, and experience — changes his sentiments, and he begins to like the town and people for their own sake. The vices and follies, the general mode of living that frightened and shocked him at first, seem natural to the climate and, after all, are by no means so very disagreeable. If he returned to settle in ultra- or pseudo-civilized and quiet states, he would surely feel himself but a "used-up" man; so he continues where he made his money, still to feel, speculate, and enjoy, to work and contend with real men in their keenest and strongest characters.

It may be thought by some that we have said many overharsh things . . . regarding our fellow citizens. We cannot help that, for the occasions seem to justify the language used. If unmingled praise or hesitating censure were adopted when talking of San Francisco, people elsewhere would not believe the tale, while those here would only laugh in their sleeve at the decent hypocrisy and cant of the writer. Better proclaim the worst at once; and then let who will find explanations, excuses, and palliations. These will be readily advanced by the wiser portion of mankind, who know the temptations that beset poor human nature and how often it falls when fatal opportunity offers. Let it be always understood that we describe the place as at particular periods and not what we think will be its grand coming destiny.

San Francisco was, at the times of which we have discoursed, and it still is, in a state of moral ferment. When the ebullition ceases, though years may elapse before that happens, the natural qualities of its adventurous and clever people will be more clearly and generously developed. The scum and froth of its strange mixture of peoples, of its many scoundrels, rowdies, and great men, loose women, sharpers, and few honest folk, are still nearly all that is visible. The current of its daily life is muddied and defiled by the wild effervescence of these unruly spirits. It may be said that nearly all came to the city only as devout worshipers of Mammon; scarcely one to find a home which might unjustly have been denied him elsewhere.

In order to accumulate the greatest heap

of gold in the shortest possible time, schemes and actions had often to be resorted to which nice honor could not justify nor strict honesty adopt. In the scramble for wealth, few had consciences much purer than their neighbors; few hands were much cleaner. Some were found out and victimized; others were wise and provoked not discussion. The few lamented, and the wise and good hoped and foresaw better things. Time, and a sounder public opinion, will cure most of the evils we have alluded to, leaving the undoubted talent, shrewdness, capacity for hard, practical work, and the original honesty, honor, and high liberal spirit of the people free to show themselves.

Cities, like men, have their birth, growth, and maturer years. Some are born Titans, and, from the beginning, promise to be mighty in their deeds, however willful and destructive. Few spring into being full armed, wise, and sedate as Minerva. San Francisco, while it can show so many enduring marvels for its few years, has also wasted much of its means in "riotous living"; but its young, hot blood will cool by and by. Then ripened years and wisdom will subdue its foolish levities and more disgraceful vices.

Meanwhile, let us treat the noble city kindly, just as we deal with the beautiful woman that offends us — look upon her face and forget her follies. We pardon the careless, extravagant, yet high-spirited youth who lavishes his substance in wild pleasure when he stops short and vows repentance; nay, even though he break out again and again, we cannot seriously feel offended with the charming gallant, so only that he hurts nobody but himself. Let us view San Francisco in something of the same gentle and forgiving if not sympathizing spirit.

110.

Edward Everett: State Funds for Harvard

In 1824 the Massachusetts legislature discontinued the allotment of state funds to Harvard. Twice during his brief tenure as the president of Harvard (from 1846 to 1849), Edward Everett requested the legislature to return to its earlier policy and give Harvard financial support. A portion of his second request, submitted in 1849, is reprinted below. Like many distinguished Americans of his day, Everett had been educated at Göttingen in Germany. There he had acquired respect for both liberal education and academic freedom. The college, he felt, should create an intellectual aristocracy to serve the nation. The legislature, the majority of which did not feel that the state should support a nonvocational institution for the elite, turned down Everett's request.

Source: *Orations and Speeches on Various Occasions*, Boston, 1850, Vol. II, pp. 605-629.

WHAT IS THE PRAYER of the colleges? It is, in a word, that the legislature would allow the revenue from the public lands, *after* the limit of $1 million assigned by law to the school fund has been reached, to accumulate for the formation of another fund, one-half as large as the school fund, to be appropriated in some fixed proportion for the benefit of the colleges.

This is our request; and I do not think it

necessary to dwell at all on what might seem a preliminary question, viz., the policy of appropriating a portion of the moneys arising from the sales of the public lands to educational purposes of some kind or other. It seems to be allowed, upon all hands, that this is their proper destination, a part of the settled policy of the commonwealth. Such appropriations seem, in fact, almost a part of the common law of the land. They have been made by the legislatures of the old states, and large reservations of the land in the new states have been made by Congress for the purpose of education. I have never heard a murmur of disapprobation at the appropriations made from this source in this state for the school fund; and I think the authors of the minority report of last year, a paper of which I wish to speak with all becoming respect, although I greatly differ alike from its train of reasoning and statement of facts, do not suggest any other than an educational destination for these funds.

Passing that topic, therefore, as one not needing argument, I will say that the bare statement of the real object of our petition is a sufficient answer to an objection which met us *in limine* last year, viz., that we asked the legislature to divert the school fund to the colleges. Not only was this statement of the object of the memorialists made in several of the public papers, but the minority of the committee use the following language: "To make, therefore, liberal appropriations to the colleges to the neglect of the common schools, richly to endow the former at the expense of the latter, the very thing which the petitioners ask, is not consistent, we believe, with a sincere desire to promote the true interests of collegiate education."

Now, with all respect to the minority of the committee, the colleges must claim to know the object and nature of their own petition, and their motives in presenting it. We have no such wish or purpose as those ascribed to us. We do not desire to build up the colleges to the neglect of the

schools; to endow the former at the expense of the schools; nor to devote one dollar of the school fund to any other purpose.

But I suppose it need not be argued that all the money in the state does not belong to the common school fund. That fund has a limit — a limit prescribed by law. The legislature, in its wisdom, fixed its amount at $1 million. This limit was not prompted nor advised by the colleges. We were not consulted, sir, on the subject; and sure I am, if we had been, no friend of the colleges with whose views I am acquainted has ever shown a wish to stint the school fund. The General Court of the commonwealth, in its wisdom . . . established $1 million as the limit of the fund; and all that we ask is, that, when that fund shall have reached the original legislative limit, from the same sources of revenue another fund, half as large, may be permitted to accrue, for the benefit of the colleges; but not a dollar before.

Well, now, sir, to say that we ask for the diversion of the school fund to the colleges, is merely to attempt to create a prejudice against us by an incorrect and invidious use of terms. It would be just as proper for the memorialists to say to those who oppose this grant, that they are trying to divert to the schools a fund that belongs to the colleges. It belongs to neither, except so far as it has been appropriated. It is not school fund beyond this, nor college fund, but state fund. A portion of it has been appropriated by the legislature to the schools; and that portion, and no more, is school fund. We ask that another portion may be appropriated to the colleges; and we submit that it is not quite fair to attempt to raise a prejudice against us, by saying that we seek to endow them richly at the expense of the schools. . . .

But, sir, we are still told, and this objection in some form or other meets us at every turn, that common school education is a popular interest, and college education is not; and that for this reason the state is

Edward Everett, photograph by Mathew Brady

bound to take care of the one and not of the other. Now, I shall not put myself in the false and invidious position of contrasting them; there is no contrast between them, no incompatibility of the one with the other. Both are good, each is good in its place; and I will thank any person who can do so to draw the line between them; to show why it is expedient and beneficial in a community to make public provision for teaching the elements of learning, and not expedient nor beneficial to make similar provision to aid the learner's progress toward the mastery of the most difficult branches of science and the choicest refinements of literature.

Sir, they all hang together; it is an abuse of ingenuity, to exercise it in showing how much can be done with one without the other. For myself I admit, if the admission is desired, that a good system of common school education is, next to religious influences, the great and solid foundation of a prosperous state. To build on anything else is to build on straw and stubble.

I honor, beyond all common names of respect, the distinguished gentleman (Horace Mann), who for twelve years has devoted the uncommon powers of his mind, and the indomitable energy of his character, to this noble cause. He will be remembered till the history of Massachusetts is forgotten, as one of her greatest benefactors. I reflect with satisfaction, that the Board of Education was established on a recommendation which I had the honor to submit to the legislature; and that I had the privilege of cooperating in its organization, in the choice of its secretary, in the establishment of the normal schools under its patronage, and in the other measures which marked its opening career and by which, under circumstances of no small discouragement, it sought to promote the objects of its institution. . . .

I know, Mr. Chairman, before this audience it cannot be necessary to argue the cause of higher education, scientific and literary, forming as it does the best preparation for all the departments of professional life; for enlightened statesmanship; and for an efficient application of philosophical principles to the great industrial interests of the community. Who does not know, sir, that there is not a yard of cotton cloth bleached or printed in the commonwealth, without assistance from the last results of chemical research; that you cannot construct a turbine waterwheel but by the aid of the highest mathematics; nor establish a uniform standard of weights and measures, without building upon a series of geometrical operations which began with Hipparchus?

The tables by which the navigator, perhaps the illiterate navigator, finds the ship's place at sea, are written in the very depths of the starry heavens; and the most learned eyes for ages have strained themselves dim, through glasses of wondrous mechanism, in deciphering the mysterious characters. The electric telegraph, which brings you the daily news, is the last achievement of a department of physical science, in which some of the brightest intellects of the last hundred years, from Franklin to Morse, have concentrated their powers of observation and analysis. This step and that may be taken by an uneducated man, may even be the work of chance, but the grand result is the product of cultivated mind, strained to the highest tension of its powers. . . .

But it is still said, the schools are for the many; the colleges for the few; the legislature must take care of the many, the few may take care of themselves; let those who want college education, the few, get it as they can. To this there are two answers. In proportion as you cheapen college education, more will be able to avail themselves of it. You thus answer your own objection, by granting the prayer of the memorial. It will become the interest of the many, if you will let it.

That is one answer, although I must say, in point of fact, I cannot think even now, that college education is unreasonably high. The charge for tuition at Cambridge, where it is somewhat higher than at the other colleges, is $75 a year. This pays for thorough and accurate instruction given by fifteen or sixteen able and accomplished men in the ancient and modern languages, in the exact, the critical, the applied, and moral sciences, in addition to general supervision three-fourths of the year.

For the instruction of a day school in Boston, five hours in the day, $100 per annum are paid. Gentlemen in practical life can say where else, for $75 per annum, they can procure such an amount of intellectual labor to be done, requiring equal talent and preparation, and involving equal responsibility. The sum of $75 per annum is, moreover, not quite half what the service costs the university. Some things, I know, are dear, however low the price. But when we give you, as you admit we do, the true thing, and that at half cost, you cannot say you have had a hard bargain.

But to the objection that school education is the interest of the many, and college education the interest of the few, my main answer is, that it is founded in a great fallacy. The man who makes that objection has not formed even a distant conception of the grounds of the duty which devolves upon an enlightened state, to educate its children. He is thinking of individuals. He forgets that it is the public, as such — the state, the great, complex, social being, which we call Massachusetts, the genial mother of us all — that it is *her* interest in the matter which creates the duty, and which gives all its importance to education, as an affair of public concernment, whether elementary or academical. It is not to teach one man's boy his ABCs, or another man's boy a little Latin and Greek, for any advantage or emolument of their own, that the pilgrim fathers founded the college, or required the towns to support each its school.

As far as individuals, many or few, are concerned, I have just as much natural right to call on the state to pay the bill of the tailor who clothes, or the builder who shelters my children, as of the schoolmaster or schoolmistress, the tutor or professor, who instructs them. The duty of educating the people rests on great public grounds, on moral and political foundations. It is deduced from the intimate connection which experience has shown to exist, between the public welfare and all the elements of national prosperity on the one hand, and the enlightenment of the population on the other.

In this point of view, I say it confidently, good college education for those who need it and want it, is just as much the interest of the many, as good school education. They are both the interest of all, that is, the whole community. It is, of human things, the highest interest of the state, to put the means of obtaining a good school education, and a good college education, within the reach of the largest number of her children.

In the nature of things there will not be

so many who desire a college education, although it is a popular error to think that everyone goes to college who can afford it; that the *few* who go to college are exclusively those who are sometimes invidiously called the "few." Very many sons of the wealthy are not sent to college. Of those who go to college, the majority are the sons of parents in moderate, narrow, and even straitened circumstances.

The demand here, as elsewhere, regulates supply. All have not the taste or talent, are not intended for pursuits which require academic training. But I maintain that, for the limited number required to meet this demand, it is just as much the interest of the community that it should be adequately and honorably supplied, as that the wider demand for school education should be adequately and honorably supplied.

It is not for the rich that the public aid is wanted. They will obtain good education, if they desire it, in one place if they cannot in another; although it is a serious evil to have to seek it abroad. As far as individuals are concerned, it is the poor student that needs cheapened education. If he cannot get that near home, he cannot get it at all. It is not that you expect to breed up everyone who goes to college into a man of eminence — an Adams, a Channing, a Bushnell, a Webster, a Prescott, a Bancroft. The lottery of life is not all highest prizes. But you do wish to train up even minds like these in a healthy, fruitful nurture; and you do wish to prepare for future usefulness in church and state the mass of average intellect.

I suppose there are not above 500 young men, natives of the commonwealth, now at college; but it is as much for the interest of Massachusetts that they should have a good education, as cheap as possible, as that the

200,000 who wish for it should have good school education. It is one great interest; but if we must draw distinctions, the son of the poor man, whose life is cast in some obscure interior village, or in some laborious walk of city life, has a deeper personal interest in the matter than the son of the affluent in town and country.

One word more, sir, and the argument, as far as I am concerned, is closed. The colleges are not pleading their own cause, on this occasion; they are pleading the cause of the people. If you grant the prayer of the memorial, you will, it is true, somewhat widen the field of usefulness of these institutions, and, if they are true to themselves, afford them, in this way, the opportunity of gaining increased credit with the community. I do not deny that, with a generous mind, this is a selfish motive, although the selfishness is of a very refined nature. But beyond this, the colleges, and those concerned in administering them, are not to be benefited.

Your bounty will not add a dollar to their salaries; it may, by increasing the number of students, add to their labors and their cares. It is the interest of the people which is to be subserved by granting the prayer of the memorial. The young man whom you will thereby enable to get an education of which he might else be deprived; the village which will have the satisfaction of seeing its promising candidate for future usefulness lifted up into the broad and cheerful field of academic training; the community whose treasures of intellect you draw out, refine, and prepare for the service of life, these are the parties to be benefited; it is these whose cause I now commend to your favorable consideration.

If this boy passes the examination he will be admitted; and if the white students choose to withdraw, all the income of the college will be devoted to his education.

EDWARD EVERETT, while president of Harvard; reply to a protest against the admission of a Negro student

111.

Charles Sumner: Segregation and the Common School

The "separate but equal" doctrine justifying Negro segregation in education and in public accommodations originated not in the South but in the North in the period before the Civil War. The doctrine was only prevalent in a section of the country where Negroes were theoretically free, but in fact forced to live as second-class citizens; until the end of Reconstruction, this was true only of the North. The first authoritative judicial statement of the doctrine occurred in the decision of Justice Lemuel Shaw in the Massachusetts case of Sarah C. Roberts v. The City of Boston *(1849). Sarah Roberts was a five year old Negro girl who had been denied admission to an all-white public school and had thereby been forced to walk a half mile to an all-Negro school. Charles Sumner argued her case before the Massachusetts Supreme Court on December 4. His plea gave American jurisprudence a new concept: "equality before the law." But, though his argument was praised by the court, the decision went in favor of the city's policy of discrimination. Portions of Sumner's plea are reprinted here.*

Source: *Charles Sumner: His Complete Works*, Statesman Edition, Boston, 1900, Vol. III: "Equality Before the Law."

Can any discrimination on account of race or color be made among children entitled to the benefit of our common schools under the constitution and laws of Massachusetts? This is the question which the Court is now to hear, to consider, and to decide.

Or, stating the question with more detail, and with more particular application to the facts of the present case, is the Committee having superintendence of the common schools of Boston entrusted with *power*, under the constitution and laws of Massachusetts, to exclude colored children from the schools and compel them to find education at separate schools, set apart for colored children only, at distances from their homes less convenient than schools open to white children?

This important question arises in an action by a colored child only five years old who, *by her next friend*, sues the city of Boston for damages on account of a refusal to receive her into one of the common schools.

It would be difficult to imagine any case appealing more strongly to your best judgment, whether you regard the parties or the subject. On the one side is the City of Boston, strong in wealth, influence, character; on the other side is a little child, of degraded color, of humble parents, and still within the period of natural infancy, but strong from her very weakness and from the irrepressible sympathies of good men which, by a divine compensation, come to succor the weak.

This little child asks at your hands her *personal rights*. So doing, she calls upon you to decide a question which concerns the personal rights of other colored children; which concerns the constitution and laws of the Commonwealth; which concerns that peculiar institution of New England, the common schools; which concerns the fundamental principles of human rights; which concerns the Christian character of this community. Such parties and such interests justly challenge your earnest attention.

Though this discussion is now for the first time brought before a judicial tribunal, it is no stranger to the public. In the School Committee of Boston for five years it has been the occasion of discord. No less than four different reports, two majority and two minority forming pamphlets, of solid dimensions, devoted to this question, have been made to this Committee, and afterward published. The opinions of learned counsel have been enlisted. The controversy, leaving these regular channels, overflowed the newspaper press, and numerous articles appeared, espousing opposite sides. At last it has reached this tribunal. It is in your power to make it subside forever. . . .

In opening this argument, I begin naturally with the fundamental proposition which, when once established, renders the conclusion irresistible. According to the constitution of Massachusetts, *all men, without distinction of race or color, are equal before the law.* In the statement of this proposition I use language which, though new in our country, has the advantage of precision. . . .

The Declaration of Independence, which followed the French Encyclopedia and the political writings of Rousseau, announces among self-evident truths, *"that all men are created equal;* that they are endowed by their Creator with certain unalienable rights; that among these are life, liberty, and the pursuit of happiness." The constitution of Massachusetts repeats the same truth in a different form, saying, in its first article: *"All men are born free and equal* and have certain natural, essential, and unalienable rights, among which may be reckoned the right of enjoying and defending their lives and liberties."

Another article explains what is meant by equality, saying: "No man, nor corporation or association of men, have any other title to obtain advantages, or particular and exclusive privileges, distinct from those of the community, than what arises from the consideration of services rendered to the public; and this title being in nature neither hereditary, nor transmissible to children, or descendants, or relations by blood, the idea of a man being born a magistrate, lawgiver, or judge is absurd and unnatural." This language, in its natural signification, condemns every form of inequality in civil and political institutions.

These declarations, though in point of time before the ampler declarations of France, may be construed in the light of the latter. Evidently, they seek to declare the same principle. They are declarations of *rights;* and the language employed, though general in character, is obviously limited to those matters within the design of a declaration of *rights.* And permit me to say, it is a childish sophism to adduce any physical or mental inequality in argument against equality of rights.

Obviously, men are not born equal in physical strength or in mental capacity, in beauty of form or health of body. Diversity or inequality in these respects is the law of creation. From this difference springs divine harmony; but this inequality is, in no particular, inconsistent with complete civil and political equality.

The equality declared by our fathers in 1776, and made the fundamental law of Massachusetts in 1780, was *equality before the law.* Its object was to efface all political or civil distinctions and to abolish all institutions founded upon *birth.* "All men are *created* equal," says the Declaration of Independence. "All men are *born* free and equal," says the Massachusetts Bill of Rights. These are not vain words. Within the sphere of their influence, no person can be *created,* no person can be *born,* with civil or political privileges not enjoyed equally by all his fellow citizens; nor can any institution be established, recognizing distinction of birth.

Here is the Great Charter of every human being drawing vital breath upon this soil, whatever may be his condition, and whoever may be his parents. He may be poor, weak, humble, or black; he may be of Caucasian, Jewish, Indian, or Ethiopian race; he may be of French, German, English, or Irish extraction; but before the constitution of Massachusetts all these distinctions disappear. He is not poor, weak, humble, or black; nor is he Caucasian, Jew, Indian, or Ethiopian; nor is he French, German, English, or Irish; he is a MAN, the equal of all his fellowmen. He is one of the children of the state, which, like an impartial parent, regards all its offspring with an equal care. To some it may justly allot higher duties, according to higher capacities; but it welcomes all to its equal hospitable board. The state, imitating the divine justice, is no respecter of persons. . . .

The legislature of Massachusetts, in entire harmony with the constitution, has made no discrimination of race or color in the establishment of common schools. Any such discrimination by the laws would be unconstitutional and void. But the legislature has been too just and generous, too mindful of the Bill of Rights, to establish any such privilege of birth. The language of the statutes is general and applies equally to all children, of whatever race or color.

The provisions of the law are entitled, *Of the Public Schools,* meaning our common schools. To these we must look to ascertain what constitutes a public school. Only those established in conformity with the law can be legally such. They may, in fact, be more or less public; yet, if they do not come within the terms of the law, they do not form part of the beautiful system of our public schools. They are not public schools or, as I prefer to call them, common schools.

The two terms are used as identical; but the latter is that by which they were earliest

known, while it is most suggestive of their comprehensive character. A "common" in law is defined to be *"open ground equally used* by many persons"; and the same word, when used as an adjective, is defined by lexicographers as "belonging equally to many or to the public," thus asserting equality.

If we examine the text of this statute, we shall find nothing to sustain the rule of exclusion which has been set up. The first section provides, that "in every town, containing fifty families or householders, there shall be kept in each year, at the charge of the town, by a teacher or teachers of competent ability and good morals, one school for the instruction of children in orthography, reading, writing, English grammar, geography, arithmetic, and good behavior, for the term of six months, or two or more such schools, for terms of time that shall together be equivalent to six months."

The second, third, and fourth sections provide for the number of such schools in towns having respectively 100, 150, and 500 families or householders. There is no language recognizing any discrimination of race or color. Thus, in every town, the schools, whether one or more, are "for the instruction of children" generally, not children of any particular class or race or color, but children — meaning the children of the town where the schools are.

The fifth and sixth sections provide a school, in certain cases, where additional studies are to be pursued, which "shall be kept for the benefit of all the inhabitants of the town." The language here recognizes no discrimination among the children but seems directly to exclude it.

In conformity with these sections is the peculiar phraseology of the memorable colonial law of 1647, founding common schools, "to the end that learning may not be buried in the graves of our forefathers." This law obliged townships having fifty householders to "forthwith appoint one within their towns to teach *all such children as shall resort to him* to write and read."

Here again there is no discrimination among the children. *All* are to be taught.

On this legislation the common schools of Massachusetts have been reared. The section of the Revised Statutes and the statute of 1838, appropriating small sums, in the nature of a contribution, from the school fund, for the support of common schools among the Indians, do not interfere with this system. These have the anomalous character of all the legislation concerning the Indians. It does not appear, however, that separate schools are established by law among the Indians, nor that the Indians are in any way excluded from the common schools in their neighborhood.

I conclude, on this head, that there is but one public school in Massachusetts. This is the common school, equally free to all the inhabitants. There is nothing establishing an exclusive or separate school for any particular class, rich or poor, Catholic or Protestant, white or black. In the eye of the law there is but *one class,* where all interests, opinions, conditions, and colors commingle in harmony — excluding none, therefore comprehending all.

The courts of Massachusetts, in harmony with the constitution and the laws, have never recognized any discrimination founded on race or color, in the administration of the common schools, but have constantly declared the equal rights of all the inhabitants. . . . It is easy to see that the exclusion of colored children from the public schools is a constant inconvenience to them and their parents, which white children and white parents are not obliged to bear. Here the facts are plain and unanswerable, showing a palpable violation of equality. *The black and white are not equal before .the law.* I am at a loss to understand how anybody can assert that they are.

Among the regulations of the Primary School Committee is one to this effect. "Scholars to go to the school nearest their residences. Applicants for admission to our schools (with the exception and provision referred to in the preceding rule) are especially entitled to enter the schools nearest to their places of residence." The exception here is "of those for whom special provision has been made" in separate schools, that is, colored children.

In this rule, without the unfortunate exception, is part of the beauty so conspicuous in our common schools. It is the boast of England that, through the multitude of courts, justice is brought to every man's door. It may also be the boast of our common schools that, through the multitude of schools, education in Boston is brought to every *white* man's door. But it is not brought to every *black* man's door. He is obliged to go for it, to travel for it, to walk for it, often a great distance.

The facts in the present case are not so strong as those of other cases within my knowledge. But here the little child, only five years old, is compelled, if attending the nearest African school, to go a distance of 2,100 feet from her home, while the nearest primary school is only 900 feet, and, in doing this, she passes by no less than five different primary schools, forming part of our common schools and open to white children, all of which are closed to her. Surely this is not equality before the law. . . .

Looking beyond the facts of this case, it is apparent that the inconvenience from the exclusion of colored children is such as to affect seriously the comfort and condition of the African race in Boston. The two primary schools open to them are in Belknap Street and Sun Court. I need not add that the whole city is dotted with schools open to white children. Colored parents, anxious for the education of their children, are compelled to live in the neighborhood of the schools, to gather about them, as in Eastern countries people gather near a fountain or a well. The liberty which belongs to the white man, of choosing his home, is not theirs. Inclination or business or economy may call them to another part of the city;

but they are restrained for their children's sake. There is no such restraint upon the white man; for he knows, that, wherever in the city inclination or business or economy may call him, there will be a school open to his children near his door. Surely this is not equality before the law.

If a colored person, yielding to the necessities of position, removes to a distant part of the city, his children may be compelled daily, at an inconvenience which will not be called trivial, to walk a long distance for the advantages of the school. In our severe winters this cannot be disregarded, in the case of children so tender in years as those of the primary schools.

There is a peculiar instance of hardship which has come to my knowledge. A respectable colored parent became some time since a resident of East Boston, separated from the mainland by water. Of course there are common schools at East Boston, but none open to colored children. This parent was obliged to send his children, three in number, daily across the ferry to the distant African school. The tolls amounted to a sum which formed a severe tax upon a poor man, while the long way to travel was a daily tax upon the time and strength of his children. Every toll paid by this parent, as every step taken by the children, testifies to that inequality which I now arraign.

This is the conduct of a colored parent. He is well deserving of honor for his generous efforts to secure the education of his children. As they grow in knowledge they will rise and call him blessed; but at the same time they will brand as accursed that arbitrary discrimination of color in the common schools of Boston which rendered it necessary for their father, out of small means, to make such sacrifices for their education.

Here is a grievance which, independent of any stigma from color, calls for redress. It is an inequality which the constitution and the laws of Massachusetts repudiate. But it is not on the ground of inconvenience only

that it is odious. And this brings me to the next head.

The separation of children in the schools, on account of race or color, is in the nature of *caste* and, on this account, a violation of equality. The case shows expressly hat the child was excluded from the school nearest to her dwelling — the number in the school at the time warranting her admission — "on the sole ground of color." The first Majority Report presented to the School Committee . . . presents the grounds of this discrimination with more fullness, saying, "It is one of *races*, not of *colors* merely. The distinction is one which the Allwise Creator has seen fit to establish; and it is founded deep in the physical, mental, and moral natures of the two races. No legislation, no social customs can efface this distinction." Words cannot be chosen more apt than these to describe the heathenish relation of caste. . . .

Boston is set on a hill, and her schools have long been the subject of observation, even in this respect. As far back as the last century, the French Consul here made a report on our "separate" school; and De Tocqueville, in his masterly work, testifies, with evident pain, that the same schools do not receive the children of the African and European. . . . Strange that here, under a state constitution declaring the equality of all men, we should follow the worst precedents and establish among us a caste. Seeing the discrimination in this light, we learn to appreciate its true character.

In India, Brahmins and Sudras, from generation to generation, were kept apart. If a Sudra presumed to sit upon a Brahmin's carpet, his punishment was banishment. With similar inhumanity here, the black child who goes to sit on the same benches with the white is banished, not indeed from the country but from the school. In both cases it is the triumph of caste. But the offense is greater with us, because, unlike the Hindus, we acknowledge that men are born equal. . . .

We abjure nobility of all kinds; but here is a nobility of the skin. We abjure all hereditary distinctions; but here is an hereditary distinction, founded not on the merit of the ancestor but on his color. We abjure all privileges of birth; but here is a privilege which depends solely on the accident whether an ancestor is black or white. We abjure all inequality before the law; but here is an inequality which touches not an individual, but a race. We revolt at the relation of caste; but here is a caste which is established under a constitution declaring that all men are born equal. . . .

The Committee charged with the superintendence of the common schools of Boston have no power to make any discrimination on account of race or color. It has been seen already that this power is inconsistent with the Declaration of Independence, with the constitution and laws of Massachusetts, and with adjudications of the Supreme Court. The stream cannot rise higher than the fountainhead; and if there be nothing in these elevated sources from which this power can spring, it must be considered a nullity. Having seen that there is nothing, I might here stop; but I wish to show the shallow origin of this pretension.

Its advocates, unable to find it among express powers conferred upon the School Committee and forgetful of the constitution, where "either it must live or bear no life," place it among implied or incidental powers. The Revised Statutes provide for a School Committee "who shall have *the general charge and superintendence* of all the public schools" in their respective towns. Another section provides that "the School Committee shall determine the number and qualifications of the scholars to be admitted into the school kept for the use of the whole town." These are all the clauses conferring powers on the Committee.

From them no person will imply a power to defeat a cardinal principle of the constitution. It is absurd to suppose that the Committee in general charge and superintendence of schools, and in determining the number and qualifications of scholars may engraft upon the schools a principle of inequality, not only unknown to the constitution and laws but in defiance of their letter and spirit. In the exercise of these powers they cannot put colored children to personal inconvenience greater than that of white children. Still further, they cannot brand a whole race with the stigma of inferiority and degradation, constituting them a caste. They cannot in any way violate that fundamental right of all citizens, equality before the law. To suppose that they can do this would place the Committee above the constitution. It would enable them, in the exercise of a brief and local authority, to draw a fatal circle, within which the constitution cannot enter, nay, where the very Bill of Rights becomes a dead letter. . . .

It is clear that the Committee may classify scholars according to age and sex, for the obvious reasons that these distinctions are inoffensive, and that they are especially recognized as legal in the law relating to schools. They may also classify scholars according to moral and intellectual qualifications, because such a power is necessary to the government of schools. But the Committee cannot assume, a priori and without individual examination, that all of an entire race are so deficient in proper moral and intellectual qualifications as to justify their universal degradation to a class by themselves. Such an exercise of discretion must be unreasonable and, therefore, illegal.

But it is said that the School Committee, in thus classifying the children, have not violated any principle of equality, inasmuch as they provide a school with competent instructors for colored children, where they have advantages equal to those provided for white children. It is argued, that, in excluding colored children from common schools open to white children, the Committee furnish an equivalent.

Here there are several answers. I shall touch them briefly, as they are included in what has been already said.

1. The separate school for colored children is not one of the schools established by the law relating to public schools. It is not a common school. As such it has no legal existence and, therefore, cannot be a *legal equivalent*. In addition to what has been already said, bearing on this head, I call attention to one other aspect. It has been decided that a town can execute its power to form school districts only by geographical divisions of its territory, that there cannot be what I would call a personal limitation of a district, and that certain individuals cannot be selected and set off by themselves into a district.

The admitted effect of this decision is to render a separate school for colored children illegal and impossible in towns divided into districts. They are so regarded in Salem, Nantucket, New Bedford, and in other towns of this Commonwealth. The careful opinion of a learned member of this Court, who is not sitting in this case, given while at the bar and extensively published, is considered as practically settling this point.

But there cannot be one law for the country and another for Boston. It is true that Boston is not divided strictly into geographical districts. In this respect its position is anomalous. But if separate colored schools are illegal and impossible in the country, they must be illegal and impossible in Boston. It is absurd to suppose that this city, failing to establish school districts and treating all its territory as a single district, should be able to legalize a caste school, which otherwise it could not do. Boston cannot do indirectly what other towns cannot do directly. This is the first answer to the allegation of equivalents.

2. The second is that in point of fact the separate school is not an equivalent. We have already seen that it is the occasion of inconvenience to colored children, which would not arise, if they had access to the nearest common school, besides compelling parents to pay an additional tax and inflicting upon child and parent the stigma of caste. Still further — and this consideration cannot be neglected — the matters taught in the two schools may be precisely the same, but a school exclusively devoted to one class must differ essentially in spirit and character from that common school known to the law, where all classes meet together in equality. It is a mockery to call it an equivalent.

3. But there is yet another answer. Admitting that it is an equivalent, still the colored children cannot be compelled to take it. Their rights are found in equality before the law; nor can they be called to renounce one jot of this. They have an equal right with white children to the common schools. . . .

In determining that the School Committee has no power to make this discrimination we are strengthened by another consideration. If the power exists in the present case, it cannot be restricted to this. The Committee may distribute all the children into classes, according to mere discretion. They may establish a separate school for Irish or Germans, where each may nurse an exclusive nationality alien to our institutions. They may separate Catholics from Protestants or, pursuing their discretion still further, may separate different sects of Protestants and establish one school for Unitarians, another for Presbyterians, another for Baptists, and another for Methodists.

They may establish a separate school for the rich, that the delicate taste of this favored class may not be offended by the humble garments of the poor. They may exclude the children of mechanics, and send them to separate schools. All this, and much more, can be done in the exercise of that high-handed power which makes a discrimination on account of race or color. The grand fabric of our common schools, the pride of Massachusetts; where, at the feet of the teacher, innocent childhood should come, unconscious of all distinctions of birth; where the equality of the constitution and of Christianity should be inculcated by constant precept and example, will be converted into a heathen system of proscription and caste.

We shall then have many different schools, representatives of as many different classes, opinions, and prejudices; but we shall look in vain for the true common school of Massachusetts. Let it not be said that there is little danger that any Committee will exercise a discretion to this extent. They must not be entrusted with the power. Here is the only safety worthy of a free people. . . .

In extenuation of the Boston system, it is sometimes said that the separation of white and black children was originally made at the request of colored parents. This is substantially true. It appears from the interesting letter of Dr. Belknap, in reply to Judge Tucker's queries respecting slavery in Massachusetts, at the close of the last century, that no discrimination on account of color existed then in the common schools of Boston. "The same provision," he says, "is made by the public for the education of the children of the blacks as for those of the whites. In this town the Committee who superintend the free schools have given in charge to the schoolmasters to receive and instruct black children as well as white." Dr. Belknap had "not heard of more than three or four who had taken advantage of this privilege, though the number of blacks in Boston probably exceeded 1,000."

Much I fear that the inhuman bigotry of caste — sad relic of the servitude from which they had just escaped — was at this time too strong to allow colored children kindly welcome in the free schools, and that, from timidity and ignorance, they hesitated to take a place on the same benches with the white children. Perhaps the prejudice was so inveterate that they could not

venture to assert their rights. In 1800 a petition from sixty-six colored persons was presented to the School Committee, requesting the establishment of a school for their benefit. Some time later, private munificence came to the aid of this work, and the present system of separate schools was brought into being.

These are interesting incidents belonging to the history of the Boston schools, but they cannot in any way affect the rights of colored people or the powers of the School Committee. These rights and these powers stand on the constitution and laws. Without adopting the suggestion of Jefferson, that one generation cannot by legislation bind its successors, all must agree that the assent of a few to an unconstitutional and illegal course nearly half a century ago, when their rights were imperfectly understood, cannot alter the constitution and the laws so as to bind their descendants forever in the thrall of caste. . . .

But it is said that these separate schools are for the benefit of both colors and of the public schools. In similar spirit slavery is sometimes said to be for the benefit of master and slave, and of the country where it exists. There is a mistake in the one case as great as in the other. This is clear. Nothing unjust, nothing ungenerous, can be for the benefit of any person or any thing. From some seeming selfish superiority, or from the gratified vanity of class, short-sighted mortals may hope to draw permanent good; but even-handed justice rebukes these efforts and redresses the wrong. The whites themselves are injured by the separation. Who can doubt this?

With the law as their monitor, they are taught to regard a portion of the human family, children of God, created in His image, coequals in His love, as a separate and degraded class; they are taught practically to deny that grand revelation of Christianity, the brotherhood of man. Hearts, while yet tender with childhood, are hardened and ever afterward testify to this legalized uncharitableness. Nursed in the sentiments of caste, receiving it with the earliest food of knowledge, they are unable to eradicate it from their natures, and then weakly and impiously charge upon our Heavenly Father the prejudice derived from an unchristian school. Their characters are debased, and they become less fit for the duties of citizenship. . . .

The whole system of common schools suffers also. It is a narrow perception of their high aim which teaches that they are merely to furnish an equal amount of knowledge to all, and therefore, provided all be taught, it is of little consequence where and in what company. The law contemplates not only that all shall be taught, but that *all* shall be taught *together*. They are not only to receive equal quantities of knowledge, but all are to receive it in the same way. All are to approach the same common fountain together; nor can there be any exclusive source for individual or class.

The school is the little world where the child is trained for the larger world of life. It is the microcosm preparatory to the macrocosm, and therefore it must cherish and develop the virtues and the sympathies needed in the larger world. And since, according to our institutions, all classes, without distinction of color, meet in the performance of civil duties, so should they all, without distinction of color, meet in the school, beginning there those relations of equality which the constitution and laws promise to all.

As the state derives strength from the unity and solidarity of its citizens without distinction of class, so the school derives strength from the unity and solidarity of all classes beneath its roof. In this way the poor, the humble, and the neglected not only share the companionship of the more favored but enjoy also the protection of their presence, which draws toward the school a more watchful superintendence. A degraded or neglected class, if left to themselves, will become more degraded or neglected. . . .

Happily, our educational system, by the blending of all classes, draws upon the whole school that attention which is too generally accorded only to the favored few, and thus secures to the poor their portion of the fruitful sunshine. But the colored children, placed apart in separate schools, are deprived of this peculiar advantage. Nothing is more clear than that the welfare of classes, as well as of individuals, is promoted by mutual acquaintance.

Prejudice is the child of ignorance. It is sure to prevail, where people do not know each other. Society and intercourse are means established by Providence for human improvement. They remove antipathies, promote mutual adaptation and conciliation, and establish relations of reciprocal regard. Whoso sets up barriers to these thwarts the ways of Providence, crosses the tendencies of human nature, and directly interferes with the laws of God.

May it please Your Honors: Such are some of the things which I feel it my duty to say in this important cause. I have occupied much time, but the topics are not yet exhausted. Still, which way soever we turn, we are brought back to one single proposition, *the equality of men before the law.* This stands as the mighty guardian of the colored children in this case. It is the constant, ever-present, tutelary genius of this Commonwealth, frowning upon every privilege of birth, every distinction of race, every institution of caste. You cannot slight it or avoid it. You cannot restrain it. God grant that you may welcome it!

Do this, and your words will be a "charter and freehold of rejoicing" to a race which by much suffering has earned a title to much regard. Your judgment will become a sacred landmark, not in jurisprudence only but in the history of freedom, giving precious encouragement to the weary and heavy-laden wayfarers in this great cause. Massachusetts, through you, will have fresh title to respect and be once more, as in times past, an example to the whole land. . . .

This is not all. The vaunted superiority of the white race imposes corresponding duties. The faculties with which they are endowed, and the advantages they possess, must be exercised for the good of all. If the colored people are ignorant, degraded, and unhappy, then should they be especial objects of care. From the abundance of our possessions must we seek to remedy their lot. And this Court, which is parent to all the unfortunate children of the Commonwealth, will show itself most truly parental, when it reaches down, and, with the strong arm of law, elevates, encourages, and protects our colored fellow citizens.

112.

CHARLES LYELL: The Relative Merits of Negro and White Labor

The great English geologist Sir Charles Lyell visited the United States in 1841 and again in 1845-1846 in order to observe firsthand the geology of the North American continent. He estimated the rate of recession of Niagara Falls, calculated the average annual accumulation of alluvial matter in the Mississippi delta, and studied the Great Dismal Swamp of Virginia; the last investigations led to several papers on the formation of beds of coal. He also wrote two books in which he commented on America from other than a geological point of view. The second of these books appeared in 1849; the selection below, in which Lyell expatiates on slavery, is taken from it.

Source: *A Second Visit to the United States of North America*, London, 1849, pp. 160-163.

I . . . REMARKED that the growth of New Orleans seemed to show that a large city may increase and flourish in a slave state; but Dr. Carpenter and Mr. Wilde both observed, that the white race has been superseding the Negroes. Ten years ago, say they, all the draymen of New Orleans, a numerous class, and the cabmen, were colored. Now, they are nearly all white. The servants at the great hotels were formerly of the African, now they are of the European race. Nowhere is the jealousy felt by the Irish towards the Negroes more apparent. According to some estimates, in a permanently resident population not much exceeding 80,000, there are only 22,000 colored persons, and a large proportion of these are free.

Over a door in the principal street of New Orleans we read the inscription, "Negroes on sale here." It is natural that Southerners should not be aware how much a foreigner is shocked at this public mode of treating a large part of the population as mere chattels. . . .

In a St. Louis paper, I read, in the narrative of a steamboat collision, the following passage: "We learn that the passengers, with few exceptions, lost all their effects; one gentleman in particular lost nine Negroes (who were on deck) and fourteen horses."

Among the laws recently enacted in Louisiana, I was glad to see one to prevent persons of color exiled from other states, or transported for some offense, from becoming citizens. In spite of such statutes the Negro-exporting portions of the Union will always make the newer states play in some degree the part of penal settlements.

Free blacks are allowed to be witnesses in the courts here, in cases where white men are concerned, a privilege they do not enjoy in some free states, as in Indiana; but they do not allow free blacks to come and settle here and say they have been compelled to adopt this precaution by the Abolitionists.

An intelligent Louisianian said to me, "Were we to emancipate our Negroes as suddenly as your government did the West Indians, they would be a doomed race; but there can be no doubt that white labor is more profitable even in this climate."

"Then, why do you not encourage it?" I asked. "It must be the work of time," he replied; "The prejudices of owners have to be overcome, and the sugar and cotton crop is easily lost, if not taken in at once when ripe — the canes being damaged by a slight frost, and the cotton requiring to be picked dry as soon as mature, and being ruined by rain. Very lately a planter, five miles below New Orleans, having resolved to dispense with slave labor, hired one hundred Irish and German emigrants at very high wages. In the middle of the harvest they all struck for double pay. No others were to be had, and it was impossible to purchase slaves in a few days. In that short time he lost produce to the value of $10,000."

113.

The Wisconsin Phalanx

The theories of French socialist Charles Fourier were popularized in the United States in the 1840s by Albert Brisbane, Parke Godwin, and Horace Greeley. Greeley was especially effective in spreading the idea of Associationism through his New York Tribune. *During the decade there were nearly fifty Fourierist phalanxes founded in Eastern and Midwestern states. These semi-utopian socialist communities all failed of their goals, sometimes within a matter of months. One of the short-lived associations was the Wisconsin Phalanx, founded by spiritualist Warren Chase, and located in Fond du Lac County. At a meeting of the members of the phalanx on November 13, 1849, the following address was presented, in which the problems that were soon to lead to the society's dissolution were discussed.*

Source: *Spirit of the Age*, December 8, 1849 [Commons, VII, pp. 263-273].

THE MEMBERS of the Wisconsin Phalanx, who retain the hope of associative life, are desirous to communicate to the public a knowledge of the present condition of the Phalanx and of the causes which have produced it; and to invite the cooperation of friends in an attempt to reconstruct an industrial and social organization on the Domain, on principles practically better adapted to a commencement in association.

The Wisconsin Phalanx was incorporated February 1845. The original members were chiefly from Southport, Wisconsin. They possessed no experience in associative life and had derived their ideas of the theory of association principally from the pamphlets and newspaper writings of the school of Fourier. By a clause in the charter of the

Phalanx, the increase in the annual appraisal of all the property, real and personal, of the Phalanx, exceeding the cost, was to be yearly divided or credited one-fourth to stock and the remaining three-fourths to labor, in such manner as the bylaws should provide.

The Domain of the Phalanx contains about 1,800 acres of prime land, prairie, oak-openings, groves and meadows, in Ceresco Township and vicinity, Fond du Lac County. This region of country is not exceeded by any part of the whole state for beauty of scenery, healthfulness of situation, and fertility of soil. No ague of local origin has ever been known here, and not one adult male member of the society, since the institution of the Phalanx, has deceased. Five women have died on the Domain during the entire existence of the society; but, before their coming to Ceresco, they were all afflicted with the diseases which proved fatal to them. Several infants and small children have died from complaints incidental to that period of life. The cause, no doubt, would be found in a want of correct knowledge and physiological treatment in regard to infants and young children; a lack of knowledge certainly not greater here than elsewhere. We are confident that no region in the whole Northwest can be found more remarkable for continued good health than Ceresco and the adjacent country.

There is a good waterpower on the Domain, the property of the Phalanx; and we have in operation a gristmill and a sawmill, the former of which is kept constantly employed. A new and commodious building, intended for a protective union store, has been erected at the private cost of some of the members, and is nearly sufficiently completed for the commencement of business. There is a good stone schoolhouse; a blacksmith shop with three fires in full employment; and buildings for the dwelling of members, one, a long, new frame house, conveniently and pleasantly arranged, several of the rooms of which are now completed and occupied, and all might be finished within a short time, and at no great expense.

Another row of frame houses, not so convenient nor strong in construction as that just referred to, was put up at the first founding of the society; and, in this latter range of buildings, the greater part of the members yet reside. There is also another row of frame buildings with a cupola and a bell, a kitchen, a bakery, a large dining room, and apartments serving for the accommodation of strangers and travelers. In addition, there is a substantial stone dwelling sufficiently large for two families living on the principles of associative life.

The most of these buildings have been constructed with a view to a unitary mode of life; they were designed for temporary use in a transitional state of society, and would principally be serviceable for the accommodation of a combined or friendly company until more suitable and comfortable dwellings were erected. They would contain altogether about thirty-five families, with the usual average number of persons to a family.

The Domain is situated 10 miles from the Fox River, a stream forming a collecting link in the great proposed communication by rivers, lakes, and canals from Lake Michigan to the River Mississippi. The intermediate ground is exceedingly well adapted for good roads, being a rolling prairie and oak-openings, without marsh. The whole of this part of Wisconsin is fast filling up with a hardy, industrious, and enterprising population. The constant influx of new settlers, while it enhances greatly the rise of real estate in these parts, affords a present market for all our productions.

Persons occupying this Domain can at once engage in profitable agricultural and other employments, with the full certainty also that each year will greatly add to the value of the premises. About 400 acres of ground are broken and under fence; and there is a nursery containing nearly 100,000 young apple trees, with some peach and pear trees. These trees are now private property, having been sold to some of the members on their own account; but their existence on the Domain, as it affords a convenient opportunity for the supply of trees for orchards, we consider an advantage. Most excellent drinking water is had in unfailing supplies by sinking wells from 10 to 30 feet; and if the attempt were made, no doubt artesian wells could be had on the Domain. Limestone, a clay suitable for brick, and a gray sandstone, of a superior quality for building, can be had in any quantity on our own premises.

The summers of Wisconsin are delightful; the autumns, serene and beautiful; the winters, cold and healthful, and not so severe as persons who have never resided here would imagine; for although the thermometer in winter indicates a low temperature, yet the air is dry, and, on this account, the cold is not so sensibly felt. The springs are generally backward; but at the beginning of summer, vegetation is as forward here as in the southern parts of New York; for vegetable growth in this soil and climate, when it commences, proceeds with great rapidity.

Wisconsin is a sure and abundant grain state, and yields also large crops of melons and summer fruits. Its favorable situation for commerce by the Lakes and the Mississippi; its rich ores; the salubrity of its climate; its highly productive soil; its intelligent, hardy, and industrious population; its wise and liberal legislation will cause it to rank second to no state in the Northwest.

It may be asked why, under all these advantages of location and healthfulness and without the encumbrance of any debt, the Wisconsin Phalanx is about to dissolve; why this appeal for the cooperation of friends to aid the members in the reconstruction of a society on the Domain? We will answer as briefly as possible, being desirous to make a candid statement, so however as not to swell our address beyond the limits of a newspaper publication.

Our charter contains a radical error. It is not just nor expedient to credit stock yearly with one-fourth of the net increase in the annual appraisement of the property. The original members acted to the best of their judgment at the time, in the organization, but sufficient knowledge, neither theoretic nor practical, was possessed by them. We do not mention this to their discredit. The subject was new and had been untried. Even had the members been better informed than they were in regard to the theory of the association which they wished to adopt, it must be now evident that the social organization of any people should be the embodiment of their inward or mental and moral preparation, and must change and advance with the mind.

A correct, practical, social life cannot be laid down fully by a philosopher in his closet; it must grow up and be developed in actual forms, as working people combined feel the wants of their situation, and as these wants suggest remedies. We do not mean to imply any reflection against the value of science and theory, and the aid of the researches of great and philosophic minds. Very far from it. But we mean that no theory or science can supply the want of experience; and, in both theory and practical knowledge, the members of the Phalanx were deficient.

We are now firmly of opinion that no dividend whatever in the nature of interest should be allowed to capital. Brotherhood and usury cannot coexist. Their tendencies are opposite and hostile. One or the other must finally sink under the antagonism. Besides, families uniting in industrial cooperation should include in their compact the principle of mutual guaranteeism, so that no deserving brother or sister may suffer from want caused by sickness or other causality. The constitution of the Wisconsin Phalanx includes no such principle of guaranteeism, but it includes an extravagant form of usury, awarding to capital yearly the one-fourth part of the increase in the annual appraisement of all property, real and personal, of the Phalanx, exceeding the cost and the last appraisement. When it is considered that the labor of the Phalanx consisted chiefly in building and in agricultural occupations, not requiring a great outlay of capital in machinery, it is manifest that this feature of injustice in the charter would eventually, if not corrected, prove fatal, by running the property into the hands of a few, and those not always the most industrious and deserving.

At the end of the first year of the Phalanx, a reappraisal was made of the real estate of the Phalanx; and the lands obtained from government, at the usual cost of $1.25 an acre, were then valued at $3. It is needless to remark that this appraisal operated for the advantage of the large stockholders, in the ratio of their stock; but we have no thought that any person was actuated by an unworthy motive in causing it to be done. The act was generally considered to be in strict justice, in conformity with the charter, and to be promotive, also, of the best interests of the society, in order that the public might perceive the rapidly increasing value of the Domain, and that persons with sufficient pecuniary means to aid in improvements and extended industrial operations might be encouraged to apply for membership.

At the same time, as the Phalanx was not in possession of capital to construct buildings for newcomers, it was deemed necessary to inform the public that applicants for membership would be expected to subscribe to the stock of the institution. This announcement, whether justly or not, created an impression abroad that the Phalanx was averse to the admission of new members, however worthy in moral character and industry, unless they were possessed also of money; and a prejudice arising from this cause, together with the advantages already enumerated as enjoyed by capital, promoted an injurious jealousy between labor and capital. Besides this, there was a real difficulty in the imperfect organization of the society, in adjusting the rates of dividend or compensation between the agricultural and the mechanical groups. The mechanics, who were in the minority, were not satisfied with the rates of dividend awarded to them. Most of them ceased to work for the Phalanx, and hired themselves out in the neighborhood, or at distant places, where they obtained, as they supposed, much better terms. Members became disheartened, and several withdrew; persons with capital, perceiving the want of harmonious action in the society, did not apply for membership; and without capital applicants were not admitted.

Some of the members who remained on the Domain, and who were influential from their business talents or the stock which they held, either because they lost confidence in the stability of the Phalanx or because they wished to make money more largely and rapidly than they could in association, engaged in enterprises on their own account, in land speculations and in merchandising. And even the products of the Phalanx, by a mistaken policy in the councils of the society, were sold to members at prices influenced by the Mexican War and the European famine, thus throwing a burden, very difficult to be borne, upon the shoulders of the members with large families and small stock, to whom the dividends were low, but the charges against them, for the support of their families, high.

While jealousies and discontents were thus increasing from causes connected with the wrong organization of the Phalanx (and we must add also from the want of sufficient moral training and experience in all the members), a new source of dismemberment arose from circumstances which, had the society been rightfully constructed at the outset, and had the members possessed a spirit of brotherhood, would have served to draw still more closely the bands of fraternal union. When the Wisconsin Phalanx settled at Ceresco, the whole of this region of country was unpeopled. Now, thriving farms are located all around us and flourishing towns are built up in our vicinity. Our own location, with its waterpowers, its quarries, excellent drinking water, its known health, and its situation in regard to a vast extent of most fertile country, is unquestionably a very eligible place for the construction of a town; and the lands of the Phalanx, before valued at $3 an acre, would now be appraised at not less than $12; and if a town were actually located here, the valuation of the premises for building lots and out lots would be immensely greater. Those members in whom the spirit of speculation exists might now be glad to have a division of the domain in the hope to advance their fortunes by individual enterprises in land transactions.

We have briefly stated the principal causes which have led to our present unfavorable condition. We have no hope to succeed as an association without a reconstruction of the society on a basis more favorable to brotherhood and equality, and better suited to the merely transitional preparation of all men in respect to social life. Brought up under the sinister antagonisms of civilization, no man or, at most, not many persons are yet fitted for the higher conditions of association. We must reach those higher forms of social life gradually.

The Wisconsin Phalanx, owing to the disagreements which we have mentioned, has already individualized personal property and the fruit trees in the nursery of the Phalanx. No part of the Domain can be sold without an act of the legislature of the state. An application, it is presumed, will be made for the passage of such an act sometime the ensuing winter.

But many of us still cling to the desire for, and the hope of, an associative life; and, under a just organization of a society, several of the members who have already withdrawn would return.

We propose that a village shall be laid out on the Domain; that members of the association shall have their own separate building lots, combining, however, according to their own pleasure, with others in dwellings, or living apart as they choose, and uniting in industrial operations; that the protective union store shall be opened and conducted in connection with the gristmill, which should be held jointly by the association, thus affording a cement for a . . . closer cooperation between the residents of the place, as their minds may be matured for a higher social life; that mutual guarantees shall exist against casualties, to be adjusted in conformity with the principles of humanity and brotherhood; that the children of all shall be educated; and that capital advanced shall be replaced, but without usury. And with an initial organization of this kind, adapted to the present imperfect state of the public mind in social science, we hope to grow up to a more true form of association, as experience and increasing knowledge and moral training shall lead the way.

We are happy to state that Ceresco, notwithstanding the impediments to our success as a Phalanx, enjoys an entire freedom from litigation and from intemperance; neither has the peace of the place ever been disturbed by unruly or violent behavior. Persons who have resided here become much attached to the spot.

The total stock of the Phalanx may be estimated at about $25,000; nearly $20,000 of this sum might be required to pay off nonresident stockholders and others who would not be willing to unite in an arrangement on the plan we have mentioned. Not more, however, than about $10,000 would be needed by the 1st of February next to buy out the shares of members making their preparations to withdraw; and the extinguishment of their rights would supersede the necessity of an application to the legislature for an act repealing the charter, until affairs could be placed on a better footing for a settlement. As there is now a general incorporation law in Wisconsin, the continuance of the present, or the grant of a new charter by the state, is not desirable, except that by the premature repeal of the act of incorporation, the Domain might pass into the hands of individuals, by purchase, who would hold it for speculation as a townsite.

The Domain is worth far more than the largest sum which we have named; and there can be no hazard in the purchase of the stock at par. Are there not friends of the cause sufficient in numbers and in pecuniary ability to buy the stock of the nonresident and going members, that, by an arrangement on the principles above suggested, this location so highly favorable for the purpose may be preserved for and consecrated to humanity and brotherhood? If not, it must and will pass into the hands of speculators and monopolists; and several fortunes will be realized by it.

114.

Anonymous: The Hardships of Farming

In spite of a growing industrialism and the increasing complexity of economic and social life, the agrarian ideals of Thomas Jefferson persisted throughout much of the nineteenth century. Transcendentalists praised the simple virtues of country life and regretted the loss of individualism associated with city dwelling. Labor associations called for distribution of public lands, so that each worker could own his own farm. City life was generally felt to be morally and physically debilitating and somehow inimical to democratic ideals. The following article, published in November 1849, attempted to explode this sentimental and somewhat unrealistic attachment to the soil. The debate stirred up was carried on through several issues of the Prairie Farmer *in which the article, signed "Practical Farmer," first appeared.*

Source: *Prairie Farmer*, November 1849: "The Poetry and Profit of Country Life."

THE POWERS OF LANGUAGE have been completely exhausted in eulogy of country life. The poets have found it a never-failing theme of song, and have portrayed its beauties in the brightest colors calculated to captivate every individual possessing the least spark of enthusiasm or romance. Politicians, too, prate about the importance of agriculture, the dependence of the other branches upon it, the dignity of labor, etc., claiming the command to "earn our bread by the

sweat of our brow" to be one of the greatest blessings ever conferred upon our race. But, notwithstanding the vehemence with which they preach, they are extremely cautious not to fret their maiden palms by too close familiarity with any implement of labor, preferring that others should practise what they preach.

The true statesman, however, regards the uncorrupted morals, unvitiated intelligence, and sterling integrity of the country population as the only hope and salvation of the nation, the chief conservators of the government. The merchant and mechanic also look forward to a residence in the country as an Elysium to their wearied and jaded spirits. All alike sigh for that independence and freedom from care supposed to exist in the country.

Alas! How many foolish, absurd, and erroneous notions have been imbibed? How many individuals and families have been deceived and disappointed, having found by sad experience, country life, instead of a bed of roses, to be one of thorns? That boasted independence to consist in an absolute denial of most of the comforts and refinements of life, indispensably necessary to maintain a creditable station in society. That much desired freedom from anxiety to consist in perplexing care, a thousand unpropitious influences to be guarded against, the best skill and utmost exertion frequently proving unavailing, vexatious disappointment, unrequited labor, loss of crops, necessity compelling the reduction of the expense of living to the lowest common denomination, obliged to practise the most rigid parsimony, thus eking out a miserable existence, the slave of toil. Is not this a true story, founded upon observation and the experience of a large majority of the operative agriculturists?

True, there are those, who, from some peculiar circumstances, manage to gain a comfortable subsistence. But allow me the question: Would not the same capital, invested in city property, yield a greater percentage and, with far less exertion, secure a larger amount of the necessaries, comforts, and luxuries of life, thereby affording more leisure for intellectual improvement and literary attainment? I answer, yes.

Such being the fact, in my humble opinion, and if the actions of men are still influenced by the strong desire for wealth and that inherent aversion to labor which have hitherto characterized them, is it not natural

and reasonable that they should pursue that course best calculated, in their judgment, to lead to results in conformity with their wishes? And why seek to prevent it by any invidious comparison or the sacrifice of truth?

Why are not the disappointment of thousands who have failed in agricultural life recorded and heralded in company with those isolated cases of success through the length and breadth of our land? Why are the beauties, pleasures, and unalloyed bliss of country life contrasted with the darkest shades of city life? Is this course dictated by philanthropy or required by necessity?

The opinion of Governor Briggs and W. C. Calhoun that "ninety out of one hundred young men who emigrate from the country to the city fail of success," is now making its second or third tour through the press and meets with universal approbation; an assertion of this kind needs to be well supported by facts, although emanating from such high authority. For my part, I am inclined to withhold my assent until better informed in regard to the premises upon which said assumption is founded. If I mistake not, when I first had the pleasure of seeing this statement, it referred to mercantile pursuits alone, but, as usual, in such cases, it has taken a wider latitude and now embraces all who emigrate.

I cannot conceive any good reason why the young man reared in the country, in industrious, frugal, and economical habits, should fail of success. My own observation convinces me that a large majority of the young men who abandon agricultural life and engage in other avocations are eminently successful, from the fact that labor is better compensated in the mechanical, mercantile, or manufacturing branches, to say nothing of the professions, than in agricultural pursuits.

True, the farmer does not lack for an abundance of the necessaries of life; he can live on less expense than the other professions; he can, if he chooses, limit his desire, contract his operations, smother every generous impulse, and become, to all intents and purposes, a complete cipher in social life, independent of all the world! But he is possessed of the feelings and desires which actuate his fellowmen; he is ambitious to maintain and support a respectable position in community; he desires the means of intellectual improvement for himself and the blessings of education for his children; he is anxious to aid and assist in the various benevolent enterprises of the day; he wants a fair and just compensation for his labor to accomplish this and to enable him to sustain that rank among the professions which the paramount importance of his own should command.

I think, Messrs. Editors, you much underrate the intelligence of the young men and women of the country in supposing that the "smooth garb, white hands, and pale countenances of their city cousins" should "warm their imaginations" for city life! Had you said they look upon the tattered garments of the farmer — his hard, careworn, and wrinkled visage marked by exposure to summer's heat and winter's cold; his frame bent and stooping by hard and incessant labor; his hopes blasted by loss of crops from various and unavoidable causes; his overexertion in the most enervating season of the year, frequently necessary in order to secure his crops, the final issue of his toil; a bare pittance, insufficient for a decent support, grudgingly meted out to him by the concentrated capital and combined action of those classes above him who are supported by his labor — had you assigned these as reasons to account for the desire of which you speak, you certainly would have guessed nearer the truth and have paid a greater compliment to the sound common sense of our young men and ladies.

Perhaps, too, the young man has not the capital necessary to conduct farming operations profitably; his health may require a less laborious occupation; the monotony of country life may not be congenial to his taste or suit his temperament; or the success of his former associates may "warm his imagination" and prompt him to flee from the hard and uncertain life of the farmer — especially so here at the present time — and seek a life of comparative ease in the city. And as far as the accumulation of wealth, the pleasures of social intercourse, the amenities of polished society are concerned, his success is equally if not more certain. Let him but practise the same restraining caution, the same rigid economy, and use the same exertion, physical and mental, absolutely necessary to gain wealth or even competence on the farm. . . .

Those who, having been bred in the city, are induced by the glowing description of some

Mad enthusiast who ne'er can rest
Till half the world is like himself possess'd,

to engage in a business and fill a station, which neither their education, habits of life, character, or disposition have fitted them — they come to teach us science. But, alas! They find, too late, that they have been "pleased with a rattle and tickled with a straw." They certainly deserve commiseration.

Why is not the same benevolent effort invoked to save them from disappointment and ruin which is so lavishly put forth on the other hand? It is for the special benefit of those who have not been victimized, but liable so to be in the absence of the knowledge of the hardship and disappointment appertaining to the farmer's life, that I have written this lengthy epistle; perhaps unadvisedly, but nevertheless in earnestness and sincerity.

Sam Houston, first president of the Republic of Texas

POLITICS AND WAR

Mexico was ready to go to war if Texas was annexed by the United States. Two decades of diplomatic errors, the emnity caused by the Texas Revolution, and border hostilities were shaping a militant resistance to the aggressive American expansionism threatening Mexico's holdings. Polk's ardent expansionist campaign in 1844 convinced Mexican leaders of the aims of American policy; they could well remember the hasty action of Commodore Jones, who had occupied Monterey, California, in October 1842 when he had mistakenly thought that the two countries were at war. Van Buren, Webster, and Clay had tried to suppress the controversy over Texas, and they delayed annexation for nearly ten years. They wished to avoid war, realizing that North and South were divided on the issue. But the spirit of Manifest Destiny was rampant. Polk's victory in the election of 1844 and Tyler's joint resolution for annexation, drawn up in his last days of office, indicated the course that the country had chosen.

Stephen Austin

Map of 1834 showing location of American grants

Texas

The Mexican government originally encouraged Americans to settle in its frontier province of Texas with generous grants such as the one given to Stephen Austin in 1823. The Americans soon outnumbered the native Mexicans and managed their own affairs as frequent civil crises in Mexico prevented effective administration of the area. In 1835, when Santa Anna proclaimed a constitution that would have tied Texas more closely to Mexico, the Texans seceded. Santa Anna's attempt to regain the area was defeated and he himself captured by an army under Houston in April 1836.

The city of Austin, capital of Texas in 1840, as it appeared in a contemporary lithograph

A pro-Harrison cartoon from the election of 1840 showing Kinder & Co. (Van Buren) robbing the U.S. Treasury

1840 Campaign

In the presidential campaign of 1840, William Henry Harrison and John Tyler were chosen to lead the Whig Party. Adopting no platform and ignoring real issues, the Whigs matched "Old Tip" against Van Buren in a "log-cabin and hard-cider" campaign designed to appeal to a populace suffering from economic depression. Harrison carried the important states, for Van Buren's Democratic Party was held responsible for the financial crisis of 1837 and the wide-spread suffering caused by the depression.

William Henry Harrison

The log-cabin, hard-cider campaign for Harrison

The campaign: rolling the ball to Washington

People's Line--Take care of the Locomotive
Sold at 104 Nassau, and 18 Division Streets, New-York.

A TIPPECANOE PROCESSION.

(Above) John Tyler; (right) Daniel Webster; (below) Lord Ashburton; who negotiated Canadian boundary dispute with Webster in 1842

Harrison died after only one month in office and the Virginian Tyler succeeded him. Once in office, he incurred the wrath of his own Whig Party by opposing their desire for a national bank and by cabinet shifts that dispensed with all Whigs and Northerners by 1844. His administration saw a settlement of the boundary dispute with Canada (Webster-Asburton Treaty) and the reorganization of the Navy. It was expansionist in character, encouraging settlement of Oregon, annexation of Texas, and warning foreign powers of America's special position in Hawaii.

The House of Representatives during a debate denouncing antislavery petitions

A cartoon of 1846 depicting U.S. recklessness in the Oregon boundary dispute

James K. Polk

The "growing conviction of America's 'manifest destiny' to expand west to the Pacific and south to at least the Rio Grande" decided the election for James K. Polk. His expansionist campaign, "Re-occupation of Oregon, Re-annexation of Texas," defeated Henry Clay, the Whig candidate, whose cautious stand on Texas in the interests of maintaining peace with Mexico offended the voters. The popular vote was close, but enough Whigs in New York State voted for Birney, the antislavery candidate, for Polk to win that state's important electoral vote.

"Polk's Dream," a cartoon labeling Polk's action as an impetuous Jacksonian venture

General Taylor's army encamped near Corpus Christi in October of 1845

(Right) Volunteers for the Mexican War. There was little enthusiasm for the war except in Texas and in the states bordering on the Mississippi; these areas provided 49,000 volunteers compared to the 13,000 supplied by the Northeast. (Below) A demonstration supporting the annexation of Texas

The Battle of Resaca de la Palma, which occurred on May 9, 1846

Mexican War

President Polk began preparing a war message for Congress when the Mexican government, in March 1846, refused to receive John Slidell, whom Polk had commissioned to negotiate with Mexico. When news arrived of a skirmish between Taylor's army, which was occupying disputed ground, and Mexican units at Matamoras, Polk presented his message, declaring Mexico the aggressor. War was declared on May 13. Taylor had already won victories at Palo Alto and Resaca de la Palma. He captured Monterrey in September and gained complete control of northern Mexico by defeating Santa Anna at Buena Vista in February 1847.

General Zachary Taylor

Taylor's army nearing Monterrey, which was captured on September 28, 1846

The Mississippi Rifles breaking up a charge of the Mexican cavalry at Buena Vista

(Above) General Wool and his staff at Saltillo, Mexico; (below) Battle of Buena Vista, the last battle of the northern campaign

The war in California: cavalry engagement at San Pasqual

Polk wanted California. Fearing that the European powers might add the area to their growing Pacific empire, he had attempted to purchase the territory from Mexico. This attempt failed, and he began making military plans. When war was declared, Fremont supported the settlers in the Bear Flag Revolt of June 14, 1846, at Sonoma, and independence was claimed. In early July naval forces occupied Monterey and San Francisco. Los Angeles was captured on August 13. But in September the Mexican residents revolted, gaining control of the interior and threatening coastal positions. A concentration of the forces of Kearny, Stockton, and Fremont defeated the resistance by January 1847, and California was securely in U.S. hands.

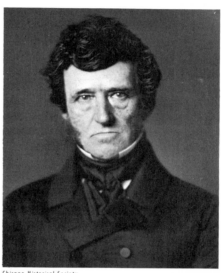

Robert Field Stockton

Sonoma, California, was placed in U.S. hands by the Bear Flag Revolt on June 14, 1846

U.S. Army under General Scott landing on the beach near Vera Cruz, March 9, 1847

Major General Winfield Scott

Polk directed Major General Winfield Scott to invade Mexico from Vera Cruz when Taylor's campaign in the north began to slow down. (Polk had also begun to worry about Taylor's popularity and political ambitions.) Scott captured Vera Cruz at the end of March and marched west toward Mexico City. After a fight at Churubusco an armistice was declared, but the Mexicans were unwilling to accept the terms that peace commissioner Nicholas Trist had drawn up. Scott's army marched on and captured Mexico City on September 17. Polk had recalled Trist after the armistice at Churubusco failed, but he remained against orders to arrange the terms of a treaty signed in February 1848.

The fortified Castle of Chapultepec, the last major obstacle on Scott's march to Mexico City

Antonio Lopez de Santa Anna, commander of the Mexican forces

Nicholas P. Trist, Polk's peace commissioner accompanying Scott's invasion army

The Grand Plaza, Mexico City, with the American flag flying from the Royal Palace

Zachary Taylor, the Whig candidate

(Above) Lewis Cass, Democratic nominee; (below) Martin Van Buren

In the presidential campaign of 1848, the Whigs selected Zachary Taylor as their candidate. Their convention left the public ignorant of the party's stand because internal division on a number of questions prevented them from issuing a platform. The Democrats chose Lewis Cass, an expansionist with Southern sympathies. The radical "Barnburners," offended by this choice, nominated Van Buren, adopted an antislavery platform, and formed the "Free-Soiler" coalition. This split in the Democratic Party gave Taylor the election.

The Democratic Funeral of 1848, a cartoon celebrating the Whig victory

115.

"Sea Gulls and Crickets"

The Mormons arrived in force in Salt Lake City in 1848, and their first winter there was especially hard because they had not had time to prepare for it. Then in the summer of 1849 their first harvest was almost devoured by vast swarms of black crickets. The harvest was saved from total destruction by a visitation of sea gulls, which glutted themselves on the crickets and left. Unaware that the sea gulls appeared annually to feed off the crickets, the pious Mormons believed they had received a special sign from God. The statue of the sea gulls in Salt Lake City's Temple Square commemorates the Mormon's gratitude. The following song tells of the events of that summer of 1849.

♫ SEA GULLS AND CRICKETS

The winter of '49 had passed,
  A winter of haunting fears;
For famine had knocked at the city gates
  And threatened the pioneers.

But spring with its smiling skies lent grace
  And cheered the hosts within;
And they tilled their fields with a newborn
    trust
  And the courage to fight and win.

With the thrill of life, the tender shoots
  Burst forth from the virgin plain;
And each day added its ray of hope,
  The blessing of ripened grain.

But lo in the East strange clouds appeared,
  And dark became the sun;
And down from the mountainsides there
    swept
  A scourge that the boldest shunned.

The crickets by tens of millions came
  Like fog on the British coast;
The finger of devastation marked
  Its course on the Mormon host.

With a vigor that desperation fanned,
  They battled and smote and slew,
But the clouds still gathered and broke
    afresh
  Till the fields that waved were few.

With visions of famine and want and woe,
  They prayed from their hearts sincere,
When lo from the West came other clouds
  To succour the pioneers.

'Twas sea gulls feathered in angel-white,
  And angels they were forsooth;
The sea gulls there by the thousands came
  To battle in very truth.

They charged down on the cricket hordes
  And gorged them day and night;
They routed the devastating foe
  And the crickets were put to flight.

All heads were bowed as they thanked
    their God,
  And they reaped while the devil raved;
The harvest was gathered to songs of praise
  And the pioneers were saved.

116.

Anonymous: Social Injustice and Civil Disorder

*The following selection is the concluding statement of a pamphlet describing the
"terrific and fatal riot" that occurred at the New York Astor Place Opera House on
the night of May 10, 1849. The riot grew out of a feud between two prominent actors,
Edwin Forrest and William C. Macready. The feud became a patriotic issue when
Forrest, an American, was allegedly snubbed by his English rival, Macready, during
a tour of England. It became a social issue as well when the partisans of Forrest
booed Macready off the stage of the Opera House on May 8, 1849, and the outraged
and wealthy patrons of the opera, headed by the author Washington Irving, protested
Macready's treatment and promised him public support if he would fulfill his
engagement despite the incident. Macready's next appearance was scheduled for
May 10, and to protect him, the mayor called out the militia. The expected riot
occurred. While police arrested offenders within the theater, the military fired
on the crowd of thousands agitating outside. More than fifty people were killed
or wounded.*

Source: *Account of the Terrific and Fatal Riot at the New-York Astor Place
Opera House,* New York, 1849: "Where Lies the Blame?"

THE DEAD ARE SLEEPING in their quiet graves. Day by day, time brings its consolations to the afflicted; but has society no lesson to learn from the horrors of which we have given as full a description as could be given, by looking at the mere surface of things? We have shown the causes which produced this dreadful sacrifice of human life — this massacre of innocent and unoffending citizens, for many of the killed were truly such. Let us endeavor to turn the terrible lesson to some useful account.

Those who were actively engaged in the scenes we have described experience different feelings in regard to it. The mob was made up mainly of well-meaning but ignorant, rash, and misguided men. The best feelings of our nature, when they are perverted, may produce the worst conse-

quences. In this case, a feeling of patriotism and a sense of justice were the ruling motives of those who violated the laws, broke the peace of the community, defied the constituted authorities, and caused the death of twenty-three human beings. They acted in all good conscience, but an unenlightened or misguided conscience is no security against wrong. Some of the worst deeds that were ever committed were done "in all good conscience." Thus Christ was crucified by a Jewish mob, and said, "Father, forgive them, they know not what they do." Thus, in all ages, the worst acts have been committed from the best of motives.

The authorities are probably satisfied with having maintained law and order, though at a terrible sacrifice, and the press has almost unanimously sustained them.

But it should be remembered that almost all men are liable to temporary excitements. Mobs are affected with a kind of insanity. The madness of a crowd seems to be infectious. These rioters may, in their calm moments, be good and quiet citizens. We have seen some of the most sober and moral communities excited into a fury of passion. At any rate, they are brethren and should be dealt with in love and kindness.

But law and order must be maintained; very true: it must be done at all hazards, but it should be done prudently and with the least possible sacrifice. Humanity has its claims as well as law; and it may not be necessary to the maintenance of public order that ignorant and misguided men, laboring under a temporary madness, should be shot down like dogs if they can be controlled by means more gentle.

The military acted naturally, under the circumstances. They were placed in an ugly position by the authorities, suffered severely for it, and obeyed their orders. No doubt they regretted the fatal necessity. Some idea of the probable feelings of those who fired the fatal volleys may be judged of from the fact that a brother of Mr. Gedney, who was shot dead at the first fire, was a member of one of the companies that fired the volleys. All men are brethren — but here was brother against brother, in a sense that the most unfeeling can appreciate.

A distinguished clergyman of this city, preaching on the subject of the riot, says of Macready and his right to act:

> Though he had been the meanest of his kind, he should have been protected here to the conclusion of his announced engagement, if an army of 10,000 men had been required to wait upon his movements, and a ship of war chartered to convey him to his native land. We have done something to vindicate order and law, and we ought to have done more.

A zeal for the rights of Mr. Macready and his friends and for the cause of law and order is commendable, but it must not be forgotten that other rights must have been violated, or this riot could never have taken place. Those ignorant men had a right to education and to such conditions of cultivation as would have made them intelligent men and good citizens. They would never have raised their hands against society had society done its duty to them. Before they committed this wrong, they had been most deeply wronged themselves; and it would be better to provide 10,000 schoolmasters to instruct people than 10,000 soldiers to prevent the result of their ignorance.

Men can be zealous and indignant about the rights of play actors, or their patrons — and we have no disposition to deny their rights or to interfere with the lawful exercise of them — but they forget in how many ways the rights of our brethren are violated and not a word is said in their behalf. Give every man the natural and social rights that belong to him and we should have few crimes and outrages to complain of, and law and order could be maintained without standing armies or ships of war.

When we go deep into the investigation of social wrongs, we shall find that society brings upon itself the very evils it attempts to subdue. Society, by an unjust distribution of the avails of industry, enables a few men to become rich, and consigns a great mass to hopeless poverty, with all its deprivations and degradations. This poverty produces ignorance, the sense of injustice, groveling tastes, and a loss of all high ambition. The only wonder is that under such circumstances of wrong and outrage, men are so forbearing, so honest, and so orderly. The only wonder is that more crimes are not committed against both property and life. Thousands of poor people know that they are robbed and plundered every day of their lives — they feel bitterly the hardships and injustice of their lot; but how calmly do they wait God's justice to set them right! How few of them comparatively attempt to right their own wrongs, and to seize upon a portion of what society withholds from them!

This terrible tragedy is a lesson to us all. None can escape its warning. We are all responsible, all guilty; for we make a part of a society that has permitted thousands of its members to grow up in poverty and ignorance, and exposed to the temptations of vice and crime. This mob is but a symptom of our social condition, and it points out a disease to which we should lose no time in applying a proper remedy.

117.

Henry David Thoreau: Resistance to Civil Government

For years Thoreau paid no poll tax (though other taxes he did pay) on the ground that it was exclusively for the benefit of a government he did not approve; and for years his delinquency was allowed to pass unquestioned. But one day during the summer of 1846 — shortly after the beginning of the Mexican War — he was arrested and put in jail. He was released the next morning when one of the female members of his household paid the tax, and at first he tended to make light of the incident. However, he discussed it in a lecture before the Concord Lyceum in January 1848, and he wrote the essay "Civil Disobedience" for the Dial *the next year. It was hardly noticed at the time; but Mahatma Gandhi read it early in his career and made of it almost a bible of nonresistance in his successful effort to free India from British rule, and on it Thoreau's present worldwide reputation as a revolutionary and prophet of revolution rests. Part of the essay is reprinted here.*

Source: *Aesthetic Papers*, Elizabeth P. Peabody, ed., Boston, 1849, pp. 189-211.

I HEARTILY ACCEPT THE MOTTO — That government is best which governs least — and I should like to see it acted up to more rapidly and systematically. Carried out, it finally amounts to this, which also I believe — That government is best which governs not at all — and when men are prepared for it, that will be the kind of government which they will have. Government is at best but an expedient; but most governments are usually, and all governments are sometimes, inexpedient. . . .

This American government — what is it but a tradition, though a recent one, endeavoring to transmit itself unimpaired to posterity but each instant losing some of its integrity? It has not the vitality and force of a single living man; for a single man can bend it to his will. It is a sort of wooden gun to the people themselves; and, if ever they should use it in earnest as a real one against each other, it will surely split. But it is not the less necessary for this; for the people must have some complicated machinery or other and hear its din to satisfy that idea of government which they have. Governments show thus how successfully men can be imposed on, even impose on themselves, for their own advantage.

It is excellent, we must all allow; yet this

government never of itself furthered any enterprise but by the alacrity with which it got out of its way. *It* does not keep the country free. *It* does not settle the West. *It* does not educate. The character inherent in the American people has done all that has been accomplished; and it would have done somewhat more if the government had not sometimes got in its way. For government is an expedient by which men would fain succeed in letting one another alone; and, as has been said, when it is most expedient, the governed are most let alone by it.

Trade and commerce, if they were not made of India rubber, would never manage to bounce over the obstacles which legislators are continually putting in their way; and, if one were to judge these men wholly by the effects of their actions and not partly by their intentions, they would deserve to be classed and punished with those mischievous persons who put obstructions on the railroads.

But, to speak practically and as a citizen, unlike those who call themselves no-government men, I ask for, not at once no government, but *at once* a better government. Let every man make known what kind of government would command his respect, and that will be one step toward obtaining it.

After all, the practical reason why, when the power is once in the hands of the people, a majority are permitted, and for a long period continue, to rule is not because they are most likely to be in the right, nor because this seems fairest to the minority, but because they are physically the strongest. But a government in which the majority rule in all cases cannot be based on justice, even as far as men understand it. Can there not be a government in which majorities do not virtually decide right and wrong, but conscience; in which majorities decide only those questions to which the rule of expediency is applicable? Must the citizen ever for a moment, or in the least degree, resign his conscience to the legislator? Why has every man a conscience, then? I think

that we should be men first, and subjects afterward.

It is not desirable to cultivate a respect for the law so much as for the right. The only obligation which I have a right to assume is to do at any time what I think right. It is truly enough said that a corporation has no conscience; but a corporation of conscientious men is a corporation *with* a conscience. Law never made men a whit more just; and, by means of their respect for it, even the well-disposed are daily made the agents of injustice.

A common and natural result of an undue respect for law is that you may see a file of soldiers, colonel, captain, corporal, privates, powder monkeys, and all, marching in admirable order over hill and dale to the wars, against their wills, aye, against their common sense and consciences, which makes it very steep marching, indeed, and produces a palpitation of the heart. They have no doubt that it is a damnable business in which they are concerned; they are all peaceably inclined. Now, what are they? Men at all, or small moveable forts and magazines, at the service of some unscrupulous man in power? . . .

The mass of men serve the state thus, not as men mainly but as machines, with their bodies. They are the standing army, and the militia, jailers, constables, *posse comitatus,* etc. In most cases there is no free exercise whatever of the judgment or of the moral sense; but they put themselves on a level with wood and earth and stones; and wooden men can perhaps be manufactured that will serve the purpose as well. Such command no more respect than men of straw or a lump of dirt. They have the same sort of worth only as horses and dogs. Yet such as these even are commonly esteemed good citizens.

Others, as most legislators, politicians, lawyers, ministers, and officeholders, serve the state chiefly with their heads; and, as they rarely make any moral distinctions, they are as likely to serve the devil, without intending it, as God. A very few, as heroes, patriots, martyrs, reformers in the great sense, and *men,* serve the state with their consciences also, and so necessarily resist it for the most part; and they are commonly treated by it as enemies. . . .

How does it become a man to behave toward this American government today? I answer that he cannot without disgrace be associated with it. I cannot for an instant recognize that political organization as *my* government which is the *slave's* government also.

All men recognize the right of revolution; that is, the right to refuse allegiance to and to resist the government when its tyranny or its inefficiency are great and unendurable. But almost all say that such is not the case now. But such was the case, they think, in the Revolution of '75. If one were to tell me that this was a bad government because it taxed certain foreign commodities brought to its ports, it is most probable that I should not make an ado about it, for I can do without them: all machines have their friction, and possibly this does enough good to counterbalance the evil. At any rate, it is a great evil to make a stir about it.

But when the friction comes to have its machine, and oppression and robbery are organized, I say, let us not have such a machine any longer. In other words, when a sixth of the population of a nation which has undertaken to be the refuge of liberty are slaves, and a whole country is unjustly overrun and conquered by a foreign army and subjected to military law, I think that it is not too soon for honest men to rebel and revolutionize. What makes this duty the more urgent is the fact that the country so overrun is not our own, but ours is the invading army. . . .

I quarrel not with far-off foes but with those who, near at home, cooperate with and do the bidding of those far away, and

without whom the latter would be harmless. We are accustomed to say that the mass of men are unprepared; but improvement is slow because the few are not materially wiser or better than the many. It is not so important that many should be as good as you as that there be some absolute goodness somewhere; for that will leaven the whole lump. There are thousands who are *in opinion* opposed to slavery and to the war [with Mexico] who yet in effect do nothing to put an end to them; who, esteeming themselves children of Washington and Franklin, sit down with their hands in their pockets and say that they know not what to do, and do nothing; who even postpone the question of freedom to the question of free trade, and quietly read the prices-current, along with the latest advices from Mexico, after dinner, and, it may be, fall asleep over them both.

What is the price-current of an honest man and patriot today? They hesitate, and they regret, and sometimes they petition; but they do nothing in earnest and with effect. They will wait, well-disposed, for others to remedy the evil, that they may no longer have it to regret. At most, they give only a cheap vote, and a feeble countenance and Godspeed, to the right, as it goes by them. There are nine hundred and ninety-nine patrons of virtue to one virtuous man; but it is easier to deal with the real possessor of a thing than with the temporary guardian of it. . . .

The soldier is applauded who refuses to serve in an unjust war by those who do not refuse to sustain the unjust government which makes the war; is applauded by those whose own act and authority he disregards and sets at nought; as if the state were penitent to that degree that it hired one to scourge it while it sinnned, but not to that degree that it left off sinning for a moment. Thus, under the name of order and civil government, we are all made at last to pay homage to and support our own meanness. After the first blush of sin, comes its indifference; and from immoral it becomes, as it were, *un*moral, and not quite unnecessary to that life which we have made.

The broadest and most prevalent error requires the most disinterested virtue to sustain it. The slight reproach to which the virtue of patriotism is commonly liable, the noble are most likely to incur. Those who, while they disapprove of the character and measures of a government, yield to it their allegiance and support are undoubtedly its most conscientious supporters and so frequently the most serious obstacles to reform. Some are petitioning the state to dissolve the Union, to disregard the requisitions of the President. Why do they not dissolve it themselves — the Union between themselves and the state — and refuse to pay their quota into its Treasury? Do not they stand in the same relation to the state that the state does to the Union? And have not the same reasons prevented the state from resisting the Union which have prevented them from resisting the state? . . .

Unjust laws exist. Shall we be content to obey them, or shall we endeavor to amend them and obey them until we have succeeded, or shall we transgress them at once? Men generally, under such a government as this, think that they ought to wait until they have persuaded the majority to alter them. They think that, if they should resist, the remedy would be worse than the evil. But it is the fault of the government itself that the remedy *is* worse than the evil. *It* makes it worse.

Why is it not more apt to anticipate and provide for reform? Why does it not cherish its wise minority? Why does it cry and resist before it is hurt? Why does it not encourage its citizens to be on the alert to point out its faults and *do* better than it

Henry David Thoreau, crayon portrait by Samuel Worcester Rowse, 1854

would have them? Why does it always crucify Christ, and excommunicate Copernicus and Luther, and pronounce Washington and Franklin rebels?

One would think that a deliberate and practical denial of its authority was the only offense never contemplated by government; else, why has it not assigned its definite, its suitable and proportionate penalty? If a man who has no property refuses but once to earn nine shillings for the state, he is put in prison for a period unlimited by any law that I know and determined only by the discretion of those who placed him there; but if he should steal ninety times nine shillings from the state, he is soon permitted to go at large again.

If the injustice is part of the necessary friction of the machine of government, let it go, let it go: perchance it will wear smooth — certainly the machine will wear out. If the injustice has a spring, or a pulley, or a rope, or a crank, exclusively for itself, then perhaps you may consider whether the remedy will not be worse than the evil; but if it is of such a nature that it requires you to be the agent of injustice to another, then, I say, break the law. Let your life be a counterfriction to stop the machine. What I have to do is to see, at any rate, that I do not lend myself to the wrong which I condemn.

As for adopting the ways which the state has provided for remedying the evil, I know not of such ways. They take too much time, and a man's life will be gone. I have other affairs to attend to. I came into this world not chiefly to make this a good place to live in but to live in it, be it good or bad. A man has not everything to do but something; and because he cannot do *everything*, it is not necessary that he should do *something* wrong. It is not my business to be petitioning the governor or the legislature any more than it is theirs to petition me; and if they should not hear my petition, what should I do then?

But in this case the state has provided no way: its very Constitution is the evil. This may seem to be harsh and stubborn and unconciliatory, but it is to treat with the utmost kindness and consideration the only spirit that can appreciate or deserves it. So is all change for the better, like birth and death which convulse the body.

I do not hesitate to say that those who call themselves Abolitionists should at once effectually withdraw their support, both in person and property, from the government of Massachusetts, and not wait till they constitute a majority of one before they suffer the right to prevail through them. I think that it is enough if they have God on their side without waiting for that other one. Moreover, any man more right than his neighbors constitutes a majority of one already.

I meet this American government, or its representative the state government, directly and face to face once a year, no more, in the person of its tax gatherer; this is the only mode in which a man situated as I am necessarily meets it; and it then says distinctly, "Recognize me"; and the simplest, the most effectual, and, in the present posture of affairs, the indispensablest mode of treating with it on this head, of expressing your little satisfaction with and love for it, is to deny it then.

My civil neighbor, the tax gatherer, is the very man I have to deal with; for it is, after all, with men and not with parchment that I quarrel, and he has voluntarily chosen to be an agent of the government. How shall he ever know well what he is and does as an officer of the government or as a man until he is obliged to consider whether he shall treat me, his neighbor, for whom he has respect, as a neighbor and well-disposed man, or as a maniac and disturber of the peace, and see if he can get over this obstruction to his neighborliness without a ruder and more impetuous thought or speech corresponding with his action?

I know this well, that if one thousand, if one hundred, if ten men whom I could name — if ten *honest* men only — aye, if *one* HONEST man, in this state of Massachusetts, *ceasing to hold slaves*, were actually to withdraw from this copartnership and be locked up in the county jail therefor, it would be the abolition of slavery in America. For it matters not how small the beginning may seem to be: what is once well done is done forever. . . .

Under a government which imprisons any unjustly, the true place for a just man is also a prison. The proper place today, the only place which Massachusetts has provided for her freer and less desponding spirits, is in her prisons, to be put out and locked out of the state by her own act as they have already put themselves out by their principles. It is there that the fugitive slave, and the Mexican prisoner on parole, and the Indian come to plead the wrongs of his race should find them; on that separate but more free and honorable ground where the state places those who are not *with* her but *against* her — the only house in a slave state in which a free man can abide with honor. If any think that their influence would be lost there and their voices no longer afflict the ear of the state, that they would not be as an enemy within its walls, they do not know by how much truth is stronger than error, nor how much more eloquently and effectively he can combat injustice who has experienced a little in his own person.

Cast your whole vote, not a strip of paper merely but your whole influence. A minority is powerless while it conforms to the majority; it is not even a minority then; but it is irresistible when it clogs by its whole weight. If the alternative is to keep all just men in prison or give up war and slavery, the state will not hesitate which to choose. If a thousand men were not to pay their tax bills this year, that would not be a violent and bloody measure, as it would be to pay them and enable the state to commit violence and shed innocent blood. This is, in fact, the definition of a peaceable revolution, if any such is possible.

If the tax gatherer or any other public officer asks me, as one has done, "But what shall I do?" my answer is, "If you really wish to do anything, resign your office." When the subject has refused allegiance and the officer has resigned his office, then the revolution is accomplished. But even suppose blood should flow. Is there not a sort of blood shed when the conscience is wounded? Through this wound a man's real manhood and immortality flow out, and he bleeds to an everlasting death. I see this blood flowing now.

I have contemplated the imprisonment of the offender rather than the seizure of his goods — though both will serve the same purpose — because they who assert the purest right, and consequently are most dangerous to a corrupt state, commonly have not spent much time in accumulating property. To such the state renders comparatively small service, and a slight tax is wont to appear exorbitant, particularly if they are obliged to earn it by special labor with their hands. If there were one who lived wholly without the use of money, the state itself would hesitate to demand it of him. But the rich man — not to make any invidious comparison — is always sold to the institution which makes him rich. Absolutely speaking, the more money, the less virtue; for money comes between a man and his objects, and obtains them for him; and it was certainly no great virtue to obtain it.

It puts to rest many questions which he would otherwise be taxed to answer; while the only new question which it puts is the hard but superfluous one, how to spend it. Thus his moral ground is taken from under his feet. The opportunities of living are diminished in proportion as what are called the "means" are increased. The best thing a man can do for his culture when he is rich is to endeavor to carry out those schemes which he entertained when he was poor.

Christ answered the Herodians according to their condition. "Show me the tribute money," said he; and one took a penny out of his pocket. If you use money which has the image of Caesar on it and which he has made current and valuable, that is, *if you are men of the state* and gladly enjoy the advantages of Caesar's government, then pay him back some of his own when he demands it; "Render therefore to Caesar that which is Caesar's, and to God those things which are God's" — leaving them no wiser than before as to which was which; for they did not wish to know.

When I converse with the freest of my neighbors, I perceive that, whatever they may say about the magnitude and seriousness of the question and their regard for the public tranquillity, the long and the short of the matter is that they cannot spare the protection of the existing government, and they dread the consequences of disobedience to it to their property and families. For my own part, I should not like to think that I ever rely on the protection of the state. But, if I deny the authority of the state when it presents its tax bill, it will soon take and waste all my property, and so harass me and my children without end. This is hard. This makes it impossible for a man to live honestly and at the same time comfortably in outward respects. It will not be worth the while to accumulate property; that would be sure to go again.

You must hire or squat somewhere, and raise but a small crop, and eat that soon. You must live within yourself, and depend upon yourself, always tucked up and ready for a start, and not have many affairs. A man may grow rich in Turkey, even, if he will be in all respects a good subject of the Turkish government. Confucius said, "If a state is governed by the principles of reason, poverty and misery are subjects of shame; if a state is not governed by the principles of reason, riches and honors are the subjects of shame." No; until I want the protection of Massachusetts to be extended to me in some distant Southern port, where my liberty is endangered, or until I am bent solely on building up an estate at home by peaceful enterprise, I can afford to refuse allegiance to Massachusetts and her right to my property and life. It costs me less in every sense to incur the penalty of disobedience to the state than it would to obey. I should feel as if I were worth less in that I have paid no poll tax for six years. I was put into a jail once on this account, for one night; and, as I stood considering the walls of solid stone two or three feet thick, the door of wood and iron a foot thick, and the iron grating which strained the light, I could not help being struck with the foolishness of that institution which treated me as if I were mere flesh and blood and bones to be locked up. I wondered that it should have concluded at length that this was the best use it could put me to and had never thought to avail itself of my services in some way. I saw that if there was a wall of stone between me and my townsmen, there was a still more difficult one to climb or break through before they could get to be as free as I was. I did not for a moment feel confined, and the walls seemed a great waste of stone and mortar. I felt as if I alone of all my townsmen had paid my tax.

They plainly did not know how to treat me but behaved like persons who are underbred. In every threat and in every compliment there was a blunder; for they thought that my chief desire was to stand the other side of that stone wall. I could not but smile to see how industriously they locked the door on my meditations, which followed them out again without let or hindrance, and *they* were really all that was dangerous. As they could not reach me, they had resolved to punish my body; just as boys, if they cannot come at some person against whom they have a spite, will abuse his dog. I saw that the state was half-witted, that it was timid as a lone woman with her silver spoons, and that it did not know its friends from its foes, and I lost all my remaining respect for it, and pitied it.

Thus the state never intentionally confronts a man's sense, intellectual or moral, but only his body, his senses. It is not armed with superior wit or honesty but with superior physical strength. I was not born to be forced. I will breathe after my own fashion. Let us see who is the strongest. What force has a multitude? They only can force me who obey a higher law than I. They force me to become like themselves. I do not hear of *men* being *forced* to live this way or that by masses of men. What sort of life were that to live?

When I meet a government which says to me, "Your money or your life," why should I be in haste to give it my money? It may be in a great strait and not know what to do: I cannot help that. It must help itself; do as I do. It is not worth the while to snivel about it. I am not responsible for the successful working of the machinery of society. I am not the son of the engineer. I perceive that, when an acorn and a chestnut fall side by side, the one does not remain inert to make way for the other but both obey their own laws and spring and grow and flourish as best they can till one, perchance, overshadows and destroys the other. If a plant cannot live according to its nature, it dies; and so a man. . . .

I do not wish to quarrel with any man or nation. I do not wish to split hairs, to make fine distinctions, or set myself up as better than my neighbors. I seek, rather, I may say, even an excuse for conforming to the laws of the land. I am but too ready to conform to them. Indeed, I have reason to suspect myself on this head; and each year, as the tax gatherer comes round, I find myself disposed to review the acts and position of the general and state governments, and the spirit of the people, to discover a pretext for conformity. I believe that the state will soon be able to take all my work of this sort out of my hands, and then I shall be no better a patriot than my fellow countrymen.

Seen from a lower point of view, the Constitution, with all its faults, is very good; the law and the courts are very respectable; even this state and this American government are, in many respects, very admirable and rare things to be thankful for, such as a great many have described them; but seen from a point of view a little higher, they are what I have described them; seen from a higher still, and the highest, who shall say what they are, or that they

are worth looking at or thinking of at all? . . .

No man with a genius for legislation has appeared in America. They are rare in the history of the world. There are orators, politicians, and eloquent men by the thousand; but the speaker has not yet opened his mouth to speak who is capable of settling the much-vexed questions of the day. We love eloquence for its own sake and not for any truth which it may utter or any heroism it may inspire. Our legislators have not yet learned the comparative value of free trade and of freedom, of union, and of rectitude to a nation. They have no genius or talent for comparatively humble questions of taxation and finance, commerce and manufactures and agriculture. If we were left solely to the wordy wit of legislators in Congress for our guidance, uncorrected by the seasonable experience and the effectual complaints of the people, America would not long retain her rank among the nations. For eighteen hundred years, though perchance I have no right to say it, the New Testament has been written; yet where is the legislator who has wisdom and practical talent enough to avail himself of the light which it sheds on the science of legislation?

The authority of government, even such as I am willing to submit to — for I will cheerfully obey those who know and can do better than I, and in many things even those who neither know nor can do so well — is still an impure one; to be strictly just, it must have the sanction and consent of the governed. It can have no pure right over my person and property but what I concede to it. The progress from an absolute to a limited monarchy, from a limited monarchy to a democracy, is a progress toward a true respect for the individual. Is a democracy, such as we know it, the last improvement possible in government? Is it not possible to take a step further toward recognizing and organizing the rights of man?

There will never be a really free and enlightened state until the state comes to recognize the individual as a higher and independent power from which all its own power and authority are derived, and treats him accordingly. I please myself with imagining a state, at last, which can afford to be just to all men and to treat the individual with respect as a neighbor; which even would not think it inconsistent with its own repose if a few were to live aloof from it, not meddling with it, nor embraced by it, who fulfilled all the duties of neighbors and fellowmen. A state which bore this kind of fruit and suffered it to drop off as fast as it ripened would prepare the way for a still more perfect and glorious state, which also I have imagined, but not yet anywhere seen.

118.

CHARLES SUMNER: War and the Common Law of Nations

In a Fourth of July oration delivered in Boston in 1845, Charles Sumner asked: "Can there be in our age any peace that is not honorable, any war that is not dishonorable?" His speech earned him the applause of many in his distinguished audience, which included a number of military men, and the enthusiastic support of reformers, whose causes Sumner thereafter espoused. In an address entitled "War System of the Commonwealth of Nations," delivered to the American Peace Society on May 28, 1849, from which the following selection is taken, Sumner developed the theme of his oration of 1845. The proposals he made for a Congress of Nations and for an associated world court had been introduced in 1840 by William Ladd, the founder of the American Peace Society, and developed by Ladd's successor, George Beckwith, in his Peace Manual.

Source: *Charles Sumner: His Complete Works,* Statesman Edition, Boston, 1900, Vol. II, pp. 329-429.

RECOGNIZING the irrational and unchristian character of War as established arbiter between towns, counties, and states, we learn to condemn it as established arbiter between nations. If wrong in one case, it must be wrong in the other. . . .

Well does John Quincy Adams say that mankind have but to *will* it, and War is abolished. Will it, and War disappears like the Duel. Will it, and War skulks like the Torture. Will it, and War fades away like the fires of religious persecution. Will it, and War passes among profane follies, like the ordeal of burning plowshares. Will it, and War hurries to join the earlier institution of Cannibalism. Will it, and War is chastised from the Commonwealth of Nations, as Slavery has been chastised from municipal jurisdictions by England and France, by Tunis and Tripoli.

To arouse this *public will*, which, like a giant, yet sleeps, but whose awakened voice nothing can withstand, should be our endeavor. The true character of the War System must be exposed. To be hated, it needs only to be comprehended; and it will surely be abolished as soon as this is accomplished. See, then, that it is comprehended. Exhibit its manifold atrocities. Strip away all its presumptuous pretenses, its specious apologies, its hideous sorceries. Above all, men must no longer deceive themselves by the shallow thought that this System is the necessary incident of imperfect human nature and thus cast upon God the responsibility for their crimes. They must see clearly that it is a monster of their own creation, born with their consent, whose vital spark is fed by their breath and without their breath must necessarily die. They must see distinctly . . . that War, under the Law of Nations, is nothing but an Institution and the whole War System nothing but an Establishment for the administration of *international justice*, for which the Commonwealth of Nations is directly responsible and which that Commonwealth can at any time remove.

Recognizing these things, men must cease to cherish War, and will renounce all appeal to its Arbitrament. They will forgo rights rather than wage an irreligious battle. But, criminal and irrational as is War, unhappily, in the present state of human error, we cannot expect large numbers to appreciate its true character and to hate it with that perfect hatred making them renounce its agency, unless we offer an approved and practical mode of determining international controversies as a *substitute* for the imagined necessity of the barbarous ordeal. This we are able to do; and so doing, we reflect new light upon the atrocity of a system which not only tramples upon all the precepts of the Christian faith, but defies justice and discards reason.

1. The most complete and permanent substitute would be a Congress of Nations with a High Court of Judicature. Such a system, while admitted on all sides to promise excellent results, is opposed on two grounds.

First, because, as regards the smaller states, it would be a tremendous engine of oppression, subversive of their political independence. Surely, it could not be so oppressive as the War System. But the experience of the smaller states in the German Confederation and in the American Union, nay, the experience of Belgium and Holland by the side of the overtopping power of France and the experience of Denmark and Sweden in the very nightshade of Russia, all show the futility of this objection.

Second, because the decrees of such a court could not be carried into effect. Even if they were enforced by the combined power of the associate nations, the sword, as the executive arm of the high tribunal, would be only the melancholy instrument of Justice, not the Arbiter of Justice, and therefore not condemned by the conclusive reasons against international appeals to the sword.

From the experience of history, and particularly from the experience of the thirty states of our Union, we learn that the occasion for any executive arm will be rare. The state of Rhode Island, in its recent controversy with Massachusetts, submitted with much indifference to the adverse decree of the Supreme Court; and I doubt not that Missouri and Iowa will submit with equal contentment to any determination of their present controversy by the same tribunal. The same submission would attend the decrees of any Court of Judicature established by the Commonwealth of Nations. There is a growing sense of justice, combined with a growing might of public opinion, too little known to the soldier, that would maintain the judgments of the august tribunal assembled in the face of the Nations, better than the swords of all the marshals of France, better than the bloody terrors of Austerlitz or Waterloo.

The idea of a Congress of Nations with a High Court of Judicature is as practicable as its consummation is confessedly dear to the friends of Universal Peace. Whenever this Congress is convened, as surely it will be, I know not all the names that will deserve commemoration in its earliest proceedings; but there are two, whose particular and long-continued advocacy of this Institution will connect them indissolubly with its fame — the Abbé Saint-Pierre of France, and William Ladd of the United States.

2. There is still another substitute for War which is not exposed even to the shallow objections launched against a Congress of Nations. By formal treaties between two or more nations, Arbitration may be established as the mode of determining controversies between them. In every respect this is a contrast to War. It is rational, humane, and cheap. Above all, it is consistent with the teachings of Christianity. As I mention this substitute, I should do injustice to the cause and to my own feelings if I did not express our obligations to its efficient proposer and advocate, our fellow citizen and the President of this Society, the honored son of an illustrious father, whose absence tonight enables me, without offending his known modesty, to introduce this tribute: I mean William Jay.

The complete overthrow of the War System, involving the disarming of the Nations, would follow the establishment of a Congress of Nations or any general system of Arbitration. Then at last our aims would be accomplished; then at last Peace would be organized among the Nations. Then might Christians repeat the fitful boast of the generous Mohawk: "We have thrown the hatchet so high into the air and beyond the skies that no arm on earth can reach to bring it down." Incalculable sums, now devoted to armaments and the destructive industry of War, would be turned to the productive industry of Art and to offices of Beneficence. As in the dead and rotten carcass of the lion which roared against the strong man of Israel, after a time, were a swarm of bees and honey, so would the enormous carcass of War, dead and rotten, be filled with crowds of useful laborers and all good works, and the riddle of Samson be once more interpreted: "Out of the eater came forth meat, and out of the strong came forth sweetness."

Put together the products of all the mines in the world — the glistening ore of California, the accumulated treasures of Mexico and Peru, with the diamonds of Golconda — and the whole shining heap will be less than the means thus diverted from War to Peace. Under the influence of such a change, civilization will be quickened anew. Then will happy Labor find its reward, and the whole land be filled with its increase. There is no aspiration of Knowledge, no vision of Charity, no venture of Enterprise, no fancy of Art, which may not then be fulfilled. The great unsolved problem of Pauperism will be solved at last. There will be no paupers, when there are no soldiers.

The social struggles, so fearfully disturbing European nations, will die away in the happiness of unarmed Peace, no longer encumbered by the oppressive system of War; nor can there be well-founded hope that these struggles will permanently cease, so long as this system endures. The people ought not to rest, they cannot rest, while this system endures. As King Arthur, prostrate on the earth, with bloody streams pouring from his veins, could not be at ease until his sword, the terrific Excalibur, was thrown into the flood, so the Nations, now prostrate on the earth, with bloody streams pouring from their veins, cannot be at ease until they fling far away the wicked sword of War. King Arthur said to his attending knight, "As thou love me, spare not to throw it in"; and this is the voice of the Nations also.

Lop off the unchristian armaments of the Christian Nations, extirpate these martial cancers, that they may feed no longer upon the lifeblood of the people; and society itself, now weary and sick, will become fresh and young — not by opening its veins, as under the incantation of Medea, in the wild hope of infusing new strength, but by the amputation and complete removal of a deadly excrescence, with all its unutterable debility and exhaustion. Energies hitherto withdrawn from proper healthful action will then replenish it with unwonted life and vigor, giving new expansion to every human capacity and new elevation to every human aim. And society at last shall rejoice, like a strong man, to run its race.

Imagination toils to picture the boundless good that will be achieved. As War with its deeds is infinitely evil and accursed, so will this triumph of Permanent Peace be infinitely beneficent and blessed. Something of its consequences were seen, in prophetic vision, even by that incarnate Spirit of War, Napoleon Bonaparte, when, from his island prison of St. Helena, looking back upon his mistaken career, he was led to confess the True Grandeur of Peace. Out of his mouth let its praise be spoken. "I had the project," he said, mournfully regretting the opportunity he had lost, "at the general peace of Amiens, of bringing each Power to an immense reduction of its standing armies. I wished a European Institute, with European prizes, to direct, associate, and bring together all the learned societies of Europe. Then, perhaps, through the universal spread of light, it might be permitted to anticipate for the great European Family the establishment of an American Congress or an Amphictyonic Council; and what a perspective then of strength, of greatness, of happiness, of prosperity! What a sublime and magnificent spectacle!''

Such is our cause. In transcendent influence, it embraces human beneficence in all its forms. It is the comprehensive charity, enfolding all the charities of all; none so vast as to be above its protection, none so lowly as not to feel its care. Religion, Knowledge, Freedom, Virtue, Happiness, in all their manifold forms, depend upon Peace. Sustained by Peace, they lean upon the Everlasting Arm. And this is not all. Law, Order, Government derive from Peace new sanctions. Nor can they attain to that complete dominion which is our truest safeguard, until, by the overthrow of the War System, they comprehend the Commonwealth of Nations —

And Sovereign Law, *the* WORLD's *collected*
will,
O'er thrones and globes elate,
Sits empress, crowning good, repressing ill.

119.

John C. Calhoun: Constitutional Government

A Disquisition on Government, from which the following selection is taken, was John C. Calhoun's most carefully reasoned statement of the principles that guided him throughout much of his political career. In it he dealt with the great problem that occupied him almost exclusively in his later years, the protection of minorities from majority rule; and in it, too, he proposed the solution that is his most enduring contribution to political thought. The minority that Calhoun represented was the slaveholding South, and his mission, as he saw it, was to discover a way for the South to remain honorably in the Union. The solution was the famous theory of "the concurrent majority." The Disquisition was begun in 1842, completed in 1849, and published, posthumously, in 1851.

Source: *A Disquisition on Government*, Richard K. Cralle, ed., New York, 1854, pp. 1-61.

IN ORDER TO HAVE a clear and just conception of the nature and object of government, it is indispensable to understand correctly what that constitution or law of our nature is, in which government originates; or, to express it more fully and accurately, that law, without which government would not and with which it must necessarily exist. Without this, it is as impossible to lay any solid foundation for the science of government, as it would be to lay one for that of astronomy, without a like understanding of that constitution or law of the material world, according to which the several bodies composing the solar system mutually act on each other, and by which they are kept in their respective spheres.

The first question, accordingly, to be considered is — What is that constitution or law of our nature, without which government would not exist and with which its existence is necessary?

In considering this, I assume, as an incontestable fact, that man is so constituted as to be a social being. His inclinations and wants, physical and moral, irresistibly impel him to associate with his kind; and he has,

accordingly, never been found, in any age or country, in any state other than the social. In no other, indeed, could he exist; and in no other, were it possible for him to exist, could he attain to a full development of his moral and intellectual faculties or raise himself, in the scale of being, much above the level of the brute creation.

I next assume, also, as a fact not less incontestable, that, while man is so constituted as to make the social state necessary to his existence and the full development of his faculties, this state itself cannot exist without government. The assumption rests on universal experience. In no age or country has any society or community ever been found, whether enlightened or savage, without government of some description.

Having assumed these as unquestionable phenomena of our nature, I shall, without further remark, proceed to the investigation of the primary and important question — What is that constitution of our nature which, while it impels man to associate with his kind, renders it impossible for society to exist without government?

The answer will be found in the fact (not

less incontestable than either of the others) that, while man is created for the social state and is accordingly so formed as to feel what affects others as well as what affects himself, he is, at the same time, so constituted as to feel more intensely what affects him directly than what affects him indirectly through others; or, to express it differently, he is so constituted that his direct or individual affections are stronger than his sympathetic or social feelings. I intentionally avoid the expression, *selfish* feelings, as applicable to the former; because, as commonly used, it implies an unusual excess of the individual over the social feelings in the person to whom it is applied; and, consequently, something depraved and vicious. My object is to exclude such inference and to restrict the inquiry exclusively to facts in their bearings on the subject under consideration, viewed as mere phenomena appertaining to our nature, constituted as it is; and which are as unquestionable as is that of gravitation or any other phenomenon of the material world.

In asserting that our individual are stronger than our social feelings, it is not intended to deny that there are instances, growing out of peculiar relations — as that of a mother and her infant — or resulting from the force of education and habit over peculiar constitutions, in which the latter have overpowered the former; but these instances are few and always regarded as something extraordinary. The deep impression they make, whenever they occur, is the strongest proof that they are regarded as exceptions to some general and well understood law of our nature; just as some of the minor powers of the material world are apparently to gravitation.

I might go further and assert this to be a phenomenon, not of our nature only but of all animated existence, throughout its entire range, so far as our knowledge extends. It would, indeed, seem to be essentially connected with the great law of self-preservation which pervades all that feels, from man down to the lowest and most insignificant reptile or insect. In none is it stronger than in man. His social feelings may, indeed, in a state of safety and abundance, combined with high intellectual and moral culture, acquire great expansion and force; but not so great as to overpower this all-pervading and essential law of animated existence.

But that constitution of our nature which makes us feel more intensely what affects us directly than what affects us indirectly through others, necessarily leads to conflict between individuals. Each, in consequence, has a greater regard for his own safety or happiness than for the safety or happiness of others; and, where these come in opposition, is ready to sacrifice the interests of others to his own. And hence, the tendency to a universal state of conflict between individual and individual; accompanied by the connected passions of suspicion, jealousy, anger and revenge; followed by insolence, fraud and cruelty; and, if not prevented by some controlling power, ending in a state of universal discord and confusion, destructive of the social state and the ends for which it is ordained. This controlling power, wherever vested, or by whomsoever exercised, is GOVERNMENT.

It follows, then, that man is so constituted, that government is necessary to the existence of society, and society to his existence and the perfection of his faculties. It follows, also, that government has its origin in this twofold constitution of his nature; the sympathetic or social feelings constituting the remote, and the individual or direct, the proximate cause.

If man had been differently constituted in either particular — if, instead of being social in his nature, he had been created without sympathy for his kind and independent of others for his safety and existence; or if, on the other hand, he had been so created as to feel more intensely what affected others than what affected himself (if that were possible), or, even, had this supposed interest been equal — it is manifest that, in either case, there would have been no necessity for government, and that none would ever have existed. But, although society and government are thus intimately connected with and dependent on each other, of the two, society is the greater. It is the first in the order of things and in the dignity of its object, that of society being primary, to preserve and perfect our race; and that of government secondary and subordinate, to preserve and perfect society. Both are, however, necessary to the existence and well-being of our race, and equally of divine ordination.

I have said if it were possible for man to be so constituted as to feel what affects others more strongly than what affects himself, or even as strongly, because, it may be well doubted, whether the stronger feeling or affection of individuals for themselves, combined with a feebler and subordinate feeling or affection for others, is not, in beings of limited reason and faculties, a constitution necessary to their preservation and existence. If reversed — if their feelings and affections were stronger for others than for themselves, or even as strong — the necessary result would seem to be that all individuality would be lost, and boundless and remediless disorder and confusion would ensue.

For each, at the same moment, intensely participating in all the conflicting emotions of those around him, would, of course, forget himself and all that concerned him immediately in his officious intermeddling with the affairs of all others; which, from his limited reason and faculties, he could neither properly understand nor manage. Such a state of things would, as far as we can see, lead to endless disorder and confusion, not less destructive to our race than a state of anarchy.

It would, besides, be remediless, for government would be impossible; or, if it could by possibility exist, its object would be reversed. Selfishness would have to be en-

couraged, and benevolence discouraged. Individuals would have to be encouraged, by rewards, to become more selfish and deterred, by punishments, from being too benevolent; and this, too, by a government administered by those who, on the supposition, would have the greatest aversion for selfishness and the highest admiration for benevolence.

To the Infinite Being, the Creator of all, belongs exclusively the care and superintendence of the whole. He, in His infinite wisdom and goodness, has allotted to every class of animated beings its condition and appropriate functions and has endowed each with feelings, instincts, capacities, and faculties, best adapted to its allotted condition. To man, He has assigned the social and political state as best adapted to develop the great capacities and faculties, intellectual and moral, with which He has endowed him; and has, accordingly, constituted him so as not only to impel him into the social state but to make government necessary for his preservation and well-being.

But government, although intended to protect and preserve society, has itself a strong tendency to disorder and abuse of its powers as all experience and almost every page of history testify. The cause is to be found in the same constitution of our nature which makes government indispensable. The powers which it is necessary for government to possess, in order to repress violence and preserve order, cannot execute themselves.

They must be administered by men in whom, like others, the individual are stronger than the social feelings. And hence, the powers vested in them to prevent injustice and oppression on the part of others will, if left unguarded, be by them converted into instruments to oppress the rest of the community. That, by which this is prevented, by whatever name called, is what is meant by *constitution,* in its most comprehensive sense, when applied to *government.*

Having its origin in the same principle of our nature, *constitution* stands to *government* as *government* stands to *society;* and, as the end for which society is ordained, would be defeated without government, so that for which government is ordained would, in a great measure, be defeated without constitution. But they differ in this striking particular. There is no difficulty in forming government. It is not even a matter of choice whether there shall be one or not. Like breathing, it is not permitted to depend on our volition. Necessity will force it on all communities in some one form or another.

Very different is the case as to constitution. Instead of a matter of necessity, it is one of the most difficult tasks imposed on man to form a constitution worthy of the name; while, to form a perfect one — one that would completely counteract the tendency of government to oppression and abuse and hold it strictly to the great ends for which it is ordained — has thus far exceeded human wisdom, and possibly ever will. From this, another striking difference results. Constitution is the contrivance of man, while government is of divine ordination. Man is left to perfect what the wisdom of the Infinite ordained as necessary to preserve the race. . . .

How government, then, must be constructed in order to counteract, through its organism, this tendency on the part of those who make and execute the laws to oppress those subject to their operation is the next question which claims attention.

There is but one way in which this can possibly be done, and that is, by such an organism as will furnish the ruled with the means of resisting successfully this tendency on the part of the rulers to oppression and abuse. Power can only be resisted by power, and tendency by tendency. Those who exercise power and those subject to its exercise — the rulers and the ruled — stand in antagonistic relations to each other. The same constitution of our nature which leads rulers to oppress the ruled, regardless of the object for which government is ordained, will, with equal strength, lead the ruled to resist when possessed of the means of making peaceable and effective resistance.

Such an organism, then, as will furnish the means by which resistance may be systematically and peaceably made on the part of the ruled to oppression and abuse of power on the part of the rulers, is the first and indispensable step toward forming a constitutional government. And as this can only be effected by or through the right of suffrage (the right on the part of the ruled to choose their rulers at proper intervals and to hold them thereby responsible for their conduct), the responsibility of the rulers to the ruled, through the right of suffrage, is the indispensable and primary principle in the foundation of a constitutional government.

When this right is properly guarded, and the people sufficiently enlightened to understand their own rights and the interests of the community and duly to appreciate the motives and conduct of those appointed to make and execute the laws, it is all-sufficient to give to those who elect effective control over those they have elected.

I call the right of suffrage the indispensable and primary principle; for it would be a great and dangerous mistake to suppose, as many do, that it is, of itself, sufficient to form constitutional governments. . . . The right of suffrage, of itself, can do no more than give complete control to those who elect over the conduct of those they have elected. In doing this, it accomplishes all it possibly can accomplish.

This is its aim, and when this is attained, its end is fulfilled. It can do no more, however enlightened the people or however widely extended or well guarded the right may be. The sum total, then, of its effects, when most successful, is to make those elected the true and faithful representatives of those who elected them, instead of irresponsible rulers — as they would be without it; and thus, by converting it into an agency and the rulers into agents, to divest government of all claims to sovereignty, and to retain it unimpaired to the community. . . .

If the whole community had the same interests — so that the interests of each and every portion would be so affected by the action of the government, that the laws which oppressed or impoverished one portion would necessarily oppress and impoverish all others, or the reverse — then the right of suffrage, of itself, would be all-sufficient to counteract the tendency of the government to oppression and abuse of its powers; and, of course, would form, of itself, a perfect constitutional government. The interest of all being the same, by supposition, as far as the action of the government was concerned, all would have like interests as to what laws should be made and how they should be executed. All strife and struggle would cease as to who should be elected to make and execute them. . . .

But such is not the case. . . . So deeply seated, indeed, is this tendency to conflict between the different interests or portions of the community that it would result from the action of the government itself, even though it were possible to find a community where the people were all of the same pursuits, placed in the same condition of life, and in every respect so situated as to be without inequality of condition or diversity of interests. The advantages of possessing the control of the powers of the government and, thereby, of its honors and emoluments are, of themselves, exclusive of all other considerations, ample to divide even such a community into two great hostile parties. . . .

As, then, the right of suffrage, without some other provision, cannot counteract this tendency of government, the next question for consideration is — What is that other provision? This demands the most serious consideration; for of all the questions embraced in the science of government, it involves a principle, the most important and the least understood; and when understood, the most difficult of application in practice. It is, indeed, emphatically, that principle which *makes* the constitution, in its strict and limited sense.

From what has been said, it is manifest, that this provision must be of a character calculated to prevent any one interest, or combination of interests, from using the powers of government to aggrandize itself at the expense of the others. Here lies the evil; and just in proportion as it shall prevent, or fail to prevent it, in the same degree it will effect, or fail to effect the end intended to be accomplished.

There is but one certain mode in which this result can be secured; and that is by the adoption of some restriction or limitation, which shall so effectually prevent any one interest, or combination of interests, from obtaining the exclusive control of the government as to render hopeless all attempts directed to that end. There is, again, but one mode in which this can be effected; and that is by taking the sense of each interest or portion of the community, which may be unequally and injuriously affected by the action of the government, separately, through its own majority, or in some other way by which its voice may be fairly expressed; and to require the consent of each interest, either to put or to keep the government in action.

This too can be accomplished only in one way, and that is by such an organism of the government, and, if necessary for the purpose, of the community also, as will, by dividing and distributing the power of government, give to each division or interest, through its appropriate organ, either a concurrent voice in making and executing the laws or a veto on their execution. It is only by such an organism that the assent of each can be made necessary to put the government in motion, or the power made effectual to arrest its action when put in motion;

and it is only by one or the other that the different interests, orders, classes, or portions, into which the community may be divided can be protected, and all conflict and struggle between them prevented, by rendering it impossible to put or to keep it in action without the concurrent consent of all.

Such an organism as this, combined with the right of suffrage, constitutes, in fact, the elements of constitutional government. The one, by rendering those who make and execute the laws responsible to those on whom they operate, prevents the rulers from oppressing the ruled; and the other, by making it impossible for any one interest or combination of interests or class or order or portion of the community to obtain exclusive control, prevents any one of them from oppressing the other. . . .

In coming to this conclusion, I have assumed the organism to be perfect and the different interests, portions, or classes of the community to be sufficiently enlightened to understand its character and object and to exercise, with due intelligence, the right of suffrage. To the extent that either may be defective, to the same extent the government would fall short of fulfilling its end. But this does not impeach the truth of the principles on which it rests. . . .

It results, from what has been said, that there are two different modes in which the sense of the community may be taken; one, simply by the right of suffrage, unaided; the other, by the right through a proper organism. Each collects the sense of the majority. But one regards numbers only and considers the whole community as a unit, having but one common interest throughout, and collects the sense of the greater number of the whole as that of the community. The other, on the contrary, regards interests as well as numbers, considering the community as made up of different and conflicting interests, as far as the action of the government is concerned, and takes the sense of each, through its majority or appropriate or-

gan, and the united sense of all as the sense of the entire community.

The former of these I shall call the numerical, or absolute majority; and the latter, the concurrent, or constitutional majority. I call it the constitutional majority, because it is an essential element in every constitutional government, be its form what it may. So great is the difference, politically speaking, between the two majorities that they cannot be confounded without leading to great and fatal errors; and yet the distinction between them has been so entirely overlooked that when the term *majority* is used in political discussions it is applied exclusively to designate the numerical, as if there were no other. Until this distinction is recognized, and better understood, there will continue to be great liability to error in properly constructing constitutional governments, especially of the popular form, and of preserving them when properly constructed. . . .

The first and leading error which naturally arises from overlooking the distinction referred to is to confound the numerical majority with the people, and this so completely as to regard them as identical. This is a consequence that necessarily results from considering the numerical as the only majority. . . .

This radical error, the consequence of confounding the two and of regarding the numerical as the only majority, has contributed more than any other cause to prevent the formation of popular constitutional governments and to destroy them even when they have been formed. It leads to the conclusion that, in their formation and establishment, nothing more is necessary than the right of suffrage and the allotment to each division of the community a representation in the government, in proportion to numbers.

If the numerical majority were really the people and if to take its sense truly were to take the sense of the people truly, a government so constituted would be a true and perfect model of a popular constitutional government; and every departure from it would detract from its excellence. But, as such is not the case, as the numerical majority, instead of being the people, is only a portion of them, such a government, instead of being a true and perfect model of the people's government, that is, a people self-governed, is but the government of a part, over a part — the major over the minor portion.

But this misconception of the true elements of constitutional government does not stop here. It leads to others equally false and fatal in reference to the best means of preserving and perpetuating them, when, from some fortunate combination of circumstances, they are correctly formed. For they who fall into these errors regard the restrictions which organism imposes on the will of the numerical majority as restrictions on the will of the people and, therefore, as not only useless but wrongful and mischievous. And hence they endeavor to destroy organism under the delusive hope of making government more democratic.

Such are some of the consequences of confounding the two and of regarding the numerical as the only majority. And in this may be found the reason why so few popular governments have been properly constructed and why, of these few, so small a number have proved durable. Such must continue to be the result, so long as these errors continue to be prevalent.

There is another error, of a kindred character, whose influence contributes much to the same results: I refer to the prevalent opinion that a written constitution, containing suitable restrictions on the powers of government, is sufficient, of itself, without the aid of any organism, except such as is necessary to separate its several departments and render them independent of each other, to counteract the tendency of the numerical majority to oppression and the abuse of power. . . .

Nor would the division of government into separate and, as it regards each other, independent departments prevent this result. Such a division may do much to facilitate its operations and to secure to its administration greater caution and deliberation, but as each and all the departments, and, of course, the entire government, would be under the control of the numerical majority, it is too clear to require explanation that a mere distribution of its powers among its agents or representatives could do little or nothing to counteract its tendency to oppression and abuse of power. To effect this, it would be necessary to go one step further and make the several departments the organs of the distinct interests or portions of the community, and to clothe each with a negative on the others. But the effect of this would be to change the government from the numerical into the concurrent majority. . . .

The necessary consequence of taking the sense of the community by the concurrent majority is . . . to give to each interest or portion of the community a negative on the others. It is this mutual negative among its various conflicting interests which invests each with the power of protecting itself and places the rights and safety of each where only they can be securely placed, under its own guardianship. Without this there can be no systematic, peaceful, or effective resistance to the natural tendency of each to come into conflict with the others; and without this there can be no constitution. It is this negative power — the power of preventing or arresting the action of the government, be it called by what term it may, veto, interposition, nullification, check, or balance of power — which, in fact, forms the constitution. They are all but different names for the negative power. In all its forms, and under all its names, it results from the concurrent majority. . . .

But, as there can be no constitution without the negative power, and no negative power without the concurrent majority, it follows, necessarily, that where the numerical majority has the sole control of the government, there can be no constitution, as constitution implies limitation or restriction and, of course, is inconsistent with the idea of sole or exclusive power. And hence, the numerical, unmixed with the concurrent majority, necessarily forms, in all cases, absolute government. . . .

All constitutional governments, of whatever class they may be, take the sense of the community by its parts, each through its appropriate organ, and regard the sense of all its parts as the sense of the whole. They all rest on the right of suffrage and the responsibility of rulers, directly or indirectly. On the contrary, all absolute governments, of whatever form, concentrate power in one uncontrolled and irresponsible individual or body, whose will is regarded as the sense of the community. And, hence, the great and broad distinction between governments is not that of the one, the few, or the many but of the constitutional and the absolute.

From this there results another distinction which, although secondary in its character, very strongly marks the difference between these forms of government. I refer to their respective conservative principle; that is, the principle by which they are upheld and preserved. This principle, in constitutional governments, is *compromise*, and in absolute governments, is *force*. . . .

A broader position may, indeed, be taken; viz., that there is a tendency, in constitutional governments of every form, to degenerate into their respective absolute forms; and, in all absolute governments, into that of the monarchical form. But the tendency is much stronger in constitutional governments of the democratic form to degenerate into their respective absolute forms, than in either of the others; because, among other reasons, the distinction between the constitutional and absolute forms of aristocratical and monarchical governments is far more strongly marked than in

democratic governments. The effect of this is, to make the different orders or classes in an aristocracy, or monarchy, far more jealous and watchful of encroachment on their respective rights; and more resolute and persevering in resisting attempts to concentrate power in any one class or order.

On the contrary, the line between the two forms, in popular governments, is so imperfectly understood that honest and sincere friends of the constitutional form not infrequently, instead of jealously watching and arresting their tendency to degenerate into their absolute forms, not only regard it with approbation but employ all their powers to add to its strength and to increase its impetus in the vain hope of making the government more perfect and popular. The numerical majority, perhaps, should usually be one of the elements of a constitutional democracy; but to make it the sole element, in order to perfect the constitution and make the government more popular, is one of the greatest and most fatal of political errors.

Among the other advantages which governments of the concurrent have over those of the numerical majority, and which strongly illustrates their more popular character, is that they admit, with safety, a much greater extension of the right of suffrage. It may be safely extended in such governments to universal suffrage: that is, to every male citizen of mature age, with few ordinary exceptions; but it cannot be so far extended in those of the numerical majority, without placing them ultimately under the control of the more ignorant and dependent portions of the community.

For, as the community becomes populous, wealthy, refined, and highly civilized, the difference between the rich and the poor will become more strongly marked; and the number of the ignorant and dependent greater in proportion to the rest of the community. With the increase of this difference, the tendency to conflict between them will become stronger; and, as the poor and dependent become more numerous in proportion, there will be, in governments of the numerical majority, no want of leaders among the wealthy and ambitious to excite and direct them in their efforts to obtain the control.

The case is different in governments of the concurrent majority. There, mere numbers have not the absolute control; and the wealthy and intelligent, being identified in interest with the poor and ignorant of their respective portions or interests of the community, become their leaders and protectors. And hence, as the latter would have neither hope nor inducement to rally the former in order to obtain the control, the right of suffrage, under such a government, may be safely enlarged to the extent stated without incurring the hazard to which such enlargement would expose governments of the numerical majority. . . .

The concurrent majority, on the other hand, tends to unite the most opposite and conflicting interests, and to blend the whole in one common attachment to the country. By giving to each interest, or portion, the power of self-protection, all strife and struggle between them for ascendency is prevented; and, thereby, not only every feeling calculated to weaken the attachment to the whole is suppressed but the individual and the social feelings are made to unite in one common devotion to country.

Each sees and feels that it can best promote its own prosperity by conciliating the goodwill and promoting the prosperity of the others. And hence, there will be diffused throughout the whole community kind feelings between its different portions and, instead of antipathy, a rivalry amongst them to promote the interests of each other, as far as this can be done consistently with the interest of all.

Under the combined influence of these causes, the interests of each would be merged in the common interests of the whole; and thus, the community would be-

come a unit, by becoming the common center of attachment of all its parts. And hence, instead of faction, strife, and struggle for party ascendency, there would be patriotism, nationality, harmony, and a struggle only for supremacy in promoting the common good of the whole. . . .

To perfect society, it is necessary to develop the faculties, intellectual and moral, with which man is endowed. But the mainspring to their development, and, through this, to progress, improvement and civilization, with all their blessings, is the desire of individuals to better their condition. For this purpose, liberty and security are indispensable. Liberty leaves each free to pursue the course he may deem best to promote his interest and happiness, as far as it may be compatible with the primary end for which government is ordained; while security gives assurance to each, that he shall not be deprived of the fruits of his exertions to better his condition.

These, combined, give to this desire the strongest impulse of which it is susceptible. For, to extend liberty beyond the limits assigned would be to weaken the government and to render it incompetent to fulfill its primary end — the protection of society against dangers, internal and external. The effect of this would be insecurity, and, of insecurity, to weaken the impulse of individuals to better their condition and, thereby, retard progress and improvement. On the other hand, to extend the powers of the government, so as to contract the sphere assigned to liberty, would have the same effect by disabling individuals in their efforts to better their condition.

Herein is to be found the principle which assigns to power and liberty their proper spheres and reconciles each to the other under all circumstances. For, if power be necessary to secure to liberty the fruits of its exertions, liberty, in turn, repays power with interest by increased population, wealth, and other advantages, which progress and improvement bestow on the community. By thus assigning to each its appropriate sphere, all conflicts between them cease; and each is made to cooperate with and assist the other in fulfilling the great ends for which government is ordained. . . .

To allow to liberty . . . a sphere of action more extended than this assigns, would lead to anarchy; and this, probably, in the end, to a contraction instead of an enlargement of its sphere. Liberty, then, when forced on a people unfit for it, would, instead of a blessing, be a curse; as it would, in its reaction, lead directly to anarchy — the greatest of all curses. No people, indeed, can long enjoy more liberty than that to which their situation and advanced intelligence and morals fairly entitle them.

If more than this be allowed, they must soon fall into confusion and disorder, to be followed, if not by anarchy and despotism, by a change to a form of government more simple and absolute; and, therefore, better suited to their condition. And hence, although it may be true that a people may not have as much liberty as they are fairly entitled to and are capable of enjoying, yet the reverse is unquestionably true, that no people can long possess more than they are fairly entitled to.

Liberty, indeed, though among the greatest of blessings, is not so great as that of protection; inasmuch, as the end of the former is the progress and improvement of the race, while that of the latter is its preservation and perpetuation. And hence, when the two come into conflict, liberty must and ever ought to yield to protection; as the existence of the race is of greater moment than its improvement. . . .

There is another error, not less great and dangerous, usually associated with the one which has just been considered. I refer to the opinion that liberty and equality are so intimately united, that liberty cannot be perfect without perfect equality. That they are united to a certain extent and that equality of citizens in the eyes of the law is essential to liberty in a popular government is conceded. But to go further and make equality of *condition* essential to liberty would be to destroy both liberty and progress.

The reason is that inequality of condition, while it is a necessary consequence of liberty, is, at the same time, indispensable to progress. In order to understand why this is so, it is necessary to bear in mind that the mainspring to progress is the desire of individuals to better their condition; and that the strongest impulse which can be given to it is to leave individuals free to exert themselves in the manner they may deem best for that purpose, as far at least as it can be done consistently with the ends for which government is ordained, and to secure to all the fruits of their exertions.

Now, as individuals differ greatly from each other, in intelligence, sagacity, energy, perseverance, skill, habits of industry and economy, physical power, position and opportunity, the necessary effect of leaving all free to exert themselves to better their condition, must be a corresponding inequality between those who may possess these qualities and advantages in a high degree and those who may be deficient in them. The only means by which this result can be prevented are, either to impose such restrictions on the exertions of those who may possess them in a high degree, as will place them on a level with those who do not; or to deprive them of the fruits of their exertions.

But to impose such restrictions on them would be destructive of liberty, while to deprive them of the fruits of their exertions would be to destroy the desire of bettering their condition. It is, indeed, this inequality of condition between the front and rear ranks, in the march of progress, which gives so strong an impulse to the former to maintain their position and to the latter to press forward into their files. This gives to progress its greatest impulse. To force the front rank back to the rear, or attempt to push forward the rear into line with the front, by the interposition of the government, would put an end to the impulse and effectually arrest the march of progress.

These great and dangerous errors have their origin in the prevalent opinion that all men are born free and equal, than which nothing can be more unfounded and false. It rests upon the assumption of a fact, which is contrary to universal observation, in whatever light it may be regarded. It is, indeed, difficult to explain how an opinion so destitute of all sound reason ever could have been so extensively entertained, unless we regard it as being confounded with another, which has some semblance of truth; but which, when properly understood, is not less false and dangerous.

I refer to the assertion that all men are equal in the state of nature; meaning, by a state of nature, a state of individuality, supposed to have existed prior to the social and political state; and in which men lived apart and independent of each other. If such a state ever did exist, all men would have been, indeed, free and equal in it; that is, free to do as they pleased and exempt from the authority or control of others as, by supposition, it existed anterior to society and government. But such a state is purely hypothetical. It never did, nor can, exist; as it is inconsistent with the preservation and perpetuation of the race. It is, therefore, a great misnomer to call it the state of nature. . . .

It follows, from all that has been said, that the more perfectly a government combines power and liberty — that is, the greater its power and the more enlarged and secure the liberty of individuals, the more perfectly it fulfills the ends for which government is ordained. . . .

The concurrent majority, then, is better suited to enlarge and secure the bounds of liberty, because it is better suited to prevent government from passing beyond its proper limits and to restrict it to its primary end, the protection of the community. But in doing this it leaves, necessarily, all beyond it open and free to individual exertions; and thus enlarges and secures the sphere of liberty to the greatest extent which the condition of the community will admit. . . .

The tendency of government to pass beyond its proper limits is what exposes liberty to danger and renders it insecure; and it is the strong counteraction of governments of the concurrent majority to this tendency which makes them so favorable to liberty. On the contrary, those of the numerical, instead of opposing and counteracting this tendency, add to it increased strength, in consequence of the violent party struggles incident to them, as has been fully explained; and hence their encroachments on liberty and the danger to which it is exposed under such governments.

So great, indeed, is the difference between the two in this respect that liberty is little more than a name under all governments of the absolute form, including that of the numerical majority; and can only have a secure and durable existence under those of the concurrent or constitutional form. The latter, by giving to each portion of the community which may be unequally affected by its action, a negative on the others, prevents all partial or local legislation and restricts its action to such measures as are designed for the protection and the good of the whole. In doing this it secures, at the same time, the rights and liberty of the people regarded individually; as each portion consists of those who, whatever may be the diversity of interests among themselves, have the same interest in reference to the action of the government.

120.

Henry Wadsworth Longfellow: "The Republic"

"The Building of the Ship," of which these lines are the conclusion, first appeared in The Seaside and the Fireside, *an otherwise undistinguished volume that Longfellow published in 1849. But this poem became immediately famous and has remained one of the best known of Longfellow's productions. It was read before the Mercantile Library Association on February 12, 1850, by Mrs. Frances Kemble, the great English actress, and "the vast multitude," a nineteenth-century editor informs us, "was stirred to its depths not so much by the artistic completeness of the rendition, as by the impassioned burst with which the poem closes, and which fell upon no listless ears in the deep agitation of the year 1850." The fate of the Union was being decided in the great congressional debate on the Compromise of 1850, and Longfellow's lines doubtless expressed the feelings of most of his Northern readers.*

Source: *Complete Poetical Works*, Cambridge Edition, Boston, 1893.

THE REPUBLIC

Thou, too, sail on, O Ship of State!
Sail on, O Union, strong and great!
Humanity with all its fears,
With all the hopes of future years,
Is hanging breathless on thy fate!
We know what Master laid thy keel,
What Workmen wrought thy ribs of steel,
Who made each mast, and sail, and rope,
What anvils rang, what hammers beat,
In what a forge and what a heat
Were shaped the anchors of thy hope!
Fear not each sudden sound and shock,
'Tis of the wave and not the rock;
'Tis but the flapping of the sail,
And not a rent made by the gale!
In spite of rock and tempest's roar,
In spite of false lights on the shore,
Sail on, nor fear to breast the sea!
Our hearts, our hopes, are all with thee,
Our hearts, our hopes, our prayers, our tears,
Our faith triumphant o'er our fears,
Are all with thee — are all with thee!

Index of Authors

representative from Massachusetts (1831-34); U.S. senator (1841-45); attorney general of Massachusetts (1853-54); leader of the Massachusetts bar. [50] See also Author Index, Vol. 9.

COLTON, CALVIN (Sept. 14, 1789-March 13, 1857), author, journalist, and politician. Worked for the *New York Observer* in England; wrote travel journals, political pamphlets, and biographies of Henry Clay. [46] See also Author Index, Vol. 5.

DIETRICHSON, J. W. C. (April 4 or Aug. 23, 1815-Nov. 14, 1883), Lutheran clergyman. Born Norway; immigrated to U.S. (1844); organized Norwegian Lutheran congregations in Wisconsin and developed them into the American Lutheran Church. [49]

DIX, DOROTHEA (April 4, 1802-July 17, 1887), social reformer and humanitarian. Founded (1821) a school for girls at Boston; started a Sunday school class in a Massachusetts jail (1841) and there began her campaign against treating the insane as criminals; reported to the Massachusetts legislature (1843); helped establish public hospitals for the mentally ill in fifteen states; superintendent of women nurses in government hospitals during the Civil War. [21]

DORR, THOMAS (Nov. 5, 1805-Dec. 27, 1854), lawyer and politician. Agitated for wider suffrage in Rhode Island (from 1834); led the People's Party in drawing a new state constitution and headed the ticket elected under it; jailed by state authorities (1844) for forming the new government; released in a year and saw a more liberal constitution enacted. [12]

DOUGLASS, FREDERICK (?Feb. 1817-Feb. 20, 1895), journalist, orator, and antislavery leader. Escaped from slavery (1838); agent (1841-45) of the Massachusetts Anti-Slavery Society; founded and edited (1847-60) the Abolitionist paper *North Star*; in Civil War, recruited Negro regiments and served as consultant to Lincoln; minister to Haiti (1889-91). [95] See also Author Index, Vol. 10.

DOWNING, A. J. (Oct. 30, 1815-July 28, 1852), architect, landscape gardener, and horticulturist. Editor (1846-52) of the *Horticulturist*; wrote *A Treatise on the*

Theory and Practice of Landscape Gardening (1841), *The Fruits and Fruit Trees of America* (1845). [100] See also Author Index, Vol. 8.

DURFEE, JOB (Sept. 20, 1790-July 26, 1847), jurist and author. U.S. representative from Rhode Island (1820-25); chief justice (1835-47) of the Rhode Island Supreme Court. [28]

EMERSON, RALPH WALDO (May 25, 1803-April 27, 1882), poet, essayist, and philosopher. Wrote *Nature* (1836) and *Essays* (1841, 1844) on his transcendentalist philosophy, and for many years kept his *Journals*; edited (1842-44) the *Dial*; lectured in England and in the U.S. on a variety of subjects, such as self-reliance, individual freedom, and abolition of slavery. [36, 79] See also Author Index, Vols. 6, 8, 9.

EVANS, GEORGE HENRY (March 25, 1805-Feb. 2, 1856), land reformer, labor leader, and editor. Edited the *Working Man's Advocate* (1829-45), the *Daily Sentinel* and *Young America* (1837-53); wrote a *History of the Origin and Progress of the Working Men's Party* (1840). [43]

EVERETT, ALEXANDER H. (March 19, 1790-May 29, 1847), author, editor, and diplomat. Editor (1829-35) of the *North American Review*; chargé d'affaires at The Hague (1818-24); minister to Spain (1825-29); first commissioner to China (1845). [52]

EVERETT, EDWARD (April 11, 1794-Jan. 15, 1865), Unitarian clergyman, orator, educator, and statesman. Pastor of the Brattle Street Church, Boston; editor (1820-24) of the *North American Review*; U.S. representative from Massachusetts (1825-35); governor (1836-40); minister to Great Britain (1841-45); president (1846-49) of Harvard College; secretary of state (1852-53) under Fillmore; U.S. senator (1853-54). [110] See also Author Index, Vols. 5, 6.

FOSTER, STEPHEN S. (Nov. 17, 1809-Sept. 8, 1881), Abolitionist and social reformer. Associated with William Lloyd Garrison in antislavery lectures and agitation; wrote *The Brotherhood of Thieves; or A True Picture of the American Church and Clergy* (1843). [17]

FULLER, MARGARET, Marchioness Ossoli (May 23, 1810-July 19, 1850), author, journalist, and social reformer. Edited (1840-42) the *Dial;* literary critic (1844-46) and first woman European correspondent (1846-50) for the *New York Tribune.* [64]

GALLATIN, ALBERT (Jan. 29, 1761-Aug. 12, 1849), financier and diplomat. U.S. representative from Pennsylvania (1795-1801); secretary of the treasury (1801-14) under Jefferson and Madison; minister to France (1816-23); minister to Great Britain (1826-27). [82] See also Author Index, Vols. 4, 5.

GIDDINGS, JOSHUA (Oct. 6, 1795-May 27, 1864), public official and diplomat. U.S. representative from Ohio (1838-59); censured by House (1842) for antislavery activities; minister to Canada (1861-64). [39]

GREENOUGH, HORATIO (Sept. 6, 1805-Dec. 18, 1852), sculptor. Among his works were a colossal statue of George Washington; "The Rescue," a large sculpture on the portico of the national Capitol; and many busts of outstanding figures. [25]

GREGG, WILLIAM (Feb. 2, 1800-Sept. 13, 1867), manufacturer. Wrote *Essays on Domestic Industry* (1845) urging that the South augment its agricultural economy with industrial development; built the first textile mill in the South (opened 1848) at Graniteville, S.C. [57]

GRISCOM, JOHN H. (fl. 1840-1852), physician. Pioneer in the New York public health movement; author of *The Sanitary Condition of the Laboring Population of New York* (1845). [45]

HALLETT, BENJAMIN (Dec. 2, 1797-Sept. 30, 1862), lawyer, editor, and politician. Editor (1821-28) of the *Providence Journal,* (1829-31) of the *Daily Advertiser,* and (1831-c. 1852) of the anti-Masonic *Boston Daily Advocate.* [93]

HAWTHORNE, NATHANIEL (July 4, 1804-May 19, 1864), novelist. Gathered material for his writing during residences in Salem, Mass. (1804-37), at Boston Customhouse (1839-40), at Brook Farm (1841), as U.S. consul in Great Britain (1853-57), and in Italy (1858-59); wrote *Twice-Told*

Tales (1837, 1842), *The Scarlet Letter* (1850), *The House of the Seven Gables* (1851), *The Blithedale Romance* (1852), *The Marble Faun* (1860). [35] See also Author Index, Vol. 9.

HENRY, JOSEPH (Dec. 17, 1797-May 13, 1878), physicist. Experimented with electromagnetism and developed an electromagnetic motor; investigated solar radiation and sunspots; discovered the nature of electric discharges; professor of natural philosophy (1832-48) at the College of New Jersey (Princeton); first secretary and director (from 1846) of the Smithsonian Institution. [90]

HONE, PHILIP (Oct. 25, 1780-May 5, 1851), businessman and public official. Pioneer in the development of canals and railroads in Pennsylvania (*c.* 1820-30); imported the first locomotive to run on American tracks (1829); mayor of New York City (1825). [11]

JACKSON, ANDREW (March 15, 1767-June 8, 1845), lawyer, statesman, and soldier, known as "Old Hickory." Seventh President of the United States (1829-37); U.S. representative from Tennessee (1796-97); U.S. senator (1797-98, 1823-25); justice of the Tennessee Supreme Court (1798-1804); major general of the state militia (1802); major general of U.S. Army (1814); governor of the Florida Territory (1821). [20] See also Author Index, Vols. 5, 6.

KIRKLAND, WILLIAM (1800-1846), educator, traveler, and writer. [42]

LAWRENCE, ABBOTT (Dec. 16, 1792-Aug. 18, 1855), merchant, manufacturer, public official, and diplomat. Founded (1845) and developed textile manufacturing city of Lawrence, Mass.; U.S. representative from Massachusetts (1835-37, 1839-40); minister to Great Britain (1849-52); financial sponsor of Lawrence Scientific School of Harvard College. [71]

LEVIN, LEWIS C. (Nov. 10, 1808-March 14, 1860), lawyer, editor, and public official. Edited (from 1838) the *Temperance Advocate* and (from 1843) a native-American organ, the *Philadelphia Sun;* U.S. representative from Pennsylvania (1845-51). [68]

Lloyd Garrison; president (1865-70) of the American Anti-Slavery Society; advocate of prohibition, woman suffrage, penal reforms, and the organization of labor. [53] See also Author Index, Vol. 10.

PITTS, JOHN W. (fl. 1843), pamphleteer. Wrote *Eleven Numbers Against Lawyer Legislation and Fees at the Bar.* [27]

POLK, JAMES K. (Nov. 2, 1795-June 15, 1849), lawyer and statesman. Eleventh President of the United States (1845-49); U.S. representative from Tennessee (1825-39) and speaker of the House (1835-39); governor of Tennessee (1839-41). [60, 66, 84]

POST, TRUMAN MARCELLUS (June 3, 1810-Dec. 31, 1886), Congregational clergyman and educator. Professor of ancient languages and of ancient history (1832-46) at Illinois College; pastor (1847-1882) of the Third Presbyterian (from 1851 renamed Congregational) Church of St. Louis, Mo. [51]

RAEDER, OLE M. (1815-1895), Norwegian lawyer and jurist. Sent to the U.S. in 1847 to study the American jury system for the Norwegian government; his impressions appeared as letters and articles in Norwegian newspapers. [91]

REMOND, CHARLES LENOX (Feb. 1, 1810-Dec. 22, 1873), Abolitionist and Negro leader. Agent (from 1838) of the Massachusetts Anti-Slavery Society; delegate to the World Anti-Slavery Conference in London (1841); recruiting officer for the 54th Massachusetts Infantry, the first Negro regiment in the Civil War. [16]

SEWARD, WILLIAM H. (May 16, 1801-Oct. 10, 1872), lawyer and statesman. Governor of New York (1838-42); U.S. senator (1849-61); secretary of state under Lincoln and Johnson. Negotiated the purchase of Alaska from Russia (1867). [1] See also Author Index, Vols. 6, 8, 9, 10.

SHAW, LEMUEL (Jan. 9, 1781-March 30, 1861), jurist. Chief justice (1830-60) of the Massachusetts Supreme Court. [13] See also Author Index, Vol. 5.

SOULÉ, FRANK (fl. 1849-1855), historian. Co-author of *The Annals of San Francisco* (1855). [109]

SUMNER, CHARLES (Jan. 6, 1811-March 11, 1874), Abolitionist and statesman. U.S. senator from Massachusetts (1851-74); leader of the antislavery faction in Congress and the first prominent official to urge emancipation (Oct. 1861); severely injured when attacked in the Senate (May 22, 1856) by Rep. Preston Brooks of South Carolina for his remarks on slavery. [80, 111, 118] See also Author Index, Vols. 8, 9, 10.

THOREAU, HENRY DAVID (July 12, 1817-May 6, 1862), writer, poet, and philosopher. Schoolteacher (1839-41) in Concord, Mass.; resided (1841-43, 1847-48) with Ralph Waldo Emerson and associated with the New England Transcendentalists; moved to a cabin at Walden Pond (1845-47) to write and to study nature; wrote *A Week on the Concord and Merrimack Rivers* (1849), *Walden; or, Life in the Woods* (1854), his *Journals* (20 vols., 1906). [29, 117] See also Author Index, Vols. 8, 9.

TYLER, JOHN (March 29, 1790-Jan. 18, 1862), lawyer and public official. Tenth President of the United States (1841-45); U.S. representative from Virginia (1817-21); governor (1825-27); U.S. senator (1827-36); Vice-President of the United States under W. H. Harrison; succeeded to the Presidency upon Harrison's death (April 4, 1841). [37]

UNONIUS, GUSTAF (fl. 1841-1858), Swedish pastor. Led a group of settlers to Pine Lake, Wis. and there established (1841) the first Swedish colony in U.S.; wrote memoirs, *A Pioneer in Northwest America.* [4]

VALE, GILBERT (1788-1866), English writer, editor, and lecturer. Edited *The Citizen of the World,* the *Sunday Reporter,* and the *Independent Beacon;* invented a globe used to teach astronomy; wrote *Life of Thomas Paine* (1841), *Fanaticism; Its Source and Influence* (1835). [6]

WALKER, ROBERT J. (July 19, 1801-Nov. 11, 1869), lawyer and public official. U.S. senator from Mississippi (1836-45); secretary of the treasury under Polk; governor of Kansas Territory (1857-58); U.S. financial agent in Europe (1863-64). [67] See also Author Index, Vol. 8.

WALKER, TIMOTHY (Dec. 1, 1802-Jan. 15, 1856), jurist, writer, and educator. Founded (1833) the Law School of Cincinnati College (now University); edited (from 1843) the *Western Law Journal;* wrote *Introduction to American Law* (1837). **[44]** See also Author Index, Vol. 5.

WAYLAND, FRANCIS (March 11, 1796-Sept. 30, 1865), Baptist clergyman and educator. President (1827-55) of Brown University, where he liberalized curriculum and enlarged the school; wrote *Thoughts on the Present Collegiate System in the United States* (1842) and *Report to the Corporation of Brown University* (1850) on educational reform. **[10]** See also Author Index, Vol. 8.

WEBSTER, DANIEL (Jan. 18, 1782-Oct. 24, 1852), lawyer, orator, and statesman. U.S. representative from New Hampshire (1813-17) and from Massachusetts (1823-27); U.S. senator from Massachusetts (1827-41, 1845-50); secretary of state (1841-43) under Tyler and (1850-52) under Fillmore. **[30, 34, 88]** See also Author Index, Vols. 4, 5, 6, 8.

WHITMAN, WALT (May 31, 1819-March 26, 1892), poet, schoolteacher, and journalist. Edited (1846-48) the *Brooklyn Eagle* and wrote (1848) for the *New Orleans Crescent;* hospital nurse (1862-64) in Washington, D.C.; clerk in U.S. Department of the Interior (1865), but dismissed by the secretary of the interior because of the "licentiousness" of his poetry; wrote *Leaves of Grass* (1855 and nine later revisions), *Drum-Taps* (1865), *Democratic Vistas* (1871). **[76]** See also Author Index, Vols. 8, 9, 10, 11.

WHITNEY, ASA (Dec. 1, 1791-June 4, 1874), manufacturer and inventor. Patented a locomotive steam engine (1840) and developed improved parts for railroad equipment. **[56]**

WHITTIER, JOHN GREENLEAF (Dec. 17, 1807-Sept. 7, 1892), poet, journalist, Abolitionist, and humanitarian. Editor (1830-32) of the *New England Weekly Review;* wrote *Justice and Expediency* and poems in behalf of the Abolitionist cause; also wrote religious works and poems of New England, including "Snow-Bound" (1866). **[31]** See also Author Index, Vols. 6, 8, 9.

WINTHROP, ROBERT C. (May 12, 1809-Nov. 16, 1894), lawyer and public official. U.S. representative from Massachusetts (1840-50) and speaker of the House (1847-49); U.S. senator (1850-51); president (1855-85) of the Massachusetts Historical Society. **[69]**